THE OXFORD ILLUSTRATED HISTORY OF ENGLISH LITERATURE

EDITED BY

PAT ROGERS

Oxford   New York

OXFORD UNIVERSITY PRESS

1990

Oxford University Press, Walton Street, Oxford OX2 6DP

Oxford New York Toronto
Delhi Bombay Calcutta Madras Karachi
Petaling Jaya Singapore Hong Kong Tokyo
Nairobi Dar es Salaam Cape Town
Melbourne Auckland

and associated companies in
Berlin Ibadan

Oxford is a trade mark of Oxford University Press

© Oxford University Press 1987

First published 1987
First issued as an Oxford University Press paperback 1990

British Library Cataloguing in Publication Data
Rogers, Pat
The Oxford illustrated history of English literature.
1. English literature—Dictionaries
I. Title
820'.3'21   PR19
ISBN 0–19–282728–6

Library of Congress Cataloging in Publication Data
The Oxford illustrated history of English literature.
Bibliography: p.
Includes index.
1. English literature—History and criticism.
I. Rogers, Pat.
PR83.094 1987   820'.9   86–8507
ISBN 0–19–282728–6

Printed in Great Britain by
Butler & Tanner Ltd,
Frome, Somerset

THE EDITOR

PAT ROGERS is DeBartolo Professor of Humanities at the University of South Florida. He is author of numerous books, including *Grub Street* (1972), and editor of the *Poems of Jonathan Swift* (1983).

THE CONTRIBUTORS

J. A. BURROW, Winterstoke Professor of English at the University of Bristol: *Old and Middle English Literature, c.700–1485*

JOHN PITCHER, Fellow of St John's College, Oxford: *Tudor Literature, 1485–1603*

PHILIP EDWARDS, King Alfred Professor of English Literature at the University of Liverpool: *William Shakespeare*

BRIAN VICKERS, Professor of English and Renaissance Literature at the Centre for Renaissance Studies, Zürich: *The Seventeenth Century, 1603–1674*

ISOBEL GRUNDY, Reader in English at Queen Mary College, University of London: *Restoration and Eighteenth Century, 1660–1780*

CLARE LAMONT, Senior Lecturer in English Literature at the University of Newcastle upon Tyne: *The Romantic Period, 1780–1830*

ANDREW SANDERS, Lecturer in English at Birkbeck College, University of London: *High Victorian Literature, 1830–1880*

BERNARD BERGONZI, Professor of English at the University of Warwick: *Late Victorian to Modernist, 1880–1930*

MARTIN DODSWORTH, Senior Lecturer in English at Royal Holloway and Bedford New College, University of London: *Mid-Twentieth-Century Literature, 1930–1980.*

THE OXFORD ILLUSTRATED HISTORY OF ENGLISH LITERATURE

EDITOR'S FOREWORD

I

'HAPPY the people', wrote Thomas Carlyle, adapting a commonplace, 'whose annals are blank in history-books!' It may be so, but one could not envy a people whose literary annals were vacant. For a nation achieves through art self-recognition, self-awareness, self-definition. In literature a race—which means here in effect a linguistic community—confronts its own aspirations and despairs. Here we shall find its conversation with itself, its quarrel with others, its inner thoughts and its outer experience, its private meditations and its public utterances. But the Englishness of English literature is not just the product of some broad political, social, or cultural influences: it is an artistic fact, a phenomenon to be explored with the help of rhetoric and criticism, just like the nature of tragedy or the essence of the fictive. A main aim of this volume is to help the reader explore the great treasury of English literature in the light of that fact.

There has been a recognizable English language since the Germanic conquests of Celtic Britain, which began during the fifth century AD and were consolidated over the next century and a half. Of course, 'Old English' or Anglo-Saxon underwent drastic changes in structure, syntax, accidence, and vocabulary after the Norman Conquest, and nothing written before the eleventh century could ever be mistaken for anything resembling Modern English. None the less, there is a basic continuity which, in the view of most scholars, overrides these differences. So the story of English literature properly begins with the first written records from the Anglo-Saxon period, which date from c. AD 700. At the other end, we have brought the story as fully up to date as is possible. We have not striven to be unduly fashionable, a sure way to become obsolete within five years, but we have all tried to take account of the most urgent debates and to write in the awareness that the world has changed since the major textbooks were written—and it is still changing.

This volume, then, will trace a measure of linguistic continuity, but also along with the richness and diversity of the literature comes an amazing capacity for self-renewal. Among the main bodies of western literature, perhaps only French rivals the English in this respect. Some of the others started late as what could be termed world powers in the field of art: Russian and, for obvious reasons, American literature are clear examples. Italian, Spanish, and Portuguese achieved great things in the medieval and Renaissance periods, but have suffered distinct troughs since that phase, whilst a fragmented German nation did not fully make its mark on the European mind until the dawn of the Romantic era. It would be an exaggeration to say that Britain enjoyed total stability in constitutional or social terms over much of its history, but there was enough sense of identity to sustain a continuing native tradition, above all in poetry. For a long time, countries tended to see the possession of a strong literary heritage as the very acme of cultural advancement: on one level this was a mere virility symbol, as pointlessly vain as running one's own national airline, but it did emphasize the centrality of the domain of letters in earlier phases of civilization.

There is one awkward issue which must not be glossed over. In speaking of the 'British' people, we slide easily across into talking about 'English' literature. A demographic dominance, and with it a political hegemony, have ensured that English has been the almost exclusive language of government, law, and most written documents for many centuries. Yet there is in addition a powerful pressure on the fringes of this metropolitan culture, exerted by Scottish and Irish forms of Gaelic and by Welsh. (This is to leave aside, as one realistically must, the tiny and practically defunct languages such as Cornish and Manx.) The Celtic tongues have their own literary tradition, and there have been moments when they made some impact on what may be termed, neutrally and descriptively, the mainstream of English literature. But these were brief and localized events, and we have not thought it either possible or desirable to include these traditions in the present book. For the rest, the groups sometimes known (with varying aptness) as 'Anglo-Irish', 'Anglo-Welsh', or 'Anglo-Scots' are present, because—however important their local roots—writers such as Walter Scott, James Joyce, or Dylan Thomas employ an expressive vocabulary which is in major respects a dialect of the vernacular tongue.

Equally, we have found it necessary to exclude writing in English outside the main geographical centre: there is no attempt to cover American, 'old Commonwealth', Caribbean, or African literature. Up to a generation or so ago, it would have been possible to pretend that Nigerian writing, for example, was a kind of colonial branch-line of the regular network. But this looks increasingly implausible, as well as patronizing, and the same applies very obviously to Australian or Canadian works. American literature is now the most widely read version of English-language writing around the world, and for at least a century has demanded an approach proper to its own distinctive concerns and techniques. Though there are interesting cross-connections to be made between all these groups (and a few ambiguous figures, such as Ezra Pound or Jean Rhys), we can no longer claim that a single frame of reference will hold them all together. Instead, we have devoted the limited space at our disposal to what could be called, by a reasonable common-sense usage, the literature in English of the British people. It is, literally, an insular definition, but if one has to draw lines somewhere, coastlines are the least arbitrary.

II

Is literary history necessary? In the strictest sense, the answer must be no: it is possible to read books with appreciation and enjoyment without cluttering one's head with dates and movements. And it is demonstrably possible to *write* great literature with little or no sense of one's place in a great tradition. Shakespeare would have had very little idea of his historical bearings, whilst Chaucer would have been bemused by most Old English poetry. Donne would have coped dismally with the 'dating' passages on which infant critics now cut their teeth and learn to nuzzle their way through a text. The truth is that literary history is a relatively modern invention, and so is the automatic sense which a modern writer such as Graham Greene must have of his location in the flow of literary time (whether or not he cares about it—and most writers do, in one way or another).

The rise of English literary history is the subject of a brilliant book by René Wellek, and this has been supplemented by an outstanding survey by Lawrence Lipking of the way in which the various arts (literature, painting, music) were 'ordered' and made sense of in the late eighteenth century.* A foreword is not the place to attempt to rival such magisterial studies, and it is enough to pick out a handful of suggestive facts. First of all, it should be recalled that many words with which we casually allocate books and writers to schools or periods entered the lexicon very late in the day. Even 'medieval' and 'Middle Ages', which seem so natural and untendentious today, had to be naturalized into English within the last two hundred years. When Coleridge wrote 'The Ancient Mariner' and Keats wrote 'La Belle Dame Sans Merci', they would not instantly have known what was meant if we had spoken to them of 'medieval' aspects to their work: the word had not arrived on cue, though the Romantic poets certainly benefited from some of the growing antiquarian lore which opened up the literary past.

Second, it is worth remembering that much of what preceded literary history, as now understood, came in the form of catalogues, collective biographies, anthologies, and compendia. Such works tend to be either encylopaedic and thus undiscriminating, or selective in an arbitrary way. None of them makes for an idea of continuity, of evolution or development. One consequence of this impaired historic sense, as it now seems, is described by René Wellek: 'Before the seventeenth century, with a few exceptions, Greece and Rome were

---

* R. Wellek, *The Rise of English Literary History* (1941, revised 1966); L. Lipking, *The Ordering of the Arts in Eighteenth-Century England* (1970).

considered as being on the same plane as contemporary England. Virgil and Ovid, Homer and Pindar, were discussed as almost contemporary writers.'

Gradually these things changed. Pope, Gray, and Coleridge all planned (but never wrote) historical schemes ordering their poetic predecessors. The crucial moment of breakthrough is usually identified with the appearance of the *History of English Poetry* by Thomas Warton (1774-81). This is indeed a deeply interesting and important book, confused and digressive though it is. But in another way Samuel Johnson, both in his *Dictionary* (1755), with its choice passages of classic writers illustrating the definitions, and in his *Lives of the Poets* (1779-81), did as much to fix a canon, and the idea of a canon. In the nineteenth century there were many dogged compilers, men of the stamp of Henry Morley who, as the critic John Gross has remarked, seemed to chart literary history with the energy and sense of mission that led other Victorians to plant railway lines around the empire. But perhaps no English work has an effect equal to that of Hippolyte Taine's *Histoire de la littérature anglaise* (1863), which was translated in 1871, and with its vivid generalities and disputable theories of art, put new emphasis on the historical and cultural milieu in which literature is written.

The twentieth century has seen a number of significant new ventures, both individual and collective. Bridging the turn of the century, though emphatically he was the heir of Victorian philological and critical study, comes the work of George Saintsbury, with primers such as *A Short History of English Literature* (1898). On a bigger scale there is the collective *Cambridge History of English Literature* (1907-16). A different plan was adopted for the later Oxford History, which consists of volumes by individual scholars on a given period: particular volumes, notably that of C. S. Lewis, remain unmatched in their insight into a phase of literature, though the plan as a whole is perhaps too loose to make for easy reference use. Meanwhile, single-volume histories of some discernment have been provided by Émile Legouis and Louis Cazamian (English translation, 1926-7), and by a team led by Albert C. Baugh (1948).

In the last decade some scepticism has been expressed about the possibilities and the utility of the form: a demand has grown up for a 'new literary history', a term which can mean a good many things but in general calls for explanation rather than mere narrative. But the narrative of the past is, if properly conducted, a species of explanation, just as a story vividly told makes us understand as well as remember its events. In this volume, strict chronology is disturbed only in the case of Shakespeare, whose unique pre-eminence requires the special attention which he is given in Chapter 3.

A final consideration relates to the way in which literary history came into being. It must be stressed that an important task had to be performed prior to any more sophisticated enterprise in the way of critical revaluation. The basic data simply had to be got right. If that seems a bald statement, consider these facts, immediately relevant to the situation in which Warton published his book. When Thomas Chatterton produced his forged poems, allegedly the work of a fifteenth-century monk, the best scholars of the day were hopelessly divided and muddled in their efforts to establish their authenticity or otherwise. Then again, it was only in this crucial decade of the 1770s that Thomas Tyrwhitt for the first time discovered the secret of Chaucer's metre (basically, the sounding of a final *e* syllable), and thus showed him to be something other than the crude and unsophisticated technician previously accepted. It was around this time that Oliver Goldsmith described *The Divine Comedy* as 'a strange mixture of good sense and absurdity . . . Dante owes most of his reputation to the obscurity of the times in which he lived'. Linguistic questions were bedevilled by ignorance of any principles of comparative philology (again things changed for the better around 1770), so that John Cleland, author of *Fanny Hill*, could seriously advance the view in 1768 that Welsh was the aboriginal tongue from which all others developed. Lastly, there is the case of James Hurdis, who maintained in 1792 that *Two Gentlemen of Verona* was among the last plays of Shakespeare, whilst the early plays were held to include *Antony and Cleopatra*, *Coriolanus*, *Cymbeline*, *The Tempest*, *Timon of Athens*, and *The Winter's Tale*—though all had been shown in 1778 by Edmond Malone, one of the first great historical scholars, to be late.

It would be graceless to sneer too readily at these blunders—Hurdis was duly made Professor of Poetry at Oxford University in 1793. Each age has its particular blind spots, and this volume might well occasion a measure of hilarity in a century or two, should the world and the book survive. And indeed, whilst we have striven to be as accurate as possible, we have not concealed our own vantage-point in the 1980s. The contributors were selected not just because of proven scholarship, but also because they maintain a vital concern with the critical ideas of the present. We do not all agree on every point, and the separate chapters have been written only within broad guidelines, so that there is room for individual emphasis or interpretation. By this means we hope to suggest some of the personal response which the encounter with great literature should always incite. We have had to leave out some figures of interest, either because their main thrust as authors belongs outside creative literature (for example, Cobbett) or because it is too early to assess their standing with posterity. Thus in the final chapter, it has been necessary to exclude many strong candidates for consideration, notably John Betjeman, Malcolm Lowry, Edwin Muir, Barbara Pym, Rebecca West, and Angus Wilson, figures of great contemporary interest who may or may not exert lasting influence. It is, after all, impossible to include everything within one pair of covers.

All the contributors passionately believe in the value of great imaginative literature, and specifically of the process by which language under the pressure of urgent experience is bent and refined in wholly unexpected ways. We have tried to keep this aspect of literature in the forefront all through the book.

This, rather than the demonstration of some abstract principle, or refutation of some academic heresy, points towards our purposes. As was the case with our notable predecessors, what we desire is to make the reading of poems, plays, and novels more satisfying because better informed, and more profound because more comprehending.

1985   PAT ROGERS

PUBLISHER'S
ACKNOWLEDGEMENTS

THE publishers are grateful to Philippa Lewis, the picture researcher, and Susan le Roux and her staff, for their great assistance with the design and selection of illustrations; to Mary Worthington, who copy-edited the text and read the proofs; and to John Vickers, who compiled the index.

CONTENTS

LIST OF COLOUR PLATES

A NOTE ON THE TEXT

QUOTATIONS from Old and Middle English texts are presented in their original form (glossed where necessary). Later passages are as a rule brought into line with modern spelling, except in a few instances where the meaning would be obscured, or archaic usage was deliberate.

Dates up to 1752 are given according to the Old Style (by that time eleven days behind the New Style in use on the Continent), but the year is taken to begin from 1 January rather than 25 March.

Dates given for plays are those of publication rather than performance or composition (except where specifically noted otherwise).

This volume is conceived as complementary to the *Oxford Companion to English Literature*, edited by Margaret Drabble, and readers are referred to that volume for more detailed information on specific topics.

Dunfermline

Edinburgh

○ Lindisfarne

Ruthwell

0   50   100 km

0   25   50 miles

•York

Wakefield •

R. Humber

Chester

The Wash

• Stafford

• Leicester   Norwich •

Areley Kings •   • Longthorpe

Wigmore •   Bury St Edmunds •

Hereford •   Worcester •   • Earls Barton

Monmouth •   Eynsham   Maldon •

Oxford •

R. Thames   London •

• Bath   Guildford •   Canterbury •

W E S S E X   • Winchester

Exeter •   • Sherborne

OLD AND MIDDLE ENGLISH LITERATURE: PLACES OF INTEREST

1. Old and Middle English

c.700-1485

J. A. BURROW

Introduction

THE periods of English literature assigned to this first chapter are together more than half as long again as all those covered by the other eight chapters taken together. They extend from 700 to about 1500, a stretch of roughly eight hundred years. For this gross disproportion in our History there are three main reasons. First, the quantities of English verse and prose actually produced during these centuries were, relatively speaking, small. The population of England in 1377, the year of the poll tax, was probably something less than three million—as against more than forty-six million in 1976. Such a great quantitative difference cannot be ignored, even though the incidence of literary talent does not rise and fall in any fixed proportion to the general population, as is sufficiently proved by the example of London in 1377, whose perhaps forty or fifty thousand inhabitants included Chaucer, Langland, and Gower. It must also be remembered that the literary efforts of this relatively small population were by no means confined to the English language. Authors who aspired to address the larger learned world regularly wrote in Latin; and Chaucer was perhaps the first Englishman deliberately to write for posterity in his native tongue. A History of Literature in England would include such Latin writers as Bede, John of Salisbury, Geoffrey of Monmouth, and Richard of Bury; but a History of Literature in English must exclude these men, together with all those subjects of the English Crown who, after the Norman Conquest, wrote in Anglo-Norman or continental French. It can therefore give only a partial account of such writers as Chaucer's friend John Gower, who wrote in all three languages: French (*Mirour de l'Omme*), Latin (*Vox clamantis*), and English (*Confessio Amantis*).

A second consideration, also quantitative in character, concerns lost literature. The amount of this can never be determined, but it is certainly much greater than in later periods. A literary work in a medieval vernacular might never get written down at all, or else, if it did, the copies may have been lost. Admittedly, one should not draw too sharp or simple a distinction between the age of

A PAGE OF OLD ENGLISH VERSE, from the Junius manuscript in the Bodleian Library, one of the four main surviving manuscripts of Old English verse, beginning 'Brand & brade ligas. swilce eac þa biteran recas.' Half-lines are here marked off by points; but Anglo-Saxon scribes did not set verse out in 'lines'. Contrast p. 28.

manuscript, with which this chapter is concerned, and the age of print, which begins for English with William Caxton's *History of Troy* (1473 or 1474). Habits of writing and reading in Anglo-Saxon England were indeed largely confined to monastic centres; but from the twelfth century onwards the production and consumption of manuscript material increased greatly, and some vernacular works of the fourteenth and fifteenth centuries survive in numerous copies. Yet even Geoffrey Chaucer is known from his own testimony to have composed works of which no copy survives (he mentions a 'book of the Leoun', for instance); and many more such losses are certainly to be reckoned with in earlier centuries. Furthermore, since verse could be composed and remembered without the use of writing, poems would not necessarily achieve even the doubtful permanence of a single manuscript copy. This consideration applies with particular force to Anglo-Saxon verse. Here, indeed, the problem for the literary historian is insurmountable, since most of the available corpus (of little more than 30,000 lines in all) survives in just four manuscript books. There is no way of estimating the number of other books which have been lost, let alone the number of poems which never got written down; nor can one assume that the contents of the four main manuscripts, all of which were compiled in monasteries, offer a representative sample of the whole.

The third consideration concerns the character and quality of what does survive. The ancient tradition that English literature begins with Geoffrey Chaucer does more than simply pay tribute to that great poet. It also recognizes an essential fact about the history of our literary language, whose modern form descends from an ancestor very like the London English which Chaucer used. A modern reader who works his way back from, say, Wyatt and Surrey through Malory to Chaucer will encounter no break in continuity, despite the undoubted linguistic difficulties which Chaucer presents. But it was only towards the end of the Middle Ages that this standard literary language emerged. Anglo-Saxon England had developed in the later tenth century its own remarkably consistent form of written English, based on the dialect of Wessex, and it is in this language that most of its literary monuments survive; but Late West Saxon is first accessible to the modern reader only as a foreign language, whose grammar and vocabulary have to be learned from books. Furthermore, when after the Norman Conquest Wessex and its language forfeited the predominance which they had enjoyed in the times of Alfred and his successors, English writers were once more reduced to using whatever form of the vernacular was current in their own part of the country. Thus, up to the fifteenth century, Middle English writings exhibit a diversity of linguistic forms which can be almost as daunting as the more remote, but also much more regular, language of Old English literature. As late as Chaucer's day, we find a great contemporary, the *Gawain*-poet, employing the vocabulary and forms of the Staffordshire or Cheshire region in which he was brought up.

It is these linguistic difficulties, more than any other factor, which prevent those medieval writers who deserve to do so from taking their rightful place, along with Chaucer, in the larger canon of living English literature. In this chapter I can attempt only to indicate who some of these deserving writers are, and what claim each may have to a place in this volume. I shall consider first Old English poetry, then Old and Middle English prose, and finally Middle English poetry.

Old English Poetry

Even if space permitted, it would not be possible to write a history of English poetry in the period before the Conquest—to display, that is, the development of a poetic tradition, tracing influences, marking changes, identifying movements and schools. The evidence is lacking. All that we have is a small and probably unrepresentative sample, most of which survives in copies made towards the end of the period. The four major poetic codices mentioned earlier all date from about fifty years either side of the year 1000: the *Beowulf* manuscript in the British Library, the Bodleian manuscript of biblical poems (including those known as *Genesis* and *Exodus*), the Vercelli manuscript (which contains *The Dream of the Rood*), and the Exeter manuscript (which includes the *Advent Lyrics*, the so-called 'elegies', and the riddles). Many of the poems were certainly written many years before these books were copied; but there is very little solid evidence for dating them and so arranging them in a chronological sequence. *The Battle of Maldon* must be late, because the event which it describes occurred in the year 991; and *The Dream of the Rood* must (in part, at least) be quite early, because some lines corresponding to the Vercelli text are to be found inscribed in runic letters on an eighth-century stone cross; but most Anglo-Saxon poetry stands grandly aloof from current affairs, and there are very few such early witnesses as the Ruthwell Cross.

In any case, considered as the product of perhaps three hundred years of poetic activity, the remains exhibit relatively few of those large variations in subject and style which might prompt literary historians to construct at least a hypothetical chronology and attempt to distinguish, as art historians are able to do with certainty, between eighth-century and tenth-century work. Indeed, reading through the surviving verse, one's first impression is of marked homogeneity. This is most obviously, and most fundamentally, a homogeneity of metrical form. All known Old English poems observe, though with some variations, the principles of alliterative verse. Such verse continued to be written in English, as we shall see, to the end of the Middle Ages, and it has been revived in modern times by poets such as W. H. Auden; but its principles, derived from a common Germanic tradition of oral poetry, present difficulties to the reader of Chaucer, Pope, or Tennyson. He must learn to forget three considerations which he has been taught to regard as fundamental: syllable

count (decasyllabic lines, etc.), recurrent patterns of stress (iambic feet, etc.), and rhyme. In their place, alliteration must be recognized as a basic formal requirement, not an optional expressive extra. The Anglo-Saxon verse line consists of two parts bound together by alliteration. Variation in the number of syllables in each half-line is (within limits) a matter of indifference, but each half will normally have two stressed or heavy syllables; and it is upon these stressed syllables that the essential binding alliteration falls. Thus:

> Þá com of móre   under místhléoþum
> Gréndel góngan,   Gódes yrre bǽr.
>
> (*Beowulf*, 710-11)

[Then came from the moor under the mist-slopes Grendel walking, he bore God's anger. þ, 'thorn', is pronounced like *th*.]

In the first half-line the alliteration may fall on either of the two stressed syllables (*more* in the first line quoted) or else on both (*Grendel* and *gongan* in the second line), but in the second half-line it must fall on the first and not the second, by a strict self-denying ordinance: a x a x, or x a a x, or a a a x, but not a a a a. The lines quoted also illustrate characteristic variations of rhythmic pattern from half-line to half-line, depending upon the positioning of the two stressed syllables in relation to the unstressed ones. These patterns represent a selection from the basic stock of two-stress phrase rhythms which spoken English still favours; and each phrase or half-line, in poetry as in common speech, is free to vary at will from the rhythm of its neighbour. Hence, in the absence of any principle of rhythmical recurrence, the Anglo-Saxon verse line approaches more nearly to the movement of conversational English than does, say, the iambic pentameter of later ages.

Yet the verse is generally far from conversational in manner. On the contrary, it displays, as archaic poetry often does, a highly elaborate and conventional language of its own, distinct from common vocabulary and idiom, such that the listening ear can clearly distinguish it as the product of a mastered art— the art of the bard, or, as Anglo-Saxons called him, the *scop*. Comparison with the alliterative verse of other Germanic peoples (German and Icelandic, for instance) shows that this poetic idiom must go back, in many of its essential features, to an early preliterate age, when the poet, exercising his skills in the very presence of his audience, relied on a stock of ready-made formulaic expressions and poetical synonyms in order to satisfy his listeners' demand for an unhesitating flow of well-formed alliterative verses. Few scholars now believe that any of the surviving Anglo-Saxon texts directly represent such an act of 'oral composition'; yet similar considerations of metrical convenience still play a large part in their poetic diction. Thus, special compounds such as *misthleoþ*, 'mist-slope', are commonly employed, as in the line from *Beowulf* quoted above, in forming a half-line of the clashing-stress type (x x // x). That instance also shows how the first element in such a compound could be varied to provide a link with different alliterating sounds in the other half-line, for

A NINTH-CENTURY BROOCH, representing the five senses: sight in the *centre*, smell *upper right*, touch *lower right*, hearing *lower left*, taste *upper left*. Compare the later representation of the same subject, p. 38.

elsewhere in *Beowulf* we meet 'under fenhleoþu' ('under the *fen*-slopes') functioning as the second half of an f-alliterating line. One typical fault in Anglo-Saxon poetry is that such variations will serve *only* their metrical purpose; but the *Beowulf*-poet's characteristically massive compounding of *mist* (not 'misty') and *hleoþ* achieves, in the eerie context of the monster Grendel's approach from the moor, much more than just a convenient alliteration.

It would, in any case, be wrong to speak as if the demands of a common metre imposed on Anglo-Saxon poets a single unvarying manner of utterance. The style of *The Battle of Maldon* is much less ornate than that of *Beowulf*, while the poet of the so-called *Later Genesis* achieves, in his version of the fall of Satan and the temptation of Adam and Eve, a remarkable freedom in the rendering of passionate speech. Here his Satan, raging in Hell, breaks off with an unspoken threat:

> 'Þæt me is sorga mæst
> Þæt Adam sceal, þe wæs of eorþan geworht,
> Minne stronglican stol behealdan,
> Wesan him on wynne, ond we þis wite þolien,
> Hearm on þisse helle. Wala, ahte ic minra handa geweald
> Ond moste ane tid ute weorþan,
> Wesan ane winterstunde, þonne ic mid þys werode . . .'

> (*Later Genesis*, 364–70)

['The greatest of my sorrows is that Adam, who was made of earth, is to occupy my mighty throne and live in bliss, whilst we suffer this torment, pain in this hell. Alas, if I only had the use of my hands and could get out of here for a time, even for just one winter's hour, then I with this company . . .']

The one unusual compound here, *winterstund* or 'winter hour', is loaded with relevant meaning—winter hours being shorter than summer ones if, as was customary, you divide daylight time into twelve. Furthermore, the common *scop*'s trick of repeating an idea in different words at the start of a following line, and so establishing a new alliteration without advancing the sense, here creates just the right effect of resentful brooding: 'ond we þis wite þolien, / Hearm on þisse helle'.

Other poets can create quite different effects. In the beautiful *Advent Lyrics* of the Exeter manuscript, for instance, the author catches in the very fullness of his English poetic idiom something of the ecstatic strangeness of an Advent invocation to Christ ('Come out by the garden gate, visit those you have redeemed'):

> Þu þisne middangeard milde geblissa
> Þurh þinne hercyme, hælende Crist,
> Ond þa gyldnan geatu, þe in geardagum
> Ful longe ær bilocen stodan,
> Heofona heahfrea, hat ontynan.

> (*Advent Lyrics*, 249–53)

[Graciously bless this earth through your coming hither, saviour Christ, and command, high lord of the heavens, that those golden gates be opened which had formerly for so long stood locked.]

These lines provide another example of the characteristic technique known as 'variation'. The two expressions 'hælende Crist' and 'heofona heahfrea' do not have the same meaning, any more than do 'wite' and 'hearm' in Satan's speech; but they both denote the same referent. Such a play of varied expressions about a single referent serves, among other purposes, to distance the language of the *scops* from ordinary language by making room for abnormal, even enigmatic, modes of expression. The set of riddles in the Exeter manuscript shows how readily and effectively the Anglo-Saxon poetic manner could be turned to the purpose of actual riddling. The skilled *scop* was adept at 'varying his words' ('wordum wrixlan', *Beowulf*, 874) and drawing on his 'word-hoard', beyond the limits of ordinary language—and even, sometimes, of ordinary comprehension. To what do the following lines refer?

> Dægscealdes hleo
> Wand ofer wolcnum; hæfde witig God
> Sunnan siþfæt segle ofertolden,
> Swa þa mæstrapas men ne cuþon,
> Ne þa seglrode geseon meahton,
> Eorþbuende ealle cræfte,
> Hu afæstnod wæs feldhusa mæst.

[A protecting shield by day, it passed across the skies. God in his wisdom had screened the sun's course with a sail, so that men could not perceive the ropes of its mast, nor could earthdwellers for all their skill see the spars or understand how that greatest of field-houses was made fast.]

The author of *Exodus* is here describing the pillar of cloud by day that led the children of Israel out of Egypt. Provoked by a subject for which the traditional word-hoard would provide no expressions, the poet refers to the pillar, riddle-fashion, as a shield, a sail, and a 'field-house' (that is, a tent).

We can see what Anglo-Saxon poetry is like at its best by looking in rather more detail at three poems: *Beowulf*, *The Seafarer*, and *The Dream of the Rood*.

The dating of *Beowulf* is still a matter of controversy. Some scholars put it as early as 700, others as late as 1000. On any possible dating, however, the poem is one of the earliest as well as one of the grandest monuments of the Germanic literatures. It is therefore not surprising that earlier scholars (many themselves Germans) looked in it chiefly for testimonies of Germanic antiquity. The main stories of the poem—Beowulf's fights against Grendel, Grendel's mother, and the dragon—yield no such testimony, for they are no more (and no less) than versions of common folk-tales; but the poet introduces many incidental stories, some of which, such as that of Sigemund, belong to the world of ancient Germanic legend. He also entangles his folk-tales and legends

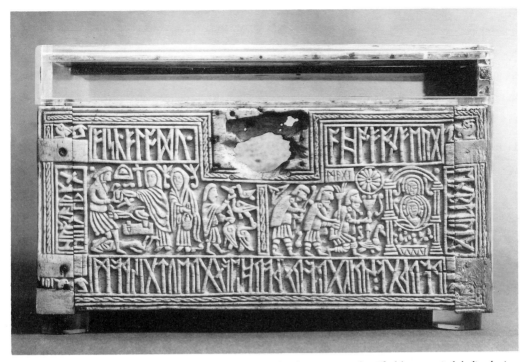

THE FRANKS CASKET, *c.*700. The right panel shows the three Magi (identified by a runic label) adoring the Christ child. On the left is a scene from the ancient Germanic legend of Weland the Smith. The runic border records the origin of the whale-bone from which the casket was made in two lines of verse: 'Fisc flodu ahof on fergenberig / Warþ gasric grorn þær he on greut giswom' ['The sea lifted the fish on to the cliff edge; the terrible lord became sad when he swam on to the shingle'].

in a web of other events, mainly set in the Baltic kingdoms of Denmark, Geatland, and Sweden; and at least one of these events (the raid against the Franks led by Beowulf's lord Hygelac, king of the Geats) can be shown actually to have occurred, in the sixth century. Furthermore, the poet's rich and leisurely portrayal of this Baltic world provides many instances of customs going back to pre-Christian times: the close relationship between lord and man in the war-band or *comitatus* (observed by Tacitus in his *Germania*), the institutions of the *beot*, or vow before battle, and the blood-feud, and the burning of the bodies of the dead. Scholarly interest in such matters naturally encouraged the supposition that the unknown author of the poem was himself a bard of the ancient type portrayed within the poem—a lord's *scop*, deep-versed in pagan tales and traditions, reciting his 'hall-entertainment' to the accompaniment of the harp (so *Beowulf*, 867 ff. and 1063 ff.).

More recent scholarship has been inclined to dismiss this image of the author as a romantic fantasy, and to substitute for it the image of a Christian poet, perhaps a monk, versed not only in old native traditions (as he must have been) but also in the culture and literature of the Latin Church, writing a poem whose chief purpose is, if not pious, at least highly moral. When *this* poet speaks of 'wyrd' or fate, he has in mind, not some archaic pagan force, but that *providentia* of which Boethius wrote in *De consolatione Philosophiae*; and his monster Grendel is not only, as the poet himself says, a descendent of Cain the first murderer, but also an embodiment, even an allegorical representative, of that evil against which the militant Christian perpetually fights.

The contrast between such views corresponds, in part, to a deliberate dichotomy within *Beowulf* itself. Medieval writers are sometimes represented as confirmed anachronists, lacking any sense of historical perspective; but this is certainly not true of *Beowulf*, any more than of *Troilus and Criseyde*. Like Chaucer, the Anglo-Saxon poet is well aware of looking back from his own Christian times to an old society with different customs and beliefs. The poem is set, as its very first line announces, 'in days gone by' ('in geardagum'); and this setting is kept actively before the reader throughout. It is, for instance, the poet and his fellow Christians who can know that Grendel and his mother belong to the race of monsters descended from Cain. For the Danish king Hrothgar, who suffers their ravages, they are totally mysterious creatures of the moor: not knowing the Bible, he cannot know their ancestry (*Beowulf*, 1355-7). Again, when the aged Beowulf is killed by the dragon, the poet can observe that his soul departs from the body to 'seek the judgement that awaits just men' ('secean soþfæstra dom', 2820). Yet the hero's people, the Geats, perform his obsequies in the pagan manner—burning his body on a funeral pyre, and burying his ashes with much treasure in a great barrow. This is what Beowulf himself commanded, in a dying speech which has all the dark pathos, but also all the grandeur, of a pagan who cannot hope for anything more than earthly remembrance after death:

> 'Hataþ heaþomære hlæw gewyrcean
> Beorhtne æfter bæle æt brimes nosan;
> Se scel to gemyndum minum leodum
> Heah hlifian on Hronesnæsse,
> Þæt hit sæliþend syþþan hatan
> Biowulfes biorh, þa þe brentingas
> Ofer floda genipu feorran drifaþ.'
>
> (*Beowulf*, 2802-8)

['Command renowned warriors to build a bright mound after my burning at the sea headland. That will tower high on Whale Cape as a reminder to my people, so that seafarers who drive their tall ships from afar over the dark waves may thereafter know it as Beowulf's Barrow.']

A noble passage such as that is itself enough to show that the Christian poet by no means adopts a polemical or derogatory attitude towards his pagan hero. The distinction between Christian and pagan could never be a matter of complete indifference; but *Beowulf*, like *Troilus*, concerns itself chiefly with human issues to which that distinction is irrelevant. The characters in the poem do not possess the Christian hope, but neither are they represented as benighted 'heathens'—a word which (with one notable exception in line 179) the poet associates with monsters not men. The men are generally portrayed as natural monotheists, who can thank God for a successful journey and live a virtuous life according to their lights. This life is overcast with regret for the past and fear of the future—it is in fact, despite bright moments, an unhappy life—but this is not because the men lack consolations available to the Christian poet. On the contrary, it is represented as a universal human condition; and the heart of the poem lies precisely in its vision of the uncertainty of all existence and in its exploration of men's responses to the changes and reversals which are their lot in any age.

It is these concerns which justify the extraordinary manner in which the *Beowulf*-poet conducts his narrative: the 'rambling, dilatory method—the forward, backward, and sideward movements' of which Klaeber speaks in what is still the best edition of the poem. In a straightforward narrative such as *Sir Gawain and the Green Knight*, neither narrator nor character will refer to past or future any more than the immediate demands of the story require; but in *Beowulf* both the characters and the narrator continually look before and after; and these digressions are so extensive, especially in the second half of the poem, that the reader sometimes finds it difficult, as the reader of Proust often does, to be sure what in the narrative present is actually happening. Hence, although the main story of the monster-fights is simple, and the thoughts and reactions of the characters are also generally straightforward, the poem as a whole presents a complex pattern, which has been compared to the intricate 'interlace' of illuminated manuscripts such as the Lindisfarne Gospels. By juxtaposing past, present, and future in this fashion, the narrative creates frequent opportunities for displaying the ups and downs of fame and fortune. Thus, after his defeat of Grendel, young Beowulf receives from his grateful Danish host Hrothgar the gift of a rich collar. Instead of describing what the collar looked like, as the author of *Sir Gawain* might have done, the *Beowulf*-poet first compares it to a collar in ancient legend (the 'Brosinga mene'), and then, looking forward, observes that it was later to be carried by Beowulf's lord Hygelac and lost by him on his disastrous raid against the Franks: 'hyne wyrd fornam' ('fate carried him off', 1205). Thus the recollected past and the anticipated future press upon and almost overwhelm the narrative present. One may see the same pattern again in the structure of the whole poem, which passes straight from the triumphs of young Beowulf in Denmark to his last battle as an old man against the dragon. The fifty winters and more which come between constitute, as it were, the poem's largest missing present, in relation to which Grendel represents a glorious past and the dragon a terrible future.

Man can come to terms with the uncertainties of life by trying to keep both past and future in view:

> Forþan biþ andgit æghwær selest,
> Ferhþes foreþanc. Fela sceal gebidan

Leofes ond laþes se þe longe her
On þyssum windagum worolde bruceþ.
(Beowulf, 1059–62)

[So understanding is always the best thing, forethought of mind. A man who is to experience life for long here in these days of strife will encounter much joy and much sorrow.]

To ignore the past or the future is at best folly, at worst wickedness. To bear them always in mind is wisdom. But true understanding, and especially a correct anticipation of future events (*foreþanc*), are things not easy to achieve in an uncertain world. Thus Hrothgar, a wise old king, who has suffered a terrible reverse of fortune at the hands of Grendel and knows from experience how cruel life can be, has long since given up all hope of relief (932–9); but he is wrong, for the hero brings relief. These ironies of *foreþanc* are most fully displayed in the case of Beowulf himself. As a young man of little experience he determines to give the unarmed Grendel a sporting chance by himself using no weapons—an imprudent decision, which proves to be a fortunate one nevertheless, since the poet reveals that Grendel, unknown to the hero, is protected by magic against all weapons. Things are going Beowulf's way.

AN EIGHTH-CENTURY ANGLO-SAXON HELMET, discovered at York in 1982. The neck is protected by chain-mail, the cheeks by hinged plates, and the nose by an elaborately decorated nose-guard, with animal motifs characteristic of the period. The bands running across the top of the helm carry a Latin inscription invoking the favour of the Trinity and naming 'Oshere', probably the original owner.

Conversely, as an old man preparing to confront the dragon, Beowulf prudently equips himself with an iron shield to resist its fiery breath; and he draws, from prolonged reflection on what he has survived in the past, the reasonable expectation that he can survive this test also. But he too is wrong: both he and the dragon are *fæge*, doomed to die. This is what the poet means when he has Beowulf say, 'Gæþ a wyrd swa hio scel' ('Fate goes ever as it must', 455). The course of life cannot be predicted with any certainty. One can hope only to foresee the foreseeable and meet the unforeseen with dignity and resolution. Such seems to be the poem's deepest wisdom.

A similar view of life is to be found in other Old English poems. In *Deor*, for instance, the speaker, a *scop* who has lost the favour of his master, recalls old stories of life's reverses and so derives from the past the wisdom to be uncertain about the future, concluding each instance with the laconic refrain, 'Þæs ofereode, þisses swa mæg' ('That passed over, and so may this'). *Deor* is not a pagan poem, any more than *Beowulf* is: it simply confines itself, as *Beowulf* mostly does, to the wisdom of the secular man. Other poems, while taking a similar view of life's uncertainties, reach out to express the hope of solid joys and lasting pleasures in a life to come. The Exeter manuscript contains, besides *Deor*, six other poems which are sometimes classified as elegies. Three of these are remarkable free-standing monologues, two for women's voices and one (in effect) for a man's, concerned with separation and loss: *The Wife's Lament*, *The Husband's Message*, and the mysterious *Wulf and Eadwacer*. None of these poems, however, offers the Christian consolation which crowns, somewhat uneasily, the two best-known 'elegies': *The Wanderer* and *The Seafarer*.

The Seafarer, known to many modern readers in the vigorous but free-wheeling translation by Ezra Pound, plunges directly into a first-person account of the hardships of life at sea:

> Mæg ic be me sylfum soþgied wrecan,
> Siþas secgan, hu ic geswincdagum
> Earfoþhwile oft þrowade,
> Bitre breostceare gebiden hæbbe,
> Gecunnad in ceole cearselda fela,
> Atol yþa gewealc.

> (*The Seafarer*, 1–6)

[I can make a true song about myself and speak of my journeys, how I have often suffered times of hardship in laborious days, endured bitter breast-sorrow, and experienced afloat many sorrowful places, the terrible tossing of the waves.]

The speaker's attitude to his experiences at sea seems unequivocal enough: they are bitter and terrible, a matter of hardship, labour, and sorrow. Yet as the poem progresses, his attitude complicates to the point of paradox. He continues to portray the hardships of sailing in graphic detail: 'Þær ic ne gehyrde butan hlimman sæ, / Iscaldne wæg' ('There I heard nothing but the pounding of the sea, the ice-cold wave'). However, he also comes to contrast sea-life with land-life in a fashion which increasingly glorifies the rigours of the former at the expense of the easy and dubious pleasures of dry land. It turns out, in fact, that the life of solitude and hardship is here, in sharp contrast to the other elegies, voluntarily undertaken, not imposed by fate. The speaker even confesses to a passionate longing for the sea:

> Forþon cnyssaþ nu
> Heortan geþohtas, þæt ic hean streamas,
> Sealtyþa gelac, sylf cunnige.
>
> (*The Seafarer*, 33–5)

[So now the beating thoughts of my heart urge that I should myself venture on the deep seas, the play of the salt waves.]

The expression 'sealtyþa gelac', 'the play of the salt waves', makes the sea sound more friendly than did the earlier 'atol yþa gewealc', 'the terrible tossing of the waves'; but in the brilliant passage of sea-fever which follows, the poet minimizes neither the hardships of the sea nor the delights of land. Spring on land is beautiful, even though the voice of the cuckoo sounds a warning of sorrow to come; and the call of the sea, though irresistible, is also harsh and frightening, like the voice of a lone-flying seabird. It is at this point that the poem takes its religious turn, with these lines:

> Forþon me hatran sind
> Dryhtnes dreamas þonne þis deade lif,
> Læne on londe.
>
> (*The Seafarer*, 64–6)

[So the joys of the Lord are more delightful to me than this dead and transitory life on land.]

Here 'land' enters into a new opposition, not with sea but with heaven; and the rest of the poem is devoted to amplifying this: on the one hand, the uncertainties and miseries of earthly life, on the other, eternal joys in a heavenly home. There is no reason to suspect here, as some scholars have done, the hand of a monkish reviser. The earth/heaven opposition is linked to what has gone before by more than a piece of word-play on 'land'. Yet this last part of the poem, despite fine things such as the description of bodily powers failing in old age, is undoubtedly inferior to what has gone before, partly because it has few of the graphic touches to be found in the sea passages, but mainly because the earth/heaven contrast, as presented here, lacks the complexity and richness of the earlier contrast between land and sea.

   Not that Anglo-Saxon religious poetry is always lacking in vividness or complexity. Indeed, the last poem to be considered in this section stands supreme in both respects. The peculiar boldness and brilliancy of *The Dream*

AN IVORY PANEL, perhaps part of the roof of a casket, carved around the year 1100. The two diving angels may have formed part of a Crucifixion scene. Ivory in this period came from whales or (as in this case) walrus, not elephants.

of the Rood derives in part from the fact that, unlike other Old English poems on biblical themes, it describes not the biblical event itself but a vision or dream in which that event, the Crucifixion, is both symbolically represented and narrated by a participant. The functions of both symbol and narrator are performed by the rood, Christ's Cross. This appears first to the dreamer as a visionary symbol of overpowering mystery and grandeur. It is a towering tree, at one moment covered in gold and jewels, at the next soaked in blood. The dreamer, himself lonely and depressed, can only prostrate himself before such supernatural strangeness: 'Syllic wæs se sigebeam, ond ic synnum fah' ('Wonderful was the tree of victory, and I stained with sins'). The opposition between the natural and the supernatural, expressed in the two contrasting halves of this alliterative line, seems unbridgeable; but then the Cross begins to address the dreamer, not as a wonderful *sigebeam* but as an ordinary tree which got involved long ago in events which passed its own comprehension. The Cross's narrative of the Crucifixion (passages from which were inscribed on the Ruthwell Cross) conveys even more forcefully than the earlier alternations of gold and blood the paradox of a death which is also a victory. Using the old language of heroic poetry, the Cross represents itself as the loyal follower of a lord who inexplicably wills his own death. In a normal battle such as that described in *The Battle of Maldon*, to obey your leader's command to 'stand fast' is to help defend his life; but for this follower, to stand fast is to serve his lord's absolute will for death by remaining rigidly upright:

'Geseah ic þa frean mancynnes
Efstan elne mycle þæt he me wolde on gestigan.
Þær ic þa ne dorste ofer dryhtnes word
Bugan oþþe berstan, þa ic bifian geseah
Eorþan sceatas. Ealle ic mihte
Feondas gefyllan, hwæþre ic fæste stod.'

(*The Dream of the Rood*, 33–8)

['Then I saw the lord of mankind hurrying with great eagerness, wishing to mount me. I did not dare to bend or break there against the lord's command, when I saw the earth's surface tremble. I could have felled all the enemies—yet I stood fast.']

Thus the Cross speaks for the bewildered humanity of the dreamer; but it also, in an entirely convincing conjunction, speaks for the suffering humanity of Christ: 'Þurhdrifan hi me mid deorcan næglum; on me syndon þa dolg gesiene' ('They drove me through with black nails; the wounds are still to be seen on me'). These words are spoken not by Christ but by the Cross. It is because the Cross so participates in Christ's suffering that it can also participate in his glory. After the Crucifixion it is first buried, like Christ, and then (in a reference to the finding of the true Cross by St Helena) raised up and honoured. The vision has come full circle back to the *sigebeam* or tree of victory of its opening; but now the dreamer can also hope to participate, as one ordinary tree has done, in that victory. The poem therefore ends in a mood of confidence which contrasts with the dreamer's prostration at the outset. He can bear solitude and the loss of friends on earth now that he sees the way open to a 'heavenly home'.

Old and Middle English Prose

The distinction between verse and prose is by no means always clear in either of the periods covered by this chapter. Anglo-Saxon scribes wrote prose and verse alike continuously to the margins of their parchment; and the metrical rules of alliterative verse (Middle as well as Old English) were such as to allow various half-measures to flourish in the no man's land between formal verse and plain prose. Yet the distinction is important to the literary historian. The study of Old and Middle English prose has lagged behind that of the poetry, and a considerable number of texts still remain unedited; but it may be possible one day to write a continuous and fairly comprehensive history of English medieval prose, such as could never be made out for the verse. Anglo-Saxon verse is the product of a tradition which, on the one hand, reached far back into pre-literate times and which, on the other, was challenged and eventually replaced after the Conquest by a quite different tradition; so the history of English poetry may be said to begin, awkwardly enough, with something more like an end than a beginning. By contrast, the earliest monuments of English prose, dating from the time of King Alfred, can claim to represent the true

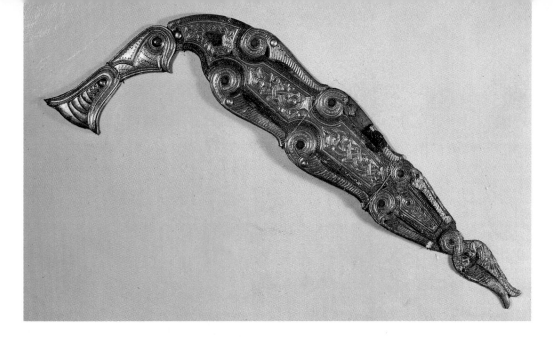

TWO SHIELD-MOUNTS FROM THE SUTTON HOO SHIP BURIAL. The funeral mound at Sutton Hoo, Suffolk, was probably that of King Raedwald of East Anglia (d. 624/5). Excavation in 1939 revealed many treasures, now to be seen in the British Museum, including the remains of a wooden shield. These two gilt-bronze mounts set with garnets were originally fitted on its leather-covered face to confront the enemy: (*above*) a winged dragon; (*below*) a bird of prey.

ye and noble prince excellent
My lord the prince my lord gracious
I humble servant and obedient
Unto your estate hye and glorious
Of whiche I am full tendir and full ielous
me recomaunde unto your worthynesse
with hert entier and spirite of mekenesse

beginnings of a tradition of written prose (and what is prose without writing?). This tradition, furthermore, can be traced, through however many turnings, in a continuous line thereafter. The scholar R. W. Chambers wrote boldly of 'the continuity of English prose from Alfred to More'. His arguments have been justly criticized for understating the new influence of French on Middle English prose; yet they contain an essential truth, as may be appreciated by anyone familiar with the King James Bible who will read the following words aloud in almost any pronunciation:

Ælc þara þe þas min word gehierþ and þa wyrcþ, biþ gelic þæm wisan were, se his hus ofer stan getimbrode. Þa com þær regen and micel flod, and þær bleowon windas, and ahruron on þæt hus, and hit na ne feoll; soþlice hit wæs ofer stan getimbrod.

This West-Saxon version of Matthew 7:24-5 was made in the late tenth century, nearly one thousand years ago; yet the sentences still go to a familiar tune.

But how many works are there, in the long and comparatively well-documented history of Old and Middle English prose, which can justly claim a place in a general history of English literature? The one kind of prose that is today universally admitted to the category of literature is prose fiction; and prose fiction is hardly to be found in the English Middle Ages. The Old English *Apollonius of Tyre* barely qualifies; nor do we find in Middle English any equivalent to the great prose compilation of Arthurian romances, the Vulgate Cycle, which occupies such a commanding position in medieval French literature—not, that is, until the work of Malory, which will be described in the following chapter. Nor, even if the chronicling of current events can count as literature, are there any English rivals to Joinville or Froissart. *The Anglo-Saxon Chronicle* is a remarkable document; but the more sophisticated historians and chroniclers of post-Conquest England wrote in Latin or French, not in English. Indeed the only work of secular prose before Malory's *Morte Darthur* which can claim a foothold in the canon of English literature is *Mandeville's Travels*—and that entertaining work is translated from the French. But with religious prose the picture is different. Works of religious instruction bulk much larger than any other type of writing in the prose corpus; and although most such writers are no more than competent at best, there are some who deserve to stand alongside Thomas More, Jeremy Taylor, and the rest. Of these I shall refer to Ælfric, Brian of Lingen, and the anonymous author of *The Cloud of Unknowing*.

The main tradition of vernacular prose makes a remarkably early start in England in the reign of King Alfred of Wessex (871-99), not only with *The Anglo-Saxon Chronicle*, but also with the group of translations made or inspired by the king himself for the instruction of his subjects, including versions of Bede's *Ecclesiastical History*, Augustine's *Soliloquies*, and Boethius's

POET AND PATRON. Thomas Hoccleve presents a copy of his *Regement of Princes* to the 'hye and noble prince excellent' Prince Hal, the future Henry V.

AN ANGLO-SAXON CHURCH TOWER, All Saints' Church, Earls Barton, Northants. The decorative stripwork is characteristic of the period. The battlements of the tower and the rest of the church belong to a later date.

De consolatione Philosophiae. However, the best of Anglo-Saxon prose was produced a century later in the age of the Monastic Revival of liturgy and learning, by the monks Wulfstan (d. 1023, best known for his *Sermon to the English*) and most notably Ælfric. Ælfric (*fl. c.*1000) spent his whole life in houses of the Benedictine order, rising in 1005 to be Abbot of Eynsham in Oxfordshire. He left a large body of vernacular writings, all devoted to the exposition of Christian faith and learning for English congregations and readers.

These include two sets of homilies known as the *Catholic Homilies*, completed in 992, and a set of Saints' Lives, completed about ten years later. Ælfric's work may be judged monastic in the most general sense, by virtue of its sober and self-abnegating (though not uncritical) concern for the propagation of orthodox belief and sound learning; but it also bears the specific impress of the great monastery at Winchester where Ælfric received his training, under one of the leaders of the English Monastic Revival, St Æthelwold. It is now believed that Winchester monks were chiefly responsible for developing that quite meticulously standardized form of written English known as Late West Saxon; and that development testifies to just the same diligent concern for correctness in vernacular writing which characterizes Ælfric's own work. Ælfric was himself a grammarian, for he wrote the first Latin grammar in English; and his own language is, as one eighteenth-century scholar put it, 'purus, suavis et regularis': 'pure, sweet, and well regulated'. The numerous manuscripts of his work bear witness to a process of authorial revision which extends to minutiae of vocabulary, grammar, and syntax; and it is typical of Ælfric, as it is of Chaucer, that he should have expressed concern lest his work be spoiled by careless copying: 'Now I beg and pray in God's name that, if anyone wishes to copy this book [the *Catholic Homilies*], he should follow his exemplar diligently, lest we be corrupted through negligent copying.'

The distinctive excellence of Ælfric's writing is both easy and difficult to illustrate: easy because almost any passage from his mature work will display his qualities, difficult because these qualities do not appear to advantage in short extracts. Here is one of his more elevated passages, from the *Lives of Saints*:

Hwæt þa, ure Hælend, þæs heofonlican Godes sunu, cydde his mycclan lufe þe he to us mannum hæfde, swa þæt he wearþ acenned of anum clænan mædene butan weres gemanan, and mann wearþ gesewen, on sawle and on lichaman soþ God and soþ man, to þy þæt he us alysde þa þe gelyfaþ on hine fram þam ecan deaþe mid his unscyldigan deaþe. Be þam we magon tocnawan Cristes eadmodnysse, þæt se healica God hine sylfne swa ge-eadmette þæt he þam deaþe underhnah and þone deofol oferswyþde mid þære menniscnysse, and mancynn swa alysde.

[So then our Saviour, son of the heavenly God, showed the great love which he had to us men, when he was born of a certain pure virgin without man's company, and was seen as a man, true God and true man in soul and in body, in order that he might release those of us who believe in him from the eternal death by his own guiltless death. By this we can understand the humility of Christ, in that the high God so humbled himself that he stooped to that death and overcame the Devil by that incarnation, and so released mankind.]

The mastery of sustained syntax in these sentences lends them an air of naturalness and ease. Yet, like most of Ælfric's mature work, this is in fact a highly artificial 'rhythmical prose', operating under metrical constraints similar to those of alliterative poetry, but looser. It consists, in fact, of a continuous series of two-stress phrases, linked together in pairs by alliteration much as are the two halves of the verse line. This pairing serves to point up the pervasive word-play, thus: 'þæt he þam deaþe *under*hnah / and þone deofol *ofer*swyþde // mid þære *menn*iscnysse / and *man*cynn swa alysde.' The linking of opposites in the first pairing (Christ gets the upper hand by lowering himself) and of similars in the second (Christ saves humanity by becoming human) both give felicitous expression to orthodox thoughts in a way entirely characteristic of this unobtrusive master, who was deservedly the first of the Anglo-Saxons to be printed, in 1567.

Turning to the first of the Middle English pieces, we find some significant differences. *Ancrene Wisse* belongs to a group of writings, also including the allegorical *Sawles Warde*, which were probably composed in the early thirteenth century at Wigmore Abbey, in that area of Norman England now known as Hereford and Worcester. This was the part of the country which most tenaciously preserved pre-Conquest traditions of prose and verse. There exist, for instance, manuscripts of Ælfric in which a thirteenth-century West Country-man, pleasingly known as 'the tremulous hand of Worcester', has glossed the difficult words. The fact that such glossing was necessary, however, itself shows how the Late West Saxon literary language had by this time become a thing of the past. The language of the *Ancrene Wisse* group already exhibits most of those simplifications in grammatical form and many of those changes in vocabulary (especially the introduction of French loan-words) which distinguish Middle from Old English. The best manuscripts of the group do indeed exhibit a consistency in forms characteristic of a written standard, regulated like Ælfric's; but this Wigmore English, unlike the earlier Winchester English, seems never to have achieved more than local currency. In this it is typical of the Middle English period, when, up until the fifteenth century, linguistic diversity and local use are the order of the day.

Comparison between Ælfric's homilies and *Ancrene Wisse* also serves to illustrate another difference between Old and Middle English writings. *Ancrene Wisse* ('The Anchoresses' Rule') is a treatise for female recluses, offering regulations for their daily life and also more general advice on resisting temptation, making confession, and the like. The book became widely popular, and was even translated into French and Latin; but modern research suggests that it was written by a canon of Wigmore Abbey, perhaps called Brian of Lingen, for certain anchoresses of his acquaintance living within a very few miles of Wigmore. This origin helps to account for the familiarity and colloquial ease of the book's manner, in comparison with which Ælfric appears very formal and impersonal. No doubt the difference also reflects changes in religious sensibility between 1000 and 1200, general changes which favoured personal devotions and spiritual friendships between individual devotees, as against the more communal and liturgical spirituality of the older Benedictines. Yet it is also true that readers who turn, as we are now doing, from Old to Middle

English literature find themselves in a world where prose-writers and poets alike do address their audience in a more familiar fashion and in a style much more hospitable to colloquial and proverbial idiom. The available sample of Anglo-Saxon work is no doubt heavily biased in this respect as in others, given the circumstance of its survival mostly in rather grand monastic copies; but it does represent a period when English writing evidently enjoyed, in some circles at least, a dignity and esteem which Chaucer and his successors were to regain only slowly towards the end of the Middle English period. In the intervening centuries the English language, always in unequal competition with Latin as the language of the learned, faced the added competition of French as the language of the powerful and the polite. The West-Saxon King Alfred was an author and sponsor of writings in English; but the Angevin King Henry II (reigned 1154–89) bestowed his patronage, so far as we know, exclusively on writers in French and Latin. The English literature of about this time frankly addresses itself to persons of less consequence—including often, as in the case of *Ancrene Wisse*, women.

The author of *Ancrene Wisse* was a scholar and a rhetorician; but his English, even at its more elevated, is lively and idiomatic, in the best Middle English manner:

For hwet makeþ us stronge forte drehe derf i Godes servise ant ine fondunges to wreastli stealewurþliche toyein þe deofles swenges, bute hope of heh mede? Hope halt te heorte hal, hwetse þe flesch drehe; as me seiþ, 'Yef hope nere, heorte tobreke'. A Jesu, þin are! Hu stont ham þe beoþ þer as alle wa ant weane is wiþuten hope of utcume, ant heorte ne mei bersten?

[For what is it that makes us strong to suffer hardship in God's service and to wrestle valiantly in times of temptation against the Devil's assaults, but the hope of a high reward? Hope keeps the heart in health, whatever the flesh suffers; as they say, 'If hope were not, heart would break'. But Jesu, mercy! How stands it with those who are in the place of all grief and misery with no hope of escape, and yet heart cannot burst?]

Here the proverbial 'If hope were not, heart would break' takes its place without incongruity in a context of rhetorical questions and high alliterative ornament. It provides the second of three couplings of *hope* with *heart* and prepares for the marvellous third, where the breaking of the heart, treated in the proverb as the feared consequence of loss of hope, becomes in hell something to be hoped for, and hoped for in vain. Heart *cannot* burst. The verb here is just a little stronger than the earlier 'break', carrying an added suggestion of intolerable pressure from within. This is one of many examples that could be given of the author's ability to convey physical sensation in a word.

The same ability is to be found, rather more surprisingly, in the mystical treatise, *The Cloud of Unknowing*. The unknown author of this work, evidently a contemporary of Chaucer, belongs to a remarkable group of late Middle English mystical writers which also includes Richard Rolle (d. 1349), Walter Hilton (author of *The Scale of Perfection*, d. 1396), and Julian of Norwich (b. 1342). Of all their works, *The Cloud* is the most esoteric, in so far as it is concerned exclusively with that advanced stage of contemplation which lies beyond devout meditations of the life of Christ, and indeed beyond all human knowledge. God himself is hidden in an eternal cloud of 'unknowing', which can only be pierced by 'a loving stirring and a blind beholding unto the naked being of God'. This 'blind beholding' of a being who cannot be known is the supreme act of the contemplative, to be achieved only by special grace; but he or she can prepare for such moments by the discipline of the *via negativa* or road of negation, which requires the blotting out of all creaturely images and categories in a 'cloud of forgetting'. Yet this demanding programme is expounded in a language which teems with creaturely images, for the author's insistence on the utter transcendence of divinity by no means involves any denial of the physicality of the created world. On the contrary, trying to be 'spiritual' in the things of this world involves essentially the same mistake as trying to conceive the spiritual in creaturely terms: both end up in the same fantastic, twilit half-way house, neither truly physical nor truly spiritual, against which the author utters many warnings. He addresses his book to a spiritual friend who, at the age of twenty-four, is embarking on the life of the solitary; and it is his unremitting effort to alert this young man to the dangers of misdirected effort ('crooked intent') and false spirituality which provides the drama of the work. In a familiar and often conversational manner, he labours to anticipate and avert the many misunderstandings to which any human being (himself included) will be exposed in such an enterprise. In the following passage, for instance, he warns against the seductively spiritual-seeming imagery of 'inwardness'. Other people, he says, might advise you to turn your attention inwards and worship God there:

Bot thus wil I bid thee. Loke on no wyse that thou be withinne thiself, and schortly withoutyn thiself wil I not that thou be, ne yit aboven, ne behynde, ne on o syde, ne on other. 'Wher than,' seist thou, 'schal I be? Nowhere, by thi tale!' Now trewely thou seist wel; for there wolde I have thee.

The simple vernacular sequence 'nowhere? . . . yes, *there*' makes the author's point with an immediacy that is characteristic of Middle English prose at its best.

Middle English Poetry

The circumstances of writers in the English vernacular changed greatly in the years after the Norman Conquest. The collapse of the written standard established by West-Saxon monks and the exclusion of English writings from

A MEDIEVAL POET AT WORK,
from a manuscript of Laȝamon's
Brut: 'There was a priest in the land,
called Laȝamon ... He took feathers
in his fingers and applied them to
book-skin.'

the main centres of power and patronage were both developments characteristic
of a period when native traditions lost much of the status which they had
enjoyed under Anglo-Saxon kings and were to recover later. By comparison
with the tenth or fourteenth centuries, in fact, the intervening period is one
in which English poetry and prose appear to have flourished mainly towards
the margins of society—in the remoter counties, or among the humbler classes.
One of the two poems which must here represent this Early Middle English
period, Laȝamon's *Brut*, illustrates clearly the relative marginality of English
in the cosmopolitan 'Channel Kingdom' of the Normans and Angevins. Geoffrey
of Monmouth wrote a Latin *History of the Kings of Britain* in the 1130s and
dedicated it to the Norman earl Robert of Gloucester, bastard son of Henry I.
The work quickly achieved popularity and was translated into French octosyllabic couplets by one of Henry II's Jersey subjects, Wace, and presented by
him (according to Laȝamon) to Henry's French queen, Eleanor of Aquitaine.
The English *Brut*, by contrast, is dedicated to no patron. Its author, Laȝamon
(*fl.* late twelfth century), was a simple priest in the remote parish of Areley
Kings, on the banks of the Severn. He made his version of Wace, about the
year 1200, in the English of his Worcestershire parish. His work survives in
only two manuscripts—as against the 20 manuscripts of Wace and the 190 of
Geoffrey.

Yet Laȝamon's *Brut* is far from being a mere slavish provincial imitation.
The English poet writes a long line of two balanced halves. Where these halves
are linked by rhyme or assonance, the effect sometimes approaches that of
Wace's couplets: 'Ærneþ ævere vorþ and vorþ; Hengest is ifaren norþ' ('Hurry
as fast as you can; Hengest has gone north'). But Laȝamon's basic rhythmical
unit is the two-stress phrase; and where these are linked together not by rhyme
but by alliteration, as they often are, the result unmistakably recalls the manner
of Anglo-Saxon poetry. The history of alliterative verse after the Conquest is

obscure. Laȝamon's Worcestershire probably still had a living tradition of alliterative composition, and the poet may also have found older models in a library such as that of Worcester Cathedral; but whatever he knew, and however he knew it, it must at any rate have included something not unlike the Anglo-Saxon poetry known to us. His battle scenes in particular recall that poetry, not only in the actual fighting ('heowen hardliche, hælmes gullen': 'thěy strike hard, helms clang') but also in the heroic speeches of resolution and scornful defiance which precede and follow the fighting. Thus the greatest of the kings of Britain, Arthur, sends a taunting message to the Romans after killing their emperor in which he speaks ironically of having now paid them the 'gavel' or tribute that they demanded, just as Byrhtnoth did two hundred years before when addressing the Viking messenger in *The Battle of Maldon*.

Laȝamon is an uneven writer, and his poem belongs to a type unattractive to present-day readers. The *Brut* is a long verse chronicle, following the line of British kings from its foundation by Brutus to its final defeat by the Saxons. Undoubtedly the most interesting part is the long account of King Arthur's reign, which occupies more than a quarter of Laȝamon's 16,000 lines. Here Arthur appears for the first time in English. Following the quasi-historical tradition established by Geoffrey of Monmouth, Laȝamon portrays Arthur as a conqueror, whose triumphs over foreign powers are brought to an end only by the treachery of his nephew Modred. The adventures of the Knights of the Round Table, as described by the French poet Chrétien de Troyes and his successors, are not Laȝamon's concern. The fictitious succession of victories over Saxon, Scot, Irish, Scandinavian, French, and Roman lacks variety as well as credibility; but it inspires Laȝamon to some of his best writing. Here, for instance, he describes how Arthur imagines his defeated enemy, the Saxon Baldulf, looking down at the corpses of his men which lie in the river Avon:

> 'Nu he stant on hulle ond Avene bihaldeþ
> Hu ligeþ i þan stræme stelene fisces
> Mid sweorde bigeorede; heore sund is awemmed.
> Heore scalen wleoteþ swulc gold-fage sceldes,
> Þer fleoteþ heore spiten swulc hit spæren weoren.'

['Now he stands on a hill and looks into the Avon, seeing how there lie in that stream steel fishes girt with swords; their swimming is at an end. Their scales gleam like gold-plated shields, their fish-spines float as if they were spears.']

Here, as often happens in heroic verse, the warrior's scorn for his adversaries finds expression in grotesque and extravagant imagery: 'steel fishes girt with swords'. Instead of comparing the soldiers to fish, Arthur treats them as though they were indeed fish and compares them with soldiers: 'their scales gleam like gold-plated shields'. The passage has no parallel in Wace. It displays an imaginative violence which is almost as remote from twelfth-century France as it is from twentieth-century England.

AN OWL MOBBED BY SMALL BIRDS. A roof boss in Sherborne Abbey. Other Sherborne bosses represent a mermaid, a pelican, St Michael killing the dragon, and a crossbowman shooting at another man's rump.

The Owl and the Nightingale, probably composed about 1200, like the *Brut*, is a poem of a quite different sort. It belongs to the genre of debate or *conflictus*, much practised by medieval Latin poets and their vernacular followers. As is customary in such works, the two disputants, an owl and a nightingale, represent diametrically opposed positions, and they use every possible argument to attack each other and defend themselves. The two birds agree only in admiring the man who is to judge between them, Nicholas of Guildford, and in deploring the fact that such a wise and good cleric should be condemned to waste his talents in an obscure Dorset parish. If Nicholas wrote the poem himself, as seems likely, then it can be read as a witty and roundabout plea for preferment, addressed to some bishop who could be trusted to enjoy it. Certainly the poem is a sophisticated and cosmopolitan piece. Unlike his Worcestershire contemporary, the Surrey poet employs the French octosyllabic couplet (very well handled), and he draws on a variety of French and Latin sources, including the fashionable poetess, Marie de France. The debate itself touches on a number of serious topics, such as the nature of divine worship; but it touches on them lightly. The balance of advantage shifts to and fro, amusingly, between the owlish owl and the amorous nightingale, as they think up ingenious arguments in their own defence and rude things to say about each other; and it is hard to know what one is meant to expect when, at the very end of the poem, the birds fly off to Portesham to receive Nicholas's judgement:

> Ah hu heo spedde of heore dome
> Ne can ich eu na more telle.
> Her nis na more of þis spelle.

[But how they fared in their judgement I cannot tell you any more. Here is no more of this story.]

The Owl and the Nightingale is, in fact, a comic poem—one of the first in English—and the wealth of bird-lore and human experience which it displays may be taken as testifying to that mature and impartial 'wisdome' which the birds both acknowledge in the man who was probably its author.

In the writings of Laȝamon and Nicholas of Guildford one can see for the first time England itself emerging as a subject of English poetry. There is very little sense of specific place in Anglo-Saxon poetry: *Beowulf* is set in the Baltic kingdoms, *The Ruin* describes Bath (if that is what it does) in a generalizing style, and the local topography of *The Battle of Maldon* is minimal. By contrast, *The Owl and the Nightingale* evokes an English countryside which is already recognizably that of Samuel Palmer and Rudyard Kipling. The debate is set in a secluded corner of a field in a 'summer valley', where the owl is perched on an ivy-clad tree-stump and the nightingale in a flowering hedge. The perches are none the less vividly imagined for being symbolically apt:

> Þe nightingale bigon þe speche
> In one hurne of one breche,
> And sat up one vaire boghe—
> Þar were abute blosme inoghe—
> In ore vaste þicke hegge
> Imeind mid spire and grene segge.

[The nightingale began the exchanges in the corner of a fallow field. She sat upon a beautiful bough, surrounded by masses of blossom, in an impenetrably thick hedge intertwined with reeds and green sedge.]

There is nothing like this lush southern landscape in the *Brut*. Laȝamon does not so much describe Britain as mythologize it, following Geoffrey of Monmouth. He tells how Stonehenge was built by the magic powers of Merlin, how London was founded by King Lud, how Cornwall took its name from the Trojan Corineus who killed the giant Geomagog, and many other similar toponymic fancies. False etymology helped Geoffrey, and Laȝamon after him, to imagine a legendary Britain, whose towns and rivers and hills were to recall, for poets as late as Spenser, Milton, and Pope, stories of the heroic past. Leicester recalls King Leir and his three daughters, the river Humber recalls the evil King Humber who drowned in its waters, and Britain itself recalls its Trojan founder, Brutus.

The trilingual literary culture to which Laȝamon and Nicholas belonged survived them by several generations. More than a hundred years later, in the 1330s, a great anthology of prose and verse made in Herefordshire, MS Harley 2253 in the British Library, includes French alongside Latin and English. The English contents of this book provide a sample of native poetry as it was towards the eve of its finest medieval flowering later in the fourteenth century.

For the first time in this survey we encounter here short poems which may without incongruity be called 'lyrics'. Some are poems of romantic passion, such as is expressed in the haunting refrain of 'Blow, Northern Wind':

> Blow, northerne wynd,
> Send thou me my swetyng!
> Blow, northerne wynd,
> Blow, blow, blow.

These 'Harley lyrics' also include religious poems, and poems on moral and political subjects. Indeed, the only English narrative poem of any note in the collection is *King Horn*, a story of love and adventure which may be taken to represent that very loosely defined genre of romance, originating in continental and insular French writings of the twelfth century, which by this time had been thoroughly naturalized. Another huge manuscript anthology contemporary with the Harley manuscript, the Auchinleck manuscript, provides a much more generous sample of the secular narrative verse of the time. It includes the two very popular English romances referred to by Chaucer in his 'Tale of Sir Thopas', *Guy of Warwick* and *Bevis of Hampton*, the fairy lay of Sir Orfeo, the polished historical romance *Kyng Alisaunder*, and much else besides. Yet it may be doubted whether even a reader of the Auchinleck collection could have anticipated the developments which were to occur in English poetry in the later years of Edward III (reigned 1327-77) and especially in the reign of his successor Richard II (1377-99). This is the remarkable 'Ricardian' period, in which, in the lifetime of Geoffrey Chaucer and John Gower, alliterative poetry flowered again in England.

The term 'Alliterative Revival' is commonly used to denote a body of mainly unrhymed alliterative verse, much of it composed to the north and west of a line running from the Wash to the Severn Estuary, which survives from the period beginning about 1350 and ending in the earlier part of the fifteenth century. This very large body of work, which is many times greater than the whole surviving corpus of Anglo-Saxon alliterative verse, includes many notable poems, among them *Winner and Waster* and *Piers Plowman*, *Sir Gawain and the Green Knight* and the alliterative *Morte Arthure*, *Pearl* and *Patience*, *St Erkenwald*, and *The Wars of Alexander*. The sheer contrast in quantity between this and the scanty remains of alliterative verse from the previous three centuries no doubt owes much to two quite general developments. The accelerating decline of French in the England of Edward III meant that readers and listeners whose tastes might previously have been satisfied by writings in that language were now increasingly turning to English. So the audience, and the market, for English poetry grew significantly both in numbers and in importance. The same period also sees a continuing increase in literacy; and the consequent development towards what is almost the mass production of manuscript copies means that poems stand a progressively better chance of surviving into modern

A PAGE OF MIDDLE ENGLISH VERSE, beginning 'To selle so precyous a prynce for penyes so fewe'. Whereas Anglo-Saxon scribes used a slow and formal script (see p. 2), late-medieval scribes wrote fast to satisfy the much increased demand for reading-matter. Hence their characteristic joined-up, 'cursive' script.

times. Yet these general changes, which between them go a long way towards explaining why there is simply so much *more* English literature of all sorts in this late medieval period, cannot completely account for the very sudden florescence of alliterative writings after 1350.

The word 'Revival' implies a deliberate and perhaps concerted effort to compose poems in a manner recently neglected but known to have been practised in the more distant past. If such an effort was ever made, we do not know by whom. Indeed, the whole question of the relation of fourteenth-century alliterative verse to what had gone before remains obscure. Alliteration itself is a pervasive feature of earlier Middle English writings, prose as well as verse; and not infrequently, as in Laȝamon's *Brut*, it is found in conjunction with the two-stress rhythm characteristic of the Old English half-line. But the poems of the Revival, surprisingly, approach nearer than Laȝamon to the classical Old English type in two important respects: they do not allow rhyme as an alternative or supplementary way of linking the two half-lines; and they generally observe the ancient ban on alliteration in the last stressed syllable of the line. Their most common pattern of alliteration is a a a x, thus:

> Ner sláyn wyth þe sléte he sléped in his ýrnes
> Mo nýghtes þen innóghe in náked rókkes
> Þeras cláterande fro þe crést þe cólde borne rénnes.
>
> (*Sir Gawain*, 729-31)

These technical resemblances, together with similarities of diction and phrasing, make it probable that the poets of the Revival inherited more of the pre-Conquest tradition than materials surviving from the years between would suggest—whether through writings which no longer survive, or through oral tradition, or a mixture of both.

In other ways, too, the Alliterative Revival is an obscure and tantalizing moment in the history of English literature. Almost everything that can be known about the authors, their circumstances, and their readers has to be inferred, more or less securely, from the texts themselves and the manuscripts (often only one) in which they survive. A case in point is the manuscript, copied in about 1400, which preserves the only surviving texts of *Cleanness*, *Patience*, *Pearl*, and *Sir Gawain and the Green Knight*. These four poems were all composed in the same dialect, located by philologists in north-west Staffordshire or south-east Cheshire; and many readers believe that they are the work of a single author—a not unreasonable conviction, given the presence of many common thematic, structural, and verbal features. But attempts to identify this '*Gawain*-poet' have not succeeded, and nothing is known about the circumstances in which he wrote. Where and what was his audience? Is it to be looked for in the area to which his own dialect belongs? Such questions may one day be answered; but in the mean time one can only say that the poetry implies an author, and probably also an audience, of more than provincial culture and learning, acquainted with a quite wide range of Latin and French writings, including such modern European classics as the prose *Lancelot* and the *Roman de la Rose*.

Whoever he was, the *Gawain*-poet ranks as one of the most brilliant representatives of that remarkable generation of English poets which may be called 'Ricardian' (after Richard II, who reigned from 1377 to 1399). His chief contemporaries were Gower, Langland, and Chaucer. With the exception of Chaucer and Gower, these writers were not, so far as we know, aware of each other's work, and they therefore cannot be said to form a true 'school'. But their poetry has certain features in common. Like so much medieval poetry, it is concerned first and foremost with narrative; but it is distinguished from earlier English narrative verse by a greater sophistication of technique and by a more articulate concern with the thematic point of stories—a moral or theological significance, often quite explicitly stated. Certainly these Ricardian poets were not too sophisticated to engage whole-heartedly in the business of story-telling (a function which in more recent times verse has largely yielded up to the novel, drama, film, and television); but their stories are controlled and directed by that kind of clear thinking about moral and religious matters which was the legacy, for educated men in the later fourteenth century, of the strenuous moral philosophy and scholastic theology of the previous two hundred years.

A perfect, though minor, example of this art is the *Gawain*-poet's *Patience*. Unlike his *Cleanness*, which labours with only imperfect success to organize several disparate Bible stories into a continuous demonstration of its moral theme, *Patience* takes a single biblical episode, of Jonah and the whale, for its narrative subject. The art of re-imagining Bible stories and retelling them in amplified form is an ancient one, going back in England to the Anglo-Saxon versions of stories from Genesis, Exodus, and other books of the Bible. Indeed, the first English poet whose name is known, Cædmon, did just this, according to Bede: having learned and pondered a scriptural story, he 'converted it into the sweetest poetry'. Seven centuries later the *Gawain*-poet does the same, converting the story of Jonah, laconically told in the Bible, into a vivid, lively, and humorous verse narrative. After the great storm at sea, for instance, Jonah is dropped overboard and falls into the whale's mouth 'as mote in at a munster dor, so mukel wern his chawles': 'like a speck of dust going into a cathedral door, his jaws were so huge': The comic shrinkage of Jonah in this simile is in keeping with the treatment of him throughout as a type of petty impatience, contrasted with the majestic long-suffering of God, both towards him and towards the Ninevites. The whole story is retold as an example or *exemplum* of the virtue which gives the poem its (modern) title and of that virtue's opposite, exemplified by Jonah. Such a formal and explicit subordination of story to theme occurs often in Ricardian poetry. The use of *exempla* was a favourite didactic device of the medieval Church in pulpit and confessional, as Chaucer's 'Pardoner's Tale' and Gower's *Confessio Amantis* both indicate; but those two poems also show how variously the poets could turn the device to their own purposes. *Patience* is more simply and seriously didactic than either; but a reader prepared to take a sympathetic interest in such a largely neglected moral idea as patience will find that this poem, like Langland's treatment in *Piers Plowman* and more than Chaucer's in 'The Clerk's Tale', can expand and enrich his sense of it, as it was no doubt intended to do. One may notice, for instance, how the narrative associates Jonah's inability to accept God's commands in patience with his inability to tell the truth, even to himself.

Pearl is in many ways very different from *Patience*. Like several poems of the period, including Chaucer's *Book of the Duchess* and *House of Fame* and Langland's *Piers Plowman*, it is a dream-poem; and the author therefore enjoys the freedom, allowed to dream-poets but otherwise rare enough at the time, to construct his own story rather than deriving it from old books. *Pearl* describes how the narrator, in his other-worldly vision, encounters a damsel who, like Beatrice in Dante's *Divine Comedy*, sets out to explain the mysteries of Paradise. The damsel, Pearl, reveals that she is the dreamer's daughter, who died in infancy and is now one of the brides of the Lamb. It is likely, though not certain, that the poem refers to an actual loss suffered by its author; and one may see in its extreme formal complexity, combining alliteration with rhyme in stanzas themselves linked together by repeated words into groups of five, something analogous to the painful intricacy of the funerary monuments of the time (see next page). Yet whatever his personal involvement may have been, this poet is also deeply interested in general truth. The case of Pearl, like that of Jonah, has a wider bearing. *Pearl* is concerned with the theology of salvation: What heavenly rewards are enjoyed by those who die as infants after baptism? The poet addresses himself seriously to this somewhat controversial question, recalling the relevant biblical passages—the Parable of the Vineyard and St John's vision of the New Jerusalem—and reasoning from them in the approved fashion. The result, even if one denies the autobiographical nature of the case, is far from frigid. The dialogue between the damsel, who, like Beatrice, has perfect knowledge as a blessed spirit, and the dreamer, who does not, is rich in the comedy and pathos of human incomprehension. How can Pearl be a queen of heaven? the dreamer asks. Is not Mary queen of heaven? Pearl explains, but the dreamer never really understands; and the dream ends as, in a final act of incomprehension, he tries to cross the stream which separates him from his daughter as if it were ordinary water.

The chronology of the works of the *Gawain*-poet is impossible to fix; but it is tempting to suppose that *Sir Gawain and the Green Knight* may be the last of them, for here the moral theme (if it can be called anything so definite) is not so much stated as suggested, most subtly and artfully, in a story of

A LATE-MEDIEVAL TOMB, with the alabaster effigy of Alice Chaucer (d. 1475), granddaughter of the poet, who married the duke of Suffolk.

incomparable richness and verve. The poem opens by introducing Arthur as the greatest of the line of British kings descended from Brutus; but this is not to be a sprawling chronicle-poem in the manner of Laȝamon's *Brut*. It belongs rather to that species of Arthurian writing ('lay', the author calls it) which picks out a single adventure from among the annals of the Round Table. In this case, it is the Adventure of the Green Chapel, undertaken by Sir Gawain in response to the challenge of the Green Knight, who rides into the hall at Camelot and offers his green head to be struck off on the sole condition that he may strike a return blow (if he survives) at the Green Chapel in a year's time. There is more to this outlandish affair than meets the eye, as the poet gradually reveals; but the restriction to a single adventure and a single year allows him a fullness and delicacy of narrative detail matched only in his day by Chaucer's *Troilus and Criseyde*. Does any other romance writer, for instance, show what it might actually feel like to wake up on the morning of a perilous tryst, as Gawain does on the stormy New Year's Day when he is due at the Green Chapel to receive the return blow?

> Now neghes þe Nw Yere and þe nyght passes.
> Þe day dryves to þe derk, as Dryghtyn biddes,
> Bot wylde wederes of þe worlde wakned þeroute.
> Clowdes kesten kenly þe colde to þe erþe,
> Wyth nye innoghe of þe norþe þe naked to tene;
> Þe snawe snitered ful snart, þat snayped þe wylde;
> Þe werbelande wynde wapped fro þe hyghe
> And drof uche dale ful of dryftes ful grete.
> Þe leude lystened ful wel, þat ley in his bedde—
> Þagh he lowkes his liddes ful lyttel he slepes;
> Bi uch kok þat crue he knwe wel þe steven.
> Deliverly he dressed up er þe day sprenged,
> For þere was lyght of a laumpe þat lemed in his chambre.

(Sir Gawain, 1998–2010)

[Now the New Year approaches and the night passes. Day comes upon the dark, as the Lord commands, but wild weather was blowing up out of doors. Clouds dropped bitter cold on the earth, with enough of a sharp north wind to hurt the unprotected flesh; snow fell fast, stinging the wild beasts; and a whistling wind swept down from the high ground, filling every valley full of deep drifts. The man listened hard, as he lay in his bed—for though he shut his eyes tight, he did not sleep much; every time the cock crew, he recognized the appointed day. He got up promptly before daybreak, for he had the light of a lamp that shone in his chamber.]

If it seems that the heroic resolution of the knight (he gets up 'deliverly', promptly and briskly) coexists somewhat uneasily with the sleepless apprehension so vividly evoked in these lines, that is no more than the deeper significance of the case requires. For in this Arthurian romance as in no other, knightly courage is exposed to something like the full strength of those forces which turn most people into cowards—and is shaken by the impact.

Gawain's integrity and honour, symbolized by his heraldic device of a pentangle, are at stake in the Adventure of the Green Chapel, and what chiefly threatens to impair them is fear of the Green Knight's axe. By arriving at the Chapel on time and submitting to the return blow, Gawain fulfils his part in the original contract and so vindicates the honour of the Round Table, challenged by the Green Knight at Camelot; but in the mean time he has pledged his word a second time on his own account, and in this second contract his good faith or *trawthe* has failed him. Staying over Christmas with a genial local lord (his adversary, unrecognized), he enters into an agreement to 'exchange winnings' at the end of each of three days; and on the last of these days he conceals from his host a green belt which has been given to him in secret by his hostess with the assurance that its magic powers can save his life. It is therefore the hero's fear of imminent death which leads him to commit his one act of cowardly *untrawthe*—a dishonourable act for which, once he understands it, Gawain reproaches himself with a ferocity of shame and remorse which takes most readers by surprise. His mortified return to a rejoicing Camelot brings the poem to a somewhat unsettled conclusion. Certainly the poet does not dissociate himself from the closing celebration at Camelot of Gawain's heroic courage and integrity. Yet it cannot be a small thing for a knight to yield to fear and break his pledged word: how could Gawain not be ashamed of that? This double view of the case is at last symbolized and fixed in the emblem of the green belt, worn henceforth by Gawain as a 'token of untruth' and a mark of shame, but adopted by the Round Table as a new badge of honour. Thus the story offers, not like *Patience* quite clearly contrasted positive and negative examples of its moral theme, but a single dubious example, in which are to be seen at one and the same time both the weakness and the strength of human nature at its best.

No other alliterative poet can match the *Gawain*-poet in his ability to meet the demands of both story and theme, sacrificing neither intellectual lucidity nor narrative richness. *The Wars of Alexander* and the alliterative *Morte Arthure* are fine and vigorous narrative poems; but in both the extended chronicling of feats of arms makes it difficult for the poet to develop his ideas. Other alliterative poets favour ideas at the expense of story. One of the best examples is *Winner and Waster*, a remarkable allegorical dream-poem probably dating from the 1350s. Here as in *The Owl and the Nightingale* two diametrically opposed adversaries engage in lively but inconclusive debate. Through the mutual recriminations of prudent Winner and big-spending Waster, the anonymous poet presents a vision of English social and economic life which anticipates, in its vivid detail and trenchant observation, the poetry of Ben Jonson more than two centuries later. But *Winner and Waster* must yield place, in a survey such as this, to the greatest and most comprehensive of its successors: Langland's *Piers Plowman*.

William Langland was a minor cleric with connections in Oxfordshire and

THE TOMB AND EFFIGY OF THE BLACK
PRINCE, d. 1376 (*above*), in Canterbury
Cathedral. In the French verses carved round
the tomb, the prince addresses passers-by:
'Such as you are, I was once; such as I am,
you will be.'

THE BLACK PRINCE'S SHIELD (*left*), hung
above his tomb together with his gauntlets,
surcoat, and scabbard. The shield is of wood.
His coat of arms declares, by quartering
English leopards with French lilies, the family
claim to the throne of France.

Worcestershire who came up to London and at one time lived with his wife, according to his own account, in a cottage in Cornhill—not many hundred yards from Geoffrey Chaucer's more comfortable accommodation over Aldgate. Langland's representation of himself as an awkward character, gaunt, poorly dressed, and 'loath to reverence lords and ladies', no doubt owes something to the literary tradition of the satirist as uncompromising outsider or bitter fool; but his life on the fringes of the London Church, earning his bread as a kind of clerical odd job man saying prayers on commission, did make him acquainted with impoverished and irregular people such as find no place in Chaucer's work, not even *The Canterbury Tales*. So far as is known, Langland wrote only one poem; but the varying states of *Piers Plowman* in the manuscripts suggest that he could never leave it alone. Modern scholars have distinguished three main versions: the unfinished A Text composed in the 1360s, the much longer B Text completed towards the end of the 1370s, and the incomplete C revision known to one unfortunate reader who was beheaded in 1388. The differences between these versions are substantial, and some scholars still believe that more than one poet had a hand in them; but most now accept that they represent the developing thought and art of a single, and a very remarkable, poet.

Considered from almost any point of view, indeed, *Piers Plowman* is a singular creation. It is an alliterative poem unlike any other in that it survives in more than fifty manuscripts, and a dream-poem unlike any other in that it consists of a long series of dreams (ten in the B Text) linked by short waking interludes. As an allegorical poem, too, it is peculiar, especially in the conduct of its action. Most allegories tell a single story, however long drawn out, and arrive at a foreseeable conclusion, as do the *Roman de la Rose* and *Pilgrim's Progress*. But in Langland's poem each of the dreams has its own narrative structure. The dreamer, Long Will, is the same in each case; but Will makes no steady progress in spiritual awareness, such as might have been looked for to provide some narrative unity for the whole. The poem's titular hero is Piers the Plowman; but he puts in only sporadic appearances at unpredictable moments: ' "Peter!" quod a plowman, and putte forth his hed.' Indeed, in the mysterious abruptness of his arrivals and in his equally mysterious departures, Piers represents the poem's narrative method at its most characteristically disrupted. These disruptions serve to express Langland's deepest sense of the elusiveness of that inner goodness and truth for which Piers himself stands.

The search for these qualities, continually frustrated and continually renewed, persists throughout the poem as a kind of pilgrimage. In the first phase of this search (the 'Visio', Prologue and Passus I–VII in the B Text), Will has two dreams of how contemporary England might be reformed, in the administration of justice and in the conduct of all classes of society, by living and acting 'truly' in accordance with the dictates of reason and conscience. But this ideal of conduct, which comes to be called 'Do Well', presents many difficulties, both because human nature is deeply perverse and also because the ideal itself seems difficult to grasp. In the second phase of the poem (Passus VIII–XIV) these problems are explored. Long Will sets out in search of Do Well. His experiences in the course of the search serve to expose the intellectual puzzles which arise when one tries to understand God's plan of salvation, and also the difficulty of submitting in patience to the apparent injustices of life. As this theme of patience modulates into that of charity, the poem enters its third and final phase (Passus XV–XX). This is primarily concerned with the history of man's salvation, and especially with God's supreme act of charity in Christ. The life of Christ, culminating in the Harrowing of Hell and the founding of the Church, leads on to the prolonged anticlimax of the last two passus. Here the charismatic beginnings of the Church under St Peter, with whom Piers now comes to be identified, are painfully contrasted with its present corrupt condition. The poems ends as it began, with a bleak view of fourteenth-century realities.

But to see *Piers Plowman* in this way one has to stand back from it so far that many of its most characteristic features are lost. Langland does not distinguish between social, moral, intellectual, and theological issues in the way that my summary suggests. For him, the Church and society are ideally coterminous; both depend for their health upon the condition of individuals; and for the individual, intellectual and moral 'truth' are inseparable. This comprehensive, though far from untroubled, vision of the world finds expression, in Langland's best passages, in a poetry which is at once sublime and ridiculous—ridiculous, that is, in its accommodation of the most commonplace images and unelevated thoughts. Here, for instance, is Lady Holy Church speaking in praise of the power of love:

> For Truþe telleþ þat love is triacle of hevene:
> May no synne be on hym seene þat þat spice useþ.
> And alle his werkes he wroughte with love as hym liste,
> And lered it Moyses for þe leveste þyng and moost lik to hevene,
> And also the plante of pees, moost precious of vertues:
> For hevene myghte nat holden it, it was so hevy of hymself,
> Til it hadde of þe erþe eten his fille;
> And whan it hadde of þis fold flessh and blood taken,
> Was nevere leef upon lynde lighter þerafter,
> And portatif and persaunt as þe point of a nedle,
> That myghte noon armure it lette ne none heighe walles.
> Forþi is love ledere of þe lordes folk of hevene,
> And a meene, as þe mair is, betwene þe kyng and þe commune.

> (B Text, I. 148–60)

[*triacle* medicine; *spice* remedy; *lered* taught; *leveste* dearest; *fold* earth; *lynde* linden tree; *portatif and persaunt* light and piercing; *lette* stop; *meene* intermediary]

In this passage the sublime paradox of a love which falls from heaven by its

A FOURTEENTH-CENTURY CHAMBER, Longthorpe Tower, Northants. The painting immediately above the fireplace shows a crowned figure (Reason?) controlling a wheel on which the five senses are represented by appropriate creatures: hearing *upper right* (a boar with pricked ears), sight *lower right* (a bird with a large eye), taste *lower left* (a monkey eating), smell *centre left* (a vulture), touch *upper left* (a spider in its web). Compare the ninth-century brooch, p. 6.

own weight and becomes light only by eating its fill of the earth reaches its conclusion in the exquisitely delicate images of the linden leaf and the needle; but it is also highly characteristic of Langland that this brilliant imagistic *tour de force* should be followed by a plain political analogy: love is like a medicine, a plant, an eater, a leaf, a needle—and a mayor.

Piers Plowman is the first poem in this survey of medieval writing which can be said to have held a place, continuously though not always conspicuously, in the canon of English poetry from the time of its composition to the present day. Whereas poems such as *Beowulf* and *Sir Gawain* had to wait to be rediscovered by scholars and antiquaries after being quite forgotten, sixteenth-century printed editions made *Piers Plowman* known to successors of Langland such as Spenser and Milton. The 'satire called *Piers Plowman*' accordingly finds a place in the first historical account of English poetry, sketched by George Puttenham in his *Arte of English Poesie*, published in 1589. For Puttenham, however, the great tradition of English poetry begins not with Langland but with Chaucer and Gower. These latter are the 'courtly makers' from whom a Tudor poet can trace his descent with pride, and before whose time 'there is little or nothing worth commendation to be found written in this art'.

Chaucer and Gower

Chaucer's life is much better documented than Langland's. He was born probably in 1343 or 1344, son of a prosperous London wine merchant. His early education is obscure, but by 1357 he had joined the household of the earl and countess of Ulster. In the French campaign of 1359–60 he was captured and ransomed. From 1367 onwards he appears frequently in records of the household of Edward III as one of the king's gentleman attendants. Between 1374 and 1386 he served as Controller of Customs in the Port of London. He was Justice of the Peace for Kent in 1385–9 and represented that county in Parliament in 1386. From 1389 to 1391 he acted as Clerk of the King's Works. He died in 1400. Historians agree that there is nothing in this career to suggest that Chaucer was anything other than a moderately successful London gentleman. Even his burial in Westminster Abbey, though it marks the beginning of 'Poets' Corner' there, was evidently no more than a common privilege for courtiers and royal officials. Chaucer was not a professional poet: indeed, one may suspect that, like T. S. Eliot and Philip Larkin in our own time, he took a secret pleasure in keeping his profession distinct from his poetry. He refers to his official career only once in his writings, with a passing allusion to his 'rekenynges' (presumably at the Customs House, *The House of Fame*, 653); and the only events in that career which can be said to have left a definite mark on his poetry are his two visits to Italy on royal business in 1372–3 and 1378, for it was presumably on those visits that he acquired his knowledge, most uncommon for an Englishman at that time, of the writings of Dante, Petrarch, and Boccaccio.

Yet this is not to say that the reader of Chaucer's poetry fails to encounter him there. On the contrary, few English poets speak more freely and (it would appear) artlessly in the first person. Chaucer speaks so, not only in short epistolary poems such as the delightful *Envoy to Scogan*, but also in every one of his major narrative pieces. The dreamer in the four dream-poems, the narrator in *Troilus and Criseyde*, and the pilgrim-narrator in *The Canterbury Tales*, all speak of what they have dreamed, read, or seen in a manner which the reader soon learns to recognize as characteristic. The Chaucer of all these poems is a retiring, bookish man, with little firsthand experience of life, least of all in the great matter of love. He can therefore do no better than report faithfully what he dreams, reads, or observes of the world and its ways. Often he is puzzled by what he finds, and at times he feels called upon to apologize for what he is obliged (for some reason) to report. Since the 'matter' of his stories is not of his own making, it cannot always be to his taste. It pains him to describe the infidelity of Criseyde, but female readers must not blame him for that: 'Ye may hire giltes in other bokes se.' It embarrasses him to report the lewd tale of the Miller, but he cannot omit it from his faithful record of the pilgrims' performances:

> for I moot reherce
> Hir tales alle, be they bettre or werse,
> Or elles falsen som of my mateere.

These are, of course, jokes; but such a comic routine has deeper implications. For one thing, it powerfully fosters the illusion of free-standing, independent reality which so many of Chaucer's poems create—a reality which surpasses the poet's own knowledge and understanding. The same illusion is created by the simple line which concludes the portrait of the Merchant in *The Canterbury Tales*: 'But, sooth to seyn, I noot how men hym calle.' How can this pilgrim be a figment of Chaucer's imagination, if the poet 'does not know what he is called'? It is not surprising that scholars have been inspired to search for the missing name in mercantile documents of the time, as if the Merchant were indeed real. Chaucer encourages the confusion, just as when in *Troilus* he claims not to be able to say whether the therefore presumably historical Criseyde had any children: 'I rede it naught, therfore I late it goon.' Such disavowals can have a further consequence, as may be seen later in Criseyde's story, at the point when, having left Troilus in Troy, she takes pity on his Greek rival Diomede:

> And for to helen hym of his sorwes smerte,
> Men seyn—I noot—that she yaf hym hire herte.

'Men say—I do not know—that she gave him her heart.' The evasion leaves a gap in the story for the reader to fill. Are we to understand that Criseyde obviously did give her heart to the abominable Greek, only Chaucer is too fond of the female sex to say so? Or perhaps that she really did not? Such uncertainties serve to hold final judgement back, allowing the events to unfold and characters to reveal themselves with a minimum of that authorial comment which might 'falsen som of my mateere'.

Chaucer's earliest major poem, *The Book of the Duchess*, shows him already master of such obliquities. He probably wrote it soon after the death of Blanche, wife of John of Gaunt, in 1368. The poem's elaborate structure allows him to celebrate the dead duchess and even hint at consolation for her husband with perfect grace and courtesy. He avoids the obsequious and the sententious by the characteristic device of saying nothing, or almost nothing, in his own person at all. Setting out on a hunt in his dream, he comes upon a man in black in a forest glade lamenting the death of his beloved. In the long conversation which ensues, the dreamer is restrained by a scruple of courtesy from admitting that he has accidentally overheard such a deeply personal utterance; and it is only when the man in black at last tells him directly of his loss that a response is called for—to be cut off at once by the sound of horns, summoning the hunt home from the forest and heralding the poem's end:

> 'She ys ded.' 'Nay!' 'Yis, be my trouthe.'
> 'Is that youre los? Be God, hyt ys routhe!'
> And with that word ryght anoon
> They gan to strake forth; al was doon,
> For that tyme, the hert-huntyng.

> [*routhe* pity; *strake forth* sound the recall]

It is a beautiful moment. Chaucer's single articulated response to the tragedy leaves, for all its inadequacy, nothing more that can be said without impertinence: 'Be god, hyt ys routhe.' And the message of the horns, capping that response with dreamlike inevitability, suggests in a pun of the utmost delicacy the only human remedy for such grief: 'al was doon, / For that tyme, the hert-huntyng.'

The Book of the Duchess displays Chaucer's command of the subtle, refined manner of contemporary French poets such as Guillaume de Machaut and Jean Froissart; but it suffers, like the poems of Froissart and Machaut, from a thinness of texture. Perhaps Chaucer felt its limitations. He seems, at any rate, to have responded enthusiastically to the richer possibilities offered by Italian poetry when he first encountered it, perhaps on his first Italian journey shortly after writing *The Book of the Duchess*. In what is probably his next dream-poem, *The House of Fame*, the influence of Dante's majestic *Divine Comedy* makes itself felt for the first time in English poetry. Yet this is essentially a light and fantastic poem, in which a bookish and reclusive Geoffrey is transported, in a dizzy space flight, to the *domus Famae* described by his favourite author Ovid, so that he may learn some 'tidings of Love's folk' in

CHAUCER RECITING HIS POETRY. This frontispiece to an early, de luxe copy of Chaucer's *Troilus and Criseyde* shows Chaucer reciting his work, as he no doubt on occasion did, to an audience of richly dressed ladies and gentlemen. The scene in the background is thought to represent an episode in *Troilus* itself.

that great clearing-house of news and gossip. Chaucer represents himself here as a keen servant of Cupid and Venus, lacking experience but anxious to learn about Love's folk and to serve them by his writings. He adopts the same role throughout the main poems of his middle period: *The Parliament of Fowls*, *Troilus*, and *The Legend of Good Women*. *The Parliament of Fowls*, probably written in the early 1380s, is an altogether more finished piece than *The House of Fame*; but it professes no greater knowledge of love's mysteries:

> The lyf so short, the craft so long to lerne,
> Th'assay so hard, so sharp the conquerynge,
> The dredful joye, alwey that slit so yerne:
> Al this mene I by Love, that my felynge
> Astonyeth with his wonderful werkynge
> So sore, iwis, that whan I on hym thynke,
> Nat wot I wel wher that I flete or synke.

Having newly abandoned the octosyllabic couplet of his two earlier dream-poems, Chaucer here displays his immediate mastery of the more spacious rhyme-royal stanza. The verse moves easily from the stately antitheses of the opening to the anticlimax of the final couplet, which expresses the poem's prevailing mood of bewilderment about the 'wonderful working' of love. After reading a book of Cicero's which represents sexual love as a lawless and selfish passion, the poet falls asleep and dreams of a licentious Venus who appears to bear out Cicero's adverse judgement. Wandering further into the garden of love, he comes upon a rival goddess, Nature, presiding over the assembly at which, every St Valentine's Day, birds choose their mates. But even love according to Nature is no simple thing. Indeed, the different orders of birds, ranging from the noble eagles to the ignoble cuckoo, display such a contentious variety of attitudes to life and love that their 'parliament' can be seen to anticipate the later assemblage of Canterbury pilgrims.

Troilus and Criseyde is one of the great poems of the European Middle Ages. Chaucer completed it in about 1385. Its main source is *Il Filostrato*, Boccaccio's youthful poem about the love-struck Troilus composed some fifty years before; but it also draws on a wide range of other writings, French, Latin, and Italian—most notably Boethius's treatise of Christian stoicism, *De consolatione Philosophiae*, a work which Chaucer was engaged in translating at about the same time. Chaucer makes no attempt to disguise the bookish origins of his 'book of Troilus'. On the contrary, frequent phrases such as 'as myn auctour seyde' and 'as I rede' plainly characterize the narrator as here not a dreamer or a pilgrim but a *reader*, retelling for the benefit of modern lovers as much of this story of ancient love as he can discover in his 'olde bokes'. Yet this most avowedly bookish of all Chaucer's works is also his most immediately vivid and absorbing—so much so that it has been described as 'the first modern novel'. What chiefly prompts this description, wildly anachronistic as it must be, is Chaucer's method of telling the story in a series of big scenes, each of which displays something of that detailed notation of setting and behaviour (benches and garden walks, coughs and glances) which we look for in Jane Austen or George Eliot. Here for instance is the beginning of the scene in which Pandarus first tells his niece Criseyde of Troilus's love:

> Whan he was come unto his neces place,
> 'Wher is my lady?' to hire folk quod he;
> And they hym tolde, and he forth in gan pace,
> And fond two othere ladys sete, and she,
> Withinne a paved parlour, and they thre
> Herden a mayden reden hem the geste
> Of the siege of Thebes, while hem leste.
>
> Quod Pandarus, 'Madame, God yow see,
> With al youre fayre book and compaignie!'
> 'Ey, uncle myn, welcome iwys,' quod she;
> And up she roos . . .
>
> (*Troilus*, II. 78–88)

[*geste* story; *hem leste* they pleased]

Chaucer here anticipates what Henry James calls the 'scenic art' of the novelist. He first selects and then extravagantly 'does' a few key scenes, whilst making the necessary economies by treating the intervening matter in summary fashion. Only *Sir Gawain and the Green Knight* among medieval English poems can rival *Troilus* in mastery of this art.

Yet Chaucer is not a novelist, least of all in that avowed dependence on old books which forces him to leave tantalizing gaps in his story: 'I rede it naught, therfore I late it goon.' This combination of the novelistic close-up with the complete blank produces peculiar effects, especially in the case of Criseyde. The motives of the poem's hero, 'that trewe man, that noble gentil knyght', are never in doubt, but those of Criseyde, both in accepting Troilus and in deserting him, are complex and partially undisclosed. What is in her mind, for instance, when she accepts Pandarus's invitation to dinner—an occasion that ends with her and Troilus in bed together? The invitation, delivered in her uncle's typical style of bullying jocosity, exerts real social pressure: 'certeynly she moste, by hire leve, / Come soupen in his hous with hym at eve.' But she is not obliged to go (she *must*, but *by her leave*), nor is she obliged to accept her uncle's assurances that Troilus is out of town. Perhaps, indeed, she sees right through them:

> Nought list myn auctour fully to declare
> What that she thoughte whan he seyde so,
> That Troilus was out of towne yfare,
> As if he seyde therof soth or no;
> But that, withowten await, with hym to go

She graunted hym, sith he hire that bisoughte,
And as his nece obeyed as hire oughte.
(III. 575–81)
[*list* pleases; *await* further ado]

The closing couplet of this rhyme-royal stanza serves to foreclose further speculation (a device unavailable to novelists): Criseyde, we are assured, is simply acting as a dutiful niece should. It is not surprising that many readers, especially women, find this protective and gentlemanly handling of the heroine profoundly equivocal. Ironies there certainly are; but the ironies do not exclude sympathy, and in the end that sympathy receives the powerful sanction of philosophic truth. For after Troilus's death an epilogue invites us to see his love for Criseyde as doomed to disappointment in any case, however she had behaved, since permanent satisfaction is not to be looked for anywhere in the sublunary world of change and decay. Only of Christ can it be said that 'he nyl falsen no wight'.

Yet women readers evidently were offended (or professed to be so), for Chaucer's next poem, *The Legend of Good Women*, offers itself as an act of reparation for this and other offences against the sex. Appearing to the poet in a mock-religious vision, the God of Love imposes upon him the penitential task of compiling a series of legends (*legenda*, saints' lives) of good women who died as martyrs for love. However, Chaucer got no further than the ninth of these legends, perhaps because his imagination had already been captured by a new idea—a setting for stories which, so far from condemning him to harp continually on a single string, allowed him the greatest possible freedom to explore the wide range of narrative genres current in his time. He began *The Canterbury Tales* in about 1387 and probably continued to work on it until the end of his life. The plan was grandiose: some thirty pilgrims, each to tell two tales on the road to Canterbury and two on the way back to London, giving a total of 120 tales in all. Of these Chaucer's literary executors found only twenty-four among the poet's papers after his death in 1400; yet the work which they evidently pieced together at that time proved an instant and lasting success, not only because of the beauty of individual tales, but also because the imaginative power of Chaucer's original idea of the Canterbury pilgrimage makes itself so commandingly felt even in the fragments that are all he left.

Even though Chaucer composed less than a quarter of his projected tales, these are enough to display his intention of matching the variety of his pilgrim company—'sondry folk, by aventure yfalle / In felaweshipe'—with a corresponding range of narrative genres, secular and religious, high and low. The two tales which follow the General Prologue, thrown together as if 'by aventure' or accidentally, stake out the range for the secular tales: at the upper end, courtly romance, represented by the Knight's tale of Palamon and Arcite, and at the lower end, the Miller's comic tale of Nicholas and Absolon. 'Romance'

CHAUCER'S SQUIRE, as portrayed at the beginning of his Tale in the Ellesmere manuscript. 'Short was his gowne, with sleves longe and wyde. / Wel koude he sitte on hors and faire ryde.'

CHAUCER'S PRIORESS, as portrayed opposite the beginning of her Tale in the Ellesmere manuscript.

must be a loose term in this context. Chaucer took no creative interest in the mainstream of French courtly romance, which is Arthurian; and the burlesque 'Tale of Sir Thopas', which he assigns to himself as pilgrim-narrator, implies a critical view of the more popular English type. 'The Knight's Tale' itself is adapted from Boccaccio's neo-classical romantic epic, *Il Teseida*; 'The Franklin's Tale' is a much elaborated Breton Lay; 'The Wife of Bath's Tale', though set in 'th'olde dayes of the Kyng Arthour', reads more like a moralized fairy-tale than an Arthurian adventure; and 'The Squire's Tale', left unfinished, has mainly oriental affinities. Yet in their different ways all these tales offer what Chaucer calls 'storial thyng that toucheth gentillesse'—examples of noble conduct and fine feeling set in a past of heroes and marvels—and so they contrast with the 'cherles tales' for which the poet disingenuously apologizes in the Miller's Prologue. The latter group, which includes the tales of the Miller, the Reeve, the Cook, the Shipman, the Merchant, and the Summoner, may appear to represent a departure from literary tradition; but these tales have in fact a formal pedigree quite as respectable as that of the 'romances', for they all more or less closely follow the tradition of the French *fabliau*. *Fabliaux* were poetic, and often highly polished, versions of comic tales. The genre was popular with French poets in the previous century, and Chaucer evidently saw in it, not only a kind of story suitable for the churls on his pilgrimage, but also an opportunity to paint contemporary life and manners. The plots of his *fabliau* tales are generally farcical and fantastic; but the people and settings are observed with minute and loving fidelity: town and gown in the Oxford of 'The Miller's Tale' and the Cambridge of 'The Reeve's Tale', merchant and monk in the suburban Paris of 'The Shipman's Tale', friar and peasant in the Yorkshire of 'The Summoner's Tale'.

Besides 'storial thyng that toucheth gentillesse' and 'cherles tales', Chaucer also speaks in the Miller's Prologue of another kind of 'storial thyng' concerned not with 'gentillesse' but with 'moralitee and hoolynesse'. Here too one can observe a loosely organized hierarchy of genres, headed in this case by the Prioress's Miracle of the Virgin and the Second Nun's Life of St Cecilia. The prologues to these holy tales, like the epilogue to *Troilus*, display Chaucer's mastery of a high religious style which owes more to Dante than to his English predecessors. To pass from the Shipman's *fabliau* of the monk and the merchant's wife to the Prioress's miracle of the murdered innocent which immediately follows it is to experience the 'sundriness' of *The Canterbury Tales* at its fullest stretch. However, not all those pilgrims who have something to do with the Church speak of 'moralitee and hoolynesse' in such exalted terms. The tales of the Friar, the Pardoner, and the Nun's Priest all draw on the clerical tradition of *exempla*—everyday stories told by preachers to illustrate

SCENES FROM CHAUCER'S 'PARDONER'S TALE' carved on a wooden chest of about 1400. The youngest reveller buys poison (*left*). He is killed by his two companions (*centre*), who then drink the poison (*right*).

moral points. These fables and anecdotes take us into worlds much like those of the *fabliaux*; and Chaucer's evident scepticism about their moral authority allows him to accommodate them easily to the prevailingly comic mood of the *Tales*. Few readers, it may be suspected, clearly remember what the stated moral of the Nun's Priest's fable of the Cock and the Fox is, and fewer still care. Yet it must be recalled that, although the plan of the *Tales*, as announced by the Host in the General Prologue, called for a festive ending back at his inn in Southwark, the work as we have it ends with a religious 'meditacioun' in plain prose—'The Parson's Tale', a formal treatise on the Sacrament of Penance.

These examples are enough to suggest the range, if not the quality, of the stories to be found in *The Canterbury Tales*. Yet it may be argued that Chaucer's most remarkable achievement of all is to be looked for not in the tales the pilgrims tell but in the narrative of the pilgrimage itself. To speak of this as if it provided merely a 'frame', or a series of 'links', for the tales is grossly to undervalue it. Even readers well acquainted with the brilliant series of pilgrim portraits in the General Prologue may fail to appreciate just how much Chaucer makes of his company of sundry folk once the pilgrimage gets under way. The introductory description of the Host, Harry Bailly, does no more than sketch a character who, once he has been appointed 'governour' of the pilgrims and judge of their tales, emerges as the central figure of the cavalcade. William Blake rightly observed that Harry 'is a first rate character, and his jokes are no trifles'. As the appointed master of mirth, he embodies the holiday spirit that is abroad in the *Tales*, genially exerting his authority whenever social or professional differences between the pilgrims break out into open hostility. Nothing in Chaucer was more original, or proved more inimitable, than the scene in the Manciple's Prologue where the Host intervenes to stop the Manciple's cruel public baiting of the Cook. All three participants in these exchanges are hauntingly vivid: the pale and stinking cook, so drunk that he can express his anger only in wordless nods; the spiteful Manciple, responding to the Host's pacific intervention by offering the Cook what he can least do with, a 'friendly' drink; and Harry himself, who knows all about drink and drunks:

> Thanne gan oure Hoost to laughen wonder loude,
> And seyde, 'I se wel it is necessarie,
> Where that we goon, good drynke with us carie;
> For that wol turne rancour and disese
> T'acord and love, and many a wrong apese.
> O thou Bacus, yblessed be thy name,
> That so kanst turnen ernest into game!'

Reading such a scene, one can endorse the judgement of one of Chaucer's many fifteenth-century admirers:

THE FIFTEEN SIGNS OF APPROACHING DOOMSDAY, in a fifteenth-century stained-glass window. Each of the fifteen scenes is accompanied by a couplet from the popular English poem *The Prick of Conscience*, e.g. in the top scene of the middle light: 'The XIIII day all that lives than/Sall dy bathe childe man & woman'.

PALATIVM REGIVM IN ANGLIÆ REGNO APPELLATVM NONCIVTZ.
Hoc est nisquam simile.

Æ̃uganit Georgius Hoefnaegius Jmmo JT Coll.

NONSUCH PALACE, SURREY: a pen and ink drawing, with brown wash and watercolour, by Joris Hoefnagel (1568). Rising from behind its walls like some allegorical dream house in the *Faerie Queene*, Nonsuch (begun by Henry VIII in 1538, acquired by Elizabeth in 1592, demolished 1680s) was a record in brick and stone of how royal power was made tasteful, even aesthetically exquisite, during the Tudor century. Despite its origins in the medieval castle—corner towers, turrets, battlements, firing-places—this palace was entirely domesticated, with stalk-like chimneys jutting up alongside elaborate plasterwork in the best Franco-Italianate style, and all its defences a sham.

His langage was so fayr and pertynente
It semeth unto mannys heerynge
Not only the worde, but verely the thynge.

The other 'courtly maker' besides Chaucer from whom Puttenham traced the lineage of English poetry, as he saw it in the age of Elizabeth I, was John Gower (d. 1408). Little is known for certain about Gower's life. He was evidently a gentleman of means, associating both with the landed gentry of Kent and with the lawyers, civil servants, and courtiers of London and Westminster. In the latter part of his life he took up residence at St Mary's Priory in Southwark. By the middle 1380s, when Chaucer submitted his *Troilus* to the correction of 'moral Gower', his friend had already produced two long didactic poems, both much concerned with the ills of contemporary society, *Mirour de l'Omme* in French and *Vox clamantis* in Latin; but much his best work is the English *Confessio Amantis* or 'Lover's Confession', first completed in 1390. Gower had evidently come to share Chaucer's interest in ways of

A LOVER'S CONFESSION, from a manuscript of Gower's *Confessio Amantis*. The lover, Amans, kneels before the priest of Venus, Genius. Courtly writers commonly imitate, though they do not challenge, the institutions of the Church in writing about love.

articulating short stories into a larger whole. The broad human comedy of *The Canterbury Tales* was beyond his powers; but *Confessio Amantis* certainly rivals *The Legend of Good Women*. The setting of both poems is a mock-religious vision in which the poet confronts a love divinity: Cupid in the *Legend*, Venus and her priest Genius in the *Confessio*. In Gower's poem the tales are told, not by the penitent narrator, but by his confessor Genius, as illustrations of the seven deadly sins. Since Gower's stories are all *exempla*, his work does not, any more than Chaucer's *Legend*, offer the pleasures of generic variety to be had in *The Canterbury Tales*. He deals mostly in 'storial thyng' drawn from the myth, legend, and history of classical antiquity, and especially from the poems of Ovid, whose *Heroides* and *Metamorphoses* were among his chief models, as they were Chaucer's. Gower has been described as 'the first English transmitter of so many of the classical themes which Renaissance poets and painters were to embroider'. Thus the confessor's first exemplary tale, illustrating sin of the eyes, is the Ovidian story of Actaeon and Diana, narrated in a mere forty-six lines yet with delicately applied touches of descriptive detail which testify to the poet's fastidious art. Gower is the first English poet who could be called 'correct'. Shakespeare's imitation of his octosyllabic couplets in the prologues of 'ancient Gower' in *Pericles* (a play drawn in part from the story of Antiochus in Book VIII of the *Confessio*) does less than justice to their polish and fluency. Ben Jonson recognized Gower's claims as an exemplar of good English by quoting frequently from the *Confessio* in his *English Grammar*; and in the eighteenth century Thomas Warton spoke admiringly of how 'by a critical cultivation of his native language, he laboured to reform its irregularities, and to establish an English style'.

Yet *Confessio Amantis* should not be read for its stories alone, admirable examples though these are of 'an English style'. The finest moments in the poem come in its closing pages, when the lover's confession is completed. Having told his last story, Genius declares that he will now turn from 'trifles' to 'truth', and advises the lover to abandon sublunary loves and 'tak love where it mai noght faile'. This priestly impulse towards a pious ending like that of Chaucer's *Troilus* is resisted by the lover, who observes that such a willed renunciation of love will seem possible only to one who has not felt its force. To this experience the lover's confessions have already done full justice; but they have failed to disclose one crucial fact, which now at last emerges when the goddess Venus herself confronts the lover with the realization that he is *old*. Hence the renunciation of love can be for him no more—and no less—than an acceptance of the natural course of things. As Venus says:

> ' "Min herte wolde and I ne may"
> Is noght beloved nou adayes;
> Er thou make eny suche assaies
> To love, and faile upon the fet,
> Betre is to make a beau retret . . .'

[*upon the fet* in the act]

It is with a 'beau retret' or dignified withdrawal from love that the poem ends, breathing an autumnal air of passion spent.

The Fifteenth Century

The dominant tradition of fifteenth-century English poetry is that established by Chaucer and Gower—a dynasty of 'courtly makers' represented by Lydgate and Hoccleve, Charles d'Orléans and James I of Scotland, Henryson, and

PILGRIMS LEAVING CANTERBURY, from a manuscript of *The Siege of Thebes*, 'ful lamentably tolde by John Lidgate; Monke of Bury' and attached by him to the unfinished *Canterbury Tales*.

Dunbar. For the literary historian the existence of such a lineage of nameable poets, each related in demonstrable ways to his predecessors, means that this century presents a picture more like that of later than of earlier times. In particular, this is the period when the condition of anonymity begins to assume something like its modern significance. Whereas anonymity is simply the normal condition of earlier English poems, to call a fifteenth-century poem anonymous is already to say something substantial about it—to mark it as popular, or folkish, or alliterative, or non-metropolitan, or non-Chaucerian, or even non-literary. Such verse merits more attention than it can be given here. One manuscript in the British Library, for instance, preserves a gathering of anonymous poetry in which the voice of English folk-song makes itself clearly heard, as in the haunting riddle-chant which begins as follows:

> I have a yong suster fer beyonden the sea;
> Many be the drowryes that she sente me.
>
> She sente me the cherry withouten any ston,
> And so she did the douve withouten any bon.

> [*drowryes* keepsakes]

This poem lived on in sub-literary tradition (ballad and nursery rhyme) until modern times, as did the mysterious 'Corpus Christi Carol', a version of which was recorded from oral tradition as late as 1908:

> Lully, lulley, lully, lulley,
> The faucon hath born my mak away.
>
> He bare him up, he bare him down,
> He bare him into an orchard brown.
> Lully, lulley . . .

This is also the century in which the traditional ballad emerges as an established popular form, distinct from the metrical romance. Among the earliest are the ballads of 'Robin Hood and the Monk' and 'Robin Hood and the Potter'. That 'old song of Percy and Douglas' which so moved Sir Philip Sidney, 'The Hunting of the Cheviot' (known in its later form as 'Chevy Chase'), also took shape in this period:

> The Perse out of Northomberlond
> An avow to God made he
> That he wold hunte in the mountains
> Of Cheviat within days three . . .

Fifteenth-century writers also played an important part in the development of vernacular drama. Like other anonymous works for which no single author is to be sought, the verse plays on biblical subjects commonly known as mystery plays cannot be satisfactorily dated. They already existed in Chaucer's day, for the parish clerk in his 'Miller's Tale' 'pleyeth Herodes on a scaffold hye'; but the four surviving cycles, from Chester, York, Wakefield, and 'N-town', seem to be mainly fifteenth-century work. These cycles present the whole history of mankind from the beginning to the Last Judgement in a selection of biblical episodes, centring on the life and passion of Christ. They were performed at the summer feast of Corpus Christi, either on pageant wagons drawn through the streets or in a playing area with fixed 'scaffolds' (as in the Oxford of 'The Miller's Tale'). Local clerics generally wrote them, but they were put on by the craft guilds, each of which took responsibility for one play. The results of such joint ecclesiastical and municipal enterprise are naturally very uneven, considered from a literary point of view. The verse is too often either flat or over-inflated; and the presentation of character and event rarely offers anything that might escape the attention of an open-air audience on a summer's day. But some of the authors had real talent, most of all the so-called 'Wakefield Master'. The two shepherds' plays which he contributed to the Wakefield cycle are justly celebrated, especially the second. This play vividly represents the world of 'sely shepardes that walkys on the moore', first in their complaints about oppressive 'gentlery men', nagging wives, and rain, and then in the farcical sub-plot of Mak the sheep-stealer. The scene where the shepherds cluster round the cradle of Mak's 'baby'—a stolen sheep, in fact—provides an original and telling counterpart to the final scene in the play, in which they worship the Christ child. In general, however, the mystery plays offer less opportunity for dramatic invention than do the morality plays. These allegorical dramas take as their subject not biblical history but the life history of an individual considered as typical, 'Humanum Genus' or 'Everyman'. The best of the surviving examples are the *Castle of Perseverance* (early fifteenth century) and *Everyman*, the latter translated from the Dutch in the early sixteenth century. *Everyman* gains greater unity by concentrating on the last days of its hero: T. S. Eliot provocatively described it as perhaps the only English example of 'a drama within the limitations of art'. The more comprehensive *Castle of Perseverance*, however, creates an equally powerful effect in performance, representing a whole life from birth to death and beyond, somewhat in the sprawling 'epic' manner of Bertolt Brecht.

The chief poets of the first generation of 'courtly makers' after Chaucer and Gower are Thomas Hoccleve (*c*.1366-1426) and John Lydgate (*c*.1370-1449). Although Lydgate was a monk of the Benedictine house of Bury St Edmunds and Hoccleve a civil servant in the office of the Privy Seal at Westminster, their literary worlds were much alike: both addressed poems to King Henry V and his brother Humphrey of Gloucester, and both acknowledged Chaucer as master. Yet they are writers of a very different sort. Lydgate's voluminous works (running to well over 100,000 lines) gained for him a public standing not unlike that of poets laureate in later times. He wrote for great occasions, and also produced gala versions of great historical subjects in his *Troy Book* (1412-20), *The Siege of Thebes* (1420-2), *The Fall of Princes* (1431-8), and *The Life of Our Lady*. These poems were read and admired long after Lydgate's day: *The Fall of Princes* was four times issued by early printers and inspired a continuation in the *Mirror for Magistrates* (1555). Lydgate, it has been observed, 'saw his role as the systematic consolidation of Chaucer's achievement in establishing a high-style poetic for English', and in this he may be said to have succeeded; yet his writing has all the faults one would expect of a one-hundred-thousand-line poet. It is diffuse and often, especially in its syntax, negligent; and the numerous Chaucerian echoes too often create effects similar to those experienced in the worst kind of concert-hall. Hoccleve wrote less and wrote better. Though he cannot be called concise, his English is generally plain and sinewy, and he displays a real command over the poetic syntax of the rhyme-royal stanza. Unlike Lydgate, he claims to have been instructed by Chaucer himself in the art of English poetry; but he recalls the master much less often than Lydgate does. Indeed he is, at his best, an idiosyncratic writer. By far his best-known work was *The Regement of Princes* (1411–12), a conventional treatise of moral counsel addressed to the future Henry V; but even this eminently public work displays Hoccleve's special aptitude for personal, autobiographical writing in its long introductory scene between the poet and an old beadsman. This aptitude is most evident in his two most interesting works: 'La Male Regle de T. Hoccleve' (*c.*1405), and the so-called 'Series' of linked pieces, beginning with Hoccleve's 'Complaint' and his 'Dialogue with a Friend', composed a few years before his death in 1426.

Neither Hoccleve nor Lydgate shared Chaucer's preoccupation with the subject of love. In this respect two poets of the next generation, Charles duke of Orleans (1394–1465) and King James I of Scotland (1394–1437), are more like Chaucer and also, as might be expected of two members of foreign royal houses, more specifically courtly. As prisoners of the English king, both came into contact with the new English poetry and were inspired to emulate it. The book of English love poetry which Charles composed during his twenty-five-year captivity consists mainly of ballades and rondeaux, but these courtly lyrics are loosely organized into a narrative, rather like later sonnet sequences. The first series of ballades, ending with the death of the lady, is followed by a vision which warns the poet, now in middle age, that the time has come for him to 'depart with honour' from love. The French duke had evidently read both *The Book of the Duchess* and the closing pages of *Confessio Amantis* with sympathetic attention. In the following section, which is more in the continental manner, the poet, now retired from love, offers other lovers a feast of 'quails and larks'—delicate rondeaux—for their delight and comfort; but a second vision, of Venus and Fortune, heralds his own renewed submission to love, which is narrated in a concluding series of ballades. Whereas the predominantly lyric character of Charles's book reflects continental taste, *The Kingis Quair* (King's Book) of James subordinates lyric to narrative in the English way. Its account of how the imprisoned poet first saw his beloved walking in a garden below his tower derives from the scene in Chaucer's 'Knight's Tale' where Palamon and Arcite first see Emily; and the vision of Venus, Minerva, and Fortune that follows belongs, like Charles's similar episode, to the tradition of philosophical love-vision represented by Chaucer's

How she þ[at] was mayden marie
And saw his soule floure and fructifie

Al þogh his lyfe be queynt þe resemblaunce
Of him hath in me so fressh lyflynesse
Þat to putte othir men in remembraunce
Of his p[er]sone I haue heere his lyknesse
Do make to þis ende in sothfastnesse
Þat þei þ[at] haue of him lest þought & mynde
By þis peynture may ageyn him fynde

The ymages þ[at] in þe chirche been
Maken folk þenke on god & on his seyntes
Whan þe ymages þei be holden & seen
Were oft vnsyte of hem causith restreyntes
Of þoughtes gode whan a þing depeynt is
Or entayled if men take of it heede
Thoght of þe lyknesse it wil in hym brede

But some holden oppynyou[n] and sey
Þat none ymages schuld I maked be
Þei erren foule & goon out of þe wey
Of trouth haue þei scant sensibilite
Passe ou[er] þ[at] now blessid trinite
Vpon my maistres soule m[er]cy haue
ffor him lady eke þy m[er]cy I craue

More othir þing wolde I fayne speke & touche
Heere in þis booke but such is my dulnesse
ffor þ[at] al voyde and empty is my pouche
Þat al my lust is queynt w[ith] heuynesse
And heuy spirit comaundith stilnesse

GEOFFREY CHAUCER. His disciple Thomas Hoccleve caused this portrait to be painted in a copy of Hoccleve's *Regement of Princes*. Chaucer's finger points at the lines in which his disciple insists on the truth or 'sothfastnesse' of the likeness.

dream-poems and Lydgate's *Temple of Glass*. Yet James writes, evidently out of his own experience, with a distinctive delicate intensity, as in his description of the heart-shaped ruby which hung on a slender gold chain round the lady's neck: 'That, as a spark of lowe, so wantonly / Semyt birnyng upon hir quhyte throte' [*lowe* fire; *quhyte* white].

The two best 'English' poets of the last part of our period also belong to Scotland: Henryson and Dunbar. The term 'Scottish Chaucerian' often applied to them registers an indisputable debt (especially in the case of Henryson) but does scant justice to their individual excellence. Little is known about the life of Robert Henryson. He graduated, probably with a degree in canon law from Glasgow University in 1462, and became master of the grammar school in the important Benedictine abbey of Dunfermline. Henryson's two major poems both have their roots in books: *The Testament of Cresseid* in Chaucer's *Troilus*, and the *Fables* in the Latin Aesop which the 'scolmaister of Dunfermling' must often have laboured over with his pupils. The *Testament* supplements Chaucer's poem by telling the 'wofull end' of Cresseid, taking up her story at a point which Chaucer would never have wished to reach:

> Quhen Diomeid had all his appetyte,
> And mair, fulfillit of this fair ladie,
> Upon ane uther he set his haill delyte.

The Roman severity of that characteristically laconic 'and more' prepares the reader for the harsh fate that Henryson invents for Chaucer's heroine: a life of promiscuity, followed by leprosy, destitution, and death. Yet the poem does more than simply avenge Troilus. A last encounter between the hero and Cresseid, now begging at the roadside, brings her to the dignity of self-realization and remorse. This is manifested in her dying 'testament' and recognized by Troilus in the inscription he composes for her tomb:

> 'Lo, fair ladyis, Cresseid of Troy the toun,
> Sumtyme countit the flour of womanheid,
> Under this stane, lait lipper, lyis deid.'

Fine as the *Testament* is, Henryson surpassed it in his *Fables*, a series of thirteen animal fables, including versions of the Cock and the Fox (reworking 'The Nun's Priest's Tale') and the Town and Country Mouse. This work is one of the masterpieces of medieval literature. The 'moralities' which conclude each story match their models, the moral ballades of Chaucer, in grave and polished eloquence; and the stories themselves, derived from Aesopic tradition and medieval tales of Reynard the Fox, are told with incomparable skill and verve. The small world of the animals, overshadowed by the fear of injury and sudden death, presents to the human reader a spectacle in which he can contemplate with some steadiness both the comedy and the horror of his own condition. Here, for instance, is a mouse in mortal fear explaining to a lion how she came to be caught dancing on his sleeping form:

'We wer repleit, and had grit aboundance
Off alkin thingis, sic as to us effeird;
The sweit sesoun provokit us to dance
And mak sic mirth as nature to us leird;
Ye lay so still and law upon the eird
That be my sawll we weind ye had bene deid;
Elles wald we not have dancit over your heid.'

[*effeird* was proper; *leird* taught]

Henryson's successor in the line of Scots 'makars', William Dunbar, died not long, perhaps, after the battle of Flodden (1513) in which his patron James IV of Scotland was killed. Dunbar was a graduate and became a priest. The range of his poetry reflects the variety of occasions, especially at the Scottish court, that prompted it: there are religious and liturgical poems, moral pieces, allegories of love and of state ceremony, petitionary poems, comic poems, and poems of abuse and insult. Dunbar's well-justified pride in his craft as a 'makar' finds expression in one of his poems addressed to James, in which he complains that his work is not rewarded like that of the king's other servants:

Als lang in mynd my work sall hald,
Als haill in everie circumstance,
In forme, in mater and substance,
But wering or consumptioun,
Roust, canker or corruptioun,
As ony of thair werkis all.

[*haill* whole, complete; *But wering* without wearing out]

The purely medieval, scholastic terms in which Dunbar claims that his poems will be long-lived, if not 'immortal', apply with precision to his own work, as they do to Henryson's. Fullness and perfection of both 'forme' and 'mater' could hardly be better illustrated than in the stanza just quoted from the latter's *Fables*, where the mouse's three excuses are effortlessly condensed into six lines of rhyme royal and clinched by the incisive rhyme of the last line. In medieval poetry, comprehensive 'wholeness' of matter is often achieved at the expense of form; but some of the best poems of the period are indeed 'haill in everie circumstance': *Beowulf*, *The Dream of the Rood*, *Sir Gawain*, Chaucer's *Troilus*, Henryson's *Fables*.

Dunbar's *Lament for the Makers* speaks of the power of death over all men (not just the 'makaris' or poets, though it is they who are listed by name). Its exhaustive catalogue of 'all estatis' is shaped and unified, like so much in Dunbar's poetry, by the metrical form—in this case, a simple stanza of two short couplets:

I se that makaris amang the laif
Playis heir ther pageant, syne gois to graif;
Sparit is nought ther faculte:
Timor mortis conturbat me.

THE FUNERAL EFFIGY OF A KNIGHT, *c.*1300. The unnamed knight wears mail coif and hauberk. His right arm is thrown across his body in the act of drawing his sword.

> He has done petuously devour
> The noble Chaucer of makaris flour,
> The monk of Bery, and Gower, all thre:
> *Timor mortis conturbat me.*
>
> [*laif* rest]

In each stanza the rhyme of the second couplet is fixed by the refrain; so every stanza reaches a moment of truth, as it were, at the end of its third line when, after the free rhyming of the first couplet, an ominous 'e' sound (faculté, thre) heralds the return of the refrain, as inevitable as death itself. It is a remarkable and characteristic union of 'forme' with 'mater'. So too, in 'Surrexit Dominus de Sepulchro', Dunbar's poem on the empty tomb, fullness of matter—in this case, the traditional imagery of the Resurrection—combines with perfection of form, metrical and syntactic, to produce what C. S. Lewis called 'speech of unanswerable and thundering greatness':

> He for our saik that sufferit to be slane
> And lyk a lamb in sacrifice wes dicht
> Is lyk a lyone rissin up agane
> And as a gyane raxit him on hicht;
> Sprungin is Aurora radius and bricht,
> On loft is gone the glorius Appollo,
> The blisfull day depairtit fro the nycht:
> *Surrexit Dominus de sepulchro.*
>
> [*dicht* made ready; *gyane* giant; *raxit* stretched]

2. Tudor Literature

1485-1603

JOHN PITCHER

Once and Future Princes

TUDOR literature begins and ends with Arthur, Prince of Britain. In one of those moments of convergence, when art meets time, the beginnings of the Tudor dynasty met with the end of the medieval Arthur. On 1 August 1485, Henry Tudor, laying claim to the crowns of England and Wales, and disputing these with Richard III, set forth from Harfleur. The day before, in the Abbey at Westminster, the publisher William Caxton finished printing a long prose romance, *Le Morte Darthur*, or 'The Death of Arthur', by Sir Thomas Malory (d. 1471). A week later Henry Tudor arrived at the Welsh port of Milford Haven, and the coincidence of art and power had begun. Down from the hills came the Welsh families to greet the prince they had waited centuries for, and whom their bards had promised them: Henry unfurled above them the flag and standard of King Arthur, the red dragon, which announced that here the sleeping lord *was* returned, that Henry, grandson of Owen Tudor, was the king who had come to claim the throne of Arthur. And a fortnight later, at Bosworth Field, on 22 August, this first Arthurian Tudor defeated Richard III and took the crown. In London, at that same time, in copies of *Morte Darthur*, Malory's first audience would have read that in many parts of England men declared that King Arthur, though slain at Salisbury, was not dead, 'but had by the will of Our Lord Jesu into another place'. And men also say, Malory continues,

that he shall come again, and he shall win the holy cross. I will not say it shall be so, but rather I will say, here in this world he changed his life. But many men say that there is written upon his tomb this verse: *Hic iacet Arthurus Rex quondam Rexque futurus.* (XXI. 7)

[Here lies King Arthur, the once and future King.]

A century later, in 1590, the last of the Tudors, Queen Elizabeth, was no less a figure in this Arthurian story. In Spenser's *Faerie Queene*—another romance, but now a hybrid of Italian Renaissance epic and English verse allegory—Prince Arthur seeks Gloriana in the forests and deserts of Faerie

Land. This Arthur, whose own story has barely begun, is making his way to the court of the Faerie princess, who, still a virgin, waits to be espoused by old Britain and its young prince. In Book II of the poem, in the vaults of Memory (Canto x), Arthur reads over the ancient history of his people, the Britons, and finds that the account ends abruptly, mid-line, with the mention of his father, Uther Pendragon. Spenser (c.1552-99) left *The Faerie Queene* unfinished, only six out of twelve books completed, but the intention was clear. His Arthur, freed from medieval Camelot and the Round Table, was to continue that old British line, and wed it to the dynasty of Faerie Land. He was to marry Gloriana (and Queen Elizabeth, whom she represents in the allegory), and so unite the Britons with the race of Faerie, the spirit people of the inner world, who were hidden from the eye, but who (in Spenser's fiction) had always existed in parallel to the Britons. The difference between English medieval and Renaissance literature can be noted here. Malory's Arthur is an old king whose death is an enigma, and whose return, or resurrection, is uncertain. Spenser's Arthur is a young man seeking nuptial, spiritual, and national joy with a princess who in real life rules the new Britain of the Tudors. Between 1485 and 1590, between Malory and Spenser, something changed irrevocably in the story of the Arthurian monarch: under the pressure of Reformation theology, the promise of the never-dying prince, a secular assurance, was made into a religious and state mystery.

The precondition for this was the work Malory had done in *Morte Darthur*. He had gathered together a variety of Arthurian tales in English and French, in prose and verse, in alliterative and non-alliterative poetry. He had translated, edited, added to, abstracted from, and remodelled his originals, giving shape to the whole chorus of medieval voices which told, piecemeal and in different tongues, the matter of Britain. At the very time he was doing this, around 1470, the authority of the medieval aristocracy was breaking up once and for all, destroyed in the madness of the Wars of the Roses. As Malory pieced together a complete new Arthurian cycle, the circumstances of the nation, and its exhaustion, made possible the Tudor take-over, and the reconciliations which followed. By 1485, fifteen years after Malory's death, the unity of stories in *Morte Darthur*, as Caxton presented them, was an image in art of how Henry Tudor, as Henry VII, had achieved a unity in the state, settling the differences between the factions and aristocratic families of England and Wales. And just as Caxton's printing had replaced the medieval manuscript, broadening the base of readership at one instant, so Henry was to devise radically new forms of royal administration reaching out from the centre. Everything conspired to make the publication of *Morte Darthur* the end of a variety of stories, just as Henry was to end the internecine turmoils of the English barons. Yet although Malory's achievement was huge and centripetal—drawing the knights Tristan and Perceval and the pursuit of the Grail in towards the king—it could not survive unchanged throughout the Tudor century. *Morte Darthur* was

HENRY VII IN REPOSE. Detail from the gilt-bronze effigy in Westminster Abbey, by Pietro Torrigiani (1512–18). After his victory at Bosworth, Henry still had much to do to consolidate his position: pretenders to dispatch, a Cornish rebellion to put down, and a Yorkist conspiracy to extinguish by executing Edward, earl of Warwick. But these efforts to establish himself were complemented by more peaceful and far-sighted moves: he married his children into the Scots and Spanish royal families, he arranged for Erasmus to visit the royal household, and he looked westward to the Americas (with his encouragement the Cabots discovered Newfoundland). In the Tudor reigns which followed there would be rebellions and suppressions, but not until 1642 would an English monarch, Charles I, again have to fight a civil war.

essentially a thing of the past, a synthesis, with nothing to say about the continuity of princes and the nation. And it is in this very question of continuity, and what it means for a prince never to die, that Spenser breaks most with Malory and overgoes him.

The pattern of succession is what sets the writers apart. In *Morte Darthur*, there is the old conundrum of how a king is to give up the crown to his son. At the beginning Uther Pendragon is maddened with desire for the wife of one of his lords, the duke of Tintagel. He besieges their castle to get at her. Through the magic of Merlin, he assumes the shape of Tintagel and is admitted to the castle. As the duke is killed fighting Uther's army outside the walls, Uther lies with Igraine and begets on her a son, Arthur. The child is spirited away by Merlin and kept hidden until after Uther's death when he undertakes the trial of the Sword in the Stone, and is acknowledged as king. In the final section of *Morte Darthur*, there is another siege, with this time Arthur himself the besieger, and his wife Guinevere and Lancelot within the castle. Once more, it is a story of sexual wrongdoing and of betrayal, and through it we are reminded that Arthur was begotten in that moment when he was and was not illegitimate, in a moment of intense sexual frenzy when his father was disguised as his mother's husband. The paradoxes are deadly, for Arthur too has fathered an illegitimate and incestuous son, Mordred, and that son will eventually kill him in the great battle at Salisbury which finishes off the Round Table. Coded here is a ritual of primitive kingship: the father, when old, will be killed by the son, who will take the kingdom, and take his mother as his bride. Malory treats his theme with decorum, but when Arthur is away in France attacking Lancelot, Mordred certainly seizes power and tries to make Guinevere marry him. This is not an Oedipal story—quite the contrary, because the son is fully conscious of his rivalry—but the story of succession, patterned in a late-medieval romance. In Malory, it is Lancelot who is Arthur's real rival, the bed-mate of Guinevere and her defender, and the knight whom no one can excel (except, as we might guess, his own son Galahad, who surpasses him in spiritual devotion). It is Lancelot who is the true 'son' of Arthur, although not of his blood, while Mordred is the untrue child who will kill him.

What matters most in *Morte Darthur* is that the king is made to see the destruction of his own achievement before he dies, and that the sexual crime in which he was born is expunged when his own line of succession fails (with his killing of Mordred). Arthur's grief nearly overwhelms him when he considers how the loss of Guinevere, and the deaths of his knights, are to be weighed. Lancelot, desperate to rescue the queen, kills Gareth and Gaheris by mischance: he 'thrang in the thick of the press; and as they were unarmed he smote them and wist not whom that he smote, and so unhappily they were slain.' It is the beginning of the end.

'The death of them,' said Arthur, 'will cause the greatest mortal war that ever was; I am sure, wist Sir Gawain that Sir Gareth were slain, I should never have rest of him till I had destroyed Sir Lancelot's kin and himself both, other else he to destroy me. And therefore,' said the king, 'wit you well my heart was never so heavy as it is now, and much more I am sorrier for my good knights' loss than for the loss of my fair queen; for queens I might have enow, but such a fellowship of good knights shall never be together in no company.'   (XX. 9)

This is the truth of it—there are many queens and many fair ladies, but only one fellowship of men, one closed circle of male love and loyalty, the Round Table. For a moment we recognize that Fortune's Wheel of succession, one king passing on authority to the next, is figured in the round of that table. But it is a circle of death, a medieval chain-gang which shackles each male prince, however great, to the bitterness of failure. In an English past long forgotten before Malory wrote—in the elegies of the Saxon invaders—there is the same heartache at the passing of the prince and his men: Oh for the bright cup, and the warrior in armour! Oh for the lord rewarding his men with the rings of gold! How they have all gone by as if they never were! Sometimes we can scarcely believe that Malory lived within a hundred years of Spenser, so grim and primitive is the picture of malehood failing, and of the anguish of death, even after the promise of Christian redemption.

Even in the early books of *Morte Darthur* there is the rattle of guilt and dead bodies behind every fancy Gothic castle and in every lady's chamber. Sir Balin fights with King Pellam and chases him into a room in which there is a bed 'arrayed with cloth of gold', and beside it a table, and on the table a marvellous spear 'strangely wrought'. Balin snatches up the spear, strikes down the king, and at once the castle collapses on to them. They lie hurt for three days, then Merlin helps Balin to his horse. The knight asks for his damsel, and the magician shows him her dead body. Balin's action has been disastrous. The spear was the one which was driven into Christ's heart on the cross, and in the bedchamber was 'part of the blood of Our Lord Jesus Christ, that Joseph of Arimathea brought into this land'. The Dolorous Stroke has cost them all dearly:

Then departed Balin from Merlin, and said, 'In this world we meet never no more.' So he rode forth through the fair countries and cities, and found the people dead, slain on every side. And all that were alive cried, 'O Balin, thou hast caused great damage in these countries; for the dolorous stroke thou gavest unto King Pellam, three countries are destroyed, and doubt not but the vengeance will fall on thee at the last.' (II. 16)

Even when the blood of Christ is invoked, it is not enough. Balin still rides out to find the streets filled with the dead, the rotting corpses of three nations, the people destroyed by a single act. This is the world inhabited by Malory's Arthur, where a king, whatever he does, even if he builds a Camelot, is only allowed a brief period of blessings before everything breaks up through lust, revenge, and greed. The remarkable thing is that the writing can contain such discoveries. As David Jones observed, everything in Malory 'is held within the restraint of an extremely economical, deceptively simple, native English prose style. The explosiveness of the content never cheapens the form or otherwise hurts the shape of the writing.' Balin's lady is a corpse crushed flat in the ruins, but Merlin says of her only, 'lo where she lieth dead'. But there is something lost in this restraint too, because the Arthurian mystery that might have been spiritual is so often only aesthetic in *Morte Darthur*, even in the Sangreal Books. When in Malory men say that Arthur is not dead, and that he is the once and future king, we are to understand it as an assurance of continuity, but nothing more. It promises that dynasties will survive, and be replaced by rightful successors (which is what the Tudor princes wanted to hear), but it edges no further to the mystery in those words, *quondam Rexque futurus*. It is left to Spenser, at the end of the Tudor century, to read in them the fulfilment of the Christian monarchy.

Spenser's meditation on Tudor kingship is as complex and multilayered as anything else in *The Faerie Queene*. In each of the six books, a knight

ENGLISH TROOPS STORMING A CASTLE, woodcut from Holinshed's *Chronicles* (1577). Not until Cromwell's New Model Army was there anything like the modern fighting force: the Tudors had no standing army, and units of men were often called up and fitted out by great landowners and aristocrats. What held such an army together was chiefly a system of personal allegiances—retainers fighting under their lord—rather than regulations and a line of command ascending ultimately to the monarch. *Henry V* touches on the tactics of infantry warfare—skills often learnt out of Roman textbooks—but the Tudors fought few major battles on foreign territory.

undertakes an adventure to release a maiden, or restore lands or justice, or free a young man from an enchantress. In the course of the narrative there emerges a play of meanings between the literal story, or quest, and its significances, political, psychological, religious, and (predominantly) sexual. In Book II, which is devoted to the virtue of temperance, Prince Arthur and Sir Guyon enter a house, which, in Spenser's allegory, represents the human body, soul and mind. There, reading a manuscript of British histories, Arthur uncovers the glories of kings past, but also the villainies of royal children and their parents. There is the lamentable tale of King Lear and his three daughters, and the ferocious story of Porrex and Ferrex, who imprisoned their old father and then fell to disagreement. Porrex tried to dispose of his brother, who attacked him with a foreign army. When Ferrex died in the battle, his mother, 'most mercilesse of women', took revenge: 'Her other sonne fast sleeping did oppresse, / And with most cruell hand him murdred pittilesse' (II. 10. 35). The wildness of the heath, the revenge of fratricides, the usurpations, the surrender to lewdness—they are all still here in Spenser, but now they are in books, or worm-eaten old papers which record the horror of successive British kings, but which are stored in a temperate body in a closed room in the turret of the mind. Not that this in any sense neutralizes the past, or renders it innocuous by shutting it away. Rather, it places public deeds, and especially British misdeeds, *within* the individual, giving him (or her) an archaic past. This is the most obvious difference between Malory's characters and those of Spenser. In Malory, it is as though the characters have no cultural past at all, as though their civilization—armour, jousts, and love trysts—were the only form of human behaviour conceivable. Lancelot may be the son of the king of France, Joseph of Arimathea may have brought the Holy Grail to Britain long before Camelot, Troy may have fallen, Arthur himself may have sacked Rome—but there is little sense that men have diverged in the ways they behave, in their courts, or in their love-making, or in their loyalties. Malory's world is as vivid, lustrous, and newly painted as a miniature from a medieval Book of Hours, but it is only at moments of great crisis (usually when sexual desire has become ruinous) that the narrator acknowledges that there have been other times, more innocent and more loving.

Spenser's world is the very opposite of this, for in *The Faerie Queene* the mutability of human endeavour and society is announced everywhere, from the Garden of Adonis in Book III, and the fleshing out of souls, age after age, to the Mutabilitie Cantos, where even the gods are challenged as impermanent. The prologue to Book V, the Book concerned with Justice, and its hero, Sir Arthegall, is given over to classical and pseudo-classical fictions of the beginnings of man, explaining how the human race and even the physical universe have decayed over the centuries:

> For from the golden age, that first was named,
>   It's now at earst become a stonie one;
>   And men themselues, the which at first were framed
>   Of earthly mould, and form'd of flesh and bone,
>   Are now transformèd into hardest stone.

This is not just a complaint, or a gesture of weariness at the prospect of degenerating even further down the scale of humanity. By tracing back to an antique time (which is one of the reasons for the ancient spellings and orthography), and back to the roots of man's first contact with the gods, it is possible, so Spenser claims, to regenerate the human spirit. During Saturn's ancient reign, there was no war or deceit or fear, and the earth was fruitful without cultivation. It was a pagan age, but God then ruled through Justice, and he gives the same sacred power to Christian princes in these fallen days, to make them

> like himselfe in glorious sight,
> To sit in his owne seate, his cause to end,
> And rule his people right, as he doth recommend.

For Spenser, it is a short step to identifying the return of Justice with Queen Elizabeth herself, the dread 'Souerayne Goddesse' who sits in the Almighty's

IMAGES OF ELIZA. Few Elizabethans outside the court and Parliament would have seen the queen in the flesh. What images her subjects had of her were generally derived from portraits, engravings, seals, coins, and medals, in which she was no more nor less than a piece of symbolic furniture. *Above*, in an engraving by van de Passe, she is a diadem, curls and head mounted on a lace disk and bell-shaped skirt. The columns—a symbol appropriated from the Spanish emperors—represent, in the iconography of the day, her transcendence of earlier limits to England's power.

But there were unofficial views. Around 1592, Hilliard's brilliant pupil, Isaac Oliver, began a miniature of the queen (*facing, left*), the fidelity of which was so devastating to her vanity that he ceased work on it (ironically, not before a version of it had been sent to van de Passe for the engraving above). Still more subversive were the caricatures circulated on the Continent. Even at home she could be satirized, though at considerable risk to the author: *facing, right*, in 'Queen Elizabeth Allegorized', a pen-and-ink drawing of around 1600 but unpublished until this century, she is attacked as a strange vain fowl, supposedly caught at Crowley in Lincolnshire in 1588.

seat of judgement handing out 'righteous doome' to her English subjects, and filling foreigners with 'awfull dread'. We can guess that this will probably all add up to iron bars, coshes, terrible beatings, prison cells, the rack and the block, and a good amount of Book V does consist of dragging everyone, innocent and guilty, back into that golden world of Justice with the help of a metal man with a metal flail who beats rebels about the head, skins the Irish, and cuts the hands and feet off women. By the mid-1590s, and after years of exile in an Ireland made vicious by the English, Spenser had come to regard man's inconstancy as the gravest of spiritual and social dangers. But it is consistent with his thinking throughout *The Faerie Queene*, and his shorter poems, that the present should be actively, if painfully, worked upon by the past.

In this there is a decidedly different notion of kingship from that in Malory, for when Elizabeth is addressed as the dreadful goddess of Justice who can restore the golden world, it is more than just a bit of slippery sycophancy. Rather, Spenser makes the queen the representative of forgotten goodness, the monarch who is still in contact with the lost virtues of Saturn's distant reign. The word we have to use for this contact, however carefully, is *sacramental*: that is, that Elizabeth is the sacramental or visible presence in Spenser's lawless stone age of the last meeting between man and his maker. Before man broke from God (and his pagan shadow, Saturn), there were no princes at all, but when man rebelled, God chose a deputy for himself in this world, a timeless prince through whom he could still be approached. Malory's prince is nothing like Spenser's because the medieval account of Arthur was transformed by a Reformation story, specifically Calvin's theology of Christ. Calvin's story, espoused by the English Puritans (of whom Spenser was one), tells of a terrible king, Jehovah, unknowable and merciless to his erring subjects, whose son, the Saviour Christ, offers his body in payment for their crimes. There is to be no pardon. Christ simply shields those whom he has chosen and will never abandon: the rest are damned. Even for the elect, though, the only way to the Father, in his unmitigable rage, is through the Son's body. For Spenser, this is the point of contact which his queen makes with the past. Like Calvin's Christ, Elizabeth–Gloriana is an undying prince who lives outside time and whose mystery redeems the chosen Christian nation and returns it to God. In Malory, the old King Arthur is a sleeping lord who represents a line of individual monarchs, each living, dying, and passing on authority. In Spenser, the young Arthur is searching for a royal lady whom he has encountered only in a vision, but who is the sacramental link with all the princes, Tudor and earlier, who have preceded her. Gloriana is Spenser's escape from that medieval circle of guilt and death, for in her there is the old Christian monarch who is reborn in every English prince.

It is tempting to dismiss this way of thinking as politically naïve, or muddled, or supinely conservative (as the poet implicitly acknowledges at the outset of Book V), and Spenser might be open to these charges if it were not for his great attacks on the male triviality and pseudo-Arthurian parts of Tudor culture. His chief target was the medieval chivalry which had fossilized in the court in the decades after Henry VII arrived in England. Year after year in the celebrations before the Tudor princes, there were the tilts, and the jousting, and the champions, and the lances, and the fights at the barriers which had been carried over from the medieval courts and in which the aristocracy participated ferociously, stimulated by elaborate rules of precedent, and the etiquette of the challenge. But for at least half a century before *The Faerie Queene* was written, all of this had been reduced to a ceremony of tin-plate suits strapped on horses, trotting around before the monarch trying to knock one another to the ground in the royal presence. It was not that the courtiers did not take the ceremonies seriously, rather they took them *too* seriously, they had become a fetish of behaviour which was longed for all the more vehemently when medieval armour and heavy cavalry were becoming useless in modern battles. Polished suits of golden armour might look good at a tournament, but they were not effective against musket-balls, and a knight could not attack a battery of cannon wearing one and hope to have much protection from gun and chain shot. In *The Faerie Queene* there are many indications of a weariness with the whole enterprise of courtly combat, and by the end of the poem, it is not only the pastoral knight, Sir Calidore, but also his author, who is desperate to get the armour off his back, and be up in the hills, piping with Colin Clout, and dancing with the rural girls. Why then does Spenser take on all the medieval trappings and traps in the first place, and put himself on the treadmill of romance allegory and on to a lexicon never heard of before or since?

One explanation might be that during the sixteenth century the English chivalric set pieces, the Accession Day tilts, the Elizabethan jousts, the whole lot, were something tediously repeated, re-enacting the death of what seemed a more simple court life of physical trials and temptations. Tudor chivalry has all the characteristics of communal obsessiveness, not to say hysteria, and the court seems to have thrived on the unreality of it all—some of Hilliard's best miniatures are of noblemen dressed for the tilt or the barriers, some of Dowland's best songs devoted to a victor in the lists. Yet Spenser was not drawn in some simple way to elaborate still further on this unreality. Rather, it was another of his attempts, as with his new Arthurian monarchy, to find

THE EARL OF CUMBERLAND, DRESSED FOR THE TILT, miniature by Nicholas Hilliard, around 1590. George Clifford, 3rd earl of Cumberland, was notorious for his infidelity in marriage and for the fortune he expended—not simply on expensive clothing and portraits, but on fitting ships for exploration and privateering. Yet his profligacy was far from unique: for a courtier, the favoured ways out of debt were either to win the monarch's favour, and hence the income from some rich monopoly, or to capture a Spanish treasure ship. Both methods were costly and hazardous, and often met with entire failure.

a way out of a dead end, to go straight for what was most unreal and most uncivilizing (because no longer alive) in his own culture. In *The Faerie Queene* there are indeed allegorical clumsinesses, moral traps, dragons laying waste to lands, archaic vocabulary, magicians, and tin-plate thumping, but they are there to be expelled, not celebrated. Spenser's energy is one which drives out the old chivalry, and replaces it with, say, Amoret's grace, or the generosity and perseverance of the lady warrior and heroine of Book III, Britomart. Significantly, passages in Spenser dealing with male or fraternal love and combat (say, Cambell's fight with the brothers, Priamond, Diamond, and Triamond at the Tournament in IV. iii) are the least engaging, whereas the memorable cantos are those in which erotic love shades into either prurience and frustration (II. xii), or into the freely-given, but unwilled sexuality of paradise (III. vi). Furthermore, we cannot fail to notice, how, throughout the course of *The Faerie Queene*, the allegorical structure breaks down time and again, and how the activity of the old chivalry, either in Sir Guyon or Sir Arthegall, gives way in interest and significance to the more complex decorum of sexual behaviour and spiritual danger (subjects discussed more fully, later in this chapter). Put simply, Spenser was trying to root a new poetic in the female, and in the vitality of the senses, and in the Calvinist notion of Grace. There could not have been a more radical attack on Tudor mock-chivalry.

Yet Spenser's attack could never have succeeded, and for an important reason. In *Morte Darthur* there is a displacement of the sexual identity of the prince as soon as Sir Lancelot arrives. Arthur becomes the grey king that Tennyson says he is, so that his energies will not rival those of the queen's paramour, and he is made ever more distant from the centre of the story as the love develops between Guinevere and Lancelot. In *The Faerie Queene* there is all manner of sexual activity, some of it beautiful and gentle (Venus and Adonis in procreation in their garden in Book III), some of it frenzied and savage (the Giantess coupling with her brother in the womb before birth, or Hellenore being ridden nine times a night by men-goats she delights to stroke and handle). But whatever the shape of the sexual need, and whatever its potency—to beget, besmirch, or bless the body—all the stories in Spenser are heading ultimately for the court of Gloriana: all that longing to seed or to despoil is making its way to the virgin princess of Faerie Land. So much for the fiction, but we cannot forget that Gloriana is also supposed to be Queen Elizabeth, the last Tudor prince, a sixty-year-old woman who will never marry the young Arthur (at least not in this life), and who is a reality of sterile spinsterhood, of dried-up old virginity, at the core of all this sexual variety, amidst the images of begetting. By 1590, as her critics have it, she was losing her teeth, her skin was yellowing slightly, she was partly bald, and she was dressed in kirtlets and lace and farthingales that might have been more fitting for a woman half her age. No matter what Spenser tried to do to regenerate the Tudor culture from within, by re-establishing its poetic in the union of the new Arthur and the eternal Gloriana, there was always at the centre of it all that sovereign goddess of untried virginity, the old woman who was the successor of the Arthurian Tudors but in whom the Tudor line itself had failed.

Origins, Lyrics, and old England

What the Tudor princes needed, as much as an Arthurian mythology, was an effective administrative class. Someone had to sort out their finances, negotiate with ambassadors, and organize the day-to-day running of the court, and so a generation or so after *Morte Darthur* (a story in which there could be no place for bureaucracy, council minutes, and civil servants), a new type of Renaissance man, and book, was to appear. He would not be a warrior, but a lawyer or a cleric; he would not need loyalty, but high principles; he would not be a pedigree aristocrat with his hounds, but a citizen Londoner with his commentary on the Gospels. And who but Sir Thomas More (*c.*1477–1535), Catholic saint and martyr, and friend of Erasmus, would bring together in his person and in his *Utopia* so many bourgeois virtues of classical learning, personal conscience, ruthless compassion and, above all, legality? *Utopia*, published in 1516, sits strangely in the history of English literature—not only because More wrote it in Latin, which was then the language of Europe, but because it was the first, and for a good while the most significant entry of Greek thought into an Englishman's writing (the next was into Spenser's poetry at the end of the century). But we must be careful not to confuse the Greek depth to the work with its polished and snobbish surface of Grecian jokes. 'Utopia', the name of the imaginary new country, is derived from the Greek and means 'no place'; Hythlodaeus, the character who tells us about Utopia, means 'nonsense-pedlar'; Anydrus, the chief river in Utopia, means 'waterless'. More's etymologies and prefatory letters and trilingual word-plays may have raised a smirk or two among the new humanists, but the real play in *Utopia* is between two types of Greek behaviour and rhetoric, between the private identity of Socrates and the social identity of Plato.

The division is made neatly between *Utopia*'s two books. In the first, which is much the shorter, More himself, while in Bruges, meets Peter Giles, a native of Antwerp, who in turn introduces him to Raphael Hythlodaeus, a Portuguese traveller, who has just returned from Brazil, via Ceylon and Calcutta, after serving with Amerigo Vespucci. The scale of travel and swirl of nations, new worlds and old, Europeans meeting each other and meeting the inhabitants of South America, funnels down in an instant to a rented house, a private conversation, and More's eagerness to hear all about Raphael's journeys: 'there in the garden we sat down on a bench covered with turf to talk together.' There are no tales of monsters or savage peoples, but a reference to the Utopians, a nation which lives on a hitherto unknown island in one of the new oceans. At this point, Raphael's account of them, which ought to follow on directly, is postponed until Book II, and instead, the attention shifts to Raphael himself, and another of his encounters, this time in England, in the very house in which, by chance, More had served as a page. It is the house of the great Cardinal Morton, the Lord Chancellor, and there Raphael meets and debates with an English lawyer. The clinches and knockdown dialogue which follow are much rougher than we are used to with Socrates (in, say, the *Symposium*), but the way of teaching and learning is much the same. Raphael's opponent,

HENRY THE REFORMER. Henry VIII's break with Rome was of much less importance, ideologically, than what was to follow: the union of Church and State under one supreme authority was still intact, only the authority was Henry and not the Pope (a substitution depicted in this woodcut). In the half-century to follow, despite Elizabeth's moderation and wiliness, the Puritans, or radical Protestants, demanded much greater changes: an end to bishops, to papist sacraments, and to prescribed religious ceremonies—an end, in fact, to the established Church itself. The consequences for the monarchy, and hierarchical rule, were clear. As Elizabeth's successor, James I, put it, 'no bishop, no king'.

although he says little, is made to look stupid, pedantic, and brutal as he clings on to English law and social order (hang all thieves, starve the peasants into submission, etc.), while Raphael, step by step, shows how needlessly vicious and economically inefficient all this repression is. The debate ends, with nothing much resolved, and in the last section of Book I, Raphael explains to More and Giles why no one like himself could counsel a prince. He would want to give advice based on Christ's teachings, or in the interest of saving soldiers' lives, or preserving the nation's peace: he would tell the king 'to look after his ancestral kingdom, improve it as much as he could, cultivate it in every conceivable way. He should love his people and be loved by them; he should live among them, and govern them kindly, and let other kingdoms alone, since his own is big enough, if not too big for him.' It would indeed be a remarkable courtier who could tell a Renaissance prince these sorts of things, and Thomas More, unlike Raphael, was of course just that remarkable. He could not bend his conscience to uphold Henry VIII's divorce from Catherine of Aragon, and so Henry had him executed in 1535.

Back in *Utopia*, there is not the same definition or finality about any single issue. Even in Book I, where much good is talked about and corruption pointed to, the personality, motives, and failings of each speaker clog up his good intentions. Raphael has the right ideas, but he despairs of being listened to, and so he will not be. The Cardinal is wise and learned, and listens carefully to Raphael, but in the end he allows his household and guests to be sycophantic, and his private audiences to applaud his suggestions alone. This is why the first book is Socratic, because it identifies truth and justice as elusive, inward virtues which men must have teased out of them, and which no one man can lay exclusive claim to. In Book II, by contrast, everything about the Utopians themselves is outward, obvious, and public—their vices just as much as their virtues. There is no poverty because there is no private wealth, and few mistakes in marriage because prospective husbands and wives see one another naked before agreeing to the match. Not surprisingly, intelligent Utopians look down their noses at religious mysteries. But equally they do not make the slightest effort to conceal their ruthless tactics in war: they use mercenaries, because they regard them as scum who deserve to be killed; they try to bribe the enemy to assassinate their own leaders; they set up death-squads to kill the enemy general in the field. If there is any perfection in the Utopians, it is not so much in moral goodness but in their invulnerability to hidden desires. They live in the world of the late Plato, the world where laws are not intended to curb passions or prurience or gluttony, but rather to drive them out into the open and leave human beings with their guilt and innocence shockingly revealed. When any individual takes a step back into privacy, and into envy, adulterous thoughts and anger, the Utopians immediately make him a slave: in other words, they exploit his body, and deny his person the moment he withdraws into it.

THE SAVAGE. The discovery of the New World and its inhabitants prompted Europeans such as Montaigne to think about their own origins, and even to ask who were the true savages: the natives, or the over-civilized Christians who slaughtered them. In 1585 the artist John White accompanied the English expedition to Roanoke Island, off Virginia, to draw and paint the indigenous people and wildlife. Engravings of these pictures, such as this one of a Roanoke medicine man, or 'conjuror', were soon published throughout Protestant Europe.

Reading the two books together, *Utopia* is as much of a hybrid as its author (libertarian and law-giver), and its medium (Latin prose, Greek derivations, and English story-telling). It is hard *and* subtle, a work in which the self is unknowably complex and yet also rigidly observable. More wrote nothing else of comparable importance (although his *Life of Richard III* has been praised by some critics), and it may be that his intellectual roots were so deeply Greek that he was unable to find a way of writing profoundly in the vernacular. What he *could* do in Tudor English, and perhaps even more in the language of the Romans, was to make something ferociously, even bitterly, laughable. When he was about to be beheaded, a barber came to cut his long hair. The barber asked whether he would be pleased to be trimmed. 'In good faith, honest fellow,' said Sir Thomas, 'the King and I have a suit for my head and till the title be cleared I will do no cost upon it.' Again, in *Utopia*, in moments which are truly Roman, we see a quality of satire rarely achieved in England until the 1590s. In one of these, Raphael is describing how aristocrats and even churchmen have been enclosing common lands for pasture. Their sheep, he says, 'that used to be so meek and eat so little' are now 'becoming so greedy and wild that they devour men themselves. . . . They devastate and pillage fields, houses and towns.' A sudden ballooning of the image, and then these fantastical, voracious sheep, straight from some medieval nightmare, are gone.

Utopia lacks only one thing, a sense of loss. Like some ship of fools, it is anchored outside the vernacular, in Greek soundings and Latin wit, and it has every reason to be confident that it is something both old and new, anciently wise and freshly conceived. For the writers who followed More, and who chose English, there could be no such confidence. In the poetry of Sir Thomas Wyatt (1503-42), who was writing in the 1530s and 1540s, there is a plangency which goes well beyond the medieval complaint and becomes a search for lost homelands. This is true whether his subject is thwarted love (the songs and sonnets), or the true man's dismay at the rapaciousness of the court (the verse satires), or the sinner's fear that he has been excluded forever from God's mercy (the paraphrases of the Psalms). Sometimes his exile is physical, and he is making his way back with 'spur and sail' for to 'seek the Thames' and the city, London, which Brutus, its first founder, had to seek by dreams. More often the poet is left behind by his lady's fickleness, and he fidgets restlessly with memories and dreams of felicity and requited love. At yet other times he is the loyal servant who recalls, in clouds of thunder, how his friends and patrons, and even his queen, were silenced by the block:

> The bell tower showed me such sight
> That in my head sticks day and night.
> There did I learn out of a grate,
> For all favour, glory, or might,
>   That yet *circa Regna tonat*.
> ('Who list his wealth and ease retain')

[*circa Regna tonat* it thunders around thrones.]

There is a combination of clarity and concealment here which is a sure sign that Wyatt has got the experience into shape. We do not see what the poet sees—the grate shuts *out* those who are free—but there is still a logic to what we are shown: the sight in his head is like the bell in the tower, but it 'sticks' in there unmoving, unlike the thunder rumbling around the throne. And his head is still *stuck* on, with the sight in it, unlike the severed head which is down in the courtyard and which we are unable to see. The lines are not evading so much as uncovering, through rips in the imagery, the entire experience—corpse, resentment, imprisonment, and all. It is easy to read Wyatt inattentively, and even unsympathetically, because the emotions of losing, grieving, and hurting, tire us quickly and make us insensitive (necessarily so, for our health's sake). The wonder of it is that there is so much variety and strength in his writing, especially in the songs, when the fictions are so

Brooke Ld Cobham.

GEORGE BROOKE, LORD COBHAM, chalk-and-ink drawing by Hans Holbein (d. 1543). From the 1530s until his death, Holbein recorded the face of the Tudor aristocracy, administrators, and upper gentry. Gathered together, as many of them are at Windsor Castle, the portraits emphasize the community of intelligence, resolution, and melancholy he saw before him at the court of Henry VIII. All the energies of the portraits are directed at the head; the eyes, often beautifully formed and slightly heavy, gaze disconcertingly beyond any audience or line of sight, even when the sitter is full face, and they tell little of what is within. Their silence perhaps testifies to the tyranny of Henry's reign.

unremittingly sorrowful. For every one of Wyatt's so-called Petrarchan conceits (galleys charged with forgetfulness, passing over seas of tears, blown by sighs, burnt on ice, frozen in fires), there are passages which ring clear like fine china, and have elegant turns and patterns:

> Is it possible
> So cruel intent,
> So hasty heat and so soon spent,
> From love to hate and thence for to relent?
> Is it possible?
>
> ('Is it possible')

Above all, in a poetry which has a relatively narrow range of vocabulary, Wyatt manages to avoid whining, and he keeps his voice firm and sure as it returns to the same vowels, alliterates, rhymes internally, and binds up sounds across the caesura:

Refrain I must, what is the cause?
Sure, as they say, 'So hawks be taught.'
But in my case layeth no such clause
For with such craft I am not caught.

('Such hap as I am happed in')

Yet for all his assurance in writing, Wyatt is none the less a troubled writer, and this may be because he has no clear idea where his poetry is coming from. Modern scholars have shown that he translates and adapts from Petrarch and certain of the Roman poets, but he is just as willing to find himself writing in ballades, carols, rondeaux, canzoni, sonnets, songs, questions, answers, imperatives sung and spoken, and even in verses which very nearly collapse from perplexity into doggerel: 'Since that I will and shall not, / My will I will refrain. / Thus, for to will and will not, / Will willing is but vain' (*The Ballad of Will*). Certainly, much can be said for Wyatt's fluency. In the epistolary satires he is the first modern English poet to master Dante's *terza rima*, and probably the last to remember the wit and speed of the exchanges in *The Canterbury Tales*. 'Peep,' calls the country mouse, who has come to visit the town,

'sister, I am here.'
'Peace,' quod the town mouse, 'why speakest thou so loud?'
And by the hand she took her fair and well.
'Welcome,' quod she, 'my sister, by the Rood.'

('My mother's maids when they did sew and spin')

But in spite of this dexterity, Wyatt is still left puzzling at whether the roots of his language are deep enough. Massed in syntax and verse, Tudor English could accumulate enough weight, but what of individual words and phrases, names and sayings—were they as distant from some unknowable origin as a lover from his unfaithful mistress, or a sinner from his God, or a subject from his prince? Perhaps the real loss was the loss of meaning, which no courtly service, or love, or intrigue, would bring back:

It was not long ere I by proof had found
That feeble building is on feeble ground;
For in her heart this word did never sound:
In aeternum.

('*In aeternum* I was once determed')

This says it all. Experience ('proof') quickly digs up a proverbial truth, in all its obviousness and feebleness (the building is as weak as its foundations), when 'this word' fails to sound in her heart. Nor should it, of course, because it is a Latin phrase, *in aeternum* ('forever'), an old fragment from a dead language instead of an English word. How can his lady promise eternal love when the very words with which she should pledge herself are not her own,

AUTHORITY AND LICENCE: HENRY VIII AND HIS JESTER, WILLIAM SOMMERS, miniature in a psalter, about 1540. Though total authority was never claimed explicitly by Tudor monarchs (and in fact Parliament steadily increased its sway during this period), the Crown did wield immense power: the lawcourts silenced religious and political dissent, the movement of individuals of the lower ranks was severely restricted, and the punishments for even trivial crimes were horrendous. In the circumstances, the Tudor holiday was an essential device for releasing social frustration. Not *all* rules were suspended, but it was possible, for at least the rich and educated, to see authority parodied and even temporarily overthrown, in masques and interludes (*Twelfth Night* illustrates such festive moments). The Tudor prince himself retained a licensed fool or jester—like King Lear's fool—to mock and criticize him.

or her lover's native speech? The problem, here in miniature but true elsewhere, is that Wyatt, no more than his lady friends, can trust his English words to mean enough. There may be large explanations for this (Henry VIII's tyrannical court or the Reformation may have broken old continuities in the language), but insecurity of meaning is what, paradoxically, holds Wyatt's poetry together.

The received view of Wyatt's near-contemporary, Henry Howard, earl of Surrey (*c*.1517–47), is that he is less of a poet than Wyatt, but a smoother one, less innovative but more precisely classical. In his translations of *The Aeneid* Books II and IV, he showed, probably to the amazement of his contemporaries, that Virgil's hexameters, and the to and fro of an unrhymed and inflected language could just about sound right when rendered in English blank verse. Before Surrey, heroic measure had only seemed possible in rhyme, but here he was, measuring the shape of Virgil's writing in English speech rhythms, and run-on. When Iarbas, Dido's former lover, is angry and contemptuous of Aeneas, he now speaks the language of Englishmen, not their books:

> That Paris now, with his unmanly sort,
> With mitred hats, with oynted bush and beard,
> His rape enjoyeth: whiles to thy temples we
> Our off'rings bring, and follow rumours vain.   (IV. 276–9)

We can still feel the shock of something new in this. The adjectives sit easily with their nouns, the subordinate clauses delay the main verb for only a line and a half, and there is little or no breathlessness. All the clauses still pause at the caesura, but the poet has succeeded in making the slight interruptions in rhythm open into moments of emphasis. The lines are not Surrey at his best, nor worst, but they give us an idea of how much the Elizabethan dramatists were indebted to him half a century later, when they wanted characters to speak blank verse on stage.

But what gives Surrey significance also takes it from him: translating Virgil, his major achievement, was too easy a choice for a poet of his talent. True, the work fitted in with the humanist ideal of reconciling ancient and modern cultures, of achieving a Renaissance of what had been best in Graeco-Roman antiquity, but it also allowed him to avoid that sense of loss which Wyatt had identified in the language itself. Instead of confronting difficulties in meaning, Surrey turned the loss away from his poetry towards the oldest of stories—the fall of Troy, and then Aeneas' betrayal of Dido for the sake of Rome. As Virgil had it, the breach in Troy's walls was the end of the Asian world and the beginning of Roman Europe, while Dido was the first of many sacrifices to Roman imperial destiny. Bringing Virgil into English, Surrey was pushing right back to the origins of a distant loss, but he substituted this, and the stories of ancient infidelity, for the more immediate and obscure loss in his own medium, the English language. This is why, in too many of his 'original' poems, Surrey's grief is all on the surface, and the words look as though they have just come into being, clumsily, a second before we read them:

> Alas, I see nothing to hurt so sore
> But time sometime reduceth a return;
> Yet time my harm increaseth more and more,
> And seems to have my cure always in scorn.
>
> ('The sun hath twice brought forth . . .')

Surrey never writes as badly as this in his Virgil, in part because he learnt much of his manner and diction from the Scots poet, Gavin Douglas, who translated the entire *Aeneid* around 1513. It is by no means unknown for English poets to recover and advance their own speech by borrowing from Scots, Welsh, or Irish writers, and in this case what Surrey got from Douglas, indirectly, was some access to the language and vigour of the master-poet, Chaucer. A line or two from Douglas makes this clear enough: 'Quharfor al thai of Troy, blyth as thai mocht, / Thair langsum duyl and murnying dyd away, / Kest up the portis and yschit furth to play . . .' The genealogy of influence in this—Virgil out of Latin out of Douglas out of Chaucer—is complicated by yet another pressure on Surrey, that of Petrarch and the Italians. Only infrequently, and this is why he is not a major poet, does Surrey bring harmony to the tongues and cultures trying to speak through him. When he does manage it, though, his sources are not only combined, but wonderfully transcended. In 'O happy dames', the opening is a medieval complaint—a grieving wife addresses other ladies—and the second stanza is a Petrarchan conceit made real (the ship, freighted with remembrance, has literally taken her husband away). But after that the poem is pure English Renaissance, and Surrey writes some very great stanzas indeed. Shakespeare apart, it is really not until the beginning of this century, in Joyce's *Chamber Music*, that we again hear lyrics of this quality and kind, where a grave monotone contains the most turbulent of passions:

> When other lovers in arms across
> Rejoyce their chief delight,
> Drowned in tears to mourn my loss
> I stand the bitter night
> In my window, where I may see
> Before the winds how the clouds flee.
> Lo, what a mariner love hath made me!
>
> And in green waves when the salt flood
> Doth rise by rage of wind,
> A thousand fancies in that mood
> Assail my restless mind . . .

It is another literary orthodoxy that the Elizabethans preferred Surrey to Wyatt, that his sweet Petrarchan manners suited them better than Wyatt's dark words and broken metres. Both poets reached the late Elizabethans (the ones who matter) through the series of anthologies published by Tottel from 1557 onwards. Their texts did not pass unhindered. Wyatt's poems in particular were tampered with to make them simpler, and easier on the ear, and this produced readings which were downright silly in some cases. The late Elizabethans also lost contact with another early Tudor writer, John Skelton (c.1460–1529), but they did this deliberately because they thought he was a crude medieval buffoon, and that his writing was a kind of grotesque *rite de passage* which poetry had to go through before it could grow up. Nothing could have been further from the truth, and the Elizabethan erasure or ignorance of Skelton's quality was philistinic and disabling. It has to be said that he is not a major writer, but he is more than a charming naïf or a dotty, hawk-flying jigster (two modern ways of placing him). When he glimpses his girl-friend's ankles, or thinks of her clothes and what is under them, the rhymes bubble with excitement, but there is no smut or guilt:

> whereto should I note,
> How often did I toot
> Upon her pretty foot?
> It rased mine heart-root
> To see her tread the ground
> With heeles short and round!
>
> (*Philip Sparrow*, 1145–50)

[*toot* peep; *rased* bruised.]

The bounce on each final syllable, and the gait and pace, *allegro non troppo*,

DRESSING FOR LOVE: in Elizabeth Vernon, Countess of Southampton, aristocratic and sexual power combine. She is vulnerable and enticing at her *toilette*—her comb bears the words 'menez-moi doucement'—but she is also the lady of authority, with ermine and jewels. Whether true or not, what is pictured is the life of silent, beautiful leisure presupposed for the heroines of Elizabethan sonnet sequences.

separates it from the medieval lyric almost as much as from the Elizabethan one, and so too do its sentiments. The girl has a rather sexy blemish, a 'scar upon her chin, / Enhatched on her fair skin,' and the thought of it, Skelton decides,

> would make any man
> To forget deadly sin
> Her favour to win. (1080-2)

Forgetting deadly sin, or rather contesting with needless or insincere shame, is one of Skelton's most serious and most attractive qualities. He rejoices in what he owes to Chaucer and Gower, taking from them without remorse, and he refuses to brood or complain self-regardingly about an affair he has with someone else's wife ('The ancient acquaintance, madam . . .'). He is more concerned that she keep mum, because her husband has a habit of bruising his neighbours' and servants' 'brainpans'. Naturally, there is a Chaucerian relish in the descriptions of rival horses, and lovers, and her riding them: 'Spur up at the hinder girth, with, "Gup, morell, gup!" / With, "Jayst ye, jennet of Spain, for your tail wags!"' Yet nothing in Skelton is ever salacious or vile— a moment's comparison with Ben Jonson assures us of how clean-minded he is. In a poem such as *Philip Sparrow*, which laments a bird's death, there are lines about the creature snuggling down between Dame Margery's breasts, but Skelton still has enough of the medieval *gentilesse* in him, and delight in the absurd, to keep the sexual temperature much cooler than in anything Catullus ever wrote.

Where Skelton is not cool is in his attacks on sham anguish, or phoney blushes, or desire which dresses itself in power and self-righteousness. Sometimes his satire seems to lose its way or be blunted in the medieval forms he has chosen (the state-as-ship allegory in *The Bouge of Court* is not as compelling as it promises to be at first), but when he goes for Cardinal Wolsey, Henry VIII's minister, the short lines hit the target, point-blank, every time: 'But this madde Amalecke, / Lyke to a Mamelek, / He regardeth lordes / No more than potshordes. / He is in suche elacyon / Of his exaltacyon, / And the supportacyon / Of our soverayne lorde, / That, God to recorde, / He ruleth all at wyll / Without reason or skyll' (*Why Come Ye Nat to Courte?*, 478-88; original spellings preserved). Just how the speed of this is made compatible with the dragging club-foot rhythm points to Skelton's special place in the history of prosody and diction. The Elizabethans would have disliked such technical roughness, but even more would they have detested his apparent unreflectiveness. The dislike would have been mutual. Skelton hated hypocritical prelates and the corrupted Church as much as Spenser and Milton did, but equally he hated the newly sublimated pride of the Protestants, who were always so concerned to make sure that God had not forgotten their very special, individual sins. Skelton died in 1529, a few years before Henry VIII's break with the Church of Rome, but he must have seen what was coming: personal conscience, and a hatred of sexuality which was to characterize even the very best things in

MEN AND PEACOCKS, from an Elizabethan embroidery. Male friendship, and the life of a courtier, were preoccupations of Tudor writers. Some of the intimacies they depicted were undoubtedly homosexual (whether explicitly or latently); but in dealing with an age that lacked privacy as we know it, we may easily confuse our standards for theirs, finding desire where there was only social custom.

Elizabethan culture. No wonder that it was Surrey, the golden aristocrat, rather than Skelton, the coarse Papist, whom the Elizabethans chose to resuscitate in the 1590s. What is only a little more surprising is the book (one by Thomas Nashe) in which the Surrey cadaver was to make its appearance.

Thomas Nashe (1567-1601), a graduate of St John's College, Cambridge, began writing in London in 1588. It was the year of the Armada when, for quite understandable reasons, English patriotism and xenophobia had a boost which lasted them a good couple of decades. The sight of all those Spanish galleons burning in the Straits, and the ones wrecked (by God's grace) off Scotland and Ireland, cheered up English hearts immensely. Hating and jeering at foreigners and smelling out foreign habits (Calvinism from Geneva, poncey clothes and daggers from Italy, piss-drunk dullards from Holland, etc.) became even more the one thing that Englishmen had in common. They might despise each other's religion, be ignorant or learned, a lord or a clerk, but all the time tugging them together was their agreement about strangers. There was nothing new about this. For centuries, Jews, or Flemish weavers, or other refugees had taken the brunt of this fear and hatred when times were bad. But in Nashe, a writer of immense wit and intellectual energy, and almost no judgement, all the ferocity and vulgarity of the mob met with Elizabethan high culture. Occasionally this was quite harmless, and even faintly amusing. In *Lenten Stuff* (1599), an essay in mock-praise of the kipper, one or two golden myths, including that of Hero and Leander, were pricked ever so gently. To shoot 'my fool's bolt amongst you', Nashe says, even 'that fable of Midas eating gold had no other shadow or inclusive pith in it, but he was of a queasy stomach and nothing could he fancy but this new-found gilded fish [i.e. smoked herring]'. Midas, according to Nashe, because he was 'unexperienced of the nature' of the kipper, 'for he was a fool that had ass's ears, snapped it up at one blow, and because in the boiling or seething of it in his maw he felt it commotion a little and upbraid him, he thought he had eaten gold indeed'. This sort of skit, featherweight in interest, can go on fizzing for pages, but it is not really what Nashe is good at. He is not writing smartly enough, nor brutally enough, although ten lines earlier he had been:

Whiles I am shuffling and cutting with these long-coated Turks, would any antiquary

TRIUMPHAL CITIES. England under the Tudors was an age of new ignorance as well as new sophistication. During the course of the century, the humanists, as elsewhere in Europe, would continue a great restoration of classical texts. Yet there was an ignorant contempt, particularly among the Elizabethans (even in Sidney), for the achievements of medieval England: its architecture, and its literature, law, and learning.

The history of Rome, from its mythic beginnings to the republic and then to the empire, was naturally a much-used example of the transitoriness of even the greatest states. *Above*, two woodcuts (to which the young Spenser added rather indifferent verse translations in 1569): the Spirit of Rome, with Tiber pouring out of his urn, and Romulus, Remus, and the wolf at his feet; and a shattered triumphal arch set beside its original intact grandeur. *Below*, one of the triumphal fronts erected in 1603 to welcome James I to London. The city's skyline is the background to a set of stagey imperial arches and niches, which dress up past and future royal power in crests, pyramids, and pseudo-classical designs.

would explicate unto me this remblere or quiddity, whether those turbanto groutheads, that hang all men by the throats on iron hooks, even as our towers hang all their herrings by the throats on wooden spits, first learned it of our herring men, or our herring men of them.

Nashe has sometimes been praised for the vividness of his images, and the way they send up and puncture the priggishness and pedantry in other Elizabethan prose. In this case, just as he is shuffling and cutting his own subject, and turning over a few neologisms and scholarly scraps, he catches sight of something—a body, or is it a fish, hanging up on a hook. Perhaps the Turks' long, hanging coats brought it to mind, but it is there in an instant, as freakishly compounded as 'turbanto groutheads' and as irreverent about hooks and spits, drying fish, and humiliating corpses, as of antiquaries and quiddities. The best one could say for this prose is that it unifies disparate things: the worst, that far from intensifying experience, it makes what is gruesome into a very literary thing, into a conceit, a clever piece of writing.

It was Nashe who brought Surrey back to life (another monstrously literary attempt) in his *Unfortunate Traveller*, published in 1594. This is a loosely constructed set of episodes, something like a picaresque novel, narrated by Jack Wilton, an English page. In France, Wilton begins his service with the earl of Surrey and together they journey down to Italy, getting in and out of scrapes, love entanglements, and knockdown practical jokes. Italy, to one half of the Elizabethan Protestant mind, was a den of iniquity, corrupt popes, and unnatural sexual desires of all kinds, so Nashe was on to a winner the moment he had got Wilton across the Alps and down to Rome. Executions, plague, Wilton locked up by a Jew, and then by the gorgeous Juliana—it is all pretty much what the 1590s audience expected. But Nashe, ever wise in these things, also gave them a touch of culture, acknowledging the justifiable English anxiety that Italy was light years ahead in the arts. For this, Nashe makes Surrey write poems to his Lady Geraldine—and very good verses they can be:

> Stars fall to fetch fresh light from her rich eyes,
> Her bright brow drives the sun to clouds beneath.
> Her hairs' reflex with red streaks paints the skies,
> Sweet morn and evening dew flows from her breath . . .

These would pass muster with much of Surrey's second-rate poetry, if not his best, and it shows how talented a writer Nashe could be. What he lacked, bundling high and low together and pulping it into an ersatz wittiness, was taste.

But Nashe's Englishness and snobberies and insularity have another side. Almost a century after Thomas More, who wrote about his new nation in Latin, Nashe, by contrast, discovered that there was an old England still waiting to be located in the native tongue. The last was as imaginary as Utopia, but no less real. Orson Welles, when asked what had attracted him to

Shakespeare's history cycle, the *Henry* plays (for his film *Chimes at Midnight*), answered that he could hear old England in them. Part of Nashe's appeal, whatever his failings, is that like Justice Shallow, Pistol, and Falstaff, he seems to speak sometimes for a culture much older, and much less orthodox than the one he is writing in. When he skipped off to Yarmouth in 1597, after writing a controversial play, he found there (and wrote about in *Lenten Stuff*) traditions, language, and history rooted securely in the fishing trade and on the coasts and even in the sands reclaimed from the sea. Perhaps it was all an illusion, but the same feeling for an England unwritten about and hidden, but always waiting to be remembered, was still alive even in the nineteenth century. Dickens, we recall, made Yarmouth and its beaches and people one of the emotional beginnings of *David Copperfield*. For poor Tom Nashe, who could not keep away from the metropolis and its insecure, sparky literary life, this England showed itself too late for him to make much of it. In all likelihood, he quickly returned to London, and died there of the plague in 1601.

Elizabethan Mysteries of Love and Power

Often, in reading a literature, we sense that there is a particular mystery, unspoken and even unconscious, which binds its writers together. On occasions, this will surface in a great dream or a vision, which is so full of grace or terror that for centuries after it has been disclosed entire communities will try to live out its secret. One such vision, dreamt in Florence in 1283 by Dante Alighieri, was a controlling mystery which persisted throughout the late Middle Ages and Renaissance. It is the secret, derived from the medieval Schoolmen, of how God entered human love and sundered man from woman to complete their salvation. In section 3 of *La Vita Nuova*, or 'The New Life', Dante describes how Beatrice, the lady whom he loves, speaks to him for the first time, after which he returns home, falls asleep and dreams of her:

In my room I seemed to see a cloud the colour of fire, and in the cloud a lordly figure, frightening to behold, yet in himself, it seemed to me, he was filled with a marvellous joy. He said many things, of which I understood only a few; among them were the words: *Ego dominus tuus* [I am your Master]. In his arms I seemed to see a naked figure, sleeping, wrapped lightly in a crimson cloth. Gazing intently I saw it was she who had bestowed her greeting on me earlier that day. In one hand the standing figure held a fiery object, and he seemed to say, *Vide cor tuum* [Behold your heart]. After a little while I thought he wakened her who slept and prevailed on her to eat the glowing object in his hand. Reluctantly and hesitantly she did so. A few moments later his happiness turned to bitter grief, and, weeping, he gathered the figure in his arms and together they seemed to ascend into the heavens. I felt such anguish at their departure that my light sleep was broken, and I awoke.

Most of the significance of this is probably lost forever to the modern mind, and yet it is the secret of Busirane's House in Book III of *The Faerie Queene*, with its bloody hearts torn from the body, and its cruel masque of Cupid, and its erotic images of divinity. And in Tudor writers less capable of its mystery, even Sidney, it becomes vain fantasy and sexual ugliness.

This is because Dante has taken a great risk. The Lord who appears to him is not only the pagan Cupid, but Christ, the divinity who can ascend to heaven—and he is not only joyful, generous, and benign, but also a second tempter, who encourages Beatrice to eat of another's body, for which he himself then suffers. Beatrice too confuses us. She is a pagan goddess in crimson veil, yet she is all innocence and hesitation as she is prevailed upon to eat the heart. Nagging at us by now are the parallels with the first making, tempting, and grief in Eden. Eve, made from a rib out of Adam's left side while he slept, was tempted to eat the apple for knowledge: here Beatrice is woken and fed the heart out of Dante's side while he sleeps. The dream is a terrible blow to orthodoxy because it looks as though Christ redeems this time through the female—by taking Beatrice to heaven and making Dante follow her there (in his *Divina Commedia*). The risk is that when God penetrates human desire in this way, sacred and profane may be confused with one another. The Lord's agony, weeping and sacrifice—his passion—may become a vicious form of sexual desire. The shock of realizing this was something which writers of later centuries spent enormous efforts trying to recover from and heal.

In *The Faerie Queene* there are many signs that this wound, divine love breaching human desire, was still open three hundred years after Dante. In Canto viii of Book VI, the Book of courtliness and courtesy, Serena, beloved of Sir Calepine, strays from her companions and is lost in the deserts of Faerie Land. Exhausted, she falls asleep and is found by a 'saluage nation', the wild men of the forests, cannibals who devour strangers. In what follows there is not simply an attempted rape, but a convergence and confusion of the three ceremonies which make up the civilization of the Elizabethans: the Eucharist, the feast, and the sexual act. The savages, overjoyed at capturing Serena, cannot decide where to begin. Should they kill her and eat her at once or save her for many meals? Their god must have her blood, but which of them will have the best bits of her flesh? 'Some with their eyes the daintiest morsels chose; / Some praise her paps, some praise her lips and nose.' Their priest washes his 'bloudy vessels' and prepares the 'holy fire'; and then the girl wakes up. Her screams are drowned by their 'whooping, and hallowing', and her clothes are torn from her. Then follow the 'lustfull fantasyes' over her body, until some of the creatures can stand it no longer and begin among 'themselues deuize, / Thereof by force to take their beastly pleasure',

> But them the Priest rebuking, did aduize
> To dare not to pollute so sacred threasure,
> Vow'd to the gods: religion held euen theeues in measure.   (VI. viii. 43)

What is human meets with what is divine here, except that the distinctions

IRISH GALLOGLAS AND ATTENDANTS, pen-and-ink drawing by Dürer (1521). Ireland made and broke a good many Tudor Englishmen—most notably Robert, earl of Essex, the queen's favourite in the 1590s, who was executed in 1601. After England's separation from Rome in the 1530s, it was inevitable that the native Irish, still Catholic, and living in a medieval, if not a heroic age, would clash with their newly Protestant overlords. Time and again, through renewed colonizing and the cruellest of repressions, the Tudors attempted to govern an island which they regarded as barbarous, but which was of major strategic importance for the sea routes to America. Only after Mountjoy had defeated the Irish cavalry at Kinsale in 1601 was the matter settled in England's favour.

between them have been lost entirely in the agony of wanting. Wanting to touch the girl, strip her naked, cut the skin off her bones, watch her struggle as she is offered up to the angry god who feeds women to men (instead of, as in Dante, a man's heart to a woman). Out in those deserts, the miracle of the sacrament, the divine banquet, becomes confused with the feast of civility, which symbolizes man's highest social achievement, and with the mystery of sexual consuming dreamt into being by Dante. Everywhere there is a muddle of mind, soul, and body, and now the priest advances towards her, and the horns and bagpipes begin to sound. In the event, Sir Calepine, her lover, rescues her, hearing her screams, once more having woken out of a sleep. By 'th'vncertaine glims of starry night', he makes out a woman, but one he cannot recognize. What he can see is someone with 'a naked knife / Readie to launch her brest, and let out loued life'. He bursts in among them, cutting down the priest first and then the others. He unties her, but in the dark still cannot see who she is, and she will say nothing in answer to his questions. Only in the daylight do her identity and nakedness become clear.

Spenser never managed to complete this particular story, but then he had not completed it the first time round, when, three books earlier (III. xii. 30–8), it had been Amoret who was cut about for the delectation of Cupid, her heart ripped open and her blood feeding Busirane's book of magic spells. In that episode Amoret was healed because another woman, Britomart, risked her own body to rescue her. The magician was forced to reverse his charms, and Amoret became whole again, but the frantic desire had not been quieted. In the story of Serena, and in many other places in the poem, Spenser was compelled to a rewriting of that single gesture and fantasy of the knife opening white female flesh, wantonly, pruriently, mocking the savagery and wild eyes with the ease of the verse, digging within to find the convulsing bag of blood. It was a terrible compulsion, yet no Elizabethan but Spenser came as close to realizing how uncarnal, how unfleshly this gesture wanted to be. It was mad, and it was hateful, but it wanted to open the female to find that she was the divine mystery herself, that within her beautiful white body, which could be eaten and raped, there was a male heart, the glowing object which had been offered to her and which she had eaten in Dante's dream. Nothing in Elizabethan lyrics is more predictable, and even tedious, than the constant verbal play on and union of harts and hearts—gentle beasts afraid and sacrificial, and the human heart—but nothing is more revealing of how deep down this sexual and spiritual agony had gone. In the episode with the cannibals, Serena is, in a real sense, the divine being and source of life-blood these monsters take her to be.

It is not that much different for Spenser himself. When the savages have first torn the clothes from her, Serena's nakedness is a shame to their eyes, but there is another shame and grief in the writing itself:

> Her yuorie necke, her alablaster brest,
> > Her paps, which like white silken pillows were,
> > For loue in soft delight thereon to rest;
> > Her tender sides, her bellie white and clere,
> > Which like an Altar did it selfe vprere,
> > To offer sacrifice diuine thereon;
> > Her goodly thighes, whose glorie did appeare
> > Like a triumphall Arch, and thereupon
> The spoiles of Princes hang'd, which were in battel won.   (VI. viii. 42)

Spenser is sometimes accused of being inexact in his language, but there cannot be any doubt about the self-awareness and precision in this passage, and the care with which the reader is implicated in the crime against Serena. There is a set of rhetorical figures which look as though they are inviting comparisons—her breasts are *like* silk pillows on a bed, her belly is *like* the white communion table, and the fork of her legs and pudenda are *like* a triumphal arch. The trope feigns a comparison—these are words, phrases, and images of victory, holiness, and bed-delights, and there is also a real girl, with whom they are compared—but the rhetoric does not allow us this comfortable division between art and life. Rather, it reminds us that Serena is made up of the bits of Renaissance poetic available to Spenser (and which he uses elsewhere to describe other heroines), and that her body is not so much like an altar, an arch, or a bed, as like a pattern of conceits in a poem. The cannibals may want to torment, humiliate, and adore Serena, but are we supposed to think that, in their incivility and shrieking savagery, this set of poetic conceits is how *they* see her? Surely not. This is the language of sophistication, of elaborate court poetry and woven comparisons, the silk and thread of an Elizabethan tapestry.

INDIANS DANCING, a ritual celebration of harvest, engraved after a painting by John White (1585). Three women, described as the fairest of virgins, dance in the middle of a circle of men and women. Whatever its significance for the Indian mind, the scene must have had an uncanny meaning for the European one: this is very much how the Three Graces are represented in Graeco-Roman mythology, and in the poetry and painting of the Renaissance (see Raphael's *Three Graces*, or Spenser's *Faerie Queene* VI. x. 24).

The connection may have been fortuitous, but it may also indicate that the Elizabethans saw what they expected to see: a group of primitives whose simplicity enabled them to inhabit in reality the innocent pastoral world that had disappeared from all but the art and philosophy of Renaissance civilization.

Disturbingly, but inevitably, the girl is traduced in the very conventions of reading and writing which are supposed to separate the audience from these eaters of female flesh. For Spenser to remind us of his own artfulness, and our complicity with it at this moment of shame, is to acknowledge that poetry too is longing for the image of woman made in man's likeness (beds, sacraments, triumphs), that poetry too wants to open up its forbidden areas of delight and find there an inner divinity.

Elsewhere in the poem, there are contraptions which can look more like women than women when the inner sanctum is manufactured, male, and diabolic. In Book III, Canto viii, the beautiful Florimell flees from the house of the witch and her brutish son. When the son learns that she has been killed by his mother's tracker-dog (wrongly, for she is not dead), he goes mad with grief, madder than he was at Florimell's rejection of him. The heart is, once more, almost out of his body (stanza 3, lines 4–6), and the courtly love code begins its strange reorganization. To pacify him, the witch makes a sex-doll for him, another Florimell 'in shape and looke / So liuely and so like, that many it mistooke'. She takes purest snow, and virgin wax for the flesh, and mingles it with a little 'vermily' to get the complexion right. Then, instead of eyes,

> two burning lampes she set
> In siluer sockets, shyning like the skyes,
> And a quicke mouing Spirit did arret
> To stirre and roll them, like a womans eyes;
> In stead of yellow lockes she did deuise,
> With golden wyre to weaue her curled head;
> Yet golden wyre was not so yellow thrise
> As *Florimells* faire haire: and in the stead
> Of life, she put a Spright to rule the carkasse dead.

What is especially grim about this False Florimell is the clumsiness, the literal-mindedness of the bits and pieces she is made of. The poetic conceits of the sonnet tradition and courtly wooing are here made banal and substantial. In Tudor lyrics, eyes are likened to burning lamps, and hair to golden wire, but this monstrosity has the real things bolted on and taped into position. Words and rhetorical figures of analogy are made into things, as if Florimell's beauty, only approachable in likenesses, could be improved on, or capped, by denying the limits of art. The vulgarity and crudity of the simulacrum, a dead carcass, is made even more dangerous by its operator. Inside the dummy sits a wicked sprite, a male demon who fell from heaven with Satan, and who 'in counterfeisance did excell, / And all the wyles of wemens wits knew passing well'. Inside this woman thing, over which the witch's son will slobber, there is certainly an immortal presence, if not a heart, and, like Dante's lord, he is a tempter as well. But it is a divinity as blockish and mechanical as the electric wire and light bulbs screwed into the dummy's head. There is no reason, and no desire to rip it open, because in it the love mysteries have all become technology, the why become the how, the lord become the servant.

The fact that Spenser can conceive of an art made substantial in this way is a departure from Dante, and indeed from much of the medieval and classical past. The Roman poet, Horace, although he was by no means the first ancient to say so, insisted that reality was not something brought into being simply by thinking. At the outset of his *Ars Poetica*, or 'Art of Poetry', he divides the constancy of Nature from the inconstancy of human inventiveness. Artists must have freedom, but they must not contradict the laws of matter, or they will be laughed at. Paint a human head on a horse's neck, or couple wild with tame (a tiger with a lamb), and no one will take you seriously. Explicit in this is the assumption that nothing can change very much in the physiological structure of the human body and Nature, and that new combinations of matter, unless they conform to what men can reasonably expect, are likely to be freakish. This is as true of poetry as it is of the body: 'the man who brings in marvels to vary a simple theme is painting a dolphin among the trees, a boar in the billows.' What many poets lack, Horace argues, is the coherence and decorum that comes only from skill *and* a total design. He puts it this way:

> The poorest smith in the area around Aemilius's school
> will render nails in bronze and wavy hair;
> The final effect eludes him because he doesn't know how
> to shape a whole . . .

In an instant we are back with Spenser, with nails and wavy hair imitated in metal, but something has gone dreadfully wrong, because in *The Faerie Queene* the freak, the impossible creation, is no longer impossible and the coherence of Nature is no longer certain. Where Horace could be sure that an aberration of form would always be regarded as monstrous, or laughable, in Spenser it often seems that there are no sure rules for making, nor for judging what has been made. C. S. Lewis, perhaps Spenser's greatest critic, does not see it this way, because for him the poem teaches its readers how to distinguish between true and false loves, between sexual naturalness and artful smut. Lewis's Christian views have been influential, and rightly so, for they are profoundly intelligent, but all the same he greatly undervalues the conjunctions in Spenser, and in other Elizabethans, between grotesque unreality and power.

A passage from the *Arcadia* by Sir Philip Sidney (1554–86) makes this a little clearer. In Book I, chapter 14 (revised version, published 1590), Pyrocles, disguised as a female warrior, recounts to Musidorus his strange entertainment by Duke Basilius, Lady Gynecia, and their daughters. Deep in the Arcadian pastoral, far from all civilities, there is still a mechanical marvel to delight his senses. It was a place, he says,

not fairer in natural ornaments than artificial inventions, wherein is a banqueting-house . . . The table was set near to an excellent water-work; for by the casting of

ACTAEON AND DIANA, an episode from Ovid's *Metamorphoses* in a late sixteenth-century needlework at Hardwick Hall. In the Renaissance, the stories in the *Metamorphoses* were as important and ubiquitous as those created by Freud in this century, and clearly bore many interpretations: as warnings against unnatural sexual feelings, as seasonal myths, as allegories of the soul, or as accounts of how man gained control over animals. Undoubtedly, there were also simpler responses.

Above, the huntsman Actaeon (*centre*) chances on the virgin goddess Diana bathing with her maids. To punish his transgression, Diana casts water over him, his head becomes a stag's, and despite his screams 'Actaeon ego sum' ('I am Actaeon') his own hounds tear him apart. Here, the narrative itself has undergone a metamorphosis, the entire episode being represented by a single plane, united by visual images (notice, for example, how the stag's antlers resemble the trees rooted in the hillsides).

the water in most cunning manner, it makes, with the shining of the sun upon it, a perfect rainbow, not more pleasant to the eye than to the mind so sensibly to see the proof of the heavenly Iris. There were birds also made so finely that they did not only deceive the sight with their figure, but the hearing with their songs which the watery instruments did make their gorge deliver. The table at which we sat was round, which being fast to the floor whereon we sat, and that divided from the rest of the buildings, with turning a vice . . . the table and we about the table did all turn round by means of water which ran under and carried it about as a mill. But alas, what pleasure did it to me to make divers times the full circle round about, since Philoclea, being also set, was carried still in equal distance from me, and that only my eyes did overtake her, which (when the table was stayed and we began to feed) drank much more eagerly of her beauty than my mouth did of any other liquor. And so was my common sense deceived, being chiefly bent to her, that as I drank the wine and withal stole a look on her, me seemed I tasted her deliciousness.

This is one of the rare times in the *Arcadia* when a technology of some kind (as opposed to a wonderful painting or costume) operates on the lives of individuals, and yet behind its trivial showiness there is an urge to make the fantastic into the powerful. The water pipes channel through the throats of artificial birds to make bird-songs, the water turns a giant cog-wheel to drive round the dining-table, and a neat cascade of water is angled just so that the sun may strike it aright for a rainbow. These are marvellous toys, the dolphins in the trees which Horace said would be preposterous—but the prose itself in the paragraph is no less of a gadget, as Sidney goes out of his way to remind us. The ratchets and hydraulic gearing are matched rhetorically by a set of clauses, locked in parallels, turning one on the other, balancing, forcing the stream of words this way, then that. The water goes down the birds' throats, the wine down his: his senses revolve towards her, as the table moves her away. Both the water-wheel and the rhetoric are fantasies of power, claiming the same control over the fluidity of the waters as over the language of the senses.

Sidney and Spenser were alive at a peculiar moment in the history of wish-fulfilment, a moment when human inventiveness was fertile but not yet potent in technology. The Elizabethans, living in a small offshore island, did not yet have a real science or empire or overseas trade or army or banking system or even an efficient way of farming. Yet they knew, nevertheless, that these things were not that far away, and that they were living at the fag end of a culture of words and dreams, Arthurian prophecies and Horatian rules. The False Florimell may be monstrous, but she is not only from a witch's cauldron. She is from Spenser's own words, from an imagination still in contact with Dante but horrified at what lies within itself, and of its prescience about the future: it knows but does not yet see how there will be calculus, contraceptives, and Adam Smith's Economic Man. This was not the first time that poets and their readers had been fascinated with bodily transformations, of course, but it was the first time perhaps that the power to change one's nature, and reorganize matter, lay in the minds of men alone. In Ovid, say, metamorphoses were accomplished by the grace, and sometimes disgrace, of the gods—the transformations were divine ones, and human beings could only wait to be liberated into (or from) this shape or that. But in England by 1600, the dream waiting to be realized, Francis Bacon's dream, was of human authority over everything, matter, mind, and soul.

Shakespeare's Ovidian Family History

The sudden quickening of literary genius at the end of the Tudor century is something which excites us to, but which defies explanation. Even the most convinced determinist would be put to it to explain why the last two decades are so crowded with special talents—Sidney, Spenser, Marlowe, Shakespeare, Ralegh, Daniel, Bacon, Donne, let alone the second-rank dramatists and the theologians. The achievements of earlier Elizabethan writers, and chroniclers, and translators will not be undervalued if we say that what distinguished them from their successors, and left them the other side of genius, was their failure to make contact with the story of Orpheus. There is nothing unusual or blameworthy in this, in fact it is the normal state of affairs for poets and readers. For most of the time the poets, whatever they say, make claims on fame, immortality, and influence over the world which no one in their right minds would believe. But then at other times, albeit infrequently, it seems that they are, *pace* Shelley, the *acknowledged* legislators, the makers of civilization. In 1590 the Orphic story arrived with the publication of *The Faerie Queene* and Sidney's *Arcadia*. The myth was disguised, but still discernible. The old Orpheus, gifted with tongue and lyre, had dared to go into the wilderness, and there, with his music and poetry, he had calmed the savage beasts, and even made the mountains move towards him in pleasure. Long before the Elizabethans, the story had been interpreted as an allegory of man's first steps towards civilization (the orator's rhetoric, or persuasive words, pacifying his unsociable wildness), but in 1590 the uncultivated desert into which Spenser and Sidney had gone was England itself. Their fame, as Daniel remarked later, was to be the first poets since Chaucer to drive 'gross barbarism', the tyrant of the North, from English shores. They had begun the task of writing a literature which would rival that of Ancient Rome and Renaissance Italy. At one stroke, what was at stake—immortality and a new beginning—had been made probable, not just possible.

There were poets like Donne who wanted nothing to do with Sidney and Spenser (dead national hero, and all-too-live Neoplatonic exile), but even they inherited from and were empowered by this Orphic charge. For others, the prospect of enduring fame brought with it almost insufferable responsibilities. Samuel Daniel (1563-1619), who published *Delia* and *The Complaint of Rosamond* in 1592, was orthodox in his allegiances to Sidney (doubting Spenser just a little, and wanting an English empire of letters as well as lands), but impatient to get at whatever would make his poetry last. He addresses sonnets to Delia in what at first looks like the old manner and for the old reason. The mistress is disdainful, cruel, and beautiful, the poet infatuated, humble, and frustrated. But it is not long before we realize just how little he wants her to reciprocate his love. 'Read in my face', he commands us, 'a volume of despairs',

> The wailing *Iliads* of my tragic woe,
> Drawn with my blood, and printed with my cares,
> Wrought by her hand, that I have honoured so.
>   Who whilst I burn, she sings at my soul's wrack,
> Looking aloft from turret of her pride:
> There my soul's tyrant joys her, in the sack
> Of her own seat, whereof I made her guide.
>
>   (Sonnet 39)

This is not so much a clamour for Delia's attention as for an audience. Daniel figures himself as a book, drawn in, made by hand, printed with care, with his face and blood becoming epic poems. By conceits derived from the physical text before us, the sonnet reminds us that we are reading, and then the image of Troy, broken into and burning, is made into a trope for Delia's possession and surrender of his soul. We, as readers, breach and enter the epic book of himself, which is handed over to us by Delia's treachery. Far from being ornamental or casually chosen, the allusion to *The Iliad* is the very prize which Daniel seeks. Because of Delia's betrayal of him (where he must write sonnets to her, and so expose himself) he becomes the site of Troy and, more important, the immortal poem in which Homer sang of Achilles' pride and the city besieged by the Greeks. This is Daniel's short cut to Orphic immortality and it is one he attempts throughout the sonnets, and indeed in all of his poetry. For him, enduring achievements are made by renewing in himself earlier poems, famous love-affairs and even the history of Britain. He translates poems by Desportes, Horace, and Petrarch, and draws them into the English self of his sonnets. He has Rosamond, the forsaken mistress of Henry II, appear to him, as Delia's poet, and tell her complaint in stanzas of rhyme royal (the form of Chaucer's *Troilus and Criseyde*). But Daniel's humanism, or his version of it, costs him dearly. By *Musophilus*, published in 1599, he is already too anxious, and almost too literal about the contacts he is making with the future. Lines of verse, written now, will be, so he claims,

> the veins, the arteries,
> And undecaying life-strings of those hearts
> That still shall pant, and still shall exercise
> The motion spirit and nature both imparts,
> And shall, with those alive so sympathise,
> As nourished with their powers, enjoy their parts.   (183–8)

The sentiments are admirable, but there is a certain leadenness here where there should be a spring. All five verbs are quite strong, but the nouns keep edging away from them just enough to deny the intactness of the body metaphor. The problem here was that Daniel was not sure, and never would be, whether the self he was communicating to posterity should be exact and constant, or open and forever redefining itself. It caused him to revise his texts, and the self in them, with a scrupulousness which verged on being obsessive. In short, where Sidney and Spenser had invented fictions, Arcadian and Faerie, in which to locate the perplexities of identity, Daniel, striving to be part of the Orphic revival, made them the very stuff of his writing.

Sir Walter Ralegh's (*c*.1552–1618) claims on poetic immortality could not have been less like those of Daniel, and the poets differed almost as much in their failings. Where Daniel at his worst can be prolix and just a little top-heavy with what Coleridge called his excellent good sense, Ralegh is often short-winded and seems restless and impatient by the time he has reached the middle of quite short poems. As befits the soldier and determined adventurer he was, he is best at the stab and thrust and at displays of extravagance followed by restraint. His big words are 'blouddy', 'boddy', 'lymes', and 'belly' (his own spellings, often plumped out, are important), and his usual technique comprises apostrophe, cryptic allusion, comparisons locked into three- or four-line parallels, and repeated word-play on liquids becoming dry, or turning to mud or dust, and vice versa. In his poems, Time, 'being made of steele and rust', turns 'snow, and silke and milke to dust', streams dry up into standing puddles, the sap is gone from the trees, and the fretting rust eats the better part of his heart-blood. Then the fires burn him, the ice melts, and his heart dissolves into wasting drops like snow pouring down from the mountains. A poetry of solidifying and liquefaction, captivity and freedom, promise and disappointment, braving the queen, then humbling himself before her—it all sounds miserably close to the gush and immurement of the Petrarchans (where the dust is learned and the tears are of boredom), but in Ralegh there is always a nakedness before language which stops any of this happening:

> But I unblessed, and ill borne creature,
> That did inebrace the dust, her boddy bearinge,
> That loved her both, by fancy, and by nature,
> That drew yeven with the milke in my first suckinge
>
> Affection from the parents brest that bare mee,
> Have found her as a stranger so severe,
> Improvinge my mishapp in each degree:
> But love was gonn. So would I, my life weare!

As ever with Ralegh, when he is taking chances, the words stick out and dare us not to read them literally. He embraces the dust which bears up the queen's body, but 'bearinge' is also life-giving, giving birth, giving suck, being naked, being understanding, being a mother. She will not carry him, expose herself to him, sustain him with her sweet fluids (we recall his dried-up sands and trees elsewhere in the poem), and she improves him with severe degrees, yet another meaning of 'bearinge'.

The lines are from *The Ocean to Scinthia*, a poem preserved in only one manuscript, Ralegh's own, which was not discovered until the last century. He probably shut it away, unfinished and uncensored, because this was just too much. The queen is not Cynthia here, some safe court goddess, but the old and yet waxenly sexy crone painted up in Zuccaro's rainbow portrait, or in the Armada pictures. This is the real Faerie Queene, the Tudor virgin mother whose child was England, and who was also supposed to bear lovers, but whose embraces would have been like dust. Ralegh was an 'ill borne creature', not one of the aristocracy, and he had got too close to Elizabeth for his poems to be respectable about what he saw. His imaginings, divine as well as secular, are often ways of averting his attention from her grisly presence. To please his senses, a lady's eyes should be of light, and she should have,

THE ARMADA PORTRAIT, painted by the sergeant-painter George Gower to celebrate victory over the Spanish Armada in 1588. The picture is composed as a pattern of globes, ellipses, and circles, from the queen's hair and whitened face—two ellipses at right angles to each other—to the globe on which she rests her hand, with its promise, since Spain's defeat, of authority over the sea lanes to the New World.

> A Violett breath, and Lipps of Jelly,
> Her haire not blacke, nor over bright,
> And of the softest downe her Belly

('Nature that washt her hands in milke')

but we may be sure that touches of beauty like these will always end up in 'age and dust' and dark silent graves. As usual, Time is made the culprit, rusting, wearing out, filing down, or even, in macabre moments, growing the hemp which 'stringes the Hangmans bagg' tied over a prisoner's head on the gibbet. But it is the queen not Time who is at the dead centre of Ralegh's poems because she is both its mistress and its victim. She is free from Time (England ages, but she does not), and yet she is all moments in one (maiden-mother, virgin-mistress, the Arthurian prince who has never died). Her own motto was *semper eadem*, 'always the same', and yet Ralegh celebrated her as Scinthia, the ever-changing moon who drew the waves of court this way and then that. But by approaching the paradox of her 'boddy'—decaying skin and bone, and eternally unplucked ripeness—Ralegh did also discover, once she was dead, a Christian truth, and even a grim Orphic one. In a poem peculiarly appropriate to him, if not by him, his persona declares:

> Seeing my flesh must die so soone,
> And want a head to dine next noone,
> Just at the stroke when my vaines start and spred
> Set on my soule an everlasting head.
>
> (*The Passionate Man's Pilgrimage*)

Everyone knows that Ralegh was beheaded in 1618, and of his courage on the scaffold, but perhaps we should also recall that it was the Bacchae, the wild virgin nymphs, who in their fury at his scorn for them, tore the poet Orpheus's head from his shoulders and cast it into the moving waters.

In 1593 Shakespeare entered this Orphic scene with deliberation and mastery. He perceived that Orpheus himself must be confronted and that the story of a man made immortal by a heavenly woman (Elizabeth and Ralegh, Delia and Daniel) was the crime and the blessing which Elizabethan poets must inherit. In Ovid's *Metamorphoses*, Book X, when he found Orpheus telling the story of Venus and Adonis, he had everything in one. Not only was there the goddess who had transformed her dead lover into a flower and so made him return eternally to her, but there was also the story-teller who was famed as the first poet, and in whom, according to Cicero, rhetoric had begun. Shakespeare had to find a way into this story, which he called *Venus and Adonis*, and so he tied it as a Gordian knot of art and sex, and then cut it. Venus, hot and capable, tries to persuade Adonis, young and chaste, to couple with her. These are some of the delights, her body as the earth, she offers:

> Sweet bottom grass and high delightful plain,
> Round rising hillocks, brakes obscure and rough,
> To shelter thee from tempest and from rain:
> Then be my deer, since I am such a park,
> No dog shall rouse thee, though a thousand bark.   (236-40)

Whatever we may think, what is really on offer here is the shape of Venus's persuasion, not the shape of her bottom. It is the reader, not Adonis, who is being tempted. The boy refuses to look at her breasts, or kiss her, although she is lying on him, because he is too well educated to be taken in by her rhetoric (he answers her point for point), and because he wants to get on with hunting the boar.

The wit in this, and it may not be to our taste now, is that the language of life and death (classical rhetoric was once used for murder trials) is in the mouths of a mythological voluptuary and her unwilling paramour. The very sober uses of rhetoric—teaching philosophy to undergraduates, swaying juries, making parliaments vote new taxes—are made to look a bit foolish when the object is to persuade a boy to give up his virginity. Everything is topsy-turvy, and that is its thrill. It was not a new pleasure (nothing much was new after the classical love poets), but in England in 1593 the urbanity and slight naughtiness of it was still novel. Around the same time, in *Hero and Leander*, Marlowe (1564-93) had caught the manner very well, especially in the jokes about how real the fiction was. Leander, swimming the Hellespont to be with Hero, is stripped to his 'ivory skin', which makes Neptune think that he is Ganymede, Jupiter's immortal boy-friend. The god seizes him and takes him down to his underwater palace, but is startled when he begins to drown:

> He heaved him up, and looking on his face,
> Beat down the bold waves with his triple mace,
> Which mounted up, intending to have kissed him,
> And fell in drops like tears because they missed him.
>
> (Sestiad II. 171-4)

Here the jaunty rhythm meets with a kissing conceit, suggestively homosexual, and Leander, a fantasy figure if ever there was one, stops short of being totally fictional when he gasps for air. The poem has no limits to its imagining (on Hero's party dress there are rejected lovers' bloodstains) and so Marlowe can wind the fiction up and down, suddenly reminding us that what we are reading is determined by his own entirely arbitrary laws.

In *Venus and Adonis* all of the rhetorical sex play is a prelude to Venus's real fear, that if she cannot have him, the boar may. The wild beast of the forest is her only rival, and when Adonis dies hunting it, she has but one way of describing their encounter. The boar, not knowing how to kiss the boy, but wanting to, sought 'to persuade him there',

> And nuzzling in his flank, the loving swine
> Sheathed unaware the tusk in his soft groin.   (1115-16)

Earlier the persuasions were conceitful, and intended for us, but now the rhetoric has gone back into the poem and with it Venus makes an ugly death into a loving thrust. Her psychology, which begins as no more than a display of tropes and erotica, becomes complex and alive. At the sight of his torn limbs she sinks to the ground, whimpering, and 'stains her face with his congealèd blood'. An artificial lady who is brought out of art into life—yes, the story shadowed here *is* that of Pygmalion's statue, and so it should be, given Adonis's family history. In Ovid, when Pygmalion had made his wonderful statue, he prayed to Venus to have a wife just as beautiful, and she gave him what he secretly wanted, the statue come to life. The child of their union was Paphos, and her son was Cinyras. From him came Myrrha, the daughter who tricked her father into incest, and from their unnatural mating, near the end of this terrible family romance, came Adonis. The goddess Venus allows art

VENUS AND ADONIS, painted by Veronese, 1580s. Whatever it gained by freeing itself from Catholic Europe, Tudor England suffered a major loss in the arts, especially the plastic and pictorial ones. There was no one to match the great Italian painters, sculptors, and architects: only Holbein and Oliver bear comparison with, say, Raphael and Titian. After Queen Elizabeth's excommunication in 1570, England became ever more isolated, and travel on the Continent was often dangerous for Protestant Englishmen. Consequently, only a few Elizabethans (Sidney among them) could have seen paintings of the quality of this one. Little wonder that in the 1590s especially, the poets (Spenser, Marlowe, Shakespeare) were constantly looking for ways, in words, to excite and satisfy the inner eye.

(the statue) to live and beget and she is punished for it three generations later: she is not able to preserve the boy Adonis, the last fruit of that begetting, except by turning his corpse into a blood-red flower.

In his version, Shakespeare excludes all of this earlier history, and Venus's part in it. He suppresses the incestuous narrative, and Pygmalion episode, and in their place he makes his own poetry breed inwardly. In one case, he takes the oldest and most trite piece of rhetoric—beauty in the red and white of a lady's face—and compounds it slowly and repeatedly throughout the poem. Doves and roses, lips red and then pale with kissing, burning cheeks, rose cheeks, 'crimson shame and anger ashy pale', lilies imprisoned in snow, and then, of course, where all of this has been heading, the sight of the boar with

> frothy mouth bepainted all with red,
> Like milk and blood being mingled both together.   (901-2)

One twist of it further, and it is Adonis's wounded body, 'lily-white / With purple tears' and then, finally, the body itself becomes a 'purple flower' sprung up, 'checkered with white'. The conceit, conventional and obvious, breeds out of itself a riot of colours, comparisons, and metaphors, and eventually, in climactic moments, it meets with the real: red and white are literally on the boar's mouth, as it charges out of the forest.

By breaking the Ovidian history, begun with Pygmalion and told by Orpheus, Shakespeare makes everything come anew out of himself. He can stop a story, begin it again where he likes (even replacing Adonis's mother, line 864), and make it evolve out of any rhetoric he chooses. By an effort of will (his own pun on his name in the *Sonnets*) he succeeds Orpheus as the primary orator, and after him civilization will never be the same again. Venus tells us as much when she announces, prophetically, that because Adonis has died, love will henceforth be cheap or unhappy, insanely jealous or raging mad. But such beginnings, whatever she says, are not in her keeping, but in Shakespeare's own. What is not entirely in his control, despite the will, is the return of Pygmalion and the ivory statue. He tries to cut away the episode but it comes back in the language. When he spurns her, Venus calls Adonis a 'cold and senseless stone', a statue 'contenting but the eye alone', and a thing 'like a man but of no woman bred'. When she embraces him she is an ivory circlet or pale, and he is ivory in her 'alabaster band'. As Shakespeare must have known, repressing the story would not suffice, although it was not until the very end of his career, in Act V of *The Winter's Tale*, that he managed to get the episode out into the open again. Only then, almost twenty years later, could Hermione, the statue queen preserved by art, get down off the plinth and walk about the stage.

Rhetorical Histories

Being shut in, cabined, cribbed, and confined, the seed unable to bud, was something which the Elizabethans knew about in more areas than just their poetic styles. The discoverers like Davis and Frobisher nosed their ships along the Arctic shores, pushing into the ice-packs, looking in vain for the north-west passage to the China Seas. The alchemists—some frauds, others crypto-chemists—scraped their limbecks and dishes, distilling and purifying, searching (again, in vain) for the residual element which would free the human body from death, make it immortal from within its immutable core. Painters tried to sketch back into the depth of the canvas along lines of perspective barely understood in this country even half a century after Dürer. For the poets, it was Daniel, characteristically alive to what hemmed him in most, who wrote, in 1594:

> O that the ocean did not bound our style
> Within these strict and narrow limits so:
> But that the melody of our sweet isle
> Might now be heard to Tiber, Arne and Po.
>
> (Preface to *The Tragedy of Cleopatra*)

Wanting to issue out of England's provincial history as well as location, Daniel's mind here moves south and back in time to 'declinèd Italy' and to the Mediterranean—only to find, in his later poems, that this too, the sea of the Romans and the Greeks, is a place of confinement, an ancient lake sealed at its African end, at Gibraltar, by the Pillars of Hercules. Only in *Musophilus* is there any way out, and there it is through the treasure of the language venting itself, moving west across the Atlantic to 'strange shores' which it may enrich. Who knows, Daniel asks,

> What worlds in th'yet unformèd Occident
> May come refined with th'accents that are ours? (961-2)

Refining, like the alchemists; forming worlds on the horizon, like the painters, explorers, and settlers; placing the emphasis, or accent, on English speech, like the poets and the colonizers—the future is an American one, in which all the movement out, in science, politics, and religion is already inherent in the language. For Daniel, the art of the Elizabethan poet is to prise open meanings hidden in the future, venting new worlds out of old poems and ancient cultures. It is one of the greatest Renaissance ideals, matched only by Walt Whitman's Romantic one, that America itself is the last epic poem.

An access to this future was so vital to Elizabethan writers that without it their work could turn dark, or precious, or puffy. In their poems and songs, Campion and Dowland, who had stretched the Tudor lyric ever more tightly across lute strings and musical disharmonies, were not far from making a lady's embrace the only light in a dismal, hellish world. Following an ancient complaint, Campion picks out, in the slightest of metrical discords, 'soon as once set is our little light, / Then must we sleep one ever-during night', while Dowland, swollen with grief (a recurrent image), wants his tears to burst out, flooding into the dark. Their limits are the musical scale itself, with the melody moving chromatically, and images sounding against the normal emotional and musical register. But where in them there is a touch of affectation and

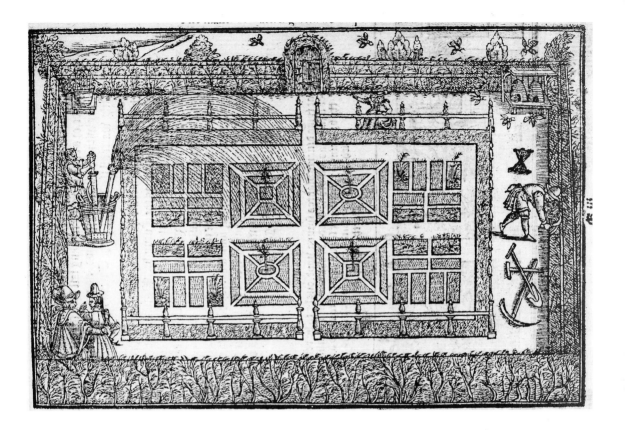

THE PLEASURES OF
CONTAINMENT, woodcuts from
Thomas Hill, *The Gardener's
Labyrinth* (1577). In the sixteenth
century, Englishmen had little
appetite for natural wildness. In their
gardens they sought an artful
command over nature, making it
gentle with scented flowers and herbs
and neat geometrical lines. Within
safe walls and gate, the Elizabethan
formal garden was a domestic
retreat—it was not until Jacobean
and Caroline times that the showier
mannerist gardens, with fantastical
hedges, statues, and big fountains,
became popular. Where the natural
world could be made an adjunct to
the social one it was praised and
exploited: where it was too bleak or
dangerous it was regarded as a
desert in which only savages or
outlaws would live (see the Arden
scenes in *As You Like It*).

self-regard about their pent-up and discordant agonies, in Shakespeare, in the *Sonnets*, what goes inward, denying its future, leads to the poet's self-contempt and abnegation, not esteem. The young man, because he closes in himself his seed, his treasure, and his rose, lives off a 'self-substantial fuel'. The poet, in love with him, knows that a body which breeds without issue, will ripen, added to out of its own fecundity, then rot, then fester. At first, the conceits are all enclosures—vials, cabinets, graves, sepulchres, eyelids closing—then they are penetrations deep into substance. The poet quizzes and accuses colours, smells, shades, and ancient poems of stealing from, but never lessening, the young man's essence:

> The forward violet thus did I chide:
> 'Sweet thief, whence didst thou steal thy sweet that smells,
> If not from my love's breath? The purple pride
> Which on thy soft cheek for complexion dwells,
> In my love's veins thou has too grossly dyed.'
> The lily I condemnèd for thy hand . . .
>
> (Sonnet 99)

Red and white, violets and lilies, death and pride, chiding and condemning—it is the language of *Venus and Adonis*, but Shakespeare has advanced beyond individual tropes which breed and reappear, and here in the *Sonnets* it is the inward turning of rhetoric itself, a history of enclosed and self-multiplying figures, which concerns him.

Appropriately, the dedication is to Mr W. H., as the 'Only Begetter of these Ensuing Sonnets', as if there were some English figure of rhetoric, the *begetter*, which made sonnets out of itself alone. Shakespeare identifies the young man's body, and then its hidden beauties and corruption, with the very substance of his poetry, which is not so much the matter of rhymes, comparisons, and vocabulary, as the space or presence in which the poet finds himself immured. In total, what Shakespeare is looking for is a passage out of that poetic core and into the young man. This is why, after his lover has disgraced him, he confesses to so many crimes: in their exchange of identities, he offers himself in sacrifice for the young man. By 'all above', he writes (in Sonnet 110), my blenches and shameful behaviour,

> gave my heart another youth,
> And worse essays proved thee my best of love.
> Now all is done, have what shall have no end:
> Mine appetite I never more will grind
> On newer proof, to try an older friend,
> A god in love, to whom I am confined.

As his heart receives 'another youth', the young man becomes 'an older friend': their ages, and their guilt and innocence, pass between them. The boy enters his poetry and becomes immortal, as Shakespeare promised, while the poet enters the boy's body, and there takes on his misdeeds. It was Sidney not Shakespeare who wrote the famous line 'My true love hath my heart, and I have his', and there it was a shepherdess to her male lover, but the sentiment is exactly right for the *Sonnets*. In the later ones we recall those times in the 1590s plays when a man so loves his friend that he is willing to stand in his place. Twice Shakespeare calls the surrogate, the older man, Antonio. 'If this young gentleman / Have done offence, I take the fault on me', says one of them in *Twelfth Night*, while the other, in *The Merchant of Venice*, is prepared to offer Christian flesh and blood to a Jew, repeating an older sacrifice, for the sake of another man.

The closing off which makes Shakespeare magnanimous, extraordinary lover that he is, turns John Lyly into a fop. Lyly (*c*.1554–1606) has some anthropological interest, like flat-earthers, or people who have transcribed the entire Bible on the back of a stamp, but he is not a great writer, and in places barely a writer at all:

I have read that the bull being tied to the fig-tree loseth his strength, that the whole herd of deer stand at the gaze if they smell a sweet apple, that the dolphin by the sound of music is brought to the shore. And then no marvel it is that if the fierce bull be tamed with the fig-tree, if that women being as weak as sheep be overcome with a fig, if the wild deer be caught with an apple, that the tame damsel is won with a blossom, if the fleet dolphin be allured with harmony, that women be entangled with the melody of men's speech, fair promises and solemn protestations. But folly it were for me to mark their mischiefs, sith I am neither able, neither they willing to amend their manners, it becometh me rather to show what our sex should do, than to open what yours doth.   (*Euphues*, *The Anatomy of Wit*)

This is from a fifteen-hundred-word monologue spoken by a lady to Euphues, a character who, like Biggles in this century, was such a hit because once his style was achieved, it could go on endlessly, episode after episode. Scholars have not discovered a story 'Euphues Flies West', but it would not be all that incongruous if they did, because the narrative—what actually happens—is of small interest in Lyly. It is the shapes of the clauses which attract us, if anything does. Above, there is a three-part structure (bulls and fig-trees, deer and apple-scent, dolphins and music), into each part of which intrudes a female weakness for figs, blossoms, and male speech. There may have been Elizabethan teachers of rhetoric who thought this was how a woman's thought proceeded, but plainly no one else could. It is not a mimetic prose, at which we look and recognize something, nor a platonic one, where these divisions and insertions shape some metalanguage. It is not algebraic (it does not add up to sense), nor investigative and dirty-minded ('figs' could mean pieces of excrement, but Lyly averts his eyes from this), nor even humorous (there is not a trace of a smile playing about behind this bull, deer, and dolphin-lore). In places the rhythm is a little confused, like the grammar, but it moves along quite happily, symmetrical and sententious.

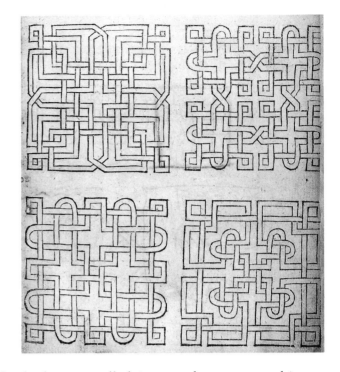

PROPER KNOTS, designs in a pattern book, which were to be traced out in gardens with 'hyssop or thyme'.

In their other arts, the Elizabethans excelled in *entrelacement*, making a motif return on itself, interweaving under and above, crossing backwards and forwards until the starting-point of the design was no longer to be seen. Threads woven in samplers and tapestries, ornate stone ridges on great houses, intricate lines of coloured soil and flowers in garden plots, polyphonic voices in the Church Mass, repeated steps and kicks in the galliard—all of them pattern-work, tracing out a fantasia of form. In Lyly, the prose is nothing more nor less than this: figures of rhetoric, winding in and out, splitting, joining up and, above all, ducking away from meaning. Poking fun at Lyly is, as Euphues might have said, wringing the proverb, a barrel in which, round and wooden as it is, and he may be, an uncourteous critic may shoot fish with much ease and eager merriment. But there may also be a serious point about the failure in this writing. During the Tudor century, although no one knew it, the rate of change in the English language was slowing down, as medieval constructions and word order settled into the modern grammatical sequences. When the Elizabethans looked back to Chaucer, and could hardly understand his grammar or vocabulary, they naturally predicted the same fate for their own language, two centuries on. But what was really happening was that there were large amounts of new vocabulary, from Italy and France, occupying relatively fixed places in the grammar. In short, the real change was no longer in the syntax (*along* lines of prose) but in the number of choices, and nuances, available in each grammatical position. It may be that Lyly's prose was so enormously popular with the Elizabethans because it defied this change, or made a show of doing so. In the convolutions of their speech and letters, his high-born characters may be using the language, unknowingly, against its historical direction, replacing an older grammatical licence with a rhetorical one. If this is so, Lyly's perversity, refusing to mean very much, is the worst form of conservatism: a style substituting for, not constituting, government of words.

It was government of the self, the passions, the nation, the language, and of the soul, which made Sir Philip Sidney such a considerable man. His father governed Ireland, Tudor England's medieval province, and Sidney himself was Governor of Flushing in the Protestant war against Spain. In both versions of his *Arcadia*, he writes about the proper duties of the prince, his counsellors and family and subjects, but it is in the revised and unfinished text (three Books, *c*.1584) that the control of rhetoric is identified with the control of others. In chapter 3 of the third Book, Lord Amphialus, enslaved by desire for his cousin Philoclea, rejoices and yet is ashamed when his mother imprisons the girl in the family castle. How should he present himself to her since she is a real prisoner, whereas he is only a prisoner of love? He looks to his wardrobe:

At length he took a garment more rich than glaring, the ground being black velvet, richly embroidered with great pearl and precious stones, but they set so among certain tufts of cypress [a rich satin] that the cypress was like black clouds through which the stars might yield a dark lustre. About his neck he wore a broad and gorgeous collar, whereof the pieces interchangeably answering, the one was of diamonds and pearl set with a white enamel so as by the cunning of the workman it seemed like a shining ice, and the other piece being of rubies and opals, had a fiery glistering; which he thought pictured the two passions of fear and desire wherein he was enchained.

The old Petrarchan rhetoric is still present here, but it longs to become seen and not heard, a picture not words. Petrarch's burning ice and freezing fires, the impossible conceits of love-madness, are what the pieces of the collar point to but try to make superfluous. Amphialus wants to dress in such a way that his appearance will speak for him, that words of persuasion will be unnecessary because meaning in pictures bypasses language, and the delays in speaking it, and goes directly to the mind. Sidney himself was fascinated by painting and the visual arts (he first saw the Italian masters on his tours of the Continent) and he returns to descriptions like this repeatedly, sometimes making up an *impresa*, where the picture, incomplete in itself, is accompanied by a motto. But where in the passage above the suit is described as both we and Amphialus see it, in what follows on, two lines later, the experience is no longer entirely mutual. Amphialus goes to Philoclea's room, and there finds her, 'because her chamber was over-lightsome',

sitting of that side of her bed which was from the window, which did cast such a shadow upon her as a good painter would bestow upon Venus, when under the trees

WOLLATON HALL, NEAR NOTTINGHAM. Built 1580–8 by the mason-architect, Robert Smythson, for the Cambridge-educated industrialist and coal-owner Sir Francis Willoughby, the house represents (with Longleat and Hardwick Hall) the very best of Elizabethan architecture. It is not securely neo-classical— its dimensions and lapses into frippery preclude that—and its defiance of nature (its water supplies had to be pumped up the hill it stands on) characterizes Elizabethan genius rather than maturity. But then this is what a prodigy-house was supposed to do: to startle the eye, and conjure admiration.

she bewailed the murder of Adonis: her hands and fingers (as it were) indented one within the other; her shoulder leaning to her bed's head, and over her head a scarf which did eclipse almost half her eyes, which under it fixed their beams upon the wall by, with so steady a manner as if in that place they might well change but not mend their object: and so remained they a good while after his coming in, he not daring to trouble her nor she perceiving him . . .

This is sensitive to light and shade, and to posture and composition, and it is meticulous about its language (notice the careful 'as it were', qualifying the 'indented' hands and fingers). In addition, the mythical precedent, Venus grieving, is discreet in its reversal: she wooed Adonis and he died; Amphialus in wooing the captive Philoclea wants the death of her honour, and she may die for it.

What we must ask is not only whether Amphialus sees the bed-scene in these terms, but whether the style, delaying ever so slightly, and making a classic line (upwards from her hands, to her shoulder, to her head and then to her eyes) is congruent with or subordinate to a visualizing of the girl. In other words, are the periods and clauses of this prose seeking to be resolved into a picture, as impatient to convey meaning as Amphialus is, or is the language supposed to stay resolutely before us, resisting absorption into its subject? Given the conjunction of the two paragraphs—Amphialus's glitter and show in the one, Philoclea's unconscious presentation of herself in the other—the only constant element which holds them together is our reading response to their differences. This is Sidney's great achievement, and it is much ahead of anything he says in his famous critical essay, the *Defence of Poetry*. He makes rhetorical awareness something which binds the reader into the narrative and makes him or her see what the characters do not. If we need a perspective on what he has managed to do, we should remember that he is writing two centuries before *Tristram Shandy*, and three before Henry James. In this case,

THE FOWLER'S TRIBUTE, Elizabethan embroidery at Hardwick Hall. Even in sylvan scenes like this, everything is purposeful and has its place. The trees give fruit for the lady of the house, the children are obedient to their nurse (*left-hand corner*), and the bare-headed fowlers present their labour respectfully. The houses at the top are divided off in size and social rank, with the horse and windmill completing the hierarchy of service and duty. Very little is purely ornamental and decorative. What bound all these creations together—some nurtured, others enforced, others made—was the teaching of the Bible. God had made Adam, with Eve his subordinate, and given him charge over Eden. For the Tudor man, to maintain an ordered society and to use the flesh of birds and beasts, was not just a matter of self-interest: it was a testimony of service to God.

where Philoclea's life is at risk, the prose is shaded in threats and danger, and Amphialus is the man in black who in his desire wants to do away with persuasion because he knows that for him it must fail. Elsewhere in the *Arcadia*, the prose is equally sensitive to comic and tragic differences and reversals—in the wild lands which were thought pacific, the foolish and the wise reverse roles, men and women do the same, aristocrats become shepherds, and clowns are taken for counsellors. But as the government of *Arcadia* goes awry, nearly tragically (the prince and his family all have mock or near-deaths), Sidney's control of the rhetoric is accomplished.

In *Astrophil and Stella*, sonnets written 1581–3 but not published until 1591, there may be another new rhetoric which points Astrophil towards Calvinist beginnings. To read the sequence as a love affair which comes to nothing except Astrophil's disappointment is probably inadequate, as are the attempts to read the poems as steps on some Neoplatonic escalator. The chiaroscuro depicted on Amphialus's garment—stars in the night, pearls on black—suggests another reading and one which is parallel to the flesh and blood trope in *Venus and Adonis*. Sidney's returning figures of light and dark are sometimes perceived by Astrophil, but more often they are not. He dreams of Stella (Latin for *star*) as a shining angel in the depths of sleep, and he sees her as a bright sun, while he is shut in dark woes, thoughts, and nights. Much of the narrative is derived from the oppositions, liberty and freedom, speech and silence, black and white, and these culminate in the songs, especially the eleventh, where in the dark night, looking out from her window, Stella finally frees herself from Astrophil. She is no longer the silent and unapproachable mistress, but a woman of light and reason who can speak and disagree. All of this prepares us for the final sonnet (108) in which not only does Stella disappear, but the conceits from earlier in the sequence are emptied of older meanings and remade for the new. Where Cupid and his bow and arrows, lead and gold, had earlier been a figure of wit, a god from the old iconography, in the last sonnet his elements are made again in sorrow's lead, in Phoebus' gold, and in 'rude despair' which, Astrophil says,

> Clips straight my wings, straight wraps me in his night,
> And makes me then bow down my head . . .

In earlier sonnets it was Cupid whose wings were clipped, but now the pagan god of love has become Astrophil's language of despair. The transmutation should worry us, and make us wonder if there has been another, more important, change elsewhere. Stella is nowhere to be seen, and there are only the figures of closed-in love: the dark furnace, the only light, and a young soul fluttering to his nest:

> So strangely, alas, thy works in me prevail,
> That in my woes for thee thou art my joy,
> And in my joys for thee my only annoy.

It is the early 1580s, Sidney is a devout and militant Protestant, and Cupid and Stella have finally been ousted from Astrophil's love. It may be that the figures of light and dark, the old conceits of passion and despair, are no longer trained on human love, and that there is a waiting here for what Sidney describes in a song in the first *Arcadia* as

> a feeling taste of him that sits
> Beyond the heaven, far more beyond our wits.

3. William Shakespeare

PHILIP EDWARDS

Shakespeare and the Elizabethan Theatre

WILLIAM SHAKESPEARE was a boy of twelve when in 1576 the first purpose-built theatre in England was opened. 'The Theatre' stood just north of the boundary of the City of London and so was outside its jurisdiction. It was built by an actor, James Burbage, whose son Richard became the leading actor in Shakespeare's plays. James Burbage had given up the trade of joiner and was a member of a strolling band of players who enjoyed the patronage of the earl of Leicester. Burbage was thus associated with another notable event of major importance in the history of English drama; in 1574 Leicester's men became the first company of actors to be granted a royal patent, entitling them to act their plays throughout the country. The queen herself became the patron of a group of actors in 1583. 'The Theatre' was the first of a long line of metropolitan playhouses that were the focus of the professional theatre in its heyday: the Curtain, the Red Bull, the Fortune north of the city, and, south of the Thames, the Rose, the Swan, the Globe, the Hope. The development of the professional drama in Elizabethan times would have been impossible without the protection and encouragement of the queen and her Privy Council. She needed companies of trained actors to supply the requirements of court entertainment. But all during her reign and for many years afterwards the 'common players' had to advance their profession in the teeth of the most determined opposition from city authorities throughout the realm and especially in London who had the strongest objections to this burgeoning activity on grounds of public order, morality, and religion. This new public professional theatre was almost crippled by the controls it was forced to operate under. The queen, the Church, and the City were all watchful for the least sign of plays and players straying beyond permitted limits, and censorship was extremely tight. But the theatre flourished, and the demand for new plays was continuous.

In what year exactly Shakespeare was drawn into the orbit of the metropolitan theatre, first as actor and then as playwright, we are not sure, but he was well

THE BRITISH SAVAGE: John White's 'Pictish Man', his skin painted with the heads of animals, monsters, and an owl, which locate his beastliness in his breast, legs, and privates. White painted a series of figures purporting to be the 'true picture' of the Picts 'which in the old time did habit one part of Great Britain', and engravings from them were published with the Roanoke series (see pp. 74, 89). However fanciful, even mannerist, some of the designs, there is perhaps an awareness of history here: of an ancestry as primitive as the savages of Virginia.

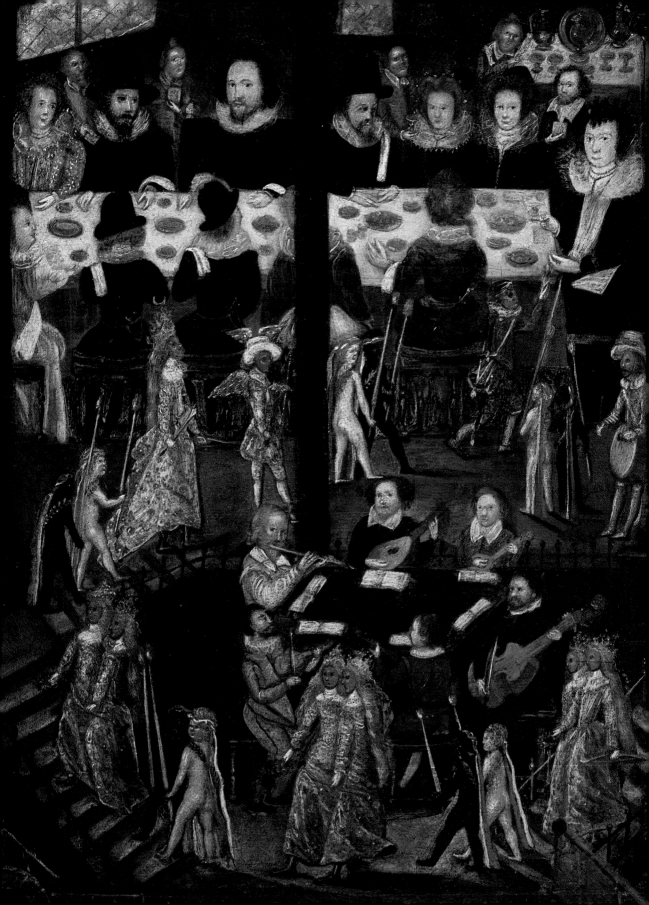

established by 1592, when he was twenty-eight. Shakespeare's father John, coming from a family of tenant farmers in the village of Snitterfield in Warwickshire, left the land and took up the glover's trade in the nearby market town of Stratford-upon-Avon. He prospered and became a leading citizen, Bailiff in 1568, Justice of the Peace and Alderman. He had thus acquired the status of a gentleman, and the right to bear arms, when misfortune fell upon him in 1577 (the circumstances are not at all clear) and he withdrew from all civic activity. His son William, born in 1564 as one of eight children, must certainly have had the formal education denied to his father, but, unlike his father, made what seems like an improvident marriage. He was eighteen when Anne Hathaway, a woman of twenty-six, became his wife. Their first child, Susanna, was born five months after the wedding (baptized May 1583). Twins, Hamnet and Judith, were born in February 1585. Before he was twenty-one, Shakespeare was the father of three young children, with a wife nearing thirty. There were no more children, and, though Stratford remained his home, Shakespeare lived his professional life in London, several days' journey away (unless you were extravagant enough to hire post-horses). His presence in London in 1592 is known from an attack on him by Robert Greene (1558–92), man of letters and playwright, who deeply resented Shakespeare coming from the ranks of the actors to undertake the writing of plays. He called him an 'upstart crow, beautified with our feathers, that with his *tiger's heart wrapped in a player's hide . . .* is in his own conceit the only Shake-scene in a country'. (The 'tiger's heart' phrase is a turning of a line from the third of Shakespeare's *Henry VI* plays.) Greene, six years Shakespeare's senior, came from a background of provincial trade very similar to his, his father being a Norwich saddler. But his distinction from Shakespeare was that he had won his way to Cambridge, and was Master of Arts of that university. He was living, disreputably enough, in London, writing romances, pamphlets, and plays—the best of which are *James the Fourth* and *Friar Bacon and Friar Bungay*—and it is in the last year of his life, in his remorseful *Groatsworth of Wit Bought with a Million of Repentance* that he spots Shakespeare as a threat to educated university men like himself as provider of plays to the young professional theatre.

Almost as remarkable a tribute as Greene's paranoia to the fact that Shakespeare had arrived is the apology which Henry Chettle felt called on to make for Greene's intemperate words. Not only was Shakespeare civil in his demeanour and an excellent actor, he said, but 'divers of worship' (that is, a number of people of considerable status) had spoken favourably of him as a person and as a writer. Just two years after this, the son of the Stratford glover, dedicating *The Rape of Lucrece* to Henry Wriothesley, earl of Southampton, spoke publicly to him of his affection. 'What I have done is yours, what I have to do is yours, being part in all I have, devoted yours.'

Of the dramatists active in London when Shakespeare began his playwriting

SIR HENRY UNTON'S WEDDING MASQUE, 1580. Elizabethan and Jacobean comedies often end with a wedding, feast, or acted entertainment (*The Tempest* with a masque, *Bartholomew Fair* with a banquet). To enact the reconciling of, and eternal divisions between, man and woman, old and young, master and servant—major comic themes—was to heighten the audience's immediate sense of social and personal harmony.

THE LONDON THEATRES (*above*).
This section of Wenceslaus Hollar's
'Long View' of London (1647) shows
two theatre buildings on the South
Bank of the Thames, west of London
Bridge. Unfortunately, the buildings
are wrongly labelled, with the Globe
(rebuilt in 1614) called 'Beere bayting'
and vice versa.

SHAKESPEARE'S BIRTHPLACE
(*right*), in Henley Street, Stratford-
upon-Avon. This water-colour by
Richard Greene (*c.*1762) is the earliest
known representation.

career, presumably in the late 1580s, the majority were university men: John Lyly, Robert Greene, Thomas Nashe, George Peele, Christopher Marlowe, Thomas Lodge. Lyly, Nashe, and Lodge were gentry, and it is noticeable that they were all three much less involved in the rough turmoil of the public theatres. (Lyly wrote his subtle and beautifully fashioned plays for companies of boy actors performing for private audiences and at court.) Marlowe's father was like Shakespeare's a respectable and substantial tradesman in a provincial town, a shoemaker in Canterbury. Of the non-university dramatists the most important was Thomas Kyd (1558–94), son of a London scrivener. There were no other actor-dramatists of note besides Shakespeare. Anthony Munday, a lesser light, began to write for the stage in the mid-1590s, followed by Ben Jonson, who was recorded as a common player in 1597. The 'university wits' did not bring to the public stage the academic canons of play construction— far from it. They infused a new richness in poetry, subjects, and passions into the popular drama; they made the public plays literary without making them academic. The vaunt of Marlowe's prologue to *Tamburlaine* is that the play will take the audience away from the 'jigging veins of rhyming mother-wits' and clownish conceits to 'the stately tent of war' where the majesty of the hero will show itself in 'high astounding terms'. It was not in the least difficult for the non-university dramatists with their grammar-school education from Stratford, Merchant Taylor's, or Westminster to keep pace with the literary manner of their more learned colleagues. Hence Greene's bitterness with the ungrateful actors: 'puppets ... that spake from our mouths', 'antics garnished in our colours'.

Shakespeare might well say of his drama what he made Jaques say of his melancholy; that it was entirely his own, 'compounded of many simples, extracted from many objects'. With so many dramatists making individual contributions to a common stock of plays not so very dissimilar in kind, it is very difficult to mark out just what Shakespeare owed to his immediate successors and his contemporaries. The indifference to the play as a literary object to be preserved, let alone printed, and the general convention of collaboration make questions of date and authorship very uncertain, and who is to be credited with innovation and who is to be seen as following whom remain enigmatic in the rapidly expanding theatre of the late 1580s and early 1590s. But there is no doubt that the work of Lyly in comedy and Marlowe and Kyd in tragedy were major influences on Shakespeare. Indeed, of Kyd and Marlowe, the great pioneers of Elizabethan tragedy, it might be said that Shakespeare was pondering over and arguing with their work throughout his career.

Kyd's main play was *The Spanish Tragedy*, easily the most famous play of its age and the great exemplar of the Elizabethan revenge tradition. It shows violent happenings at the Spanish court watched over by the ghost of a dead man and his guide from the spirit world; the ghost is to be shown a process of satisfaction for his own untimely death. These watchers see Hieronimo find the body of his murdered son and search for the murderers. They see him go mad with the burden of his quest and take the law into his own hands, exacting wild vengeance under cover of a court play before committing suicide. The ghostly observers note with satisfaction that in this passion and carnage Hieronimo has also paid the scores which *they* wished to settle. Kyd's complex web of relationships and interconnecting aspirations, and the perpetual irony with which he handles all human endeavour, could not be farther removed from Marlowe's concept of drama, in which a single individual hero carves out his own path through obstacles and objectors, or like Icarus soars near the sun before his wings melt and he dives to earth. Marlowe's irony is very different from Kyd's. For Kyd, a grim control of the universe by forces capricious in their favours makes all human pretension and struggle vain. Marlowe's restless scepticism sardonically surveys the values and assumptions

The Spanish Tragedie:
OR,
Hieronimo is mad againe.

Containing the lamentable end of *Don Horatio*, and *Belimperia*; with the pittifull death of *Hieronimo*.

Newly corrected, amended, and enlarged with new Additions of the *Painters* part, and others, as it hath of late been diuers times acted.

LONDON,
Printed by W. White, for I. White and T. Langley, and are to be fold at their Shop ouer againft the Sarazens head without New-gate. 1615.

The Tragicall Hiftoy of
the Life and Death
of Doctor Fauftus.

With new Additions.

Written by *Ch. Mar.*

LONDON,
Printed for *Iohn Wright*, and are to be fold at his fhop without Newgate, at the figne of the Bible. 1620.

ELIZABETHAN REVENGE TRAGEDY. The title-page of Kyd's *Spanish Tragedy*, in a later version containing additions to this immensely popular play. The woodcut shows Lorenzo (*right*), with blackened face, hustling Bel-Imperia away from the scene of the murder of her lover, Horatio, whose hanged corpse is discovered by his father Hieronimo (*centre*).

DOCTOR FAUSTUS. The title-page of the sixth printing of Marlowe's play, showing the hero experimenting in conjuring spirits, and a devil rising from the trapdoor.

which men traditionally live by and sends his heroes out to discover some new foundation for existence, which always fails. Kyd's characters are trapped because everything has been mapped out for them. Marlowe's characters are trapped because they cannot discover a map.

In *Tamburlaine*, Marlowe shows a mere shepherd working his way to world conquest by sheer force of personality. He has a vision of a life of superlative richness in which power and possessions are transmuted into spiritual majesty. But at the end of two long plays, beauty and royalty are words that have lost their radiance; the underlying substance is coarse and ugly. Both *The Jew of Malta* and the important historical tragedy *Edward II* explore in their different fashions the consequences of defying convention and seeking a new salvation. It is the hero of *Dr Faustus*, however, who most extensively rejects the values of society and suffers most for doing so. Faustus is indeed modern man impatient with traditional values, but his ambitions are a strange blend of intellectual aspiration and personal greed. Mental courage is accompanied by physical fear of the devils to whom he sells his soul, and the alternative heaven which he seeks gets sadly confused with the sexual embraces of a simulated Helen of Troy. Marlowe had extraordinary power to exhibit both the absurdity of conventional beliefs and the impossibility of replacing them. What we see in his plays and what we know of his short violent life suggest a deep religious sensibility beneath a contempt for prevailing religious beliefs and practices.

It is sometimes said that the deaths of Greene, Marlowe, and Kyd in the early 1590s—all of them young when they died—left the playwriting field free for Shakespeare to occupy. He learned his trade among that remarkable group of dramatists, the 'university wits', and as he forged his own profoundly original drama their influence never abated. When at the age of forty-six or so he wrote *The Winter's Tale*, memories of Peele's *Old Wives Tale* of c.1590 were sharp in his mind.

In 1592 severe outbreaks of the plague broke up playing in the public theatres for two years. It is not clear which company or companies Shakespeare had been attached to and had written for before this disaster of the plague years broke up the existing company formation. In 1594 Shakespeare appears with William Kempe and Richard Burbage as one of the leading men of a new company of actors under the patronage of Lord Hunsdon, the Lord Chamberlain. This became the most stable, the most prosperous, and the most famous acting company of its times. Shakespeare wrote for no other group.

The Early Comedies

The title given to the collection of his plays which Shakespeare's colleagues published after his death was *Mr William Shakespeare's Comedies, Histories and Tragedies* and it is still helpful to divide the plays into those three large categories in which they were originally printed, while making some provision for the different periods of his writing career. In looking first at the earlier comedies, those which Shakespeare wrote before 1602, we are impressed as much by their dissimilarity one from another as by their family likeness. We might think that the typical Shakespearian comedy is easy to describe: a setting in Italy with a duke, a clown, a heroine disguised as a boy, misadventures in a woodland, and an ending with young love duly rewarded. But in fact there is no single formula for a Shakespearian comedy. *The Comedy of Errors* is a very Roman sort of play, chiselled like a crystal, with the action moving at high speed. *Love's Labour's Lost* is expansive, literary, witty, satirical. Plot is everything in *Much Ado About Nothing* but of negligible importance in *As You Like It*. The major figure of Shylock in *The Merchant of Venice* has no parallel in the other comedies. *The Merry Wives of Windsor* is unique in its English bourgeois setting. For all that they have in common, each of

Mr. WILLIAM
SHAKESPEARES
COMEDIES,
HISTORIES, &
TRAGEDIES.

Publiſhed according to the True Originall Copies.

LONDON
Printed by Iſaac Iaggard, and Ed. Blount. 1623.

THE FIRST FOLIO. Unlike Ben Jonson, who published his *Works* in 1616, Shakespeare did not collect his plays for publication, though some were published separately (with or without his authority) during his lifetime (see p. 133). His colleagues Heminges and Condell set themselves to collect his plays after his death, the result being the 'First Folio' of 1623, with the title-page reproduced here. Eighteen of the plays were printed for the first time. The 'portrait' is by Martin Droeshout.

Shakespeare's earlier comedies is a new experiment, and in looking for what is centrally Shakespearian in them we have to be careful not to iron out the sharp individuality of each.

Shakespeare clearly took immense pains with these early comedies. He owed less than usual to his sources. There is no known source for *Love's Labour's Lost*, *A Midsummer Night's Dream*, or *The Merry Wives*. If he pillaged translations of Italian *novelle* or plays for ideas, he transmuted what he found into entirely new substances. Traditions of every kind are visible in the plays, Roman comedy, the popular Italian *commedia dell'arte*, the English court comedies of Lyly, and so on, but his comedies are not within any single tradition. Shakespeare never wrote *better* plays than the best of his early comedies; they are almost perfect in their own kind, intricate, witty, lyrical plays which amazingly combine an airy nonsensicality with a profound *sotto voce* on the nature of life, love, and art. They are mostly lighthearted fantasies, but there are few areas of human experience they do not touch.

Their cheerful disclaimer of any serious intention is something of a trap. Shakespeare makes rather too much of the triviality of his intentions. Those casual titles! *Much Ado About Nothing, Twelfth Night, or What You Will, A Midsummer Night's Dream, As You Like It.* The plays are always calling attention to themselves as unlikely fabrications. 'If this were played upon a stage now,' says Fabian, winking at the audience during the gulling of Malvolio, 'I could condemn it as an improbable fiction.' When at the end of *Love's Labour's Lost* the lovers are dismissed for twelve months, Berowne cries, 'That's too long for a play!' *A Midsummer Night's Dream* is particularly mischievous in making fun of its own credibility. The absurdities of Peter Quince, Nick Bottom, and the other 'mechanicals' in preparing the play they want to perform at court parody the efforts of the Lord Chamberlain's Men in the play at large. 'The best in this kind are but shadows,' says Theseus, watching the blunders of the mechanicals. ('Shadow' could mean actor as well as shadow.)

Why does Shakespeare so regularly break theatrical illusion to remind us that his plays are only fictions? When Jonson breaks theatrical illusion it is to remind us that we must never forget the great reality outside the theatre. Shakespeare seems to have a double purpose. On the one hand, certainly, he is insisting that art is art because it is not life, and that, as Touchstone said, 'the truest poetry is the most feigning'. But Macbeth said that 'Life's but a walking shadow.' In *The Tempest* Prospero paralleled the sudden ending of the little masque he had contrived with the transience of all the happenings in the 'great globe'. Let Shakespeare mock his art as he will, we know as he knew that even his lightest comedies are images of life, and not least in suggesting the flimsiness, the insecurity, the evanescence of what we assume to be the firmer realities of our everyday lives. It is in one of these earlier comedies that Shakespeare gives Jaques his superb rendering of the time-honoured commonplace, 'All the world's a stage.' Shakespeare's self-mockery in his comedy is double-edged. In emphasizing the insubstantiality of the plays he hints at the insubstantiality of our lives. It is not only art that can seem 'an improbable fiction'.

But the primary function of Shakespeare's comedies is to entertain the audience, to 'take them out of themselves', to perform the therapy of dissolving the cares of 'this working day world' into 'holiday foolery', to use the words of *As You Like It.* In Christopher Sly, the drunken tinker in *The Taming of the Shrew*, we find an unkind portrait of ourselves as audience. As a joke he has been taken up and dressed in fine clothes, and he wakes to the sound of music—and a new identity. To entertain him 'a pleasant comedy' is performed, as recommended by doctors to cure melancholy. What Sly witnesses is a remarkable fantasy of masculine achievement, in which Petruchio dominates his termagant bride and reduces her to manageable docility. Curiously, the rather beautiful epilogue, in which Sly wakes up in his own clothes and staggers home to try out Petruchio's methods on his own wife, is found only in a secondary version of the play (*The Taming of A Shrew*) and is omitted in the primary text.

Laughter alone is not enough to make the healing power of comedy work; the laughter has to be generated within an action that moves the characters from discord, separation, and unhappiness to peace, unity, and concord. Most of the comedies begin with a strong scene of loss or enmity. One of the earliest, *The Comedy of Errors*, has a fine symbolic first scene of the banning of trade and communication between two cities, and a Syracusan, searching for his lost sons, condemned to death in Ephesus. In *As You Like It* brother's hand is against brother; in *A Midsummer Night's Dream* Hermia is being forced to marry a man she hates. In some of the comedies there is an escape from the initial unhappiness into a never-never land, a place of confusion, bewilderment, and transformation where difficulties eventually melt away. Then from this 'green world' of absurdity the characters return reinvigorated to the court of the first scene. This is the procedure of both *A Midsummer Night's Dream* and *As You Like It*. In *The Merchant of Venice* there is a kind of shuttle service

A

Midſommer nights

dreame.

As it hath beene ſundry times pub-
likely acted, by the Right Honourable, the Lord Chamberlaine his
ſeruants.

VVritten by VVilliam Shakeſpeare.

Printed by Iames Roberts, 1600.

A MIDSUMMER NIGHT'S DREAM. The title-page of the first edition of the play, published some five years after its first performance. Unlike some unauthorized publications with poor texts (the 'bad quartos'), this provides an excellent text, presumably based on Shakespeare's own manuscript, or a fair copy of it.

between the grim constraints of the Rialto and the world of gratuitous blessings at Belmont. Other plays dispense with the symbolic change of location but they insist on confusion as an intervening state between misery and happiness. The confusion is intense in *The Comedy of Errors* with two sets of identical twins, and in *Twelfth Night* with the mistakes caused by Viola's male disguise compounded by her resemblance to her twin brother.

We may well ask who or what controls the movement of the characters from pain through confusion to pleasure. Certainly, with the exception of the ruthless Petruchio, it is not the characters themselves. Ardent, intelligent, and determined as they are, heroines such as Viola and Rosalind do not achieve their destinies by thought, hard work, and virtue. The best people win, but not because of their strength, or their weaknesses. In later plays there are semi-divine figures such as Prospero to control the action, but these are not developed in the earlier plays—unless we fancy seeing Portia, with her power to release her friends from the clutch of evil, as a surrogate of the divine. Only in *A Midsummer Night's Dream* is there evident a machinery of control in the king and queen of the fairies, Oberon and Titania. They act as a comic and irreverent parody of divine providence, a witty 'non-explanation' of the control of human destiny. Voyages towards happiness such as we find in the comedies defy rational explanation. But even in this cheerful evasion of the tyranny of the possible, the plays manage to make their comment on the mystery of an uncontrollable and unpredictable future.

It is strange how frequently there is some flaw in the happy ending in Shakespeare's earlier comedies. 'Love is ever matter of comedies' said Francis Bacon (scornfully enough), and what brings happiness in these plays is, naturally, the sexual relationship. But only in *As You Like It* is there a feeling of completeness, as Hymen bestows his ceremonial blessing on the wedding to come. At the end of the *Dream* we wonder whether Demetrius would have returned to Helena without the potent spell of Oberon on his eyelids. In *Love's Labour's Lost* the unsteady movement of the French nobles towards their ladies is finally thwarted by the women's insistence on a twelve-month cooling-off period. In *Much Ado* the final wedding of Claudio and Hero is a repair of the earlier marriage brutally broken off when he denounced her at the altar. *The Shrew* goes on beyond marriage; however compliant we judge Katherina to be at the end, Lucentio has acquired in Bianca a bride whose compliance has not survived the wedding. The pairing-off at the end of *Twelfth Night* has its uneasiness. Viola wins the man she loves, but only at the very last minute when Orsino has to give up Olivia—who has married Sebastian, believing him to be someone else.

If there is some hesitation in the endings of the comedies, in so far as they are hymns to the victory of true love, it is because there is a good deal of hesitation in the plays about the whole matter of sexual attraction. The love with which the comedies are concerned is a fulfilment of the self in a relationship

THE COMEDY OF ERRORS as staged by Komisarzhevsky at the Shakespeare Memorial Theatre in Stratford-upon-Avon in 1938. This brilliantly inventive production was criticized by some for burlesquing the play.

which is not exclusively or primarily a sexual relationship. The quest in *The Comedy of Errors* is for the reintegration of a divided family. The moving reunion of Viola with her brother Sebastian in *Twelfth Night* presents none of the problems which the final pairing gives us. There is love between the sexes, love between members of a family, love between friends of the same sex. Montaigne, in his great essay 'Of Friendship' said that love generated by desire or dependent on family relationship was as nothing compared with the free affection between friends. In Shakespeare's very last play, *The Two Noble Kinsmen*, sexual love is a tyranny which breaks up the ideal companionship of Palamon and Arcite, and of Theseus and Pirithous. There are some striking hymns to friendship in the last plays, but the earlier comedies also contain many gestures indicating the strength and the rights of friendship, particularly in the figures of the two Antonios, one in *The Merchant* and the other in *Twelfth Night*, with their friendships for Bassanio and Sebastian, and in Hermia and Helena in the *Dream*, and above all in *The Two Gentlemen of Verona*.

Two sworn friends find themselves falling in love, Proteus with Julia and Valentine with Silvia. Unfortunately, Proteus feels Silvia to be more attractive, and by an act of treachery gets Valentine out of the way and tries to force her love. When Valentine arrives in the nick of time to rescue her, Proteus begs for forgiveness, which Valentine readily grants, taking him back without further question. And Silvia? Valentine says

> that my love may appear plain and free
> All that was mine in Silvia I give thee.   (V. iv)

Like Julia, who is standing nearby disguised as a page, we find this generosity extreme. Fortunately, this reappearance of Julia saves Valentine from the consequences of his offer; the final pairing of Proteus/Julia and Valentine/Silvia saves the situation and the friendship. The ending of *The Two Gentlemen* is certainly awkward, but that is not because of the immaturity of Shakespeare's art; it is the awkwardness of the problem itself, the competing claims of friendship and sexual love. Valentine's reckless offer, in a bid to save a friendship which he values above the love of women, is *his* solution of the problem, not Shakespeare's. What the play does testify to is Shakespeare's deep consciousness of the importance of friendship and the fact that the inevitable progression to sexual love is not always a move into maturity and good sense.

'Love is merely a madness', says the love-sick Rosalind. In the liveliest and wittiest comedy scene that Shakespeare wrote, Act IV Scene i of *As You Like It*, Rosalind, in the liberation of her disguise as a young man, mocks everything that lovers hold sacred—particularly the depth and the permanence of the emotions which seem all-in-all to them. But, resuming her own person, she can only say, 'O coz, coz, coz . . . that thou didst know how many fathom deep I am in love!' Sexual love in the comedies is an irrational and inexplicable compulsion, as destructive as it is bountiful. In men in particular, desire is unstable and shifting. Women are more constant and true in their affection. 'Varium et mutabile' applies to the male sex. No one is immune; those who scoff at love fall quickly and heavily, like the sworn celibates Benedick and Beatrice in *Much Ado* and the royal entourage in *Love's Labour's Lost*. Whether Elizabethan writers learned of the power of love to possess and transform people from their own lives or from Ovid, they constantly turned for ideas and language to the great passions of the *Metamorphoses*. Medea's helpless cry as she falls in love with Jason, 'Video meliora proboque, deteriora sequor', may seem further away from the comedies than it is. Olivia, sworn to mourn her brother in celibacy but unable to repress her passion for Cesario—whom mercifully she does not know to be a woman—says under her breath, 'A fiend like thee might bear my soul to hell.' What does Oberon's spell symbolize as Titania moons over and takes to her bed a creature with a human body and a donkey's head?

It is indeed that commonest of Renaissance topics, the transforming power of love, which Shakespeare harps on in the comedies. 'So full of shapes is fancy . . .' says Orsino. The resourceful Berowne apologizes to the ladies for the absurd behaviour of himself and his colleagues: 'Your beauty, ladies, Hath much deformed us.' That love may be both deformity and self-realization is a contradiction which the openness of Shakespearian comedy makes no attempt to resolve. Many of the lovers seem to find their true destination only by a sort of dislocation of the self. This is often shown or symbolized by a period spent in disguise. The most startling of these temporary transformations is of course that of Bottom, degraded to a beast in order to be upgraded to consort of a goddess.

The comedies are full of transformations, and they are not always connected with the pursuit of love. Much of the laughter and much of the profundity of the plays lie within these transformations. New identities are acquired by disguise or are foisted on to a character by the spell of an inefficient Puck or mistakes in recognition. Great gifts can come from the grafting of these new identities, as Sebastian found when he was swept off to church to marry Olivia. But not all are so lucky. In *The Shrew*, Petruchio's psychological warfare makes life a nightmare for Katherina, and in *Twelfth Night*, while Sebastian is marvelling at his new existence, Malvolio is in despair with *his*, fooled into believing he is loved by Olivia then locked away and taunted as a madman.

In *Much Ado* new identities are imposed on their victims by tricksters both good and bad. Because of Don John's contrivances, Claudio and Don Pedro take Hero to be a whore; but Claudio, Don Pedro, and Hero, victims of that deception, have taken a ready part in the deception by which Benedick and Beatrice are tricked into believing that each is in love with the other. When we are watching a comedy, the bewilderment of characters who are in some way lost or at cross-purposes can be very funny indeed, but this twinning of the deceptions in *Much Ado*, one wicked and one well-meaning, helps us to see that the abounding insecurity of personality in the comedies is not too far distant from the insecurity of the characters of tragedy who suddenly find that the ground they stand on has begun to shift beneath their feet. If there is a lesson in the comedies apart from the lesson that laughter is a great blessing it is a lesson complementing the view that 'all the world's a stage', teaching us that the self which always seeks its completeness through love of others is an unfixed, indefinite, wandering thing. The comedies suggest that we are all very tentative as persons, ready enough to try to alter the lives of others but with precious little control over ourselves or our destinies.

The structure of a Shakespearian comedy is a harmony of seemingly incompatible voices. *A Midsummer Night's Dream* is famous for its polyphonic construction. Scene by scene the different elements whose blending is to compose the play are introduced: Theseus and the Athenian court, the young lovers, the stage-struck working men, the fairy creatures of the forest. In *As*

HENRY IRVING AND ELLEN
TERRY as Shylock and Portia in the
trial scene of *The Merchant of Venice*,
pictured in the *Sketch*, 31 July 1880.
This famous production at the
Lyceum had run for 250 consecutive
nights since its opening in November
1879.

You Like It the ponderous satire of the non-joiner Jaques chimes with and
clarifies the wittier tones of Rosalind and Touchstone—and those two are very
different from each other. *Twelfth Night* is a miracle of the twining together
of different voices, of Sir Toby Belch, of Orsino, and the mocking voice of the
unfathomable Feste. But the great triumph in the successful mingling of
discordances is in *The Merchant of Venice*. To bring Shylock into a comedy
was the most daring thing Shakespeare did in that genre. There are indeed
villains in other comedies, such as Oliver in *As You Like It* and Don John in
Much Ado. These are characteristic Shakespearian villains in the gratuitousness
of their mischief. 'Born under Saturn' (Don John's phrase), they can hardly
explain to themselves the instinctiveness of their hatred. But Shylock is different.
He knows why he hates. He comes on the stage in the third scene with
assurance, dignity—and passion. During the course of the play hatred masters
him; but Shakespeare keeps this absurd and vindictive member of a persecuted
race so vividly alive as a person that it is impossible for us to share the delight
of the Christian characters in finally crushing him, destroying his wealth, his
religion, his family. There is no point in saying that the values of Shakespeare's
age were not ours, and that in our interpretation of Shylock we attribute
to him a sensibility not then existing. He was expecting us. He was content in
that same play to present a stereotype of the tawny Moor in the Prince of
Morocco, but his Jew was no stereotype. *The Merchant of Venice* is an
'improbable fiction' indeed, and it needed a stage villain to be hissed off the

stage at the end. In making that villain a Jew whose malice is qualified by a perception of the history of his race, Shakespeare brilliantly demonstrates how his comedies, which are trifles light as air, can be as thoughtful as the tragedies.

The Histories

History plays are perhaps the most remarkable contribution which the Elizabethans made to world drama. Great though the best of their comedies and tragedies are, it is the 'history play' that is their most distinctive innovation, and it was a striking legacy to other nations which in later centuries set out to create a national literature.

Its origins are not as dignified as they might be. Hard-pressed dramatists in the period of the Armada, dependent on an advance from the playhouse owner for their next meal, looted the chronicles of Holinshed and others for plots which might be used to appeal to the patriotism of a London audience. But it is not in Shakespeare's plays alone that are found the deeper values of a national historical drama. These plays about Saxon and Norman kings, about King John, or Edward III, or Henry V, were a form of national self-discovery, defining the new England in a not wholly uncritical scrutiny of its past. Shakespeare was among the pioneers of the history play along with Peele, Munday, Greene, Marlowe, and others whose names are lost. As a young actor of twenty-four or twenty-five Shakespeare had the temerity to conceive the idea of a sequence of four plays on the Wars of the Roses, terminating with the coming in of the Tudors at the battle of Bosworth in 1485. Marlowe had written a sequence of two plays on the exotic history of Tamburlaine. Here was to be a sequence twice as ambitious on matters nearer at hand for Englishmen than the adventures of a foreign potentate. There is little doubt that the whole sequence was in Shakespeare's mind from the start. The 'tetralogy' as it is often called is in the shape of a single symphony, of which the individual plays are related movements. Whether a unit of four plays covering the events of sixty years is a good idea is another matter. When we think of the briskness of each of his well-wrought comedies, Shakespeare's first history plays seem laboured and ponderous. It is very serious drama indeed. The continuous exchange of very long speeches must have been taxing for the actors (especially the boys taking the parts of women such as Queen Margaret) and something of a strain for the audience. Shakespeare's commitment to recording in poetry the mighty pageantry of plots and counterplots, sieges and battles, fallen kings and widowed queens, takes him sometimes beyond what can easily be translated to the bare boards of his stage. But if we get the impression that the stage was sometimes a restriction for him there is no doubt that he saw history as drama and presented it as drama, not as narrative or description. And in any case there is no question about the success of these first history plays on the stage. Philip Henslowe, the playhouse owner, recorded many performances of 'harey the vj' in 1592 and in the same year Thomas Nashe wrote eloquently of the effect on London audiences of the death of 'brave Talbot, the terror of the French' in *1 Henry VI*.

The first part of *Henry VI* deals with the loss of Henry V's French empire. With the new king a child, the relatives of the old king bicker for supremacy and fail to support the embattled Englishmen whose courage is not enough to hold out against French forces fortified by Joan of Arc. Shakespeare's Joan is a very interesting figure, distinctly Marlovian in her lowly birth, her cynical wit, and her great aspirations and her confidence in her destiny. But of course she is on the wrong side, and Shakespeare betrays her in an infamous last scene in which she disowns her father and her virginity. The second and third parts of *Henry VI* are really rather horrifying plays showing the wresting of power from the saintly king and the milestones along the violent road to civil war. Every battle, St Albans, Wakefield, Towton, Tewkesbury, is marked by some new spectacle of horror. Ritual killings follow one another in a retaliatory cycle. Clifford kills York's son, then York himself, cornered by the king's forces, is forced to undergo the abuse and ridicule of Queen Margaret, to which he replies with magnificent defiance, before he is killed. The Yorkist sons, Edward, Richard, and Clarence, take their revenge by a ceremonial murder of King Henry's son in the presence of the queen. The last of the many killings in the plays is the stabbing of Henry VI in the Tower by Richard of Gloucester.

Richard, with his hunchback and withered arm as emblems of his social deformity, emerges during *3 Henry VI* as a product of the internecine savagery of his times and, in the final play of the series, *Richard III*, he goes on to create history in his own image in his determination to be king. This witty, crooked, ugly man is Shakespeare's answer to Marlowe's majestic, handsome hero Tamburlaine as the embodiment of insatiable ambition. The cool, amused insolence of his great opening speech makes clear the attraction which the role has for every great actor (though for almost two centuries it was Colley Cibber's reorganized version of the play that was performed). Richard III is the great actor-king. He sees history lying before him as a malleable mass to be given shape, and it is all to be done by duplicity and pretence. Misrepresentation is a way of life. He clothes his total callousness and contempt for others in a hundred masks, and the zest and energy with which he plays his roles are at the heart of the play's appeal and power, placing it with *The Spanish Tragedy* and *Dr Faustus* in the trinity of early Elizabethan tragedies. His monstrous and macabre game comes to an end when at last he gains the coveted crown. All his resourcefulness cannot stem the conventional recompense and poetic justice which was all Shakespeare could offer his brilliantly unconventional villain. The play (and the tetralogy) concludes with the new Tudor king's invocation of reconciliation and peace for the wounded country.

King John, which belongs to no sequence, was written some time in the mid-1590s; its isolation may indicate some indecision on Shakespeare's part before he embarked on his second great sequence, *Richard II* to *Henry V*. *John* is an important and often underestimated play. At its centre is one of Shakespeare's most splendid creations, the Bastard Faulconbridge. He begins as a figure of subversive irresponsibility, wittily puncturing everyone's pretensions and self-esteem, and ends by saving England, by sheer force of personality, from the disaffection of its nobles and a French invasion. In this play Shakespeare's conception of kingship becomes more mystical than hitherto. Though the play ends with the resounding cry of the Bastard, 'Nought shall make us rue, / If England to itself do rest but true', its burden is that the health of the kingdom depends on knowing and possessing its true king—who, like Godot, is never to be found.

At any rate, when Shakespeare launches into his new sequence of plays on the three reigns preceding the Wars of the Roses, he brings with him a new imaginative view of kingship which quite transforms the brutal struggles for power which we have witnessed in the plays on the Wars of the Roses themselves. Shakespeare must have been anxious to get the first of the plays, dealing with the reign of Richard II, into exactly the right shape. It was the keystone of the massive arch which he had begun to build with the first of the *Henry VI* plays and which he would finish, almost a decade later, with *Henry V*. The unseating of the last truly legitimate king in the Norman line in 1399 was, everyone accepted, the basic cause of the troubles of the century that followed. Shakespeare's Richard II is indeed the true king, a real feudal monarch whose right is not disputed; but his autocratic and irresponsible ways, particularly in engineering the death of his uncle Woodstock, have alienated the great nobles. His strongly developed view of the sanctity of his office is disastrously associated with an idea of his personal invulnerability; but as the army of the banished and dispossessed Bolingbroke, Duke of Lancaster, builds up against him, he adjusts himself to the realities of political power while coming to believe more and more in the holiness of regal office. In a series of marvellous speeches he shares with whoever will listen his bitter discoveries about himself, kingship, and the political situation. We like the king the more as he moves towards the dethronement and death which he knows await him. If *Richard II* is a history play, it is also one of Shakespeare's finest political tragedies.

The first part of *Henry IV* follows a quite different dramatic method; indeed, its structure reminds us of the interwoven texture of *A Midsummer Night's Dream*. Falstaff, Hotspur, Prince Hal, and Bolingbroke (now king) are strongly differentiated strands which combine into a richly achieved unity. The purpose of such a structure is clear. Hal was by indefeasible legend a wild young profligate who became England's hero-king. Shakespeare wanted to show him having to choose his way of life from among competing claims upon the human spirit: self-indulgence, idealistic commitment, and calculating self-control. Alas,

SHAKESPEARE ON THE SCREEN. Henry V receives the French envoy at the battle of Agincourt. A scene from the most famous film of a Shakespeare play, Laurence Olivier's wartime *Henry V* (1944).

the choice is made all too early in the play; Hal dedicates himself to the caution and self-protection of the successful ruler, and he never wavers from his decision. So it is we, and not Hal, who are tempted by the enthusiastic recklessness of Hotspur and the unbuttoned humour of Falstaff. Hal wins through to the triumph over Hotspur at Shrewsbury, and, in the second part of *Henry IV*, to the long-awaited rejection of Falstaff.

When he is crowned, Henry V becomes, like his father, an efficient ruler and not a medieval priest-king; he has no interest in the sacramental or mystical idea of kingship. The stain of the deposition of Richard II is something to be worn away by time and good government. England is powerful in his reign; Shakespeare views it as an anticipation of the imperial future offering itself to his country in his own day. It is extraordinary, however, what risks Shakespeare took in presenting his warrior-hero, exposing him to challenges which later ages have found all too strong. The rejection of Falstaff is politically unavoidable but morally unpalatable. Falstaff's death, his heart 'killed' by the king, is movingly reported in the uneducated language of Mistress Quickly. At the height of Agincourt, Fluellen launches into a comparison between Henry, who turned away Falstaff 'in his right wits and good judgement', and Alexander the Great, who killed his best friend when he was drunk. Falstaff's followers, Pistol, Bardolph, and Nym, compose a vivid anti-heroic group in Henry's army. Pistol's intention to pillage in France, 'like horse-leeches, my boys, / To suck, to suck, the very blood to suck', is in awkward mimicry of Henry's imperial ambitions. ('I love France so well that I will not part with a village of it.') A voice more compelling than the manic bluster of Pistol is that of Michael Williams, who challenges the disguised Henry on the night before Agincourt with his responsibility for those who die in battle if the king's cause 'be not good'. Henry has no difficulty in demonstrating that the state of a soldier's soul is the soldier's responsibility, but he does not answer that part of Williams's question which concerns leading men to their death in an unjust war.

The play of *Henry V* ends as *Richard III* had done in a military victory which is supposed to put an end to the weary blood-letting, heal the wounds of division, and promote peace. It is not unnatural that in concluding the story of Henry V the Chorus should remind the audience that what followed his reign had already been shown on the stage in the *Henry VI* plays. This reminder of the anarchy and self-destruction during Henry VI's reign comes like a drench of cold water after the blessings and prayers for peace and unity which we have just heard. The rapid alternation between a promise of the future and a recollection of past misery is characteristic of the histories. The whole majestic cycle of these plays suggests that Shakespeare's pride in his country and his belief that the Tudors had led England out of the wilderness coexisted with a strong feeling that the quest for stability and peace never ends. Society is shown bewildered and divided, lacerating itself as it looks for the true leader who never seems to turn up. The hope at the end of one play is dashed by the events of the next. Perhaps this makes Shakespeare's histories sound gloomy and pessimistic. Certainly they are unrelenting in showing cruelty, selfishness, suffering, betrayal, and failure as the common condition of life. But the creation of characters like Richard III, the Bastard, and Falstaff witness to the imaginative vitality which raises Shakespeare's ten-year-long portrayal of the sombre centuries well above the merely depressing and gives it as a whole a strength akin to tragedy.

The Theatre at the Turn of the Century

Henry V was written in 1599. His next play, *Julius Caesar*, marks the beginning of the cycle of major tragedies which Shakespeare wrote in the ensuing eight years. The year 1599 also marks the building of the Globe theatre, the Lord Chamberlain's Men's own building, south of the Thames on Bankside near Southwark Cathedral. The company already had the best dramatist and no doubt the best actors; they now had the best theatre. Shakespeare was one of the chief shareholders in the property, and he was now becoming a person of substance. He was able to buy one of the finest houses in Stratford, New Place, in 1597. In documents he is described as William Shakespeare of Stratford-upon-Avon, gentleman. His family now had its coat-of-arms. The Lord

SHAKESPEARE'S COAT OF ARMS. Shakespeare's father applied for a coat of arms in the years of his prosperity, but the application was not followed up until his son's years of prosperity (1596). Six years later York Herald made the sketch (*left*) to indicate his disapproval that a grant of arms had been made to a mere 'player'.

Chamberlain's Men were unwittingly involved in the Essex rebellion of 1601 when some of the conspirators paid them to put on the old play of *Richard II* on the day before the abortive rising. The year 1603 witnessed a major change in the company, for James I on his accession brought all the major acting companies under the patronage of members of the royal family. The Lord Chamberlain's company became the King's Men. They were much more often called upon for court performances than they had been under Elizabeth.

The most important of Shakespeare's fellow dramatists at the turn of the century were Thomas Dekker (*c.*1572–1632), George Chapman (*c.*1559–1634), John Marston (1576–1634), Thomas Heywood (*c.*1574–1641), and Ben Jonson (1572/3–1637). Not one of these had the same exclusive commitment to writing for the theatre that Shakespeare had. True, none of them had Shakespeare's enviable job-security as resident dramatist for a major company. But that is not the whole story. Ben Jonson did not regard the theatre as the true environment for his writing; he did not want to be dependent on it for his livelihood. He sought private patronage, was the major provider of masques for the royal court in James's time, and produced entertainments for the great nobility. This was Jonson's life as the public theatre was Shakespeare's life, though Jonson was never able to 'leave the loathèd stage' (as he put it) completely. His stage plays he regarded as literature to be read, and so he published their full texts, with growls at the audiences and the actors. He published his collected plays, poems, and masques in 1616 as his 'Works'. Shakespeare, on the other hand, though the Sonnets show some restiveness with the condition of working for the theatre, may be said never to have published a single one of his plays. Some of his plays appeared in reasonably good texts in his lifetime, but it is extremely unlikely that he in any way oversaw their publication even if he agreed to it. His indifference to the preservation of his writings is mysterious. Jonson was vociferous about the central role of the poet in society; did Shakespeare have no such views? His ideas on the authority of the poet have to be gleaned and inferred from his writings, from the Sonnets, from *Timon of Athens*, from *The Tempest*, for example. They are subtle and far-reaching, but full of self-mockery; and no doubt it is the vein of scepticism about the value of his own art, which is constantly observable, that made him leave it to others to preserve his writings, if they wished to.

The contributions made to comedy by Chapman, Dekker, Shakespeare, and Jonson at this richest period of Elizabethan drama are extremely diverse. Chapman's original and intelligent comedies have received much less attention than his pensive tragedies, of which *Bussy D'Ambois* (1607) is the liveliest. Dekker's work, often in collaboration, speaks of the haste of the public theatre, but it is always fresh, energetic, and well written. His talent for rendering the life of the common people, shown also in his many vigorous pamphlets, is apparent everywhere, and nowhere better than in his best-known play, *The Shoemakers' Holiday* (1600). Ben Jonson's comedy is rooted in satire as Shakespeare's is rooted in romance. *Every Man in His Humour* (1598), later rewritten to change its setting from Italy to England, is a straightforward enough guying of affectation, but the 'comical satires', *Every Man Out of His Humour, Cynthia's Revels*, and *Poetaster* (1599-1601), are difficult, fantastic plays, in which the brilliance of Jonson's invention and the shrewdness and pungency of his satiric barbs are in danger of being strangled in complexity. To this period belongs his one great tragedy, *Sejanus* (1603), a grim study in the tyranny of a police state, which, like so much of Shakespeare's writing, seems inexplicably to belong more to our times than to theirs.

The comedies on which Jonson's later fame chiefly depends all belong to the Jacobean theatre: *Volpone* (1606), *Epicoene, or The Silent Woman* (1609), *The*

BEN JONSON, after Abraham van Blyenberch. This portrait was acquired by the National Portrait Gallery in 1935.

Alchemist (1610), and *Bartholomew Fair* (1610). In these great satires the contest is three-cornered, between rogues, fools, and authority. The rogues win handsomely. It is the habit of Jonson to direct his plays towards the exposure of folly and vice, and to the need for civilized, restrained, and ordered living, and to sabotage that purpose by the sheer vigour and gusto with which he portrays his tricksters and parasites, whose supply of victims will last as long as the cupidity of man and the ineffectiveness of venal authority. Jonson's work is full of such paradoxes. The beautiful and learned court masques on which he worked in uneasy harness with Inigo Jones in the winter of each year seem to flatter a complacency in their audience and performers which his acerbic intelligence would normally delight in puncturing.

Shakespeare and Jonson are often correctly seen as antithetical spirits. Many times Jonson was critical of Shakespeare's imperfect standards in his art and his want of learning, though he said he 'loved the man . . . (on this side idolatry)' and wrote that Shakespeare was 'not of an age, but for all time'. If these two major figures in the Elizabethan and Jacobean drama are antithetical, it could also be said that they are complementary, the giver and the restrainer, Dionysus and Apollo.

The Tragedies

Shakespeare's tragedies begin and end with Roman themes. The arc goes from the fantastic and gruesome fiction of *Titus Andronicus* of the early 1590s to the spare and craggy study of *Coriolanus* in 1608. In spite of the diversity of tragic subjects, Rome remains a constant preoccupation, inspiring the two major works, *Julius Caesar* (1599) and *Antony and Cleopatra* (1607). These two plays on historical subjects underline the ready transference between 'history' and 'tragedy' and the strong political element to be found in nearly all the tragedies. *Hamlet* (1601), a play directing intense light on the recesses of personality, is all the same a play about the state of Denmark, its government and its relations with neighbouring states. *King Lear* (1605) has the political stability of England at its centre. *Macbeth* (1606), drawn like the histories from Holinshed's chronicles, is concerned like the histories with rebellion, civil war, foreign invasion, and usurpation. And even in *Romeo and Juliet* (1595) and *Othello* (1604), which no one could call political, the relationship between the individual and the community is organic, and is essential to the play. *Timon of Athens* (date unknown) combines the story of the hero with a major political crisis centring on Alcibiades.

Generalizations about Shakespearian tragedy are hazardous, so distinctive is each one in its purpose, its atmosphere, its very language. Of course, all the tragedies contemplate loss, defeat, disappointment, failure, death—but even here we must be careful if we want to include *Troilus and Cressida* (1602), for both Troilus and Cressida are alive at the end of the play. In an endeavour to find thematic groupings in the tragedies we might begin with revenge, a major issue in one of the greatest of the plays, *Hamlet*, and one without much claim to greatness, *Titus Andronicus*.

Titus Andronicus may well have been one of Shakespeare's very first plays. It is the kind of work an 'upstart crow' might write, trying to outdo both Kyd and Marlowe and make everyone sit up and take notice of the author. It dresses action of the wildest savagery in an elaborate lyricism. When Titus's

AN EARLY SKETCH OF *TITUS ANDRONICUS*. This drawing of Tamora pleading with Titus for her sons' lives, thought to be by Henry Peacham, may well be based upon a contemporary performance of the 1590s. Aaron the Moor is on the *right*. Titus's Roman garb is in strong contrast with the solidly Elizabethan dress of the soldiers.

daughter Lavinia stands on stage, 'her hands cut off, and her tongue cut out, and ravished', Titus's brother says,

> Alas, a crimson river of warm blood,
> Like to a bubbling fountain stirred with wind,
> Doth rise and fall between thy rosèd lips,
> Coming and going with thy honey breath.   (II. iv)

First a victim of revenge himself, Titus is next the avenger of his own abused or dead children, labouring for justice in a Rome that he calls 'a wilderness of tigers'. The play ends in an absurdity of carnage, including Senecan pie when the queen of the Goths eats a dish in which Titus has cooked her sons' limbs. Aaron the Moor is a powerful figure, perhaps conceived in emulation of Marlowe's Barabbas, the Jew of Malta. He is an alien cynically enjoying the crumbling of Roman society—mostly as a consequence of his own devilish practical jokes. He has a disarming affection for the black love-child which the queen of the Goths has borne to him.

Titus Andronicus was perhaps a stage rival to the popular pre-Shakespearian play of *Hamlet* (possibly by Kyd) whose ghost shrieking for revenge was celebrated. In 1601 Shakespeare, who had just achieved the orderly dignity of *Julius Caesar*, returned to the wildness of the revenge convention and remodelled the old Hamlet play. By so doing he composed his most subtle, complex, searching, enigmatic tragedy, which each successive age thinks the most modern of his plays. But though Shakespeare was revolutionary in exploiting the potentialities of the revenge theme for radical doubt and self-questioning, he did not discover them. Even in the midst of its sensationalism, while 'the croaking raven doth bellow for revenge', as Hamlet put it, the revenge play had been concerned with the problem of justice and the responsibility of the individual in achieving it. The long life of the revenge play, going back much earlier than Kyd and achieving a new life on the Jacobean stage, cannot be explained simply by the attraction of the grotesque horrors it revelled in— ghosts, skulls, insanity, poisonings, and so on. Some intelligent dramatists, such as Marston, who wrote *Antonio's Revenge* in 1601, were unappreciative of the deeper implications of revenge, but Kyd, Chapman, Webster, Tourneur, Beaumont, and others make it clear that the nerve-centre of the revenge play is not the thrill of vindictiveness but the trauma of trying to obtain justice in an unjust and indifferent society. And so it is in Shakespeare's *Hamlet*.

To Hamlet, totally alienated from Danish society, the voice of the Ghost asking for revenge gives meaning to a life that had lost all meaning. His conception of his mission extends beyond killing Claudius into the cleansing of Denmark, and includes what was specifically forbidden by the Ghost, the moral rescue of his mother. Disabling doubts about the authenticity of the Ghost, and about the value of any act (in the 'To be or not to be' soliloquy), alternate with the exultation of conviction, and the impulsiveness of the sword-thrust that kills the wrong man, Polonius. So Hamlet becomes the object of a counter-revenge, Laertes seeking requital for the murder of *his* father. By the last act of the play, after his adventures at sea, Hamlet is utterly convinced

GIELGUD AS HAMLET at the Old Vic, 1929-30. This was John Gielgud's first Hamlet, at the age of twenty-five, and it was widely acclaimed. Gielgud wrote, 'Most actors tried to whitewash the unpleasant aspects of Hamlet's character ... I tried to find the violent and ugly colours in the part.'

of the rightness of his cause and the necessity of killing Claudius, whom he describes as a cancer in society. He sees himself as a humble instrument of heaven, and to fail his duty in removing that cancer would be at the peril of his own soul. But it is too late; Laertes wounds him fatally before he at last kills the king. The Denmark that he had sought to preserve from the odious Claudius passes into the hands of the foreigner Fortinbras. *Hamlet* ends in both victory and failure. The possibility that a man has been picked out to do a deed which society condemns but which a higher, divine authority sanctions is balanced against the possibility that the Ghost led Hamlet into delusion and error, and (to steal Yeats's words) bewildered him till he died.

Revenge has to do with hate. Our second major issue in the tragedies is love, which is the inspiration of four plays: *Romeo and Juliet*, *Troilus and Cressida*, *Othello*, and *Antony and Cleopatra*. In each of the plays everything is staked upon a love-relationship which to a greater or lesser extent is unpalatable to society; in each play, though for vastly different reasons, the love fails to abide and ends disastrously.

Romeo and Juliet is Shakespeare's love tragedy of youth as *Antony and Cleopatra* is his love tragedy of middle age. To Juliet, a girl of fourteen, hedged around by nurse and parents and a family feud, comes the liberation of first love—which Shakespeare enshrines in a sonnet shared between Romeo and Juliet when they kiss. The plot moves forward by a simple mechanism of ironic reversals which mark the stages of a clear path of 'responsibility' for the tragic outcome. Romeo's love for a Capulet leads into his killing Juliet's cousin; the Friar's good offices for the lovers lead into the tragic mistiming at the tomb. If there is less than full tragedy at the end, it is not because of too much coincidence and bad luck, but because, for all their impetuousness, the young lovers in their desperately sad conclusion are simply victims—not of fate, but of their elders and betters. There is nothing of that fatal collaboration in one's own destruction which is so marked in the great later tragedies. Intense pity, little terror. 'Catharsis' there certainly is in *Romeo and Juliet*, however, in our feeling that the lovers, completing their union in death as they could not complete it in life, are at least *safe*; and in our feeling that such love as theirs, passionate and sexual though it was, was a dedication to a higher scale of values than obtained in the violent commerce of the worldly society they lived in.

This must surely be the case in *Othello* too. To the wealthy citizens of Venice, epitomized in Desdemona's father Brabantio, Othello is a totally undesirable match; it is against 'all rules of nature' for her to fall in love with a black man, and Othello must have used spells for her to do so. It is a common view that Desdemona did not really know Othello. She did; she knew the Othello who existed before Iago began to twist and corrupt him. She knew, approved, loved; and she committed herself in as definite and courageous an act as is to be found in the tragedies. It was of course a fatal consecration.

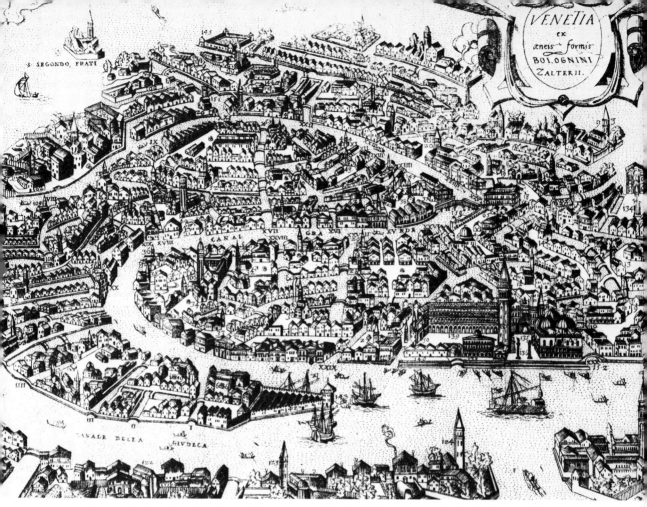

VENICE, the setting for *The Merchant of Venice* and *Othello*. Shakespeare probably had no greater personal knowledge of the city than is afforded by pictures like this contemporary woodcut. The Rialto bridge is in the centre.

For Othello, this love, after a career of soldiering, is a miracle of happiness. But Iago was born to oppose happiness. He is the sheerly satanic in man, bound by the acute malevolence that is his nature to wreck and destroy. The strength of the love between Othello and Desdemona is an offence to him. He cannot corrupt Desdemona, but he can corrupt Othello into misconceiving her very goodness:

> So will I turn her virtue into pitch,
> And out of her own goodness make the net
> That shall enmesh them all.   (II. iii)

There is no more painful scene in drama than that in which Iago begins his work, crumbling Othello's confidence in his wife's chastity and fidelity and stirring up that unappeasable jealousy which ends in his killing a totally innocent woman. Iago works on Othello's sense of inferiority, his blackness,

OTHELLO STRIKES DESDEMONA: an eighteenth-century view. Francis Hayman's painting of *Othello*, Act IV, was engraved by Gravelot for Hanmer's *Works of Shakespeare* (1743-4).

his foreignness, his ignorance of cultivated society. That Othello has not sufficient faith in Desdemona to withstand the attack is terrible; but the attack is a manifestation of evil that almost by definition cannot be withstood. At any rate Desdemona's dedication of herself is cruelly betrayed. Disowned by her family, she is brutally rejected and ceremoniously murdered by her husband. *Othello* is the grimmest of the tragedies, though in these days a lot of its tragic effect is lost on those who, confident in their ability to deal with such a situation as the play presents, have patronized Desdemona and despised Othello.

In *Antony and Cleopatra* we have once again the old soldier finding a haven in love. But the soldier is now the great sharer of Rome's imperial rule, and the woman is not the virginal daughter of a wealthy citizen. To standers-by Antony's neglect of the claims of office and empire for the seductive sensuality of Cleopatra is simply shameful—

> The triple pillar of the world transformed
> Into a strumpet's fool.

Antony himself veers from protesting that 'the nobleness of life' is within Cleopatra's arms to the sharp disgust at the enchantment that has ensnared him, the 'strong Egyptian fetters'. It seems a straightforward *Either/Or*. The love of Cleopatra means the decline of his power, disorder within the empire, and the abandonment of the codes of honour and responsibility by which he has lived. As he leaves Cleopatra to reassert himself in the affairs of Rome, it might seem that we have a tragedy of choice between love and honour, like the famous choice of Hercules, Antony's supposed ancestor, who came to a fork in the road, one path leading to duty and the other to pleasure. But there is no choice in this play, and no one is free, not even Caesar who, though he seems to have choice, has only drive. Octavius Caesar's progress towards sole rule is remorseless. Shakespeare strongly contrasts the youth and asceticism of this brisk and efficient man with the hedonistic, warmer nature of the older man, Antony. Cleopatra is Antony's only refuge. As he comes to ruin and death the basic question of the play asserts itself as what quality of refuge the love of Cleopatra provides for Antony. It is certain that in military ventures Cleopatra fails Antony again and again. But Antony fails Cleopatra again and again. Her famous question, 'Not know me yet?', after the great row over Caesar's messenger kissing her hand, echoes to the moment of Antony's death.

It is often said that Shakespeare presented Cleopatra with a kind of double focus: sometimes we see nobility, sometimes we see coquetry. This is not so; she is all of a piece. She is continuously a strumpet. Her life is to win men and to hold them as long as she wants, to make love, to enjoy herself, to be flattered, to lie her way out of problems, to be jealous, unfair, hot-tempered, very loving, or very cool as her advantage dictates. And all this in a woman in whom regal magnificence combines with unequalled attractiveness. The mystery of Cleopatra, which Antony never quite discerns, is the way in which her royalty transcends the gold and silk of her 'burnished throne'. Enobarbus follows his description of the royal barge on the Cydnus with his account of her hopping forty paces through the public streets; thereby she makes 'defect perfection'. It is this power to make defect perfection that leads to his astonishing remark that 'the holy priests / Bless her when she is riggish'—that is, acting like a whore. The problem in understanding Cleopatra is not to decide whether she is noble or meretricious but to follow the daring of Shakespeare in investing meretriciousness with something greater than 'nobility'.

It takes an Antony to create Cleopatra fully; not to change her but to fulfil the rich complexity of her nature. But there is no possibility that the relationship can prosper, or even survive. Antony's death is a miserable confusion. He is convinced that Cleopatra has betrayed him in the last sea fight. 'The witch shall die!' he vows. To cool his anger Cleopatra sends word that she has died—'and bring me how he takes my death'. On hearing this Antony tries to kill himself, but fails to do it cleanly. As he dies in Cleopatra's arms he does not say one word about their love—only that she should save herself and remember him in his earlier, Roman, greatness. It is not love that is uppermost in his mind at the end, but the past. For Cleopatra, on the other hand, their love is her totality. She has no thought of outliving him, but before she dies there is a stillness in which she can contemplate their love. There is no higher hymn to love in Shakespeare than in the ecstatic imagery of her adoration of the dead Antony.

There was never any future for the love of Antony and Cleopatra in worldly terms. She chokes him like entangling weeds pulling a swimmer down. That is because the world is what it is. 'The holy priests', however, bless her in her very sexuality, and it is Octavius of all people who utters the amazing words that even in death she looks ready to 'catch another Antony / In her strong toil of grace'. A toil is a snare or trap. The captivation which fetters her 'victims' is a toil of grace, a captivation which bestows something rare and spiritual, no sooner glimpsed than lost.

To move from the exalted mood of the ending of *Antony and Cleopatra* to the reductiveness of *Troilus and Cressida* is hardly fair. *Troilus and Cressida* does not recognize the existence of love, only sex. Troilus's feeling for Cressida is a self-regarding infatuation that never properly focuses its object. If he feels himself unspeakably let down by Cressida's defection, he really has only his own injudiciousness to blame. The whole Trojan War is seen as a demonstration of the two motive-forces in human life, lust (in the seizure of Helen) and

MODERN-DRESS SHAKESPEARE. Pandarus, Helen, and Paris in Act III, Scene i of *Troilus and Cressida*, directed by Tyrone Guthrie at the Old Vic, 1955-6. Early experiments in 'modern-dress' Shakespeare had been made by Barry Jackson at the Birmingham Repertory theatre after the First World War.

aggression (in the war which followed). *Troilus and Cressida* as a whole is a bitter, deflationary play, cornering and stabbing every ideal of love or honour. It is anti-heroic in the extreme in its portrayal of the famous worthies on the Greek side, and even Hector does not escape. It seems certain that if we have to include *Troilus and Cressida* among the tragedies because it will not go anywhere else there is nothing truly tragic about its mood. The great merits of this powerful and sardonic play lie in another realm. Perhaps there should be a separate category of Shakespeare's works called 'Ironies', and this should be the one play in it.

We have been looking at tragic heroes in terms of their commitment to revenge and to love. There is another type of commitment, to a political course of action, and this brings together two very different plays in which the hero assassinates the ruler of the state: *Julius Caesar* and *Macbeth*.

Julius Caesar was an anticipation of *Hamlet* in exploring the problems of an intellectual, a bookish man who is something of a philosopher, who in order to purge and reorder society undertakes an act of violence against the head of the state. The texture of the plays is quite different, but each play illuminates the other. Brutus is invited to join the conspiracy against Caesar by Cassius, who has a fierce personal and ideological hatred for the autocratic behaviour of Caesar. Brutus has no 'personal cause' against Caesar but persuades himself that it is his civic duty to assassinate the man. In his high-mindedness he makes political mistake after mistake, and Shakespeare makes a strong point of contrasting his public-duty rhetoric with the physical butchery of Caesar. The old republicanism which Brutus wishes to restore is not really a political possibility for Rome but in the first place it is Brutus's great errors of judgement which allow Mark Antony to take the initiative, exploit civil disorder, and sweep the conspirators out of existence. Antony, who can afford to be generous at the moment of victory, gives Brutus a fine eulogy: 'This was the noblest Roman of them all.' He acted, he says, 'in a general honest thought' and for 'common good to all'. It is the depressing truth. Brutus is the best man we see in Rome, thoughtful, gentle, altruistic, affectionate, acting for principle and not personal advantage. It is his personal qualities which make his political career so frightening. It is not alone that he was too 'nice' to succeed in the rough and tumble of political life, but that his attempt to phrase political violence within the language of highly principled conduct turns him into a pharisaical prig and makes certain the failure of a political cause which even an Elizabethan could view with a certain sympathy.

In *Julius Caesar*, *Hamlet*, and *Macbeth* the hero aims at the heart of existing society, intending to change that society by killing the prince or governor. In both *Julius Caesar* and *Hamlet* the endeavour is to restore the moral order of a past society. Macbeth's aim in assassinating Duncan seems entirely selfish. Yet curiously he is impelled by nothing like Richard III's lust for power. Royalty is a misty dream of magnificence, as vague to Macbeth as it is to us:

'the swelling act / Of the imperial theme'. Macbeth and his wife share in a guilty fantasy of becoming king and queen of Scotland. It is a hardened loyal soldier, capable of the bloody suppression of rebels, who is a prey to these strange imaginings, which seem to torment him as much as they give him pleasure. When the weird sisters on the heath hail him as the future king, they have pierced to the secret life of his thoughts. Banquo sees him start with fear. The life of this mental world is as real to Macbeth as the tangible world around him. After the witches have spoken he almost collapses under the

THE WEIRD SISTERS GREET MACBETH as portrayed in Shakespeare's source, Holinshed's *Chronicles*. 'It fortuned as Makbeth & Banquho iourneyed towarde Fores ... there met them .iij. women in straunge & ferly apparell, resembling creatures of an elder worlde...' (1577 edn.).

pressure of the 'horrible imaginings' in which he sees himself in the act of murder. Later in the play, the dagger which he sees before him in the air—what he calls 'a dagger of the mind'—is 'in form as palpable' as the dagger he then draws from its sheath. After the assassination he *hears* a voice crying 'Sleep no more!' Most terrifying of all these 'palpable' fancies is the bloody corpse of Banquo, sitting in his chair at the feast.

Tempted by the prophecy of the witches and taunted by his wife, Macbeth turns his vivid dream of majesty into reality by murdering the king, Duncan. He is in a state of horror before, during, and after the murder—when, unable to sleep, he says he would rather be dead

> Than on the torture of the mind to lie
> In restless ecstasy.

Macbeth has to live not only without the glory he thought would come with kingship but also with entire knowledge of what it is that he has done. He cannot avoid facing it, and he cannot face it. 'To know my deed,' he says, ''twere best not know myself.' His fierce wife succumbs first. The reality which the pair of them created out of their dreams reinvades her dreams, and in her sleep she is forced to re-enact the murder. 'Who would have thought the old man to have had so much blood in him?' Macbeth's fate is different. When he hears 'the cry of women' within, he realizes that his interior, sentient life has gone dead: he cannot even be afraid any more. And when he is told that

BLAKE INTERPRETS 'PITY' (c.1795).
Macbeth's words, contemplating the murder of Duncan, are

—pity, like a naked new-born babe,
Striding the blast, or heaven's cherubin horsed
Upon the sightless couriers of the air,
Shall blow the horrid deed in every eye...

By 'sightless couriers of the air', Shakespeare meant the invisible winds. But Blake's Shakespeare evidently had the eighteenth-century emendation 'coursers' for 'couriers', and, supposing that 'sightless' meant without sight, he drew blind horses.

MACBETH SEES THE GHOST OF BANQUO. Charles Kean's production at the Princess's theatre, 1853. Kean was renowned for his spectacular staging, which quite dwarfed the rendering of the text.

Lady Macbeth has died, the terrible conviction comes over him that the exterior world is also without life, meaningless, inert.

> It is a tale
> Told by an idiot, full of sound and fury,
> Signifying nothing.

The man whose every experience was made doubly alive by the workings of a powerful imagination now finds only deadness in both imagination and reality.

To body forth the intensity of Macbeth's inner life, Shakespeare gave him a poetry whose metaphoric richness is unsurpassed among the tragic heroes. The power of the poetry draws us in to share this inner life of Macbeth's. We may be reluctant to be so drawn but we have little chance of holding back. The play shows us how a man who is not evil brings himself or is brought to do evil. By the empathy which Macbeth's poetry forces us into, we are made to share his heart of darkness.

Every hero we have looked at makes a commitment—to love, or revenge, or political violence—and this commitment is seen as the key to a new existence. What commitment does King Lear make? He proposes to divide his kingdom between his three daughters and retire from a long life of ruling, looking forward in particular to finding rest in the 'kind nursery' of his beloved Cordelia. He does indeed commit an act, the violent, peremptory act of disowning and banishing Cordelia for not openly professing her love for him, but for the rest of the play, though it is the consequence of his act that he suffers from, he endures rather than acts. *King Lear* is more of a 'passion' than the other tragedies. The closest resemblance is with *Richard II*. Both plays show us the painful process of the collapse of the hero's world, and of the self that fitted that world, and the equally painful process of learning a new identity. The questioning of himself, his values, the nature of society, and of the meaning of existence, which adversity forces Lear to undertake, is not confined to his individual predicament. The suffering of Gloucester through the malice of his illegitimate son confirms that Lear's bitter experience is not unique or unrepeatable; and with the tremendous orchestration of the storm scenes challenge and protest become a universal chorus. The outcries of the mad king, the songs and snatches of the shivering Fool, the manic chatter of Poor Tom combine into an extraordinary and unsatisfied interrogation. 'Is man no more than this?' The climax of evil is not on the heath or in the hovel but in Gloucester's own castle, where Gloucester is bound to a chair, cross-questioned and abused by Regan, and has his eyes put out by Regan's husband, Cornwall.

This terrifying scene is the extreme edge of cruelty and inhumanity in the tragedies, and it is balanced by another scene in which the power of love is more profoundly shown than anywhere else in Shakespeare. It is a humble

'THOU HAST HER, FRANCE: LET HER BE THINE.' King Lear banishes Cordelia (I. i). This water-colour (1866–72) by Ford Madox Brown deeply impressed Henry Irving, who asked the painter to design a production for him. A painting of Irving in this first scene, by Partridge, shows him in very similar garb and attitude.

Lear who emerges from his insanity to be reunited with his daughter Cordelia. They are defeated in battle and led away to prison. The prison becomes a symbol of the pressures of the social and political world from which Lear feels himself totally liberated simply by being with Cordelia.

> Come, let's away to prison.
> We two alone will sing like birds i' th' cage.
> When thou dost ask me blessing, I'll kneel down
> And ask of thee forgiveness. So we'll live,
> And pray, and sing, and tell old tales, and laugh
> At gilded butterflies, and hear poor rogues
> Talk of court news; and we'll talk with them too—
> Who loses and who wins, who's in, who's out—

> And take upon's the mystery of things
> As if we were God's spies; and we'll wear out
> In a walled prison packs and sects of great ones
> That ebb and flow by the moon.   (V. iii)

If the transfiguring power of love, which can only exist as an opposition to the values of worldly society, is never more shiningly apparent than in this speech, the retribution of the world is never more cruelly shown than in the ending of the play. Cordelia is hanged, and the old king makes his final entrance with the dead girl in his arms.

> Thou'lt come no more,
> Never, never, never, never, never.

The god of Shakespeare's tragedies is indeed a hidden god. Those who like Albany in *King Lear* expect his intervention or manifestation are disappointed. It is the devil who is in full view all the time. The witches in *Macbeth*, 'instruments of darkness', tempt and mislead the hero; Othello becomes convinced that Iago is a devil and has brought him to do an act for which he is eternally lost; Hamlet is deeply conscious of the traps waiting to ensnare the soul into hell and damnation. Although the viciousness of Goneril, Regan, Cornwall, Edmund, and Iago does not exceed the documented record of human cruelty and malice, there seems no doubt that in them Shakespeare wanted to portray an operation of evil that is more than a matter of ill will and sadism. 'Is there any cause in nature that makes these hard hearts?' asks Lear in the crazy 'arraignment' of Goneril. The answer is no; the cause is supernatural. Evil is a presence lying in wait below the surface of human life, ready to erupt in the most unsuspected places, in one's trusted lieutenant, one's affectionate daughter, one's loyal general, one's own brother.

> Rank corruption, mining all within,
> Infects unseen.

The idea of an indomitable corrupting force in life is strong also in *Timon of Athens*, a play which Shakespeare seems to have left unfinished. Timon is a rashly generous host who gets through everything he owns and in adversity can get no help from those who have enjoyed his bounty. In fury he turns away from society altogether, and in the wilderness rages against the ingratitude of men. His curses take on the generality of Lear's tirades in the storm.

> There's nothing level in our cursèd natures
> But direct villainy. Therefore be abhorred
> All feasts, societies, and throngs of men.
> His semblable, yea himself, Timon disdains.
> Destruction fang mankind!   (IV. iii)

The fierce misanthropy of Timon is not 'authorized' by the play as a whole;

TIMON'S CAVE. Henry Fuseli, surely the most imaginative of all artist interpreters of Shakespeare, depicts the visit of Alcibiades and the two whores to the misanthrope Timon in his cave in the woods (*Timon of Athens*, IV. iii). The drawing dates from 1783.

but the forgiveness and compassion of the play's ending, so wonderfully imaged by the tide washing Timon's grave, cannot cancel, any more than in *Measure for Measure*, the endemic rottenness they confront.

Shakespearian tragedy is concerned as much with displacement as with death. The conflict between the generations is a terrible warfare in *King Lear*; in some of the tragedies, especially *Antony and Cleopatra*, the tussle of the older person to hold on and assert his right to exist is fused with the movement of history. New epochs are coming into being, brashly ousting a more cultivated and humane but incompetent past. We see that Hamlet, a young man, allies himself with the older, simpler, chivalric values of his father, and tries to unseat a usurping régime, one of whose marks is, characteristically, a brisk administrative efficiency. Coriolanus is another who binds himself to the past and tries to stem the tide of advancing history. Brought up to believe that the patrician class he was born into was by nature a superior group responsible for guiding and protecting the Roman people, Coriolanus is supreme in the uncomplicated skill of saving Rome from attacking armies. His heroic mould is brittle, and cannot adjust itself to the requirements of a developing new urban society, in which the people demand a voice in the affairs of state. In spite of his youth and impetuosity he is really a relic of the past thrown up and stranded on a shoal. Banished by the city which he has given his whole life to defending, he has only one solution, the military solution of destroying the city whose new configuration he cannot bring himself to accept. It is his mother, who fashioned him into his rigid shape, who has now to undo her work, and turn him aside from his vengeance. But to let the new Rome live is to let Coriolanus die, and the Volscians kill him for failing them. So the tragedy of supersession is not confined to those who are old, or growing old, like Lear and Antony, but includes those who are in one way or another identified with obsolescence, like Richard II, Hamlet, and Coriolanus.

The 'tragic flaw', that weakness of character or fatal error of judgement which since Aristotle's time has seemed a prime constituent of tragedy, is less important than the tragic commitment. Within the hero's course there are all sorts of moral weakness, wrong decisions, and character deficiencies. But these do not initiate the tragic impetus; they accompany it and direct its course. In his or her consecration to revenge, or love, or political violence, or political resistance, each of the heroes is in some way defying society, asserting a primordial dissatisfaction with things as they are. The freedom which each hero seeks is different, leads to a different kind of disturbance, and ends in a different kind of failure. But in every single tragedy the audience is left with a balance of conflicting emotions as regards the hero, the bid for liberation, and its cost. And in that equilibrium lies much of the power of tragedy.

The Tragicomedies

'Tragicomedy' is not a common classification for Shakespeare's plays, but it is a useful term for distinguishing the later from the earlier comedies. There are two groups: the 'problem comedies' of 1602-5, *All's Well That Ends Well* and *Measure for Measure*, in which there is an extended treatment of serious moral problems with the threatened tragic consequences bypassed, and the 'Romances' of 1608-13, *Pericles Prince of Tyre*, *The Winter's Tale*, *Cymbeline*, and *The Tempest*, the highly experimental plays of Shakespeare's last years, in which the tragic crisis occurs but death is averted and loss is miraculously made good.

The two 'problem comedies' feature strong and determined heroines, Helena and Isabella. Passionate love in the one and passionate asceticism in the other precipitate the crisis. In *All's Well*, the lowly Helena is infatuated with the aristocratic Bertram, and her desperation drives her to bargain with the king that if she cures him of his disease, as none other can, she may choose a husband from his court. When she succeeds and makes her choice, she is as appalled by Bertram's contemptuous repudiation of her as Bertram is by being chosen. In trying to get out of each other's way, they both turn up in Florence. There, by substituting herself for the girl Bertram is trying to seduce, Helena makes herself indeed his wife. This most improbable of folk-tale motifs, the 'bed-trick', is also at the centre of *Measure for Measure*. In each play the man is prevented from carrying out his 'wicked meaning' of deflowering a virgin by the secret replacement of his intended consort by a woman who ought to be his wife, whom he has repudiated. So 'wicked meaning' is converted into 'lawful deed'. Both Bertram and Angelo are saved from sin by women who value them rather more than the audience does. Misdirected fornication becomes consummation. It is a curious way of symbolizing moral rescue, and it continues to make audiences and readers uneasy.

The unease is probably greater in *Measure for Measure* in which, although the plot is redolent of folk-tale, the substance of the action is intensely realistic, and the crisis too painful and unsettling for us to be content with the tragicomic devices necessary for the fortunate outcome. None of the tragedies explores moral problems more deeply than *Measure for Measure*, problems of permissiveness, law and justice, the scope of political authority, and so on, and these moral problems are explored by means of individuals in passionate conflict, often a fight for survival. Pleading for her brother's life, forfeit under severe new sex laws, Isabella brilliantly translates the arid legalism of Angelo into the truths of human weakness and divine mercy.

> Go to your bosom,
> Knock there, and ask your heart what it doth know
> That's like my brother's fault.   (II. ii)

She is all too successful. In a sudden access of lust for her, Angelo promises her her brother's life in exchange for sex. Isabella, a novice in an order of nuns, refuses to surrender her chastity even when her brother pleads with her to accept the bargain. Here the disguised duke steps in to stage the devices, including the bed-trick, by which Angelo is outwitted and Claudio saved. The end of the play is superb, but the cost of its contrivance is almost too great.

Several years later, having written in the mean time some of the greatest tragedies the world has ever seen, Shakespeare returned to the problem of fashioning a play which would allow situations of intense seriousness to emerge in happy endings. His solution was not to increase the sense of likelihood and verisimilitude, but to decrease it. In his final plays he advertises the improbability of the rescuing devices, emphasizing that these fortunate ends of difficult situations are only make-believe. He cradles scenes of beauty and terror in narratives which call attention to their fictiveness; thus persuading us of the truth of his art even as he assures us that (in another sense?) it is not true. Part of his technique is to dip heavily into the least realistic of genres, traditional romance. *Pericles Prince of Tyre* is a problem play indeed, since it was not included in the First Folio and has come down to us only in an exceptionally corrupted text. Probably the original was not wholly by Shakespeare; but there is every sign that the original play was a remarkable Shakespearian innovation. The story is a very ancient romance and it is brought to the audience by a 'presenter', the medieval poet Gower, who insists on the antiquity of his fare

SHAKESPEARE'S HANDWRITING. It is generally thought that three pages of the manuscript of an unacted play on the life of Sir Thomas More (by several authors) are in Shakespeare's hand. A portion of the text is reproduced here, part of a speech by More protesting against the 'inhumanity' of Londoners in persecuting immigrant workers.

SHAKESPEARE'S SIGNATURES.
(a) from the conveyance of the Blackfriars property, March 1613;
(b) from Shakespeare's will, March 1616.

and its power to please in generation after generation. It is a very episodic story, full of marvels, disasters, and wonderful coincidences. Its power is not in the development and solution of crisis, but in the individual acted scene. Even through the disfigurement of the extant text we feel the *power* of Marina's struggle for her chastity in the brothel scenes, and the *power* of the reunion of the father with the daughter long presumed dead:

> O, come hither,
> Thou that beget'st him that did thee beget.

The Winter's Tale does not declare itself as a somewhat similar kind of far-fetched romantic story until half-way through, when we have landed on the sea-coast of Bohemia with the infant princess, and Antigonus has gone off 'pursued by a bear'. Before that, we have had the intense micro-tragedy of Leontes' abrupt, reasonless, and paranoid persecution of his wife for her 'infidelity', ending in the death of his son, his wife, and the casting out of his infant daughter. Now a strange figure emerges to usher in Act IV; he is dressed as Time, and tells us that this is *his* tale, and that he can do anything. We jump over sixteen years to the pastoral happiness of the sheep-shearing feast and the love of Florizel and Perdita, their flight to Sicily, and the amazed discovery by Leontes of his cast-out daughter. In both *Pericles* and *The Winter's Tale*, a lost daughter and a wife are returned to the hero from the dead. In *Pericles* all the emphasis is on the reunion of father and daughter; in *The Winter's Tale* on the reunion of husband and wife. The very first audience would not have guessed that Hermione was still alive; their amazement as the statue stepped down from its pedestal would have rivalled that of Leontes. The miracle of *The Winter's Tale* is not that Hermione is still alive—she never died—but that successive audiences, who know the story perfectly well, are beguiled into sharing Leontes' joy at the restoration of his supposedly dead queen, though we know that her 'preservation' has been the contrivance of Paulina. Thus 'we are mocked with art', as Leontes says when he thinks he sees the eyes of the 'statue' move. *The Winter's Tale* consists of three strong 'movements': Leontes' jealousy, the sheep-shearing scene, the statue scene, all of which the supreme dramatic verse of Shakespeare's late years brings to glorious life. These three movements are strung together in a narrative whose improbability the showmaster seems eager for us to recognize.

The improbabilities of *Cymbeline* were too much for Dr Johnson. 'To remark the folly of the fiction . . . and the impossibility of the events in any system of life, were to waste criticism upon unresisting imbecility.' He noted, however, that the play had 'some natural dialogues, and some pleasing scenes'. The play is an astonishing medley of genres, adding the history play to comedy and tragedy. The characters themselves are chameleon-like, changing their shape as they move through the genres. Cloten, for example, is the typical booby-suitor of Jacobean comedy, then a sturdy patriot, and finally an ugly, sadistic psychopath. Imogen herself, another calumniated wife, is a spirited and intelligent woman who has to don boy's clothing and wander out of tragedy into a pastoral play in which she comes across mountaineers who are in fact her brothers, abducted from court in infancy. Before the quite remarkable denouement, a very stagey divine vision appears to the imprisoned hero, Posthumus. 'Jupiter descends in thunder and lightning, sitting upon an eagle; he throws a thunderbolt.' The vision reminds us of the masques of the Jacobean court. A scene of divine intervention is standard in the Romances, but it seems wrong to jump to the conclusion that these theophanies indicate Shakespeare's belief in a providence that eventually rewards the true deserver. Their staginess, in *Cymbeline*, *The Winter's Tale*, and especially *The Tempest*, makes them not images of revelation but images of the fabrications which humanity makes in its longing for divine assistance and protection.

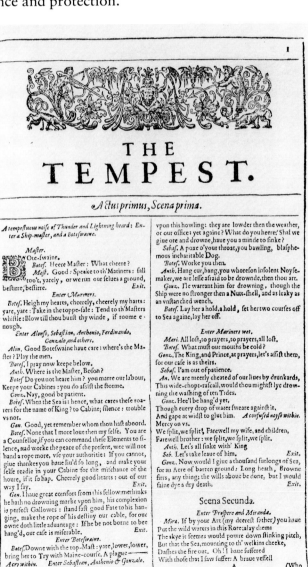

THE TEMPEST. The opening of the play as printed in the 'First Folio' of 1623. Although it was one of the very last of Shakespeare's plays, *The Tempest* was given special prominence as the first play in the volume, printed from a manuscript carefully prepared by Ralph Crane, a scrivener for Shakespeare's company.

In the last and greatest of the Romances, *The Tempest*, Shakespeare eschewed the 'anti-dramatic' features of confusion of genres, sprawling narrative, and geographical expansiveness. *The Tempest* is the most tightly knit of all the plays in its unity of tone and action. Yet it contains everything that its straggling fellow plays have been asserting. It too uncreates the reality it creates; by making the whole sequence of events the contrivance of a magician. Prospero's endeavours to bring happy conclusions from the base deeds of men are constantly likened to the endeavours of a dramatist.

The tragic issue which is to be turned to a fortunate conclusion is not this time within the play, except by report; it is the Cain and Abel scenario, brother's hand against brother, by which Prospero was usurped as duke of Milan by his brother Antonio years before. Prospero of course is a kind of usurper himself on his island, having taken it over from Caliban, whom he has reduced to serfdom. Shakespeare preserves an almost maddening fair-mindedness in showing us the rights and wrongs of Caliban, who represents natural man, instinctively poetic and instinctively brutal, longing for independence and manufacturing his own servitude.

Prospero by his art brings his enemies to his island. His idea of building the future lies not in the negativeness of punishment but in uniting Naples with Milan through the marriage of his daughter Miranda with the king of Naples' son, Ferdinand. He makes Ariel bring them together and watches them fall in love.

> Fair encounter
> Of two most rare affections. Heavens rain grace
> On that which breeds between 'em.   (III. i)

He arranges an elaborate masque, a 'vanity of mine art', to convey to them *his* sense of the divine blessing that should fall on this couple. But he brings it to an abrupt conclusion as he remembers the plot of Caliban upon his life. In one of the most renowned speeches in all the plays, he reassures Ferdinand and Miranda that what they have been watching was only a play—and suddenly goes on to say that its sudden end was in keeping with the fleeting and transient nature of everything in the world.

> Like the baseless fabric of this vision,
> The cloud-capped towers, the gorgeous palaces,
> The solemn temples, the great globe itself,
> Yea, all which it inherit, shall dissolve
> And, like this insubstantial pageant faded,
> Leave not a rack behind. We are such stuff
> As dreams are made on, and our little life
> Is rounded with a sleep.   (IV. i)

The time-honoured identification of Prospero with Shakespeare, and of this speech with Shakespeare's own thoughts, is very hard to resist. For it is this

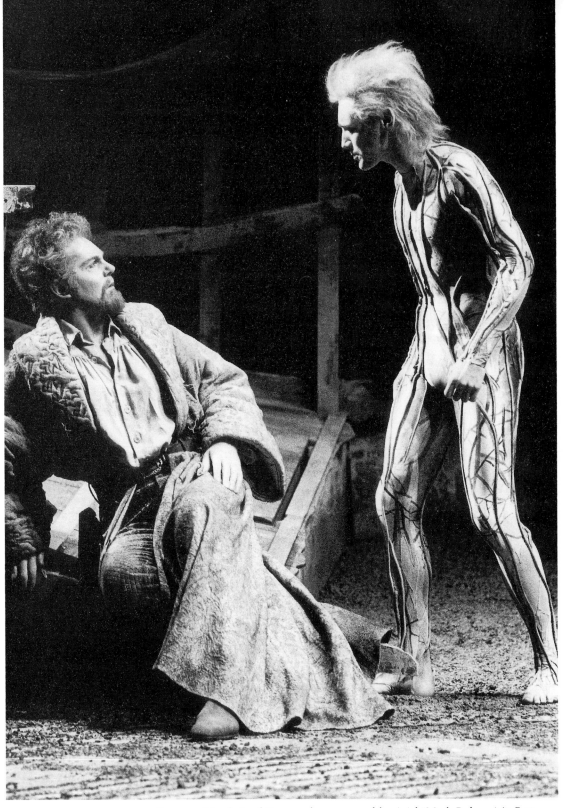

A MODERN PROSPERO. Prospero (Derek Jacobi) somewhat overawed by Ariel (Mark Rylance) in Ron Daniels's production of *The Tempest* at the Royal Shakespeare Theatre, Stratford-upon-Avon, 1982.

speech that explains the direction and the seriousness of the last plays, with their perpetual insistence on make-believe, fantasy, improbability. These romantic tragicomedies contain images of life as potent, and to audiences and readers as *true*, as anything in Shakespeare. Yet in general they are not sustained within a prolonged, coherent, and satisfying plot development, but handed to us as the momentary triumphs of the poetic imagination (like the masque in *The Tempest*). Yet the reality of our ordinary life and everyday experience, by the standard of which these moments are mere figments of make-believe, is shown to be as illusory, shadowy, and transitory as the fictions are. Shakespeare balances the 'untrue' images of art against the uncertain 'truths' of reality. His last plays deal with the age-old debate on the relation between art and reality with a brilliance and a lightness of touch that make all attempts at summary sound ponderous and pretentious. He asserts nothing, and offers everything. If you wish, in any way, to take his plays as truth, you have his permission; but he claims nothing for them.

Conclusion

Shakespeare died in Stratford-upon-Avon in April 1616. His great monument is the folio collection of his *Comedies, Histories, and Tragedies* brought together by his fellows in the King's Men and published in 1623. Eighteen of his plays were here published for the first time. He was succeeded as chief dramatist of the company by John Fletcher, with whom he had collaborated in his last two plays, *Henry VIII* and *The Two Noble Kinsmen*. Fletcher preferred collaborative work, writing first with Francis Beaumont and then with Philip Massinger, who took over as chief dramatist on Fletcher's death in 1625. Fletcher's output was enormous, chiefly in romantic tragicomedies; the best tragedy in the 'Beaumont and Fletcher' collection, *The Maid's Tragedy*, is largely Beaumont's work. Though Fletcherian tragicomedy was the staple fare of the Jacobean and Caroline stage, we think more highly of the tragedies of the period by John Webster (*c*.1578–*c*.1634), Thomas Middleton (1580–1627), and John Ford (1586–1639); and the citizen comedies of Marston, Middleton, and Massinger. The lurid plots of Jacobean tragedy, heavy with lust and violence in corrupt Italian courts, are vehicles for the strong sense of displacement and instability which the dramatists breathed in the English air about them at a time of rapid social, economic, and political change. The alienated intellectual, especially Webster's Flamineo (in *The White Devil*, 1612) and Bosola (in *The Duchess of Malfi*, 1614), searches vainly for a more relevant and up-to-date moral code as well as a livelihood, while the women, such as Vittoria in *The White Devil* or Bianca in Middleton's *Women Beware Women* (1621), test out the ancient prohibitions and warnings against unchastity. Ford's uncompromising treatment of incestuous love in *'Tis Pity She's a Whore* (1632) is the summation of the tragedy of challenge and defiance. Erring women

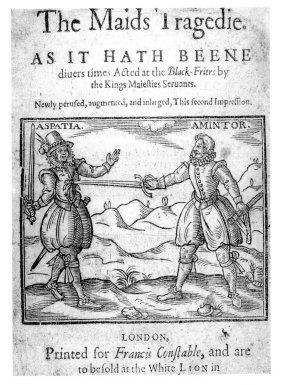

BEAUMONT AND FLETCHER. The title-page of the 1622 edition of *The Maid's Tragedy*. The woodcut shows part of the violent ending. Amintor is provoked into a duel by a stranger claiming to be the brother of Aspatia, whom he has wronged. But it is Aspatia herself in disguise, seeking her own death.

SHAKESPEARE'S MONUMENT above his grave in Holy Trinity Church, Stratford-upon-Avon. This painting by Sir William Allan of Sir Walter Scott visiting Shakespeare's grave is a token of the legacy of the dramatist to all succeeding writers.

dominate Jacobean and Caroline tragedy; one of the finest portraits is the shallow soul of Beatrice-Joanna in Middleton's *The Changeling* (1622). But Webster's Duchess of Malfi is a notable exception, persecuted to a terrible end by her brothers for no worse a crime than a secret marriage to her steward.

Citizen comedy, again, is informed and vitalized by the feeling of rapid social change, particularly the upward mobility of tradesmen seeking gentility and coveting the land and titles of an impoverished gentry. Marston's vintner Mulligrub in *The Dutch Courtesan* (1604) or the ridiculous goldsmith Yellowhammer in Middleton's *A Chaste Maid in Cheapside* (1613) become the rapacious tycoon Sir Giles Overreach in Massinger's *A New Way to Pay Old Debts* (1625). The later social comedy of Richard Brome (d. 1652), the protégé of Jonson, and James Shirley (1596–1666), links the vigorous scorn of Jacobean city comedy with the élitist wit of Restoration comedy, showing English social comedy of the seventeenth century to be of one piece. To say that, however, is not to minimize or underestimate the devastation caused to the traditions of English drama by the closing of the theatres by Parliament at the outbreak of the Civil War in 1642.

From the opening of the Theatre in 1576 to the closing of all the theatres in 1642 is sixty-six years, during which the professional companies, equally at home in the big public open-air theatres, the more refined 'private' theatres, and in the courts of three successive monarchs, performed plays by generations of dramatists which taken together comprise one of the greatest achievements of English literature and one of the wonders of world drama. This chapter has been about Shakespeare and not the drama as a whole because for the richest twenty-five years of that sixty-six-year span Shakespeare's plays dominated the London stage, and because his achievement is so extraordinary that if any English writer is to have the tribute of a chapter to himself, it should be William Shakespeare.

4. The Seventeenth Century

1603-1674

BRIAN VICKERS

Elizabethan to Jacobean

LITERARY history does not always lend itself to tidy divisions. The accession of King James I in 1603 inaugurated 'the Jacobean age', but such period divisions reflect no dramatic change of mood, and few scholars would now accept the old concepts of 'Jacobean melancholy' or 'Jacobean mutability'. There was in fact much rejoicing when James came to the throne, after the uncertainties of Elizabeth's last years, and while disillusionment and frustration at the king's political tactlessness grew, this was an entirely separate reaction to those minor voices proclaiming the decay of the world. We need to see the late Renaissance in England—from Sidney and Spenser to Milton and Marvell—as a whole movement, punctuated by changes of government but obeying its own internal logic. Political events do impinge on literature, nowhere more dramatically than in the closing of the theatres in 1642, but the introduction, development, and ultimate decline of literary modes or genres follow their own laws, depending on the innate vitality of a form or the inventiveness of the writers using it. In the older generation of writers, those born in the 1550s or 1560s, such as Sir Walter Ralegh (*c*.1552), George Chapman (*c*.1559), and Francis Bacon (1561)—contemporaries of writers who did not live to see the new reign, such as Sidney, Spenser, and Nashe—we find a mixture of older and newer forms and attitudes.

Ralegh's *History of the World* (1614) ignored the new developments in historiography coming from the Italian Renaissance and harked back to two medieval traditions, the *De casibus* or 'fall of princes' as the subject-matter of history, and the *De contemptu mundi* approach to life, stressing human depravation. Ralegh's view of God, man, and history seems backward-looking, stressing evil, guilt, and punishment to the exclusion of human goodness or divine grace, ignoring the Renaissance reassertion of the dignity of man. A poet more in tune with newer attitudes extolling human value was George Chapman, author or co-author of more than twenty plays, and translator of Homer. In his plays Chapman could create heroic characters, in the Stoic mode, who suffer adversity nobly, arousing our admiration and emulation. But in translating Homer this desire to produce single states of virtue or vice falsifies the original. Following a long tradition of allegorical interpretation Chapman turns Ulysses into a type of Renaissance hero, overcoming temptation and yielding examples of such abstract virtues as prudence or fortitude. This moralizing simplification of Homer's more complex poem can result in serious misunderstandings. Where Homer records splendid feasts as signs of guest-friendship, so important in ancient Greece, Chapman presents them disapprovingly as instances of greed or self-indulgence. Even more alien is his treatment of the Greek gods, reducing their discordant polytheism to Christian monotheism, and importing into the text such anachronistic concepts as patience, submission, and divine grace. The result is a strange hybrid of Renaissance philological scholarship with a totally unhistorical attitude to classical culture.

Chapman's Homer is problematic, too, as a translation. In the *Odyssey* (1614-15), as in the *Iliad* previously (1598-1611), modern scholarship has shown that Chapman (who, like many Elizabethans, knew little Greek) translated not from the original but from a contemporary Latin version. Not only is Greek rendered via neo-Latin, but Chapman actually includes in the text of his translation footnotes and glosses from the commentators, as if they were the very words of Homer. His Latinate diction derives verbatim from the commentators, and he also coins fantastic compound epithets, attempting to imitate Homer's style, such as 'They honey-sweetness-giving-minds-wine filled', or 'wise-in-chaste-wit-worthy wife'. He introduces elaborate periphrases, often to bring out a point which he feels is not clear enough in Homer, and dislocates syntax with an awkward word order that creates ambiguity and confusion. Although there are occasional passages of simple and flexible movement, Chapman has learned nothing from the revolution in English verse made by Sidney, Spenser, Marlowe, Shakespeare, and Donne. Despite his desire to appeal to a learned élite Chapman revealed a lordly disregard for the integrity of the text. He despised 'word-for-word traductions', but many of his contemporaries had different standards of accuracy, as we can see from the hostile marginalia that Ben Jonson wrote in his copy. For the modern reader it is difficult to know what Keats saw in Chapman's Homer.

Chapman founded no school of poets, provoked little imitation. Francis Bacon (1561-1626), by contrast, was the most influential writer of the whole century, with an enormous impact on the scientific movement. He wrote on a remarkable range of topics: ethics, philosophy, all the sciences, mythography, history, politics, law, a total of over seventy works, only twenty of which were published during his lifetime. 'I have taken all knowledge to be my province,' he wrote at the age of thirty-one, and few Englishmen, even in that period of heroic endeavour, achieved so much. Bacon's most obviously 'literary' works are the *Essays* (first version 1597, much enlarged in 1612 and 1625). But his commitment to the Renaissance concept of the *vita activa*, the life dedicated to serving society, meant that he took the classical injunction to mix 'profit and delight' seriously. The *Essays* are not mere discursive jottings, but fill the need that he had noted in *The Advancement of Learning* (1605) for more studies of 'moral knowledge' (the influence on men's *mores* and behaviour of such factors as age, health, sickness, riches), and 'civil knowledge' (such topics as government, negotiation, conversation). Bacon's intention was to analyse cause and effect in social and psychological terms. He praised Machiavelli and other moderns for describing what men do rather than what they should do, that is, for producing descriptive accounts of life rather than prescriptive-didactic ones. But it is wrong to call Bacon a Machiavellian, as if he believed in success at any cost, or ruthless dissimulation. The *Essays* are full of statements of fundamental ethical principles: 'power to do good is the true and lawful end of aspiring'; 'Riches are for spending, and spending for honour and good actions'; 'goodness of nature', or *philanthropia*, 'of all virtues and dignities of mind is the greatest; being the character of the Deity; and without it man is a busy, mischievous, wretched thing; no better than a kind of vermin'. Dr Johnson praised the *Essays* as 'the observations of a strong mind operating upon life'. They show not only strength of mind but imagination, in the striking metaphors, often opening an essay: 'Suspicions among thoughts are like bats among birds, they ever fly by twilight', or closing one: 'For a crowd is not company; and faces are but a gallery of pictures; and talk but a tinkling cymbal, where there is no love.'

These imaginative qualities are prominent in *The Advancement of Learning*, Bacon's first published work on the intellectual reforms to which he dedicated so much of his life. Scientific research in the Renaissance still laboured under the stigma of 'forbidden knowledge', the Church viewing with suspicion man's attempt to pry into the movements of the heavenly bodies or the secrets of the Creation. In the first book Bacon set out to defend the pursuit of knowledge from these and other charges, describing its benefits for individual and society. Education teaches us to weigh both sides of a question, prevents the mind from becoming 'fixed or settled' in its defects, makes it still 'capable and susceptible of growth and reformation'. This capacity for unending development is not limited to the individual but characterizes learning itself, which persists through the ages, even though monuments decay:

the images of men's wits and knowledges remain in books, exempted from the wrong of time and capable of perpetual renovation. Neither are they fitly to be called images, because they generate still, and cast their seeds in the mind of others, provoking and causing infinite actions and opinions in succeeding ages.

This conclusion to the first Book goes on to describe 'letters' or written texts as ships that 'pass through the vast seas of time', a metaphor that became a

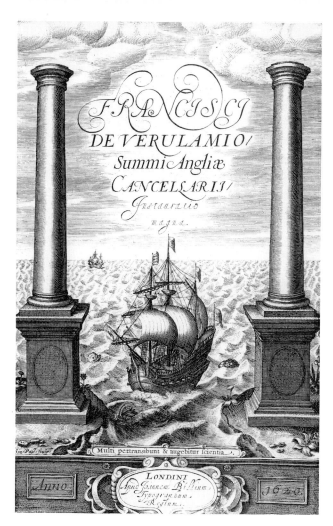

symbol used in the frontispiece of his later scientific works, where a ship sails past the pillars of Hercules, out into the unknown waters of discovery.

Bacon's faith in the 'perpetual renovation' of knowledge, expressed in such inspiring language, had a tremendous influence on the seventeenth-century scientific movement. Although not himself a scientist of the first rank, Bacon grasped some of the important principles of the scientific revolution. Science can no longer be derived from the books of Aristotle or Pliny but must result from firsthand observation and experiment. Instead of being isolated, scientific disciplines should cross-fertilize each other. In the *Novum organum* (1620), a title challenging comparison with Aristotle's old 'Organon' of logical treatises, Bacon outlined a new scientific method, not deductive from fixed premises, as in classical logic, but inductive, working up from individual observations to general laws. And in the *Sylva sylvarum* (1626) and the various 'natural histories' published in the 1620s, he attempted to provide collections of raw material, pure observations of physical reality. This range of works, although flawed in many ways, was the first attempt in any language to provide a complete programme for the rebirth of science. Bacon was a pioneer, too, in seeing the need for scientific co-operation. His *New Atlantis* (1624) is a Utopian fable describing 'Salomon's House', an imaginary scientific institute which has underground laboratories to study coagulation and refrigeration; observatories; pressure-chambers; acoustic laboratories; devices to 'convey sounds' over long distances, to make waterproof fire-bombs, submarines, and much else. Scientists are arranged in groups, descending from theoretical geniuses to technologists and engineers, their collective goal being 'the knowledge of causes . . . and the enlarging of the bounds of human empire, to the effecting of all things possible'. It was entirely appropriate that when the Royal Society of London was founded in 1660 it honoured Charles II as patron and Bacon as its inspiration.

A FLEA: from Robert Hooke, *Micrographia* (1665), one of the first fruits of the Royal Society (founded 1660). The success of Hooke's work owed much to these beautifully executed plates (this one on a vast and frightening fold-out), some of them drawn by Christopher Wren, which gave the first accurate illustrations of what the microscope revealed. The initial response to the new science in literature was satirical, as in Shadwell's play *The Virtuoso* (1676), and Swift's *Gulliver's Travels*, Book Three.

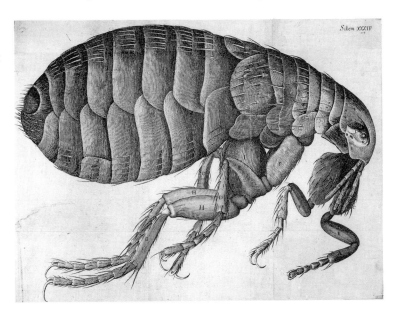

The Masque

Although Bacon got through an enormous amount of work he believed in the importance of play and refreshment, ritual and ceremony. In the 1590s he composed three 'devices' or proto-dramatic entertainments, and he was instrumental in organizing several masques for important state weddings. In his essay 'Of Masques and Triumphs' Bacon wrote with obvious affection of the combined attractions of the masque: 'Dancing to song is a thing of great state and pleasure;' 'the alterations of the scenes . . . are things of great beauty and pleasure.' The masque indeed encouraged a remarkable union of the arts. The music was composed by such leading figures as Alfonso Ferrabosco and Giovanni Coperario; the dances were choreographed by specialists such as Jacques Cordier, who supervised rehearsals for several weeks; the stage sets, full of spectacular effects, were often designed by England's greatest architect,

THE MASQUE, from John Ogilby, *The Fables of Aesop Paraphrased in Verse* (1651), 'the masque of apes'. As in the masques presented in the Banqueting House, Whitehall, the king as chief spectator sits on the throne, with distinguished foreign ambassadors and members of the court forming the privileged audience. There is a large space for the dancers, while the actors and musicians perform on the stage, which is graced with elaborate 'scenes and machines'.

Inigo Jones, while the texts were provided by such poets as Chapman, Beaumont, Campion, Middleton, and above all—he being responsible for twenty-one of the thirty-three main masques performed at court between 1605 and 1640—Ben Jonson. The leading artists were paid handsomely, £40 per masque (multiply by twenty or more for a modern equivalent).

The sudden vogue for the masque was due to the new ruler, or rather his wife, Queen Anne of Denmark, who not only encouraged poets and provided ideas (as for Jonson's *Masque of Blackness*) but took part in many of them as the chief dancer, in a costume whose splendour outshone all the others. Although the musicians and choreographers were professional, as were some of the actors, the main performers in the dances, which were for many spectators (not least James I) the chief attraction, were the lords and ladies of the court. James's favourite, the duke of Buckingham, was an outstanding dancer, who saved one flagging performance, when the king cried out in a loud voice (as reported by a Venetian observer) 'Why don't they dance? What did they make me come here for? Devil take you all, dance!', by a brilliant impromptu display. These were events performed by the court, for the court, attendance in the Banqueting House being limited to that privileged group and to foreign ambassadors. They were produced for great marriages or on feast-days, and were given once only, apart from a special repeat performance. The cost was phenomenal. Being official expenditures, detailed accounts were kept and show that bills of £1,000 to £3,000 for one night were common (Bacon is said to have paid £2,000 from his own pocket), enough money to buy a substantial country house. Specifications for individual costumes reveal a lavishness of material and care of design exceptional in any age. The masque can be seen as conspicuous consumption, a sign of decadence, or as the apotheosis of the arts.

The texts of the masques are short, often slight, setting up an allegorical or mythological framework which provided an occasion for the dances or the spectacle. The theme, predictably enough, was often the glorification of nobility, or right rule. The allegorical personages were provided with costumes and attributes derived from popular Renaissance mythology books, such as Cesare Ripa's *Iconologia*, and described with a full panoply of scholarship. Jonson was the only writer who attempted more than providing a scenario for the dancers and designers, indeed he resented the ever-increasing success of Inigo Jones's scenes and machines.

One of the few substantial masques is his *Pleasure Reconciled to Virtue* (1618), staged on Twelfth Night as the first masque in which Prince Charles took part. Appropriately, the main character is Hercules, 'active friend of

A LADY MASQUER, Lucy Harrington, countess of Bedford, by Johann de Critz, in Jonson's *Hymenaei* (1606). The designer was Inigo Jones, and the matching costumes were fitted out lavishly, with gold and silver cloth, plumes, diamonds, rubies, and pearls. The earl of Rutland paid over £100 for his wife's jewels in this masque (multiply by 20 for a modern equivalent).

Both, woo'd my *Youth :* And, both perſwaded ſo,
That (like the *Young man* in our *Emblem* here)
I ſtood, and cry'd, *Ah ! which way ſhall I goe ?*
To me ſo pleaſing both their Offers were.
VICE, *Pleaſures* beſt Contentments promiſt mee,
And what the wanton *Fleſh* deſires to have :
Quoth VERTVE, *I will Wiſdome give to thee,*
And thoſe brave things , which nobleſt Mindes doe crave.
Serve me ſaid VICE, *and thou ſhalt ſoone acquire*
All thoſe Atchievements which my Service brings :
Serve me ſaid VERTVE, *and Ile raiſe thee higher,*
Then VICES *can, and teach thee better things.*
Whil'ſt thus they ſtrove to gaine me, I eſpyde
Grim *Death* attending VICE ; and, that her Face
Was but a painted *Vizard,* which did hide
The foul'ſt Deformity that ever was.
LORD, *grant me grace for evermore to view*
Her Vglineſſe : And, that I viewing it,
Her Falſehoods and allurements may eſchew ;
And on faire VERTVE *my Affeĉtion ſet ;*
    Her Beauties contemplate, her Love embrace,
    And by her ſafe Direĉtion, runne my Race.

THE CHOICE OF HERCULES, from George Wither, *A Collection of Emblemes, Ancient and Moderne* (1635). As usual in England, the plates were taken over from a continental emblem book, here the *Nucleus emblematum selectissimorum* by Gabriel Rollenhagen (Utrecht, 1611?, 1613).

virtue', and the work recounts the exceptional peace proclaimed for this night only, ''Twixt virtue and her noted opposite, / Pleasure'. Since classical antiquity *virtus* and *voluptas* had been conceived of as mutually exclusive opposites, as in the fable of Hercules, offered the choice at a crossroads between two paths, one leading up a steep and stony path to a distant hill with the temple of honour, the other down a broad and flowery path to hell. The motif of choice and discrimination fundamental to this masque, and to Renaissance ethics, is skilfully translated into the artistic medium by having Daedalus lead the masquers through complex dances representing the labyrinths of beauty and love, first uniting then separating virtue and pleasure. While the noble actors have been permitted 'To walk with Pleasure, not to dwell', they must henceforth return to the hard life and steep hill of virtue: ''Tis only she can make you great, / Though place here make you known.' However extravagant and ephemeral these 'spectacles of state', at their best, when music, dance, scene, and text combined, they must have offered a unique aesthetic experience.

James's queen was certainly the dominant influence on a form that flourished briefly, disappearing in the 1640s as the public crises grew. In other areas the decisive redirection to many literary forms had been given in the 1590s, indeed the two decades spanning the turn of the century saw the birth of many genres. In verse there is the sudden maturity of formal satire, as in the work of Joseph Hall, John Donne, and John Marston. A specific verse form largely connected with satire was the epigram, which William Camden described in his *Remaines* (1605) as 'short and sweet poems, framed to praise or dispraise', in which 'our country men now surpass other nations'. The roll-call of English epigrammatists writing either in the vernacular or in Latin (where some enjoyed a European reputation) is distinguished. In drama this period saw the importation from Italy of the tragicomedy and pastoral play, besides the masque. In prose a whole series of genres appeared, foremost being the essay and its related genre the paradox or mock-encomium. The religious counterpart to the essay was the meditation, sometimes concluding with a 'resolve' or resolution to amend one's behaviour. The wit of the prose paradox and verse satire found special expression in the prose 'Character', or satiric character-sketch of typical human vices and virtues, sometimes generalized and abstract, but often particularized as recognizable contemporary types.

The genres that appeared in such profusion between 1590 and 1610 did not appear from nowhere, of course. They were imported from continental Europe, either from classical antiquity or from the contemporary vernaculars, especially French and Italian. Englishmen were keen students of the classics, since the introduction of the teaching methods and values of Renaissance humanism into the curricula of grammar schools and universities in the early sixteenth century was being consolidated all the time. The number of schools founded in the period 1610–30 marked a high point in English philanthropy. All the writers of this period had had a school and university education based largely on Latin, with Greek sometimes added later. English was used for translation exercises, but was otherwise forbidden under pain of punishment. Remarkably thorough routines of parsing, construing, and memorizing ensured that the texts learned at school were never forgotten. Every writer could count on most of his readers being able to recognize quotations or allusions from Ovid's *Metamorphoses*, some books of the *Aeneid*, Cicero's *De officiis*, or the moral works of Seneca. Many of our major poets wrote Latin verse: Donne, Jonson, Herbert, Crashaw, Milton. All writers were trained in rhetoric and logic, with an extensive knowledge of the techniques of composition, the use of the figures and tropes to illuminate the discourse and to move the audience's feelings. Their readers were also able to recognize deliberate abuses of logic and rhetoric, witty or speciously sophistic manipulations of argument, misuses of the laws of reasoning. Being able to count on the knowledge and reactions of your readership is the sign of a restricted culture but also of a homogeneous one. The modern reader must always strive to re-create a context that readers of the time could take for granted.

Englishmen read contemporary European literature, history, philosophy, science, and all other subjects in neo-Latin or in the vernaculars. We know from library catalogues of the period, both institutional and private, that continental books circulated freely in England, Protestants and Catholics making equal use of each other's learning, despite doctrinal differences. Many writers travelled abroad, either for self-improvement or in the service of the government or a nobleman, while great institutions such as the Frankfurt book fair ensured a steady two-way movement of ideas. Some of the newly imported genres can be traced directly to continental models: the essay to Montaigne (although none of our writers ever attempted his large autobiographical scope), the paradox to Ortensio Lando, the character to one book, Casaubon's Latin translation of Theophrastus. In this as in every period the bookseller and the librarian were essential to our culture, often anonymous 'middlemen' in an endless process of education and discovery.

Writers, too, are middlemen, at a higher level, where specific credit can be given. Of the writers associated with new genres three names stand out, one minor, two major. Few readers today know the work of Joseph Hall (1574-1656), but he can claim the record as the most successful pioneer or importer in our literature. In *Virgidemiae* (1598, eight further editions by 1639), Hall was the first to attempt truly Juvenalian satire in English, at least the first in print, as he proudly announced: 'I first adventure: follow me who list, / And be the second English Satirist.' Between 1605 and 1611 he published *Mundus alter et idem*, an imaginary voyage satirizing human credulity; three books of *Meditations and Vowes Divine and Morall*; *Characters of Virtues and Vices*, the first formal collection of characters; and *Epistles in Six Decades*, inaugurating another 'fashion of discourse, by Epistles; new to our language, usuall to others'. Hall also published twenty-one books of *Contemplations*, together with sermons, panegyrics, and occasional works. While undoubtedly a respected writer in his day, who did much to shape contemporary taste, Hall never succeeded in leaving his mark on any of the genres he imported. He could seize an opportunity to innovate, but his personality was not strong enough to make something individual out of it.

John Donne

The other two pioneers who spanned the turn of the century were much greater individualists, indeed John Donne (1572-1631) and Ben Jonson (1572/3-1637) were two of the most forceful and influential writers of the century. Donne's *Satires* may have ante-dated Hall's, since like all of his early poems they circulated in manuscript. Writers in the sixteenth and seventeenth centuries can be divided into professionals and amateurs. The first group published their work without shame, as it were, receiving payment from the printer and, in money or in presents, from the patron to whom they dedicated it. The amateurs, often writers of a higher social class, preferred not to write for money, only enduring 'the stigma of print' when their work was issued in unauthorized editions, or after their death. Donne comes into the second class, referring in his letters to the prospect of being 'brought to a necessity of printing' his poems, of 'descending' and 'declining' into print. Luckily this dreaded prospect was spared him, his poetry and other prose works being published posthumously in 1633, by his son. From internal and other evidence we can assign to the late 1590s his *Satires, Elegies, Paradoxes and Problems*, and some of the poems in his *Songs and Sonnets*, arguably the greatest collection of lyric poems in English. These poems, too, circulated in manuscript copies: we still have no less than forty collections devoted wholly to Donne, and he figures in over a hundred manuscript miscellanies mostly dating from 1610 to 1630.

Donne's individual handling of inherited forms appears very early on. Where Hall had gone through the imitation of Juvenal in a bookish way, castigating fashionable vices in London yet without ever establishing the credibility of his role as moralist or the reality of the figures he attacks, Donne immediately involves himself and us in the urban scene. The first and fourth satires are set in London, and are full of finely observed detail of vanity and vice, while the fifth exposes corruption in office with a sober disgust. Most memorable is the third satire, surveying the chaos of conflicting religious beliefs. Donne argues the search for a truth transcending sectarian difference, perfectly adapting verse-movement to meaning:

> Doubt wisely: in strange way
> To stand enquiring right is not to stray;
> To sleep or run wrong is. On a huge hill,
> Cragged and steep, truth stands, and he that will
> Reach her about must, and about must go;
> And what the hill's suddenness resists, win so.

If the seriousness of the *Satires* sometimes masks the element of play, the *Paradoxes* are mock-serious discussions which use logical techniques for wholly playful ends. The paradox derives in part from the debate tradition in schools and universities, where students had to argue for or against a topic in order to show their proficiency in logic and rhetoric. The defence could often take the form of praising an unworthy subject—baldness, or smoke, or folly (as in Erasmus's *Moriae encomium*)—or reversing contemporary attitudes. Donne is clever enough to argue in 'defence of women's inconstancy' while simultaneously satirizing it; can invert a standard theme to show 'that the gifts of the body are better than those of the mind'; and can bring a reader up short by arguing 'that virginity is a virtue', so unsettling the reader who knows, or thinks he knows, that that belief is generally shared. The working out of these paradoxes is a series of pseudo-logical arguments fired off like popguns. Arguing that women ought to use cosmetics, he begins, 'Foulness is loathsome: can that be so which helps it?' That of course does not meet the case against cosmetics, but the author knows that, and knows that you know it. The method works by piling up arguments that are seen to be specious yet have a tenuous connection with the facts: 'If in kissing or breathing upon her the painting fall off, thou art angry: wilt thou be so if it stick on?'

This argumentative technique, both serious and mocking, is found in the love poems. Compare 'Break of Day', spoken by a woman to a man who wants to leave her bed because day has dawned: 'Why should we rise because 'tis light? / Did we lie down because 'twas night?' Donne uses paradox to question some of the traditional ideals of love poetry, replacing them with more realistic models. This is a frequent procedure in the *Songs and Sonnets*, which collectively challenge or invert many received traditions. In most sixteenth-century love poetry the mistress is remote, unattainable, approached by the poet from time to time only to be rebuffed, at which point he laments his misfortune, accuses her with a mixture of love and resentment, and finds continuing inspiration from his frustration. Donne breaks with all this. Where other poets place their mistress on a pedestal, he puts her in bed, next to him. In 'The Sun Rising' the lovers watch the sun breaking through the bedroom curtains, and send him off to more suitable tasks: 'go chide / Late schoolboys, and sour 'prentices.' The sun has no business disturbing them, since lovers are subject to no laws or duties but their own:

> Love, all alike, no season knows, nor clime,
> Nor hours, days, months, which are the rags of time.

Yet, having been sent off, the sun is summoned back just as imperiously: 'Shine here to us, and thou art everywhere.' Where the aubade or dawn-song can be a serenade by a lover under his mistress's bedroom window, in Donne 'The Good-Morrow' is spoken in bed, their 'little room' becomes 'an everywhere' through the power of love. Where some poets use the pronouns 'I' and 'she', implying a distance between man and woman, and others 'I' and 'thou' or 'you', implying direct address, perhaps in separation, Donne fuses both pronouns into 'we', 'us', 'our'. He can wonder 'what thou and I / Did, till we lov'd? were we not wean'd till then?' The riddle of the phoenix gains extra meaning from their case: 'we two being one, are it.' This sense of forming a unit brings a feeling of security. In 'The Anniversary' they are both kings and subjects, and

> Who is so safe as we? where none can do
> Treason to us, except one of us two.

The lovers form a unit outside time, outside the world, in one sense above it. One of the great insights of Donne's new attitude to love is that a love-relationship constitutes an experience knowable only by the two people involved in it. Other people's judgements are of no relevance, indeed everything else pales into insignificance compared to the value that the lovers have in each other's eyes:

> She is all states, and all princes, I,
> Nothing else is.
>
> ('The Sun Rising')

With the same eye for the logical implications of an argument that he showed in the *Paradoxes*, Donne pushes the distinction 'lovers / rest of the world' to its absolute, infinity against zero. Further, by a bold, sometimes outrageous development these lovers become the definition of true love, its only authentic exponents. In 'Twickenham Garden' the poet invites other lovers to test his tears ('love's wine'), and so the authenticity of his love, 'For all are false that taste not just like mine'. Being so far above all other lovers they take on the status of cult-objects: ''Twere profanation of our joys / To tell the laity our love' ('A Valediction: forbidding Mourning'). In 'A Valediction: of the Book' their love-letters are to be used by future historians to write for 'love's clergy' an authentic record of love, where 'Love's divines' will preserve all human knowledge. Donne pushes this religious comparison to its ultimate, blasphemous stage. In 'The Relique' he is 'Love's martyr', and their bones dug up from their grave will become sacred relics. In 'The Canonization' other lovers will sing hymns to them, 'canonized for love', and he ends by inviting us to 'Beg from above / A pattern of your love!' If Catholics pray to saints to pray for them, Donne and his mistress are now intermediaries between us and God.

Donne regenerated love poetry by describing love consummated, and he developed a very individual line in turning the lovers into saint-figures. No less original was the opposed procedure, the cynical rejection of love. In this mode constancy is mocked as being pointless or impossible, both in women ('swear / Nowhere / Lives a woman true, and fair') and in men: 'I can love both fair and brown . . . / I can love any, so she be not true.' As Venus is made to say in this poem ('The Indifferent'), 'she heard not this till now', Donne drawing attention to his originality. Now a man can appeal to Love that it should 'let my body reign, and let / Me . . . snatch, plot, have, forget, / Resume my last year's relict' ('Love's Usury'), newly irreverent ways of behaving with women— seize at one go, mount a long campaign, enjoy, abandon, take up a cast-off. This casual, flippant attitude was a refreshing challenge to the stock worship of the woman, and like all his other ideas Donne carried it to its absolute, as in the conclusion to 'Mummy: or Love's alchemy', where even at their best women 'are but Mummy, possess'd'—that is, 'mere lumps of dead flesh', once you've had them. Equally shocking is the end of 'Community':

> Changed loves are but changed sorts of meat;
> And when he hath the kernel eat,
>   Who doth not fling away the shell?

The *Songs and Sonnets* show a great variety of poses or attitudes in love, including wholly original versions of the seduction poem or 'invitation to love' ('The Flea'; 'The Ecstasy'), and vital energizings of traditional poems of parting or loss ('Twickenham Garden'; greatest of all, perhaps, is 'A Nocturnal upon St. Lucy's Day'). His originality extends to poetic form, also: he uses a great range of stanza forms, forty of them being invented by him, and he seldom repeats a form. In the religious poems he is more conventional in form. The *Holy Sonnets* have some of the same qualities that we find in the love poems,

such as the insistent imperatives: 'Batter my heart, three-personed God', and
the development of an idea to its absolute, as in the ending of this sonnet:

> Take me to you, imprison me, for I
> Except you enthral me, never shall be free,
> Nor ever chaste, except you ravish me.

That startling paradox, chastity co-existing with rape, both strong metaphors
for the union of the individual soul with God, is exceptional in the sonnets,
which are usually less witty. Perhaps the regularity of the form and its brevity
did not give Donne enough scope and variety, or perhaps he conceived these
'Divine meditations' as more serious theological essays.

The greatest of the religious poems are 'Good Friday, 1613. Riding Westward',
a poem of forty-two lines in couplets, and the three hymns, each in stanzaic
form. In these poems Donne creates a more personal sense of relationship with
God, an immediate involvement in Christ's suffering:

> What a death were it then to see God die?
> . . . .
> Could I behold those hands which span the poles,
> And turn all spheres at once, pierced with those holes?

DONNE IN HIS FUNERAL SHROUD
(1631). In his *Life of Donne*, Izaac
Walton recorded that a monument to
Donne was to be erected and a
painter came to make a sketch.
Donne stripped, put on his winding-
sheet, 'so tied with knots at his head
and feet, and his hands so placed as
dead bodies are usually fitted to be
shrouded and thus put into their
coffin or grave. Upon this urn he thus
stood with his eyes shut, and with so
much of the sheet turned aside as
might show his lean, pale, and death-
like face, which was purposely turned
towards the East, from whence he
expected the second coming of his and
our saviour Jesus. In this posture he
was drawn at his just height, and
when the picture was finished he
caused it to be set by his bed-side,
where it continued, and became his
hourly object till his death.'

The conclusion to this Good Friday poem is another imperative appeal: 'O think me worth thine anger, punish me, / Burn off my rusts, and my deformity', until God's image in man be restored to its true shape. In the poem on his sickness, probably the serious illness of 1623, which also gave rise to a remarkable prose work, the *Devotions upon Emergent Occasions*, we find the grim conceit of his fever being a quick passage to a new world, a 'south-west discovery', yet the ending accepts 'that he may raise the Lord throws down'. In 'A Hymn to God the Father' the poet lists his sins in asking forgiveness, punning on his name: 'When thou hast done, thou hast not done, / For I have more.' In the final stanza the fear of extinction after death is checked by the appeal to God that his 'son [also "sun"] / shall shine as he shines now', for then 'thou hast done, / I fear no more.' With a remarkable sense of timing Donne ended his last poem on that note of confidence in the mercies of God. Outer and inner form cohered.

In the last seventeen years of his life Donne wrote little poetry, most of his creative energies going into his weekly sermon. Ordained in 1615, he became six years later Dean of St Paul's Cathedral, and preached there to a devoted congregation. In 1631 he produced *Death's Duel*, his own funeral sermon, having practised a mortification of the flesh verging on the macabre. Donne left some 160 sermons, delivered by all accounts with enormous spiritual and emotional conviction. The modern reader, even if religious, does not always find it easy to recapture the keen interest that seventeenth-century church-goers took in sermons. Diarists usually noted the biblical text which the priest selected, recording, too, whether he had 'done well' or not; others took down the main points in their notebooks, sometimes in shorthand. Sermons lasted between one and two hours, and were keenly followed by the congregation, who took both a professional and a personal interest. Professional, in so far as they were educated men with a wide knowledge of theology and divinity; personal, since they relied on their pastor to preach 'comfortable words' for the good of their souls. Sermons formed the largest category of printed books in this period, with important political and social implications.

For much of the time Donne, like any preacher of that age, performed an exegesis of the biblical text, which the modern reader may not need. We are also unlikely to share the Church of England's hostility towards Catholics, Turks, or Nonconformists. Where we can respond to Donne is in his intense concern with human sin, divine grace, and the urgent need for salvation. Although man may feel 'terror' from his 'inherence and encombrance of original sin . . . there is a holy charm, a blessed incantation', by which we are 'invulnerable unto death'. By 'incantation' Donne means faith, but the term can serve as a description of his own preaching style, which ranges eloquently between the extremes of joy and despair, hope and fear. He reminds his congregation that although there is only a minute's sand left in his hour-glass, it remains open whether God 'shall bless you for your acceptation, or curse you for your refusal of him this minute'. While willing to remind us of death as the 'contemptible vilification, the most deadly and peremptory nullification of man', Donne is equally ready with inspiring visions of heaven. In both phases his writing makes much use of rhetorical repetition, in passages of great incremental power (like the ending of Mahler's third symphony, say):

in the agonies of death, in the anguish of that dissolution, in the sorrows of that valediction, in the irreversibleness of that transmigration, I shall have a joy, which shall no more evaporate than my soul shall evaporate, a joy that shall pass up, and put on a more glorious garment above, and be joy superinvested in glory. Amen.

One can well believe contemporary accounts of Donne 'weeping sometimes for his auditory, sometimes with them'.

Donne's sermons appeal to the ear, the mind, and the emotions. A very different style of sermon was produced by his great contemporary, Lancelot Andrewes (1555–1626). In his *XCVI Sermons* (1629) Andrewes certainly addresses his congregation, but rather through a sustained scrutiny of the chosen biblical text. Where Donne expands outwards, Andrewes contracts inwards, into the heart of scriptural meaning. As T. S. Eliot wrote, he 'takes a word and derives the world from it; squeezing and squeezing the word until it yields a full juice of meaning'. This intensity gives a heightened perception of language, but Andrewes also shows great powers of imagination in taking a biblical text and re-creating the whole scene, as a Renaissance painter would do. On Christmas Day 1622 he preached on the Magi's coming to the new-born Christ, *'venimus'*: 'we have seen his star in the east, and *are come* to worship him.' In their coming he considers first the distance ('many a hundred miles'), secondly the way ('vast and desolate', through deserts infested with thieves). Last,

we consider the time of their coming, the season of the year: just the worst time of the year to take a journey, and specially a long journey in. The ways deep, the weather sharp, the days short, the sun farthest off *in solstitio brumali*, the very dead of winter.

T. S. Eliot was inspired by that passage to write *The Journey of the Magi*, responding precisely to this reconstruction of landscape and feelings. From the text Andrewes moves out to the congregation, since he shared St Augustine's belief that the only true praise of a sermon is its incitement to good. So he juxtaposes the Magi's willingness to travel with the average man's reluctance: 'With them it was but *Vidimus, Venimus*: with us, it would have been but *Veniemus* at most . . . Come such a journey, at such a time? No! but fairly to have put it off to the spring of the year. . . .' As he remarks later, 'all considered, there is more in *Venimus* than shews at the first sight.' The individuality of Lancelot Andrewes lies in his sensitivity to words and their full implication, etymological and spiritual.

Jonson, Herbert, and the Emblem

The individuality of Donne expressed itself in terms of language, argument, poetic form. While the speaker of the religious poems may be Donne himself, the 'I' of the love poems is, as in all lyric poetry, an imagined speaker, a *persona* or 'mask' of the poet, who takes up various poses, various moods, not to be identified with the poet himself. Donne sets his mark on each of his poems, but does so through his handling of language and form rather than by self-revelation. In Ben Jonson's poetry, by contrast, the 'I' is always Jonson himself, a figure of massive authority and consistency, who maintains in his three collections of poems a constant attitude to life, language, and poetry. Jonson shared the fundamental belief of Renaissance humanists that the 'good poet' must first be a 'good man', an educator and guardian of morality. He must have eloquence and facility in verse-writing, but also 'the exact knowledge of all virtues, and their contraries; with ability to render the one loved, the other hated, by his proper embattling them'. That is, the poet's subject-matter is primarily the innate opposition between virtue and vice.

Jonson alludes here to an important branch of rhetoric, linked to ethics since Plato and Aristotle, known as epideictic. This mode concentrates on the procedures of praise and blame, the basic assumption being that a good man will praise virtue, make it admirable so that we imitate it, and attack vice, making it loathsomely deterrent. Virtually the whole of Jonson's poetry can be placed in these two categories of praise and blame. In a poem to William, earl of Pembroke (*Epigrams*, CII), Jonson praises his 'true posture' in 'this strife / Of vice, and virtue; wherein all great life / Almost, is exercised'. In 'To Katherine, Lady Aubigny'. Jonson presents himself as actively involved in this battle, as a good poet should be, 'in love / with every virtue', and 'at feud / With sin and vice, though with a throne endued'. This ethical poetry has a solidity of purpose derived from its conviction that the greatest of all human assets is virtue,

> Without which, all the rest were sounds, or lost.
>   'Tis only that can time, and chance defeat:
> For he that once is good, is ever great.
>
> (*Forest*, XIII)

Where such simple, declarative sentences occur in Donne, their subject is likely to be love; in Jonson, virtue.

The danger of such a programme for poetry is that it can result in either violent vituperation that ultimately alienates us from the poet himself (as happens with Marston's satires), or pious hymns to abstract virtue. Jonson avoids both dangers. In attacking evil he deploys a mixture of contempt and irony, as in this short poem 'On Court-Worm' (*Epigrams*, XV):

> All men are worms: but this no man. In silk
> 'Twas brought to court first wrapped, and white as milk;

JOHN DONNE in the pose of a melancholy lover, *c*.1595. The Latin inscription implores his lady, to whom he owes a saint-like devotion, to lighten the shadows which envelop his love-sick misery.

PREACHING AT OLD ST PAUL'S CATHEDRAL (*c.*1616). In the foreground is Paul's Cross, from which a bishop is preaching to the king, the court, judges, and other officers. This is probably an imaginary scene.

> Where, afterwards, it grew a butterfly:
> Which was a caterpillar. So 'twill die.

The courtier who arrived dressed in silk is dismissed by being identified with a butterfly, emerging from its cocoon only to enjoy a brief life. The dismissal is given more force by the juxtaposition of tenses ('afterwards, it grew . . . which was . . . So 'twill'), suggesting an inevitable progress to oblivion. This poem also illustrates Jonson's preferred verse form, the couplet, especially when 'broken', that is, where the unit of sense does not coincide with the two rhyming lines but moves on by the pressure of thought or argument. The play of sound against sense, rhyme against syntax, creates a nervous energy in his verse, an elliptical movement that can observe the formal rules of poetry while giving the freedom of the speaking voice. So in 'To Fine Lady Would-Be', (*Epigrams*, LXII), Jonson wonders why this court lady should prefer to have abortions rather than bear children:

> Is it the pain affrights? That's soon forgot.
> Or your complexion's loss? You have a pot,
> That can restore that.

Instead of writing two regular lines coinciding with the couplet rhyme, Jonson tends to split them into a half, a whole, and a half-line, the sense moving diagonally across the form:

> What should the cause be? Oh, you live at court:
> And there's both loss of time, and loss of sport
> In a great belly.

Yet he can exploit the symmetry and sonority of rhyme when it suits him, as in the biting concluding paradox:

> Write then, on thy womb,
> Of the not born, yet buried, here's the tomb.

That icy irony is much more effective than violent denunciation, for it condenses a whole range of ethical responses into measure and control.

Jonson does not really 'embattle' virtue and vice in this early collection, which divides blame from praise, devoting separate poems to celebrating examples 'Of honour and virtue'. In the later collections praise and blame are fused in the same poem, made to make fundamental discriminations about good and evil in society, in such major works as those addressed to Sir Robert Wroth, the countess of Rutland, and Lady Aubigny. The 'Epistle to a friend, to persuade him to the wars' (*Underwoods*, XVII), is Jonson's major satire, of a Juvenalian dimension and force.

Given his conception of poetry as being to 'correct [the commonwealth] with judgments', it is not surprising that Jonson wrote so little in the two most popular genres of this period, love poetry and religious poetry. Jonson's muse is

OBDVRANDVM ADVER-
sus urgentia.

The more contrary Windes *doe blow,*
The greater Vertues *praise will grow.*

RENAISSANCE EMBLEMS FOR VIRTUE presented it as a quality that could overcome all obstacles: a palm-tree laden with a weight continues to grow, the flame of virtue endures the blasts of envy.

True Vertue, firme, *will alwayes bide,*
By whatsoever suffrings *tride.*

By Labour, Vertue *may be gain'd ;*
By Vertue, Glorie *is attain'd.*

VIRTUE was heroic in its resistance to opposition, yet it was not socially exclusive: anyone who worked hard could win the crown of glory.

a civic muse, dedicated to the good society, and to his role in it. He was aware
of his limitations, setting out in verse 'Why I write not of love' (*Forest*, II), and
presenting himself in a comic light as an elderly, clumsy, overweight lover ('A
Celebration of Charis', and 'My Picture Left in Scotland': *Underwoods*, II, IX).
It is hard to conceive of Jonson's massive personality ever giving itself over
to another person, and when he writes love poems the convention of the
mistress on a pedestal returns (*Underwoods*, XX, XXI, XXIV). In the few
religious poems, however, we do find a personal involvement, as in 'To Heaven'
(*Forest*, XV), which starts from an immediate sense of guilt and sin:

> Good, and great God, can I not think of thee,
>   But it must straight my melancholy be?

With this sense of sin there is the fear of being 'exiled' from God, who only
now 'stoops' to reclaim him: 'Dwell, dwell here still', he implores.

The individual's relationship with God is the subject of three or four poems
by Jonson, but for George Herbert (1593–1633) it is the centre and circumference
of his whole existence as a poet, and as a country priest (for the last three
years of his life). His collection of 167 'Sacred Poems and Private Ejaculations',
entitled *The Temple*, was published after his death in 1633. Herbert called the
collection 'a picture of the many spiritual conflicts that have passed betwixt
God and my soul, before I could subject mine to the will of Jesus my master:
in whose service I have now found perfect freedom'. Many of the poems derive
from this pattern of struggle and acceptance. Herbert resembles both Jonson
and Donne in his dramatization of the Christian's dread of alienation from
God, as in 'The Collar', which begins from a note of frustration with a life
of virtue and service being apparently unrewarded: 'I struck the board [table],
and cried, No more. / I will abroad.' 'Deniall' starts from a crisis, the poet
being unable to reach God through prayer, and so experiencing 'fears / And
disorder'.

Both poems present separation from God as a state of confusion, and in
'Deniall' this dislocation of feeling finds its counterpart in the form of the
poem, for 'then was my heart broken, as was my verse': the last line of each
stanza does not rhyme. This striking effect, new in English poetry, shows
Herbert's sensitivity to form as the expression of content. As the poem develops
through the next four stanzas the unrhymed line sticks out like an excrescence,
creating and representing discord. Yet Herbert seldom ends his poems on a
note of frustration. The harmony of the poet and his work comes from a sense
of harmony with God, and the end of the poem prays, confidently, that God
will 'tune my heartless breast', so that His favours 'and my mind may chime, /
And mend my rhyme'. In 'The Collar' the discord lies rather in the movement
of feelings, the poet reaching a low point of depression in his sense of being
excluded from God's blessings: 'Is the year only lost to me? / Have I no bays
to crown it? / No flowers, no garlands gay? all blasted? / All wasted?' From

this stage of despair the poet resolves to abandon ethics and religion, catch up with 'double pleasures' for all he has missed, in future serve his own needs rather than other people's. Just at this point of hedonism and egoism the crisis is resolved, from above:

> But as I raved and grew more fierce and wild
> At every word,
> Me thought I heard one calling, *child*:
> And I replied, *My Lord*.

In Herbert the poem contains its experience, and one often has to wait for the last line to discover the resolution, or at times the discord, as in 'Grief', where after twelve anguished lines describing his sighs and tears Herbert turns against poetry itself:

> keep your measures for some lover's lute,
> Whose grief allows him music and a rhyme:
> For mine excludes both measure, tune, and time.
> Alas, my God!

That anguished cry, all that is left as the poem breaks down, is a striking effect, but not one that could be repeated. In fact Herbert followed the examples of Sidney and Donne in inventiveness, using some 111 different stanza forms, 98 of them being original to him.

The attitude of man to God in Herbert's poems is one of reverence, but also of love, a close and mutually sustaining relationship. Herbert must be one of the few poets who can call God 'my dear' without seeming presumptuous. In 'The Flower' he celebrates the recovery of divine grace after a period of alienation: 'How fresh, O Lord, how sweet and clean / Are thy returns!' His 'shrivelled heart', blasted by God's anger at his sins, is like the root of a flower, apparently killed by frost. Yet God can 'quicken' as well as kill, as Herbert records in one of the most perfectly simple and spontaneous stanzas in English poetry:

> And now in age I bud again,
> After so many deaths I live and write;
> I once more smell the dew and rain,
> And relish versing: O my only light,
> It cannot be
> That I am he
> On whom thy tempests fell all night.

If Herbert can dedicate his poems to God as 'my first fruits . . . / Yet not mine neither: for from thee they came, / And must return', he repaid the gift generously. This sense of talents being given to be used, of love as a gift-exchange, occurs in many of the poems, most memorably, appropriately enough, in the last poem of all, 'Love (III)': 'Love bade me welcome: yet my soul drew back, / Guilty of dust and sin.' God invites the Christian to partake of His grace in the Eucharist (which means 'thanksgiving') yet he feels himself unworthy: 'I the unkind, ungrateful? Ah my dear, / I cannot look on thee.' His misgivings finally disposed of, the poet wants at least to wait at table:

> 'My dear, then I will serve'.
> —'You must sit down,' says Love, and 'taste my meat':
> So I did sit and eat.

It is hard to imagine a more fitting conclusion to a collection that has shown in so many ways Herbert's faith in the reciprocal relationship of man and God.

In his harmonizing of form with content and feeling Herbert showed his originality yet also his debt to a tradition, that of the hieroglyphic or emblematic poem. Within the main section of *The Temple* the first poem is called 'The Altar', representing by its typography the shape of an altar. In 'Easter-Wings' the two stanzas reproduce the shape of a pair of wings, probably those of angels. Both poems allude to their shape and to their meaning. Herbert, drawing on a European tradition going back to the *Greek Anthology*, has fused visual and verbal planes: the language both describes and represents the image. In the tradition of emblem poetry these resources were handled

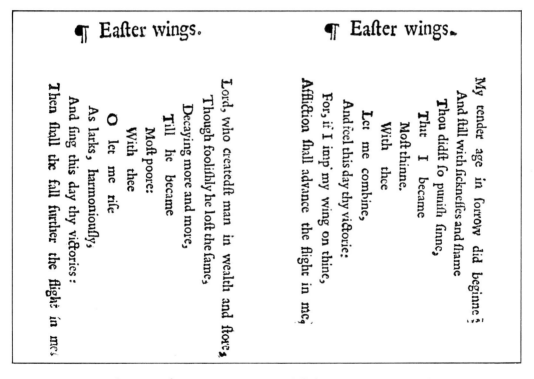

PATTERN POEMS: George Herbert, 'Easter Wings', modelled on 'Wings' by the Hellenistic poet Simias of Rhodes.

Quàm sordet mihi terra, dum cælum adspicio!

Dum Cælum aspicio, Solum despicio.

THE ENGLISH EMBLEM BOOKS, almost wholly adapted from continental models. Here Quarles and his engraver, William Marshall, have taken the image of St Ignatius Loyola standing on the globe, commemorating the Spanish missionaries to America, from a Dutch Jesuit emblem book *Typus Mundi* (Antwerp, 1627) and replaced it with the poet's soul regarding the sun, the bag of treasure and the Cupid on which she lies symbolizing her rejection of worldly vanities for higher things ('majora canamus'). The coat of arms hanging on the blasted tree, next to the poet's crown of laurel, is Quarles's, while the English villages named are the homes of Quarles (Roxwell) and his great friend the poet Edward Benlowes (Finchingfield).

separately. The emblem normally consists of three parts: a motto, a picture, and a verse. The motto was a proverb or *sententia*, usually of a single line; the picture represented the idea contained in the motto; and the poem brought out the relationship between the two. Emblem-books first appeared in England in the Elizabethan period, drawing on Italian and Dutch sources, and reached their peak of popularity in the seventeenth century. The *Emblems* (1635) and *Hieroglyphicks of the Life of Man* (1638) of Francis Quarles (1592–1644), reprinted together, formed the most popular book of poetry in the whole century. The popularity of the form was not due to its excellence, either as poetry or painting, indeed in some cases one feels we have the worst of both arts. The Christian emblem was valued for devotional and meditative purposes, the secular emblem because of its usefulness in inculcating moral lessons. 'For the emblem', as one writer put it, 'is properly a sweet and moral symbol,

Invidiosa Senectus.

which consists of picture and words, by which some weighty sentence is declared.' As in Jonson's poetry, or in the whole of Renaissance moral philosophy, Christian or secular, the heroic figures are types of virtue overcoming vice. The fable of Hercules at the crossroads was frequently represented as an allegory of all human ethical choice. The images, recurring throughout Europe in hundreds of collections, were simple, easily grasped: the laurel symbolizing crowns for victors or poets, the olive peace; the pelican feeding its young from its own breast as an emblem of Christ's self-sacrifice for us; the geometrical compass representing prudence or judgement; the palm-tree burdened with a heavy weight yet still flourishing as a symbol of perseverance, virtue overcoming opposition.

These images and their associations were familiar to all readers, and poets could invoke a whole chain of meaning by a brief allusion. In 'The Bunch of Grapes' Herbert draws on that symbol of Christ's sacrifice and Eucharist, while in 'Hope' he alludes to the familiar image of the anchor for Christian hope, 'spes fides', adding other symbols which take on meaning from their context—a watch, a prayer-book, a telescope, a vial of tears, unripe ears of corn, a ring. The thought of the poem is expressed through the images, but is not translated out explicitly. Other emblem writers, Quarles for instance, are prone to divide up their emblem into units which are then laboriously spelled out. In an emblem of the human soul being saved from shipwreck in the sea of the world by Divine Love, there is a simple series of one-to-one correspondences: ship = body; unfaithful pilot = the will; rope = prayer; anchor = hope, bucket = repentance; pump = his eye; cargo = corruption. The poem glosses the picture, but it does not develop an argument or form of its own.

A more successful use of the emblematic mode was made by Henry Vaughan (1621/2–95). His third collection, *Silex Scintillans* (1650) has a complex engraving of a hand (evidently of God) reaching down from the clouds holding a thunderbolt which has just struck a heart made of stone, from which flames ascend and tears drop down. In the Latin verse that follows Vaughan describes how God, out of love, has smashed his stony heart, turned it back into flesh,

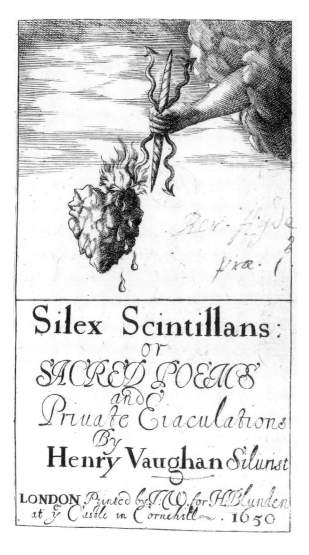

THOMAS VAUGHAN, emblematic frontispiece to *Silex Scintillans* (1650).

so that he is once more open to grace and to new life. 'The Palm tree' is a meditation on the traditional emblem of the tree which is 'pressed and bowed' with 'weights (like death / And sin)', but 'the more he's bent / The more he grows'. Vaughan then relates it to the palm-tree used in the building of Solomon's temple, the tree of immortality, the crowns of palm for the victors in the fight against evil, and with 'the patience of the Saints', which tree 'Is watered by their tears'. The basic image thus expands to create a larger meaning. In other poems the reference can be to a specific emblem illuminating just one stage. So in that lyric with the beautifully simple opening, 'They are all gone into the world of light! / And I alone sit lingring here', the contrast between darkness and light that runs through the poem is expressed in the eighth stanza in a new image. Here Vaughan draws directly from an emblem

Verità non può star sepolta.

AN EMBLEM FROM JACOB CATS, *Spiegel van den Ouden ende Nieuwen Tijdt* (s'Graven-Hage, 1632) taken over by Vaughan in 'They are all gone into the world of light!':

If a star were confined into a Tomb
    Her captive flames must needs burn there;
But when the hand that locked her up, gives room,
    She'll shine through all the sphere.

by the influential Dutch emblematist, Jacob Cats, to illustrate the belief that 'truth cannot be hid'.

Vaughan's individual voice emerges most strongly in poems dealing with childhood, where his desire to recapture that innocence may owe something to the Neoplatonic idea of the soul losing its purity by the descent into the body: 'Happy those early days! when I / Shined in my Angel-infancy' ('The Retreat'). There his soul had 'a white, celestial thought', and in contemplating a cloud or flower would 'in those weaker glories spy / Some shadows of eternity'. He longs 'to travel back' to the promised land, but as a later poem called 'Childhood' says, 'I cannot reach it; and my striving eye / Dazzles at it, as at eternity.' Vaughan wrote few wholly successful poems, although he is capable of striking openings, such as 'I saw Eternity the other night', and can at times sustain a complex argument. Yet too often inspiration vanishes, a poem runs out of ideas. His verse-movement, too, can be stiff and jerky, the flow of syntax being chopped up into long and short lines unanimated by any inner rhythm. Even in such interesting poems as 'Regeneration', 'The Resolve', or 'Church-Service' the movement of the iambics is too regular, too heavily stressed. Reading Vaughan we often recall Herbert's superior lyricism and organization.

The Schools of Jonson and Donne

Vaughan's homage to Herbert in *Silex Scintillans* was echoed by many poets who imitated the two great original voices. (Formerly these poets were grouped together under the title 'Metaphysical', a vague classification derived from the Augustans which erodes individuality.) Jonson did his own mythologizing in his lifetime, presiding over gatherings of younger poets in London taverns, even writing a poem to 'One that Asked to be Sealed of the Tribe of Ben' (*Underwoods*, XLVII). Of the ten or twelve poets who professed themselves his disciples the most considerable was Robert Herrick (1591–1674), a country parson who in his long career produced some 1,400 mostly short lyrics. In 'His Prayer to Ben Jonson' Herrick asks his patron to 'Make the way smooth for me' in his verse, and smoothness and grace are its abiding qualities. Herrick never wrote an ugly line, and if his lyrics are those of a miniaturist who seldom attempts larger issues, they satisfy by their coherence and poise. In the dedicatory poem to *Hesperides* (1648) he reveals an unusually self-aware delimitation of subject-matter to pastoral themes: 'I sing of brooks, blossoms, birds, and bowers . . . / I sing of May-poles, hock-carts, wassails, wakes . . . / I sing of times trans-shifting.' His world is a cosy one, of fires and meals indoors, harvest and summer festivals, with an agreeable sense of being looked after. His creature comforts are innocent pleasures, his friendships without ambition or pomp. There are many poems on the transience of flowers, and few poets mention death so often, or so lightly. The Englishness of setting and idiom can be deceptive, for Herrick was a diligent imitator of classical poets, from the 'terse muse' of Catullus to relaxed bucolics. A more passionate rhythm and a more urgent feeling are found in the religious poems in *His Noble Numbers* (1647), especially 'His Litany to the Holy Spirit'.

Jonson's influence made itself felt both in style and in subject-matter. In 'To Penshurst' Jonson virtually invented the genre of 'the country house poem', of which notable imitations are Herrick's 'The Hock-Cart, or Harvest Home', and 'To Saxham' by Thomas Carew (1594/5-1640). Carew's finest poem is his Elegy on Donne, a generous and perceptive tribute to one 'who ruled as he thought fit / The universal monarchy of wit'. Although notionally a follower of Donne, Carew still prefers themes of rejected or frustrated love, with titles like 'Ingratefull beauty' and 'Disdain returned', where Petrarchan attitudes reappear. The Cavalier (or royalist) poets, such as Sir John Suckling (1609-42), could imitate both Jonson and Donne, reproducing the former's asymmetrical verse-movement, as in 'For love grown cold or hot, / Is lust, or friendship, not / The thing we have'. In other poems this produces a jerkiness, while Donne's inversion of Petrarchan submission gestures turns coarse. 'If of her self she will not love, / Nothing can make her: / The devil take her', sounds like an oath at a drinking party. Suckling still retains Donne's combination of lyricism and cynicism: 'Out upon it, I have loved / Three whole days together; / And am like to prove three more, / If it prove fair weather.' But in the conclusion he sounds more like Don Giovanni: had it not been for her lovely face, 'There had been at least ere this / A dozen dozen in her place'. In the extension of this mode by Richard Lovelace (1618-58), the time-scale has been reduced further: 'Have I not loved thee much and long, / A tedious twelve hours space?' By the time of Rochester (1648-80) the duration of male constancy has been reduced to 'this live-long minute'.

In 'To Lucasta going beyond the Seas' Lovelace echoes Donne's movement but cannot reproduce the pressure and tension in the language or in the thought. Imitation could work in short bursts, but the poets of this period failed to evolve a style or mode of their own. Edmund Waller (1606-87) has a welcome simplicity in the shorter lyrics, with a tighter, more functional use of language than Carew, but in a longer poem, the 'Panegyrick to my Lord Protector', language and thought become vapid and flaccid. In elevating Cromwell he demeans both himself and poetry, for without the saving grace of irony as practised by Marvell, Waller becomes fatuous. In panegyric, patriotism is not enough. It is in the celebratory poems, especially the elegies, that the failure of inspiration and originality are most striking. In the work of Abraham Cowley (1618-67), a prolific poet who failed to write a single memorable poem, the elegy on William Harvey is a mass of clichés and unconvincing melodramatic gestures, that on Crashaw abounds (perhaps appropriately) in incredible hyperboles. Cowley's range was wide, from love poems, such as *The Mistress* (1647), a collection lacking wit, surprise, or feeling; to the *Pindaric Odes*, where Cowley adapts his usual diction and sentiments to the irregular and poorly understood stanzaic structure of Pindar; to the *Davideis, A Sacred Poem of the Troubles of David* (1656). In this worthy biblical pastiche, as in *Gondibert* (1650) by Sir William Davenant (1606-68), we see how a genre like the Renaissance epic can persist beyond its time, and be practised without conviction or need. It took the genius of Milton to show that the form was not wholly dead, but the more prophetic example was that of Samuel Butler, who in *Hudibras* (1663) brought new life to epic through parody and the mock-heroic (see chapter 5).

Butler's heirs were Swift and Gay; Denham and Waller were acknowledged as models for Dryden and Pope, so that in the death of one mode can lie the birth of others. But some literary modes failed to survive the slow transition from Renaissance to Restoration. Few poets have had such little impact as Richard Crashaw (*c.*1613-49), whether in his early love poems, *The Delights of the Muses* (1646) or in his religious poetry, *Carmen Deo Nostro* (1652). Crashaw's religious sensibility, his Anglo-Catholic ecstatic and exclamatory manner on such topics as the adoration of martyrs, must be shared if his poetry is to be enjoyed. Crashaw's intensity of feeling allows the reader no soft option, we too must celebrate 'mystick deaths', apostrophize a 'sweet incendiary!', ecstasize over St Teresa being martyred. She is 'love's victim' and his 'dart' or arrow will bring a welcome death: 'How kindly will thy gentle heart / Kiss the sweetly-killing dart!' The problem is that Crashaw's own reverence for the subject and her blessed state turns images of physical suffering into pleasing, or even erotic experiences, in a form of oxymoron or union of contraries: she shall 'complain / Of a sweet and subtle pain', the 'intolerable joys' of death. Yet Crashaw's control of language is not great enough to persuade or compel the reader to share his experience. Death will hold St Teresa 'close in his embrace', hugging 'Those delicious wounds', while her soul will melt 'Like a soft lump of incense, hasted / By too hot a fire'. The conceits seem intellectual, diagrammatic consolations, not felt human experiences. It may help to understand this poem by comparing it with Bernini's sculpture of St Teresa in ecstasy, and to relate both to the Baroque, but in Crashaw there are also traces of metaphysical wit without the energy needed to make it convincing.

The sense of a loss of coherence in religious poetry in the mid-seventeenth century is not limited to Catholicism. In Thomas Traherne (1637-74), a Church of England priest whose work was only discovered in the 1890s, we find a similar gap between the writer's convictions and his ability to render them convincingly. His worship of God and His creation is too often expressed in long series of exclamations, as in 'Love': 'O Mine of Rarities! O Kingdom Wide! / O more! O Cause of all! O Glorious Bride! / O God! O Bride of God! O King! / O Soul and Crown of evry Thing!' This ecstatic note becomes tiring, as do the lists of marvellous attributes of the godhead ('The Vision', 'Eden', 'Thoughts (II)', 'Christendom'). The law of diminishing returns dilutes our enjoyment of his excitement. Traherne's poetry gives the impression of having been written at great speed, out of a spontaneous consideration of a single topic. There seems to be little planning; his poems are not 'through-composed' but exist as a series of statements, each stanza often consisting of a single sentence or one long breath, divided across lines of varying lengths. At times only the rhymes remind us that we are reading poetry. There are very few memorable stanzas, or even lines.

Significantly Traherne is much more convincing in prose, where he can sustain a thought without having to worry about metre or rhythm. His *Centuries of Meditations* (groups of one hundred paragraphs) are in the didactic tradition of the meditation and resolve, analyses of a topic concluding in an admonition or resolution. But the third Century begins with a remarkable passage of autobiography and Neoplatonism, recalling an infant's pristine vision (of Herefordshire, in his case):

The corn was orient and immortal wheat, which never should be reaped, nor was ever sown. . . . The dust and stones of the street were as precious as gold. The gates were at first the end of the world. The green trees when I first saw them through one of the gates transported and ravished me; their sweetness and unusual beauty made my heart to leap, and almost mad with ecstasy, they were such strange and wonderful things.

Yet the child soon learns a wholly false set of values. The 'tinselled ware upon a hobby horse', 'a drum, a fine coat, a penny, a gilded book' represent the degraded worship of 'silly objects': 'so that with much ado I was corrupted, and made to learn the dirty devices of this world'. The 'celestial, great, and stable treasures' to which he was born were 'as wholly forgotten, as if they had never been'. With the help of religious meditation and poetry Traherne hopes to regain that pristine vision.

Autobiography

Traherne is not writing a straight autobiography, but a reflective-didactic treatise ('By this let nurses and parents learn . . .', 'By this you may see . . .'), in the exemplary tradition inaugurated by St Augustine's *Confessions*. The events recorded may be real or fictitious, their real purpose is to represent the aspirations and backslidings of a Christian for the benefit of readers who may meet the same problems and learn how to cope with them. The seventeenth century saw an outpouring of autobiographies (some two hundred have been counted, compared to fourteen in the previous century), many of them self-justifying works on behalf of the religious sects or political groups, and an equally dramatic rise in the number of diaries kept. This period marked a great step forward in self-analysis. One major influence was the Calvinist-Puritan stress on calling the self to account, keeping stock of one's spiritual and material state, those 'talents' given by God (following 2 Corinthians 13: 5: 'Examine yourselves, whether ye be in the faith; prove your own selves').

The most dramatic example is *Grace Abounding to the Chief of Sinners* (1666) by John Bunyan (1628-88), a 'relation of the work of God upon my own soul . . . wherein you may perceive my castings down, and raisings up'.

His work falls into the conventional three-part pattern of conversion narratives: conversion; calling; ministry. The greater part is given to his struggle to defeat the devil, who is presented as a fully realized physical presence, disturbing Bunyan at prayer as if he were pulling his clothes to make him stop. Bunyan describes his oscillations between faith and despair with unequalled vividness, being 'assaulted and perplexed' by doubt, his mental agonies affecting his body: 'my conscience now was sore, and would smart at every touch; I could not now tell how to speak my words, for fear I should misplace them.' Another time he has been ready to 'hold my mouth from opening' lest it speak sinfully, or 'leap with my head downward, into some muckhill hole or other'. His sense of the critical moments in life, of salvation or perdition, comes out best of all in the account of what might seem to us a harmless game, tip-cat:

But the same day, as I was in the midst of a game of cat, and having struck it one blow from the hole, just as I was about to strike it the second time, a voice did suddenly dart from heaven into my soul, which said, wilt thou leave thy sins and go to heaven, or have thy sins and go to hell?

Although he could see 'with the eyes of my understanding . . . the Lord Jesus looking down upon me', Bunyan continued to 'take my fill of sin', until the desire to reform came upon him again.

This narrative of success and failure, advance and backsliding, makes compulsive reading through the urgency and simplicity with which it is told. Yet 'great sins do draw out great grace', and when Bunyan discovers 'the love and mercy of God' his ecstasy, too, is conveyed with a directness that many poets might envy: 'I could not tell how to contain [it] till I got home; I thought I could have spoken of his love, and of his mercy to me, even to the very crows that sat upon the ploughed lands before me, had they been capable to have understood.' Gripped as we are by the marvellously intense and physical rendering of experience, we do not at first notice the extreme vagueness of the setting. There are virtually no names of counties, towns, places; people are referred to as 'a young man', '3 or 4 poor women'; there are two references to 'my wife', one of them to her being in labour, yet we never learn whether she gave birth, or what sex the baby was. Bunyan consciously chose not to diminish the applicability of his experience to other Christians facing similar struggles. The individual soul must make its own settlement with God, and the conclusion records both the joy of a 'dead and dry' heart being reclaimed by Christ and the 'insufficiency of all inherent righteousness', the need for a continual struggle. Yet the seventeenth-century religious autobiography never records failure: it is, by definition, a success story.

In secular narratives contemporary readers also expected something of general application, of use to them in their own lives. When Sir Thomas Browne (1605–82) published his *Religio medici* in 1643, Kenelm Digby criticized him for 'making so particular a narration of personal things, and private thoughts of his own; the knowledge whereof cannot much conduce to any man's betterment'. The criticism is true, but misplaced, since Browne set out not to be exemplary but wholly idiosyncratic. As he wrote, 'the world that I regard is my self; it is the microcosm of my own frame that I cast mine eye on; for the other, I use it but like the globe, and turn it round sometimes for my recreation'. Browne is 'averse from nothing', can 'sympathize with all things', believe in witches, spirits, or anything else, one sometimes thinks, just as long as it is difficult or paradoxical enough:

As for those wingy mysteries in divinity, and airy subtleties in religion, which have unhinged the brains of better heads, they never stretched the *pia mater* of mine. Methinks there be not impossibilities enough in religion for an active faith. . . . I love to lose myself in a mystery, to pursue my reason to an O *altitudo!*

Although Browne sets out to declare his religious faith, he does not attempt to justify it in the usual ways, by argument, by citation of biblical texts, or by a narrative of his own conversion. He writes instead of the pleasure he gains from losing himself in mysteries, finding it a 'solitary recreation' to consider the 'involved enigmas and riddles of the Trinity, with incarnation and resurrection'. In celebrating 'the humour of my irregular self', rather than being self-analytical, Browne becomes self-regarding. Yet his egotism is so naïve that it is impossible to be cross with a man wholly unaware of his wish to stand out: 'my desires only are . . . to be but the last man, and bring up the rear in heaven.'

Unique in personality, Browne is so in style, developing a way of writing that is equally flexible. Sentences and paragraphs are constructed on the principle of parataxis (adding on items with an 'and' or 'also') not hypotaxis (subordinating minor clauses to the major ones), and this aggregative manner allows Browne to follow his thoughts wherever they take him. Human life is fragile, he writes, 'it is in the power of every hand to destroy us, and'—the co-ordinating conjunction conceals the paradox—'we are beholding unto every one we meet, he doth not kill us'. (That is typical of Browne's pursuit of an idea.) This paratactic movement cumulatively gives each sentence a separate existence, as if they too, like their maker, were anxious to retain their independence. In general the style of *Religio medici* is informal, apparently unstudied. More elaborate effects are provided by *Hydriotaphia. Urn-Burial or a discourse of the sepulchral urnes lately found in Norfolk* (1658), especially the fifth chapter, a meditation on death that has been praised by critics since Lamb for its 'music' and 'sonority', compared to Isolde's Liebestod or to purple robes. There are flashes of plangency and pathos, but the content of thought is out of proportion to the elaboration of the style, while the meditative pose produces a meandering collection of self-contained sentences, each aspiring to the oracular or enigmatic.

Burton and Hobbes: Chaos and Order

The reader of Browne may often exclaim 'more matter, and less art!' The reader of *The Anatomy of Melancholy* (1621; revised in the five following editions up to 1651-2) by Robert Burton (1577-1640) may well wonder if any art at all has been lavished on this prose style, which teems with lists, names, Latin quotations (up to ten per page), book and chapter references, and flaunts

ROBERT BURTON, *Anatomy of Melancholy* (1628). Each panel represents emblems of the symptoms or attributes of melancholy. In the upper row, *left*, is *Zelotipia* or sexual jealousy, including two fighting cocks. In the *centre* is Democritus of Abdera meditating, surrounded by the skins of animals which he has anatomized to find 'the seat of black choler': in the sky is the sign of Saturn, 'Lord of Melancholy'. On the *right* is *Solitudo*, the symbolic animals including a sleeping dog, a hare (timorous and melancholy) in the 'desert', and owls hovering over 'shady bowers' in 'melancholy darkness'. *Centre left* a lovesick melancholic, with the traditional folded arms and hat pulled over his eyes, the 'lute and books' as 'symptoms of his vanity'; *centre right* the hypochondriac melancholic, chin resting on his hand (sign of inactivity), pots and glasses from the apothecary all around him. *Lower left* is a superstitious and idolatrous monk telling his beads; *lower right* a madman in rags shackled to the floor. Below them are the herbs borage and hellebore, 'sovereign plants to purge the veins ... and chear the heart' of its black fumes. The portrait is of the author as Democritus Junior, intending to revive and complete the work of his great predecessor. (Quotations are from the poem Burton wrote to gloss the engraving.)

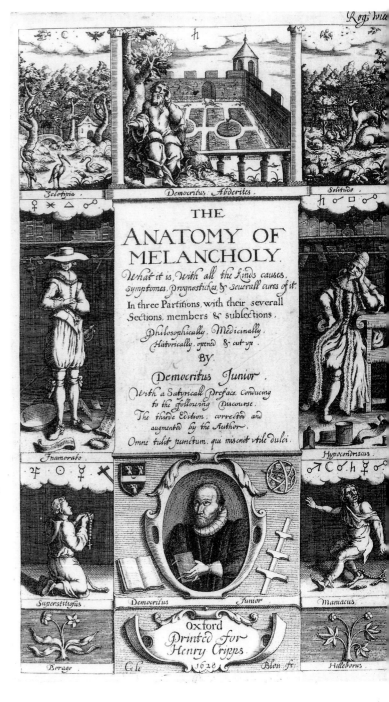

its lack of design. In the 'satirical preface' (itself as long as *Religio medici*), under the *persona* of 'Democritus junior' Burton gives a devastatingly candid account of his own style:

And for those other faults of barbarism, Dorick dialect, extemporanean style, tautologies, apish imitation, a rhapsody of rags gathered together from several dunghills, excrements of authors, toys and fopperies, confusedly tumbled out, without art, invention, judgment, wit, learning, harsh, raw, rude, phantastical, absurd, insolent, indiscreet, ill-composed, indigested, vain scurrile, idle, dull and dry, I confess all ('tis partly affected) thou canst not think worse of me than I do myself.

Despite the attempt to deflect criticism (''tis partly affected') that remains an accurate account of Burton's style. His work is organized clearly in outline, the 'anatomy' being carried out through an elaborate sequence of division into partitions, sections, members, and subsections, but in texture it lacks all design. Burton's *Anatomy* is a perfect example of the virtues and vices of the Renaissance commonplace-book technique, in which readers indexed their reading by subject. The wider the reading, the larger the notebooks—in Burton's case they must have been huge—but the more discipline and judgement needed if the author is not to give the impression of having emptied his notes on to

JOHN EVELYN, aged twenty-eight (in 1648), painted by Robert Walker. Evelyn is shown as an aesthete and philosopher in idealized dress, his head resting on one hand in the classic melancholy pose, the other touching the emblem of mortality. Above is a motto in Greek reading 'Repentance is the beginning of philosophy'. His *Diary*, kept between 1631 and 1684, is an invaluable record of events, especially contemporary religion, politics, and science.

paper. Burton does have some passages of his own composition, but here the imagery is often negative, the attitudes coarse and abusive. The *Anatomy* remains an important source of information for Renaissance ideas about melancholy, but in the history of English prose style it is a dead-end.

After Burton's sprawling collection it is a relief to turn to *Leviathan* (1651) by Thomas Hobbes (1588–1679), a work of remarkable lucidity. Here a unified subject-matter produces a unity of form and style, as a few basic assumptions are developed by almost geometrical reasoning to create a whole philosophy of man and society. For Hobbes human beings are inherently acquisitive, acting solely by self-interest with no thought of love, altruism, or ethics. Given man's selfish and warring instincts he must be restrained by civil society from lapsing into a state of 'mere nature' or anarchy, where life would be 'nasty, brutish, and short'. Given the need for a state, it must have a hierarchy controlled by a sovereign with absolute power, to whom the Church is wholly subordinate. The individual, having once opted for membership of this society, must resign himself absolutely to the king and his officers. The subordination of the individual to the whole is symbolized in the great central image of the book, society as a living organism, whose head is the ruler. Like the emblem-writers, Hobbes spells out each part of the analogy. The Leviathan or commonwealth is 'an artificial man', sovereignty is its soul, the magistrates are its joints, 'reward and punishment, by which fastened to the seat of the sovereignty every joint and member is moved to perform his duty, are the nerves that do the same in the body natural'. Concord is its healthy state, 'sedition, sickness, and civil war, death'. His use of this old idea or allegory, which goes back to the Greeks and was common in medieval political thought, is a perfect example of the persuasive or coercive power of metaphor, even though Hobbes rejected metaphor as deception. Similarly, although he attacked absolutes, advocating moral relativism, his own system is as absolute as could be. True, it would eliminate controversy and dissent; but it would also eliminate all political activity, reducing the individual to a mute presence in society. Peace can be preserved at too high a cost.

John Milton

Hobbes was a royalist, and wrote *Leviathan* during his exile in Paris with the court of Charles II. The rigidity of his system shows his fear of discord, his wish to re-establish authority being so strong that it could not tolerate

THE ALLEGORICAL FRONTISPIECE TO *LEVIATHAN*, evidently designed by Hobbes himself. The ruler, literally made up out of the bodies of his subjects, appears beneath a text from the Vulgate (Job 1:24), 'There is no power on earth which can be compared to him.' The panels contain illustrations corresponding to the emblems of civic and ecclesiastical power that he holds, the sword and the crozier. On the *left*, a castle, a coronet, a cannon, a trophy of arms, and a battle; on the *right*, a church, a bishop's mitre, and a thunderbolt. In the fourth panel is a trident lettered *Syl./logis./me*; a bull's horns lettered *Di/lem/ma*; one fork *Spiritual* and *Temporal*; another *Real* and *Intentional*. As an extension of these logical terms the bottom panel represents a disputation. While the ruler's face has been thought to resemble both Charles I and Oliver Cromwell, it has recently been claimed to represent Hobbes himself.

disagreement. A totally different response to those troubled times, expressing courage and boldness, was *Areopagitica, a speech for the liberty of unlicensed printing, to the parliament of England* (1644), by John Milton (1608–74). Between 1641 and 1660 Milton produced at least eighteen major prose works on behalf of the Puritan rebellion, supporting its cause, vilifying its enemies. His active involvement in political and religious controversy shows him accepting the ethos of the *vita activa* (which the commonwealth party embraced with much more fervour than the royalists). In his defence of free speech Milton deploys a range of resources greater than that of any other prose-writer of his age, from inspiring metaphors to coarse abuse. In place of restrictive censorship, which would mean 'a perpetual childhood of prescription', Milton appeals to God's gift of reason to man 'to be his own chooser', for 'reason is but choosing'. Since 'good and evil . . . in the field of this world grow up together almost inseparably', then we need to know evil in order to be able to reject it by a deliberate act of will:

He that can apprehend and consider vice with all her baits and seeming pleasures, and yet . . . prefer that which is truly better, he is the true warfaring Christian. I cannot praise a fugitive and cloistered virtue, unexercised and unbreathed, that never sallies out and seeks her adversary, but slinks out of the race, where that immortal garland is to be run for, not without dust and heat.

Milton's concept of life 'in this world of evil' is one of struggle and testing: any praise for 'well doing' would be destroyed if people were protected from temptation. Human beings are responsible for their actions, as are nations. The intellectual ferment in contemporary England would stagnate if knowledge were to be subject to strict controls like broadcloth or woolpacks. The condition of all intellectual progress is 'liberty, the nurse of all great wits', the free exchange of ideas. The final sentence sums up Milton's argument memorably: 'Give me the liberty to know, to utter, and to argue freely according to conscience, above all liberties.' The strength of utterance of this work, its grasp of colloquial English style coupled with resonant rhetorical appeals, makes it outstanding in Milton's prose. In the other works, although one can detect a falling-off of imaginative vitality in the 1650s (Milton had gone blind in 1652, and it is much harder to dictate and correct prose than poetry), the modern reader willing to re-create something of the contemporary context will find in the works of the 1640s a massive intellect serving its chosen cause in prose whose unpredictable energies have yet to be fully appreciated.

In all his writings Milton was able to draw on an extensive education—or, as he would regard it, preparation for becoming a poet. Seven years at Cambridge, seven years' further study, a year's travel in Italy, all this time devoted to the Bible and theology, literature and philosophy, in Latin, Greek, Italian, and English, constituted a deliberate course of self-shaping for the task. Yet, despite his vast knowledge Milton was a determinedly English writer. His learning had been properly 'digested', and does not obtrude in the form of quotations in foreign languages or self-display. The linguistic spectrum of the prose works, from withering sarcasm to inspirational eloquence, is a sign of the appropriate fitting of style to subject-matter, or decorum, which he called 'the grand masterpiece to observe'. In poetry the eloquent end of the spectrum was developed with an easy lyricism and natural movement that generations of poets were to envy and imitate.

His first considerable poem in English, 'On the morning of Christ's nativity' (written 1629), draws on a wide range of models and absorbs other poetic influences, yet creating a distinctly English music. While not without some awkward conceits, and a lack of invention in syntax (such as the co-ordinating use of 'and' at the beginning of lines, used 34 times in 31 stanzas) the 'Nativity Ode' establishes a lyrical mode that was extended in 'L'Allegro' and 'Il Penseroso' (*c.*1631). This pair of poems juxtaposes the cheerful and the thoughtful man, the one rejoicing in mirth, dance, pastoral landscape, feasting, and comedy; the other in melancholy, contemplative withdrawal, study, tragedy, and a solitary existence. While notionally opposed, as in the debate or dispute tradition, the two are really complementary, dividing all legitimate pleasures into the public and private spheres. Both give great prominence to music.

Milton never lost his love of music, but the 'sweetness' or pleasure enjoyed here came to be tempered with sterner attitudes, given the Renaissance opposition between virtue and pleasure. This opposition is one of the clues to the right interpretation of *Comus. A Masque presented at Ludlow Castle* in 1634. In this, his longest poem so far (just over 1,000 lines) Milton presents the evil world of Comus, offspring of Bacchus and Circe, who haunts an 'ominous wood'. He lures travellers into drinking a magic potion that turns them into monsters who abandon their friends and 'roll with pleasure in the sensual sty'. Comus has many of the stock attributes of the tempter figure, specious reasoning (''Tis only daylight that makes sin'), a debased eloquence that can deceive the unwary, and a degraded conception of the human body as made only for sensual pleasure. His rhetorical question,

> Wherefore did Nature pour her bounties forth,
> With such a full and unwithdrawing hand
> . . . .
> But all to please, and sate the curious taste?

has deceived some critics into making him the hero of the piece, but a Renaissance reader would regard that and his other arguments (virginity is but a name; beauty must not be hoarded but enjoyed with me, here and now) with contempt. The Lady, captured and tempted by Comus, rejects his 'false rules' and specious arguments with no difficulty. Nature's abundance is meant for those who live 'according to her sober laws', while his bestial indulgence is set below 'the sage / And serious doctrine of virginity', that is, chastity and

WILLIAM BLAKE, illustration for Milton's *Comus*: 'Comus and his Revellers', water-colour, made for Thomas Butts, probably about 1815. Blake clearly responds to Milton's juxtaposition of innocence and corruption, giving Comus and his transformed animals a sinister grace.

marriage. *Comus* embodies the ethic of *Areopagitica*, that praise of God's providence, who 'pours out before us even to a profuseness all desirable things, and gives us minds' that can choose temperance and justice.

The temptation of pleasure is central to *Comus*, but only one element in Milton's next major poem, *Lycidas* (1637), published with other elegies to the memory of Edward King, a friend and colleague who had drowned on a journey to Ireland. Milton casts his compressed monody (193 lines) in the form of pastoral lament, with several deliberate echoes of Theocritus and Virgil. As in the earlier pair of poems, Milton is able to modulate from natural to literary pastoral ('Meantime the rural ditties were not mute, / Tempered to the oaten flute'), while developing a more resonant register that looks forward to the later verse. The fairly loose form allows Milton to introduce two episodes, in the first of which, like Herbert in 'The Collar', he questions the value of dedication to one's task. Why should one 'strictly meditate the thankless muse', instead of indulging in amorous pleasure? The poet's answer is the orthodox Renaissance humanist belief that 'Fame is the spur that the clear spirit doth raise . . . / To scorn delights, and live laborious days'—but with the bitter addition that before we can attain it on earth death will destroy us. To settle this mood of despair, where Herbert had invoked God, Milton introduces Apollo to remind us that the ultimate rewards for virtue must come in heaven not on earth. The second episode brings on a figure designed to provide not consolation but criticism, St Peter taking on the role announced in the subtitle of foretelling 'the ruin of our corrupted clergy then in their height'. The saint attacks the corrupt bishops of the Laudian Church, and Catholic proselytism, threatening them both with the 'two-handed engine' of retribution. These messages delivered, Milton returns to the pastoral mode with a sequence of images that reverses the pattern of sinking and drowning in the first part of the poem, with a vision of Lycidas rising, like the stars, to heaven. And then, in a daring extension of the conventions of pastoral, Milton adds a final eight-line stanza in which he himself, 'the uncouth swain' figures, having turned his 'eager thought into Doric lay', rising in the evening light in his blue gown (the colour of hope) before moving on, 'Tomorrow to fresh woods, and pastures new'.

The pastures of poetry that lay before Milton were not rich: a number of Latin poems occasioned by his Italian journey, and a series of twelve sonnets between 1642 and 1658 inspired by contemporary politics. It was not until 1667 that Milton published his masterpiece, following twenty years of service to the commonwealth, after more years of study and preparation—his wife and daughters reading aloud to him and taking down his poetry from dictation. Here again temptation plays a major role, in the figures of Satan, Adam, and Eve. If we classify *Paradise Lost* as an epic, in Renaissance terms it is anomalous, for according to contemporary theory epic should present heroic deeds in order to inflame its readers to virtuous emulation. The myths of the fall of the angels and the fall of man left very few admirable roles, and it is perhaps for this reason that Milton originally conceived it as a tragedy. In Christian terms the fall of man is a tragic disaster, and Milton dramatizes Eve's sin on a terrestrial scale. When she plucks the apple 'Earth felt the wound', nature groans at the loss (IX. 780). Yet it is also only a stage in a longer narrative that culminates in Christ's Crucifixion and redemption. While choosing to end with the expulsion of Adam and Eve from paradise Milton allowed himself sufficient narrative freedom to introduce Christ interceding with God on behalf of man (XI. 20 ff.), and opened up vistas of space and time that break through all literary categories.

Paradise Lost is an epic without a hero. Some modern critics, following the anti-authoritarian remark of Blake ('Milton was of the devil's party without knowing it') have turned Satan into the poem's hero. But this is to miss a hundred places where the language and the action show Satan to be another Comus figure, only more dangerous. Like Comus, Satan is given 'well-placed words of glozing courtesy / Baited with reasons not unplausible', but now

Milton constantly undermines his *persona*. Satan is discovered at the opening of Book I lying in hell with 'his horrid crew . . . vanquished . . . Confounded', tormented by thoughts 'of lost happiness and lasting pain'. Milton sets up a double, ironic perspective, giving us an observer's view of his painful and humiliated condition together with Satan's specious versions of it. What we see as 'obdurate pride and steadfast hate' (I. 58) he describes as a 'fixed mind / And high disdain' (97–8). His defiant words sound heroic but ring hollow, since the fallen angels' consignment to Hell is irrevocable:

> What though the field be lost?
> All is not lost; the unconquerable will,
> And study of revenge, immortal hate,
> And courage never to submit or yield.   (I. 105–8)

Satan moves from the glamour of their attack on God to the glamour of their defiance, missing out the unpleasant details of defeat, 'the apostate angel . . . / Vaunting aloud, but racked with deep despair' (I. 125–6). Like all Renaissance writers, Milton expects his readers to recognize evil and detest it, but he adds his own moral judgements to reinforce ours. Since the fallen angels represent the greatest evil in God's creation, their resolution—'ever to do ill our sole delight' (I. 160)—only makes them the more vicious.

In his inversion of normal epic, Milton uses a whole repertoire of devices to make evil look both sinister and ridiculous. The fallen angels' rhetoric is feeble and empty, a manipulation of words with no power over deeds. Their arguments are shown up as being based on the misuse of logic. 'Better to reign in hell than serve in heaven' (I. 263) sounds grand, but it is only making the best of a bad job. Satan even argues that in hell, 'where there is . . . no good / For which to strive', there will be no strife (II. 30–1), a conclusion that only shows up the awful fate embodied in the premiss. The assembly of rebel angels is a marvellous mixture of degradation, absurdity, futility, all with a patina of false grandeur. Their speeches are riddled with logical fallacies, as when Moloc says that although the descent from heaven was hard, 'ascent is easy', (II. 81), recalling to many of his readers a famous passage in the *Aeneid* which says exactly the opposite. Belial is first dismissed by Milton, invoking the standards of the *vita activa*, for recommending 'ignoble ease and peaceful sloth', and then wholly exposed as 'false and hollow' (II. 111). Mammon is rapturously received, 'Advising peace: for such another field / They dreaded worse than hell' (II. 292–3). This comic, anti-heroic conclusion, an inversion of all the responses to heroic speeches in Homer, Virgil, or Shakespeare, typifies Milton's remarkably sustained deflation of these evil beings.

True, Satan is described in epic similes, but only to give a delusive appearance of greatness. Milton describes 'his ponderous shield' in terms reminiscent of Homer's Achilles, but to Satan, defeated warrior who will never fight again, it is useless. His spear, tall as a Norwegian pine, is no longer a weapon but an improvised walking stick, 'to support uneasy steps / Over the burning marl' (I. 295-6). Greater, and more absurd discomfort awaits Satan when he seizes the role of main actor in the plan to seduce mankind. He brings the debate to an abrupt end (before anyone else can steal the limelight!) and sets off towards earth. His journey starts on a heroic note: 'his sail-broad vans / He spreads for flight'—but he is soon at the mercy of the elements, sinking in an airpocket some 60,000 feet, 'fluttering his pennons vain' (II. 927-33). Recovering, he has to pass through quick-sands, bogs, and other obstacles that reduce his progress to a desperate scramble, using whatever part of his body he can:

> O'er bog or steep, through straight, rough, dense, or rare,
> With head, hands, wings or feet pursues his way,
> And swims or sinks, or wades, or creeps, or flies.   (II. 947-9)

As a pseudo-hero Satan is always deflated by being set against the epic form. The comic bathos there points on to the mock-heroic vein of the Augustans, and was imitated for the debased athletic contests in Pope's *Dunciad*.

Satan is still an evil and dangerous figure, although Milton reminds us of the wider perspective of God's plan to redeem mankind's sin through the sacrifice of Christ. The fall of man is presented in two stages, Books IV and IX, the action being interrupted by God's sending Raphael to warn Adam and to remind him of what is at stake, so as 'to render man inexcusable' should he still believe Satan. The interruption in the action destroys the drama, but allows Milton to widen the theological and historical span. The narrative of Adam and Eve shows this blind poet's powers at their fullest, in the luxuriant description of paradise, embodying 'nature's whole wealth' of trees, flowers, herbs, animals. Yet this paradise already contains its invisible worm, for Satan has entered, 'as when a prowling wolf, / Whom hunger drives . . .'—the epic simile now has no trace of even the mock-heroic—'So clomb this first grand thief into God's fold' (IV. 192). Here we see the whole sequence through Satan's eyes, which register anguish at being excluded from this 'enormous bliss', and a wish to destroy their fragile joys. The presence of Satan on this second night of creation is a vicious counterpoint to the poet's apostrophe to 'wedded love' and his own protective intervention: 'Sleep on / Blest pair.' The guardian angels protecting paradise come too late, finding Satan 'Squat like a toad, close at the ear of Eve', pouring his evil into her 'phantasms and dreams' (IV. 799 ff.). When Eve tells Adam her dream next day Milton marvellously recreates Satan's temptation, insinuating and insistent in its specious repetition of such words as 'sweet', 'taste', 'fair', 'gods', 'good', 'happy', 'life' (V. 50 ff.), the vocabulary of Comus and all other corrupters.

It is not until Book IX that Milton changes his 'notes to tragic' and takes up again the temptation. Satan returns, delighted to find 'Eve separate', and urges that breaking God's command would be a 'petty trespass' which would show 'dauntless virtue' and make them 'be as gods'. His words, 'replete with

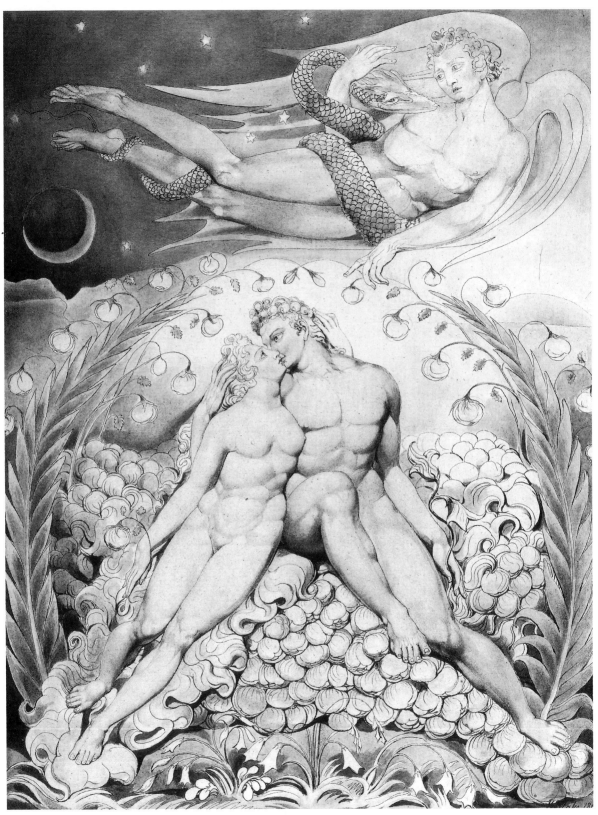

WILLIAM BLAKE, illustration for *Paradise Lost*: 'Satan watching the endearments of Adam and Eve', water-colour, made for Butts in 1807. Satan embraces the serpent, gazing wistfully at 'the loveliest pair / That ever since in love's embraces met ... so lively shines / In them divine resemblance.'

guile / Into her heart too easy entrance won' (like Comus, able to deceive 'the easy-hearted'), and in a masterly sequence (IX. 745 ff.) Milton gives Eve a soliloquy in which she rephrases in her own words the gist of Satan's speeches, full of false premisses and conclusions, leading to the fatal act, as she greedily 'engorged without restraint, / And knew not eating death'. Returning with 'bland words' to Adam, she reveals what she has done, being met with his shocked lament for her, 'on a sudden lost, / Defaced, deflowered, and now to death devote'. Out of love Adam, in full knowledge of what he is doing, 'not deceived' by Satan but—Milton adds, allocating responsibility—'fondly over-come with female charm', eats the fruit. As with Eve's transgression, 'nature gave a second groan' at this 'completing of the mortal sin / Original'. Now the fall is only too visible. Where they had that night celebrated 'the rites / Mysterious of connubial love', now they 'cast lascivious eyes' on each other, burning with lust. Nor is the discord reserved to the human plane. Our first view of them was idyllic, sitting at their 'supper fruits' while 'About them frisking played / All beasts of the earth' (IV. 325 ff.). In savage contrast, 'Beast now with beast gan war, and fowl with fowl', leaving off grazing herbs to devour each other (X. 707 ff.). Chaos has come again.

Paradise Lost succeeds where Milton is able to address great events and great issues in an immediate, concrete way. The scenes with Satan and the fallen angels, the temptation in Eden, offer material which is vividly dramatic, yet could not have been treated so effectively in drama. The presence of Milton as narrator and producer, simultaneously directing events and retelling them, becoming at key moments an impassioned but helpless spectator, as in his outburst when Eve goes off to do her work, promising to return by noon—

> O much deceived, much failing, hapless Eve,
> Of thy presumed return! Event perverse!
> Thou never from that hour in Paradise
> Found'st either sweet repast, or sound repose . . .   (IX. 404-7)

—this involvement of the poet in the poem adds a level of meaning that would be lost in the theatre. Equally, the use of Satan as both character and point of view, a technique more like that of the novel, justifies Milton's decision to write an epic poem. Such a vast creation is not always equally inspired, but, as Dr Johnson defended it, 'a palace must have passages'. For many modern readers the least successful parts are the war in heaven (Book VI), a sequence where a failure of imagination or judgement produced much that now seems grotesque, and the sections of didactic exposition or recapitulation. Milton's ultimate purpose was 'to justify the ways of God to men', and his defence of the divine plan in every instance creates problems. Nevertheless, it remains the greatest single achievement of the seventeenth century, and has inspired much outstanding scholarship and criticism in our time. Few poems more deserve, or more repay, prolonged study.

Milton treated temptation and fortitude in two other long poems, *Samson Agonistes* (date uncertain; 1647–53?) and *Paradise Regained* (1667–70), both based on relatively short biblical texts (Judges 16: 4–31; Luke 4: 1–13). But in both the heroes, Samson and Christ, triumph, and belong more to the exemplary pattern of normal Renaissance epic, even though the first is written in the form of a classical tragedy. Samson has suffered a tragic reversal, once 'great deliverer' of his people but now 'Eyeless in Gaza at the mill with slaves'. His betrayer Dalila returns with feigned repentance but is rejected, an episode that shows Samson's constancy. His fortitude is shown in the encounter with the giant Harapha, while in his destruction of the temple with all the Philistines his readiness 'to destroy and be destroyed' proves his strength and courage. The judgements passed on his act are all approving. His 'virtue given for lost . . . Revives, reflourishes'; he 'heroicly hath finished / A life heroic'. Yet the unanimity points up one of the weaknesses of this poem, its programmatic nature, lacking inner tension or complexity.

The same demonstrative, exemplary intent is announced at the opening of *Paradise Regained*, to celebrate Christ's rejection of the devil's tempting: his 'firm obedience' tested, 'the tempter foiled / In all his wiles'. Satan—the word means 'adversary' in Hebrew—appears to Christ in the wilderness disguised as an old man, but Christ immediately sees through the pretence, thus unfortunately ruining the dramatic possibilities and reducing the poem to a debate or battle of wits. Milton undercuts Satan in various ways, but without the brilliant ironies of *Paradise Lost*, and he nowhere reaches the dangerous level of his corruption of Eve. The basic weakness is again a lack of conflict, for we never think for a moment that Christ will yield, and the successive humiliations of Satan turn him into a butt, rather like the Falstaff of *The Merry Wives of Windsor*. At the opening of Book III Satan has been made speechless by Christ's reply, 'confounded . . . confuted and convinced / Of his weak arguing'. At the opening of the next book he is again 'perplexed' by his 'bad success', his 'persuasive rhetoric', that had deceived Eve, now powerless. Satan is even made, somewhat unconvincingly, to praise Christ as being 'Proof against all temptation as a rock / Of adamant'. When Satan took Christ up to the 'highest pinnacle', Christ it was who stood while Satan 'fell' (the word five times repeated), dropping back into hell as Christ ascended to heaven, where 'angelic choirs / Sung heavenly anthems of his victory'. The reader's verdict on this temptation must be 'no contest', since for our involvement with a hero to take place there must at least be the possibility of danger and defeat. In the end these poems even fail in the exemplary mode, for the heroes are too far beyond our scope. Few of us can hope to emulate Samson, or Christ.

Bunyan and Marvell

Paradise Lost ends with the expulsion of Adam and Eve from paradise. The other great religious work of the seventeenth century reverses this movement, in *The Pilgrim's Progress from This World, to that which is to come: Delivered under the Similitude of a Dream* (1678). Bunyan's book, written while he was in prison as a Baptist preacher, involves the reader to a degree that Milton never achieved in his two lesser epics, for the characters are ordinary human beings, like ourselves, and their goal of saving their souls is one that every individual can share, even if only in the 'willing suspension of disbelief' needed when reading works based on a creed not our own. The events are recounted by a narrator, the dreamer figure from medieval allegory, but the story is vivid and universal. This allegory does not work on multiple levels, with the literal level representing a series of abstractions, rather, each episode has a moral significance. Bunyan introduces personified types—Mr Worldly-Wiseman, Mr Facing-Both-ways—but his story never loses its grasp on everyday reality. It begins dramatically, with 'a man clothed in rags', 'a great burden on his back' (human sin, we subsequently learn), trembling and weeping as he reads a book,

THE CHRISTIAN PILGRIM AND HIS GUIDE. Frontispiece (by Francis Barlow) to William Denny's *Pelecanicidium: or the Christian Adviser against Self-Murder* (1653).

Wise Traveller through Wildernesse does lead
The Christian Pilgrim, teaching where to tread?
From Feind in World's Way Foes he warnes his Freind.
Through Deepe, up Steepe, shewes Heav'n's his Journeys end?
F. Barlow fecit.

and asking '*What shall I do to be saved?*' He is Christian, previously called Graceless, who has learned from the Bible that the world will be destroyed at the last day, and wants to find heaven. He decides to set off in its quest, leaving behind his wife and children, since they are in love with this world and its 'foolish delights'. (This is the right action in theological terms, since each individual must save his own soul, but some may have found it heartless, for Bunyan published a sequel in 1684 showing how Christian's wife and children followed him.)

Christian's journey is both external and internal. It lies through a realistically imagined landscape, at once actual and symbolic (the Slough of Despond, the Hill Difficulty, the Valley of Humiliation, Doubting Castle, the Delectable Mountains, the Celestial City), a landscape full of people. There are fellow pilgrims, some of whom fall away since they lack dedication, cannot learn right behaviour, or are caught by the traps of evil. Then there are the adversaries and obstacles, both human (Mr Worldly-Wiseman, who knows only the difficulties involved, or Discontent, who distorts the truth of God's mercy and benevolence), and superhuman (Apollyon, the Giant Despair). But as well as harmers there are helpers and fellow pilgrims who give essential information, moral support, or rescue: Evangelist, Interpreter, Good Will. The presence of danger keeps up the tension, making us read on, since we want to know who will succeed, and how.

In addition to the external level of landscape and adversary there is the internal dimension, since Christian talks to everyone he meets, good and bad. There are also recapitulations of an episode just over, and longer flashbacks when a character tells his life-story with its successes and failures. The importance of this internal level of conversation is that the reader, like the main actors, becomes involved in a prolonged analysis of the qualities needed to defeat sin and death. The Christian needs to know what he should do or be before he can make his pilgrimage, which is a journey of knowledge and self-knowledge. Some expository-analytical episodes may well be static at the level of the journey, but they are dynamic in terms of the discriminations made, the knowledge gained. In any case none of the episodes is very long (there are about forty in all, averaging three to five pages each), and they are all varied in form and style. *Pilgrims Progress* remains such a gripping book to read because the hero knows no more than we do. He meets Mr By-ends, or Mr Talkative for the first time, has to size him up, and can be right or wrong. So can we.

Our experience of reading *Pilgrims Progress* is one of direct confrontation with characters and their dilemmas, a series of tests which have to be passed if they are to go on. The reader is helped by the narrator, who tells us what he saw in his dream and brings out further meaning. When Christian passes through the Valley of the Shadow of Death, almost overcome by fiends, the narrator records a subtle form of psychological warfare. Christian was so confused that he no longer knew his own voice, for 'just when he was come over against the mouth of the burning pit, one of the wicked ones . . . stepped up softly to him, and whisperingly suggested many grievous blasphemies to him which he verily thought had proceeded from his own mind'. That is an excellent instance of the power of 'suggestion' then attributed to the devil.

While Christian reaches heaven, thanks to others' help and his own fortitude, one of the true pilgrims does not. In the most brilliant episode, set in Vanity Fair, that world where everything is for sale, the pilgrims are beaten, put into a cage, and tried. Since their beliefs are 'diametrically opposite' to the people of the Fair, their captors' inverted values dominate at the trial, a travesty of logic and justice. Bunyan re-creates the proceeding in marvellously varied styles, most concise in the jury's summing-up: 'And first Mr. Blindman, the foreman, said, "I see clearly that this man is an heretic" . . . "He is a rogue", said Mr. Liar. "Hanging is too good for him", said Mr. Cruelty. "Let's dispatch him out of the way", said Mr. Hatelight.' Faithful is then 'put to the most cruel death that could be invented', yet a chariot carries him off to heaven. At the very end Christian also reaches the Celestial City, a passage in which Bunyan adds to his economy and colloquialism a new register for this triumphant vision (recalling Traherne's): 'behold, the City shone like the sun, the streets also were paved with gold, and in them walked many men with crowns on their heads, palms in their hands, and golden harps to sing praises withal . . . which when I had seen, I wished myself among them.' Bunyan could have ended there, but he adds a brief episode in which Ignorance, whose intentions are good but who has no idea what it means to become a Christian, is rejected, and sent to hell. We have met Ignorance in two previous episodes, observing his failings at some length, so that we are not surprised to see him join the other would-be pilgrims who failed to acquire the qualities needed to be saved. Selection implies judgement, therefore exclusion of the unqualified. Rather than undermining the whole book, as a recent critic has complained, the rejection of Ignorance proves the coherence between the book's story-line and its value-system. The dreamer wakes, the book ends, but *Pilgrim's Progress* succeeds in convincing its readers of the reality and coherence of the world that has been dreamed into being.

Despite the very different nature of the works they produced, Bunyan's ethos resembles that of Milton—not surprisingly, given the Puritan background from which they both started. There is the same emphasis on individual salvation, on life as a test of one's virtue, 'celestial glory' now being the reward that is 'worth running the hazards' to obtain. As Evangelist says to Christian, 'the crown is before you, and it is an incorruptible one; so run that you may obtain it'. The same ethos inspired another writer, one who produced a smaller *œuvre* than Milton or Bunyan, Andrew Marvell (1621–78). Marvell had a similar background to Milton: education at Cambridge, travel and study abroad, return to public office. Marvell became Latin secretary (on Milton's recommendation) in 1657, survived the Restoration by demonstrating his loyalty to the returning monarch, and served as MP for Hull for eighteen years, also acting as a political agent abroad and adviser to Trinity House on their maritime affairs in London. Marvell's output was largely in verse, but it was verse in the lyric not the epic mode. While Marvell's lyrics include religious poems, pastorals, love poems ('To his Coy Mistress' is one of the most powerful of all invitations to love), and satires, his enduring works are all concerned with the dialectic between private and public life.

THE EXECUTION OF KING CHARLES on 30 January 1649. This popular early print, although dramatic, has several inaccuracies. A seventeen-year-old boy remembered as long as he lived the reaction of the crowd, 'such a groan as I never heard before, and desire I may never hear again'.

COLLECTORS OF ART became active in the years before the Civil War. Here, Daniel Mytens portrays Thomas Howard, earl of Arundel, pointing to the sculpture gallery of Arundel House, and the statues bought on his trip to Italy in 1614. Most of the rich collections amassed under James and Charles I were dispersed during and after the Civil War, confiscated or sold to raise money for the commonwealth.

GARRICK AS RICHARD III awakening from his dream before the battle of Bosworth Field, painted by Hogarth (1745). 'O coward conscience, how dost thou afflict me!' (V. iii.). Garrick was acting Colley Cibber's much-altered version of Shakespeare's play; when asked to revive the original, he 'would not hear of it'.

'An Horatian Ode upon Cromwell's Return from Ireland' (1650) begins—as *Lycidas* ends—with the poet linking himself with the subject of the poem:

> The forward youth that would appear
> Must now forsake his *Muses* dear
> Nor in the Shadows sing
> His numbers languishing.

The implicit criticisms of the poet there—'Shadow' describes an ignoble retreat from the world (as in *Lycidas*: 'To sport with Amaryllis in the shade'), instead of emerging into the sun where the tests of life take place—turn to praise for Cromwell, who gave up 'the inglorious arts of peace', left 'his private Gardens,

THE KING AS MARTYR, the frontispiece to *Eikon Basilike. The Pourtraicture of his Sacred Majestie in his Solitudes and Sufferings* (1649), which went through thirty-six editions in one year. It was produced as the work of the king but is now known to have been put together from his notes by John Gauden, who was made a bishop by Charles II. The king kneels like Christ in the Agony in the Garden, and takes up a crown of thorns, intermediate between the earthly crown that he has discarded and the heavenly one that awaits him. If the iconography on the right is Christian, that on the left is secular, the two emblems of virtue being copied from well-known models (see p. 178, *top*). Of the many commemorative medals the best known has the king's head on one side, and on the other a hammer striking a diamond with the inscription 'Inexpugnabilis' (see p. 178, *bottom*).

THE PROTECTOR LEGITIMIZED: from the engraving after William Faithorne for *The Emblem of England's Distraction* (1658). Cromwell, attended by Fame, tramples on Error and Faction. In the *top-left* corner is the Ark on Mount Ararat, and below it Abraham about to sacrifice Isaac; in the *top right* are Scylla and Charybdis, with the ark of state sailing between, past the obstructive remora (see p. 163). The right-hand column represents Anglia, Scotia, and Hibernia kneeling in homage with garlands. As with the illustration on p. 209, later artists were able to draw on the emblematic tradition to synthesize pictorial meanings.

where / He lived reserved and austere', and set his mark on history. Although managing to express in the same poem admiration for the king's courage at his execution, Marvell's hero is Cromwell, who exemplifies the ideal union of theory and practice: 'So much one man can do, / That does both act and know.'

'Upon Appleton House, to my Lord Fairfax', a long, discursive, and at times whimsical poem, is dedicated to an ex-hero, Edward Fairfax, one of the outstanding commonwealth generals, who had retired from the army in disgust at Cromwell's policies in Scotland. Fairfax's career is the reverse of Cromwell's, and Marvell delicately jokes about his patron's new hobby, gardening, where his military background reappears in the tidy way he plants his flowers. The tribute is also a lament, for Fairfax, had he continued in office, 'Might once have made our gardens spring / Fresh as his own and flourishing'—only he preferred to cultivate 'Conscience, that heaven-nursed plant, / Which most our earthly gardens want'. While praising Fairfax as an ex-hero, Marvell includes in his poem an anti-hero, namely the narrator or poet himself, who has retired 'careless' into the wood, to become an 'easy philosopher'—that is, a philosopher of ease, or leisure, an ambivalent concept in the ethos of the *vita activa*. Ease, or *otium*, as the reward for service, was legitimate, but Marvell makes it clear that what this poet is practising is sloth and self-indulgence:

> Then, languishing with ease, I toss,
> On pallets swollen of velvet moss
>
>   .   .   .   .   .   .
>
> Abandoning my lazy side,
> Stretched as a bank unto the tide.

From this self-indulgent reverie he is awoken, with a guilty reflex ('Hide trifling youth thy pleasures slight'), by the arrival of Maria Fairfax, who represents virtue, and the glorious future of the Fairfax line. By the placing and structuring of this episode Marvell reminds us of many classical and Renaissance poems where a messenger from heaven appears in order to recall a straying hero to his task. Since, for Marvell as for Jonson, the poet's duty is to praise virtue, the poem ends with the celebration of Maria.

In the seventeenth century gardens were ambivalent places. They were legitimate settings for religious contemplation or secular refreshment after, or in alternation with, achieved work. But they could be seen as refuges for the idle or disaffected. Marvell's most famous poem, 'The Garden', begins with its speaker rejecting the whole ethos of the active life:

> How vainly men themselves amaze
> To win the palm, the oak, or bays;
> And their incessant labours see
> Crowned from some single herb or tree.

He rejects the three types of crown (for victors in war, rulers, poets), as he

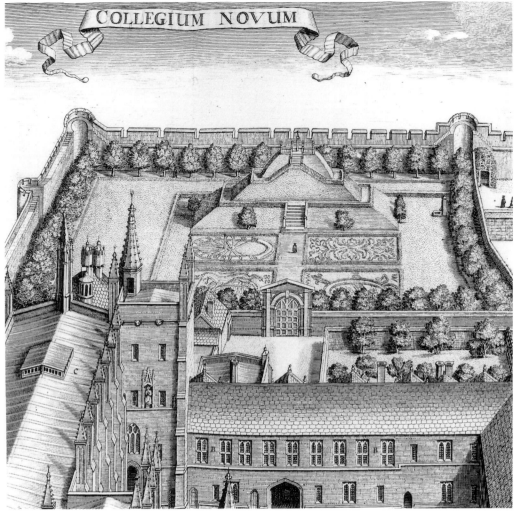

COLLEGIUM NOVUM

MARVELL'S 'GARDEN' refers to a formal garden with a floral sundial, such as the one in New College, Oxford, from David Loggan, *Oxonia Illustrata* (1677): 'Where from above the milder Sun / Does through a fragrant Zodiack run.'

would the incorruptible crowns of Milton or Bunyan. He dismisses society as 'rude' or uncivilized(!); he rejects women, in favour of trees; he revels in the pleasures of the senses, passive while nature presses her riches on him ('The luscious clusters of the vine / Upon my mouth do crush their wine'); he withdraws into a reverie, from which his soul looks forward to its flight to heaven. At every stage the *persona* of this poem is violating some cherished belief of Renaissance writers. Like the poet at Nun Appleton he is guilty of laziness and self-indulgence, but he is aggressive, rejecting the works of man, and indeed of God: 'Such was that happy Garden-state, / While Man there walked without a mate.' Where God had said, 'It is not good that the man should be alone; I will make an help meet for him', Marvell's *persona* knows better: woman ought not to have been created, pure solitude would be the true paradise. But, any schoolboy could object, the consequence of such a belief would be sterility, and death. The ninth and last stanza juxtaposes the *persona*'s solipsism with 'th'industrious bee', flying around a floral sundial, which works, pollinates, and procreates, so that life can go on. The *persona* concludes with a vacuous exclamation at the beauty of it all, not seeing that the bee is a reminder of time and work, both of which he is neglecting. The subtlety of Marvell's method is such that his character—like all those who praised retirement as against involvement—is allowed to see only his own selfish ends, while the rest of us are reminded of the existence of society, love, virtue, and self-fulfilment. That delicate balance is typical of a period in which men were taught to argue both sides of a case, while knowing that virtue means choosing.

Marvell is an appropriate writer with whom to end. He is, first, a Renaissance poet, heir to a tradition going back to Virgil and Horace, Cicero and Plato, a tradition of involvement with the state in ethical and political terms. For him, as also for Milton, or Sidney, or Spenser, the poet has a responsible role in society, to encourage and celebrate 'well doing'. He also follows Donne in blending lyricism with wit and paradox. But, while inheriting and revitalizing a tradition, he heralds a new age. His prose satire, *The Rehearsal Transprosed* (1672–3) looks on to Swift, while his satiric couplets in *The Last Instructions to a Painter* (1667) show that—like Haydn learning from Mozart—he has absorbed the new style of Oldham and Dryden. Marvell sums up the ability of seventeenth-century literature to find fresh forms for new experiences.

THE BEE, symbol of work and fruition: from Henry Hawkins, *Partheneia Sacra* (1633). 'And, as it works, th'industrious Bee / Computes its time as well as we.'

5. Restoration and Eighteenth Century

1660–1780

ISOBEL GRUNDY

THE eighteenth century in English literary history generally opens with the Restoration period as a kind of preface, which is held to prolong itself until the new century dawns. There are reasons for this. The political U-turn of the Restoration itself was matched by changes in literature: the drama took on a new lease of life, prose fiction modulated into the novel proper, and poets turned more and more to the heroic couplet and to effects of clarity, balance (sometimes parallelism and antithesis), and pointed but unflamboyant wit. The period is sometimes labelled the Age of Reason (reason was indeed much

praised and valued, but chiefly because writers respected and feared the power of unreason), or the Augustan Age (several writers drew the parallel between their own age and that of Augustus Caesar, but they differed widely in their estimate of that age). On the whole labels only obscure the variety of what was written in these four generations of accelerating change.

The Restoration

Poets rushed to work at the news—hinted, leaked, denied, restated—of Charles II's imminent return. A memorable verse welcome would be a useful career move, and the imagery appropriate to royalty—the sun, lions, eagles; England as a traditionally white-clad female penitent for unchastity—exerted its own attraction. Edmund Waller, who had twice praised Cromwell in verse, compensated with an address to Charles on his happy return. John Dryden (1631–1700), who had commemorated Cromwell's death in heroic stanzas (1659), came forward with *Astraea Redux*, a poem of grandiloquent conceits in which, as the king's ship draws near, the land moves from its place to receive him.

The history of the Interregnum was soon being written and interpreted. Samuel Pepys (1633–1703) foresightedly began his diary on New Year's Day 1660. John Evelyn was already keeping his; John Aubrey started about 1667 to amass materials for a work he never finished, *Brief Lives*, whose gradual publication began a century later. Samuel Butler (1613–80) lampooned the

HUDIBRAS (1662), by Hogarth (1726). The London populace, just before the Restoration, signify their disgust with the Rump Parliament by burning rumps (and Hudibras in effigy) at Temple Bar, which is shown adorned with two heads and a leg from recent execution and quartering of traitors.

Puritans (but probably not, as was long believed, his ex-employer) in his mock-heroic *Hudibras*, published in two parts (1662 and 1663). This rollicking narrative attributes to the Presbyterian side the irrationality of debate by force (to 'prove their Doctrine Orthodox / By Apostolic *Blows* and *Knocks*'). Its witty handling of all strong opinions plants some doubt as to whether the struggle, when 'men fell out they knew not why', could have been worth while for either side. But the poem was all the rage. Pepys, having bought the first part, found it 'silly' and sold it—at a loss—all on the same day, had to conform to the fashion and buy another copy.

True history with sufficient style to qualify as literature was slower to appear. Lord Clarendon's *History of the Rebellion* saw print (to the profit of the Oxford University Press) only in 1702–4. Before it came the duchess of Newcastle's 'heroical history' of her husband, who 'did act a chief part in that fatal tragedy' (1667). Not published till the nineteenth century were Lucy Hutchinson's balancing life of *her* husband (a parliamentary general), and various personal memoirs like those of Ann, Lady Fanshawe, which catch the flavour of gallant, under-rewarded loyalty through appalling trials. All these memorialists looked back to pre-Restoration fervour; in a cooler age George Savile, marquess of Halifax, defended the middle way against political extremes in *The Character of a Trimmer* (1688).

Dryden had been a schoolboy at Westminster when Charles I was beheaded hardly more than a stone's throw away. His writing evinces strong interest in topical matters, care for political security, vivid historical-literary sense, and concern for the expanding glory of his nation and his age. *Annus Mirabilis*, 'an historical poem' (1667), celebrates two national defensive victories: against the naval attack of the Dutch, and against the havoc wrought by the Great Fire of London. Its preface examines the problems presented by heroic writing in a modern age. Dryden aggrandizes the Dutch war with elaborate classicizing images, and likens the fire to some mythological ravaging monster. He gives a key role to the king, who offers to sacrifice himself for his people, and is associated, though indirectly, with the divine decision to end the fire with a heavenly extinguisher. The poem closes on a fine image of London restored: once a shepherdess, now a maiden queen to whom the whole world brings the offerings of trade.

Annus Mirabilis effectively modernizes and domesticates ancient epic, with Charles II and his admiral succeeding the Greek heroes. Its alternately rhyming quatrains offer conveniently demarcated space for similes to punctuate the action. Its diction ranges from the grandiose to touches of satire and to the much-disputed technical terms such as *calking-iron* and *tarpawling*. It was a mode of the heroic soon to be superseded: *Paradise Lost* appeared later the same year, and Dryden was quick to recognize its greatness.

Dryden never fulfilled his ambition to write an epic, 'the greatest work which the soul of man is capable to perform'. The restored king lost no time in granting licences to two theatre companies, which demanded a constant flow of lesser work: beginning with *The Wild Gallant* (1663) Dryden produced more than twenty comedies, tragedies, and operas in twenty years, as well as prologues and epilogues for others' works, and the seminal *Of Dramatick Poesie, An Essay* (1668), which uses four separate characters to dramatize the conflicting viewpoints which new theatrical activity had produced.

Men and women of the theatre inevitably generated alliances, rivalries, and disputes: in about 1678 Dryden wrote his first major satire, a personal attack on his Whig competitor Thomas Shadwell, entitled *Mac Flecknoe*. He avoids emphasis on party feeling, however, by fantastically linking Shadwell with the Roman Catholic Richard Flecknoe (whom Marvell had already trounced for bad poetry and whose death probably coincided with Dryden's writing). Dryden makes Flecknoe an anti-monarch, ruling over 'all the Realms of *Non-sense* absolute', who hands on his power, in an absurdly pompous ceremony of procession and coronation, to his son Shadwell, or 'Mac Flecknoe'. The poem is the direct progenitor of Pope's more savage and serious *Dunciad*.

Dryden sets up Flecknoe and Shadwell in order to knock them down again.

THE GENUINE STATE OCCASION: the newly-arrived George I goes in procession to St James's Palace, 1714.

He opens the poem with a resounding aphorism, a distillation of timeless wisdom.

> All human things are subject to decay,
> And, when Fate summons, Monarchs must obey:
> This Flecknoe found . . .

The terms of his description vigorously endorse that quality of stupidity which it is usual to despise: 'But *Sh*——'s genuine night admits no ray, / His rising Fogs prevail upon the Day.' The scene is actual Restoration London, the arena of the theatres and the book trade where inferior writers struggle for survival. Casualties are mentioned with reverence: unsold books put to culinary and hygienic purposes are 'Martyrs of Pies, and Reliques of the Bum'. The fun lies in a dignified mocking of pretensions to dignity. Dryden did not print *Mac Flecknoe*, but allowed it to circulate in manuscript—a usual step at the time, when readers assiduously garnered bundles of their own copies or filled handsome commonplace-books. It got into print apparently behind his back in 1682; later he implicitly acknowledged it.

By then he had published another highly partisan, highly controversial combination—in rather different proportions—of poetical grandeur and mockery: *Absalom and Achitophel* (1681), on the burning question of the succession. Charles had no legitimate child; his brother the duke of York—the future James II—was a rigid, aggressive, and unpopular Roman Catholic; the Whigs wanted legislation to set him aside in favour of Charles's handsome, popular, Protestant bastard the duke of Monmouth. The king, who supported his brother, requested Dryden to write on this delicate issue. Dryden, like others before him, used the Old Testament for a topical parallel, making Charles the biblical King David, facing and overcoming the rebellion of his beloved son Absalom. (Not till later did the historical Monmouth rebel, against James II.)

Dryden begins by facing squarely the issue of Monmouth's illegitimacy, in terms which appeal to his age's ribald temper and also its distrust of religious fervour.

> In pious times, ere Priestcraft did begin,
> Before Polygamy was made a sin;
> When man on many multiplied his kind,
> Ere one to one was, cursedly, confined . . .

In this sexually liberated version of the Golden Age, David begat Absalom, the brave and beautiful child of nature. These paradoxes suggest too much good humour for party quarrels, on which Dryden's 'sober part of Israel' look back 'with a wise affright': only the ignorant and hot-headed, held up for our contempt, will risk reopening those scars.

Dryden is not this time threatening the dignity of any leading character. Drawing on *Paradise Lost* to paint the conflict between good and evil, he introduces Achitophel (the Whig leader Lord Shaftesbury) with his supporters

Come Sirs, and view this famous Library,
Tis pity Learning should discourag'd be :
~res Bookes (that is, if they were but well Sold)
~ maintain't are worth their weight in Gold

THE
COMPLEAT
AUCTIONER

Then bid apace, and break me out of hand :
Ne'er cry you don't the Subject understand ;
For this I'll say –howe'er the Case may hit,
Whoever buys of me.-I teach 'em Wit.

A PORTABLE BOOKSTALL, from a print of about 1700. It offers the library of a scandalous figure lately deceased, with pornography as well as books of fiction, travel, and medicine.

like fallen angels around him, and makes him encounter Absalom in a scene heavy with verbal reminiscence of Milton's Satan. Absalom, like Eve, resists but then succumbs. Once Absalom in his turn has tempted the populace, Dryden has brought his allegorical tale up to the moment of writing; the usefulness of the David parallel is exhausted. True to his persuasive purpose, he gives the king a closing statesmanlike speech, endorsed by the Almighty. His prophecy of an ideal future, however, lacks the convincing detail of that in *Annus Mirabilis*.

Dryden's other satirical works (including *The Medall* and the wicked character sketches which were his only contribution to Nahum Tate's *Second Part of Absalom and Achitophel*, both 1682) are of less account. His abiding interest in principles of authority and methods of government went into two poetic statements of his religious creed—or creeds. *Religio Laici, or A Layman's Faith* (1682), a piece of direct argument, supports the Church of England, while the longer *The Hind and the Panther* (1687), a beast fable of a kind reminiscent of the Middle Ages, makes the Church of Rome its 'milkwhite Hind, immortal and unchanged', and the Church of England her rebellious daughter the panther: intelligent, carnivorous, feline, and spotted.

His change of faith, just as a Catholic king succeeded, has given Dryden a bad press. But he held to his change when James was ousted. The Anglican *Religio Laici*, too, already reveals a longing for the restfulness of absolute authority. A Church which could claim to solve all problems, it says, if such existed, *would* be worth commandments and creed put together. Its opening beautifully likens the uncertain, glimmering light of Reason to 'the borrowed beams of Moon and Stars' which fade and die away in the sun of Religion (one of the first of many feeling complaints from the so-called Age of Reason about Reason's shortcomings). The later poem redirects this imagery: 'My manhood, long misled by wandering fires, / Followed false lights.'

Dryden's rendering of Virgil's pastorals and *Aeneid* into English poetry was a boon to readers without classical education. He also had an important hand in versions of Ovid and Juvenal; his last collection, *Fables* (1700), shows him still improving as a translator. His heroic couplet became the foundation of poetry for a hundred years or more. He fully earned the title 'father of English criticism' though his critical works are chiefly essays tacked on the front of plays, single poems, or collections. His vigorous mind grasped and ordered the issues involved in every kind of writing he practised: the epic, drama, satire, narrative poetry, and translation.

Till recently Dryden was the only Restoration verse satirist widely known (Marvell's vigorous, sometimes scorching, and always inventive satire being, unlike his lyrics, little read). We have now mustered courage to admire the poetry of John Wilmot, earl of Rochester (1647-80). Rochester dazzled the court, burned himself out, and retained the limelight with a spectacular death-bed repentance encouraged and later reported by Gilbert Burnet. The legend of his life has obscured the mastery of his poetry: his Puritan mother and Cavalier father, his drunkenness 'for five years together', his philosophical atheism, his duels, disguises, love-affairs, and public pranks which epitomize the rakishness of the Restoration court. The canon of his work is highly problematical: his reputation ensured that every anonymous piece either bawdy or scurrilous was at once ascribed to him. But his known poems secure him a high place. Both satires and lyrics, they cover almost every imaginable aspect of love and sex—meeting, parting, masturbation, premature ejaculation, riddling idealism, and brutal lechery—and a few other subjects as well.

A verse letter from 'Artemisia' describing town life to Chloe [?1675], opens a vein of satire on fashionable, financial, and marital pursuits which Dryden touched only in comedies: the female persona serves to present a series of deliberately off-beat judgements. 'A Satyr against Reason and Mankind'—or simply 'against Mankind'—opens with uncompromising rejection of human rationality. There follows a kind of thinker's progress, which translates mental exploration into a nightmarish journey through topography suggesting Spenser or Bunyan. The follower of so-called Reason (a phoney sixth sense for which he rejects the natural, honest five) 'climbs with pain / Mountains of whimseys, heaped in his own brain' and 'falls headlong down / Into doubt's boundless sea'. The will-o-the-wisp, deceitful Reason, leaves him not as Dryden had imagined, to be rescued by the light of Religion, but

> to eternal night.
>
> . . . .
>
> Huddled in dirt the reasoning engine lies,
> Who was so proud, so witty, and so wise.

If he could find even one Christian of sincere faith and 'pious life', the poet concludes, that would be enough to make him recant and join the 'rabble' majority of believers; but his tone expresses his scepticism as to this possibility.

Rochester, without the repentance, was said to have sat for the hero of Etherege's *The Man of Mode*. Restoration drama kept close touch with the off-stage lives of its participants, abounding in characters tailored to particular actors, in direct flattery or abuse of audiences, in witty references to the nature or the limitations of dramatic illusion, and in in-jokes of all kinds. With only two licensed theatres, an audience drawn chiefly from select court circles, and the same plays revived briefly year after year, a highly self-referential comic style developed.

Tragedy meant larger-than-life passions, clashes of Love with Fate or Duty, the fall of empires, formal rhetoric, and statuesque gesture. These conditions help to explain why Restoration heroic tragedy, though now making some critical come-back, is unlikely ever to commend itself to many readers, actors, or producers. Of the comedies only a tiny proportion remain in our repertory, but those are still full of life.

Although Shakespeare and other inherited plays dominated, the two theatres had a voracious appetite and kept many writers busy. Shadwell was prominent mainly in comedy, as was Aphra Behn. Nathaniel Lee and Elkanah Settle specialized in tragedy; so did Thomas Otway and Thomas Southerne, who both also wrote problematical, socially critical comedies. Among many modernizers of Shakespeare, Nahum Tate perpetrated a *King Lear* (1681)—not wider of the mark than the most provocative twentieth-century interpretations, but no substitute—which held the stage for most of the eighteenth century. Only Dryden, in *All for Love* (1677), made a durable new play from a Shakespearian original (*Antony and Cleopatra*). He himself said he had fitted his plays, glittering comedies and ranting tragedies, to the audience's bad taste; *Mac Flecknoe* makes fun of his own megalomaniac hero Maximin in *Tyrannick Love*.

Today's common reader (if not the common teacher) has selected for

STAGE SET FOR *THE EMPRESS OF MOROCCO*, a tragedy by Elkanah Settle, as performed by the Duke's Company at Dorset Garden theatre, 1673. The tragedy is full of set-piece spectaculars like sea-battles and prison scenes, and the splendour of the stage is well represented in one of the unprecedented, grandiose illustrations to the printed play—illustrations which apparently caused Dryden a pang of jealousy. Later, however, Settle's reputation declined: his role as official City Poet was mocked by Pope in the *Dunciad* and his indigent old age pitied by Johnson in his life of Dryden.

attention five dramatists from the period: Sir George Etherege (*c.*1636–?1692), William Wycherley (1641–1715), Sir John Vanbrugh (1664–1726), William Congreve (1670–1729), and George Farquhar (*c.*1677–1707). The first four were gentlemen with independent incomes. Etherege wrote three comedies, Wycherley and Congreve four; of Vanbrugh's only two are much known. Only Farquhar among these was a professional, with an acting career and six comedies achieved when death cut him short.

Their plays, though far from carbon copies, have much in common, notably the influence of Thomas Hobbes's *Leviathan*, published in 1651. (Indeed, its materialist philosophy, and psychology based on the endless competitive pursuit of power, seem to permeate the mental and literary climate of the Restoration just as John Locke's *Essay concerning Human Understanding* (1690), with its scrupulous examination of the workings of reason and the associative faculty, permeates that of the eighteenth century.) Typically, the comedies portray the London life of hedonistic young men who fill their leisure with drinking, whoring, theatre-going, extravagance, and wit, who need money but have no resources for earning it except marriage to an heiress. The young women's necessarily conflicting plans and interests are also shown. Names encapsulate traits. Middle-aged, middle-class, or sexually unattractive people of both sexes, unchaste women, widows, cuckolds, and unsuccessful pretenders to wit are in general fair game. The heroes seek sex (sometimes discriminatingly) and money; the heroines seek a say in choice of a marriage partner. All are judged on abilities—'wit'—rather than moral qualities, but the penetration and self-knowledge that go with wit are given a positive moral value. In this comedy a younger generation repudiates past rules and chooses freedom: of speech, belief, and action (though it never questions the rule that heroines can be sexual free-*thinkers* only).

Etherege and Wycherley began as playwrights very soon after the Restoration. Etherege's first was staged in 1662, Wycherley's (written long before, he said) probably in 1671. If Wycherley's *Love in a Wood, or St James's Park* was written before his *The Gentleman Dancing-Master* (which is uncertain), then each man followed a rather confusing and over-energetic first play with a more polished and unified second; Etherege also began, in *The Comical Revenge, or Love in a Tub*, with an incongruous mixture of every level from low plot (treatment for venereal disease) to high plot (pure-minded lovers speaking in heroic couplets).

Each of the pair attained the peak of a rapid technical development in the mid-1670s. Etherege's final play, *The Man of Mode* (1676), like his earlier ones, adroitly bypasses moral judgement. From the first its hero, Dorimant, divided critics as to how far we are meant to admire or endorse him, and one may ask the same of other characters. Within the play Dorimant both sheds one mistress and seduces and abandons a second before being caught for marriage. The successful heroine's steely purposefulness contrasts with Bellinda's clear-eyed capitulation to a desire which she knows will bring instant punishment. The play's butt, Sir Fopling Flutter, arbiter of tailor's dummy style as Dorimant is of personal panache, cannot be admired except by himself, but remains cheerfully impervious under the wits' disdain.

Unlike Etherege, Wycherley has a string tuned to emotion and another to violent satire. Horner, central figure of *The Country Wife* (1675), has achieved perpetual sexual one-upmanship behind the camouflage of a report that disease has ruined his potency. He thus becomes the playwright's instrument for exposing society's hypocrisy, but his triumphs, unlike Dorimant's, do not even tempt our acclaim. He has indeed tapped an endless supply of willing duplicitous females, but must conceal his triumph from his old friends the rakes as well as from the money-minded husbands who use him with contempt as an unpaid, unthreatening wife-sitter. Sexual activity has disengaged itself in Horner from every human concern.

Wycherley, satirist and moralizer, gave some of his own traits to Manly, hero of his last play, *The Plain Dealer*, acted 1676, which is based on but much altered from Molière's *Le Misanthrope*. (The soubriquets 'Manly' and 'The Plain Dealer' stuck to him for the rest of his life.) Yet the play severely handles Manly, who rages self-righteously against social peccadilloes yet becomes an easy dupe to real evil. He is saved only by the love of Fidelia, disguised as a boy—a figure even more incongruous in this world than himself.

While Etherege and Wycherley lived on after their latest plays, the 1690s saw another comic flowering. Congreve had two plays put on in 1693, when he was twenty-four; in his *Love for Love* (1695) and *The Way of the World* (1700) the comedy of wit reaches its apogee. 'One's Cruelty is one's Power; and when one parts with one's Cruelty, one parts with one's Power; and when one has parted with that, I fancy one's Old and Ugly,' says his heroine Millamant, affectedly repeating the affected word 'one', and yet also scoring an intellectual point by reference to Hobbes on the pursuit of power. Congreve delights in language for its own sake: in Valentine's satirical diatribes in the guise of Truth, in Lady Wishfort's tirade against her treacherous servant or in her self-dramatizing renunciation of a cruel world, every phrase falls into its place like poetry. All his characters, servants included, are sharply differentiated through speech.

Trickery and deception rule in these plays. In *Love for Love* Mrs Frail and Tattle marry each other in disguise as nun and friar—each thinking she or he is securing a matrimonial catch. In *The Way of the World* the elderly widow Lady Wishfort is falsely wooed by Mirabel's supposed uncle, really his servant under orders to get from her the key financial documents in the case. Yet each of these humiliated victims retains some dignity and humour.

MRS FRAIL: Ah, Mr Tattle and I, poor Mr Tattle and I are—I can't speak it out.
TATTLE: Nor I—but poor Mrs Frail and I are—
MRS FRAIL: Married. (Act V)

'THE JUBILEE BALL AFTER THE VENETIAN MANNER, Or Masquerade at Ranelagh Gardens' on 26 April 1749, in belated celebration of the Peace of Aix-la-Chapelle. Horace Walpole called it 'nothing Venetian . . . but . . . the prettiest spectacle I ever saw'. Rhyming couplets below the print comment on the figures, among which is Miss Chudleigh making her famous undress appearance as Iphigenia. Fielding, Richardson, and other novelists used the masquerade as dramatists had used disguise, for suggesting ambiguity, mistaken identity, extravagance, and licentiousness.

Heroes and heroines are often the greatest tricksters. Angelica, an heiress with cause to fear a purely mercenary suitor, dissimulates her love till she has exhaustively tested Valentine. 'Never let us know one another better,' she says, 'for the Pleasure of a Masquerade is done, when we come to shew our Faces'; not till the last ditch does she admit 'I have done dissembling now'. On the other hand, Mirabel and Millamant in Congreve's last play, still reticent, are not quite so secretive with each other. In the celebrated scene where they lay down guidelines for their married relationship, Mirabel's provisos all concern

Millamant, and all are negative: prohibitions of those vices that had been immemorially the staple of anti-feminist attacks—gossip, secret tippling, grotesque make-up. Her demands are newer: for the securing of personal liberty.

The Way of the World failed on stage, for reasons now hard to assess. Its plot is convoluted, but hardly more than those of other comedies. It has unsavoury aspects (a hero pretending love to an older woman in order to cheat her, who has married his former mistress, on her supposed pregnancy, to a scoundrel), but again not exceptionally so. In any case, Congreve took its bad reception as reason or excuse to give up writing plays.

Between Congreve's last two comedies, his friend Vanbrugh staged two, with plots remarkably alike: a married heroine is severely tempted to infidelity between an unkind husband and an assiduous genteel would-be lover, but resists—just. In *The Relapse*, produced first though written second, the husband and wife are reworked from someone else's play. Colley Cibber (1671–1757), dramatist and future hero of Pope's *Dunciad*, had a success in January 1696 with *Love's Last Shift, or The Fool in Fashion*, which ends with the rake Loveless reformed by his wife's faithful love, about to live happy ever after. Its explicit moral point prepares the ground for sentimental comedy. Ten months later Vanbrugh put that marriage back on stage after years of blissful country retirement, the husband already suffering from unacknowledged boredom and ripe for London and infidelity, the wife also soon to be tempted. Vanbrugh's problematic marriages carry more conviction, and give more amusement, than his vindications of virtue.

The 1690s also heard rumblings of discontent with the ethos of the stage, as Societies for the Reformation of Manners reactivated various ancient objections to plays and their effects. Some favoured reformation and some abolition. In 1698 the blow was struck by Jeremy Collier in *A Short View of the Immorality and Profaneness of the English Stage*. Collier, a high Anglican and high Tory, objected especially to stage blasphemy and to the depiction of the clergy (including pagan priests), the upper classes, and females, as anything but admirable. It will be seen from this that he had no brief for—indeed, no comprehension of—either naturalism or satire. Pamphlet warfare waxed furious; Congreve, Vanbrugh, and a host of others wrote against Collier, and were matched by a host in favour. Plays were mechanically brought into line by dropping expletives like 'O Jesu!' and 'O Pox'; Sir John Brute in Vanbrugh's *The Provoked Wife* (1697), who had hitherto frolicked drunkenly dressed as a clergyman, now did it in women's clothes instead (becoming in time one of David Garrick's favourite roles). But Collier spoke for a powerful pressure group, and caused far-reaching as well as ludicrous change.

Farquhar's first comedy took the stage in December of Collier's year, when he was twenty-one, and he developed rapidly. His two last plays, *The Recruiting Officer* (1706) and *The Beaux Stratagem* (1707), leave London for provincial towns (Shrewsbury and Lichfield) and introduce not only new stage types but also interesting and never finished theatrical experiments in subject-matter, plot, and attitudes. In each play visitors from the capital come to prey on the countryside: to transform yokels into cannon-fodder or to marry money under an assumed identity. Though he has some swashbuckling heroes (and heroines), Farquhar's humour sometimes verges on pathos: when Tummas Apple-Tree tries vainly to warn his friend against taking the queen's shilling; when Mrs Sullen, like Lady Brute before her, complains of the oppression of her marriage; when Aimwell, about to marry his heiress in the confidence of pretended riches of his own, breaks down and confesses his destitution and deceit.

To achieve a happy ending, Farquhar willingly resorts to sleight of hand. In each of these plays an off-stage brother is snuffed out so that his sibling may inherit his money. The Sullens' marriage is dissolved in a mock contract:

SQUIRE SULLEN: Yes—To part.
MRS SULLEN: With all my Heart.
SQUIRE SULLEN: Your Hand.
MRS SULLEN: Here.
SQUIRE SULLEN: These hands joined us, these shall part us—away—
MRS SULLEN: North.
SQUIRE SULLEN: South.
MRS SULLEN: East.
SQUIRE SULLEN: West—far as the Poles asunder.
COUNT BELLAIR (*a minor character*, *French*): Begar the Ceremony be vera pretty.

(V. v.)

For a moment this fantastically suggests that the personal may prevail over the institutional. The joke is still not over, for the pretty ceremony founders on the question of financial settlement. But another solution is found. Farquhar remains suspended between realism and surrealism. His Aimwell, repentant and rewarded, is more in tune with the spirit of the times than his Archer, happily hardened to pursuit of more than one woman at a time, or his Mrs Sullen, miraculously delivered. The theatre as school of morality was to continue to suffer periodical irreverent irruptions: from John Gay and his friends, for example, and later from Henry Fielding. But sentimental and improving comedy predominated, enjoying a run of fifty years between Farquhar's death and the muted challenge from Goldsmith and Sheridan.

Scriblerians and Others

London remained the focus of early eighteenth-century literature, despite Farquhar, despite Swift's—predominantly—Irish domicile, despite Defoe's splendid regional reportage in *A Tour Through the Whole Island of Great Britain*, first published in 1724-6. Our vivid mental image of London literary life under Queen Anne is chiefly due to Joseph Addison (1672-1719) and Sir Richard Steele (1672-1729). These very different men had in common an almost

QUEEN ANNE'S LONDON, central detail from a huge panorama by Johannes Kip (1710) with the court as its focal point. As if standing above the later Buckingham Palace, we see St James's Church, Square, Palace, and Park in the foreground. In St James's Park the lake, still as straight-edged as the Mall beside it, stretches towards Horseguards Parade (its traffic featuring several sedan chairs), Inigo Jones's Banqueting Hall, and what we know as Whitehall. The Strand links Westminster with London: south of it lie palatial mansions, northwards and eastwards the dubious frontier area of theatres and Grub Street bohemia. The City proper holds Sir Christopher Wren's new churches and St Paul's, the Monument, and London Bridge (still the only one in the metropolis). A windmill stands on the South Bank near the site of the present National Theatre.

lifelong friendship and an interest in the theatre: Steele wrote much dramatic criticism and several comedies of sentimental tendency; Addison wrote *Cato*, a tragedy deeply admired by his contemporaries although today it seems frigid and static. Between them they invented a new literary genre, in their periodicals the *Tatler* and the *Spectator*.

In April 1709, while Addison was away in Ireland, Steele began the *Tatler*. He started in something like newspaper format: political items from St James's coffee-house, theatrical from Will's (where Dryden used to preside) and so on, with a general-interest item 'From my own Apartment'. He wrote under the name of 'Isaac Bickerstaff, Esq.', which Swift had recently used in a pamphlet hoax. Gradually, however, complete essays 'From my own Apartment' came to predominate, and a tone emerged which was very different from Swift's.

The *Tatler* ran for twenty-one months, with 271 numbers, two-thirds by Steele—more than four times as many as Addison's. It is sometimes forgotten how far the new form was Steele's brain-child, since in the *Spectator*, which ran 1711-12 with a short second life in 1714, Addison took an equal part. Indeed, in the later series it was he who mostly established innovations and new directions, and he made less use than Steele of contributions solicited from others. The *Spectator* makes more of its fictitious author (withdrawn from action, sharply observant, his 'short face' no doubt borrowed from Steele's actual appearance) and his club, especially Sir Andrew Freeport the embodiment of the new, polished, confident Whig merchants, and Sir Roger de Coverley the country Tory, eccentric, lovable, but not a mind whose political judgements one would care to endorse. To centre a periodical on sustained fictional characters became a pattern for later essayists such as Fielding.

These essays, accurately reflecting the spirit of their age, promote a type of gentleman most unlike the Restoration hero: he believes in reason and control, values correct opinion higher than anarchic wit, and is less ready to call a spade a spade; he is civic-minded, moderate, Christian, instead of aristocratic, libertarian, sceptical. He admires women for moral and supportive qualities rather than for drive, initiative, or sex; he has noticed that they are badly educated and wishes to raise their standard of knowledge as well as behaviour. Steele was susceptible to and fascinated by women, Addison more fastidious and critical. They have been at least sufficiently congratulated for improving the status of women; today it is easy to react too far in condemning them for condescension. Both care deeply about minute points of social convention; both mix more than a touch of complacency with their humour. But what range of interests they have, what eye for detail, what constant novelty and variety!—letters, short stories, criticism (Steele on drama, Addison on *Paradise Lost*, on ballads, on true and false wit). Though Addison's style has been justly praised, his hand cannot be distinguished from all the others which contributed to these essays. A new kind of prose, direct, familiar, and flexible, had come within the grasp of a whole social group.

The reputation of the *Tatler* and *Spectator* has eclipsed Defoe's *Review* (written single-handed, weekly from 1704 to 1713), a great achievement in its way but thoroughly political and historical rather than all-embracingly cultural. Swift was a crack periodical essayist too, in his fiercely partisan *Examiner*

ALEXANDER POPE. One of the most frequently portrayed authors of any age, he often sat to his friend Jonathan Richardson the elder. This drawing, of early 1734, gives him both the 'critic's ivy' and 'poet's bays' to which his *Essay on Criticism* referred, and bears an inscription by the artist, with one word altered by his sitter.

papers (1710-11). He and Pope, who dominated the literature of the early eighteenth century, both contributed to the *Tatler* and *Spectator*.

Jonathan Swift (1667-1745), born in the Restoration period, reflects it in his verbal violence, hyperbole, and explicit sexual and excretory terms. Other influences on him were his birth after his father's death, his upbringing as a poor relation, his stress on his Englishness despite the way others saw him as Irish, his nevertheless increasing outrage at the oppression of Ireland, and his oddity as a priest with zero tolerance for humbug and little for human weakness.

Swift was already writing in the 1690s, as secretary to the statesman and writer Sir William Temple. He went in for elaborately constructed and figured Pindaric odes (one addressed to Congreve), while his prose was unclassically exuberant. His mock-heroic *Battle of the Books*, begun in 1697, gives literal form to the literary conflict between ancients and moderns, embodying authors as volumes or as soldiers. The ancients include not only the Greeks and Romans but more importantly those who at the present day honour and learn from them; since the original ancients copied direct from Nature, the new ancients range a wider field than do the moderns. Swift makes this clear through the subsidiary episode (these were an important feature in epic) of the spider and the bee. The spider like a modern spins dirt and poison out of his own entrails; the bee draws from every flower honey and wax, which furnish sweetness and light. (Thus literal is that famous phrase in its first use.)

At about the same time he satirized the abuses of Christianity in *A Tale of a Tub*: he published the two together in 1704. The central *Tale* is a riotous burlesque ecclesiastical history, enwrapped in brilliant etceteras like—Swift's simile—a nest of boxes. It presents a maze of ironies and mocking rhetoric, as remote as possible from classical form, and the inexhaustible puzzle of how to relate Swift's views to those of the penurious, pompous, and particularly *modern* writer to whom he attributes it.

The central fable is a transparent allegory. Three brothers are left by their father a coat apiece and a Will instructing them on coat care and other matters. The eldest brother, Lord Peter, clearly signifies, from the Apostle, the Roman Catholic Church; the others, Martin and Jack, imply Luther, parent of Anglicanism, and Calvin. Peter and Jack ruin their coats, while Martin's is only somewhat spoilt. To uphold the middle way is doctrinally impeccable; but the sharp and damaging judgements on the Churches' combined record— the brothers' sophistry in interpreting the Will, the ludicrous yet apt metaphors for theological opinions—suggest a mind more sceptical than orthodox.

The allegory, thickly hedged with digressions, can only begin at all after multitudinous preliminaries. The fifth edition (1710) increased these to include the following: a satirical list of forthcoming works by the supposed author; a straight, defensive 'Apology', dated 1709 ('some of those Passages in this Discourse, which appear most liable to Objection, are what they call Parodies . . .');

then items attributed to the book's publisher: a note professing bafflement about the whole work, and a dedication which, as if unintentionally, exposes all the hypocrisy of dedications. From his bluff tone we move back to the ingratiating, insecure yet boastful voice of the supposed author, in an address to 'His Royal Highness Prince Posterity', and a preface and introduction (both elaborately, analogically, polysyllabically devoted to telling us what the work *will* be like). Only then do we reach 'Once upon a Time'.

After that, Swift quickly regathers bewildering momentum. Proliferating digressions alternating with the story aim at various satirical targets (critics, the modern mode, digressions themselves, and madness). They make up a running commentary on the *Tale* and how to read it, pillorying its stylistic and technical devices and disguising its opinions as their opposite. In a work which is constantly affording us glimpses of unpalatable truth, the supposed author declaims against any investigation below the surface (adducing in argument the woman whose appearance deteriorated so much when she was flayed), and urges on us (in an echo of Rochester's Artemisia) the option of remaining '*well deceived*; The Serene Peaceful State, of being a Fool among Knaves'. Swift, as Johnson said, never wrote anything quite so extraordinary again. But the mental agility and cunning which a reader develops in wrestling with the *Tale* remain the most useful preparation for his other, simpler but always devious, writings.

Between December 1707 and May 1714 Swift, though based in Dublin, spent most of his time in London (three separate protracted stays), deeply involved in politics and Church affairs. Pamphlets, poems, satires, reports, and proposals flowed from his pen. During his first visit, as a Whig, he met Addison and Steele; on the second he moved gradually from Whig to Tory circles; the third saw the brief lifetime of the Scriblerus Club, which was to shape the course of English writing for a generation. Its other members were the Tory leader Oxford (anxiously anticipating Queen Anne's death), Arbuthnot (her personal physician, as well as a writer), and Parnell, Pope, and Gay, writers pure and simple. The Scriblerians exchanged social and convivial verse, planned a satirical biography of an all-purpose learned fool to be called Martinus Scriblerus, and laid the foundations in parody, mock-learning, laughter, and serious gloom about the human condition, for the future *Gulliver's Travels*, *The Beggar's Opera*, and *The Dunciad*.

Swift recorded these activities, day by day, morning by evening, in his *Journal to Stella*. She was Esther Johnson, fourteen years his junior, who had met him as a child in Temple's household, was taught by him, and moved to Ireland to be near him (but probably never, despite persistent rumours, to marry him). His continuous journal-letter is rich in minute detail, and in unparalleled power of verbally creating intimacy. The same appetite for minutiae produced two later works: *Polite Conversation*, a short version of a pompous title (1738), a choice tissue of inanities, and *Directions to Servants*

(1745), an ingenious and sometimes stomach-turning advocacy of employers' nightmares.

Swift is always ready to lose his own identity in fictional ones created for the occasion. Writing on the issue of tolerance for Dissenters, he produces *An Argument Against Abolishing Christianity*, another abbreviated and modified title (1708), which with fulsome servility assumes that the whole governing establishment is bent on abolition, and has barely the temerity to breathe a hint about some possible advantage in keeping up nominal Christianity—the *real* or primitive kind being of course unthinkable. Mobilizing opposition in 1724 to a plan to coin copper halfpence for Ireland, he becomes M.B., a

Exegi Monumentum Ære perennius. Hor.

JONATHAN SWIFT, esteemed the saviour of Ireland by his *Drapier's Letters* campaign of 1724 against William Wood's copper halfpence, sits enthroned, as Dean rather than draper, outside St Patrick's Cathedral. The quotation from Horace says, 'I have achieved a monument more lasting than brass!' This was the frontispiece to Swift's *Works* of 1735, vol. iv.

public-spirited Dublin draper, author of acute and racy letters to everyone from the Lord Lieutenant down to the common people. Swift attained a national heroism, and the endless sufferings of Ireland drew from him *A Modest Proposal* (1729), ostensibly promoting a plan to get the destitute Irish back into national economic life by urging them to breed and fatten their babies, their only actual or potential asset, as delicacies for English tables. Swift carefully conceals his shock suggestion until the psychological moment; it must be one of the worst-kept secrets in literature, but pre-acquaintance with it cannot shield a reader from the lightning glare in which the essay bathes the workings of the cash nexus.

What we know as *Gulliver's Travels* appeared in 1726, distanced from its author as *Travels into Several Remote Nations of the World*, by Lemuel Gulliver, whose portrait is affixed. Under this humble disguise—low-church, not over-successful ship's surgeon, and writer in the crude and undemanding genre of first-person travel narrative—Swift addresses the condition of and prognosis for the human race.

In parts one and two the little and big people, so clearly versions of ourselves, show us the relativity of our standards. Gulliver, another version of us, shows the relativity of our motives too. In Lilliput, while effortlessly admired and respected, he nonchalantly performs heroic exploits and insists on preserving a conquered people's liberty. In Brobdingnag, persecuted by pets and servants, he becomes a show-off eager to see a people's liberty crushed by cannon. Part three hits out in several directions: at colonial power, pedantry, and abstract learning. Gulliver reaches impasse when he meets the Struldbruggs, people exempt from natural death: he has heard of their existence rapturously, as a longed-for means of improving or perfecting the human lot (only, of course, it is his own potential gain that he rhapsodizes over), and once disillusioned he has nowhere else to turn.

Part four presents us with beings which look human but are loathsomely subhuman, and beings which look like horses but which offer the lure of a new ideal. The Houyhnhnms' perfect rationality is genuinely impressive, but they are also funny, with their neighing language and gawky equine *politesse*. Gulliver has never appeared so ludicrous on his earlier voyages as here, from the beginning when he is frisked by an enquiring hoof to the end when he signalizes his new adoption of perfect reason by loving the *smell* of English horses. We leave him convinced he has attained a nature above the human: in that belief his refusal to let his wife and children 'touch my Bread, or drink out of the same Cup', brings him into direct contrast with Christ, the more-than-human who voluntarily descended to human nature and is represented in bread and wine. Gulliver, while remaining inescapably human, has become a parody and a contradiction of the only superhumanity which Swift believed in.

Swift's poetry has only recently received its due. His mature poetic voice breaks upon us (after his early pindarics) in 'Verses wrote in a Lady's Ivory Table-Book' (1698): the snappy octosyllabic line, the focus on contemporary detail, the merciless judgement, the sharp and literal physical embodiment of the moral and spiritual, and the play of two modes against each other. This poem opposes the inflated courtly language addressed to the lady—'Here in Beau-spelling (*tru tel deth*)'—with her own impoverished jargon of shopping-list and beauty care.

Such collisions recur in Swift's later poems. His 'Descriptions' of the morning and of a city shower, both first printed in the *Tatler*, apply to urban squalor the knowledgeable eye which Virgil's *Georgics* had turned on rural scenes. His annual birthday poems to Stella glorify the humdrum; *Cadenus and Vanessa*, probably written in 1713, which justifies his own behaviour in an even more problematical relationship, involves Venus and Pallas in daily human social routines. His 'Verses on the Death of Dr Swift', written in 1731, speak many tongues: those of himself urbanely enforcing the truth of La Rochefoucauld's maxim that we enjoy our friends' distresses; the friends, complacently gossiping about his decline, censuring his bequests to charity, unable to encompass grief—'The Dean is dead, (*and what is Trumps?*)'; the publisher hustling last year's wares to oblivion; and the mysterious 'One quite indifferent in the Cause' who movingly speaks Swift's vindication.

The Lady's Dressing Room and related poems from the early 1730s turn on the violent clash between two myths of the female or the bodily: on one hand, vapid pastoral names and idealization; on the other, revolting physical detail of spit and snot and worse. (This opposition now stands revealed as more traditional, less unique to Swift, than had been supposed.) Sense-perception denies the idealized myth. Cassinus, who runs insane at the fearful discovery that '*Caelia, Caelia, Caelia* sh[its]', has foolishly supposed this crime to be hitherto 'unknown to Female Race'. Swift none the less blocks any comforting interpretation of these poems as simply enforcing equilibrium, recognizing corporeality. The message—and *each* of the opposed myths—is more disturbing than that.

Swift's poems constantly press the existing conventions into the service of new genres. The Scriblerians loved mock forms, and his two 'Descriptions' inaugurated a carnival of mock-epic and mock-pastoral. Pope, Gay, and Lady Mary Wortley Montagu accommodated urban matter to classical form: Lady Mary and Gay in a group of town eclogues each; Gay also in the tragi-comi-pastoral farce *The What D'Ye Call It* (1715), with collaborating friends, and in the town georgic *Trivia, or The Art of Walking the Streets of London* (1716); Pope in *The Rape of the Lock* (1712 and 1714). Of this briefly gathered triumvirate, Lady Mary (1689-1762) was and remained an amateur and dilettante poet; John Gay (1685-1732) was an adept at that balancing act which can blend pathos, laughter, and a glimpse of the serious. His *Shepherd's Week* (1714) sets the classical eclogue form (usually involving highly literary shepherds and shepherdesses) among bulls and pigswill, porridge and nappy ale. Gay's laughter at the self-conscious simplicity of Ambrose Philips ('Namby Pamby') is nevertheless full of rustic charm.

Pope wrote gleefully of *The What D'Ye Call It* that the audience doubted whether they were meant to laugh or cry. *Trivia* seems to relish the dirt and crime of eighteenth-century London streets, but also ornaments them with delicate classical echoes, mythological digressions (to explain, for instance, the origin of shoe-blacks, sprung from the Goddess of Sewers and a mortal scavenger), and a mock-dissertation on the walker's moral superiority to the rider in a flashy coach. *The Beggar's Opera* (1728), Gay's masterpiece, exploited a fertile parallel between politicians and petty crooks. It gives the Prime Minister, Sir Robert Walpole, two aspects: the swashbuckling highwayman and the more sinister figure who makes his largest profits betraying the thieves he employs. It also perfectly parodies the conventions of the Italian opera, that expensive, non-intellectual, cliquy art-form which writers of the period so despised.

Alexander Pope (1688–1744) used the mock form superbly in *The Rape of*

POPE'S TWICKENHAM VILLA and ideal literary retreat was a favourite subject for artists. This water-colour, done a few years after his death, is particularly atmospheric.

the Lock, which saw print in two cantos in 1712, and reappeared in a deeper and subtler form in 1714. This version adds the sylphs which parody the militant gods of epic, and the uncannily Freudian Cave of Spleen episode, an underworld visit which links fashionable vapours with society's distortion of natural instinct. In 1717 Pope added a speech (based on one in Homer's *Iliad* in praise of the heroic code) urging Belinda to rely on good humour, not beauty which, 'alas! . . . must decay'. By such echoes Pope miniaturizes the epic world of vaunting and conquering (a curl in place of Helen or the city of Troy), and indicates his ambivalence towards the 'beautiful people' he depicts. The high style unweariedly restores itself after hints at that of Restoration comedy, as when Sir Plume puts his oar in:

> 'My Lord, why, what the Devil?
> 'Z—ds! damn the Lock! 'fore Gad, you must be civil!
> 'Plague on't! 'tis past a Jest—nay, prithee, Pox!
> 'Give her the Hair'—he spoke, and rapped his Box.

> It grieves me much (replied the Peer again)
> Who speaks so well should ever speak in vain.
> But by this Lock, this sacred Lock I swear,
> (Which never more shall join its parted Hair. . . .)   (IV. 127–34)

Pope's range is far beyond that of Gay. *The Rape of the Lock* is the only substantial satire he wrote during the earlier part of his career. This falls conveniently into two phases, the first culminating in his issue of collected *Works* (1717) (an act of some presumption in a poet not yet thirty). Busy translating Homer and editing Shakespeare, he then published no major original poems till the earliest version of *The Dunciad* (1728): in his second phase *An Essay on Man* is the only important *non*-satirical work.

Before the revised *Rape*, Pope had already arranged his early poetic steps to progress from pastoral to epic, like those of Virgil and Spenser. His four *Pastorals*, 'Spring', 'Summer', etc., composed very young and printed in 1709, paint with intense lyricism and technical virtuosity a picture of human life in tune with the natural world.

Windsor Forest, published in 1713 though, like most of Pope's works, it was long in gestation, turns from eclogue to georgic to celebrate the scenes of his adolescence. Public rather than private in feeling, it not only pictures the forest ('Thin Trees arise that shun each other's Shades') but also gives it the perfection of Milton's Paradise,

> Not *Chaos*-like together crushed and bruised,
> But as the World, harmoniously confused:
> Where Order in Variety we see,
> And where, though all things differ, all agree.   (13–16)

This cultivated fertility reflects Queen Anne's just regime as the game-preserves

WINDSOR FOREST by Paul Sandby (*c.* 1763). The trees could almost be the 'thin' ones which 'shun each other's shades' in Pope's poem, published fifty years before this drawing; the presence of George III on a private ride picks up Pope's themes of retirement and royal associations.

of the Norman kings once reflected their unjust one. The poem's conclusion, bowing towards the end of European war in the Tory party's Peace of Utrecht, calls up Father Thames to foretell a wealthy, mercantile future in which the foes of peace will be triumphed over as in a masque or allegorical painting. The poet closes by retreating from public scenes to the forest, from prophecy to a modest and circular farewell, reusing like Virgil the first line of his first pastoral to complete his last.

Balance or harmony is one of Pope's early themes; the other is *literary* ambition. *An Essay on Criticism* (1711), as well as surveying abuses in reading and writing, makes a heartfelt plea for generous, constructive criticism. *The Temple of Fame* (1715), modelled distantly on Chaucer's *House of Fame*, distributes praise and blame with magisterial hand and disclaims any but an honest fame.

Pope's physical disability later involved, as Johnson gently suggests, a humiliating contrast between his stature as greatest living English poet and his inability to dress or undress without help. He was healthy till his teens, when he developed a tubercular spine which restricted his height to four foot six, with progressive curvature. His experience as a youth cossetted by elderly parents fostered both sympathy with and yearning for the other sex: his epistle to Miss Blount 'With the Works of Voiture' deplores the social restraints set on women; the one 'On her leaving the Town, after the Coronation' charmingly depicts the poet in town dreaming of the girl in the country, who dreams in turn of 'lords, and earls, and dukes, and gartered knights'.

The 1717 *Works* included Pope's two most 'romantic' poems, 'Eloisa to Abelard' and 'Elegy to the Memory of an Unfortunate Lady'. The former imitates Ovid's *Heroides*, a collection of verse letters both passionate and self-analytical, of which those from betrayed women to their lovers proved most popular. Pope's Eloisa (several removes from the historical one) struggles amid 'grots and caverns shagged with horrid thorn' to sublimate her frustrated erotic feeling to religious renunciation, and succeeds only in making religious fervour erotic. Her violent, contradictory swings of feeling, both theatrical and likely, set a long-lasting style for literary handling of passion. The 'Elegy' seems to commemorate an actual woman, of whose story we can gather only that her love brought her condemnation, ostracism, and suicide. Pope hinted at real-life sources, but in fact he had invented a vehicle for the feeling he wished to embody in poetry.

Pope's translation of Homer was by now winning him both fame and money. Barred by his Roman Catholicism from landownership (compare his youthful translation of Horace's lines on the blessing of *paternal* acres), from university education, and other civil rights, he took pride in his achieved self-sufficiency. He had early become enmeshed, however, in literary feuds even beyond

F. Hayman inv. et del.   C. Grignion Sculp.

THE DYING ALEXANDER POPE is attended in his Twickenham grotto by his great predecessors Milton, Spenser, and Chaucer, and a female deity, on the title-page of *Musaeus* (1747). This monody—one of the many verse laments for Pope—was written by the minor poet William Mason, in imitation of Milton's *Lycidas*.

Dryden's. Some jovial lines in *An Essay on Criticism*, on the touchiness of the critic John Dennis, provoked a brutally crushing retort. Other quarrels followed. By 1725, it seems, Pope was at work on a satirical poem intended to demolish, more comprehensively than the *Essay* or the *Temple of Fame*, all false pretenders to the dignity of literature. *The Dunciad* opposed, in Swiftian spirit, many contemporary trends which dismayed and enraged Pope: a suspected general decline in standards through expansion of the reading public; the influence on high art of popular themes and styles (despite the involvement in this of his friends Swift and Gay); the jostling of straight plays by afterpieces, opera, pantomime, song and dance; the multiplication of petty writers under contract to newspaper or publishing entrepreneurs, who confessedly aimed at a living, not at either art or fame; and the corrupt, pragmatic, extremely durable hegemony of Sir Robert Walpole, employing the wrong and less talented side in party hackwork.

Of all Pope's meticulously revised and re-revised works, *The Dunciad* has the most complicated publishing story. Its earliest, three-book version appeared in May 1728, anonymous and allegedly unauthorized. This prepared the ground for *The Dunciad Variorum* (1729), which adds a heavy load of burlesque scholarship: prefatory material with critical quotations, pseudo-learned notes and appendices, much of it supposedly by Martinus Scriblerus. Here Pope furthered his revenges and his attack on pedantry and misuse of intellect, as well as providing help towards identifying the poem's characters. He published in 1742 a separate fourth book, more sombre and broader in scope, and in 1743 a completely recast version of the whole: *The Dunciad, In Four Books*, with a new hero and new conclusion. The poem therefore both ushers in and closes his later career.

His other work of this phase comprises three sequences of individual related poems: *An Essay on Man*, in four epistles published separately (1733-4) but all addressed to his friend Lord Bolingbroke, *Moral Essays* (four epistles to different friends, published 1731-5), and the *Imitations of Horace* (1733-8), including some poems not *directly* from Horace. Each group tackles one of his major concerns during the 1730s: social morality in the *Moral Essays* (also, confusingly, called *Epistles to Several Persons*), philosophy in *An Essay on Man*, and a personal defence, drawn from Horace, of his trade of satire. Almost every poem, of whatever group, addresses some particular personal ally.

An Essay on Man approaches the study of humanity scientifically, in relation to the cosmos:

> Placed on this isthmus of a middle state,
> A being darkly wise, and rudely great
>
> .   .   .   .
>
> In doubt to deem himself a God, or Beast;
> In doubt his Mind or Body to prefer,
> Born but to die, and reasoning but to err.   (II. 3-10)

SAMUEL JOHNSON. After years of Grub Street obscurity, Johnson became a close friend of Sir Joshua Reynolds, who painted him several times. Here, about 1775, Johnson is shown mistreating a book, as he regularly did; he objected to this picture as emphasizing the 'defect' of his sight—'I will not be *blinking Sam*'—but it catches his urgency of attention as well as his reliance on one substandard eye.

RURAL LABOUR. Art and literature of the later century increasingly included toiling rustics, generally more or less prettified, in its depiction of the landscape. The emphasis given in Stubbs's *Reapers* (1791) to a watchful landowner and female gleaner suggests an illustration to the romantic story of Palemon and Lavinia in Thomson's *Autumn*.

Certainty being thus limited, Pope voices a satirical scorn equal to Rochester's at the presumption of human claims to fathom the mysteries of the universe. But unlike Rochester he is confident that meaning can be found. Creation is a 'mighty maze! but not without a plan'. He was soon accused of Deism for ignoring Christian doctrine and of complacency for concluding (in capitals for emphasis) that 'WHATEVER IS, IS RIGHT'—of which it can be said that the mystics would agree, and that Pope's context prevents this acceptance from sounding facile.

If nothing is wrong in God's creation, plenty is wrong in human society. More than a year before *An Essay on Man* began to appear, Pope had issued *An Epistle to Lord Burlington*. (It became the fourth *Moral Essay* when the series was reordered to follow the *Essay on Man*.) What became the first (*To Cobham*) investigates the maze of individual personality (of which the ruling-passion theory explains all the apparent inconsistencies), the second the

POPE THE SATIRIST is given a monkey's body (because lampooners suppressing part of his name made him 'A. P—E'). The donkey resembles the one which the frontispiece to his own *Dunciad Variorum* had just shown bearing a load of his enemies' works. Under the insulting inscription at the bottom stand Pope's own lines on Thersites (the deformed, insulting cynic among the Greeks at Troy), and the Latin motto at the top reads 'know thyself'. This print, frontispiece to a pamphlet on 'Pope Alexander' (1729), was also sold separately.

subspecies female personality, the third and fourth the use of riches to promote public prosperity and high culture. The *Epistle to a Lady* depicts atrocious women traditionally but with unparalleled brilliance, and concludes by advocating the ideal (so much narrower than the patriotism of the other three!) of unobtrusive domestic rule through apparent submission. Mistaken identification of the satiric butt in *To Burlington* caused accusations of ingratitude, and so helped to provoke the self-defensive Horatian poems.

Pope wrote these imitations, printing Horace's Latin opposite his English updated equivalents, more rapidly and with less revision than usual. They vary widely in topic (an exposé of contemporary food snobbery; a history of English poetry ironically addressed to George II, glaringly deficient modern counterpart of the cultivated Roman Augustus) and in tone (encompassing relaxed chat and passionate denunciation). They unite, however, in presenting a backdrop of officially sponsored humbug and corruption, and against it the beleaguered, rueful, often inadequate, but stubbornly truth-telling and ultimately heroic poet.

The series closes with two dialogues jointly entitled *Epilogue to the Satires*

BARTHOLOMEW FAIR, Smithfield, engraved from a drawing on a fan of 1721: it shows stalls for trinkets, refreshment, tumbling, rope-dancing, and fortune-telling. A harlequin and other mountebanks perform a tragedy featuring Judith's murder of Holofernes; a peepshow man presents *The Siege of Gibraltar*; rides are offered on a little cart for children and a crude ferris wheel (Richardson's Lovelace was to use one of these to image a young woman's risk of 'falling'). The caption to the engraving coyly identifies a figure on the right as the Prime Minister, Sir Robert Walpole. Pope's *Dunciad* makes this boisterous and non-intellectual milieu the home base of his goddess Dulness.

(1738), which swing the balance away from jest towards apocalypse. In each Pope argues, as Horace often does, with a cautious, protective friend who wishes him to save his skin by toning down his criticism on the government. The friend provides a few smiles and even has the last word in the second dialogue; but each poem climaxes in a picture of licensed evil bearing down all opposition. In the second Pope stands with his drawn pen as last survivor on the field of defeat; in the earlier one the goddess Vice (drawn with an eye on Walpole's mistress Molly Skerrett, who once married had been granted the accolade of instant court reception) makes a triumphal progress through a submissive land—a reversal of *Windsor Forest*'s end, a foretaste of the *Dunciad*'s.

The final form of that work gives the goddess Dulness a realm which cannot, as in Dryden's *Mac Flecknoe*, coexist with that of wit, but has expansionist ambitions. Perversions of literary culture—smut, libel, plagiarism, pantomime—which have long held sway at lower-class saturnalia are now invading the churches, the theatres, the educational system, the court. The hero, once Lewis Theobald (type of that old bogey, the pedant) is now Colley Cibber (patcher-up of plays, stage portrayer of fops, derided Poet Laureate, and in his recent autobiography a vivid analyst of the way economic forces control one branch of culture, the drama). He and his goddess-mother become comically debased antitypes of Christ and the Virgin Mary, recalling Milton's Satan and Sin; the dunces' writings become a kind of chaos or anti-creation. The fun and mockery, schoolboy obscenities, riddling paradoxes, and protean transformations end in the yawn of Dulness, by which she effects her triumph over the defeated Arts and Sciences:

> Lo! thy dread Empire, CHAOS! is restored;
> Light dies before thy uncreating word:
> Thy hand, great Anarch! lets the curtain fall;
> And Universal Darkness buries All.   (IV. 653-6)

Stupidity reverses the process which opens St John's Gospel: 'the Word was with God, and the Word was God. . . . All things were made by him.'

Non-satirical Poetry

Pope, a satirist dominating a satirical age, was also, through much of his early work, significant in the second stream of eighteenth-century poetry: that of natural description, philosophical meditation, and personal introspection. This tradition is sometimes labelled 'pre-Romantic' but is more usefully seen in relation to the seventeenth century.

Anne Finch (1661-1720)—her name till her husband's peerage made her Lady Winchilsea in 1712—exemplifies the breadth of this stream. She explored everything from full-blown classical tragedy and Pindaric ode (and satire) to songs and colloquial fables. Her personal lyrics celebrate friendship, deplore the price exacted for her presumption from a woman who 'attempts the pen', exorcize depression, and paint the beauties of nature or more particularly the response they awaken in the attentive observer. Like Pope in his *Pastorals* she seeks in nature the timeless and universal; yet she values particularity, like the foxgloves fading in dusk and the momentarily startling appearance of a grazing horse in 'A Nocturnal Reverie'. This expresses pleasure in the nightly release of nature and beasts from 'Tyrant-*Man*'—a feeling characteristic of a later age.

The work of James Thomson (1700-48) is far more formal and ambitious. As an Edinburgh student he succeeded in replacing his native lowland Scots (no longer a literary language) with standard English. His blank verse imitates Milton, who—unlike Pope—often proved a dangerous model, and makes of his towering splendour a cultured elegance which is only occasionally pompous. Thomson came south in 1725 and published in 1726 a poem of 405 lines called *Winter*, which uses the georgic mode for natural description—floods, snow, frost, and gales, probably coloured by homesickness—and contrasts fleeting Time with approaching Eternity. He followed this poem, at first complete in

itself, with *Summer*, *Spring*, and finally the four *Seasons* together, chrono-
logically arranged, in 1730.

He continued to revise and expand them all his life, till they total, with a
concluding 'Hymn', about 5,500 lines. The loose structure accommodates
almost anything: up-to-date scientific explanations of weather, political comment, praise of friends and patrons. Yet interweaving of recurrent themes
makes the whole a unity. Each poem begins by invoking the personified deity
of the season with attendant spirits. Each describes seasonal effects (spring
flowers, nesting birds, etc.) and stages in rural labour (ploughing, sheep-
shearing), and narrates some human incidents, many with touches of pathos.
Winter now includes a shepherd dying in a snowdrift while his wife and 'little
Children' await him vainly and the 'gay licentious Proud' pursue their pleasures
untouched by sympathy; a robin driven indoors by hard weather

> Eyes all the smiling Family askance,
> And pecks, and starts, and wonders where he is:
> Till more familiar grown, the Table-Crumbs
> Attract his slender Feet.   (253–6)

BOOK ILLUSTRATION. William
Kent designed four frontispieces for
James Thomson's complete *Seasons*
(1730). Each presents two planes of
activity: mythological and allegorical
figures above, nature and human
beings below. Here, beneath the
zodiac signs of Summer, animals seek
shade, corn stands in stooks, and
Damon spies on Musidora bathing,
as in the poem.

Each relates the bounties of the British fields and climate to patriotic pride, and nature's apparent cruelty (in vividly depicted storms for every season) to its beneficial effects. Like Pope in *An Essay on Man*, Thomson means to show how the earth declares the glory of God: as the 'Hymn' puts it, 'the rolling Year / Is full of Thee.' He found like Pope that his emphasis on natural religion drew accusations of Deism or of confusing Nature with God. Simple, pious, unbookish people, however, recognized the piety of *The Seasons* and gave it a circulation comparable only to that of *The Pilgrim's Progress* and *Paradise Lost*.

Thomson sometimes appears as a figure in his own landscape: the contemplative man whose eye composes the scene around him, the retired man who endorses labour but ranks his own way of life higher. In his other major poem, *The Castle of Indolence* (1748), he plays a larger but more elusive role. The work imitates Spenser in stanza and in allegorical narrative: passers-by are lured by the enchanter Indolence with promises of ease, luxury, and aesthetic delight, then consigned to a dungeon where they languish in apathy and impotence until the Knight of Arts and Industry dissolves the spell. The poem's imagery enacts its ambivalence: it paints indolence as not only delightful but also morally superior to the busyness of 'ant-hill earth', so that the Knight's rescuing anti-magic suggests destruction and devastation as much as release and renewal.

Thomson's death was movingly if rather fantastically lamented by William Collins (1721–59) in an ode beginning 'In yonder Grave a Druid lies'. The notion of poet as druid goes well beyond Thomson's choice of elegant retirement and patriotic virtue. Collins, like Anne Finch and Thomas Gray (1716–71) a sufferer from depression, is like them a poet of mood and emotional atmosphere. Gray and Collins between them established the ode as the usual poetic vehicle for these purposes: the virtuoso, irregular Pindaric ode beloved by the seventeenth century gave way to a form of lyric stanzas, regular and simple in structure but with formalized diction revolving round personification. Collins personifies feelings (pity, mercy, peace) or outer settings (spring, evening) as deities to invoke. Each prayer-poem conjures up, as in an allegorical painting (or the opening of one of Thomson's *Seasons*) visual attributes of its presiding power: clothing, expression, and details like fingers or eyelids.

Collins's writing career was cut short by insanity, as was later that of Christopher Smart (1722–71), whose poetry ranged from the conventionally Augustan, via the hymn-like roll-call of creation's glories in *A Song to David* (1763), to the private mythology and long irregular lines of *Jubilate Agno* (published only posthumously). Gray's work is more highly wrought than either of theirs. In June 1742 he sent his school friend Richard West an 'Ode on the Spring' poignantly expressing his alienation from youth, liveliness, and natural enjoyment. West had died before it arrived, and it became the first of several poems which freight traditional, even elaborately formal diction with

GARDENING. One of a series of views which Balthazar Nebot painted for the Leé family of their seat at Hartwell, Bucks., about 1738. The gardening style is old-fashioned, with vistas radiating in French *patte d'oie* style and vegetation formally clipped to emulate masonry.

tortured personal feeling. Its action resembles a masque: the scene is set by the Hours and Zephyrs, observed by·the poet and his attendant Muse, and cheekily interrupted by one of the ephemeral insects who had seemed mere passive objects for moralizing. The poet wryly mocks his own isolation by first voicing and then undermining the thinker's feeling of superiority to merely physical, mindless being.

This self-exposure presupposes a sympathetic and even intimate listener. Gray responded to the news of West's death in a sonnet: 'I fruitless mourn to him, that cannot hear, / And weep the more, because I weep in vain.' Wordsworth, dispraising this sonnet in his preface to *Lyrical Ballads* (1798), singled out these lines and three others as the only part of any value, because simple. But the aureate diction of the opening lines sets up a painful contrast, displaying a panoply of traditionally perceived relationships between natural world and human feeling from which the poet now finds himself excluded.

In his famous *Elegy written in a Country Church-Yard*, completed a few years later, Gray adopts a measured and public tone, yet here too he depicts himself at the end as alienated from the simple life he has been celebrating, inexplicable to the villagers except under the inadequate headings of insanity or unrequited love. Only in the 1750s, with *The Progress of Poesy* and *The Bard* (which move back, with scholarly precision, from the stanza to the irregular ode form) and in later Norse- and Celtic-influenced pieces, does Gray substitute wholly public for implicitly personal feeling.

Gray, in his Cambridge college, sounds more guarded about the pleasure of retirement (a growing cult, combated by Johnson almost alone) than do Thomson or William Cowper (1731-1800). Growing up in London, Cowper belonged to the Nonsense Club, whose members Robert Lloyd and Charles Churchill were later known for poetry of a decidedly metropolitan flavour. Cowper's London period ended abruptly in the winter of 1762-3, when the stress of facing a purely nominal interview for a safe sinecure drove him first to a bizarre, unconvincing series of suicide attempts and then into frenzied and raging conviction that he was damned. A conversion experience in 1764 completed his cure, and Cowper was compelled to country retirement by his obvious unfitness for anything else. Later the certainty of damnation returned as a lifelong implacable companion, so that retreat in his writing has a more than normal overtone of refuge.

Cowper's poems fall into several distinct groups. The *Olney Hymns*, drawn from him by a forceful friend and named after the village where he lived, include continuing favourites like 'God moves in a mysterious way' as well as others more emotionally self-abasing; his translation of Homer aims (besides the therapeutic purpose it shared with all his writings) at superseding Pope's; he used discursive couplets and blank verse, and every kind of metre for occasional poems. These, which some think his best, capture the small beer of his daily life, creating vignettes of pathos about felled trees or a plundered raven's nest, of humour about John Gilpin (that supremely incompetent horseman) or a cat which involuntarily tastes retirement when shut in a drawer by mistake. His frequent lightness of touch contrasts with naked despair in poems about his damnation, like 'The Castaway' and the sapphic stanzas (a most resistant metre in English) written in madness. Their emotional force is that of perfectly direct statement, both in parable—as the sailor washed overboard drinks 'The stifling wave, and then he sank'—and even when Cowper abandons analogy: 'But I beneath a rougher sea, / And whelm'd in deeper gulphs than he.' (The poem effectively survives its now familiar misuse by Virginia Woolf's Mr Ramsay.)

Even Cowper's major work, *The Task*, six books of blank verse published in 1785, can be seen as occasional. As its title implies, the undertaking was imposed: Cowper complained of lacking a subject, and his friend Lady Austen retorted, 'you can write upon any—write upon this sofa!' Accordingly, he begins by detailing the pedigree or evolution of this piece of furniture from cruder and less civilized seating arrangements, fusing through ironic humour his pride in modern elegance with nostalgia for lost austerity.

The poet of *The Task* does not speak, like Pope or Thomson, as public conscience or as explicator of cosmic design. He comments as occasion arises on matters of politics or social morality, but does so with the air of a gentleman in private conversation. The seasons, the weather, farm and garden labour play a large part in *The Task* as in *The Seasons*, but here as part of the poet's own experience rather than of the general human scheme. Cowper excels in individualized, momentary glimpses—the woodman's dog, 'half lurcher and half cur', gambolling in the snow, withered grasses standing coated with frost.

RURAL SPORTS. This engraving (1769-71) after George Stubbs shows gentlemen engaged in shooting, which held its popularity throughout the century. It was made to represent tranquillity in Pope's *Windsor Forest* and to occasion sensational accident in various novels late in the period.

'EUROPE HE SAW, AND EUROPE SAW HIM TOO' was Pope's comment on a young gentleman on the Grand Tour in *The Dunciad*, Book IV. This drawing by David Allan, of 1776, shows 'The Arrival of a Young Traveller and his Suite' in the Piazza di Spagna, Rome, during the annual Carnival before Lent. In it the traveller and his entourage are tempted to part with money for food, entertainment, and pictures. On the left may be seen the Caffè degli Inglesi, a resort for British artists and visitors.

He is a major character in his own poem, projecting a sensitive yet narrow personality, compassionate towards hunted animals and generously enraged at slave owners, whimsical over his own mock-heroic toil at the manure heap, but querulous or sweepingly censorious about whole modes of life (urban or less than rigorously pious) which contrast with his own.

Cowper's talents for playfulness, for intimacy at a distance, and for giving pleasure, have won him, as they did for Gray and his friend Horace Walpole (1717–97), fame as a letter-writer. The dearth of English familiar letters which Johnson complained of in the *Rambler* (1751) looks to us like profusion. The spirit of the age favoured friendship, discreet self-revelation, and enjoyment of reported detail. Letter-writing was often called 'talking upon paper'; formal style was rejected for 'undress'; personal and domestic topics ranked higher than previously as ingredients in friendship. The journals of Fanny Burney and James Boswell are sometimes indistinguishable from letter form; thousands of poems, essays, and novels were couched in it, and had in their turn some influence on actual letters. Practice in this mode helped Hester Piozzi, formerly

THE TRIBUNA OF THE UFFIZI (1772–8). The painter John Zoffany was commissioned by Queen Charlotte 'to paint for Her, the Florence Gallery'. Zoffany chose to paint the Tribuna, the chief room in the Uffizi where the Grand Dukes of Tuscany kept their distinguished art collection. Most of the works of art in the painting can be identified, although Zoffany caused the canvasses to be rehung, and arranged a profusion of objects in the foreground. The completed painting did not please its royal patron, however, because of the number of English travellers—many of them identifiable—included in the composition.

Mrs Thrale, to arrive at the radically novel, informal style of her *Observations and Reflections* on continental travel (1789).

Lady Mary Wortley Montagu excelled at most things which the letter does well: affectionate private joking, society gossip with a touch of savagery, intense self-analysis during courtship, torrid emotion during a middle-aged love-affair, sharp-eyed reporting on travels, and mature musings, some serene and some vividly reflective of moods and annoyances. Her sometime correspondent Pope is disappointing in this genre; the carefully posed self-portrait which crowns his satires is unwarranted in letters. Swift, less apt to conciliate either correspondent or wider audience, writes pungent letters apart from the *Journal to Stella*. Gray and Walpole crossed the Alps together in 1739 and reported

SNOWDON (between 1757 and 1774), by Richard Wilson. As mountains came into favour late in the eighteenth century, more and more novels and poems were set in Wales. This painting shows the influence of Italian landscape.

in letters the first stirrings of the human race's love-affair with mountains before turning their talents to the academic and fashionable scene respectively. Walpole's correspondence, maintained throughout his long life with fanatical care, is one of the most entertaining as well as bulkiest surviving from any period. It succeeds in combining acidity, name-dropping, and the savouring of eccentricity with that element of routine and banality which is daily epistolary bread. Lord Chesterfield's letters, despite their fame, read more like a treatise on correct behaviour published in instalments than like the offhand artistry of a true letter-writer.

Much of the most enjoyable reading of the age is to be found in letters, sometimes unexpected ones from unknown names. Probably the best of all are

Johnson's, especially those to Hester Thrale, which show him always strongly conscious of the obstacles to sharing individual experience, always strongly creative in making the letter itself a means towards such sharing.

The Novel

We must now retrace some chronological distance. In Queen Anne's reign and that of the *Tatler* and *Spectator*, the 'novel' meant a short story for popular reading, often issued in collections. Many dramatists wrote them, notably Aphra Behn (1640-89), whose tale *Oroonoko* (1688) is perhaps her most powerful work, rich in sex, violence, and sentiment, its hero an African prince and romantic lover sold into slavery. The young William Congreve theorized, in the preface to his lively and deliberately contrived *Incognita* (1691), that while romances feature 'Mortals of the first Rank', novels should deal with matters 'more familiar'.

This type of story is only one ancestor of the novel. Others are the essay, which often dealt in fiction, and those various prose narratives which purported to be non-fictional, primarily travels, biographies, and collections of letters. The historians Clarendon and Gibbon each wrote autobiography as well; the novelists Smollet and Goldsmith wrote history; the historical memoir takes on many novelistic features in Lord Hervey's *Memoirs of George II*, unpublished till the nineteenth century, where Queen Caroline's courageous death is flanked by her comic-grotesque family relations.

Of several claimants to the title of our first true novel, the strongest is *The Life and Strange Surprizing Adventures of Robinson Crusoe* (1719) by the fifty-nine-year-old Daniel Defoe (1660-1731), who had himself known many adventures in the financial and literal senses. He apparently meant to pass off as genuine these memoirs of a shipwrecked sailor, as he had already done with a short ghost story. Crusoe's tale has many different levels: the trial of the castaway's practical ingenuity and emotional resilience, a spiritual progress based on repentance for the sin of leaving home against the paternal wish, and the individual's re-enacting of species' slow progress from primitivism to productivity and order. It combines the exotic with the prosaic or familiar, but it is the exotic calculated to appeal to citizens of a mercantile and colonial country.

In his last twelve years Defoe produced at least ten more novels, or full-length narratives purporting to be autobiographical. They are the climax to an immense productivity: Defoe's experience of writing essays, travels, didactic dialogues, political pamphlets, and satirical verse, was all there to be drawn on. Each novel focuses on an individual's struggle for survival in a competitive world; each has a certain topicality. *Memoirs of a Cavalier* (1720), *A Journal of the Plague Year* (1722), and *Memoirs of Captain George Carleton* (1728), which read like reconstructed documentary accounts, dramatize medical and military perils of the previous century. *Moll Flanders* (1722) and *The Fortunate Mistress*, better known as *Roxana* (1724)—most of the original titles are longer and more descriptive than those we use—have the added attraction of female central characters. These provide an unarguable reason to include plenty of sexual incident, and reflect Defoe's interest (recorded in non-fictional works) in redrawing the limits set to women's permissible activities in commercial and public life.

Defoe, in some ways a careless writer, nevertheless took some pains to distinguish his heroes and heroines from each other. Moll is less troubled by conscience than Roxana (who once financially secure is prone to asking herself the disturbing question, 'Why was I a whore *now*?'); Moll identifies success chiefly with wealth, Roxana with fashion as well. But there is a clear family resemblance. All lean strongly to the main chance (most pressed hard by necessity), yet wish uneasily to be able to defend their moral conduct to themselves. All are adept special pleaders—which clearly makes for psychological truth to nature, while also effecting a necessary compromise between improving purpose and gripping story. All exist outside, or move outside, the secure middle-class world of most of Defoe's readership, who, deep in business and hopeful of rising in status, were anxious to see conventional religious constraints upheld and the self-indulgent (perhaps sinful) pastime of reading

READING BY CANDLELIGHT. When Lady Mary Wortley Montagu wished she had 'relays of eyes', she was voicing a complaint made at one time or another by almost every reader of the period. This young lady of *c.*1770 was probably nothing like as short-sighted as Johnson (see colour plate) but she reads with head bent, book held close, and candle and apparatus for trimming it near at hand.

fiction justified by a claim to be, like other reading matter, beneficial. The rapidly increasing breed of novelists needed, like Restoration lampooning poets, to vindicate their *métier*, and for this they turned to moral and practical rather than aesthetic arguments.

Novel-reading probably increased as reading of plays declined and a leaner period in drama followed that entitled the 'Restoration'. Addison, Steele, and Gay all coupled dramatic with non-dramatic success. So did a briefly more notorious dramatist, Henry Fielding (1707–54), who with Samuel Richardson (1689–1761) dominated the novel in the mid-century. Where Defoe had essentially repeated with variations a highly successful formula, these two, more conscious and ambitious artists, were constantly learning from each other to conquer new worlds.

Their lives could have been conceived as antitheses. Richardson, born to lower-middle-class parents and to limited schooling, was apprenticed to a printer and flourished in that trade. Fielding, born to a well-connected but impoverished army officer and educated at Eton, turned to the stage for a living, and goaded Walpole with ingenious and sophisticated dramatic satires until the Licensing Act of 1737 (attacked the following year in a Swiftian pamphlet by the young Samuel Johnson) blocked that avenue and flung him into law and journalism.

At this stage the printer Richardson was asked to compose an elementary letter-writing manual. He got so interested in a group of these model letters (from a father advising his maidservant daughter on how to fight off sexual harassment) that he laid them aside to write, at white-hot speed, a different book. *These* fictional letters, from Pamela Andrews to her honest, poverty-stricken parents, give a breathless, blow-by-blow account of how she resists her master's first advances, his bribes, his psychological pressures, and finally her own growing response to him; how when once he has learned (from her letters, how else?) to appreciate and respect her nature, he proposes marriage in earnest. The story does not end there: Richardson's didactic purpose requires Pamela to prove by her behaviour in her married state that she was exceptional enough to deserve her exceptional promotion.

Pamela (1740) caused a furore. It went beyond Defoe in naturalism, and depicted a prolonged instant of temptation, with resistance yet unassured. In subtitling it *Virtue Rewarded*, Richardson played into the hands of those who saw how Pamela's virtue becomes a valuable commodity to her, and saw this as damaging the novel's moral purpose. They included Fielding, who riposted with the anonymous satirical skit *Shamela* (1741), whose anti-heroine, a girl of purely tactical 'vartue', is engagingly open about her predatory purpose in letters to her patron-bawd.

Fielding did not rest there. He may or may not have already completed *Jonathan Wild the Great*, published 1743, an elaborately, even heavy-handedly ironical tale in which the writer consistently lauds the 'greatness' of his hero, a criminal and scoundrel, and pours scorn on the innocent Heartfree. In any case, the germ which *Pamela* planted in his mind grew into a more complex work, *The History of the Adventures of Joseph Andrews* . . . (1742). This sets out from as straightforward a reversal as *Jonathan Wild*. Joseph (Pamela's brother), resisting the lures of his employer, is a bald but effective device for making fun of chastity (male) as a heavy moral issue. Something less schematic, however, emerges. Unjustly dismissed and travelling homewards with Abraham Adams, a poor clergyman who actually lives by undiluted Christian teaching, Joseph comes into bruising contact with most of the assumptions, values, and practices of worldly or self-styled virtuous society.

To read *Pamela* and to read *Joseph Andrews* call for two different mental exercises. In *Pamela*, despite the caution that sophisticated criticism very properly imposes, our experience remains essentially that of feeling for the heroine's emotions, assessing her responses, judging her self-analyses, and responding to her fictional letters as to a mind in contact with our own. Fielding constantly reminds us that an authorial hand has shaped the trail, leaving clues here and dead-ends there, planting rewards, disappointments, and surprises. We are justified in requiring verisimilitude from Pamela and her associates—and, when we have allowed for the effect of her naïve and self-centred angle on events, that is what we find. But Fielding often points up what is emphatically, traditionally fictional, like the hilarious confusion of one bedroom with another, or the persistence against experience of Adams's faith in human goodness. He presents events and characters not as examples of life but as comments on it, comments aimed at subverting a Richardsonian, bourgeois, self-protective, profit-and-loss, commandment-keeping morality, and substituting self-forgetfulness, warmth of feeling, and sympathy with others.

The debate went on to a second round. Richardson published in separate instalments his *Clarissa* (1747-8), which unlike *Pamela* (or its sequel, 1742), took long consideration and revision, and marks an immense stride in technique. Whereas Pamela's voice carried on her story almost alone, so that the reader lacks any yardstick by which to corroborate or modify her views, Clarissa leads an orchestra of communing and conflicting voices, in which her earnest tones are often contradicted or qualified but in the end, for most readers, thoroughly vindicated. Like Pamela, she defends herself against sexual take-over, but this time the stakes are higher: total extinction of personal autonomy. The story pits female against male, resistant weakness against encroaching strength, the uphill struggle to be accurate against irrepressible and ultimately destructive fantasizing. Each central character finds the other's world view deeply threatening, and is bent on disproving it. Clarissa believes she can 'convert' Lovelace. He believes he can reveal her to be, as woman, a purely sexual and not a morally responsible being. Both are destroyed, but Clarissa's death is vindication while Lovelace's is defeat.

Richardson agonized as to whether he had made his moral points clear

F. Hayman, inv.

H. Gravelot sculp

ILLUSTRATIONS TO *PAMELA*. In 1742 Richardson published his larger, octavo edition of the novel—the first to bring together in four volumes the original story and its sequel, *Pamela in her Exalted Condition*. In it he aimed to assert his heroine's purity and gentility against the tone of Fielding's *Shamela* and of unauthorized continuers of his tale. Rejecting an earlier idea of illustrations by Hogarth, he chose Francis Hayman and Hubert Gravelot to produce a series of refined, rococo images. *Above* Mr B. purloining Pamela's very first letter and reading it half-written.

At about the same time Richardson's friend Joseph Highmore painted another complete Pamela narrative series. *Below* his summer-house scene from letter xi, where the heroine receives—modestly and unwillingly—her first kiss. His Pamela bears a remarkable physical likeness to that of Hayman.

enough: as the early volumes of the novel were succeeded by later volumes and later editions, he further blackened Lovelace to save his readers from succumbing to the magnetism which he had so aptly represented as boisterous creative wit. But no tinkering could efface the ambiguities and contradictions of Clarissa's position, as she seeks to shoulder moral responsibility without disobeying a code of submission, and pursues perfection while teetering on the brink of spiritual pride.

Because of its almost impossibly demanding length, this wonderful book remains little read, and bald plot-summary is more than normally inadequate to its intricately woven plot, in which no emotional situation remains the same from letter to letter or even from paragraph to paragraph.

Fielding sent his rival (a friend of his novelist sister Sarah) a letter of generous praise for *Clarissa*. He also, however, sought in *Tom Jones* (1749) to counter its method, its structure, and its assumptions about character. Where Lovelace expands ordinary rakishness to include as much evil as one human being can do another, Fielding comically reduces it in Tom to good looks, ready instincts, and an inability to say no (often seduced, he never once seduces). Where Clarissa pursues perfection and is lacerated by the inadequacy of the social code, Sophia undertakes disobedience (and physical risk) lightly, and makes a virtue of submission only when it will gain her unadmitted ends.

There has been argument over whether or not *Tom Jones* is meant to inculcate prudence and whether or not we see Tom learning it. Fielding mentions prudence both with respect and with heavy irony in his explicit authorial utterances (which, both concentrated in the essays introducing each of the eighteen books and scattered in the course of the story, play a large part in directing and spicing it). What Tom does learn is how to take wise and effective action in the interest of others. As a boy he gets his friend Black George into trouble; as a man he saves his friend Nightingale from despicable though socially acceptable meanness, and Nightingale's Nancy from ruin. He even says no to a woman, eligible and moneyed Arabella Hunt.

Clarissa casts her influence on Fielding's last novel, *Amelia* (1751), which presents a feminine counter-ideal, and Richardson's own last, *Sir Charles Grandison* (1753-4), which presents a complementary masculine ideal. Each occupies new fictional territory: *Amelia* that of 'low' domestic subject-matter, *Sir Charles* that of the loving circle of moral, emotional, and psychological scrutinizers.

The methods of Richardson and Fielding are poles apart: on one hand a series of letters from which the author excludes himself; on the other the 'comic Epic-Poem in Prose', a formally structured narrative with the author in close attendance. What they share is their strong grasp on actuality. Johnson remarked in *Rambler* no. 4 on the fidelity with which the new genre reflected life; but few novelists had so far abandoned (like Richardson) or subjugated (like Fielding) transparent fictional or didactic devices.

Mr Richardson reading the MS History of Sir Cha. Grandison at North End | Mr T. Mulso | Mr E. Mulso | Miss Mulso now Mrs Chapone | Miss Highmore now Mrs Duncombe | Miss Prescott now Mrs Mulso | Mr J. Duncombe

SAMUEL RICHARDSON, drawn by Susanna Highmore (1751) in his private, expanded-family literary circle. As his art became more complex and ambitious, he came to rely more and more for the process of composition on his friends' critical support, though he reacted against their advice as often as he accepted it. Here he reads his last novel, *Sir Charles Grandison*, in manuscript; among those present are the artist and her future husband (both significant minor writers) and Hester Mulso (to Richardson a sprightly and provocative critic; later, as Mrs Chapone, a highly conservative bluestocking author).

Tobias Smollett (1721–71) followed Fielding in life-stories of high-spirited young men, with much physical combat and a range of comic minor characters, but with less depth and artistry. When his heroes reach final refuge from the world of dog-eat-dog, their reward tends to include a rich and sentimental heroine singularly lacking in character or role in the action. Slices of documentary or non-fictional matter are roughly inserted. His first novel, *Roderick Random* (1748), scarifyingly depicts the carnage and sheer mismanagement of the naval expedition to Cartagena. His last, *Humphry Clinker* (1771), adopts the epistolary mode and benefits from the resulting multiplication of viewpoints although, since each character writes to a confidant outside the story, the letters generate no dramatic conflict. It also shifts the novel's usual concerns towards those which interest Smollett, drastically limiting the love interest and giving centre stage to the crotchety, benevolent, elderly hypochondriac Matthew Bramble.

In 1759 the novel form was hit by a bombshell, all its developing and still youthful conventions exploded, in the first two volumes of *The Life and Opinions of Tristram Shandy*, by Laurence Sterne (1713-68)—his only novel except the slighter *Sentimental Journey* (1768). *Tristram* continued to come out in two-volume instalments until the ninth and last in 1767. Its hero-narrator recalls as he begins volume seven that he had promised to keep it going for forty years if he were only granted health and spirits, and goes on with characteristic obliquity to say that his *spirits* are satisfactory. Whatever Sterne had intended, a rapid decline in his own health probably affected the novel as we have it.

The title 'Life and Opinions' is ironic, since much of the story pre-dates Tristram's birth. Sterne digresses freely backwards and forwards in time as the

LAURENCE STERNE. Thomas Patch depicts him (1766) as on bowing terms with Death, like his hero Tristram, who thanks his good spirits that 'when Death himself knocked at my door—ye bad him come again; and in so gay a tone of careless indifference, did ye do it, that he doubted of his commission—' (*Tristram Shandy*, vol. vii, ch. 1).

topics of discourse (mostly related to his characters' respective hobby-horses) drag it, always avoiding what would normally be central and highlighting incongruous peripheral detail. Tristram is conceived while the reader's attention is diverted, just as surely as his father's is by his mother's query about winding the clock. The birth itself happens in volume three while all eyes are elsewhere, the novelist busy writing a long-deferred 'author's preface' and his principal characters asleep: even when they wake, semantic confusion about other matters keeps the birth long unannounced. Still the mixture remains the same: the free-floating narrative alights now and then in the novel's present tense to mention Tristram's various disasters—to his nose, his name, his brother, his education, and (perhaps) his masculinity. But from volume seven the narrative settles down into one period at a time, first the present tense (now Tristram's adulthood, in which he is tearing across Europe in flight from Death), and finally the remote past of Uncle Toby's courtship, before Tristram was thought of.

The novel's extremely complex time-scheme produces a sense of timelessness; its endless cross-purposes about the senses of words threaten meaninglessness; Lockean chains of often imaginary association compete with chains of cause and (unpredictable) effect; its memorable characters paradoxically reinforce the contention of David Hume's *Treatise of Human Nature* (1739–40), that identity is unstable, a constant flux of perceptions. But although the narrator disclaims any control over his material, he drives his digressions so that each one drops him off at the spot at which he had clearly planned to arrive. Despite the impotence all around him, we know he prefers his story's jagged outline to the straight line beloved by cabbage-planters.

As a popular form, and one in which a living could be respectably made, even by women, the traditional novel went its steady way despite such experiments. Frances, or Fanny, Burney (1752–1840), later Mme d'Arblay, had before the age of fourteen drafted a story related to her future *Evelina* (1778). This, like all her novels, looks at the world through the eyes of a young girl facing the limbo between dependence on elders and dependence on a husband: who can do nothing to increase her own worth, consequence, or value, but may easily be guilty of all kinds of actions from the trivial to the worse-than-death that would diminish these things. This summarizes the practical side of Evelina's situation, but it also has a symbolic, fairy-tale side: rejected by her powerful father because of slanders on the reputation of her actually pure, victimized, and now dead mother, Evelina as innocent scapegoat represents her sex.

Fanny Burney, lumbered with a wish at all costs not to offend, progressively damped her liveliness and satiric wit. Evelina writes delightfully sharp and witty letters, but hampers action by her passivity. This grows more pronounced in the heroines of *Cecilia* (1782), a wealthy heiress, of *Camilla* (1796), an impulsive girl subject to violent fault-finding by her family and the mentor-hero,

VAUXHALL, famous from Restoration times as New Spring Gardens, reopened with a new design and new name in 1732; it figures in innumerable plays and novels, though Ranelagh, opened in 1742, was to become more fashionable. Canaletto drew the scene for this mid-century print, captioned in both English and French, showing the Grand South Walk, Triumphal Arches, Roubiliac's statue of Handel, and patrons clearly of quality. Owners of pleasure gardens wished them to be popular yet also exclusive; novels by Smollett and Burney were to deplore the mixture of classes there.

and of *The Wanderer, or Female Difficulties* (1814), who tries vainly to earn a living while destitute and anonymous. Each proves her moral purity by an absolute need for others to act and think for her and by an intense capacity for suffering—qualities which have dated more than Clarissa's passion to act rightly.

Suffering was rife in novels written under the sway of 'the sentimental'—an idea so compelling for a time that almost no field of literature in the later eighteenth century can be understood without some reference to it. The word did not imply, as it does to us, exaggeration or falsity of feeling, but merely intensity, which was made a touchstone of moral worth. Whereas Richardson tends towards the sentimental in our sense of tear-jerking, Fielding is more so in eighteenth-century terms, since he centres goodness in feeling above all else.

Fielding stresses sympathy for others' joys as well as sorrows. A later generation preferred fictional characters who seem to us wildly excessive in susceptibility to others' woe. Tears flow copiously in Henry Mackenzie's *The Man of Feeling* (1771); characters shedding them are consoled with a sense of belonging to a natural élite. Jane Austen, while still a teenager, said the last word on this fashion, whose influence on literature was (her parodies always excepted) largely malign.

The craze for Gothic—the ancient, the primitive, the magical—was on balance another dubious influence. Horace Walpole is often credited with its invention in his remarkably influential *The Castle of Otranto* (1764), but it is better seen as rooted (like Pope's 'Eloisa') in pre-novelistic romance. Ruins or ancient buildings, ghosts either authentic or suspected, became almost essential ingredients even in novels whose main emphasis lay elsewhere. The leader in true Gothic was Ann Radcliffe, whose work is discussed in the next chapter. Her literary techniques draw on those of other arts: she uses visual settings of mountains and forests as if they were paintings or scenery, and distant glimpses, appearances and disappearances, sudden contrasts of light with darkness and noise or music with silence as if on a stage. The nineteenth century was to learn from these techniques as well as from those of *Sir Charles Grandison*.

Johnson and his Circles

Samuel Johnson (1709-84) became during his lifetime the very centre of English literature and of a number of fertile literary groupings gathered by himself. He looked an unlikely prospect for rising out of Grub Street to eminence: son of a provincial bookseller, afflicted with several congenital diseases, who had to abandon his university career for lack of funds, who then wasted several years in lethargy, depression, and a series of stopgap teaching jobs, who came almost penniless to London leaving his much older wife temporarily behind. He brought with him his half-completed heroic tragedy, *Irene*, but was soon engaged in writing of much lower status: jobbing journalism for Edward Cave, owner of the first monthly review, the *Gentleman's Magazine*. Johnson wrote biographies of the famous, occasional poems, anti-Walpole satires, and—a massive compound work of great historical interest—reports of parliamentary debates, which since the government forbade recording of its proceedings amounted to a work of political fiction.

Two writings stand out from Johnson's early years: *London* (1738), a verse satire in imitation of Juvenal (a poet more sombre and biting than Pope's Horace) and the *Life of Richard Savage* (1744), in which he memorialized not a hero but a hack writer, personal friend, and centre of scandal. Writing in the lingering shade of Swift and Pope, Johnson shares their moral outrage at the jungle aspect of contemporary society, but neither Pope's readiness to prescribe remedies nor Swift's to proclaim despair.

London paints an environment equally inimical to talent and to integrity, its violence so extreme as to be comical: 'Prepare for Death, if here at Night you roam, / And sign your Will before you sup from Home.' Yet the poem's gusto and energy suggest the germ of the famous love of London which was to come. *Savage* is the first of many lives by Johnson to divide the critics as to its intention and effect: attack or defence? lampoon or apology? Johnson lays bare Savage's self-importance, his paranoia, his incapacity to get to grips

'THE DISTRESSED POET'. William Hogarth captioned his print of 1736 with lines from Pope's *Dunciad Variorum*, to which it could almost be an illustration. In the painted original, this struggling hack had pinned on his wall a caricature of Pope (see page 242 above); in this state of the print it becomes a picture of Pope beating the unscrupulous publisher Edmund Curll, and in the print's second state an aid to fantasy: 'A View of the Gold Mines of Peru'. Working on a poem here entitled 'Poverty' (in the later state 'Riches'), he tries to console himself for domestic squalor. For many, the profession of authorship amounted to sweated labour.

with any unpleasant reality, yet also proclaims his kinship with general human nature, with what the honest reader must recognize from self-examination. In poetry and prose, these two works establish the Johnsonian style, massive yet succinct: pressing constantly towards the finality of axiom yet as constantly unmaking conclusions with modification and questioning; enlivening abstract propositions with the play of half-revealed imagery.

Johnson wrote usually under financial pressure, always with mental effort and strong self-criticism, applying his professional skill both to long-term corporate projects and memorable trifles on the price of corn and the building of bridges. After *London* he wrote only one more major poem, *The Vanity of Human Wishes* (1749), again in imitation of Juvenal—though where the Roman poet inclines to laugh at human folly, Johnson carefully weighs this attitude and does not endorse it. The poem's message—that we know ourselves so little that we desire what is bad for us—is explored through a series of examples.

In these, individuals who are exceptionally gifted (with political or military power, knowledge, long life, or beauty) explore to the bitter dregs the insufficiency of these things to human satisfaction. People dream of having 'the Doom of Life reversed' for their special selves, but all experience the same pattern: 'They mount, they shine, evaporate, and fall.' The poem shows this parabola repeating itself over a wide field (not limited, like Pope's, to one age or nation) of struggle and danger. Its religious conclusion attempts to relinquish wishing except in accordance with the rulings of God: it conveys some sense of equilibrium, but precarious and effortful.

Some fine short poems aside, Johnson hereafter wrote prose. In 1746 he contracted to produce a *Dictionary of the English Language*, for which he not only composed definitions (grouped to display related meanings) but also illustrated them with quotations from the best writers of the previous couple of centuries. Published in 1755, it is a surprisingly entertaining compendium of knowledge and opinion.

During his *Dictionary* years Johnson wrote the *Rambler* (1750-2). Though it follows the *Spectator* tradition, it differs from earlier essays in its steady maintenance of a non-frivolous tone. Johnson ponders religious and psychological processes such as self-delusion and procrastination; literary-critical matters such as biography, pastoral, and the new novel form; and social and topical issues such as marriage, prostitution, and rural retirement. He is much concerned with the exceptional individual: outlets for talent, outcome of ambition. He often uses fiction, sometimes fables or allegories but more often mini-biographies tracing the growth of some trait into obsession or of intention into experience. The comic side of these essays reveals itself gradually, the reader smiling wryly and with surprise.

Johnson followed the *Rambler* with contributions to a rather similar periodical, the *Adventurer* (1753-4), and with another series of his own, the *Idler* (1758-60). Here he assumes the persona of the kind of trivializer he despises; the essays, therefore, although shorter, more topical, and often very funny, have a bleakness absent from the *Rambler*. His oriental tale (not really a novel) *Rasselas* (1759), collects, reshapes, and surveys many of the concerns of his essays. A group of characters, including some quite ignorant of the world though already dissatisfied with an artificial paradise, attempt to exercise 'choice of life'. Like those of Fielding's *Joseph Andrews*, they wander from one encounter to another, but Johnson raises abstract issues of life and death, chance, choice, and freedom, instead of Fielding's specifically English and contemporary ones. *Rasselas* keeps its reader constantly on the stretch to evaluate the attitudes being set against each other, but compels us in the end to rest content without any prescription for happiness.

Johnson's *Dictionary* and *Rambler* brought him, as the rewards of fame, a royal pension (his first financial security) and the acquaintance of James Boswell (1740-95). Although from Scotland, although thirty years younger than Johnson,

Boswell lost no time in pressing the friendship to intimacy. He was already keeping an unusually full and open journal of his own every move and mood, with close attention to a varied collection of role-models; Johnson was his most exciting trophy yet.

When Johnson met Boswell in 1763, many of his major works were still to come. Like his earlier ones, they span several genres, homogenous only in the stylistic manner which reflects the characteristic bent of his mind. The notes in his edition of Shakespeare (1765) make a new step in the direction of particularity in criticism. The preface begins by questioning, not assuming, its subject's status as established classic. Challenging established critical assumptions, commenting on Shakespeare's imperfections and on the role of editors, it sketches an acutely sensitive map of the writer's position relative to the flux

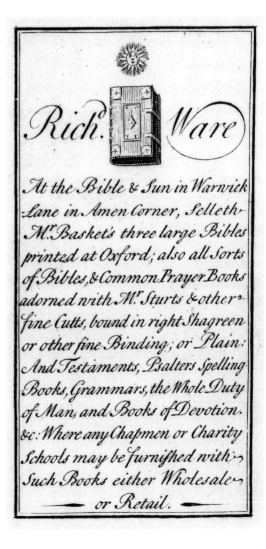

A BOOKSELLER'S TRADE CARD. Throughout the period publishers were generally known as 'booksellers': the two trades had not diverged. Trade cards like this one normally featured the sign by which the shop was known (as pubs are today), and often listed subjects or authors' names, or mentioned the 'Cutts' (illustrations) or fine bindings of the stock. The latter were unusual: most books were sold unbound for purchasers to deal with themselves according to choice and purse.

Rich. Ware

At the Bible & Sun in Warwick Lane in Amen Corner, Selleth M.ʳ Basket's three large Bibles printed at Oxford; also all Sorts of Bibles, & Common Prayer Books adorned with M.ʳ Sturts & other fine Cutts, bound in right Shagreen or other fine Binding; or Plain: And Testaments, Psalters Spelling Books, Grammars, the Whole Duty of Man, and Books of Devotion. &c. Where any Chapmen or Charity Schools may be furnished with Such Books either Wholesale or Retail.

of life which offers itself as subject-matter and to the processes of critical evaluation. Through the grandeur of nature (rivers, mountains, forests, the outline of the planet itself) it images the splendour of those works which continue to live.

Johnson's various groups of political essays (from the late 1730s, the 1750s, and the 1770s) chart a different kind of relationships, and his changing attitudes to them. The middle group takes a remarkably non-jingoistic attitude to the English–French war in what is now Canada; the 1770s group—unusually for Johnson—assails several targets with scornful disparagement: warmongers in *Falkland's Islands* (1771), and in the rest, less comfortably to modern sensibilities, demagogues or popular leaders. The most famous, *Taxation no Tyranny* (1775), is so because it treats the issue of American independence, trenchantly and entirely without sympathy.

Having realized a long-standing plan to travel to the Hebrides with Boswell, Johnson published in 1775 his *Journey to the Western Islands of Scotland*. This makes, like many of his works, unusual demands on readers' capacity for serious enquiry. While the focus of travel books was shifting from cities, antiquities, and works of art towards landscape, Johnson investigated human social institutions. He had hoped to step back in history in visiting an area barely (and involuntarily) emerging from tribalism, acquainted for only about thirty years with the wheel and with submission to central government. Instead, he found the turmoil of rapid change, in which familiar ways were dead and the new not yet functioning. His account holds a fine balance between scientific enquiry and emotional involvement.

Last came the *Lives of the English Poets*, first published in 1779–81 as *Prefaces, Biographical and Critical* to an ambitious collection of the poets' works. Here Johnson was combining personal biography, literary history, and analytical criticism. Again he maps a series of relationships: that of great writings, generously praised, with other works either worthy or unworthy of respect; that of the great writers' achievement with the unfulfilled aims and stalled aspirations of petty writers; and that of books with their authors. Johnson portrays the works of the imagination as transcending their creators, who remain in their non-literary lives all too ordinarily human.

Johnson's tone in the *Lives* is pre-eminently judicial: constantly evaluating, constantly placing. Boswell learned much from Johnson's practice, but his own biographical method depends on partisanship, on proudly asserting his subject's superiority. His journal methods, his hero-worship, his flair for publicity, and his close though intermittent social contact with Johnson qualified him especially well to cater to his age's growing appetite for published detail about famous people. Boswell first began to purvey Johnson's talk in his *Journal of a Tour to the Hebrides* (1785). In the *Life* (1791), talk becomes itself a literary genre, in which a host of sharply differentiated characters now explore a range of topics with passionate and open-minded intellectual curiosity and now break

JAMES BOSWELL, having just published his *Journal of a Tour to the Hebrides* (1785) as a sort of test run for his projected life of Johnson, is caricatured in Collings and Rowlandson's *Picturesque Beauties of Boswell* (1786): 'The Journalist, With a View of Auchinleck or the Land of Stones' makes him a Highland barbarian in a prohibited plaid; his ancestral seat is a hovel, its name a *double entendre*.

into verbal sparring, scoring points in rapid repartee. Boswell's Johnson, conversational champion, is a permanent fixture now in the corporate English-speaking imagination.

Johnson's circles produced many other accounts of him: the snapshots in Fanny Burney's *Diary*, the intimate domestic portrait in Hester Thrale's *Anecdotes*, the stiff, grudgingly respectful tribute in Sir John Hawkins's *Life*, and innumerable scattered comments elsewhere. The Literary Club was the most intellectually productive of his succession of sociable think-tanks; he tried all his life to make writing a less solitary activity. Apart from the general, unquantifiable influence of his mind on the creative minds of others, he was instrumental in the writing or publication of many literary milestones: various experiments in biography; the first investigation of Shakespeare's sources, by Charlotte Lennox (1753-4); Sir Joshua Reynolds's *Discourses* delivered to the Royal Academy (1769-90); Goldsmith's novel *The Vicar of Wakefield* (1766), which, nearly four years before its eventual publication, he sold on behalf of its penniless author for ready cash.

Oliver Goldsmith (?1730–74), at once stimulated and overshadowed by Johnson, was like him active in many fields: essays, poems, plays, and novel, besides miscellaneous journalism. His poem *The Traveller*, published in 1764, surveys the European nations and his own feelings while travelling through them. *The Deserted Village* (1770) turns from foreign parts to home—though its village, which scholars long sought to identify, is clearly a country of the mind. In it everything is reassuringly, even cosily, in its long-established and proper place, but whereas the Thames Valley Golden Age of Pope's *Pastorals* never existed and could not therefore be lost, Goldsmith presents an idealized historical village where, he says, he 'still had hopes, my long vexations past, / Home to return—and die at home at last'. That he cannot do so is not because of its obviously fictional aspects, but because it has been destroyed by a rapacious landlord. So increasing consciousness of the imperfections of rustic life feeds the legend of a lost ideal.

This almost cloying sentiment contained by humour and by closely observed detail is typical of Goldsmith. A recurrent figure in his work (derived apparently from childhood memories of his father, and well matched to the age's passion for sentiment and benevolence) is the man so naturally generous that he urgently needs to learn self-protection. The Man in Black in Goldsmith's *Citizen of the World* essays (1760–1), which employ the innocent eye of a visiting cultured Chinese to expose the less rational aspects of English life; Sir William Thornhill (alias Mr Burchell) in *The Vicar of Wakefield*; and Honeywood in his first play, *The Good Natured Man* (1768): all these supply money to friends in want until, and even after, they have none left to give, and only learn through agonizing reappraisal that they cannot attend to the needs of others without first attending to their own.

Goldsmith saw himself as striving to reintroduce humour into a world which had rejected it for sentiment and for the fastidious avoidance of anything 'low'. This monosyllable, he wrote in an early essay, had 'almost got the victory over humour amongst us'. (He might have added that it had served to damn *Amelia*.) His plays are funniest when most closely engaged with the low. *The Good Natured Man* includes several separate parodies of the high-flown sentimental language *de rigueur* for conversation between eligible young ladies and gentlemen: in one the hero sits with his beloved over tea, attended by two bailiffs whose presence he has attempted to hide by dressing them as extra servants. They refuse to be excluded from the intellectual-literary conversation, and play havoc with it by seizing on those few words they understand and reapplying them like characters from *Tristram Shandy*.

This scene, which a modern audience is likely to find the cream of the comedy, was hissed at the first performance and had to be dropped: it was unacceptable to foist the company of such low characters on genteel ones, or on the audience. Goldsmith returned to the attack in *She Stoops to Conquer* (1773). Not only has the subsidiary heroine to endure being called by her

BLOOMSBURY SQUARE, a mezzotint of 1787 showing the Palladian buildings and railed centre which date from the first half of the century and express the new fashionable ideal of seclusion, even in town. Yet the upper classes share their space with picturesque representatives of the lower.

boisterous half-brother Tony Lumpkin 'as loud as a hog in a gate', but distaste for lowness is portrayed on stage as an attitude of the lowest class: Tony's boon-companion 'fellows' at the Three Pigeons all agree to 'damn anything that's *low*, I cannot bear it'.

Goldsmith's ineffectual father-hero in *The Vicar of Wakefield* (whose dithering self-complacency has, surprisingly, aroused the respect as well as affection of a long-term majority of readers) was succeeded by two ineffectual lover-heroes in his plays. Neither is any match in force of personality to the girl he loves, who in each case puts him through an embarrassing re-education before bestowing herself as reward. These plays show the inhibiting effect of polite society's elaborate conventions; Marlow's terror of Kate Hardcastle dressed as a lady (contrasted with his forwardness to her dressed as a woman) needs the backing of stage costume to conceal the human being in forests of feathers, miles of ribbons, acres of lace.

Goldsmith's fellow Irishman Richard Brinsley Sheridan (1751–1816) also aimed to redirect the theatre away from weeping and towards laughing comedy. Although twenty years Goldsmith's junior, he wrote his plays so young that the works are nearly contemporary. Sheridan's first, *The Rivals*, staged in 1775 and cut and polished after the first performance, fairly teems with action. One of each of its two pairs of lovers is sentimental, but in very different ways. Lydia Languish, whose imagination has been formed by the sentimental novelists among whom Sheridan's mother, Frances, was a leader, dreams of elopement ('so amiable a ladder of Ropes!—Conscious Moon—four horses—Scotch parson') so that her eligible suitor has had to pretend to be ineligible in order to win her. Faulkland, in love with Julia, has digested the sentimental equation of love with emotional pain: for him any moment of cheerfulness in the beloved's absence must be a betrayal, and so is any rational esteem that might sully the gratuitousness of love: 'I have often wished myself deformed, to be convinced that I owed no obligation *there* for any part of your affection.' Whereas Lydia inflicts on her lover nothing worse than colds caught in nocturnal attendance beneath her window, Faulkland is an ingenious tormentor, obsessively devising an endless succession of tests for Julia's love. Their

CIRCULATING LIBRARIES. An early one was set up at Bath in 1725. By the 1780s they were everywhere, from the great municipalities (solidly intellectual) to the resorts and spas (less wholly frivolous than their reputation suggests). Sermons and works of self-education were popular, yet public opinion identified the libraries overwhelmingly with female (by implication, therefore, second-rate) writers and readers of fiction.

relationship, perfectly to the taste of the contemporary audience, makes for us a dark spot in an otherwise sparkling comedy.

The School for Scandal (1777) also has its dark side. Here the sentiment attacked is that of the *sententia* or improving maxim: Joseph Surface, the man of sentiment, is exposed as a self-seeking hypocrite, while his brother Charles is assumed to be a good fellow though he does virtually nothing but drink, run up debts, and sell his family portraits, never attempting the personal dominance of the Restoration comic hero. The force of the villainous brother and feebleness of the good one produce an effect of imbalance.

Sheridan and Goldsmith looked back to the earlier comedy, but they avoided its cutting edge. Their elderly characters, for instance, tend to be lovable rather than grotesque. Goldsmith twice ends with a father or father-figure arranging matters for the young couples with a benevolence unthinkable on the Restoration stage. Sheridan's Sir Anthony Absolute and Sir Peter Teazle only toy with the roles of tyrannical father and husband: they may lose their tempers, but their affection for son and wife is clear, vividly unlike the paternal rage, resentment, and rivalry of Congreve's Sir Sampson Legend. We are invited to look with sympathy as well as amusement on the marriage of elderly Sir Peter and young Lady Teazle, to hope that mutual affection will surmount their incompatible tastes, to rejoice when Lady Teazle after all remains faithful, and to ignore the question of her sexual satisfaction, which a Restoration play would have made the focus of cynical interest. Mrs Hardcastle and Mrs Malaprop do obstruct young love, but they are made foolish and ludicrous, not hateful or contemptible.

These comedies approach the earlier ones most closely in the way they exploit the resources of language. Fantasy creeps in with Bob Acres's invention of 'sentimental swearing' ('Odd's Blushes and Blooms!' for comment on Julia's beauty and health) and Mrs Malaprop's assertion of absolute dominion over the dictionary (priding herself on her 'nice derangement of epitaphs'). The famous screen scene and the scandal school's commentary on it exemplify the two sides of Sheridan's genius, for staging and language. When extrovert Charles throws down the screen, exposing his brother's double bluff and compromising Lady Teazle in front of her husband, four characters stand transfixed, confronting—apparently—an appalling truth. When Lady Sneerwell's school gets hold of the story they elaborate it thus: an affair of Lady Teazle with *either* one or other brother, a duel in which Sir Peter is dangerously hurt, and the extraordinary detail that the bullet struck a bust of either Shakespeare or Pliny (Sheridan's many revisions often left competing versions extant) 'that stood over the chimney piece—grazed out of the window at a right angle—and wounded the Postman, who was just coming to the Door with a double letter from Northamptonshire'.

Despite this exuberant absurdity—plentiful also in Sheridan's *The Critic* (1779), a farce on theatrical topics—the sentimental and morally improving element triumphed for the moment in both drama and the novel. At the

'THE KING OF BROBDINGNAG, AND GULLIVER.' This print by Gillray was one of many designed to arouse patriotic contempt for France during the threat of invasion in 1803. George III inspects Napoleon, a dwarf figure under a large plumed hat. It is reported that the king on seeing it exclaimed, 'quite wrong quite wrong no bag [-wig] with uniform'.

THE TRAVELLERS' BREAKFAST, by Edward Rippingille (1824). The scene shows a circle of writers with the family of Sir Charles Abraham Elton, taking breakfast in an inn in Bristol. At the table Coleridge is seen handing Wordsworth an egg, apparently for him to sniff. The lady on his left with folded hands is Dorothy Wordsworth. To the right of her the poet Robert Southey admires Julia Elizabeth Elton as she pours tea (her father stands behind her grinning). To the left of Wordsworth Charles Lamb hands the bill to the artist, Rippingille. The scene is fictitious, drawing on the earlier association of the writers portrayed with Bristol, and was probably painted to compliment Elton, himself a poet, who lived nearby at Clevedon Court.

THE NEW DRURY LANE THEATRE, by the Adam brothers, opened in 1775. Throughout this period there was always a Theatre Royal, Drury Lane, but it had several incarnations.

century's close the most interesting developments in fiction involved its harnessing to competing political ideologies, particularly in the radical novels of Mary Wollstonecraft (*Mary*, 1788, and *The Wrongs of Woman*, published posthumously, 1798), William Godwin (*Caleb Williams*, 1794), and others; and those works might have been better if their protagonists' practical and social problems had been presented through a less dense veil of agonizing emotion. The non-fictional polemics of these two, with Edmund Burke's *Reflections on the Revolution in France* (1790) on one hand and Thomas Paine's *Rights of Man* (1791) on the other, subordinated literary skills to practical intentions. The sense of turmoil in late eighteenth-century writing, where development of the individual voice often seems subsidiary to alignment with the right team, sets the stage for a complete change.

6. The Romantic Period

1780–1830

CLAIRE LAMONT

Introduction: Romantics and 'the Romantic'

FOR the common reader the poetry of the English Romantic poets—Blake, Wordsworth, Coleridge, Byron, Shelley, and Keats—has created a concept of what poetry is, just as for the common listener the symphonies of Beethoven, their contemporary, has supplied an ideal of music. Why should that be?

The Romantic period in Europe saw the end of the dominance of the Renaissance tradition. It saw the fragmentation of consciousness away from the cultural authority of classical Rome. One result was the rediscovery of local cultures, and a flowering of vernacular literatures. Romantic literature is strong in many of the vernaculars of Europe, and indeed is most clearly seen in the literatures which it more or less creates, notably German and Russian. In this sense it draws on one of the strands of meaning in the complex word 'romantic' which derives from Old French *romans*, meaning a vernacular language descended from Latin. In Britain, where there had been a strong vernacular literature for several centuries, this fragmentation of consciousness was a less sudden affair. There were many pointers to it in the eighteenth century: Thomas Gray, for instance, had explored those literatures, other than the classical, which had influenced English, notably Celtic and Norse. There was no need to look to other languages. One could look at those sections of society where the classical inheritance had had little influence, in ballads, folk-songs, and the literature of the common people. Or one could look back in time, to the non-classical medieval world, as in the vogue for the 'Gothic'. Or one could turn to the inspired utterance of Europe's other tradition, the biblical.

Although the adjective 'romantic' derives ultimately from the word that gives us the expression 'the Romance languages' it came to mean more than a language; it meant also the quality and preoccupations of literature written in those languages, especially 'romances' and stories. By the seventeenth century in English the word 'romantic' had come to mean anything from imaginative or fictitious, to fabulous or downright extravagant. It was often used with overtones of disapproval; as the eighteenth century progressed, however, it was increasingly used with approval, especially in descriptions of pleasing qualities in landscape. The use of the term 'romantic' for the poetry of the period from 1780 to 1830 has this bunch of meanings behind it.

It is hard to see the significance of the 'romantic' without looking at what it was reacting against. The Romantic period saw changes in philosophy, politics, and religion, as well as in the arts of literature, painting, and music, changes which the English Romantic poets both articulated and symbolized. In philosophy the Romantic period saw a reaction against the rationalism of the eighteenth century. It was a reaction against a view of the physical world increasingly dominated by science, and of the mental world by the theories of Locke. The attack on the adequacy of reason in literature had started with the Augustan satirists; it was the Romantics who tried to capture and explore what was missing. The Romantic poets rebelled against the emphasis on the material and on 'common sense' which had dominated the preceding period. For most of them there was a more real order, only to be glimpsed but which commanded their faithful allegiance. It is Wordsworth's 'something far more deeply interfused . . .'. The more visionary Romantic poets are concerned with something more than what is derived from everyday observation, or the sanction of the majority view.

The Romantic period in literature coincided with the French Revolution which was to some extent a political enactment of its ideas. It too, in its idealistic early stages, involved breaking out of the restrictive patterns of the past. The two generations of English Romantic poets were each affected by it. The older generation, Blake, Wordsworth, and Coleridge, were young men in 1789 and were fired with revolutionary ideals. In *The Prelude* (1850) Wordsworth eloquently recalled that time:

> France standing on the top of golden hours,
> And human nature seeming born again.   (VI. 340-1)

What followed, the Terror and the rise of Napoleon, all too easily caused disillusionment. Although some of these poets retreated into reaction in later life they were lucky to have lived through a period which offered something to match the idealism of youth. The younger generation of poets, Byron, Shelley, and Keats, were less fortunate. They grew up in a society dominated by the repression of a series of Tory governments apprehensive that every request for freedom might open the floodgates of revolution.

It was galling for writers to think how, under threat of an invasion that never came, the country could do itself so much damage. Blake was the poet who most memorably exposed the 'mental chains' with which his countrymen were bound. One respect in which the Romantics differed from their predecessors was in their attitude to society. The eighteenth century had regarded society as a great work of man, ideally holding all ranks together in mutually

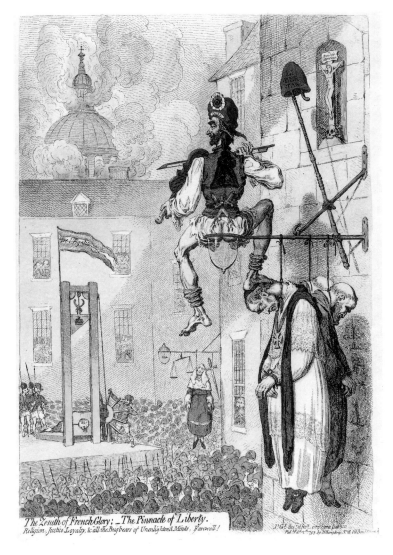

THE EXECUTION OF LOUIS XVI.
News of the execution of the French
king on 21 January 1793 drew this
cartoon from James Gillray. A
Jacobin fiddler, 'sans culottes', with
the opening words of a revolutionary
song ('Ça ira') on his cap, sits in
lewd triumph over the work of the
mob. The hanged figures of a bishop,
two friars, and a judge, a burning
church, and the grim ingenuity of
the guillotine specially adorned for
the king, combine to show the
response of most Englishmen to that
event.

The Zenith of French Glory; _ The Pinnacle of Liberty.
Religion, Justice, Loyalty, & all the Bugbears of Unenlighten'd Minds, Farewell!

supporting harmony. For the Romantics society had become an evil force
moulding and stunting its citizens. It was not merely that so many people were
foolish, greedy, and vain—the eighteenth-century satirists had seen that more
clearly than anyone else—it was that society itself came to be regarded as a
dark, repressive cloud, limiting action and obscuring perception.

Of the many consequences of these ideas for the poets one was the flight
from the city. Classical literature had been metropolitan, associated with the
Greek cities, with Alexandria, and with Rome. It is the boast of English
classicism that London may be worthily added to this list, and the late
eighteenth century saw comparable claims made for Edinburgh. The Romantic
poets on the whole fled from the city. As Shelley remarked, 'Hell is a city much
like London.' Wordsworth, looking at London from Westminster Bridge, did
declare that 'Earth hath not anything to show more fair', but that was when

the city was asleep in the early dawn. Awake it was a prison to those pent up inside it, from which he retreated to the English Lakes. Among the Romantic poets only Blake's vision was of a regenerated city.

Of the many social evils of the late eighteenth and early nineteenth centuries—the slave trade, the treatment of the poor, press-gangs—one was beginning to be recognized as a new and growing threat: industrialization. In the Preface to his poem *Milton* (1804), there appeared Blake's famous question, 'And was Jerusalem builded here / Among these dark Satanic mills?' Blake no doubt had factories in mind here; but he usually uses the word 'mill' in its primary sense of something that grinds. He frequently uses the image of the mill for the repetitive churning and grinding of oppressive philosophies. By and large the description of mass industrialization is a feature of mid-nineteenth-century literature. But the description of the cast of mind that causes it to happen—to borrow a distinction from Dickens's *Hard Times*, the Gradgrind rather than the Bounderby—was first recognized for what it was by the Romantics.

It is hardly surprising therefore to learn that the Romantic poets turned to nature. This is not to imply that their predecessors did not write about the natural world. They did, but they tended to appreciate different things there. In a rural retreat of happy contemplation for the Augustans, Windsor Forest, Pope rejoiced that 'Here Ceres' gifts in waving prospect stand, / And nodding tempt the joyful reaper's hand'. What the Augustans liked to see in nature was man and nature working together productively, reflecting good government and a benevolent Creator. Nature needed the help of man if she was to fulfil herself. The Romantics describe many different kinds of natural scene, and they are if not 'wild' at least independent of man. Many of the poets of this period found their deepest experiences in nature. For them it was nature, rather than society, that was man's proper setting: man needed the help of nature to fulfil himself.

The Romantic period saw also a shift in religious ideas. This is not surprising as so many of the areas of debate were precisely those where man in the past would have looked for answers from the Church. It is the first period in English literature when many writers failed to find Christianity satisfying. Although there was in the period a pronounced streak of rationalistic atheism, influenced by writers of the French Enlightenment, there is noticeable among the Romantic poets a search for a spiritual reality. The problem was that orthodox Christianity did not appear to supply it. Some writers, instead of being attracted to heaven by Christianity, celebrated the glorious excesses of hell. But this inversion, though useful to project an extreme state of mind, was not enough. The more visionary writers of the Romantic period, drawing on other traditions, particularly Platonism and Neoplatonism and various forms of dissenting Christianity, propound a personal search for the spiritual, and many of their poems are built round this search.

In the search for a spiritual truth the Romantic poets used two faculties

SIR ISAAC NEWTON by Blake (1795).

> Nature, and Nature's Laws lay hid in Night.
> God said, *Let Newton be!* and All was *Light*.

That was Alexander Pope's epitaph for Sir Isaac Newton (1730). Blake's *Newton* shows Newton doubled over the task of measuring and calculating, in the Romantic period's most succinct condemnation of scientific rationalism. Newton is apparently under water, the symbol, according to the Neoplatonists, of materialism.

which rationalism had tended to discredit: feelings and the imagination. Keats made a large claim for both of these when he asserted, 'I am certain of nothing but of the holiness of the Heart's affections and the truth of Imagination—'. The imagination in the Romantic period was raised from being simply the faculty for creating fictions, pleasing perhaps, but not necessarily true, to a method of apprehending and communicating truth. The result was that the search for spiritual truth became one in which the poet played a greater role than before. The imagination, the peculiar gift of the poet, was now enlisted in man's most important endeavour.

The poet ceased to be a man of letters and became an artist. But how is the artist to fit into an increasingly bourgeois society? The eighteenth century had seen the growth of the system of supporting a writer through the marketing of his product by the booksellers. Of the poets of this period only two met with commercial success, Scott and Byron. Most of the others survived through inheritances or the help of friends. In his *Elegy written in a Country Church-Yard* Thomas Gray, drawing inspiration from his own temperament, had painted a picture of the misfit poet suffering an untimely death. The submerged implications of suicide in that poem were enacted in real life in the tragic case of Thomas Chatterton (1752–70). Chatterton, inspired by medieval documents in the church of St Mary Redcliffe in Bristol, wrote poems in the name of a fictitious fifteenth-century monk, Thomas Rowley. It was an age used to fictitious authors, but Chatterton confused the issue by also contriving imitation medieval manuscripts and allowing it to be believed that he had found the real thing. His poems, their breath-taking lyricism hidden to the casual eye under his 'medieval' spelling and vocabulary, were not recognized, and he drove himself to a death that appeared to be suicide in 1770, at the age of seventeen. Chatterton became for the Romantics a symbol of the poet: a youthful genius, driven by poverty and lack of recognition to a tragic death; and this was long before the early deaths of the second generation of Romantic poets.

But it is time to enter a caveat. The use of the term 'Romantic' obscures the many differences between the poets of this period. It is salutary to recall that though the term was used by German critics at the very end of the eighteenth century to describe features which they found in their own literature, it was not at the time used in Britain in that way. The term 'Romantic', to describe the poets writing roughly between 1780 and 1830, did not come into currency until the second half of the nineteenth century. It may be a useful term, so long as it does not imply more in common among the writers than there is, or more in common with literary trends on the Continent.

The Poets: the Older Generation

William Blake (1757–1827) was the son of a hosier in London; he became an engraver. As a child he saw visions, from which he drew inspiration all his life. Blake supplemented his training as a painter and engraver by wide reading, especially in the Bible and the works of Dante, Shakespeare, and Milton. Some of Blake's other reading is more surprising unless one recalls his intellectual background, in political radicalism and religious dissent. In particular he was influenced by the religious writings of Jacob Boehme and Emanuel Swedenborg and by the work of Thomas Taylor, the translator of Plato and his Neoplatonist followers. What Blake particularly responded to in such reading was the assertion of the central importance of a spiritual world, and of the presence of the divine in man.

From an early age Blake had been writing poetry, and his two arts, of poetry and engraving, came together triumphantly for the first time in 1789 with the publication of his *Songs of Innocence*. The volume was illustrated and printed by himself. *Songs of Innocence* is an evocation of that paradise which Milton had declared lost. Blake was the first poet to locate innocence not in the race's childhood but in the individual's childhood, and his book is a collection of short poems influenced in style by children's songs, ballads, and hymns. Poems such as 'Nurse's Song' and 'The Ecchoing Green' present the joys of childhood in a natural and protected world. The same delight is expressed in the illustrations. These consist of little scenes showing children playing, as well as decorative trees and foliage framing the poem, with often little tendrils sporting

THE TITLE-PAGE OF *SONGS OF INNOCENCE* (1789). The lower part of the plate is a naturalistic scene of children reading, suggesting a children's book. In the upper part the branches of a tree turn into the flame-like letters of the word *Songs*, among which are birds and joyful figures. The figure playing a pipe leaning against the *I* of *Innocence* is probably Blake himself, the piper of the first song.

'THE CHIMNEY SWEEPER' FROM *SONGS OF EXPERIENCE* (1794). A solitary child walks barefoot in the snow with his bag of soot, 'crying weep, weep'. This and the illustration to the poem 'London' are the only two urban scenes in Blake's *Songs*.

between the lines of verse. The world of *Songs of Innocence* is a pastoral world, but it is Christian pastoral rather than classical. From the immemorial occupation of watching sheep there arises, naturally and without anxiety, a religious question. In 'The Lamb' the speaker, a child, asks, 'Little Lamb who made thee?'

These poems conjure up clear, intense pictures; but there are others where the response is more ambiguous. In 'The Chimney Sweeper', Blake faces one of the social outrages of his day, the use of little boys as chimney sweeps.

> When my mother died I was very young,
> And my father sold me while yet my tongue,
> Could scarcely cry weep weep weep weep,
> So your chimneys I sweep & in soot I sleep.

The child is so young that he can scarcely say 'sweep'; so with terrible irony it comes out 'weep weep weep weep'—incidentally compelling the ear to abandon the metre of the stanza. One is forced to ask what has happened to the concept of innocence when one of the songs presents this great wrong perpetrated against children. But Blake proclaims an innocence which can, miraculously, survive the most appalling conditions. The little chimney sweep is not complaining at his situation; what has interested him is a dream in which 'by came an Angel who had a bright key, / And he opened the coffins & set them all free'. The child can argue only from within the situation; he cannot stand outside and protest that it should never have been allowed to happen. The child may be a limited reasoner, but he can see angels. It is a feature of Blake that he too could see angels, and he was capable also of scathing social criticism.

Five years later, in 1794, Blake produced another sequence of poems entitled *Songs of Experience* in which he wrote of things unknown or only hinted at in *Innocence*. Here the child and young adult are impeded by social and religious oppression, with a sickly consciousness of it. The illustrations show death, weeping, menace, and desolation. Here we have the angry tone of protest:

> Is this a holy thing to see,
> In a rich and fruitful land,
> Babes reduced to misery,
> Fed with cold and usurous hand?
>
> ('Holy Thursday')

We have also the cynical reasoning of the world of Experience:

> Pity would be no more,
> If we did not make somebody Poor . . .
>
> ('The Human Abstract')

Repression in *Songs of Experience* is not necessarily from without. 'Mind-forged manacles' are not always forged in someone else's mind, as Blake points out in a series of poems on inhibition, secretiveness, and hypocrisy. Many of the most memorable of these poems consist of a slight episode or a single image presented as an enigmatic symbol of a psychological state. 'The Sick Rose', for instance, is one image in words and illustration:

> O Rose thou art sick.
> The invisible worm,
> That flies in the night
> In the howling storm:
>
> Has found out thy bed
> Of crimson joy:
> And his dark secret love
> Does thy life destroy.

The rose and the worm suggest sexual symbolism, but no specific interpretation removes the general implication of the taint which affects all life's dearest values. This is the terrible vision of Experience.

Some of the poems in *Songs of Experience* parallel songs in *Songs of Innocence*. One of these is perhaps Blake's most famous poem, 'The Tyger'.

> Tyger Tyger, burning bright,
> In the forests of the night;
> What immortal hand or eye,
> Could frame thy fearful symmetry?

It recalls the question put to the Lamb, 'Little Lamb who made thee?' It is a theological question, about who made the world. Looking at the tiger the poet asks, working up from creature to creator, who could make thee?

> What the hammer? what the chain,
> In what furnace was thy brain?

The imagery at this point is from metal-working: the hammer, the furnace, the anvil. Are we, on the basis of the tiger, to posit an artificer God, a suggestion drawing on all the traditional fear of metal-working? In 'The Lamb' the world is united with its maker; in 'The Tyger' the poet reflects, 'Did he who made the Lamb make thee?' The poet of 'The Tyger' can only ask questions. There is no reassuring answer, only in the last stanza a reframing of the initial question

> What immortal hand or eye,
> Dare frame thy fearful symmetry?

In the difference between these two poems can be seen in embryo two important strands in Blake's later work. Blake distinguishes between the distant creator God, variously at odds with his creation, and whom he came to call Urizen, and the divine figure in 'The Lamb'. He who made the lamb shares a name with his creature; he is Jesus, or 'the Divine Humanity', the regenerative figure of Blake's later poems.

Blake printed his own works by a method devised by himself of relief etching. After printing each plate would be touched up and coloured by hand. Visually Blake's books hark back to medieval manuscripts in providing a rich marriage of text and illustration. Blake was a total artist, undertaking many roles usually separated. He was poet, painter, engraver, printer, publisher, and bookseller. In the last unfortunately he failed, and his poems found few readers in his own day. The fact that the etcher uses an acid bath to isolate the lines on his plate was of significance to Blake. In *The Marriage of Heaven and Hell* (1790-3) he describes his method of printing as 'melting apparent surfaces away, and displaying the infinite which was hid'. Blake came to see himself as a prophet, a man of inspired utterance.

We have already seen that Blake's penetrating observation of evil led him to speculate on its origin. Blake shared the Neoplatonist view that the evil in the world is inherent in 'generation', in being born into the natural world. The result of 'generation' is to confine man in his five senses, woefully limiting his capacity for perception. Man can be freed only by the operation of the Poetic Genius, or Imagination, the capacity to apprehend realities beyond the prison of the senses. From this belief stemmed Blake's dislike of the 'Philosophic & Experimental' which had dominated the thought of the preceding century. Enquiry based on the evidence of the 'natural or bodily organs' would always tend to deny the existence of what it could not perceive—hence in Blake's view the neglect of the 'infinite' world. Blake believed this profoundly, and he chose no petty target when he made his most memorable indictment an engraving of Isaac Newton, leaning forward engrossed in a diagram he is drawing with the aid of compasses.

In Blake's earlier prophetic works he was inspired by current affairs: a radical in politics, he celebrated the independence of the American colonies and the French Revolution; and in *Visions of the Daughters of Albion* (1793) he denounced the subordination of women. In his later works such topical references become less frequent as he expounded his beliefs about the world and his hopes for its regeneration in a series of prophetic books for which he developed his own mythology. It is a vast system, continually evolving. He tackles the question of the origin of evil in *The Book of Urizen* (1794). This book, whose title imitates a book of the Old Testament, is Blake's version of Genesis, his account of creation. In Christianity the creation is an act of heroic power. For Blake the creation of the world is a wilful and tragic mistake on the part of his tyrant God, Urizen. Urizen, one of Blake's most consistent mythological creations, is associated with law and with dividing and measuring. In the illustrations he is an old man, bearded and wrinkled.

Blake's later works are difficult for the reader. The characters are confusing,

URIZEN EXPLORES HIS WORLD. Blake's *Book of Urizen* (1974), plate 22. Urizen with 'a globe of fire lighting his journey' explores the world he has created and finds it 'teemd vast enormities'. He is sickened at what he finds, 'for he saw / That no flesh nor spirit could keep / His iron laws one moment'.

the structure perfunctory, and one can feel that the emotions are too few and too extreme. Blake had scant sympathy with such criticism: 'But you ought to know that What is Grand is necessarily obscure to Weak men.' Blame for his obscurities must be divided between the demands of his visionary imagination and the isolation of the unrecognized artist bent over his laborious art. In even his most difficult works, however, the reader is rewarded with passages of gnomic splendour and a note of prophecy not heard again until the work of W. B. Yeats and T. S. Eliot. In his last years Blake produced some of his finest engravings, illustrating the Book of Job, Virgil's *Pastorals*, and the works of Dante. He died 'Singing of the things he saw in Heaven'.

Wordsworth and Coleridge are the only two of the Romantic poets who worked, for a time, in collaboration, and their early careers show a number of parallels. William Wordsworth (1770-1850) was born in Cockermouth, Cumberland; Samuel Taylor Coleridge (1772-1834) was the son of the vicar of Ottery St Mary, Devon. They both went to Cambridge University. Wordsworth was in France in 1791-2 and mingled with republicans and saw the ruins of the Bastille; the subsequent excesses of the triumphant Jacobins caused him acute suffering. The young Coleridge wrote and lectured in the republican cause, and, turning from political to social revolution, was involved in an ill-fated project to create an ideal society, a Pantisocracy, on the banks of the Susquehanna in Pennsylvania. In 1797 the two were living near each other in Somerset. The result was one of the most important publications of the Romantic period, a collection of *Lyrical Ballads, With a Few Other Poems*, published in Bristol in 1798. According to Coleridge, in his *Biographia Literaria* (1817), the plan of the *Lyrical Ballads* was that he should supply poems whose subject-matter was supernatural, while Wordsworth's would deal with ordinary life. Coleridge honoured his part of the bargain with 'The Ancient Mariner', which appeared as the first poem in the collection. Of the remainder the greater number were by Wordsworth. A second edition in 1800 contained more poems and a 'Preface' by Wordsworth in which he expounded his views on poetry.

Wordsworth's 'Preface' is best read as a statement of his own practice:

The principal object then which I proposed to myself in these Poems was to make the incidents of common life interesting by tracing in them, truly though not ostentatiously, the primary laws of our nature . . .

It is important to notice what is new here. The ambition to trace 'the primary laws of our nature' would have been shared by many of his Augustan predecessors. What is new in Wordsworth is to look for them in 'common life'. Appropriately to his subject-matter the language of Wordsworth's poems was to be 'a selection of the language really used by men'. In making such a claim Wordsworth was declaring his opposition to the convention of 'poetic diction' which he thought had rendered the language of poetry artificial. It is possible that these points gain too easy assent today, and to recognize the impact of Wordsworth's ideas it is necessary to recall the hostility of many of the early reviews which found the simplicity of his style and subject-matter shocking and 'unpoetical'.

Wordsworth's contributions to the *Lyrical Ballads* commonly explore the submerged tragedies in society, the sufferings of old age, poverty, and desertion, which have often left their victim half-crazed. He writes about basic relationships, especially that of parent and child, where the emotions are intense and instinctive. Some of his poems take the form of monologues overheard by the poet, such as 'The Female Vagrant' and 'The Mad Mother'. Others are shaped round an encounter between the poet and another person. The other person is usually very old, like 'The Old Cumberland Beggar', or young, like the child in 'We are Seven', or otherwise unable to command the situation. In the poem the poet's thoughts proceed from external description to a moment of illumination as he reflects on the true nature of the life he is observing. A third sort are tales, often founded on some slight incident or anecdote that Wordsworth had heard. Of these the best known is 'The Idiot Boy'. The poem recounts the heroic ride undertaken by Johnny, the idiot son of Betty Foy, to summon the doctor to a sick neighbour. Much of the attention of the poem is on Betty as she waits with the invalid for Johnny's return. Her mood changes from pride and confidence, to anger at his tardiness, to fear for his safety. When in the end she makes the journey to the doctor herself, so anxious is she for her child that she forgets the original reason for the summons. Wordsworth gave the best description of the aim of such a poem: 'it is to follow the fluxes and refluxes of the mind when agitated by the great and simple affections of our nature.' What cannot be followed, however, is Johnny's journey. All we have is his enigmatic account of his glorious adventure, the couplet which had fired Wordsworth's imagination in the first place:

'The cocks did crow to-whoo, to-whoo,
And the sun did shine so cold.'

For some readers the narrative sophistication of this deceptively simple poem is not sufficient compensation for banality of style, leading at times to bathos. Few will deny, however, that Wordsworth here finds subject-matter where few earlier poets had sought it, and responds without sentimentality.

The reason for the strength of humble life was its closeness to nature, for Wordsworth's poor are the rural poor. The major theme of Wordsworth's poetry was the influence of nature on man, and as well as exploring it socially he explored it autobiographically. As a child he had felt the influence of nature very strongly. It brought intense haunting pleasure, and also exerted over him a tutelary power. On one occasion he borrowed a shepherd's boat, 'an act of stealth', and rowed it out into the lake (it was Ullswater). As he rowed out a huge cliff, previously hidden from view, became visible, climbing more

VIEW IN LANGDALE. The popularity of the English Lakes increased after Thomas Gray's visit in 1769. John Constable, a native of Suffolk, went there in 1806, and met Wordsworth. This water-colour shows the view from Langdale up Oxendale to Crinkle Crags. Although Constable found there 'the finest scenery that ever was', he is reported to have said 'that the solitude of mountains oppressed his spirits'.

menacingly over him with every stroke. He turned back, and as the rhythmical strokes took him closer to where he could return the boat the cliff receded. The passage in which Wordsworth describes this, in Book I of *The Prelude*, is a perfect example of the union of the natural scene, the mental state of the child, and the poetic description.

In much of Wordsworth's autobiographical poetry he explores those moments of intense awareness which he referred to as 'spots of time'. One concern that preoccupied him was the question of holding on to his experiences. Could they bear fruit when he was away from the scenery that inspired them? Could they be sustained when the 'dizzy raptures' of youth gave way to maturity? A poem which deals with these themes is his 'Lines composed a few miles above Tintern Abbey', which appeared as the last poem in the *Lyrical Ballads*. The poet is aware that his response to nature has changed in character with the years:

                    For I have learned
            To look on nature, not as in the hour
            Of thoughtless youth, but hearing oftentimes
            The still, sad music of humanity,
            Not harsh nor grating, though of ample power
            To chasten and subdue. And I have felt
            A presence that disturbs me with the joy
            Of elevated thoughts; a sense sublime
            Of something far more deeply interfused,
            Whose dwelling is the light of setting suns,
            And the round ocean, and the living air,
            And the blue sky, and in the mind of man,
            A motion and a spirit, that impels
            All thinking things, all objects of all thought,
            And rolls through all things.

This poem takes us to the heart of Wordsworth. It has his characteristic tone of dignified tranquillity, recognizing loss and admitting recompense. It is in his most successful metre, blank verse of an austere majesty. The poet is describing visionary experience, and doing so outside any religious code which might have supplied vocabulary and images. On occasions like this one ceases to ask about 'the language really used by men'; the miracle is that the language will express it at all.

In 1799 Wordsworth returned to the Lakes, where he lived until his death in 1850. It was a fruitful homecoming, made vivid to us from the journals of his faithful sister Dorothy. Shortly before his return he had started the long autobiographical poem tracing 'the Growth of a Poet's Mind', which was published posthumously as *The Prelude*. He published a collection of poems in 1807 and a long poem called *The Excursion* in 1814. Wordsworth went on writing poetry all his life, but seldom in later years recaptured the visionary intensity of his youth. The move to the Lakes gave him the resolution of his problem as a young man. He renounced the principles of French republicanism to find an answer that was more suited to his temperament in rural life, especially as symbolized by the Cumbrian shepherd. A sturdy independent figure, like the hero of his poem 'Michael', the shepherd was preserved in natural innocence, and bound to the land and to the community by ties of simple piety. The subtitle of 'Michael' is 'A Pastoral'. A realistic poem, it apparently has little in common with the outmoded literary convention of pastoral. But in another sense it achieves the same thing: it presents an alternative order founded on country life, alternative not to a corrupt court, but to the corruptions of the expanding commerce and industrialization of the cities.

His years of collaboration with Wordsworth were the happiest of Coleridge's life, and the most productive of poetry. At about the time they met Coleridge devised a poetic form for autobiographical exploration which encouraged a

WORDSWORTH ON HELVELLYN (1842). The background of this portrait by Benjamin Robert Haydon may have been suggested by the lines on Wordsworth in Keats's sonnet 'Great spirits now on earth are sojourning', which he sent to Haydon in 1816. Wordsworth mentions Helvellyn in several poems.

quiet ruminative style. Usually called the 'conversation poems', they are blank verse monologues in which there is a silent or envisaged hearer. In these poems Coleridge starts from a domestic situation—his cottage, his wife, friends, and baby—and moves out into the landscape surrounding his Somerset home. These poems lead out to some point of illumination and back again. One such is 'This Lime-Tree Bower my Prison'. Coleridge addressed the poem to Charles

Lamb. As a result of an accident the poet is unable to join Lamb and the Wordsworths on a walk. Confined to a 'lime-tree bower' he follows in his mind the walk his friends are taking. He envisages Lamb's feelings on seeing the sun set gloriously over the ocean, feelings beyond normal bodily sensations, accompanying an experience of the presence of 'the Almighty Spirit'. Certain ideas in this poem Coleridge shared with Wordsworth—for instance, the healing and revelatory power of nature, and its power in the memory. But although they both agree on the importance of nature, they do not take an identical view. Nature for Wordsworth is a more autonomous force than it is for Coleridge. Coleridge usually celebrates the one Life or Spirit which animates both man and the natural world.

Coleridge's conversation poems of the 1790s, despite the anxiety in some of them about political events, are written in a tone of optimism. In a poem written in 1802, 'Dejection: an Ode', that tone has gone. The domestic setting has become painful as the poet suffers a life of physical pain and marital unhappiness. He describes a mood of despair, or what we should now call depression. In this 'unimpassioned grief' he derives no pleasure from nature, and concludes, 'I may not hope from outward forms to win / The passion and the life, whose fountains are within.' His afflictions have robbed him of the faculty which enabled him to respond to nature; and worst of all they have robbed him of his 'shaping spirit of Imagination'.

As the imagination was so important a faculty for the Romantic poets it is perhaps desirable to ask what it was thought to be; what, for instance, was Coleridge's 'shaping spirit of Imagination'? For eighteenth-century theorists the imagination was simply a faculty for reordering former sense impressions: the perceiving mind and the perceived object were separate. For the Romantics the imagination had a larger contribution to make to the record of experience. Its value became for many of the poets an article of faith, and they mention it with reverence. But while Blake and Keats give their view of the imagination in magnificent affirmations and *aperçus*, it is to Coleridge that we must turn for a reasoned account of it. Much of Coleridge's philosophy is scattered in notebooks, still being published; but his central ideas on the imagination are set forth with reasonable conciseness in chapter XIII of *Biographia Literaria*. There Coleridge divides the imagination into two, the primary and the secondary. The primary imagination is the first act of self-consciousness, which makes knowledge and perception possible. It is 'a repetition in the finite mind of the eternal act of creation in the infinite I AM'. 'I AM,' whether said by God or man, unites the perceiver and the perceived in one act. The secondary imagination, which is the poetic imagination, brings that fusion of perceiving mind and perceived object out into the world. The poetic imagination is a faculty of the mind, involving 'deep feeling and profound thought'—perhaps what we should call 'insight'—which interprets, shapes, and re-creates its experiences. It was because Coleridge's secondary imagination was so closely analogous to the primary creative acts of the universe that its possession in a poet was so important, and its loss, in his 'Dejection' ode, so grievous.

These ideas continued to haunt Coleridge's thought throughout his life. Coleridge was poet, philosopher, theologian, critic, journalist, and playwright. As a philosopher he introduced to Britain the work of the German idealist philosophers. He spent the last years of his life from 1816 until 1834 in the house of Dr Gillman in Highgate, where he was able to think and write in a friendly and protective environment.

As a poet Coleridge is best known for a small number of poems, of which the most outstanding are 'The Ancient Mariner' and 'Kubla Khan'. 'The Ancient Mariner' was the nearest in the *Lyrical Ballads* collection to a true ballad. It tells a story, with the stress on action rather than character; and its form probably derives from the eighteenth-century fashion for the ballad imitation. In accordance with his agreement with Wordsworth, Coleridge's tale was supernatural.

'The Ancient Mariner' owes much to Coleridge's reading of Renaissance travel literature. No objective is stated for the mariner's voyage, but on entering the Pacific he says, 'We were the first that ever burst / Into that silent sea.' As the first European to sail into the Pacific was Magellan in 1520 the poem may be assumed to be set in the early sixteenth century. 'The Ancient Mariner' is a tale of a voyage beyond the limits of the inhabited world, with a strong sense of global geography; it is a tale of death, nightmare, and hallucination. On the

'THE ICE WAS ALL AROUND'. Coleridge's description of the south polar sea in 'The Ancient Mariner' drew on accounts of the far north, including Frederick Martens' *Voyage into Spitzbergen and Greenland* (1694). This plate illustrates a chapter 'Of vast Mountains and Fields of Ice, and the great difficulty of sailing'.

most rational level of interpretation it is a story—not unknown in travel accounts—of a voyage in which after extreme sufferings there was one sole survivor. That survivor, partly deranged, tries to make sense of his experiences. In particular, did he 'deserve' his fate?

The mariner's ship had sailed south, into the south polar regions, where the only living thing to appear was an albatross. After days in which the bird shared the life of the sailors, in an action for which he could offer no explanation, the mariner shot the albatross. The ship was then driven north into the Pacific and becalmed. The sailors suffered extremities of drought. His crewmates, looking for a scapegoat, blame the mariner and 'Instead of the cross, the Albatross / About my neck was hung.' They die cursing him, but the mariner is spared to suffer 'Life-in-Death'. He looked between the 'rotting sea' and his dead crewmates with a 'heart as dry as dust'. Then after seven days he looked again at the creatures of the sea:

> A spring of love gushed from my heart,
> And I blessed them unaware . . .

At this blessing the albatross fell from his neck, the drought gave way to rain, and the mariner was brought mysteriously home.

In justifying his use of the supernatural in his poems, Coleridge explained that its function was to express elements from 'our inward nature'. The use of the supernatural was for Coleridge a technique of psychological revelation; it allowed the poet to bring into play in his poem the hidden forces of the mind. In 'The Ancient Mariner' the chief of these is guilt, especially as it exists in the mind to some extent independent of cause. The mariner's experiences include transgression and apparent retribution, but there is a discontinuity between them. 'The Ancient Mariner' is one of several distinguished literary works on the phantasmagoria of crime and punishment. In the poem events which we suppose to need motive take place without motive. The mariner does not know why he shot the albatross; likewise he blesses the living creatures of the sea 'unaware'. His regenerative acts bring about only partial restoration. He remains a frightening figure, the impact of whose experiences unsettles ordinary life: the Wedding-Guest to whom he tells his tale turns stunned from the feast, and the Pilot's boy who greeted him 'now doth crazy go'.

'Kubla Khan', despite marked differences from 'The Ancient Mariner', also takes its initial inspiration from a travel book. 'Kubla Khan' is thought to have been written in 1797, but it was not published until 1816 at the persuasion of Byron. On publication Coleridge prefixed to it a note about its composition which has become as famous, and as controversial, as the poem. According to the note he fell into an opium-induced sleep over an early seventeenth-century collection of voyages, Samuel Purchas's *Pilgrimage*. (Coleridge had started taking opium, as was usual at the time, as a pain-reliever and tranquillizer.) In his sleep he composed two or three hundred lines. On waking he started to write them down, until, after about fifty lines, he was interrupted 'by a person on business from Porlock'. When he returned to his task he found he could remember scarcely any more. Coleridge called the poem 'A Fragment', in what is now usually assumed to be an unnecessary apology.

'Kubla Khan' is strange and enigmatic. It is full of images that have the clarity and inexplicability of dream. It is apparently about artistic creation, and its mysterious and frightening power. The first thirty-six lines describe Kubla Khan, a thirteenth-century Mongol emperor about whom Coleridge had just been reading in Purchas. He built by decree 'a stately pleasure-dome' in a paradisal garden. Through the garden ran Alph, the sacred river. The river has a source, a chasm where it erupts in violent bursts, and a destination 'Through caverns measureless to man / Down to a sunless sea'. Coleridge presents symbols of his deepest intuitions, where Wordsworth would proceed reflectively. Kubla Khan appears to symbolize the all-powerful artist. He created a beautiful pleasure-dome and garden; through the garden a river ran its mysterious course. The sacred river, bursting forth and then disappearing unfathomably, is a symbol of the artist's inspiration. Kubla Khan's pleasure-dome and the river may be taken as a symbolic presentation of the interaction of what we should now call the conscious and the unconscious in the act of creation.

At line 37 we turn from the creation of an eastern potentate to another and more accessible kind of artist, a damsel with a dulcimer. Surely, the poet asks, if he could revive her 'symphony and song' he could create in emulation of Kubla Khan? And were he to do so the bystanders should beware. What follows is the most famous Romantic description of the artist, a description, deriving details from Plato, of the poet whose inspiration has driven him mad. Poetry like this, which proceeds by image and symbol, will always elude interpretation. Criticism may suggest the source of the images, but it cannot explain their power.

The Scottish Poets

The late eighteenth century saw a shift away from the dominance of the metropolis over the literary culture. Evidence of this may be found in the important books which were published outside London. The *Lyrical Ballads* was published in Bristol. Three years earlier, in 1786, there had appeared *Poems, Chiefly in the Scottish Dialect* by Robert Burns, published in Kilmarnock. Poems like these, which arose from the speech and experience of his native Ayrshire, helped to break down the geographical limitations of eighteenth-century literature. The traditional view of town versus country and the assumption that the relationship between man and nature could be satisfactorily determined in the Thames Valley, which had dominated since the Restoration, gave place to a wider discovery of the variety of Britannia's domains. The poems of George Crabbe describe the villages and small ports of Suffolk; the world of agricultural Northamptonshire is brilliantly evoked in the poems of John Clare. This is clear enough in England. It is clearer still when the muse is found north of the Border.

Robert Burns (1759–96) was born in Alloway, son of a tenant farmer. On the success of his first volume of poems in 1786 he spent some months in Edinburgh where he was praised and patronized as a 'ploughman poet'. Thereafter he returned to farming. In a period of economic hardship in agriculture he failed, and spent his last years as an excise officer in Dumfries. In terms of English literature Burns may be seen as the greatest of the eighteenth-century 'rustic' poets; for the early nineteenth century he was a successor to Chatterton as a type of the poet victimized by a hostile world.

Such ideas, however, give too narrow a view of Burns, for he was a Scottish poet and best seen in that tradition. At the end of the eighteenth century we see a blending of the Scots and English traditions in literature in the works of Burns and Walter Scott. The eighteenth century had had Scottish writers— James Thomson, Smollett, Boswell—but though they sometimes reveal their origin in their writing they did not receive much from the Scots literary tradition. Burns, on the other hand, wrote within that tradition which had flowered in the fifteenth century in the works of William Dunbar and Robert Henryson, and which had its best-known exponents in the eighteenth century in Allan Ramsay and Robert Fergusson. Burns's poems are frequently comic and satiric, and in them the doings of the small town of Mauchline gain their place in literature. His most savage satire is 'Holy Willie's Prayer', a dramatic monologue by a church officer in which the hypocrisy of the speaker and the vengefulness of his Calvinist religion are revealed. The sober and virtuous aspect of Scottish rural life and religion is presented in the 'genre-painting', 'The Cotter's Saturday Night'. Burns often writes about local Ayrshire superstitions, and in such poems fear of the supernatural is shot through with an especial terror of Auld Nick, the Devil. The best known of these is 'Tam o'Shanter', a magnificent and warmly humorous account of Tam's vision of a supernatural company, in which the objectivity of the vision is called in question by the drunkenness of the spectator.

Burns is frequently, at least once a year, celebrated for his defence of freedom and the rights of the common man, and for his sympathetic observation of nature. It is typical of him that he should sympathize with the mouse whose nest he has destroyed ('To a Mouse'), and that he should use the occasion to point up some truth with overtones of proverbial wisdom: 'The best laid schemes o' Mice an' Men / Gang aft a-gley.' The most distinguished of his poems in celebration of freedom is his cantata *Love and Liberty* (published under the title *The Jolly Beggars* in 1799). This cantata draws on *The Beggar's Opera* and a whole tradition of vagabond literature. The ebullient songs of the motley band at Poosie Nansie's gain in vigour because they celebrate not only Liberty in the late eighteenth-century political sense, but also the freedom of the untrammelled life of the road. Burns had a genius for song. He spent the last years of his life collecting Scottish songs and song fragments. He wrote words to Scottish tunes, and 'mended' fragments of song. His skill at this activity has kept many of these songs not simply as recorded pieces of folk poetry, but as songs which are still sung.

The same genius for folk poetry was also found in Burns's fellow countryman, Walter Scott (1771-1832). Scott was of Border descent and spent much of his childhood in Roxburghshire. He was a young lawyer in Edinburgh when he started to search out the Border ballads that he had heard in his youth. The result was *The Minstrelsy of the Scottish Border*, which was published in Kelso in 1802-3.

Although Scott is now best known as a novelist he first became famous with a poem, *The Lay of the Last Minstrel* (1805). His minstrel's tale of love and war is set in the Borders in the sixteenth century. Its success caused Scott to produce further verse romances, *Marmion* (1808) and *The Lady of the Lake* (1810). Readers responded to his heroic characters, and to his romantic landscape descriptions reflecting the moods of man and history. His popularity may be gauged from a remark on changing fashions in poetry in Jane Austen's *Sense and Sensibility*, published in 1811. Elinor Dashwood says to her sister, talking of her new acquaintance with Willoughby,

You know what he thinks of Cowper and Scott; you are certain of his estimating their beauties as he ought, and you have received every assurance of his admiring Pope no more than is proper.

The Poets: the Younger Generation

The importance that the Romantic period accorded to the working of the imagination has tended to make readers overlook those poets whose particular virtue is the accurate observation of the world round them. One such is George Crabbe (1754-1832). A native of Aldeburgh, clergyman, poet, and botanist, Crabbe is a figure who complicates many generalizations about poetry in this period. He is the oldest of the poets mentioned in this chapter, but much of his finest work appeared when he was in middle age. He is best known for *The Borough* (1810), and his collections of tales built round small but significant episodes in ordinary life, *Tales* (1812) and *Tales of the Hall* (1819). Beside the major Romantic poets Crabbe has suffered the indignity of claiming no special inspiration, and his work shows the social and psychological realism that has come to be associated with the novelist rather than the poet. His verse has much in common with that of his Augustan predecessors; his morality is that of the vignettes in Johnson's *Rambler* essays, but with the parish clergyman's closeness to the lives he describes. The poet who was still closer, however, to the countryside he wrote about was John Clare (1793-1864). Clare was the son of a thresher, and such a living as he was able to make was by the various skills of a farm labourer. When he started to publish poems he experienced tensions similar to those of Burns with the literary world. His *Poems Descriptive of Rural Life and Scenery* appeared in 1820, *The Village Minstrel* in 1821, and *The Shepherd's Calendar* in 1827. His was a life of difficulty and tragedy, and he spent his last twenty-three years in the General Lunatic Asylum in Northampton. The enclosure of land in Clare's native village of Helpston in his early manhood combines with his sense of the loss of youthful happiness in poems in which one can detect the influence of Goldsmith's *The Deserted Village*. But there is another note in Clare's poetry that is peculiarly his. He is one of the foremost poets of nature in the English tradition because of his precise observation of the natural world, especially birds, which he presents in language which is vivid with local words and expressions. When he writes of enclosures Clare recognizes the affront to nature involved in a further intrusion of the man-made into nature's domain. His lament for the old village structure of Helpston is on behalf of the poor labourers depossessed of their rights, but it is also on behalf of the beasts who will not now be able to wander at large over the common ('The Mores'), and on behalf of each field, moor, and tree. In his later poems written in the asylum Clare produced lyrics of a startling visionary quality, such as 'A Vision' (1844):

> I lost the love, of heaven above;
> I spurned the lust, of earth below;
> I felt the sweets of fancied love,—
> And hell itself my only foe.

If there is any poet with which to compare him in such poems it is his contemporary Emily Brontë (see chapter 7).

In his madness one of Clare's repeated delusions was that he was Byron. There is pathos in this association between the poet with the lowest worldly fortunes and his flamboyant contemporary. George Gordon Byron (1788-1824) was the son of a dashing but spendthrift father and the Scottish heiress whom his father had married to restore his fortunes. At the age of ten, on the death of a great-uncle, he became Lord Byron and owner of Newstead Abbey in Nottinghamshire. He was educated at Harrow and Cambridge. Byron was a handsome young man, though with a deformed foot of which he was acutely conscious. He had an aristocratic bearing, with a liking for action; he affected to despise 'scribbling and scribes'. 'Who', he asked, 'would write, who had any thing better to do?' Nevertheless he soon entered the arena: he published in 1809 a satire on the current literary scene, *English Bards and Scotch Reviewers*. In the same year, at the age of twenty-one, he set out to travel abroad. The war with France influenced his route; he travelled to Portugal and Spain, and

'THAT BEAUTIFUL PALE FACE IS MY FATE' (Lady Caroline Lamb). Byron drawn by George Henry Harlow, engraved by H. Meyer (1816). The calculated negligence of the open-necked shirt set a fashion.

thence to Albania and Greece. In Greece he started to write a poem, in Spenserian stanzas, on his travels. The first two cantos were published after his return to England under the title *Childe Harold's Pilgrimage*. Descriptions of Portugal and Spain were of topical interest in view of the Peninsular War; Albania introduced the exotic. His first acquaintance with Greece established Byron's love for that country and its despoiled places which was to remain with him all his life. But it was not those things which caused *Childe Harold's Pilgrimage* to create a stir on its first appearance on 10 March 1812.

'I awoke one morning and found myself famous,' was Byron's comment. In Childe Harold (the title 'Childe' alludes to a way of styling the hero found in ballads) we meet for the first time the character who has come to be known as the 'Byronic hero'. His qualities were summed up by Macaulay, 'a man proud, moody, cynical, with defiance on his brow, and misery in his heart, a scorner of his kind, implacable in revenge, yet capable of deep and strong affection'. The character owes something to Milton's Satan, to the dauntless figures of contemporary German literature, and to the dark and discontented heroes of the Gothic novel—with the added *frisson* of self-portraiture. It had a delirious effect on the European public. In the following years Byron produced further poems: *The Bride of Abydos* and *The Giaour* appeared in 1813, and *The Corsair* in 1814. In them we find the same towering heroes, and plots involving crime, infatuation, and death. If we may use Jane Austen's characters again as witnesses to popular taste in poetry, we may note that by the time she came to write *Persuasion*, in 1816, Byron had come to rival Scott. Captain Benwick's conversation included

trying to ascertain whether *Marmion* or *The Lady of the Lake* were to be preferred, and how ranked the *Giaour* and *The Bride of Abydos*: and moreover, how the *Giaour* was to be pronounced . . .

[*Giaour* meaning infidel, unbeliever, is pronounced to rhyme with 'hour'.]

In England Byron was a Whig nobleman, and in one of his few speeches in the House of Lords he spoke eloquently in defence of the Luddites; he was a Regency debauchee, described by Lady Caroline Lamb as 'Mad—bad—and dangerous to know'. In 1815 he married, and from then on his life started to enact aspects of his poetic hero in earnest. He was separated from his wife the following year, and left England amid rumours of an affair with his half-sister. He never returned.

In 1817, from Italy, he published *Manfred*, a metaphysical verse drama, set in the Alps, which is plainly autobiographical. Its satiated hero, a voluntary outcast rebelling against the human condition, 'half dust, half deity', seeks only oblivion.

In 1818 Byron began what was to be his major work, *Don Juan*, which was unfinished in over sixteen cantos at his death. It is not surprising that he should have been interested in the libertine hero; but his interest does not embrace the traditional conclusion, the descent to hell. His casual attitude to the conclusion he did not reach is expressed in a letter to his publisher, John Murray, '. . . I had not quite fixed whether to make him end in Hell, or in an unhappy marriage, not knowing which would be the severest'. Like Childe Harold Don Juan may be said to wander; but he is less indebted to Cain than to the heroes of the picaresque novel. Instead of the brooding Byronic hero, in *Don Juan* we have a buoyant hero with zest for experience and sensation, but with little definable character, the latter being supplied by the cynical and witty voice of the narrator.

Don Juan is in Byron's most successful and characteristic metre, the *ottava rima*, deriving from Italian poetry. It is demanding in terms of rhyme, and Byron's virtuosity and flippancy in using it, especially in the final couplet of the stanza, are an important part of the impact of the poem. This stanza, with its capacity for dignity but aptness for deflation, is a ready vehicle for Byron's comic purpose. Don Juan is taken on a series of outlandish adventures. His arrival in England at the end of Canto X is an opportunity for satire—satire on Britain, the 'False friend, who held out freedom to mankind, / And now would chain them, to the very *mind*'. In such passages *Don Juan* is an unromantic poem. It is a reminder of the early eighteenth-century satirists whom Byron admired,

Oh! that the Desert were my dwelling place!!!!!.....

Byron.

BYRON MANIA, in a sketch by Olivia de Ros (*c.*1820). The quotation at the foot is from *Childe Harold's Pilgrimage*, IV. 177. The picture (*top right*) shows Almack's, fashionable assembly rooms in St James's, at some remove from a desert.

> Thou shalt believe in Milton, Dryden, Pope;
>   Thou shalt not set up Wordsworth, Coleridge, Southey ...   (I. 205)

But although his criticism of society has something in common with Pope's, Byron's voice is not that of the Augustan consensus, that of all right-thinking people; it is rather the solitary voice, angry and mocking, of the aristocratic exile.

In the second generation of Romantic poets we find a turning away from the dark, illiberal north to the warmer and more generous climate of the Mediterranean. The poets were not all attracted in the same way. Keats, who was hardly to experience the warm south in person, responded to the beauty of mythological Greece. His deepest feelings were called forth by a country and period 'When holy were the haunted forest boughs'. For Keats perhaps sensation was enough; for Byron it was not. He saw nothing but oppression and hypocrisy in English society after Waterloo; but the southern countries that he loved, Italy and Greece, were not free either. The subjection of northern Italy to the Austrians and Greece to the Turks gave Byron scope for positive action that he had not found in England. His evocative lines on 'The Isles of Greece' in Canto III of *Don Juan* are a great hymn to national freedom. His death of a fever at Missolonghi in 1824 while preparing to fight in the cause of Greek independence gave stature to his reputation as embodying the finest qualities of the Romantic hero.

Percy Bysshe Shelley (1792-1822) was born in Sussex, eldest son of Timothy Shelley, a Member of Parliament and heir to a baronetcy. He was educated at Eton. As a young man Shelley absorbed the political radicalism of William Godwin, author of *Political Justice* (1793). In 1810 he went up to University College, Oxford. Two terms later he was expelled for refusing to satisfy the college's enquiries concerning a pamphlet he had published entitled *The Necessity of Atheism*. 'I have experienced tyranny and injustice before, and I well know what vulgar violence is . . .' Shelley declared to the Master. He was eighteen. He was fervently opposed to the tyranny of king, Church, and family; and he devoted his life to his vision of liberty.

In 1811 he made a run-away marriage with a sixteen-year-old, Harriet Westbrook, and established a life in which he attempted to put his ideas into practice. He wrote and campaigned on the radical issues of the day. In 1813 he published his first long poem, *Queen Mab*, a statement of his views, with forthright prose notes. In 1814 he abandoned Harriet and their two children and eloped with Mary, the daughter of William Godwin and Mary Wollstonecraft. Two years later he published a volume of poems in which the title poem was *Alastor*, a dream-like allegory in which the poet-hero pursues a visionary beloved. In 1818 Shelley left England for Italy, and never returned. Like Byron he left behind him a considerable reputation: he had excited the interest of government spies by his radical pamphleteering; he had offended society with his atheism; he was held to account for the suicide of Harriet, and a court deemed him unsuitable to have custody of their children. Godwin's liberalism did not extend to Shelley's running off with his daughter; and the young man always overspent the money grudgingly allowed him by his irate father.

It is hardly surprising that a poem Shelley wrote shortly after arriving in Italy should express unhappiness. In his 'Lines written among the Euganean Hills' he gives a description of Venice in the sunrise which reminds one that Shelley is the poet who most invites comparison with Turner, in the rendering of brilliant light effects. The sun rises out of the ocean

> And before that chasm of light,
> As within a furnace bright,
> Column, tower, and dome, and spire,
> Shine like obelisks of fire . . .

Mer de Glace ——— Sea of Ice ——

'DUMB CATARACTS AND STREAMS OF ICE' (*The Prelude*, VI, 530). The vale of Chamonix, and the Mont Blanc range above it, inspired poems by Coleridge and Shelley as well as Wordsworth, and became increasingly popular with tourists. The Mer de Glace, the setting for this mocking cartoon of 1821 by George Cruikshank, is a glacier above Chamonix. The inscription at the top, from Virgil's *Aeneid*, II, 429-30, reads 'Neither your great piety nor the fillet of Apollo protected you as you slid.'

As Shelley looks down on Venice his own misery is mingled with that of the city whose republic had been overthrown by Napoleon in 1797. Wordsworth had written a sonnet paying tribute to what Venice had been, 'Once did she hold the gorgeous east in fee . . .'. It is not in Shelley's nature to be purely elegiac, and he rouses the Venetians to resist their conquerors and restore the 'Sun-girt City' to her ancient state. In the last paragraph he hopes that his little community may establish themselves in Italy in some 'healing Paradise'. The poem ends on a brief prophetic note: the influence of such a paradise, spreading beyond themselves, would be such that earth itself would 'grow young again'.

Residence in Italy did not remove Shelley's interest in English politics. The occasion of his best-known political poem was the receipt of the news of the Peterloo Massacre, which took place in St Peter's Field, Manchester in August 1819 when militia dispersed a large crowd gathered to listen to a speech in favour of parliamentary reform, leaving at least eleven dead and a large number injured. Shelley responded with *The Mask of Anarchy*. The second half of that poem contains a long speech by a dauntless spirit called Hope, who gives an eloquent account of what constitutes freedom. But how are the people to fight for that freedom? Shelley's answer is particularly interesting:

> 'Stand ye calm and resolute,
> Like a forest close and mute,
> With folded arms and looks which are
> Weapons of unvanquished war.'

It is a suggestion of peaceful resistance, though there is some threat in the ringing declaration with which the poem concludes, 'Ye are many—they are few.' Shelley sent his poem to Leigh Hunt for publication in the liberal periodical the *Examiner*, but Hunt did not dare publish it. This was the fate of much that Shelley wrote in Italy, both poems and prose works. Because they were plainly hostile to government no publisher would take them on with the author out of range of reprisal. *The Mask of Anarchy* was finally published in 1832, the year in which some measure of parliamentary reform was achieved.

Because their eighteenth-century predecessors were so clearly influenced by classical writers—largely the epic poets and the Roman satirists—it is often overlooked that the Romantic poets also owed much to the ancient world, particularly to the Greeks. This was most true of Shelley: far more than Byron, who died for contemporary Greece, he owed his ideas to classical Greece. He looked on Greek civilization as, with some admitted exceptions, a fount of ideas of freedom whose progress had been destroyed by the authoritarian cultures of later centuries. In his search for a philosophy behind the manifestation of human affairs, personal and political, Shelley was attracted to the works of Plato. In the summer of 1818 he translated Plato's *Symposium*. Shortly afterwards he began his greatest work, a lyrical drama entitled *Prometheus Unbound*. The subject was suggested by a lost play of Aeschylus, successor to his *Prometheus Bound*.

Prometheus appealed to Shelley because, having defied Zeus in bringing man the gift of fire, he represented a champion of mankind against a tyrannical god. According to the myth Zeus punished Prometheus by chaining him to a rock in the Caucasus. It is with the chained and suffering Prometheus that Shelley's drama begins. Prometheus and Jupiter (Zeus) are in conflict, yet Prometheus' first action is to repent the curse which he had formerly hurled at his oppressor. 'I wish no living thing to suffer pain,' he explains. In a manner Shelley was to advocate in *The Mask of Anarchy* Prometheus offers peaceful resistance. The beginning of *Prometheus Unbound* takes up the point made in *The Mask* and presents it on a universal scale. Prometheus undergoes ages of staunch endurance, refusing to bargain with Jupiter for his release. Mary Shelley recorded of her husband that

. . . the subject he loved best to dwell on was the image of One warring with the Evil Principle . . . a victim full of fortitude and hope and the spirit of triumph emanating from a reliance in the ultimate omnipotence of Good.

If the victim's only weapons are fortitude and hope how is the triumph of Good brought about in *Prometheus Unbound*? In many ways *Prometheus Unbound* is a pendant to Blake's *Book of Urizen*. Blake's book probes the source of tyrannical evil; Shelley's drama enacts its overthrow. The ideas behind it are Platonic: good overcomes evil in the long run because of the radiant attractiveness of good, and the self-destructiveness of evil. Jupiter, the tyrant, is overthrown, as the original myth hinted, by his own progeny: Demogorgon, the son, represents 'fate' or 'time' (he calls it 'Eternity'). The positive side of the overthrow of Jupiter is wrought by Asia, representing Love, the invincible power of good. No summary can do justice to Shelley's ecstatic vision of the defeat of tyrannical evil. His poetry takes on a sublime lyricism as it celebrates Love:

> Child of Light! thy limbs are burning
>   Through the vest which seems to hide them;
> As the radiant lines of morning
>   Through the clouds ere they divide them;
> And this atmosphere divinest
> Shrouds thee wheresoe'er thou shinest.   (II. v. 54-9)

Such passages, where the sheer splendour of Platonic ideas is expressed, contrast with passages describing experience more nearly human, the sufferings imposed by the tyrant, and the paradisal freedom enjoyed after his defeat. Shelley projects his philosophy through ethereal characters and spiritualized landscapes; earth, ocean, and all nature share both the suffering and the triumph. *Prometheus Unbound* is a difficult work; its imagery is abstract and its symbolism often seems unattainable. The poet's thoughts are perhaps in the empyrean for too long; but the drama presents a magnificent vision of a universe on the side of good. It is Milton's *Comus* on a cosmic scale.

Shelley shares with almost all the Romantic poets a skill in the brief lyric. He is, however, happier with more extensive verse forms which allow for his profusion of thoughts and images. An example is his 'Ode to the West Wind', written in the Autumn of 1819. In it Shelley's torrential style is curbed by a highly organized structure and a demanding rhyme scheme, the *terza rima*. An address to the west wind is an appropriate subject for Shelley's favourite imagery, of clouds, vapours, and atmospheric effects. Shelley's Ode may be compared with poems by Wordsworth and Coleridge that lament the loss of an original spontaneous vision. In his invocation to the wind Shelley recalls his boyhood 'when to outstrip thy skiey speed / Scarce seemed a vision'. Now his plea is 'Be thou, Spirit fierce, / My spirit!' Shelley's thoughts are, as usual, directed towards 'unawakened earth'. This poem is not in the triumphal key

JOHN KEATS. A pen-and-ink drawing by Benjamin Robert Haydon (1816). Haydon used Keats's profile for one of the crowd in his large canvas *Christ's Entry into Jerusalem* (1817).

of *Prometheus Unbound*; the poet's prayer is that though 'chained and bowed' he might yet be able to contribute to the great movement of the earth towards regeneration. 'If Winter comes, can Spring be far behind?'

When Shelley died by drowning while sailing in the Gulf of Spezia in 1822 there was in his pocket a volume of poetry by Keats. John Keats (1795–1821) was born into a family which ran an inn and stables in London. He went to school in Enfield and in 1811 was apprenticed to a surgeon and apothecary. Perhaps his experiences in a surgical ward contributed to his describing his other world, that of poetry, as 'golden'. Although he became a Licentiate of

'RUIN SEIZE THEE, RUTHLESS KING!' *The Bard* (1817) by John Martin, inspired by Thomas Gray's poem *The Bard* (1757). The last of the Welsh bards hurls defiance at Edward I from a rock towering over the river Conway. Gray's bard, who followed his prophecy of the destruction of Edward's race by plunging from the rock to his death, provided for the Romantics a resonant image of the poet.

'TOWERS BEHOLD/QUIVERING THROUGH AERIAL GOLD'. Venice from the steps of the Europa Hotel by J.M.W. Turner, first shown in 1842. The domed building on the left is S. Giorgio Maggiore; the building on the right is the Dogana, or customs house. Turner knew Shelley's description of Venice, and used some of its images in his own verse.

the Society of Apothecaries in 1816, Keats decided shortly afterwards to abandon medicine and devote his life to poetry. He joined the liberal literary circle associated with Leigh Hunt. In 1817 he published a small volume of *Poems*, and the following year a long poem called *Endymion*. *Endymion* is based on a mythological subject, the shepherd Endymion's love for the moon and his journey in search of her. The theme of pursuit has something in common with Shelley's *Alastor*, but the terrain is entirely Keats's—of nature observed at ground level, of thicket and glade and 'Rain-scented eglantine'. The poem starts with an elevated utterance revealing Keats's deeper thoughts, 'A thing of beauty is a joy for ever'.

Endymion fell foul of the reviewers. The early nineteenth century had seen the foundation of several new reviews and magazines which took regular notice of literary works. Their articles usually contained extensive extracts from the works under review as well as forthright critical judgements. For the author there was, however, a negative side: each periodical had a pronounced political allegiance, and, of course, at any time a writer might find himself the victim of some irresponsible squib from a reviewer hiding in semi-anonymity. The Tory *Quarterly Review* mocked the luxuriance and immaturity of *Endymion*, and *Blackwood's Edinburgh Magazine* included Keats in its 'Cockney School of Poetry' (a disparaging phrase coined on analogy with the 'Lake School'). *Blackwood's* reviewer, John Gibson Lockhart, added social snobbery to political bias in his remarks on Keats: 'It is a better and a wiser thing to be a starved apothecary than a starved poet; so back to the shop Mr John . . .' Lockhart went on to marry Scott's daughter and to be his biographer; he wrote his review of Keats before he had imbibed any of his father-in-law's humanity.

Keats died in Rome at the age of twenty-five, and Shelley in an elegy, *Adonais* (1821), implied that his death had been brought about by the reviewers. Although Keats was naturally hurt, he was as a poet fairly robust. He was not to be 'snuffed out by an article', to use Byron's witty but misleading phrase. The cause was tuberculosis, which had already killed his mother and brother.

In 'Sleep and Poetry', written at the outset of his poetic career, Keats asks with typical exuberance for 'ten years, that I may overwhelm / Myself in poesy'. In the event most of his best poetry was written in one year, between September 1818 and September 1819. The result was one of the most distinguished volumes of poetry ever published, *Lamia, Isabella, The Eve of St. Agnes, and other poems*, which appeared in 1820. Among the 'other poems' were most of Keats's Odes.

The major subject of Keats's poetry is absorption in love and beauty, and the problems these ideals meet in the real world. 'The Eve of St. Agnes' may illustrate this. It is a narrative poem in Spenserian stanzas which presents a succession of sensuous effects. The poem starts with a Beadsman in an icy chapel, and then shifts quickly to the 'argent revelry' of the Baron's halls. Doors shut out the music, and attention is fixed on one room, Madeline's

THE FLIGHT OF MADELINE AND PORPHYRO DURING THE DRUNKENNESS ATTENDING THE REVELRY by William Holman Hunt. This painting, inspired by the last stanzas of 'The Eve of St. Agnes', was exhibited at the Royal Academy in 1848, where it was admired by Dante Gabriel Rossetti. Hunt regarded it as an illustration of 'the sacredness of honest, responsible love and the weakness of intemperance'.

bed-chamber, rich with the colours of jewels and stained glass. In his descriptions Keats was influenced by paintings and medieval architecture; it is hardly surprising that his poetry in turn provided subject-matter for the Pre-Raphaelite painters. This is the poet who advised Shelley to ' "load every rift" of your subject with ore'.

To say no more than that is to overlook the narrative. The poem is based on a folk superstition, that if on St Agnes' Eve young girls should observe certain ceremonies on going to bed they would 'soft adorings from their loves receive / Upon the honeyed middle of the night'. It is the tale of a girl who decides to observe this superstition. As she does so her lover arrives at the castle, and, with the help of old Angela, is hidden in her chamber. It is Porphyro's 'stratagem' to make Madeline's dream come true. This for Keats is a challenge, inviting consideration of the relation between dream happiness and happiness in the waking world. Madeline *does* dream of her lover, and at that moment Porphyro attempts to waken her. As she opens her eyes she experiences the abrupt juxtaposition of his pale figure and her dream of him. The disappointment is painful, until it is dispersed as 'Into her dream he melted . . .'. Love is achieved, but it is not exempt from the conditions of ordinary life. The noise of sleet on the window wakens the lovers; 'St. Agnes' moon hath set.' Porphyro has entered a dream; Madeline now has to enter the waking world. The realities of that world are that he is in an enemy castle, and she is a 'deceivèd thing'. The poem is rescued from tragedy a second time by Porphyro's initiative.

> Awake! Arise, my love, and fearless be!
> For o'er the southern moors I have a home for thee.

The lovers escape, and the reader is left feeling the preciousness of love won against such difficulties.

Successful love is not common in Keats's poems. In the months following the writing of 'The Eve of St. Agnes' he wrote again on the subject of illusion and reality in love. In 'Lamia' and 'La Belle Dame Sans Merci' the male protagonist is bewitched by a supernatural lover. The use of the supernatural helps to convey the uncanniness of love. Lycius in 'Lamia' is deceived by a snake-woman. He can enjoy love *à deux*, but when he wants to rejoin society by inviting his friends to a wedding-feast his beloved cannot withstand the gaze of an uninvited guest, the 'philosopher' Apollonius. 'La Belle Dame Sans Merci' is an enigmatic ballad lyric. There are debts to many of Keats's favourite poets in the phrasing, but the laconic narrative seems to derive from two themes from ballad and folk-tale, the love of a fairy woman, and the vision of an enthralled underground community. When the knight in the poem wakes from his dream 'On the cold hill side' it is with the debilitating knowledge that he too is 'in thrall'. He does not die, like Lycius; but he is condemned to death in life 'Alone and palely loitering', and that against deft suggestions of the coming of winter, 'The squirrel's granary is full, / And the harvest's done.'

If one of the themes of Keats's narrative poems is enquiry into the 'truth' of ideal visions, a common theme of his Odes is their lack of permanence. Most of the Romantic poets wrote odes. Keats made the form a ceremonious address, in lengthy stanzas, developing a theme at a stately pace. His famous 'Ode to a Nightingale' follows a procedure common to many Romantic poems, that of pursuing a mental experience of the poet through identification with a circumstance in the natural world, for instance the coming of a storm, the singing of a bird, or the movement of the moon in the sky. In the Ode the poet hears a nightingale singing and decides to follow the bird into the forest 'on the viewless wings of Poesy'. The poet joins the nightingale in the dark, fragrant stillness of the forest. As he evokes the immortality of the nightingale's song through a profusion of images he suddenly finds that the spell is broken by a single word—'forlorn'. 'Forlorn! The very word is like a bell / To toll me back from thee to my sole self!' Can we say what has happened? To ask that is to pose a question which, as we have seen, exercised several of the Romantic poets. Are the experiences which the poet feels in the natural world received from nature, or created by his own mind? On returning to his 'sole self' the poet first rounds on his imagination, using the synonym which had become for the Romantics pejorative, 'The fancy cannot cheat so well / As she is famed to do, deceiving elf.' But it is unfair to blame the loss entirely on his imagination. In Coleridge's terms the poetic imagination fuses the perceiving mind and the perceived object—and in this case the object is the nightingale, which is flying away

> Past the near meadows, over the still stream,
>   Up the hill-side; and now 'tis buried deep
>   In the next valley-glades . . .

As Coleridge also knew, the imaginative vision cannot be sustained long. The 'Ode to a Nightingale' enacts such a vision and its loss, and the poet is left at the end wondering which state is the truer, 'Do I wake or sleep?'

Keats was also a magnificent letter-writer, and in his letters we can trace his thoughts on life and on poetry, and even see his poetry in the making. There is one topic in Keats's letters that seems to lead to the heart of his poetry, and perhaps to offer a key to the sensuousness of its imagery. Keats frequently expressed suspicion of philosophical systems, and he disliked poetry 'that has a palpable design upon us—'. 'Axioms in philosophy are not axioms until they are proved upon our pulses,' he wrote. That respect for what is 'proved upon our pulses' explains the concern with individual experience which we find in all the Romantic poets, even those more interested than Keats in philosophy and in politics. For Keats the great poets are those who, like Shakespeare, most fully absorb and respond to life. For this quality he coined the term '*Negative Capability*', 'that is when man is capable of being in uncertainties, Mysteries, doubts, without any irritable reaching after fact & reason—'. Out of this creative indolence the imagination is the active quality: 'What the imagination seizes as Beauty must be truth—whether it existed before or not—'. For Keats it is a Platonic article of faith that Beauty is Truth.

Keats wanted a poem to have 'intensity' rather than argument. In a letter of 27 February 1818 he wrote of poetry (the verbal irregularities are Keats's own):

Its touches of Beauty should never be half way therby making the reader breathless instead of content: the rise, the progress, the setting of imagery should like the Sun come natural natural too him—shine over him and set soberly although in magnificence leaving him in the Luxury of twilight . . .

The best example of such poetry is in Keats's ode 'To Autumn', an evocation of autumn, with only the slightest movement from the luxuriance of late

summer and the harvest to anticipations of winter. The question of imper-
manence is briefly raised, but only to be dismissed. Addressing autumn the
poet asks

> Where are the songs of spring? Aye, where are they?
> Think not of them, thou hast thy music too . . .

The poem is poised in a rich appreciation of the present, and is not searching
after anything else. It was Keats who wrote to a friend, 'I scarcely remember
counting upon any Happiness—I look not for it if it be not in the present
hour—'.

If the poetry of the Romantics has tended to have a special place in the
hearts of readers, it is because those poems which are most clearly Romantic
are those which particularly defy explication and are in the supreme sense
'poetic'. Romantic poetry pushes experience to the utmost point, where there
is no direct reference to the ordinary world. Like the nightingale's song it has

> Charmed magic casements, opening on the foam
> Of perilous seas in fairy lands forlorn.

It may be that we respond to the poetry of the Romantics also because we are,
curiously, in a position not unlike theirs. Shelley's words in his *Defence of
Poetry* (1821) are still true:

We have more moral, political and historical wisdom, than we know how to reduce
into practice; we have more scientific and economical knowledge than can be
accommodated to the just distribution of the produce which it multiplies. . . . We
want the creative faculty to imagine that which we know; we want the generous
impulse to act that which we imagine; we want the poetry of life: our calculations
have outrun conception; we have eaten more than we can digest. The cultivation of
those sciences which have enlarged the limits of the empire of man over the external
world, has, for want of the poetical faculty, proportionally circumscribed those of the
internal world; and man, having enslaved the elements, remains himself a slave.

Over the gulf of almost two centuries of progressive scientific rationalism,
which has reduced man to a speck in deserts of time and space, we respond
to the humanism of the Romantics. For them man, however burdensome his
journey, still came 'trailing clouds of glory'.

The Drama and its Critics

It is natural to ask whether the Romantic period was as distinguished in other
genres of literature as it was in poetry. On turning to the drama one's first
impression is disappointing. Many of the Romantic poets tried their hand at
plays, usually in verse, but none was really successful on the stage. The poet
with the most success as a playwright was Byron, despite his inability to
'conceive any man of irritable feeling putting himself at the mercies of an

EDMUND KEAN in *A New Way to Pay Old Debts* by the Jacobean dramatist Philip Massinger, by George Clint (1820). Kean had immense success as the extortioner Sir Giles Overreach. The last scene, in which the villain meets defeat with raving fury, overwhelmed both the audience and the other actors. Byron recorded that Kean's performance 'threw me into convulsions ... the agony of reluctant tears—and the choaking shudder which I do not often undergo for fiction'.

audience'. His *Marino Faliero*, a political play set in medieval Venice, was produced in 1821, and several of his other plays reached the stage after his death, in the 1830s.

Although the best writers were not playwrights the early nineteenth century was, paradoxically, an exciting period in the theatre. The London theatre was still dominated by the two houses operating under patent, Drury Lane and Covent Garden, and the vulnerability of the buildings to fire enabled them both to be rebuilt with increased capacity in these years. The period can boast many famous actors: John Philip Kemble, his sister Sarah Siddons, Edmund Kean, and William Charles Macready. The theatre was popular, and the appetite for plays was partly satisfied by productions of the classics of the past, pre-eminently Shakespeare. Mrs Siddons was celebrated for thrilling and impressive performances in tragic roles such as Lady Macbeth, and Volumnia in *Coriolanus*. Many besides Hazlitt compared Kemble and Kean in the part of Hamlet: 'Mr. Kean's Hamlet is as much too splenetic and rash as Mr.

Kemble's is too deliberate and formal.' The abrupt and passionate style of acting which appeared with Edmund Kean is summed up in Coleridge's comment that watching him was 'like reading Shakespeare by flashes of lightning'. The theatre was influenced by the requirements of the actors. Plays were cut and altered to produce suitable parts—but at least great plays were attempted. New plays, on the other hand, were sentimental comedy and farce, and what Wordsworth dismissed as 'sickly and stupid German tragedies'. The German playwrights supplied themes for melodramatic tragedies: Schiller's *The Robbers*, for instance, put on to the English stage many a robber and outlaw, a cross between Satan and Robin Hood. The shortage of new plays may explain why Scott's novels were dramatized almost as soon as they appeared.

Although the Romantic period did not produce good plays it did produce dramatic criticism, much of which drew on experiences in the theatre. An example is 'On the Knocking at the Gate in *Macbeth*' by Thomas de Quincey (1785-1859). De Quincey meditates on the awful effect of the knocking which succeeds the murder of Duncan: 'it makes known audibly that the reaction has commenced; the human has made its reflux upon the fiendish . . .' There was among some critics, however, a feeling which even the most famous actors could not remove, that Shakespeare at his greatest was too great for the stage. Hazlitt said of *Hamlet*, 'There is no play that suffers so much in being transferred to the stage.' Lamb was particularly doubtful about *King Lear*: 'But the Lear of Shakspeare cannot be acted.' He shrewdly accounted for the alterations made by Nahum Tate which had been observed in dramatic productions since the Restoration: 'Tate has put his hook in the nostrils of this Leviathan . . . to draw the mighty beast about more easily.' (The 'happy ending' of *King Lear* was not abandoned in the theatre until Kean did so in 1823; Macready restored the Fool in 1838.) 'The truth is,' wrote Lamb explaining his doubts about dramatic performance, 'the Characters of Shakspeare are so much the objects of meditation rather than of interest or curiosity as to their actions . . .' The character who was the chief object of meditation for the Romantics was Hamlet. The intellect, the irresolution, and the *tedium vitae* which they found in Hamlet they recognized in themselves. As Coleridge remarked innocently, 'I have a smack of Hamlet myself, if I may say so.'

William Hazlitt (1778-1830) was the foremost critic of his day. He used the popular forms for criticism, the lecture, the review, and the essay, and his work on earlier writers is so extensive that it in some sense constitutes a critical history of English literature. He described his procedure as a critic thus: 'I have endeavoured to feel what was good, and to "give a reason for the faith that was in me".' Hazlitt is good at capturing the flavour of an author or a work. This quality is reflected in the title of one of his best books, *The Spirit of the Age*, a criticism of his contemporaries, drawing on his own recollections of many of them, which appeared in 1825. The book is lively and prejudiced, and in it the Romantic period interprets itself. Hazlitt is an eloquent writer;

a quieter, whimsical tone is found in the work of Charles Lamb (1775-1834). In the *Essays of Elia*, which appeared in the *London Magazine* in the 1820s, Lamb reflects on his childhood, on quiet pleasures, and on the small change of London life. They include, too, some pieces of dramatic criticism. In a period which saw itself as having an affinity with tragedy it is interesting to observe those critics who are sensitive to comedy. Hazlitt defended the Restoration dramatists in his *The English Comic Writers* in 1819. Perhaps the most celebrated defence of the comedy of manners is by Lamb. In 'On the Artificial Comedy of the Last Century', in his usual mixture of the tentative and the assertive, he defends Restoration comedy from the condemnation of an over-earnest age. Such plays, so far from transcending the stage, scarcely exist outside it. They are for Lamb a 'happy breathing-place from the burthen of perpetual moral questioning'.

The Novel

The drama as it existed in the theatre was, of course, a popular form; but by far the most popular form in the period from 1780 to 1830 was the novel. In the last decades of the eighteenth century there was a large increase in the number of novels published. They were still expensive to buy—Jane Austen's *Emma* and Scott's *Waverley* both cost 21s. (£1.05) on their first appearance— but the thirst for fiction was satisfied by the development, increasing throughout the eighteenth century, of the 'circulating libraries'. Much of what they circulated was poor stuff, and ready access to books was not everywhere approved. As Sir Anthony Absolute pronounced, in Sheridan's *The Rivals* (1775), 'A circulating library in a town is an ever-green tree of diabolical knowledge!' A particular feature of this explosion of fiction is that many of the writers were women; indeed this is the first period in which women were, and were acknowledged to be, large contributors to published literature.

Some of the ideas which we associate with the Romantic may be seen in the popular novel. One of these is the cult of the feelings, which is known as 'sensibility'. Sensibility had an honourable history: it arose out of a reaction against the sheer brutality of eighteenth-century life, and it drew on philosophical beliefs in the innate goodness of man. Eighteenth-century fiction saw an increase in characters whose response to life was charged with emotion. To the native breed, the characters in Richardson and Sterne, and Henry Mackenzie's *The Man of Feeling*, were added important examples from abroad in the characters in Rousseau's novels and Goethe's *Werther*. Sensibility was expressed in human relations and in response to nature and art. It became a fashionable attribute; but the rage did not make the world at large any nicer and by the 1790s novelists were warning heroines of the danger of sensibility. The fashion which in a man might be civilizing and emotionally enriching tended to make a woman dangerously feeble and vulnerable. Emily St Aubert, the heroine of

Ann Radcliffe's famous *The Mysteries of Udolpho*, is warned by her dying father to avoid the dangers of sensibility, 'the pride of fine feeling, the romantic error of amiable minds'. Jane Austen, whose early novels are an index of contemporary fashions in the novel, entered the debate in her first published work, *Sense and Sensibility*, begun in the 1790s and published in 1811. Jane Austen's criticism of sensibility is not only that it is dangerous to its possessor—and her heroine Marianne joins the heroines of sensibility in an illness that brings her close to death—but that it is a self-centred emotion which makes its possessor unwilling to recognize the claims of others.

The interest in non-rational experience, which was part of the Romantic reaction against eighteenth-century rationalism, took many forms. In some writers it led outwards in pursuit of a spiritual reality; in others it led inwards to the exploration of a personal and social underworld. One area of interest was the world of dreams, especially the heightened dreams induced by opium. De Quincey's *Confessions of an English Opium-Eater* (1821) describes the phantasmagoria of such dreams, as well as discussing the slavery to the drug which tormented Coleridge.

The world of nightmare became to some extent institutionalized in the Gothic novel, mentioned at the close of the previous chapter. These novels, set in a vague 'medieval' world, explore the more lurid emotions of terror, guilt, and horror. Gothic novels use the medieval settings of castle and convent, in their ugly aspect as prisons, physical and emotional. These buildings are the settings for extreme manifestations of physical power and moral outrage. Their dark and 'irrational' architecture and labyrinthine passages have been taken as analogues of what Coleridge called 'The unfathomable hell within'. The Gothic castle usually occurs in a sublime, mountainous landscape; it is often in northern Europe or the Alps, but if in the Mediterranean world (and the most famous, that of Udolpho, is in the Apennines) one may be sure that it is far away from liberal Hellenic sunshine. The Gothic villain is similarly sublime, exercising a sadistic power over a helpless heroine. (These works are contemporary with those of the Marquis de Sade (1740-1814), although a direct influence cannot usually be traced.) The most famous of the Gothic novelists was Ann Radcliffe (1764-1823). In *The Mysteries of Udolpho* (1794) the heroine is under the power of a wicked guardian, Montoni, until after many terrifying adventures she is free to marry the hero of sensibility, Valancourt. Gothic novels were calculated to keep a fearful reader awake at night. Many readers must have shared Catherine Morland's excitement to know what lay behind the black veil: 'what can it be?—But do not tell me—I would not be told upon any account. I know it must be a skeleton . . .'

A certain delicacy in Ann Radcliffe's works, despite her subject-matter, is absent from a more notorious work, *The Monk* (1796), by Matthew Gregory Lewis (1775-1818). In his presentation of a monk who rapes a young girl in a charnel house he is dealing not simply in terror, but in that fear combined

THE GOTHIC VOGUE satirized by Gillray (1802). Tension mounts as a group of women read *The Monk*. Something of the content of the book is indicated by the ornaments in the room. Another work by M. G. Lewis, a collection of Gothic verse tales called *Tales of Wonder* (1801), gave the print its title.

with moral and physical recoil which we might rather term horror. It is probably significant that in Jane Austen's novel about the Gothic craze, *Northanger Abbey*, it was only the less admirable John Thorpe who claimed to have read *The Monk*. Jane Austen takes an astringent view of the Gothic as she had of sensibility. Her young heroine, Catherine Morland, on her first visit from home, is so full of her Gothic reading that she interprets life at Northanger Abbey in Gothic terms, only to be seriously embarrassed later by the discrepancy between her Gothic imaginings and reality.

Although the clichés of the Gothic were looking somewhat outworn by the beginning of the nineteenth century the vogue turned out to have considerable powers of renewal. The Gothic villain may be detected behind Mr Rochester in *Jane Eyre* and Heathcliff in *Wuthering Heights*. As the Gothic occurs in later periods the conventional trappings of castles, ghosts, and bleeding nuns came to be replaced by other settings and occasions for irrational emotions and dark fantasy. The beginning of the extension of the Gothic in different directions may be seen in the Romantic period. Crabbe occasionally uses imagery that borders on the Gothic. His *Peter Grimes* is a tale about a brutal fisherman who adopted orphan children and treated them so cruelly that they died. His own death is haunted by visions of the dead children leading him to a hell of 'tortured guilt'. Such use of the Gothic to express wickedness and guilt in a realistic setting perhaps reached its high point in the novels of Dickens.

There were plenty of mocking references to the tribe of 'lady novelists' who supplied the circulating libraries. There is no less appropriate object of such a gibe than Mary Shelley (1797–1851), the founder of what might be called the

FANNY BURNEY, by Edward Francesco Burney (1782). Fanny Burney commented, 'Never was Portrait so violently flattered. I have taken pains incredible to make him *magnify* the Features, & darken the complection . . .' Edward Burney was her cousin, who had taken the manuscript of her first novel, *Evelina*, to the printer in 1777.

MARY SHELLEY, by Richard Rothwell (c.1840). After her husband's death Mary Shelley returned to England, where she continued to write novels, and accounts of her travels. In 1838 she brought out an edition of Shelley's poems with valuable notes.

'scientific Gothic'. She had in any case an intellectual tradition behind her which would have kept her from sentimentality and sensationalism. Her father was William Godwin, the radical philosopher and also novelist, author of *Caleb Williams* (1794); her mother was Mary Wollstonecraft. Mary Wollstonecraft was one of a group of radicals, which included William Blake, whose hopes of the French Revolution included freedom for women in society, and especially freedom from subordination in marriage. In 1790 she published *A Vindication of the Rights of Men* (the year before Thomas Paine's *Rights of Man*). She followed it in 1792 with *A Vindication of the Rights of Woman*, which is one of the milestones in the history of feminism.

Mary Shelley was nineteen when she wrote *Frankenstein*, which was published in 1818. It originated in a plan to write ghost stories, formed by Byron, Shelley, and herself while they were staying on Lake Geneva in 1816. Hers was the only one to be completed. Frankenstein is a scholar who is obsessed with the desire to find the 'principle of life'. We recognize the modern world in the replacement of Faustus's study by a laboratory. Frankenstein gives life to a creature, gigantic and hideous, and, as it turns out, with needs that he has not anticipated and cannot satisfy. The mountains above Chamonix, which had been for the Romantic poets the 'glorious presence-chamber of imperial Nature', are the scene of a meeting in which the creature makes his demands, his arguments fortified by a reading of *Paradise Lost*. The early part of the book is concerned with the responsibilities of a creator; in the latter half the centre of interest shifts. When the monster, in revenge at Frankenstein's refusal to supply him with a mate, haunts him and destroys those he loves he seems to be an evil familiar, operating as some sort of psychological reflection of aspects of his creator.

This *Doppelgänger* effect is present also in another novel of the period, James Hogg's *The Private Memoirs and Confessions of a Justified Sinner* (1824). The protagonist of this novel is possessed by the devil, the atrocious deeds which he allegedly commits being 'justified' according to his perverted form of Calvinism. The novel uses the Gothic for extreme religious mania. *The Confessions of a Justified Sinner* has an enigmatic structure, with abrupt narrative shifts, which appears to be a feature of the 'psychological Gothic' and looks forward to *Wuthering Heights*, and, in our own century, the techniques of the Gothic film.

So far in this chapter different aspects of what one might agree to call Romantic have appeared more or less without challenge. It is misleading, however, to imply that no challenge was offered. They did not escape mockery by Thomas Love Peacock (1785-1866), author of a series of prose tales in which the fashionable ideas of the day were satirized. Peacock's usual procedure, devised in *Headlong Hall* (1816) was to establish a large house full of guests, each of whom was a spokesman for some topical trait or enthusiasm. Most of the famous writers of the day appear, thinly veiled, in Peacock's books. Literary satire is perhaps most prominent in his *Nightmare Abbey* (1818) in which Shelley and Coleridge are caricatured, and the plot parodies features of the Gothic novel. Criticism of the Romantic was not, however, confined to the satirist. There is much in Crabbe that is anti-Romantic. We have seen that in two early novels by Jane Austen heroines who espouse the fashionable enthusiasms of sensibility or the Gothic are driven by painful circumstances to abandon them. There are clearly currents in literature tending in the opposite direction, away from the Romantic.

Jane Austen (1775–1817) was the daughter of a Hampshire clergyman. Her life was externally uneventful; but besides one sister she had six brothers, whose more active lives gave her some knowledge of the greater world. Two of her brothers, for instance, entered the navy, and to them are owed the sympathetic accounts of the navy in *Mansfield Park* and *Persuasion*. Her family was on visiting terms with what one might call the gentry of Hampshire, which supplied her with the parties and outings on which many scenes in her novels are based.

Jane Austen was writing before she was twelve years old. Her first attempts to get a work published, however, were unsuccessful, and she was thirty-five when *Sense and Sensibility* appeared in 1811. Thereafter she published *Pride and Prejudice* (1813), *Mansfield Park* (1814), and *Emma* (1816). These were the only novels she published herself. She died at the age of forty-two, leaving to appear posthumously *Persuasion* (with the early *Northanger Abbey*), and an unfinished novel usually referred to as *Sanditon*.

Catherine Morland, the heroine of *Northanger Abbey*, woke up from her Gothic fantasies with the reflection that

Charming as were all Mrs. Radcliffe's works, and charming even as were the works of all her imitators, it was not in them perhaps that human nature, at least in the midland counties of England, was to be looked for.

Human nature, as manifested in an ordinary English setting, was precisely Jane Austen's subject-matter as a novelist. Once when giving advice to a niece who was attempting to write a novel she wrote, '3 or 4 families in a country village is the very thing to work on'. Jane Austen's heroines are all young girls at the outset of adult life. By the end of the novels they have made the commitment which will determine their occupations and happiness for the rest of their lives—marriage. The abstract nouns which occur in several of the novels' titles indicate the qualities to be reckoned with as the heroines are educated for marriage. In writing novels with a realistic setting about the reconciliation of the claims of the individual and of society, and in which the concluding marriage is a symbol that that harmony has been reached, Jane Austen was in a tradition of the English novel which lasted throughout the nineteenth century to die out, if indeed it has, only in the modern period.

GODMERSHAM in Kent, from J. P. Neale, *Views of the Seats of Noblemen and Gentlemen . . .* (1826). Godmersham, built in the early eighteenth century, was inherited in 1797 by Jane Austen's brother Edward. Jane Austen associated it with 'Elegance & Ease & Luxury— . . . I shall eat Ice & drink French wine, & be above vulgar Economy.' One of Edward's daughters recorded that when she was staying there she would 'suddenly burst out laughing, jump up, cross the room to a distant table with papers lying on it, write something down, returning presently and sitting down quietly to her [needle-] work.'

'It is a truth universally acknowledged, that a single man in possession of a good fortune, must be in want of a wife.' That is the famous opening sentence of *Pride and Prejudice*. The word 'universally' is an ironic exaggeration which may easily slip past the reader's defences. If it does the reader is quickly in the world of the first speaker, Mrs Bennet, the business of whose life 'was to get her daughters married; its solace was visiting and news'. Few novelists have had Jane Austen's economy and mastery of tone, nor her sense of structure in a novel. In *Pride and Prejudice*, for instance, the heroine, Elizabeth Bennet, resists her mother's pressure and refuses to marry the odious Mr Collins. Three days later Mr Collins is accepted by Charlotte Lucas. Elizabeth's reflections on her friend's action are worthy of a Romantic heroine: 'she could not have supposed it possible that . . . she would have sacrificed every better feeling to worldly advantage.' The reader, however, has seen the matter briefly from Charlotte's point of view. She was twenty-seven, 'without having ever been handsome', and at her engagement her brothers 'were relieved from their

MILSOM STREET, BATH, by J. C. Nattes, from *Bath, illustrated by a Series of Views* (1806). Bath had risen in popularity in the eighteenth century as a watering-place and fashionable resort. The town was extensively rebuilt in handsome Georgian terraces and crescents. Jane Austen, however, did not care for it; like her heroine Anne Elliot she dreaded 'the white glare of Bath'. In Milsom Street, Isabella Thorpe in *Northanger Abbey* saw 'the prettiest hat you can imagine', and Anne Elliot in *Persuasion* met Captain Wentworth while sheltering from the rain in Molland's, a confectioner's at No. 2.

apprehension of Charlotte's dying an old maid'. Jane Austen's world is an unromantic place where, whatever is allowed to the sparkling heroine, Charlotte Lucas has to make the best of Mr Collins. A Jane Austen novel surprises the reader by the neatness with which commonplace topics are illuminated from different points of view. Jane Austen was the first real artist to devote herself to the novel; and she once wrote, 'an artist cannot do anything slovenly'.

There are two criticisms which have sometimes been directed at Jane Austen's work. The first is that her range is too narrow—you would not know, so the charge goes, that the Napoleonic wars were in progress when she wrote. The second may be best expressed by Charlotte Brontë, who was not particularly impressed by her reading of Jane Austen: 'the Passions are perfectly unknown to her; she rejects even a speaking acquaintance with that stormy Sisterhood.'

Perhaps these criticisms might be considered in relation to *Emma*. *Emma* is unusual among Jane Austen's novels for having no military men among its characters; but it is worth remembering the history of Jane Fairfax. She is an orphan, because her father, Lieutenant Fairfax, had been killed in action abroad. Such references to a wider world go almost unnoticed in a Jane Austen novel. The second charge is that 'the Passions are perfectly unknown to her'. *Emma* certainly starts at a low point where the passions are concerned. In the first chapter Emma and her father spend a disconsolate evening after the wedding of her former governess. (This is a subtle opening in view of the miseries of a governess's life described in the rest of the novel, and in many later nineteenth-century novels.) The emotions in Jane Austen are often the more muted ones, like boredom, embarrassment, and mortification. The happier

A CANCELLED CHAPTER OF *PERSUASION*. The only manuscript to survive from Jane Austen's completed novels is a first version of the conclusion to *Persuasion*, begun on 8 July 1816. The passage over which Jane Austen had second thoughts was the reunion of Anne Elliot and Captain Wentworth. In the first version it took place in Admiral Croft's house; in the published novel (1818) that was replaced by a scene in the White Hart Inn, Bath.

emotions are delight in the family, and satisfaction at self-control and doing one's duty. The 'stormy Sisterhood' may be detected when Jane Fairfax breaks off her secret engagement, and, in *Mansfield Park*, when Maria Rushworth runs away with Henry Crawford. Such intense passions are on the periphery in Jane Austen's work.

Jane Austen said of Emma that she was 'a heroine whom no-one but myself will much like'. She is a rich and rather snobbish young girl who amuses herself by planning marriages for other people. The plot of *Emma* consists of a series of appearances which turn out to be false. The experience of reading the novel is that of recognizing how hard it is to understand either the events before one's eyes or one's own heart. The early Jane Austen novels had heroines whose minds were carried away by fashionable ideas. We reach the mature Jane Austen when she no longer needs a fashionable idea to blind her heroine—sheer wilfulness will do it.

Jane Austen's novels were not particularly popular, and only two of them reached a second edition in her lifetime. There was too much subtlety, and not enough sensation, in her novels for the majority of popular novel readers; but she had some gratifying admirers. Scott reviewed *Emma* favourably, and the novel was dedicated to the Prince Regent at his request. Jane Austen's reputation rose throughout the nineteenth century, until she became established as one of our major novelists and the first woman writer in the English literary tradition who is unassailably in the first rank.

In July 1814 there appeared anonymously *Waverley; or 'Tis Sixty Years Since*. The attempt at anonymity was not successful and in a couple of months Jane Austen was complaining to her niece,

Walter Scott has no business to write novels, especially good ones.—It is not fair.—He has Fame and Profit enough as a Poet, and should not be taking the bread out of other people's mouths.—I do not like him, & do not mean to like Waverley if I can help it—but fear I must.

Scott had started *Waverley* as early as 1805, but had been discouraged and had abandoned it during the decade when he established his fame as a poet. Once published, however, it was instantly successful, and he followed it with many more novels: *Guy Mannering*, *The Antiquary*, *Old Mortality*, *Rob Roy*, *The Heart of Midlothian*, *The Bride of Lammermoor*. These are the early novels, mostly historical and set in Scotland. In 1819 he extended his range with a medieval novel, *Ivanhoe*, which is set in England in the twelfth century; *Quentin Durward* (1823) is set in France in the fifteenth century. He returned to Scotland and the eighteenth century with *Redgauntlet* (1824). Despite the fame that the various titles have had in the past those most highly regarded now are the Scottish novels, about a country and society he knew. Scott's novels are famous for the portrayal of Scottish life—the clans of the Highlands and the lairds and peasants of the Lowlands. They present various trades and professions, shopkeepers, fishermen, farmers, and lawyers; and also a range of eccentrics on the edge of the social scene, the beggar, the village idiot, the smuggler, the gipsy—the best known of the last being Meg Merrilies, who caught the imagination of Keats. Scott's novels are wide-ranging in theme and setting, the opposite of the deliberately restricted world of Jane Austen. The series, in deference to the supposed anonymity, became known as the Waverley Novels, after the first of them, but each novel in the series is self-contained.

Scott became rich through his pen: he was paid unprecedented sums for his works by his publisher, and he was a partner in the firm which printed them. Of all the writers of the period he was the one who gained most in terms of worldly recognition. He was offered, but refused, the post of Poet Laureate on the death of Henry James Pye in 1813. (It went to Robert Southey.) His novels were immensely popular, were translated into most of the languages of Europe, and were waited for avidly in America. He was awarded a baronetcy by the Prince Regent. The triumph did not last: in 1826 an economic recession brought about the collapse of Scott's publisher and it jeopardized the position of the printing firm of which Scott was a partner. Scott was ruined. In the attempt

WALTER SCOTT. A study (1818) for a painting of the discovery of the Scottish Regalia, by Andrew Geddes. A chest containing the Scottish Regalia, forgotten since the seventeenth century, was opened in Edinburgh Castle in Scott's presence in 1818. He meditated a novel on the subject, but did not write it.

to stave off bankruptcy he decided to go on writing to pay off the debts incurred. There followed bitter years, which he recorded in his *Journal*, the most moving of his works. He wrote on, dogged by ill health, and had written enough ultimately to pay off the debts by his death in 1832.

Scott is usually said to have created the historical novel. The most obvious requirement of a historical novel is that it should be set in the past. But *Waverley* was not the first such novel; most of the Gothic novels were set in the past. In the Gothic novel, however, the setting in the past is only a way of avoiding the present; it is an escape to a time when brigandage and terror might be supposed to flourish unchecked, and its accuracy was probably of little concern to the author. Scott, on the other hand, was a historian, and the periods in which he set his novels were of significance in themselves. The vividness with which Scott re-created earlier periods in his fiction actually influenced the writing of history in the nineteenth century.

Scott gave the novel tradition, however, more than an interest in the past; he gave it a sense of history, that is, an awareness of the flow of history. His novels are the first in which we see people consciously conditioned by the historical and political circumstances of their birth. His characters have an ancestry which imposes a tradition which they have either to follow or reject, and such a decision is the central situation in his novels. Edward Waverley has to decide where to commit himself between Hanoverian and Jacobite at the outset of civil war. Jeanie Deans in *The Heart of Midlothian* has to decide whether to save her sister's life at the cost of perjuring herself, thus denying the strict religion in which she had been brought up.

Many of Scott's novels are set in what one might call the fairly recent past—*Waverley* for instance is set at the time of the Jacobite Rising of 1745. One theme of novels set in the recent past is the exploration of how the present situation has come about. Several of Scott's novels are concerned with the development of modern Scotland. Novels set in the distant past cannot usually shed light on the present in quite the same way, but they may offer analogies of present situations, or even an inspiration to the present. In his medieval novels Scott rescued the Middle Ages from the obscurantism of the Gothic, and by allowing the Middle Ages idealism—faith, nobility, chivalry—he inspired the medievalism associated with the religious movements of the nineteenth century.

The origin of Scott's view of history was in the Scottish Enlightenment, which pioneered the study of the development of societies, yet at the same time in the presentation of it in his novels there is much that is Romantic. As we have seen in Jane Austen the Romantic tends to be at odds with the realism of a realistic novel. One way that the two can come together in a novel is when a romantic character seeks to impose his mental ideas on the real world. That is what happens in *Waverley*. Young Edward Waverley dreams of love, honour, and loyalty. He becomes a soldier in the Hanoverian army, although

'STILL, AS OF YORE, QUEEN OF THE NORTH!' 'Edinburgh, March of the Highlanders' by Turner (*c*.1835). Turner made a series of illustrations to Scott's poems. This picture has a different origin: it is based on a sketch made by Turner during George IV's visit to Edinburgh in 1822, and shows Edinburgh Castle from Calton Hill. The composition, however, may owe something to the description of the Highland army below Arthur's Seat in chapter 44 of *Waverley*. It was published in G. N. Wright's *Landscape-Historical Illustrations of Scotland and the Waverley Novels* (1836-7).

the traditional loyalty of his family is Jacobite. When he visits a Highland clan preparing to take up arms in support of the Stewart line, Waverley, in a rush of loyal emotion, joins them. The consequence is that he takes part in an ugly civil war, and in the end has to wake up to the irresponsibility of his actions. The plot of *Waverley* has a pattern similar to the early Jane Austen novels— it submits romantic ideas to the test of hard experience and finds them wanting. That, however, is not all. Many readers of Jane Austen have found in her work, despite the fact that her heroines come to terms with an unromantic world, a considerable hostility to a society that demands such conformity to its values. In Scott that undertow is much stronger. It may be that Edward Waverley has to grow out of his idle dreams, but the conflict between Hanoverian and Jacobite is larger than can be reflected in the education of one man. At the end of the novel the reader's attention is on the stature of the losers—the heroic chieftain Fergus MacIvor, and the eccentric idealist, the Baron of Bradwardine. The contrast between two conflicting sides, especially when one of them may be regarded as more progressive than the other, is common in Scott's novels. He writes about Saxon and Norman, Roundhead and Cavalier, Covenanter and Episcopalian. A Scott novel may ostensibly end happily, but the prevailing tone is often, none the less, elegiac, because of what is lost in revolution or the march of progress. Idealism may not succeed in the world, but Scott will not allow that it does not exist. Scott is at odds with the anti-heroic mood that is usually associated with realism. He is a Romantic novelist because he will not abandon idealism, however unpromising the circumstances for its fulfilment.

At the outset of this chapter the Romantic was defined in terms of a reaction to the prevailing rationalism of eighteenth-century culture. The Romantic, it was implied, occurred at a certain time. As we consider the literature written between 1780 and 1830, however, it appears that features which might be regarded as Romantic are as much a matter of temperament as of date. By the end of the period there had come to be recognized a distinction between the Romantic and the Classical, a distinction which has been found useful ever since for the description of the biases of human nature and art. It is the optimism of the utterance rather than its substance which parts the modern reader from the host in Peacock's *Crotchet Castle* (1831), who makes this announcement at the breakfast table:

The sentimental against the rational, the intuitive against the inductive, the ornamental against the useful, the intense against the tranquil, the romantic against the classical; these are great and interesting controversies, which I should like, before I die, to see satisfactorily settled.

THE LAST CHAPTER. R. B. Martineau's painting exhibited in 1863, shows a woman reader gripped by the final chapters of a new novel. The picture is in part a tribute to the popular success of the mid-century 'sensation-novels'.

7. High Victorian Literature

1830-1880

ANDREW SANDERS

Reviews and Readers

IN its first year of publication the *Athenaeum* printed a series of articles on the state of periodical literature by the journal's editor, Henry Stebbing. As Stebbing noted in 1828, the existing range of British periodicals had struck one foreign visitor as 'the most powerful literary engine in Europe'. It was an engine which was to mark the nineteenth century as forcefully as the steam locomotives which two years later began to ferry passengers between Manchester and Liverpool. To suggest a link between the periodicals and the new technology is not merely a convenience, for both seem to have struck contemporaries as outward and visible signs of 'the spirit of the age'. When, thirty years later, Wilkie Collins remarked that he lived in 'the age of journals' his phrase was not ill-chosen; he was expressing something of the power of a press which had harnessed energy, and narrowed distances between classes and cities, and between town and country, almost as vigorously as had the new railways. Even in 1828 Henry Stebbing considered that the periodicals possessed an unparalleled influence and that periodical literature acted 'with an imperceptible power on the minds of all classes', gave 'publicity and popularity to themes which, but for it, would have remained the property of the learned', raised into 'busy and active zeal multitudes that would otherwise have been buried in indifference', and propagated 'notions of right and wrong' which had 'no other sanction but its authority'. Literature published in the weekly, fortnightly, monthly, or quarterly periodicals, novels in cheap monthly parts, or poetry in illustrated annuals, were to have an unprecedented influence largely because of unprecedented social circumstances. An increase in the population automatically seemed to imply an audience; a steady expansion of education, both for the poor and the rich, ushered in what appeared to many to be an age of enhanced political and cultural awareness; above all, the efficient application of technology meant cheaper printing, lower prices, and speedy circulation.

The *Athenaeum* had not chosen its name idly. In ancient Athens, the temple of Athene had become a meeting-place for scholars, teachers, philosophers, and poets; its name was readily usurped by British institutions anxious to promote learning, discussion, or simply common interests amongst members. The name 'Athenaeum' could be applied to a patrician club as much as to a provincial self-improvement society for working men, but both expressed, like Stebbing's weekly journal, a unity of learning and a community of knowledge shared by the learned. As the century progressed that sense of community gradually diminished. The years 1830–80 were perhaps the last period in which it was assumed that a poet like Tennyson should know his astronomy; that an art critic like Ruskin should be *au fait* with geology and economics; that a biologist like Darwin should have read recent poetry as a part of his education; or that there was nothing incongruous in the fact that a clerical mathematician like Lewis Carroll should have written the greatest of all English children's books. Although the ancient English universities long resisted the introduction of degrees in natural science, it still seemed proper for Henry Stebbing to see a tripartite division in the 'literary' concerns of his new journal. The 'works of the imagination' would now probably be exclusively classed as 'literature', but Stebbing proposed two further categories, that of works of an 'investigatory moral nature' (by which he meant history, philosophy, and theology), and 'those which are composed from the results of philosophical enquiry into natural causes' (by which he meant all disciplines which we would class as 'science').

Although this chapter will concentrate on a twentieth-century understanding of literature, it is important to stress the sophistication of an educated nineteenth-century reader. Victorian periodicals embraced a vast range of subjects largely because they assumed that sophistication and because they saw themselves as the focus of the major intellectual concerns of the century, the divisions and contradictions as much as the confident belief in progress which seems to many modern observers to be a characteristic of the age. Obviously, not all of the journals aimed at a highbrow readership. The literary Annuals associated with Lady Blessington in the 1830s seem principally to have been directed at middle-class, middle-brow women, though they did provide a notable vehicle for the upsurge of the (often sentimental) women's poetry of the period. Journals such as *Ainsworth's Magazine* (edited by the popular historical novelist, William Harrison Ainsworth) and Charles Dickens's *Household Words* provided fiction as well as articles for readers Dickens himself once described as 'common-place'. The more heavyweight, even monumental, periodicals tended to follow the anonymous style established by the *Edinburgh Review* (founded 1802) and its early rival the *Quarterly* (founded 1809). Certainly, the initially Benthamite *Westminster* (1824) maintained the principle of substantial unsigned articles and reviews, but both *Blackwood's Magazine* (1817) and *Fraser's Magazine* (1830) included new fiction and, occasionally, poetry. The epoch-making *Cornhill Magazine*, first published in 1860 under the editorship of Thackeray, was always illustrated by the finest English artists

THE HEART OF THE EMPIRE. Niels Lund's panorama of London, taken from the roof of the Royal Exchange and looking westwards to St Paul's and Westminster (1901). A guidebook of 1850 proudly declared London to be 'the richest and largest, best-lighted and best-drained, city in the world'.

available and proved able to attract most of the best working novelists to its pages (most notably Thackeray himself, Trollope, Elizabeth Gaskell, George Eliot, and later George Meredith). The *Cornhill* also published Charlotte Brontë's fragmentary unfinished novel *Emma*, poetry by Tennyson, Arnold, and Elizabeth Barrett Browning, a series of major critical essays by Arnold and Ruskin's radical *Unto This Last* (so radical that protests obliged Thackeray to discontinue publication).

Charles Dickens, who was notable for his absence from the *Cornhill*, chose to serialize several of his novels in his own journals. *Hard Times* appeared in *Household Words*; then *A Tale of Two Cities* launched *All the Year Round* in 1859, to be followed in 1860 by *Great Expectations*. As an editor Dickens proved quick to discover and exploit other talents; he tried, but failed to recruit

THE RUSH FOR THE MONTHLY PARTS OF DICKENS'S *MASTER HUMPHREY'S CLOCK*. Richard Doyle's sketch from his Journal of 1840 of the Booksellers' men laden with bundles of the new serial leaving Chapman & Hall's London offices.

George Eliot, though he published Elizabeth Gaskell's *North and South* and *Cranford*, Wilkie Collins's *The Woman in White*, and later managed to persuade his old friend, the highly esteemed historical novelist Edward Bulwer Lytton, to write *A Strange Story* for him. Although she generally disliked serial publication, George Eliot agreed to publish *Romola* in the *Cornhill* and her first fictional experiments, the *Scenes of Clerical Life*, had come to public notice through their appearance in *Blackwood's Magazine*. These important links between the major creative writers of the period and the periodicals are further reinforced by the fact of the participation of many of the same writers as members of editorial boards, or, more vitally, as editors themselves. Both Harrison Ainsworth and Bulwer Lytton ran their own journals, a principle followed by Dickens in *Household Words* and *All the Year Round* once he had tested the ground as editor of *Bentley's Miscellany* in the 1830s and as founder editor of the *Daily News* in 1846. Thackeray, an early contributor to both *Fraser's* and *Punch*, proved a highly successful editor of the *Cornhill* from 1860 to 1862, and Trollope, who had once argued against publishing fiction in periodicals but found himself outnumbered by other members of his board, acted as editor of *St Paul's* during its brief existence. Equally noteworthy was the editorship of George Eliot's husband, G. H. Lewes, of the *Fortnightly Review*, and George Eliot's own work for the *Westminster* (1850-3).

The great Victorian journals, and latterly, the newspapers, provided a public forum for the discussion of domestic and foreign politics, for debates over religious certainties and religious difficulties, for speculation on the banes and blessings of contemporary society, and, above all, for detailed and extensive criticism of the state of literature. To some extent they projected the preoccupations of another Victorian institution, the public lecture, into the relative intimacy of the library, the club, and the drawing-room. Two of the most influential figures of the 1830s, Macaulay and Carlyle, first concentrated their energies into articles and reviews in the *Edinburgh* and *Fraser's*; George Eliot's and Thackeray's work as critics of fiction appeared in the journals with which

THE UNION OF ART AND SCIENCE. W. H. Fox-Talbot's pioneer calotype of the new Hungerford Bridge across the Thames, photographed in 1845. This image of Victorian London captures its smoky atmosphere, its working river, and Brunel's superb suspension bridge, demolished in 1860.

they were associated before they had written novels of their own, and Mill's and Matthew Arnold's later prose works emerged from essays or reviews first published in periodicals. Scholarship and argument were thus public property, not necessarily the preserve of an élite.

The 1830s opened with a vigorous debate about Reform, which, when the Reform Bill was rejected by the House of Lords, exploded into arson and the apparent danger of blood-letting in the streets. When the Reform Bill was finally passed in June 1832 it appeared to some observers to be the corner-stone of a pattern of reforming legislation designed to deflect a revolutionary tide through channels of reasoned and determined change; to others it seemed to be the beginning of the end of the old Constitution of Church and State. Later in the century George Eliot would look back on the period in both *Felix Holt* and *Middlemarch* as a key to the understanding of what had happened since, and as a means of grasping some of the implications of the second Reform Bill of 1867. The ostensibly more radical Dickens proved a more sanguine immediate observer, pouring scorn on the workings of Parliament throughout his career after a brief period in the 1830s as a parliamentary reporter, and forcefully attacking the workings of the 1834 Poor Law in his *Oliver Twist*.

Religion, Society, and the Novel

The so-called age of reform made the Church shudder as much as the State. The bishops who had voted against the bill in the House of Lords were publicly, even physically, abused in a way that indicates a widespread and uncommon anticlericalism. This opprobrium extended beyond the prelacy to an attack on what were assumed to be the fat endowments of the Church as a whole, an attack which is deftly suggested in Trollope's *The Warden* (1855). Once Parliament had set its house in order with the abolition of rotten boroughs and the redistribution of seats, it was naturally accepted by rational reformers that the Church would follow suit, either of its own accord or by force. Literary evidence of a spiritual reaction against an earlier complacency through the impact of Evangelicalism can be found in the last of George Eliot's *Scenes of Clerical Life*, but it was State interference in Church government that stimulated a very different reaction in the University of Oxford in 1833. In that year, a former Professor of Poetry in the University, the Revd John Keble (1792–1866) preached the Assize Sermon, directing his observations against what he saw as misguided reform, a reform which constituted an example of 'national apostasy'. Although other leaders of what was to be called the 'Oxford Movement' saw this sermon as marking the opening of a long and influential campaign against secularism, Keble himself stood in a strong but placid enough Anglican tradition. He was a high churchman in the manner of George Herbert, and he was a poet who sought to remould Herbert's tradition for the nineteenth century. Keble's *The Christian Year* (1827) contains poems for each Sunday and each major Festival in the Anglican Calendar, and he had modestly aimed to establish through it 'a sober standard of feeling in matters of practical religion'. This often flat and unadventurous volume of verse was to achieve an influence not always connected with its limited poetic merits, for it became hallowed as a spiritual call to order and its many editions throughout the century testify to its effect. The worst kind of narrow piety it inspired is suggested by the atmosphere of Sue Bridehead's Oxford lodgings in the early chapters of Hardy's *Jude the Obscure* (1895); more profitably it gave an impetus to the gradual revival of interest in seventeenth-century religious verse, and it set a pattern for a new generation of Christian poets and hymnologists, most significantly for a poet of the stature of Christina Rossetti, for lesser talents like those of Henry Lyte and Isaac Williams, and for the excellent translations from the Greek of J. M. Neale and from the German of Catherine Winkworth.

By far the most significant figure amongst the leaders of the Oxford

Movement, in both the historical and the literary sense, is John Henry (later Cardinal) Newman (1801–90). Newman's precision, in matters spiritual as much as personal, suggests an inheritance from his Evangelical youth; politically and ecclesiastically he was a conservative; it was, however, the essence of Newman's precision and conservatism that obliged him to take radical action and which led him inexorably from the Church of England to the Church of Rome. He was always well aware of the power of argument expressed in clear and subtle prose. The Oxford men found an early platform in the *British Magazine*, but it was Newman who dominated the series of doctrinal and historical pamphlets produced under the title *Tracts for the Times*, and it was Newman who brought the series of ninety Tracts to a conclusion in 1841 with a publication which created a national furore. There is, however, an earnest continuity between Newman's work as both an Anglican and a Roman controversialist and a line of developed thought which links his impressive Oxford sermons and his greatest theological statement, *The Grammar of Assent* of 1870. He was to describe the process of conversion three times, twice in fiction and later in the careful justification of his life and opinions in *Apologia pro vita sua* of 1864. *Apologia* was initially provoked by an attack on his integrity by Charles Kingsley (a religious controversialist of a very different stamp), but much of the debate in response to Kingsley's misrepresentation of him was reordered once Newman shaped his material into one of the great, if elusive, autobiographies of the century. *Apologia* traces 'that great revolution of mind' which he saw as the characteristic of himself and his times, and attempts to analyse 'the multitude of subtle influences' which had worked on him. His two novels, *Loss and Gain* (1848) and *Callista* (1856), are both propagandist in intent but despite some fine descriptive passages and some excellently alert dialogue they are also remarkably wooden. The earlier book offers an interesting account of Oxford in the 1840s; *Callista*, in part a response to Kingsley's *Hypatia*, is set in third-century North Africa. It offers a 'sketch' of the period through an evocation of the spiritual progress of a pagan towards Christianity but it also contains pointed reflections on the parallels between dissent from a modern establishment and modern complacency and those of the ancient world. Newman's poetry at times shares the clarity and argumentative precision of his prose. His *The Dream of Gerontius*, which was later to provide the basis of Elgar's oratorio, effectively combines a lyric intensity with a liturgical patterning in its description of the passage of a soul from earth to afterlife.

The Oxford Movement and what Newman called the 'Second Spring' of the English Roman Catholic Church offered a kind of certainty and an assertion of tradition, to a nation increasingly beset with uncertainty and the consequences of progressive change. What both offered, however, had little appeal either to those who found 'the Protestantism of the Protestant religion' (to use the phrase reiterated by Arnold) a satisfying code of belief and action or to those who espoused progress or who, like Dickens, distrusted the ecclesiastical 'dandies' who 'would make the Vulgar very picturesque and faithful, by putting back the hands upon the Clock of Time, and cancelling a few hundred years of history'. That sentiment of Dickens's almost certainly derives from the vigorous opinions of the second great preacher-controversialist to emerge in the 1830s, Thomas Carlyle (1795–1881). Carlyle was, however, no Tractarian, no Churchman, and no graduate of Oxford. He was a product both of a rugged Scottish Presbyterianism and of the more refined, but equally censorious, world of the Edinburgh Enlightenment and the *Edinburgh Review*. Like the Oxford men he recognized the power of the printed word and the influence of the journals and of pamphlet propaganda. Carlyle's earliest published work relates to what was to prove a continuing passion for German literature, philosophy, and history, and in particular to the dominant figure in recent German letters, Goethe. Carlyle translated *Wilhelm Meister* into English in 1824. His first real impact on his contemporaries, however, came through the commission of the editor of the *Edinburgh Review*, Francis Jeffrey, for a series of essays the most notable of which is 'Signs of the Times' of 1829, an essay in which Carlyle attempted to characterize his age. Rejecting epithets like 'Heroical', 'Devotional', and 'Moral' he lit on the description 'the Mechanical Age', the age of machinery 'in every outward and inward sense of that word'. The essay tellingly developed the consequences of a machine-dominated society and machine-inspired ways of thinking and acting. Although national wealth had increased, so had the divisions between the rich and the poor in the industrialized cities. Far worse, an external world might be efficiently regulated by machinery, but men, mechanical in head and heart, had begun to apply mechanical definitions to relationships, attachments, and opinions.

Through a steady stream of essays, pamphlets, and lectures Carlyle emerged as the dominant social thinker of early Victorian England. He obliged his contemporaries to face the evident enough contradictions within their civilization and to attempt to make some sense of the disorder around them. The conflict he identified was not simply that of faith and doubt, of tradition and innovation, or of conservatism and reform, but of a gulf between the rich and the poor. National despair needed to be countered by social energy, the 'Everlasting Nay' of the spiritual desert by the 'Everlasting Yea' of determined action. *Sartor Resartus*, from which those phrases come, appeared serially in *Fraser's Magazine* between 1833 and 1834 in the form of a supposed commentary on a German treatise on the 'philosophy of clothes'. Despite its presumed German base the essays gradually expand into observations on a particularly English problem and a particularly English sham, 'dandyism', which ignores the real and pressing condition of the nation.

The variety, contradictoriness, and bluster of much of Carlyle's mature writing, and the aggressive inventiveness of his prose style, have tended to render him an unsympathetic figure to modern readers. The figure who broods

THOMAS AND JANE CARLYLE AT HOME, by R. S. Tait (1857-8). The 'Sage of Chelsea' in his modest but comfortable house in Cheyne Row. A typical enough middle-class interior of the period.

so conspicuously in the midst of Ford Madox Brown's painting *Work*, however, remains crucial to our understanding of Victorian intellectual enterprise and energy. Carlyle was revered as both sage and prophet by his many disciples and echoes of his voice can be heard in much of the literature of the first half of the century. In the 1840s his public protestations became all the more urgent, most notably in his lectures *On Heroes, Hero-Worship and the Heroic in History* (in which he sought new definitions of heroic action appropriate to his times) and in *Past and Present* (which bears on its title-page a quotation from Schiller expressing the vital Victorian sentiment that 'life is earnest'). *Past and Present* effectively restates the theme that had run through all of Carlyle's work to date: 'England is full of wealth, of multifarious produce, supply for human want of every kind; yet England is dying of inanition.' Like the *Heroes* lectures which preceded it, the volume moves towards the idea of a hero who transcends the 'shams' and 'quackery' of the times, and whose will and action is capable of galvanizing society and forcibly moving history forward. Although he was ready enough with definitions of the heroes of the past, he remained vague about the precise nature of what the present demanded. Half-quoting

Tennyson's newly published poem 'Ulysses', he none the less urged progressive movement through uncharted seas 'towards that haven' to which Supreme Powers were driving: 'let all true men, with what of faculty is within them bend valiantly, uncessantly, with thousandfold endeavour, thither! There, or else in the Ocean-abysses, it is very clear to me, we shall arrive.'

In *Past and Present* one can detect what Robert Browning meant when he remarked that Carlyle's bitterness was only melancholy and his scorn sensibility. The vexation, rage, and frustration evident in its pages seem to rise from a peculiar sensitivity to present problems seen in a historical perspective. The book does not look back nostalgically to a lost golden age of medieval perfection (though there is a heartfelt tribute to the twelfth-century Abbot Sampson), but instead offers readers a charged awareness of a present which holds in it 'both the whole Past and the whole Future'. This sense of historic pressure, and the need actively to seize a historical moment informs his most substantial and least read works, the two great histories of *The French Revolution* (1837) and of *Friedrich II of Prussia, called Frederick the Great* (1858–65). Despite their schematization and the constrictions imposed by the direction of their arguments, both are masterpieces of narrative innovation. Carlyle used certain historical sources, most notably diaries, memoirs, letters, and printed ephemera, with great imaginative skill, bringing many voices to bear upon his narrative and telescoping often myopic eyewitness accounts into a larger interpretative overview. Carlyle's histories, especially that of the *French Revolution*, are the epics of their age.

Like his contemporary, T. B. Macaulay (1800–59), Carlyle made Victorian England acutely aware of its place in a pattern of progressive advance. For Macaulay that advance was determined by constitutional precedent and by a confident espousal of a future guided by the principles of Whig democracy. Carlyle, increasingly pessimistic as the century advanced, posited examples from the past more as warnings than as plans of action, ranted at inaction, and cultivated the cause of the strong man. Nevertheless it was he who spurred so many of his fellow writers into a direct response to the 'condition of England' in the 1840s and 1850s. The urgency of much early and mid-Victorian 'social' fiction cannot simply be explained away by a dutiful attraction to the cause of the poor, or by an acute attack of middle-class guilt. It was rather an awareness that a deeply divided nation needed to face its problems head on. Easy answers and social panaceas, were, as Carlyle reminded them, unlikely to be immediately forthcoming. Earlier in the century the Waverley novels had demonstrated that social crises could be the proper and serious matter of fiction; the Victorian social novelists moved from the past to the present, confronting divisions which threatened to imperil the prospect of a steady future advance.

Benjamin Disraeli's famous division of the England of 1845 into 'two nations—the rich and the poor' is perhaps too startlingly rash to be anything

A VISION OF THE REVIVED MIDDLE AGES. The title-page of A. W. N. Pugin's *Glossary of Ecclesiastical Ornament* (1844). Though an attempt to proclaim the splendour of a lost age of faith, Pugin here spectacularly used the new art of coloured lithography to propagate his stylistic ideas.

The Glossary of Ecclesiastical Ornament

MONUMENTAL CLASSICISM FOR THE MACHINE AGE. P. C. Hardwick's perspective of the Booking
Hall at Euston Station (1846–9), a view dominated by the statue of the great engineer, Robert Stephenson.
The hall was demolished in 1962 by another progressive generation.

more than a debating point. It did, however, reflect much of what Carlyle had been preaching for more than a decade. Disraeli (1804–81) produced a trilogy of socio-political novels, *Coningsby* (1844), *Sybil* (1845), and *Tancred* (1847), which stem, however, not simply from a politician's sense of the currency of an issue but also from an experienced Romantic novelist infected by social concern. Disraeli's arguments in his novels are sometimes as strikingly effective, as is his evocation of exotic and charged settings, but his solutions are generally evasive. His novels are witty, paradoxical, contradictory, and excitedly imaginative, qualities which also render the later *Lothair* (1870) particularly effective, but they scarcely expound a serious political programme. They evoke issues and focus attention on them largely through the effect of clever juxtaposition and aphoristic dialogue.

The contrast between Disraeli's account of Wodgate in *Sybil* and Charles Kingsley's disturbing picture of the London slums in *Alton Locke* is telling.

THE EMIGRANTS' LAST SIGHT OF HOME. Richard Redgrave's painting of 1858 captures something of the result of economic pressures, and economic hopes, which obliged so many Victorians to emigrate. This was the various fate of the Micawbers, of Mary Barton, and of many disgruntled Chartists, all hoping for something to turn up in a new world.

Kingsley (1819–75) is observing from personal experience and using his observation to evoke more than an occasional effect. *Alton Locke: Tailor and Poet* appeared in 1850 in the form of the supposed autobiography of a self-educated, politically alert Chartist, a working-class radical stirred into action by the despair, disease, and squalor of contemporary London. Kingsley's sympathy with what was, by 1850, the dying fire of Chartism is evident throughout the story, but, in moving his narrator towards an acceptance of Christian brotherhood rather than class confrontation, his own espousal of Christian Socialism shapes the conclusion. It is a Christian Socialism informed with the spirit of Carlyle, a character who figures in the novel in the form of a Scottish bookseller who acts as Alton's guide, philosopher, and friend.

Although he was later to dissociate himself from Carlyle's pessimism and agnosticism, Kingsley followed his mentor in cultivating both a taste for history and a penchant for the kind of heroes to whom the soubriquet 'Muscular Christians' has been affixed. Kingsley's later novels certainly suggest a relish for dynamic and often bloodthirsty action. His historical novels, *Hypatia* (1851–3), *Westward Ho!* (1855), and *Hereward the Wake* (1865) tend to see the historical process in terms of Old Testament struggles between positive rights and positive wrongs (a tendency which contributed to his blundering encounter with Newman and to his unfortunate tenure of the Chair of Modern History at Cambridge). Although Kingsley had ostensibly abandoned the confusion of modern social problems for the relatively simply explained divisions of the past it was essentially because he saw the key to the present in an understanding of history. His most sustained achievement, *Hypatia*, a novel set in fifth-century Alexandria, has the subtitle 'New Foes with an Old Face'; it reflects modern religious problems by picturing, without a modicum of flattery, the unfortunate state of Patristic Christianity. The novel is surprisingly balanced in its argument and contains both a forceful evocation of the deserts, ruins, and cities of Egypt and some vivid and eccentric characters. The two later historical novels celebrate the strong man struggling against the forces of evil and proclaim a somewhat naïve faith in providential advance and the advantages of Protestantism and Teutonism. Kingsley's much neglected *Two Years Ago* (1857) returned to a contemporary setting and to the problems of sanitation and disease which had haunted him in his own parish.

By far the most persuasive and observant of the early Victorian social novelists is Elizabeth Gaskell (1810–65), the wife of a prominent Unitarian clergyman and, with Friedrich Engels, the most memorable contemporary observer of what Carlyle called that 'sublime' 'prophetic city'—Manchester. Although her *Mary Barton* (1848) bore a quotation from Carlyle on its title-page, and begins with a contrast of past and present, two factors seem to have determined the nature of the novel: a personal grief and an equally personal stimulus to describe the lives of 'some of those who elbowed me daily in the busy streets of the town'. *Mary Barton* began as a therapy after the death of

THE INDUSTRIAL NORTH. A view of the railway viaduct at Stockport, Cheshire about 1850. This could equally be Dickens's Coketown, 'a town of machinery and tall chimneys, out of which interminable serpents of smoke trailed themselves for ever and ever, and never got uncoiled'.

her infant son; it became an urgent reminder to middle-class novel readers, especially those of the North of England, of the distress of the poor which it was all too easy to ignore. As Engels had noted of contemporary Manchester, social classes lived physically apart; they saw little of each other and seemed to care less. With the growth of class consciousness in the 1830s and 1840s, especially amongst factory workers, divisions, suspicions, and antagonisms grew more apparent. Elizabeth Gaskell's frankness about the prejudices of both mill-owners and mill-workers in *Mary Barton* seems initially to have ruffled feathers; the *Manchester Guardian* (not then an especially liberal-minded newspaper) accused her of sinning against truth 'in matters of fact . . . beyond her sphere of knowledge', and a correspondent later complained that she had misrepresented the conduct of the masters and had disguised from the men 'the fact that their surest remedy lay in self-help'. They are scarcely justifiable complaints, for few citizens of Manchester knew its urban problems as intimately and few had attempted to picture the unhappy human consequences of the city's economic successes and slumps. Many twentieth-century critics of the novel have, however, taken a radically different line of complaint. *Mary Barton* has been seen as lacking political edge, of providing graphic evidence but of reaching inadequate conclusions. It is a criticism which must also be qualified in the light of evidence. The year of the novel's publication, 1848, effectively marked the climax of one kind of working-class politics, Chartism, but with the ebbing of Chartist energy the new phase of political consensus which marks the 1850s was beginning. *Mary Barton* is a retrospect, looking back on the 'Hungry Forties', on middle-class indifference, emigration and the distress which occasioned it, from the viewpoint of a new optimism which united rather than divided classes. As the *Westminster Review* noted, the novel embodied 'the dominant feeling of our times . . . that ignorance, destitution and vice . . . must be got rid of. The ability to point out how they are to be got rid of, is not a characteristic of this age. That will be the characteristic of the age which is coming.'

The 1850s were to prove a more prosperous, more consolidated, and co-operative decade in politics and economics than were the divided 1840s. It is a factor which determines the argument of Elizabeth Gaskell's second great industrial novel, *North and South* (1855). When the novel was serialized in Dickens's journal, *Household Words*, it bore a statement of intent in its epigraph from Tennyson, which ends with the words, 'for some true result of good / All parties work together'. *North and South* is set chiefly, like its predecessor, in Manchester (here represented under the name 'Milton North-ern'), though the novel exploits the distinction drawn at the beginning between rural, deferential, traditionally stratified southern England and the industrial, pushy, class-conscious North. The Hale family moves between one England and another, and the move proves traumatic. Mr Hale, a clergyman who has abandoned his orders, becomes a private tutor to John Thornton, a self-made mill-owner anxious to obtain the education if not the attitudes of a gentleman. Hale's daughter, Margaret, one of Elizabeth Gaskell's most distinctive and intelligent heroines, seeks out a very different realm of action in becoming a succourer and supporter of the poor. The relationship which develops between Thornton and Margaret is not simply a continuation of the juxtaposition of North and South, it also comes to suggest a profitable synthesis of the attitudes of a determined master and those of an equally determined sympathizer with his men. Both parties adjust to one another, forging new responsibilities, and new and interdependent relationships.

Elizabeth Gaskell's industrial novels have of late tended to overshadow the rest of her work, and especially her two late, subtle masterpieces, *Sylvia's Lovers* and *Wives and Daughters*. She had tackled a somewhat different social problem in *Ruth* in 1853, dealing with charity and understanding with the problem of a 'fallen woman', but it was through the once vastly popular *Cranford* (1853) that she relaxed with a series of tales which explore the nuances and details of private life. The interlinked tales centred on the town

THE HUB OF THE 'SUBLIME CITY'. Alfred Waterhouse's perspective of the new Manchester Town Hall of 1868. A superb monument to northern civic pride, memorable as much for its vigorous Gothic as for its excellent planning. Its architect saw it as 'essentially of the nineteenth century'.

of Cranford were first published in *Household Words* in 1851-2 and suggest a community flourishing away from the new industrial cities but linked to a larger world of international trade and travel. Elizabeth Gaskell's finest study of a tight trading community is that of Monkshaven (a fictionalized Whitby) in *Sylvia's Lovers* (1863). The town, cut off from the rest of England by moorland on one side and the North Sea on the other, is seen with its whaling ships and their crews threatened by the incursions of the naval press-gangs during the Napoleonic Wars. The town's resistance to the press-gang and the disappearance of one of Sylvia's lovers provides the spring of the 'saddest' story the novelist ever wrote; it is also her most gripping. The strong Yorkshire dialect of the characters, and the extraordinary vitality of the details of everyday life suggest something of the impact of Elizabeth Gaskell's researches at Haworth for her *Life of Charlotte Brontë* (1857). Her last novel, *Wives and*

Daughters, was serialized in the *Cornhill* and left marginally unfinished at the time of her death in 1865. Like her many short stories, *Wives and Daughters* relates a meticulous observation of domestic affairs outward to a wider context and demonstrates the individuality and distinction of her genius for representing what many other writers have neglected as merely commonplace. Although she had moved away from the propagandist fiction with which her name is most readily associated, her later novels reveal a profound, if sometimes tragic, grasp of the complexity of human relationships, the true quality of which still remains to be acknowledged.

Although Charles Dickens (1812–70) enthusiastically promoted her novels in his journals, the somewhat vexed editorial relationship between the two writers suggests a divergence in their literary predilections and styles. It is a divergence which is evident in the contrast presented by the two most important novels to appear in the pages of *Household Words*, *North and South* and Dickens's own *Hard Times* (1854). Elizabeth Gaskell carefully and delicately recalls the industrial North of England which she knew at first hand, shaping a plot around unspectacular, but alert, characters. Dickens's novel seems vividly impressionistic beside it. *Hard Times* offers an imaginative variation on landscape and character which he saw as an outsider, albeit an exceptionally observant one. Both writers had been spurred by Carlyle, but Dickens seems to have reacted more directly to the premiss that the 'Mechanical Age' had carried hearts and minds as well as mills. His 'Condition of England' novel is in many ways his most schematized work of fiction, presenting a shaped attack on the 'philosophy of facts' while still allowing for the ultimate triumph of an innate human goodness. *Hard Times* is Dickens at his baldest and sharpest.

Dickens, Thackeray, and the Brontës

John Ruskin, who praised the sharpness of *Hard Times*, did so at the expense of Dickens's other novels which he seems to have found exaggerated in their representation of the contemporary world. It is a complaint which still surfaces from readers who admire strict verisimilitude or who respond best to fiction which has moved furthest from the roots of popular story-telling. When Dickens himself responded to the criticism, in a preface to *Martin Chuzzlewit*, he drew a distinction between the long-sighted observer and the myopic one; 'what is exaggeration to one class of minds and perceptions', he wrote, 'is plain truth to another'. That 'plain truth' consisted of shaping a highly diverse and multifarious vision of life into stories. Fiction became for Dickens a means of making sense of a disordered, increasingly anarchic world in which sanity and madness, banality and eccentricity, love and cruelty, coexisted and tangled with each other. His fictional shapes may often seem conventional, but they contain within them not an exaggerated vision but a sense that humanity cannot really be contained, let alone tidied and explained.

Dickens's intensely funny early fiction, from the *Sketches by Boz*, to *Martin Chuzzlewit*, suggests the degree to which he was loosely but happily working in the literary tradition which he had inherited from Fielding and Smollett. His eighteenth-century characteristics were evident from the first to Sydney Smith who in 1837 recognized the extent to which the soul of a third great artist, Hogarth, had 'migrated into the Body of Dickens'. Significantly though, he was also the quintessential artist of a new era, the Victorian writer best equipped to transform the age's restless urban civilization into art. Dickens was a best-seller at a time when the term 'best-seller' did not automatically imply second-rate fiction and a sensation-craving public. He became an efficient exploiter of a popular market with *Pickwick Papers*, but in his subsequent thirty-three years of successful response to his public he never lost the ability to appeal to a vast range of readers from the highbrow to the semi-literate. Dickens's peculiar genius, like Shakespeare's in an earlier period, renders him the central consciousness of his age. He is the foremost Victorian artist simply because he best reflects the complexity, the excitement, the fertility, and the often confusing abundance of contemporary England. Other writers deal more persuasively, probingly, or movingly with aspects of the age to which Dickens merely gestured (the life of the intellect, for example, or the condition of woman) but he has a totality, and range and a freedom which eludes all but the greatest of artists. If Dickens's novels have struck certain critics as vulgar, random, inconsistent, or simply as too prolix, it is because those are leading characteristics of the age itself. Dickens took a popular art-form, the comic novel, and gave it a distinctive wit, energy, and variety. He is the artist of 'many voices', but he is also, as T. S. Eliot recognized, an artist like Shakespeare who can 'with a phrase make a character as real as flesh and blood'. His many voices are also the echoes of the contradictory and clamorous noises of the century.

Dickens was the first great writer to tackle the essentially modern problem of the discontents of an urban civilization. His London, unlike the great manufacturing cities of the Midlands and North, had not suddenly boomed; it had steadily expanded as a commercial centre, a port, and the hub of government, the law, finance, and fashion, to become the great metropolis, the largest and richest, if not the most splendid, of European cities. Dickens drew his characters from the breadth of this social and commercial spectrum, but, as his career developed, his vision of the city became increasingly threatening. In *Pickwick Papers*, or *Oliver Twist*, or *Nicholas Nickleby* London is a city of stark contrasts, but it can still be escaped; in the later fiction, most notably in *Little Dorrit* and *Our Mutual Friend*, it is encroaching and unrelieved, a microcosm of a weary, stale, and unprofitable world in which the only hope for the future lies in individual regeneration.

THE MODESTLY PROSPEROUS LONDON CLERK. The first plate of George Cruikshank's teetotal propaganda, *The Bottle*. Though intended to show the dire effects of indulgence in alcohol, the engraving also gives an excellent picture of small luxuries now affordable by a family of this class in the 1840s.

COLD MISERY AND WANT DESTROY THEIR YOUNGEST CHILD. A graphic demonstration of the often narrow division between prosperity and destitution. It is the same room as the one above but is now devoid of its ornaments, its furniture, even of its grate.

Although the novels that succeed *Dombey and Son* (1847–8) are far more concentrated in their commentary on society they are also far darker and gloomier than the stories which first established Dickens's successful rapport with his readers. All of his novels, however, share the same sense of fun and determining optimism. His plots are rarely tight-knit (though *A Tale of Two Cities* is distinctive here) but each tends to trace the destinies of his central characters and to move them towards an enlightened fulfilment. The traditional devices with which novels end, marriage or a crock of gold, are not eschewed, but they become for Dickens an expression of a comic world-view in which dislocation and pain are answered by order and a modicum of happiness. This is not simply fortuitousness, sentimentality, or a sop to undiscriminating readers, but a way of coming to terms with confusion and a potential anarchy. The structure of Dickens's narratives, from the relatively simple *Oliver Twist* (1837–8) to the masterfully complex *Bleak House* (1852–3), allow him to give full rein to individual eccentricity, to social and mental deviation, even to murder and madness, while still moulding circumstances into a kind of resolution. In the later fiction, and especially in *Great Expectations* (1860–1) or *Our Mutual Friend* (1864–5), virtuous, or potentially virtuous, characters survive by the skin of their teeth, but the very fact of their survival suggests a positive assertive gesture in the face of the negatives of their environment.

It is this optimistic control which partly explains the nature of Dickens's so-called sentimentality and his lurches from high comedy and absurdity to the lachrymose. Largely because he was so close to his readers' responses, through the very nature of the monthly-part serialization of his novels, he readily responded to what he felt they wanted of him. Death-bed piety, simpering children, and angelic child-wives were scarcely Dickens's invention, but in incorporating such elements of popular contemporary culture into his novels he has continued to embarrass certain of his twentieth-century readers. His own period of acute unhappiness as a child seems to have given him a special sympathy with the sufferings of children and a sensitivity to happy, nuclear families (especially when gathered around a Christmas hearth). His individual ideal of womanhood, developed yet again from existing literary stereotypes, seems also to have determined his homeward-looking, upward-pointing domestic angels from Rose Maylie to Agnes Wickfield and Esther Summerson. These are aspects of Dickens's work which require a sympathetic understanding of the culture of his age in order to be given their proper context. *The Old Curiosity Shop* (1840–1), his tribute to saintly girlhood, having once briefly reigned as his supreme novel, is now perhaps his most misunderstood. His death-beds, especially Nell's unconscionable time a'dying, having once been hailed as rivalled only by Shakespeare's tragic ends, are only just receiving the kind of sympathy which they require of readers alert to Dickens's emotional range and variety. Having reacted violently against 'Victorianism' twentieth-century culture has been disinclined to allow Dickens not simply Homeric nods, but also the passages of sentiment which are integral to the nature of his art.

In one vital area of the immediate background to Dickens's work, the theatre, we are, however, beginning to recover a fuller sympathy. Dickens was steadily drawn to the stage, both as an actor and a dramatist and as a reader of his own novels. He had once contemplated becoming a professional actor, and as the Thespians and would-be Thespians of his fiction vividly suggest, he retained a sure grasp of theatrical mannerism and performance. He was also pulled by the steady magnet of Shakespeare and by the taste of his contemporaries for melodrama. Much of his dialogue, particularly his passionate and amatory dialogue, can be readily related to the kind of expression found on the Victorian stage. His readings from his novels, which became so notable a feature of his career, also indicate the degree to which his novels are *performable*. His observation of character, like that in the novels of the eighteenth century which he so admired, or in the drama, is largely external; he interprets the inner life, like a dramatist, through action and speech rather

CHARLES DICKENS THE ACTOR. C. R. Leslie's painting of Dickens as Captain Bobadil in Ben Jonson's *Everyman in his Humour* as performed in 1845. The picture serves to stress the links between Dickens and his literary forebears, especially those who worked in the theatre.

than by an analysis of thought and motive. To say that Dickens is a novelist in the dramatic tradition of Shakespeare and Jonson is not to imply that he was a playwright *manqué*, but to note that he was able to choose the art of the novel over that of the theatre. The novel of his time had triumphed as the supreme art-form of the age, but for Dickens it was also a medium which related to the immediacy and effect of a performance in acknowledging the relationship between reader and writer, and between performer and audience.

Dickens's creative career ended dramatically enough with his *Mystery of Edwin Drood* left suspended and unfinished at the time of his sudden death in 1870. There have been many attempts to finish the novel and to solve its mystery, not least among them being theatrical ones. Perhaps the only contemporary of Dickens with sufficient flair to unravel its threads satisfactorily was his former protégé, Wilkie Collins. Collins somewhat huffily declined to do so, perhaps because he was vexed by the fact that Dickens had been imitating the kind of novel that he had made distinctively his own. Collins (1824–89) remains the greatest English master of the mystery story, the unrivalled exponent of what was known in the 1860s as the 'Sensation Novel'. *The Woman in White*, which had been serialized in *All the Year Round* in 1860, is a *tour de force*, both a disturbing treatment of insanity and a clever narrative structure. It also contains Collins's finest villain, Count Fosco, an Italian with a murky background in secret political societies and a habit of playing disconcertingly with his white mice. *The Moonstone* (1868) has a yet more sophisticated series of narrators, each adding clues towards the unfolding of the mystery and it shows an interest in the unconscious mind under the influence of drugs which may well have inspired Dickens's plot for *Edwin Drood*. Collins's middle novels, most memorably *No Name* (1862) and *Armadale* (1866), though scrupulously plotted, suggest that he was not always at home with the serial form and the expansive narrative. His characters, and his often flat style, do not quite sustain the dramatic intensity which marks his best work.

To their contemporaries the only writer seriously to challenge Dickens's supremacy as a novelist was William Makepeace Thackeray (1811–63). Dickens had firmly established himself with his public with the green monthly parts of *Pickwick* in 1836–7. Thackeray had to await the success of the yellow parts of *Vanity Fair* ten years later. The rivalry between the two men was not purely circumstantial, for Thackeray had been preparing himself as a critic and as an experimenter with small-scale fiction for some time; it also seems to have been based on an unstinted admiration for Dickens's genius. When, for example, he had finished the fifth number of *Dombey* (in which little Paul dies) he told a friend, 'there's no writing against such power as this . . . it is unsurpassed—it is stupendous'. Such generosity of spirit when, as the author of *Vanity Fair*, he *was* trying to write against such power, was typical enough of a writer proud of his own profession, but prone to witty self-deprecation. It was a generosity which his friends sometimes found puzzling, even when the rivalry further expressed itself in competing novels, annual Christmas Books, and travel books.

Writing to a deadline and for serial publication was not new to Thackeray, but the launching of *Vanity Fair* indicates a quite distinctive literary ambition. He had struggled as a journalist since the late 1830s and had produced some of the funniest and sharpest occasional pieces in English. His first substantial masterpiece, *Barry Lyndon*, had appeared serially in *Fraser's Magazine* in 1844, but he seems not to have held this brilliantly disquieting story in much esteem and did not republish it until 1856. It was through *Barry Lyndon*, however, that he found the mastery of narrative control which marks his later work. Barry's 'memoirs' of his varied life as a soldier, gambler, and playboy are

THE FIRST SOCIAL REGENERATOR OF THE DAY. This portrait of the young Thackeray in 1832 by Daniel Maclise captures something of the energy that Charlotte Brontë so admired in the author of *Vanity Fair*.

presented as being 'edited' by one of Thackeray's many personae, one G. S. FitzBoodle, and it is this same FitzBoodle who functions as the narrator of the digressive *Book of Snobs* ('by one of themselves') which appeared in *Punch* (1846-7). *Vanity Fair* develops directly out of these two earlier works, the one providing him with the model of a raffish story set in the recent past, the other with an amused, even slightly cynical narrator. *Vanity Fair* is like *Barry Lyndon* a masterpiece of tone, constantly challenging a reader's assumptions about characters and situations, and questioning motive and judgement. His great 'novel without a hero' is not, however, the work of a cynic; it is rather the book of a particularly vigorous moralist who disconcerts by asking his readers to reassess their preconceptions. Reading Thackeray we have to be perpetually alert not just to his comic variety, but to a questioning intelligence and a narrative method which bids us scrutinize the very nature of the story and its telling.

Thackeray's later novels have been unjustly criticized for a supposed lack of the sardonic edge of *Vanity Fair*. They are, in fact, developments of the narrative mastery he discovered in his earlier work and they raise equally subtle questions about reader response. *Pendennis* (1848-50) and *The Newcomes* (1853-5) view mid-Victorian society as quizzically as had *Vanity Fair* the laxer, less earnest Regency world. Their relative sobriety is less a reflection of Thackeray's acceptance of convention than a response to changed social conditions. They represent a teasing of a would-be respectable, self-confident society. Thackeray's characterization and his wit are just as brilliant, and the juxtaposition of scenes and attitudes just as challenging. What has altered is a desire to grant his characters a degree of achieved maturity, happiness, and security. Thackeray's second great masterpiece, *The History of Henry Esmond* (1852), is, however, radically different from *Vanity Fair*. Like *Barry Lyndon* it has a first-person narrator, not one we immediately recognize as a lying braggart, but one whom we also learn to question and qualify. Esmond is a melancholic, an unhappy and lonely child who grows into an unhappy lover and a gauche and isolated dabbler in national politics. The novel, set in the England of Queen Anne, describes the clumsy and unfortunate manœuvres of the Jacobites, but, as we readily sense, there are many pretenders and yet more pretences. Everything is seen from the narrator's point of view; he flatters, distorts, broods, and attempts to make sense and a shape out of his confused experience. *Henry Esmond* struck Anthony Trollope as one of the three greatest novels in English; its present relative neglect is perhaps best seen as symptomatic of Thackeray's power to disconcert.

Esmond is one of a loose group of novels published in the 1840s and 1850s in the form of fictional autobiography. The vogue was perhaps re-established by a spate of diaries, letters, and memoirs (most notably those of Pepys, Evelyn, and Horace Walpole) which began to appear in the 1820s. The roots of *Barry Lyndon* certainly lie here, but it was Charlotte Brontë's *Jane Eyre* which seems

IN THE SERVICE OF HER MAJESTY QUEEN ANNE. Augustus Egg's painting of 1857 of a scene from *Henry Esmond*. The novel helped to establish a growing fashion for eighteenth-century artifacts and the architectural style loosely labelled 'Queen Anne'.

to have stimulated contemporary novelists into their own experiments with first-person narratives. Dickens's *David Copperfield* and *Bleak House*, Kingsley's *Alton Locke*, Thackeray's *Esmond*, Anne Brontë's *The Tenant of Wildfell Hall*, and Charlotte Brontë's *Villette* can all be seen as a direct response to a particularly demanding way of story-telling; Tennyson's *Maud* and Elizabeth Barrett Browning's *Aurora Leigh* suggest that the form offered a parallel challenge to contemporary poets.

When it was published in 1847 *Jane Eyre* created a sensation parallel to that of the contemporaneous serialization of *Vanity Fair*. The difference lay in the fact that Charlotte Brontë's equally disconcerting novel seemed to have exploded suddenly, as if from nowhere. G. H. Lewes, enthusiastically reviewing the book in *Fraser's*, proclaimed it 'an utterance from the depths of a struggling, much-enduring spirit'; he was later to greet the second edition (dedicated, incidentally, to Thackeray) in the *Westminster* as 'decidedly the best novel of the season'. What seems to have added to the sensation of the pseudonymous novel's first appearance was the awareness that the unknown 'Currer Bell' had discomposed and irritated more conservative readers. J. G. Lockhart, the editor of the *Quarterly* noted privately that the novel's heroine was 'rather a brazen Miss' and the *Christian Remembrancer* found its message burning with 'moral Jacobinism'. The seriously alarmed Elizabeth Rigby blustered, 'the tone of the mind and thought which has overthrown authority and violated every code human and divine abroad, and fostered Chartism and rebellion at home, is the same which has also written *Jane Eyre*.' Such vituperation is more than faintly ridiculous in its overstatement, but it does serve as an acknowledgement of the power of the narrative, of its political relevance, and of its proclamation of personal integrity and independence. In Chapter XII, for example, Jane is allowed a now celebrated stirring of revolt from the lot of the oppressed: 'Women are supposed to be very calm generally; but women feel just as men feel . . . they suffer from too rigid a constraint, too absolute a stagnation.' The adult Jane has channelled her sense of injustice into an assertion of her selfhood; the persecuted child has become a woman matured by experience and self-discipline who is capable of testing circumstances, companions, and lovers. *Jane Eyre*, though now regarded as a classic variation on a traditional enough love story, is in fact the narrative of a far from conventional heroine who never recedes into passivity or mere observation.

When Charlotte Brontë (1816–55) was asked for her opinion of Thackeray's *Esmond* she responded with the words 'admirable and odious'. They are qualities which are perhaps reflected in *Villette* (1853), a story in which (according to Mrs Gaskell) a particular action of M. Paul's is based on one of Thackeray's. As with *Esmond*, a reader is bidden to question the motives, the expression, and the self-analysis of the narrator. Charlotte Brontë's heroine, Lucy Snowe (originally Lucy Frost), has to struggle and endure as much as does Jane Eyre, but she is denied true fulfilment and her happiness seems fleeting. As her creator remarked, 'I never meant to appoint her lines in pleasant places.' The novel offers an often disturbing evocation of a character seeking assurance in an encroaching and suspicious environment, and it subtly transposes elements of the Gothic novels of fifty years before into a modern setting in investigating the effects of loneliness and confinement on an impressionable woman. *Villette* also transforms autobiographical material, relating to the novelist's own experiences as a teacher in Brussels, which she had more clumsily dealt with in her first novel *The Professor* (published posthumously in 1856). *Jane Eyre* had, however, been immediately succeeded in 1849 by *Shirley*, a novel written under the strain of tending the dying Anne Brontë. It is an ambitious experiment, combining a troubled industrial background (which relates it to the 'Condition of England' novels) with studies of women in love, women who are not loved, and of women who, like Jane and Lucy, feel, think, and act with resolve intermixed with passion. The distinctive character of Shirley Keeldar was, Elizabeth Gaskell affirmed in her *Life of Charlotte Brontë*, partly based on Charlotte's conception of her sister, Emily.

All of the novels of the Brontë sisters, mostly written in the cramped parsonage at Haworth, share an interrelationship which is as much literary as it is biographical. The three sisters, with their brother Branwell, had composed highly romantic fiction as children; as adults they seem to have stimulated and animated each other as novelists and poets. The younger sister, Anne (1820–49), is by no means the shadow of her sisters, a role in which she is often cast by critics. Admittedly her first novel, *Agnes Grey*, is an unpretentious study of the life of a governess which seems slight beside *Wuthering Heights* (with which it was published as the third of three volumes in 1847), but *The Tenant of Wildfell Hall* (1848) exhibits very individual merits. It has a complex narrative structure and an impressive range of characters, the most memorable of whom, the dissolute Huntingdon, seems to have been modelled on that of Branwell Brontë (she claimed in the second edition that the painful 'brutality' had been carefully 'copied from the life'). The novel reveals something of the impact of *Wuthering Heights* on one of its first readers but it also has a delicacy and power of its own.

In her 'Biographical Notice' appended to the new edition of *Wuthering*

THE BRONTË PARSONAGE AND HAWORTH CHURCHYARD. The village, wrote Elizabeth Gaskell, 'is situated on the side of a pretty steep hill, with a background of dun and purple moors, rising and sweeping away yet higher than the church which is built at the very summit of the long narrow street'.

Heights and *Agnes Grey* in 1850, Charlotte Brontë remarked on a tendency to 'morbidity' in Anne's work which she related to a 'tinge of religious melancholy' which had cast a 'sad shade' over her short life. Charlotte's comments on Emily (1818-48) point, not to melancholia, but to a deep and religious attachment to the high moorland scenery which surrounds Haworth. Of *Wuthering Heights* she noted, 'It is rustic all through. It is moorish, and wild and knotty as a root of heath.' Such a comment does not indicate much affection for the novel, but the word 'knotty' suggests that she had recognized the relationship of its complex structure to its theme. The violence explicit in the story derives directly from a powerful feeling for wild nature filtered through a controlling imagination. *Wuthering Heights* bears a family resemblance to the work of Charlotte and Anne, but it is not really *like* it, nor is it really like any other novel of its time in its disturbing evocation of passion and instinctive freedom. The word 'strange' echoes through many of its original reviews, and many early readers found it disjointed, baffling, and odd. Even as unconventional and enthusiastic a reader as D. G. Rossetti found it 'a fiend of a book', with its action laid in hell '—only it seems places and people have English names there'. By the mid-twentieth century, however, it was acclaimed as the supreme Brontë novel, albeit alternatively bowdlerized for the cinema and extravagantly praised by critics who had little taste for more conventional Victorian fiction. Its multiple narrative structure, which expresses the passing of time through a variety of viewpoints, still renders it an especially challenging book. What often seems repressed in Charlotte's novels, breaks out, often destructively, in *Wuthering Heights* as a sense of passionate delight in freedom and alternative awareness of the transience of life and of seasonal and generational change.

The Poets

'Liberty', Charlotte wrote, 'was the breath of Emily's nostrils; without it she perished.' As her poems make startlingly clear, that liberty was most often associated with the 'bleak solitude' she enjoyed on the moors. Emily's verse stands out from the *Poems* published by 'Currer, Ellis and Acton Bell' in 1846. Charlotte's poetry occasionally exhibits themes we more readily associate with her novels (aspects of feminist assertion in 'Pilate's Wife's Dream', for example, or the loneliness of a governess in 'The Teacher's Monologue') but her verse is bland compared to the rapt precision of Emily's. Her passionate response to the liberty she found in empty, wild landscape is evident in many of her lyrics (such as 'The Bluebell', 'The Night-Wind' or 'Shall earth no more inspire thee') and her dialogue poems like 'The winter wind is loud and wild', reflect the narrative invention of her novel. Some poems also look forward yearningly for a death which brings with it a release into a wider natural scheme, as does 'No coward soul is mine' and 'Riches I hold in light esteem' with its link of a desire for a finer liberty to the prayer for 'a chainless soul, with courage to endure'. Life, in its ardour, opens to a death which frees the soul into ecstasy.

Emily Brontë's intense, romantic landscape poems contrast vividly with the use made of place by the greatest Victorian lyric poet Alfred Tennyson (1809-92). The joy in wildness and loneliness is replaced by a fusion of character, spirit, and landscape which expresses a sense of hypnosis, entrapment, and annulment. Tennyson's early work is introspective; his characters dream of death not as release but as expressions of the very dreaminess of life. What delivers Tennyson's early poetry from the charge of reiterated morbidity is its quite extraordinary melodic and verbal skill, a fluency which is both poignant and exquisite. His metrical gifts were recognized immediately by the critic of the *Athenaeum* who reviewed his long undergraduate prize poem 'Timbuctoo' in 1829. The age which had seemed to suggest that poetry itself was passing away with 'the great generation' of poets (Byron, Shelley, Keats) who had recently died, had now, 'in a most decided Manner' contradicted the assumption. The young Tennyson, he concluded, was possessed of a 'really first rate genius'. The poet was not to remain as fortunate in his critics and two especially bad reviews of his 1833 *Poems* (which included 'The Lady of Shalott', 'Oenone', and 'The Lotos Eaters') deeply wounded the hyper-sensitive Tennyson. Both J. W. Croker in the *Quarterly* and Bulwer-Lytton in the *New Monthly Magazine* remarked on what seemed to them a damning relationship with the poetry of Keats. Croker, who had been so scathing of *Endymion* in 1818 had even declared that he was determined 'to make another Keats' of Tennyson by killing his growing reputation. Bulwer too blustered at what he saw as 'affectation' and Keatsian 'effeminacies'. These links back to the poetry of an earlier generation are doubly interesting. They suggest the degree to which the dominant 'Victorian' poet grew out of the still far from established modes of the early century, and they serve as a reminder that Keats's own reputation was only to become secure in the late 1840s, at the very time of the acceptance of Tennyson as the major poetic voice of a new generation. What is remarkable about his volumes of 1830 and 1833 is not simply the luxuriant musicality of the verse, but also the indications in the later volume of a rejection of introspection and an alternative movement to responsibility and social action.

The year 1833 was to prove emotionally traumatic for Tennyson; one of the major effects of the trauma was to reinforce the new social direction of his poetry. In October he received the news of the sudden death of his undergraduate friend, Arthur Hallam. It was a bereavement which also deprived him of a steady and observant supporter of his art. Hallam seems also to have been an important influence on his response to contemporary social and intellectual issues. Tennyson's first poetic reaction was an expression of his grief in a series of short elegiac lyrics which acted, as he later put it, as 'dull narcotics, numbing pain'. Some of these lyrics were later to be shaped into the early sections of *In Memoriam AHH* (1850). This was also the period of very different tributes to Hallam, the two great progressive monologues 'Ulysses' and 'Tithonus' and a preliminary investigation of an Arthurian theme, the superbly bleak 'Morte d'Arthur'. These three long poems were published in 1842 in a two-volume collection which also reprinted the best of the earlier lyrics. *In Memoriam* had a far longer genesis. The metrical expressions of acute grief, the 'mechanic exercises', only gradually seem to have found their place in a long memorial poem, tracing a slow change from a drained emptiness and doubt to an acceptance of transience. Such suggestions of extended development derive both from the events which lie behind the poem (Hallam died in Vienna in September 1833, but was not buried in England until January 1834) and from a decision to move from an essentially private elegy to a public one, from private desolation to a public assertion. The passage of time described in the poem allows for the poet's own extended period of mourning and for an acceptance of change and decay in nature. Tennyson was not merely making reference to seasonal succession or to annual rites and calendar events (like the Christmasses, New Years, or to the wedding with which the poem ends) but also incorporating

THE PENSIVE LAUREATE. Julia Margaret Cameron's romantic portrait of Alfred Tennyson (1865). The poet irreverently christened this photograph 'The Dirty Monk'.

into the poem many of the parallel scientific and social ideas espoused by Hallam himself. Thus the theory of progressive development, in the genetic as much as in the spiritual sense, becomes central to the structure and argument. Tennyson takes the passage of time to stand both for a personal growth in understanding and for a wider acceptance of evolutionary change in nature. The theme of doubt and unbelief, which he had handled somewhat clumsily in the early 'Supposed Confessions of a Second-Rate Sensitive Mind', now found a subtle expression; doubt is as much psychological and scientific as it is religious. *In Memoriam* moves, nevertheless, towards an apocalyptic vision of the transfigured Hallam waiting, smiling, beyond the ravages of human history and measured time as an emblem of humanity rendered divine by the fact of its advance in enlightenment. Hallam, 'known and unknown', looks on benignly, testifying in his smile to the wisdom that time renders all things well. Below him, though, doubting mortal eyes still wonder at a 'brute earth' which is potentially 'compass'd by the fires of Hell', an intrinsic Hell of its own making.

Despite its deep ambiguities *In Memoriam* struck Charles Kingsley as the 'culmination of all Tennyson's efforts and the key to many difficulties in his former writings'. With Wordsworth's death in 1850, Tennyson now seemed 'our only living great poet' and a natural enough choice as his successor as Poet Laureate. The purposeful anti-introspective theme which Kingsley most admired in *In Memoriam* was also evident in the long poem which had immediately preceded it, *The Princess* of 1847. The poem bore the descriptive subtitle 'a medley', a description which partly suggests the poet's difficulty in coping with a substantial verse tale that has both a vaguely medieval setting and a distinctively modern theme. The poem's structure was also to be tampered with once it had appeared in print and the exquisitely memorable songs were only added to its third edition. Tennyson's intention of sympathetically describing a woman's university presided over by the emancipated Princess Ida (a direct reflection of a new concern with the higher education of women), is hampered, even bodged, by the fact that he cushioned his narrative with a modern prologue and undermined Ida's determination by insisting on her final surrender to the role of wife and mother. *The Princess* is an awkwardly flawed experiment relieved by superb evocations of landscape and eroticism. The equally innovative *Maud* of 1855 is a far greater success. Its varied verse rhythms, often startling imagery, and its disturbing account of an anguished mind render it a poem of exceptional power, beauty, and originality. The narrator, a lover torn between conflicting emotions, expresses rage both at himself and at the corruption of society around him. The poem veers between passages of positively Carlylean spleen to equally passionate imaginings of and addresses to the elusive beloved and eventually moves to a violent resolution in the narrator's energetic acceptance of the justice of the British cause in the Crimean War.

THE ARTHURIAN IDYLL. William Dyce's Raphaelesque fresco of Sir Galahad (1851), which decorates the new Houses of Parliament, indicates the importance the Arthurian legends held in Victorian literature and iconography.

Conflict and emotional division dominate Tennyson's underrated later work, from *Enoch Arden* of 1864 to the slow realization of the long Arthurian cycle, the *Idylls of the King* (1842, 1859-85). The 'Morte d'Arthur', written in 1833, which was to form the climax of the new cycle, had originally presented a buttress to the story of the king's end with a modern prologue which gave, as Edward Fitzgerald noted, 'a reason for telling an old-world tale'. From 1859 onwards, once Tennyson had embarked on his cycle, that reason seemed less pressing much as it did to another Arthurian poet of the age, R. S. Hawker (the author of the remarkable 'Quest of the Sangraal'). The *Idylls* generally eschew the verbal richness and metrical invention of Tennyson's early and middle years, but they exhibit a new sobriety of expression and a calm grandeur which is particularly effective in the representation of the nobility of the betrayed and isolated Arthur. The *Idylls* do not suggest a poet of ideas grappling with an intellectual crisis, but they are Tennyson's response to what he recognized as the dissolution of earlier patterns of morality, order, and faith.

The phenomenal sales of his late poems also indicate that his readers shared, or at least accepted, something of his pessimism.

Tennyson's late experiments in verse drama also exhibit a similar darkness of vision. His plays are not to modern theatrical taste, and despite Henry Irving's relish for the title role in *Becket* (1884), they did not make a significant mark on the Victorian stage. That a poet should be drawn to writing for the stage, and to costume drama in particular, is scarcely surprising given the aspirations of the writers of the first third of the century, but like them Tennyson was to prove ill at ease in the medium. He found it difficult to shake off the mantle of Shakespeare and to find an alternative dramatic shape appropriate to the nineteenth century and its poetic energy. Where the Victorian theatre was notably inventive, as in its penchant for comedy, or its pantomime, or the evolving music-hall, or even in the careful revival of formerly neglected Shakespeare plays, the door seemed to be shut to the modern tragic poet.

Like that of Tennyson, the genius of Robert Browning (1812–89) was dramatic but not distinctively theatrical. Throughout his early career, however, he wrote for the stage, and his *Strafford* (1837) at least achieved a modest commercial success. It is in his four major collections of verse, *Dramatic Lyrics* (1842), *Dramatic Romances and Lyrics* (1845), *Men and Women* (1855), and *Dramatis Personae* (1864) that his energies found expression beyond the confines of the theatre. Browning is generally at his most subtly fluent and concentrated writing in the form of the 'dramatic monologue', a form in which a given speaker addresses a listener, a listener both implied by the poem and who is, by extension, the reader. Unlike a soliloquy, we do not assume that the speaker is alone or that he tells the truth; Browning's characters do not necessarily articulate their minds or their natures, rather, they betray something. Character is suggested both by what is said, and by how it is said, by inference, a reference, a turn of phrase, a rhythm, an image, or a reiteration. In perfecting the form, from the relatively simple, ironic use of it in the 'Soliloquy of the Spanish Cloister' (1842) to the subtle suggestiveness of 'Andrea del Sarto' (1855) and the expression of transitory experience in 'Abt Vogler' (1864) Browning moved beyond the far vaguer representation of character in Tennyson's parallel poems, 'Ulysses' and 'Tithonus'. He was also using each poem to concentrate on particular aspects of human experience, an experience which, as Browning's mature poetry indicates, he seems to have found fascinatingly diffuse.

This diffuseness seems to have rendered Browning a 'difficult' poet to his contemporaries (though it was a quality which endeared him to some modernist writers). When George Eliot reviewed *Men and Women* in the *Westminster* in 1856, for example, she contrasted the poet's 'robust energy' with his 'subtle penetrating spirit'. Even so, her evident unease with some of the verse occasioned her own awkward choice of an image; the 'tough piquancy' she detected in Browning struck her as rather like that of a russet apple, strong in form but sharp to the palate. When John Ruskin complained of 'obscurity', Browning replied that he could not begin writing poetry until his imaginary reader 'had conceded licence' to him; all poetry, he believed, was 'a putting the infinite within the finite'. His characters are defined individuals, glimpsed attempting to justify themselves, or musing on problems, or off their guard, but through what they say about themselves they suggest a much larger range of conditions, references, or artefacts beyond them. Browning is not exactly an encyclopaedic poet, but he does seek to suggest a world larger than the confined verbal framework of a poem by a sometimes startling, sometimes brash, accumulation of detail. Thus it is scarcely surprising that so many of his narrators are artists (such as Andrea del Sarto, Fra Lippo Lippi, the 'Pictor Ignotus', or Abt Vogler), or connoisseurs (such as the duke in 'My Last Duchess', or the bishop ordering his tomb). His theologians too speculate about the spiritual from a firmly physical base, like Bishop Blougram with his 'worldly circumstance', or Rabbi ben Ezra, or the meditating Johannes Agricola or even the 'natural theologian', Caliban. Art for Browning epitomizes a difficult and multifarious world, and, as for Abt Vogler in his 'structures brave' it contains opposites which are at once manifold and transitory, diffuse and elusive.

Given the parallels Browning drew between himself and other kinds of artists in his dedication of *Men and Women* to his wife ('One Word More'), it was perhaps natural that so much of his inspiration came from Italy, a country which was also to draw so many other Victorian writers. He had first visited Italy in 1838; he returned in 1844 (the year of Dickens's residence in Genoa) and it became his home from the time of his marriage to Elizabeth Barrett in 1846 until her death in 1861. Florence in particular became a source of subjects, ancient and modern, and as a means of detachedly reflecting back on his native England from a distance. In contrast to some other contemporaries, most notably to Clough, Browning comparatively rarely refers to the *Risorgimento*. Indeed, the paired poems 'An Italian in England' and 'An Englishman in Italy', seem to indicate that he saw himself as equally detached from modern politics both at home and abroad (though keenly alert to the nature of Italian patriotism and English sympathy with it). Browning's Italy, as George Eliot's was later to be, was essentially that of the Renaissance. Through his representation of complexity and paradox in the past he does, however, focus attention on the problems of the forging of a modern Italian state out of historical division. Browning's Italy is as violent as it is colourful; it is as contradictory as are many of the poet's own prejudices about it, and it is always glimpsed through patterns of sound which remain robustly English.

It is through his grasp of point of view, shifting perspective, and his alert detachment that we can best understand Browning's most substantial work, *The Ring and the Book* (1868-9). In 1860 the poet found an 'old yellow book' on a Florentine stall containing various documents relating to the seventeenth-century trial of Count Guido Franceschini. This chance discovery both fascinated and stimulated Browning: 'bit by bit I dug / The ingot truth, that memorable day / Assayed and knew my piecemeal gain was gold.' The documents required him to search for evidence, to sift truth from falsehood and white lies from black ones. The complex poem which emerged from the process reflects this initial stimulus to 'dig' and 'assay' for it presents a series of subjective views of the events surrounding a murder. The observers and participants in the event offer a multifaceted picture and the voices in their monologue contribute to a diverse and demanding narrative development. *The Ring and the Book* is the climax of Browning's poetic career. It is also an indication of the extent to which he had moved from his early theatrical aspirations towards the form of the verse novel.

A similar impulse is evident in the major achievement of Elizabeth Barrett Browning (1806-61), her verse-novel *Aurora Leigh* (1857), which was extrava-gantly praised by Ruskin as 'the greatest *poem* in the English language'. Ruskin's enthusiasm may well have been based on a distaste for Robert Browning's verse, but although it is hard to defend his critical judgement it ought to be stressed that *Aurora Leigh* remains a landmark in women's verse. It treats in epic form, the dawning and growth of a woman writer's conscious-ness, and it deals impressively with the process of the education of both the mind and the emotions. As befits a poet who had shown an active interest in social and political problems in her early verse, Elizabeth Barrett Browning moves the argument of her poem from the comfortable, landed background of Aurora's childhood, through an involvement with the poor, to the wretched career of Marian Erle. It ends in Italy with Aurora having established her reputation as an artist. Of her 'poetic art-novel' she commented: 'If it is a failure, there will be the comfort of having done it as well as I could.' The 'failure' of the poem has all too often been taken for granted and it has consequently been unjustly neglected. Despite its tracts of dullness, *Aurora Leigh* remains an outspoken feminist statement of considerable literary and historical merit. Elizabeth Barrett Browning's love poetry, notably the forty-four *Sonnets from the Portuguese*, is emotionally highly charged and often shows a lack of refinement both in language and sentiment; *Casa Guidi Windows* (1851), however, suggests an alert awareness of the nature of contemporary Italian nationalism, albeit glimpsed from the detached viewpoint of an Englishwoman's casement.

A far more versatile and subtle woman lyric poet, Christina Rossetti (1830-94), emerged from a background equally steeped in Italian culture and politics. Her own poetry is, though, informed with an intense Anglican devotion and with reference to seasonal and climatic variation which is essentially English. Her religious poetry draws from the placid devotion of Herbert and Keble but it also reflects the often highly coloured ritualism of the Tractarians. In 'From House to Home' she rises to a visionary intensity, but much of her devotional verse is commonplace in comparison with the secular lyrics in which she developed and redeveloped themes over a considerable period. Her verse is usefully characterized by what her brother noted as 'a modest but not the less definite self-regard', a quality especially in evidence in her expressive, nervous but determined comments on the failure of relationships between men and women. Some of the early lyrics, like the Tennysonian 'Dream Land', fit well into the narcotic world of the young Pre-Raphaelites (they were published in the PRB's short-lived journal the *Germ*), but her real distinctiveness emerged in *Goblin Market and Other Poems* of 1862 and *The Prince's Progress and Other Poems* of 1866. The longer narrative poems, like the title poems in these volumes, show considerable originality in their use of alliteration, assonance, and half-rhyme, and in their odd combination of irregular metre and sing-song rhythms. 'Goblin Market' in particular has an uncanny power, largely derived from its accumulation of images and sounds. The elusive, slightly whimsical lyric 'Winter my Secret' uses similar devices to suggest an uneasy, teasing evasiveness. Christina Rossetti dealt frequently with death, both as the door to a flower-bedecked Paradise and a ghostly afterlife and as an intrusion between lovers. It is not always an undesired or brutal intrusion. The famous sonnet 'Remember', the song 'When I am dead my Dearest', and the

THE FRONTISPIECE AND TITLE-PAGE TO *GOBLIN MARKET*. Dante Gabriel Rossetti's startlingly original decorations to one of his sister's finest collections of verse.

question-and-answer 'Up-Hill' suggest a stoic acceptance tinged with a longing for resolution in dissolution. Their technical and verbal control eschews the decorativeness so often associated with Pre-Raphaelite verse but their simplicity of expression retains a telling ambiguity.

Christina's elder brother, Dante Gabriel Rossetti (1828–82), seems to have drawn far more from his family's Italian heritage. He was especially attracted to what was then deemed the strangeness of early Tuscan painting and poetry, dedicating a good deal of energy to translations from, and variations to, Dante. Most notably he seems to have found in Dante the figure of a woman, both fleshly and divine, both the beloved and the redemptrix, who figures constantly in his art. The faces of women which occur again and again in his richly erotic canvases relate closely to his best-known poem 'The Blessed Damozel', a poem centred on a leaning female figure surrounded by emblems. Rossetti's poetry can be decorative in the best sense; at its worst it can be glutted with images and hypnotic in its languor. 'The Blessed Damozel' had first appeared in the *Germ* in 1850, a journal which also contained his prose narrative 'Hand and Soul', the story of a thirteenth-century Pisan painter blessed with a vision of his own soul, materialized in the form of a golden-haired woman with a mouth 'supreme in gentleness'. In virtually all his work Rossetti attempts to intermingle a medieval courtly-love tradition of deference to a mistress with a passionate, erotic evocation of her presence. This is especially true of the sonnet sequence, *The House of Life*, a sequence which forms an interesting parallel to the verse novel *The Angel in the House* by a fellow contributor to the *Germ*, the uxorious Coventry Patmore. For both poets sexual love becomes sacramentalized and sanctified, and the wife/mistress is pressured into the transcendental role of an angel, as idealized as she is adored. The most interesting exception amongst Rossetti's poems is the remarkable 'Jenny' a plainly told musing on a passionate response to a woman of the streets, beautiful as a bedfellow, yet held back from transcendence by her very earthiness.

The younger poet, Algernon Charles Swinburne (1837–1909), was for a time a central member of the bizarre menagerie of writers, painters, and artists' models which surrounded Rossetti at Chelsea. Despite Rossetti's promotion of his protégé, both the thrilled, pulsating rhythms of Swinburne's early verse, and his highly individual choice of subjects, render his poetry distinct from 'Pre-Raphaelitism'. Swinburne was an early admirer of Blake and Baudelaire (though his own poetry lacks the pithy lucidity of both); he was receptive to the ideas of the marquis de Sade, and he had adopted a vigorous republicanism and a no less strident distaste for Christianity. His female figures are sensual and desired, but they are also lamias, exquisite tormentors, and penal hierophants. Perhaps only Swinburne could have written a love lyric in the form of an address to England's tiny native carnivorous plant, the sundew. In his pro-Italian verse, in particular the *Songs before Sunrise* (1871), he writes, however, with a political passion worthy of Shelley, albeit a coagulated Shelley. His achievement has always proved difficult to assess. He was, naturally enough given his subjects, abused by his first critics and acclaimed by those of the last years of the nineteenth century. His luxuriant vocabulary has all too often deflected readers from a proper appreciation of his dramatic effects, his metrical inventiveness, and the keen ear for sound evident in his variation on Greek tragic form *Atalanta in Calydon* (1865) and in his first major collection *Poems and Ballads* (1866).

Plainness of expression was one quality William Morris (1834–96), a friend of Gabriel Rossetti, strove for throughout his life; it generally eluded him. As a poet his besetting sin is dullness, despite a strong feeling for narrative and a vigorous pursuit of a Chaucerian method. From Chaucer he took the loose

IRON AND COAL. William Bell Scott's picture of industrial life on Tyneside. It also includes a working drawing of a steam locomotive and a newspaper of 1861 which advertises a panorama of Garibaldi's Italian campaign.

structure of his longest work, *The Earthly Paradise* (1868-70), in which he intermingles stories from northern and southern European traditions, often effectively using legend to suggest mysterious areas of the unconscious, but more often dreamily rewriting stories in a sub-Tennysonian manner. 'If a chap can't compose an epic poem while he's weaving tapestry', he later frankly remarked, 'he had better shut up.' To Morris, all of his creative work, be it poetry or prose, designing or weaving, printing or illumination, expressed a unity of art and craft. When he moved to translations of the Norse sagas (he was amongst the first modern tourists to Iceland) he revealed himself steeped in romance; in shrinking from 'rhetoric', as he called it, he left himself not the plain, unadorned frankness of the originals but awkward, folksy, and oddly archaic English. Morris's youthful dream of a medieval Utopia, shaped by a Gothic which was as much Victoria's as Edward III's, was, however, transformed both by his experience as an artist and by a new political edge. From the 1870s the body of social and artistic theory he had imbibed from Ruskin was reinvigorated by strong draughts of Marxian socialism, pushing Morris into the forefront of revolutionary politics. 'Demos' who so terrified those who had benefited from the reforms of the 1830s, fired Morris with enthusiasm. His notion of a co-operative community in which the barons have been driven out by the craftsman and the maker reached its apogee in his two most successful prose narratives, *A Dream of John Ball* (1888) and *News from Nowhere* (1891). Unlike his earnestly jolly 'Chants for Socialists', these two visions of a commonweal in which past and present have been purged of their shortcomings, powerfully evoke a future society free of smoke and machines where ordinary men and women find self-expression in individual creativity.

Moral and Social Critics

John Ruskin (1819-1900), from whom Morris had learned to articulate his view of the relationship of art and work, did not share his political optimism. Ruskin's mind was both too tortuous, and by the 1880s too tortured, to see the answer to the problems of society in the inevitability of the triumph of socialism or in any other social and political panacea. In a sense, everything that Ruskin wrote is an attempt to understand human beings in a complex natural and industrial environment. If his work strikes modern readers as dislocated, digressive, or dissolved in a plethora of detail, it is in part a consequence of his awareness of his inadequacy for the task he had set himself. He was both a victim of the explosion of knowledge in his century and one of the few who made the attempt to grasp the meaning of its totality. His emphasis on careful and meticulous observation as an analytical tool was finally to push him from an awed sense of wonder into an equally awful despair. When, in the early volumes of *Modern Painters* (1843-60), he moves backward and forward in the history of landscape painting, he also recognized

the necessity of explaining the formations of clouds, the geological structure of marble and the massing of mountains; as an observer of plant form he was later to turn to an analysis of the 'organic' forms of architecture (in his influential *The Seven Lamps of Architecture*, 1849); having formed a theory of good and bad building he moved, in *The Stones of Venice* (1851–3), to a commentary on how and why a particular historical society produced a style and how both the style and the society declined. Like Carlyle, he saw modern instances in historical decline and fall and in the series of essays biblically entitled *Unto this Last* (1860–2) asked social questions with a devastating directness. Despite this provocative forthrightness (which proved too strong for many middle-class stomachs), Ruskin's influence was pervasive, stretching from an opening of Victorian eyes to formerly unperceived beauty, to an awakening of both an environmental and moral conscience. When he attempted to explain himself autobiographically in *Praeterita* in the 1880s much had to remain unsaid, perhaps because it caused too much pain to Ruskin's now unsettled mind. *Praeterita* is, however, one of the great confessional narratives in English, a moving and delicate account of the process of the recall of things past. Ruskin's shapely, rhythmical style here has a fine lucidity as his climaxes melt into a calm concentration on the object in hand.

Ruskin's horrified aversion to middle-class, middle-brow philistinism to some extent parallels Matthew Arnold's increasingly urgent commentary on the shortcomings of nineteenth-century English culture. Arnold (1822–88) shared with Ruskin a deep moral conviction of the necessity of the struggle for truth amidst the ravages of 'the fierce intellectual life of our century' but he did so not as an Olympian outsider but as a well-travelled Inspector of Schools and as the son of an eminent Victorian headmaster. In his later criticism, most notably in the essays which became *Culture and Anarchy* (1869), he argued wittily for an idea of culture which both contained within it the sum of past achievement and at the same time fostered progressive improvement. Education for Arnold meant the moulding of the individual and a wider hold on the advanced ideas of his time, a resistance to smug insularity, and an openness to change. In responding to what he saw as the threat of popular anarchy, he promoted the concept of a culture which embraced both poetry and religion and which could act as a catalyst to the uneasy advances of modern democracy. *Culture and Anarchy* has as its motto a quotation from the Sermon on the Mount commanding the ideal of perfection; the essays interpret the ideal not simply as an attribute of God, but as an expression of Hellenistic values shot through with an Hebraic earnestness. The habit of perfection entailed the directing of a divided society towards a 'true and satisfying ideal', a culture of intellectual sweetness and moral light. Arnold's 'culture' was not the preserve of an élite, but the common inheritance of human experience and discovery; he sought neither a new Jerusalem nor a second Athens, but a secularized kingdom of heaven within every human breast shaping a future which might have to do without religion.

His proclamation of this gospel grew from a clear awareness of the divisions of his age, divisions not only in social class and in class attitudes, but also in the ferment of ideas and in the decline of conventional religious belief. In an earlier periodical essay, revised under the title 'The Function of Criticism at the Present Time' (1864) he indicated why his own age had seemed unpropitious for the creation of 'master-works' of literature and why he himself moved from poetry to criticism. 'The power of the man' and 'the power of the moment' he believed had to coincide, but *Zeitgeist* had militated against a fully achieved literature; even in the first third of the century 'the creative power of poetry wanted, for success in the highest sense, materials and a basis'. His criticism of Wordsworth, Shelley, and Keats is often as perceptive as it is demanding, but his comments on his immediate contemporaries suggest a dissatisfaction which can nowadays be seen as wilful blindness (his dismissive comments on Dickens, for example, suggest that he saw him as little more than a philistine writing for philistines). 'The confusion of the present times is great,' he wrote in the preface to his *Poems* of 1853, and a young writer needed both 'a hand to guide him through the confusion' and a voice 'to prescribe to him the aim he should keep in view'. Having found no obvious guide himself, Arnold the critic took on a distinctly prescriptive role. The demanding standards of his criticism derive from his own wide reading of European literature, ancient and modern, but many of his attempts at definition continue his complaints about the unproductive confusion amongst his contemporaries. What he found wanting in modern English letters was an intellectual and philosophical grasp comparable to what he admired in recent German poetry and French criticism. In literature as much as in education he insisted that the English were smugly content with the second-rate.

Arnold's own uncertainty about the role of the poet in modern society is suggested by the publishing history of his most substantial poem, *Empedocles on Etna*. It was published in the 1852 volume, but then suppressed until 1867 when it reappeared in a volume bearing an epigraph which suggested that his Muse had departed. This metrically varied dramatic poem describes the musings and ultimate suicide of an ancient philosopher, but it was imbued, Arnold stressed, with 'modern feeling'. Empedocles 'becomes the victim of depression and overtension of mind, to the utter deadness to joy, grandeur, spirit and animated life'. An empty age, either in the past or the present, leads inexorably to alienation and self-destruction. In suppressing the poem, albeit temporarily, Arnold seems to have considered that its morbidity undermined the more positive feeling for life in some of his other poems. When he approvingly quotes Schiller's aspiration to an art 'dedicated to joy . . . which creates the highest enjoyment' in his 1853 preface, he also seems to be seeking for an affirmative poetry. Certainly his finest narrative verse ('Balder Dead' or 'Sohrab and Rustum', for example) celebrates life even while evoking a tragic mood. The restless, disillusioned spirit of a latter-day Empedocles continued to haunt him, both in the remarkably tender but elusive 'Marguerite' poems and in the stoic later verse such as 'Rugby Chapel' or the much anthologized 'Dover Beach'. Despite final confident gestures, there remains a sense of a world that has to survive without 'joy, love, light, certitude and help for pain', a world which lacks the refuge once provided by the faith of a 'strong soul' like his father Thomas Arnold.

Dr Arnold's Rugby had also marked the development and disillusion of Matthew's friend Arthur Hugh Clough (1819-61). Matthew Arnold mourned Clough's untimely death in 'Thyrsis', an elegiac extension of his meditation on the decay of youth and hope in 'The Scholar Gypsy', but his celebration has often served to distort perspectives on Clough's work as a poet. His verse

RUGBY CHAPEL. Arthur Hughes's illustration to *Tom Brown's Schooldays* shows the novel's hero returning in pilgrimage to the tomb of his mentor, Thomas Arnold. Tom Brown was merely one of a remarkable generation of Rugbeians educated by Arnold.

does not suggest a 'too quick despairer', nor does it necessarily sound 'the stormy note of men contention-tossed'. Clough clearly did address himself to the intellectual issues of his time, and his education had given him an urgent honesty, but honest admission of doubt did not lead to a poetry of the 'modern feeling' of despair. Certainly, as the Epilogue to his various Faustian poem *Dipsychus* suggests, Dr Arnold was the product of an age which had over-excited the religious sense and the result had been an 'irrational, almost animal irritability of conscience'; Clough's own conscience, and his urge to truthfulness and duty, obliged him to admit to an agnosticism which could not provide an excitable moral alternative to religion. His poetry echoes his religious doubt and an acceptance of the residual positives of action and conviction, but it rejects moral certainties. Clough accepted, as Matthew Arnold appears not to have been able to do, a potential anarchy of systems which no revitalized idea

'DEATH IS A FEARFUL THING', Holman Hunt's painting (1850–3) of *Measure for Measure*, III. i. Isabella has just told Claudio that Angelo is willing to free him in exchange for her virginity. Claudio's resolution begins to weaken. 'The Shakespearian scenes which fascinate Hunt are those in which are displayed a strong sense of sin and sexual guilt' (Timothy Hilton).

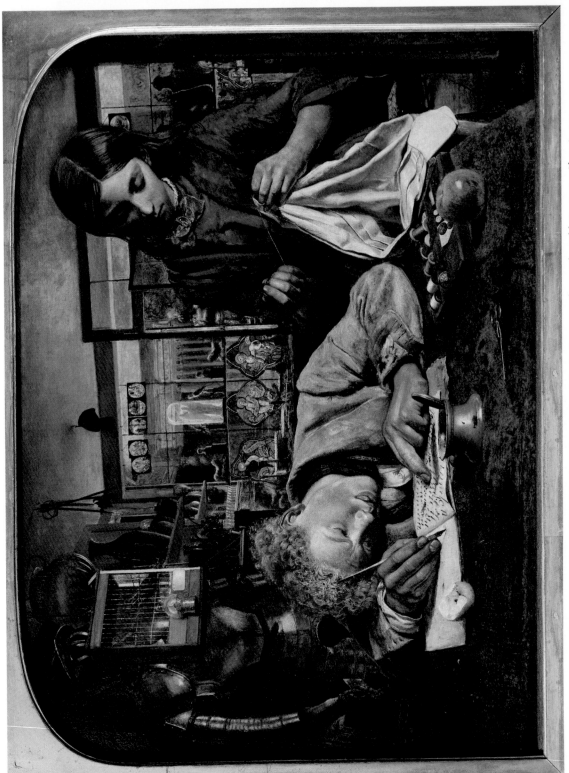

KIT'S WRITING LESSON. R. B. Martineau's painting (1852) of a scene from *The Old Curiosity Shop* is one of many contemporary representations of characters from Dickens's novels. The picture also usefully suggests something of the spread of literacy in the period.

of 'culture' could stem. He had also accepted the permanency of doubt as a way of thinking, and not, as it had become for Tennyson, a way of believing. Many of Clough's most impressive lyrics, like 'Easter Day: Naples 1849', or 'Bethesda: A Sequel', resemble 'hymns, but not hymns' (to cite the title of another poem), religious songs about having no religion. Nevertheless, as his best-known lyric puts it, the struggle *did* avail, and one particular struggle, that for Italian independence and unification, is impressively celebrated in poems like 'Peschiera' and 'Alterem Partem'.

The sense that it is 'better to have fought and lost than never to have fought at all' also runs through Clough's most impressive narrative poem 'Amours de Voyage' (1858). The poem translates the doubt, introspection, and self-love evoked in its epigraphs into a profound examination of character in action and inaction. The use of hexameter, often awkward in English, allows the poet to echo speech rhythm and to suggest the easy flow of conversational exchange. The epistolary form of the poem also gives glimpses of emotion and contemplation, and subtly suggests the shifting perspectives of a failed love-affair set against the background of the Roman Republic of 1848-9. 'Amours de Voyage' opens with an expression of disappointment, moves to an account of the stirring of amatory and political action, and ends with an evocation of a profounder disappointment. Its melancholy renders it distinct from Clough's earlier experiment with narrative, *The Bothie of Tober na Vuolich* (1848), the story of the romance of an Oxford radical and the daughter of a Highland farmer during a long-vacation reading party.

Clough's candid agnosticism, and his unconventional treatment of social relationships, has often been interpreted as strikingly un-Victorian. The extent to which it *was* characteristic of its period, at least amongst certain avant-garde writers, is stressed in the title of George Meredith's (1828-1909) sequence of poems, *Modern Love*, published in the year following Clough's death, 1862. The fifty sixteen-line 'sonnets' describe the tensions and frustrations of a disintegrating marriage. Many of the poems also capture the distinction between private awareness of mutual alienation and deception and the pressures additionally imposed by public exposure. *Modern Love* is not a consistent success, for Meredith can prove awkward in striving for an image or a rhyme-word, but the best poems in the sequence form an interesting counter-balance to the considerable body of Victorian verse which celebrates love, or more conspicuously, elevates the beloved. Its subject, though undoubtedly 'modern', was still *risqué*, just as Meredith's first novel, *The Ordeal of Richard Feverel*, gave sufficient moral offence to be banned from Mudie's Circulating Library. Its subject, like that of a French novel referred to in *Modern Love*, may have seemed 'unnatural' to the conventional guardian of morality, but it reflected a truth in life, 'and life, they say, is worthy of the Muse'. It was largely on his fiction that Meredith's later considerable reputation was based. His novels reveal a complex range of interests, from an excellent characterization of exceptional women (particularly in *Diana of the Crossways*, 1885) to able analytical comments on the workings of contemporary politics, both at home (in *Beauchamp's Career*, 1875, 1876) and abroad (tangentially in *Sandra Belloni*, 1864 and more directly in its sequel *Vittoria*, 1866). Meredith had a real penchant for substantial dialogue scenes, a talent finely displayed in *The Egoist* (1879), a novel regulated by the 'Comic Spirit' which delves into and exposes character through verbal exchange, both idle and pointed.

Trollope and George Eliot

Meredith's clever iconoclasm came to be admired by those late Victorians and Edwardians who chafed against mid-Victorian moral corsets. Although the ironic intelligence which informs his best work is distinctive, his restless anti-earnestness can be seen to reflect a new questioning of values in the literature of the 1860s and 1870s. The year of *Richard Feverel*, 1859, proved remarkable for its crop of influential books, not merely from established writers like Dickens, Thackeray, and Tennyson but also from a new star, George Eliot, the author of what was proclaimed the novel of the year by the *Saturday Review*, *Adam Bede*. Charles Darwin's *On the Origin of Species by Natural Selection* was, however, to prove the most dense and disorienting of the new books of 1859; it was to intensify the so-called Victorian crisis of faith, and for those readers who readily responded to Darwin's radical conclusions, and then assimilated them, it began a process of reassessment which embraced matters of morality, class, and politics as much as biology and religion. Not only had God been toppled from his heaven by an argument from nature, but Man had been thrown from his pinnacle as the climax of creation. Darwin's impact on his adherents, both direct and indirect, was essentially one of dislocation; it then became, to use his own terminology, one of adaptation.

The importance of Darwinism to Victorian literature can be overstated (working writers such as Dickens or Trollope seem to have been largely untouched by its influence) but arguments from *The Origin of Species* seem genuinely to have accentuated an existing intellectual, social, and political restlessness. The social and political consensus of the 1850s, like its confidence, was gradually breaking down to be succeeded by a mood of increased questioning of established values and institutions. The second Reform Bill of 1867 was an acknowledgement not simply of the necessity of extending the franchise but also of the advent of a non-deferential, politically responsive proletariat. The implications, and later the supposed threat, of socialism were to haunt the late Victorian imagination. In the 1860s Arnold's *Culture and Anarchy* represents one uncertain espousal of a basis for progressive, educative change; George Eliot's *Felix Holt* represents another; Trollope's *Phineas Finn* and Disraeli's *Lothair*, somewhat less cautiously, suggest others. The period was only marginally another 'age of reform', rather it was a time of re-forming

AN ARABIAN FANTASY IN LEICESTER SQUARE. The 'Panopticon' opened in 1854 'to exhibit and illustrate, in a popular form, discoveries in science and art' became in 1858 the Alhambra Music Hall, the most splendid of its kind in England.

and reshaping ideas about morality, sexuality, society, and the future of society. It saw the emergence of the so-called 'new woman' as much as of a new democracy.

The tensions evident in John Stuart Mill's thought in the 1850s and 1860s are in many ways central to the developing political debate, much as his own intellectual development reflects many of the leading ideas of the century. Mill (1806–73) was born the eldest son of a prominent disciple of Bentham's, a philosophical radical founder of the *Westminster Review*. His immediate background and the strict, intense education imposed upon him as a boy, provided him both with a firm foundation on which to build his own systems and with a rigidity of thought against which he sought to react. As he also noted in his *Autobiography* (1873), he was one of the 'very few examples in this country who has not thrown off religious belief, but never had it'. This inherited atheism led to an inability to grasp the nature of anything numinous,

THE MAN ON THE FLYING TRAPEZE. Richard Doyle's observant and witty illustration from the *Cornhill Magazine* shows a performance by the famous Leotard at the Alhambra in 1861. Casual visitors to the spectacle stand on the stage; indifferent patrons eat and drink at tables; the less affluent in the galleries seem fascinated.

and a tendency to see religion merely as a set of moral propositions; it also seems to have left him open to a peculiar 'religious crisis'. His equivalent of an experience of sudden grace came not through the Bible, but through poetry, and in particular through Wordsworth who became 'medicine' to him during a severe bout of nervous depression at the age of twenty. Wordsworth seemed to provide a necessary counterbalance to the barren rationalism of the Utilitarians, allowing the boy to acknowledge a 'culture of the feelings', or more especially, the vitality of an 'internal culture of the individual'. For Mill the struggle for mental and emotional autonomy, so effectively described in the *Autobiography* (1873), determined the nature of his later arguments about the freedom of the individual. As both *On Liberty* (1859) and *The Subjection of Women* (1869) demonstrate, he remained convinced of the paramount social importance of individual liberties, rights, and obligations and of the role of individuality in an egalitarian society. His espousal of the cause of female suffrage ('men as well as women do not need political rights in order that they may govern, but in order that they may not be misgoverned') was the proper extension of his acceptance of progressive constitutional change and of the need to secure an informed and responsible electorate. Although he was also to recognize the challenge to the idea of individuality (or of an individualist élite) presented by a future mass democracy, he rested his argument in *On Liberty* on the premiss that 'a State which dwarfs its men, in order that they may be more docile instruments in its hands even for beneficial purposes—will find that with small men no great thing can be really accomplished.' Mill's political argument, uniting the rational with the emotional as equal expressions of human totality, was to provide subsequent British liberalism with a lucid theoretical basis.

No Victorian novelist better caught the nature of untheoretical political action than Anthony Trollope (1815–82). Trollope could scarcely be called an intellectual or philosophical novelist, nor, as his own unhappy attempts to enter Parliament suggest, was he a remarkably practical politician, but he was the prime contemporary commentator on how institutions of government work, or rather on how individuals make them work. His characterization of himself (using the new party terminology of his day) as an advanced Conservative-Liberal suggests why he has seemed to his admirers an ideally balanced analyst and to his critics a flabby compromiser. Although he excels as a writer about how pressures bear upon the holders of, or aspirants to, power, he is also deft at suggesting how larger social issues work on political processes and how, for example, a scandal, the influence of the press, or public opinion affect the evolution of a particular character or a series of events. In one of his earlier novels, *The Warden* (1855), he somewhat heavy-handedly defined his own expository method by satirizing those of Carlyle ('Dr. Pessimist Anticant') and Dickens ('Mr. Popular Sentiment'). A determinedly reforming literature, he implied, resorted to prejudice and preconception; his own required sympathy, balance, and tolerance. Trollope seems to have distrusted Dickens's heightened colouring as untruthful; his own portraits of individuals were, he later claimed, 'created personages impregnated with habits of character which are known'. Like his adored Thackeray, he aspired to a fiction without heroes and without obvious saints and sinners.

Trollope's view of himself as a novelist can be glimpsed not only in his excellent critical study of Thackeray (1879) but also in his comments on the history of the English novel in his *Autobiography* and his lecture on 'English Prose Fiction as a Rational Amusement'. His account of his own method of composition (he wrote, almost mechanically, on trains, in his club, even in the midst of Mediterranean sea-squalls and bouts of sickness) has rendered him vulnerable to the criticism of those who held far higher views of the art of the novel than he did himself, but he none the less delighted in the act of creating. A novel he said, 'should give a picture of common life enlivened by humour and sweetened by pathos'. It is a flat enough formula, but it is one that is only slightly amplified elsewhere when he argued that love-stories are the mainstays

THE COUNTRY MEETS THE TOWN.
J. E. Millais's woodcut frontispiece to
Trollope's *Orley Farm* (1861) shows
the novelist's own boyhood home on
Harrow Hill.

of prose fiction and that any other 'attractions' hang round and depend on that love-story 'as the planets depend upon the sun'. It is, of course, a disarming and self-deprecating comment on his approach to his plots and his characters. His definition might work well enough when applied to shapely, slow-moving, placid narratives such as *Doctor Thorne* (1858) or *The Small House at Allington* (1864), but it is inadequate as a way of approaching his more complex and acerbic social studies such as *Phineas Finn* (1869), *Phineas Redux* (1874), or *The Last Chronicle of Barset* (1867) or, above all, his masterpiece of comic disillusion, *The Way We Live Now* (1875) (a *Vanity Fair* for the 1870s).

To interpret Trollope's work by his own canons is, as his variable critical reputation suggests, not especially helpful. When, for example, he characterizes the Englishness of *Framley Parsonage* (1861) by remarking 'there was a little fox-hunting, and a little tuft-hunting, some Christian virtue and some Christian cant. There was no heroism and no villainy,' he is obviously seeking to place himself in a Thackerayan tradition of irony. As his comment also suggests, he is adapting Thackeray's methods by softening them and turning them to individual ends, tied more to the country than the town, and to traditional institutions, like the Church or the Law, than to a broad spectrum of society. Trollope has often struck his admirers as reassuring in his analysis of snobbery, or politicking, or antagonism within the framework of enduring social conventions. As his best work suggests, he was equally alert to change and to social fragmentation. In the Barchester novels, from *The Warden* to *The Last Chronicle*, and in the 'Palliser' series, from *Can You Forgive Her?* (1864) to *The Duke's Children* (1880) he is not simply observing the process of ageing, or the ossifying of characters' attitudes, but also more radical social and ideological shifts, and changes in the old order, which are taking place both in Barsetshire and beyond its borders. The less Trollope is viewed as a reassuring fence-sitter and the more he is seen as sharing something of Thackeray's power to disconcert, the more justly will he be allowed his place amongst the great Victorians.

Despite the substance, the range, and the popularity of Trollope's fiction, the dominant English novelist of the 1860s and 1870s was George Eliot (1819–80). With Thackeray's death in 1863 and Dickens's in 1870, she emerged, as Leslie Stephen later observed in the *Cornhill*, as 'the greatest living writer of English fiction . . . probably . . . the greatest woman who ever won literary fame, and one of the very few writers of our day to whom the name "great" could be conceded with any plausibility'. Stephen was, to be sure, drawn by George Eliot's intellectual prowess, but his critical judgement of her work was also conditioned by the feeling that an era closed with her death. Her novels, he believed, marked 'the termination of the great period of English fiction which began with Scott'. To modern commentators it has often appeared less of a termination than a culmination of the dense social, moral, and historical direction given to the nineteenth-century novel by Scott. At the beginning of George Eliot's independent literary career she reveals herself as a spirited critic of fiction steeped in Scott's work. These early critical essays in the *Westminster* also suggest something of a further determining influence on her own fiction, modern German literature. Her debt to German thought is clear too in her translations of standard works of what was known as the 'Higher Criticism', reasoned challenges to Christian orthodoxy through the application of new historical methods to the Gospels. Before Marian Evans adopted the pseudonym 'George Eliot' in 1857 she was already an experienced, and exceptionally well-read writer. She had come to terms with the nature of her own religious de-conversion; she had made a modest living as an editor of the *Westminster* and she was established as the companion of a married man, one of the most

THE RACE FOR WEALTH. The first painting in W. P. Frith's series (1880) which comments on the precarious nature of financial speculation. Here the Spider, a corrupt speculator, woos prospective clients who include a widow, a clergyman, and a squire. This is very much the atmosphere of *The Way We Live Now*.

gifted intellectuals of the day, George Henry Lewes. After the success of the *Scenes of Clerical Life* in 1858 and the acclaim accorded to *Adam Bede* a year later, 'George Eliot' the intensely moral novelist, steadily eclipsed the immoral and Godless Miss Evans.

In a sense that eclipse sprang from the very nature of her fiction. The unconventional woman upheld convention in her work. George Eliot's lack of faith was not particularly evident to readers of her first clerical stories (one critic assumed that they were the work of a 'scientific clergyman'), and her liaison with a married man seems scarcely to have touched the treatment of sexuality and marriage in her fiction. G. H. Lewes the thinker, the immediate inspirer and first critic of her novels, may have been of cardinal importance to her development as a writer, but the nature of their relationship is never reflected in the norms of conduct accepted by her characters. The 'new woman' does not figure in George Eliot's novels unless she can be recognized in Romola

VICTIMS. The third scene in the 'Race for Wealth' series. The clergyman, who has been entrapped by the Spider, now learns from his morning newspaper that he and his family are ruined. Frith's picture shows a well-furnished professional home of the period.

Bardi, an educated, independent, un-Christian protector of a family which is not technically her own, but separated from the 1860s by three and a half centuries. When Maggie Tulliver, the heroine who springs most directly from the novelist's own roots, steps beyond narrow moral conventions, her freedom is not celebrated, it becomes tragically awkward. This is not to argue that George Eliot rejoiced in convention in her books because she allowed fiction to represent her own unease with unconventionality, but to suggest that in seeking to establish a new basis for moral action she was first determined not to offend her readers by touching raw nerves. She became a major naturalistic novelist because she was able to present so impressive and observant a picture of ordinary, and often conventional, men and women. She is a great moral novelist because she sought to explain and give substance to a personal morality which can function without a supernatural *fiat*.

Adam Bede is set in a deferential, stratified England of peasants, artisans, farmers, clergymen, and squires. It describes an 'organic' society, working co-operatively at a distance from industry, war, power, and politicians, and although its order is briefly disrupted, calm returns at the end when passion is spent. The world of the novel was, as the narrator is at pains to suggest, a lost one to most readers of 1859. George Eliot was not necessarily being nostalgic about a historical past, nor, in *The Mill on the Floss* (1860), was she sentimentally dwelling on a lost childhood, but in her first two novels she was both commenting on the workings of pre-industrial provincial England and relating the 'organism' she observed to a scientific model. In her later fiction both the model and the rural, pastoral idyll are broken. However much her readers, then and now, responded to her evocation of stability and social order, George Eliot seems to have recognized that the range and subjects of her fiction had to expand in order to express more of the complexity and variety of the nineteenth century. Deference and complacency no longer held, either in the social or the intellectual sense. In her underrated historical novel, *Romola* (1862–3), she turned from the English provinces and the recent past to a highly charged, violent, politically unstable, Renaissance city-state, but she was not escaping into a world of emblems and artefacts, she was attempting to see in the divisions of the past a parallel to modern fragmentation. Romola's spiritual progress from paganism to an independent moral faith was meant, in part, to stand for a larger, modern pattern of exploration. In both *Felix Holt* and *Middlemarch* she returned to England in the 1830s studying provincial life both in terms of its interwoven human relationships, and with supreme skill in *Middlemarch*, a series of developing individual destinies. *Middlemarch* (1871–2) has long been recognized as her most substantial and carefully controlled narrative. Its successor, *Daniel Deronda* (1876), is the most restless and ambitious of her prose works. Its theme, imagery, its intellectual reference, and its epic structure have struck some readers as strained but, as its modern setting indicates, it was also George Eliot's most direct expression of her growing unease with dislocating influences, both scientific and social, working upon her. The contemporary, cosmopolitan world of the novel is one in which a centre no longer seems to hold. The very structure of the novel, plunging *in medias res*, with a series of questions, in the midst of a game of chance, seems to suggest the extent to which the novelist was attempting to move her art towards an expression of 'the vast mysterious movement' which was the unknown future. 'Extension', she remarks in her novel, 'is a very imperfect measure of things.' For all its imperfections, *Daniel Deronda* attempts measurement by combining tradition and innovation, convention and exploration. It was for a new generation of writers to take its implications further.

8. Late Victorian to Modernist

1880-1930

BERNARD BERGONZI

Fin de siècle

WE may not be sure what the spirit of an age is, but we can usually tell when it is giving way to something else. What G. K. Chesterton called, in a book title, the 'Victorian Age in Literature' seemed to be at its zenith when Dickens died in 1870; but ten years later, at the death of George Eliot, the signs of change were unmistakable. The High Victorian was becoming Late Victorian. The phrase *fin de siècle* came into common use, pointing to a preoccupation with what the end of the century might portend. John Gross has summed up the shifting mood in *The Rise and Fall of the Man of Letters*:

Whatever one puts it down to—economic difficulties, foreign competition—it is undoubtedly possible to detect by the 1880's a widespread faltering of Victorian self-confidence, a new edginess and uncertainty about the future. Among writers, such a climate might have been supposed to favour a mood of determined realism, and so, in some cases, it did. But the commonest reaction was withdrawal, a retreat into nostalgia, exoticism, fine writing, *belles-lettres*.

There are interesting signs of changing attitudes in the correspondence of two Victorian clergymen of literary inclinations; one, the Jesuit Gerard Manley Hopkins (1844-89), was a poet of genius, though unrecognized in his lifetime; the other, Richard Watson Dixon, was a canon of the Church of England and a talented minor poet of Pre-Raphaelite affinities. Hopkins and Dixon lived obscure lives, remote from the main currents of Victorian culture; but they were widely read in the literature of their time and had decided opinions about it which they exchanged in letters. In January 1879 Dixon commented on the defects of Tennyson's widely admired 'Locksley Hall', finding in it 'only a man making an unpleasant and rather ungentlemanly row. Tennyson is a great outsider.' In his reply Hopkins tries to defend Tennyson—'Come what may he will be one of our greatest poets'—and praises the pure achievement of the early poems and *In Memoriam*. But he is scathingly dismissive of the *Idylls of the King*, which was the crown of Tennyson's public reputation: 'He should have called them *Charades from the Middle Ages* (dedicated by permission to

H.R.H. etc.).' Hopkins agrees with Dixon about 'Locksley Hall' and adds to the indictment: 'not only *Locksley Hall* but *Maud* is an ungentlemanly row and *Aylmer's Field* is an ungentlemanly row and the *Princess* is an ungentlemanly row.' A few years later in 1885 another of Hopkins's correspondents, the Catholic poet Coventry Patmore, wrote as if the decline of Tennyson's reputation was generally recognized: 'A great popularity always produces a reaction—such as is setting in now against Tennyson.' An idol may not have toppled, but he was being undermined. Elsewhere in the letters, one finds Hopkins making highly unappreciative comments on other High Victorians, such as Browning and George Eliot. Such observations are the signs of a shift in literary consciousness.

In 1873 Walter Pater (1839-94) published his *Studies in the History of the Renaissance*, a work which was to be influential for many years. Pater was a shy, reclusive Oxford scholar but he was quietly subversive of Victorian certainties and assumptions. His book, whose name was later shortened to *The Renaissance*, is perhaps most famous for the passage of poetic prose describing Leonardo's *Mona Lisa*, beginning 'She is older than the rocks on which she sits.' But the Epilogue was the most influential part of the book, and is almost as celebrated. Pater was a historical relativist, sceptical about all fixed positions, doctrines, or theories; human life was fleeting and uncertain and instead of pursuing inaccessible ultimate truths man should strive to refine and purify his sensations and passing impressions:

To burn always with this hard, gemlike flame, to maintain this ecstasy is success in life. In a sense it might even be said that our failure is to form habits: for, after all, habit is relative to a stereotyped world, and meantime it is only the roughness of the eye that makes any two persons, things, situations, seem alike. While all melts under our feet, we may well grasp at any exquisite passion, or any contribution to knowledge that seems by a lifted horizon to set the spirit free for a moment, or any stirring of the senses, strange dyes, strange colours, and curious odours, or work of the artist's hands, or the face of one's friend. Not to discriminate at every moment some passionate attitude in those about us, and in the very brilliancy of their gifts some tragic dividing of forces on their ways is, on this short day of frost and sun, to sleep before evening.

It is in art, Pater believes, that the finest sensations are to be found and where we have the best hope of preserving the intense but fleeting moments of experience. This doctrine made Pater a revered master for the aesthetic poets and writers of the closing years of the century. In *De Profundis* Oscar Wilde recalled how he read *The Renaissance* in his first term at Oxford, calling it 'that book which has had such a strange influence over my life', while the poet and critic Arthur Symons wrote that *The Renaissance* 'even with the rest of Pater to choose from, seems to me sometimes the most beautiful book of prose in our literature'. Pater developed the ideas of *The Renaissance* in *Marius the Epicurean* (1885), a historical novel about a Roman gentleman, a virtuous pagan who is fascinated by the beliefs and rituals of a gracious community of early Christians but resists conversion. *Marius* is a book which expounds the importance of a ritual approach to life, and what became known as the religion of art.

Pater's influence among the young poets of the *fin de siècle* expressed itself in the vogue of the brief lyric poem recording a fleeting moment of experience, and in a taste for ritual living divorced from religious commitment. The influence continues in the tougher-minded context of early twentieth-century modernism, where the Paterian 'moment' is transformed into the 'image' of Ezra Pound and the Imagist poets and the 'epiphany' of James Joyce.

Hopkins was in a position to have been directly influenced by Pater, who was his tutor for a time when he was an undergraduate. But Hopkins was a convinced Christian, who had converted from Anglicanism to Catholicism at

GERARD MANLEY HOPKINS at the age of eighteen. A photograph taken by Hopkins's uncle, George Giberne, a few months before he went up to Oxford. His life as a Jesuit priest and his posthumous fame as a poet lay ahead of him.

Oxford, and he rejected Pater's intellectual scepticism and moral relativism, though he liked and respected him as a man. It is not certain how much Hopkins took from Pater, but his strong lyrical feelings before God and Nature have affinities with Pater's conviction of the need to live at maximum intensity. Hopkins's idiosyncratic critical terminology of 'inscape' and 'instress' may well owe something to the Paterian 'moment'; these terms are sometimes obscure but the underlying idea is of a unique perception and penetration into the life of a phenomenon or object. Again, Pater's emphasis on the uniqueness and singularity of the fleeting aspects of experience seems to have been given a Christian dimension by Hopkins, in his use of the concept of *haecceitas* or 'thisness', taken from the fourteenth-century Franciscan philosopher Duns Scotus.

Nearly a hundred years after his death Hopkins is regarded as a major poet. But in his lifetime he was invisible as a writer; his poems were unpublished and circulated only in manuscript among a few friends; when he died at the age of forty-four he was known only as a learned but eccentric member of the Jesuit order and Professor of Greek at University College, Dublin. His friend Robert Bridges, himself a poet and eventually Poet Laureate, had only an imperfect understanding of Hopkins's genius, but he treasured both his memory and his manuscripts. When he judged the time to be finally ripe he published an edition of Hopkins's poems in 1918. It was several more years before they aroused any interest but by the early thirties Hopkins had been recognized as a poet of great and original gifts, and indeed as a modern poet writing long before his time. Later critics have reacted against this judgement by emphasizing the Victorian aspects of Hopkins's work. The truth is that he is too original to fit easily into any category; he is both Victorian and modern; or neither. Hopkins was moved and excited by the natural world, like many Romantic and Victorian poets before him, but he saw Nature not as a surrogate for God but as a shining manifestation of his glory and creative power; as in such well-known poems as 'Spring' and 'God's Grandeur'. The lyrical intensity of Hopkins's poetry is unmistakable, but it is controlled by a strong intellectual power. His principal ancestors are the religious Metaphysical poets of the seventeenth century, particularly George Herbert, whom Hopkins much admired. His later poems, especially the so-called 'terrible sonnets' written in Dublin, enact a condensed psychological drama, when the soul fears that it has been abandoned by God and grapples with despair; we may be reminded of Herbert's religious dialectics, though the struggle is more racking. These poems represent the pinnacle of Hopkins's poetry, though they are less immediately inviting than his earlier, more lyrical poems.

Hopkins's essentially paradoxical and original quality is evident in his language, which he subjects to great and deliberate strain, somewhat reminiscent of the stresses and distortions of Baroque sculpture and architecture. He has often been praised for his closeness to the speaking voice, for his ability to convey the rhythms and intonations of English. That quality is undoubtedly present; but against it one has to set an aspect of his work that is decidedly artificial or unnatural: the distortions that he imposes on ordinary English syntax, and his invention of compound epithets that would never occur in everyday speech. Hopkins was prepared to take many liberties with language in the interests of expressive vividness; in particular, like Milton before him, he wanted to use English with the flexible word order of an inflected language like Latin. It is perhaps significant that he professed an equal regard for the 'natural' Shakespeare and the 'artificial' Milton.

Though Hopkins was a poet of great sensuous power he was a highly speculative thinker and theorist, and the tension between the sensuous and the conceptual runs through his poetry. The theoretical and critical reflections scattered in his notebooks and letters are of the highest interest. In a note on poetry he outlines a position that has some affinities with the contemporary ideas of the French Symbolists, but which was not to be fully developed until well into the twentieth century:

Poetry is speech framed for contemplation of the mind by way of hearing or speech framed to be heard for its own sake and interest even over and above its interest of meaning. Some matter and meaning is essential to it but only as an element necessary to support and employ the shape which is contemplated for its own sake.

This was later to become a basic tenet of modernist poetics as developed by Pound and Eliot, and given its most extreme form in the Russian Formalists' insistence that the content of a literary work was never more than an excuse for the poetic 'devices'.

William Butler Yeats (1865-1939) met Hopkins in Dublin in 1886; Yeats was a young student, Hopkins was a professor of Greek, and neither of them took much interest in the other, though Hopkins had read one of Yeats's poems with mild appreciation. Yeats came from the Protestant minority in Ireland, a small but influential social group who have produced many writers over the centuries, including Yeats's contemporaries, Oscar Wilde and Bernard Shaw. Yeats described himself as a man who was naturally religious but whose Christian belief had been overturned by the scientific rationalism of the nineteenth century. In response he invented his own mythology, drawn from Irish legend and folklore, and in his early years as a poet he withdrew into an ideal world of myth and imagination. To his Irish sources he added an interest in Indian legends, and in magic and theosophy. At this stage in his career Yeats was thoroughly representative of the aesthetic attitude to life as expounded by Pater. The title of one of his early prose books, *The Celtic Twilight* (1893), indicated a subject and a state of mind that appealed to other young writers, for Irish themes were becoming fashionable. What distinguished Yeats from his lesser contemporaries was whatever mysterious quality we mean by 'genius'.

W. B. YEATS (1908). Sargent's drawing of the younger Yeats emphasizes almost to the point of caricature his deliberate self-presentation as a late-Romantic poet.

His early work is the minor poetry of a man who was later to emerge as a major poet.

After the turn of the century Yeats broke out of the *fin de siècle* mood. He was increasingly involved with the movement for Irish national culture, though he always refused to be a propagandist. He founded the Irish National Theatre Company, which was housed in the Abbey theatre in Dublin, where Yeats took an active part in day-to-day management. His prolonged love for the beautiful Irish revolutionary Maud Gonne inspired some major love poetry, or poetry where love and politics are in tragic conflict. Yeats's poetic style became harder and barer, though he continued to be a myth-maker; in his poetry he mythologizes his friends and enemies and his native land. Yeats despised the middle classes, and his ideal Ireland was divided between a hard-riding Protestant aristocracy of fine artistic tastes and a devout Catholic peasantry, full of instinctive wisdom and preserving a living folklore. In later life Yeats realized with some bitterness that the clerical and bourgeois Free State set up in 1922 bore little relation to his dreams.

In the 1890s Yeats was a member of a group of young poets in London called the Rhymers' Club, whom he later mythologized as a lost generation of decadents. They were minor but dedicated artists, more concerned to withdraw from life than to live it, and they tended to die young. Their lyrics pursued the fleeting Paterian moment and they were inspired by Catullus and the Elizabethan song-writers and Paul Verlaine. Their muses and subjects were often the prostitutes and music-hall dancers of London and Paris, and in this respect their poetry showed a post-Victorian spirit. One of the most attractive and talented of these doomed young men was Ernest Dowson, whose famous poem, 'Non sum qualis eram bonae sub regno Cynarae', with the refrain, 'I have been faithful to thee, Cynara! in my fashion' is a haunting and resilient instance of the decadent love poem. (It was drawn on for such titles as

TWO DRAWINGS BY AUBREY BEARDSLEY. (*left*) A cover design for Ernest Dowson's drama, *The Pierrot of the Minute* (1897); the pierrot was a favourite image of the *fin de siècle*. (*right*) Beardsley's drawing for his own accomplished translation of a poem by Catullus (1896). Beardsley's art was very literary in inspiration and he was himself a gifted writer of verse and prose.

COVER DESIGN. FROM "THE PIERROT OF THE MINUTE," PUBLISHED BY JOHN LANE

Margaret Mitchell's *Gone with the Wind* and Cole Porter's 'Always true to you, darling, in my fashion'.)

A. E. Housman (1859–1936) was a few years older than the Rhymers and he was never associated with them. But the poems in his *A Shropshire Lad*, published in 1896, are products of the *fin de siècle* mood. A 'here/there' opposition recurs, as the poet in middle age looks back to a golden age of youth and freedom, where 'Shropshire' is not so much an English county as an image of the lost ideal time and place. Like Pater, Housman was preoccupied with the fleetingness of things: 'Youth's a stuff will not endure' is the central motif of his lyrics. *A Shropshire Lad* lacks the slight exoticism pursued by the Rhymers; its themes and subjects are English and rural, though Housman, who was a professor of Latin, controls his potentially disturbing feelings with classical formality. The book became a poetic best-seller; the homosexuality which underlay Housman's poetry was sufficiently obscured not to be found troubling by his many readers.

The two most important Anglo-Irish contemporaries of Yeats were Oscar Wilde (1854–1900) and Bernard Shaw (1856–1950). They were born in Dublin within a year or two of each other; both made major contributions to English drama, were masters of witty paradox, and regarded themselves as socialists. In all other respects their attitudes to life and art were totally different. Shaw's public career was also very much longer, for he outlived Wilde by fifty years. Wilde, a disciple of Pater, was a quintessential aesthete, cultivating an extravagant style of living and defying conventional opinion with his wit. Wilde wrote in all the main literary forms; fiction, poetry, drama, essays, but he said that he put his talent into his writing and his genius into his living. As a result Wilde survives as a myth, a legend of pure style that ultimately turned to tragedy, rather than as a conventional man of letters whose work can be assessed in the ordinary way. His novel *The Picture of Dorian Gray* (1891), heavily influenced by a famous text of the French Decadence, J.-K. Huysmans' *A Rebours*, is a melodramatic and lurid exploration of the idea that art has nothing to do with morality, and that it endures while life passes. *Dorian Gray*, once notorious, is now something of a period piece. Wilde's art has lasted far better in his comedies of manners, where the stagecraft is impeccable and the wit arresting. His greatest work for the theatre, *The Importance of Being Earnest* (produced 1895, published 1899), transforms the inanities of fashionable social life into an inspired farce, a pure pastoral, where wit triumphs over reality. Wilde's brief and brilliant career ended in ruin, when he was sentenced to two years' imprisonment for homosexual practices. Out of this experience Wilde wrote *The Ballad of Reading Gaol* (1898), his one work in poetry with a hint of greatness.

Bernard Shaw was not particularly interested in art; he was much more concerned with ideas, and he freely used his plays as a vehicle for his social thinking. He made a false start as a novelist before turning to drama, and he

FANCY PORTRAIT.

QUITE TOO-TOO PUFFICKLY PRECIOUS!!

Being Lady Windy-mère's Fan-cy Portrait of the new dramatic author,
Shakspeare Sheridan Oscar Puff, Esq.

["He addressed from the stage a public audience, mostly composed of ladies, pressing between his daintily-gloved fingers a still burning and half-smoked cigarette."—*Daily Telegraph.*]

OSCAR WILDE. A *Punch* caricature from 1892, after the success of *Lady Windermere's Fan* made Wilde a fashionable dramatist. His disgrace and imprisonment lay three years in the future.

was also an acute critic of music and theatre. He was well known, too, as a political journalist and edited *Fabian Essays* (1889). Shaw was much influenced by Ibsen, and his book *The Quintessence of Ibsenism*, published in 1891, explained Ibsen to English readers and upheld Ibsen's use of the drama as a force subverting accepted social attitudes. A year later, Shaw's play *Mrs. Warren's Profession*, which looked at some of the ignored realities of contemporary sexual exploitation, was banned by the censor. By degrees Shaw's startling provocations, which stopped short of being downright offensive, and his admirable sense of the theatre, made him a respected dramatist of an 'advanced' kind, though his radicalism was a matter of content not of form. His *Plays Pleasant and Unpleasant*, published in two volumes in 1898, helped to establish his reputation; his highly articulate dramatic writing was readable as well as actable. Audiences responded to Shaw's witty, paradoxical presentation of social problems, but they enjoyed the long expository speeches he gave his characters—Shaw regarded them as operatic arias—as performance rather than as argument. This was Shaw's fate throughout his long subsequent career as a leading dramatist; he was never taken as seriously as he wished, though he also expanded his ideas in lively prefaces to his plays.

During the early 1900s Shaw became a dominant presence on the London stage, with such provocative but popular plays as *Man and Superman* (1903, first produced 1905), *Major Barbara* (1907, produced 1905), and *Pygmalion* (1916, produced 1913). Meanwhile his fellow countryman, Yeats, who was the

HENRY STRAKER (*left*). The chauffeur in Shaw's *Man and Superman* is an early version of the technocrat, the man who has power because he knows about machinery.

PETER PAN (*right*). Stephanie Stephens as J. M. Barrie's androgynous, ageless figure. *Peter Pan* was written in 1904 and is a steadily popular Christmas theatrical entertainment for children, rivalling the more ancient pantomime.

antithesis of the rationalistic Shaw in his literary and dramatic beliefs, was attempting a very different kind of drama as playwright and manager of the Abbey theatre in Dublin. Yeats wrote a series of poetic dramas on Irish legends; he regarded these plays, which were not very popular at the time, as contributing to the development of national consciousness by making dramatic speech from the inherently poetic language of the Irish peasantry. His friend J. M. Synge (1871-1909) had a similar ideal, which inspired *The Playboy of the Western World* (1907), and which he explained in his preface to the play: 'in countries where the imagination of the people, and the language they use, is rich and living, it is possible for a writer to be rich and copious in his words, and at the same time to give the reality, which is the root of all poetry, in a comprehensive and natural form.' *The Playboy of the Western World* has become a classic, though the poetic speech of its peasant characters is more stylized and literary than Synge or Yeats might have wanted to admit. Synge's play was noisily rejected on its first production in Dublin in 1907, much to the disgust of Yeats, who responded with a bitter poem, 'On Those that Hated "The Playboy of the Western World"'. Yeats's ideal Ireland was divided between peasants and aristocrats, and in time he moved closer to the aristocratic pole, as exemplified in Noh drama, the 'noble plays of Japan', to which Ezra Pound introduced him in 1913. Yeats's later concept and practice of drama became hieratic, ritualized, and remote from everyday living.

The New Fiction

In fiction the *fin de siècle* mood of withdrawal from everyday reality and the pursuit of a higher world of myth and art and imagination led to a taste for fictional romances, evident, for instance, in the short stories of Wilde and Yeats. Robert Louis Stevenson (1850-94) made a cogent defence of fictional romance as a superior mode to the realistic novel that tried to capture 'life' itself: 'Life is monstrous, infinite, illogical, abrupt and poignant; a work of art, in comparison, is neat, finite, self-contained, rational, flowing and emasculate.' But art could also improve on life by offering images of possibilities that for most people were unattainable in realistic terms. Stevenson's idea of fiction as art was quite other than that of the aesthetes and decadents; he found it best expressed in adventure stories, where human beings escape from the trivial contingencies of social life and are caught up in primitive and archetypal forms of action, such as 'fighting, sailing, adventure, death or child-birth . . . These aged things have on them the dew of man's morning . . .' Stevenson is still enjoyed as a master of adventure fiction, such as *Treasure Island* (1883) and *Kidnapped* (1886), which appeal to young readers, but not only to them. In *The Strange Case of Dr. Jekyll and Mr. Hyde* (1886) he presents the archetypal image of the *Doppelgänger* in the guise of a horror story. Stevenson's interest in evil and duality appears at greater length in *The Master of Ballantrae* (1889),

a memory of Henry James and
Joseph Conrad conversing at an afternoon party—
circa 1909.

max
1926

HENRY JAMES AND JOSEPH CONRAD, by Max Beerbohm (1926). Beerbohm published affectionate parodies of the mannered prose of both these masters in *A Christmas Garland*.

which is as much a novel as a romance, with complexity of form and considerable psychological insight.

Whatever the claims made for romance, the novel proper, which deals with the ordinary world of action and desire, was taking new directions in the 1880s. A century later, Stevenson's friend Henry James (1843-1916) appears to us as a novelist of greater stature than he was accorded by his contemporaries. James was an American who preferred to live and write in England, and he now occupies a pre-eminent place in both English and American literature. One should note, incidentally, that in James's lifetime no such distinction was made; in the present essay the prominence of Irish writers means that 'English' literature refers to language rather than nationality. James's expatriation meant that he never completely belonged anywhere, which some might see as the essential condition of the late-Romantic artist. Although much attached to English life and culture, James continued to think and feel like an American (he finally became a British subject during the First World War, not long before his death). James's fiction of the 1870s and 1880s focuses on the adventures and misfortunes of Americans in Europe—though in one novel, *The Europeans* (1878), the pattern is reversed and the Europeans go to America—and it has become a critical cliché to say that James's theme is the collision of American innocence and European experience. This is too simplifying and reductive a formula; expatriation in James is metaphorical as well as literal, and pervading his fiction is a strong sense of human loneliness; the community of the High Victorian novel has ceased to exist. Nor is James much interested in the close rendering of the multiplicity of things and appearances that has always been central in the appeal of realistic fiction; in James the physical world is no more than a backcloth for the drama; and drama is central to James's art; he has a wonderful ability to render the subtleties, and the pain and the dismay, that exist in the mutual relations of human beings. Joseph Conrad called him the 'historian of fine consciences', and in Conrad's Gallic English 'conscience' echoes the French *conscience*, 'consciousness'. Yet no interpretation of James is definitive or final; this is ultimately true of all literature that is worth returning to, but it is more immediately and obviously true of the modernist masterpieces of the early twentieth century, and it is in this illustrious company that we now see James. If one way of reading James stresses the underlying themes of alienation and betrayal, another can detect a predilection for the melodramatic, while another emphasizes James's sense of humour and the fine social comedy that he extracts from the mutual misunderstandings of Americans and Europeans; or, indeed, Americans and Americans.

All these aspects are apparent in *The Portrait of a Lady* (1881), one of James's most satisfying novels and one of his most popular. Most of the action takes place in England and Italy, but all the characters, apart from Lord Warburton, are American. At the centre of things is the heroine Isabel Archer, an attractive and headstrong embodiment of American innocence from the placid provincial backwater of Albany, New York. The dangers of a certain kind of aestheticism provide a central theme of the novel, illustrated in Isabel's tragically wrong-headed marriage to a shallow and corrupt connoisseur of art, Gilbert Osmond. James believed in the importance of art, but he regarded art and morality as ultimately indistinguishable, unlike Wilde, for whom they were totally opposite. In his presentation of Isabel James certainly took something from Dorothea Brooke in *Middlemarch*. But overall the two novels are very unlike each other. *The Portrait of a Lady* is open-ended, offering no finality or assured conclusion. Isabel goes back to Osmond, and in the book's last words Henrietta Stackpole says, ambiguously, to Isabel's long-time suitor Caspar Goodwood, 'Look here, Mr. Goodwood, just you wait!'

Thomas Hardy (1840–1928), who was patronizingly referred to by James as 'the good little Thomas Hardy', was born three years before James. Both men began to publish novels in the 1870s and both represent a departure from the familiar forms of Victorian fiction: they show us central figures who are or become alienated from their society and are never reintegrated with it. Beyond

A SHEEPFOLD IN THE EVENING (1890), by Sir George Clausen. This painting recalls Hardy's *Far From the Madding Crowd*, where sheep are a valuable property, as well as a traditional emblem of pastoral.

this, comparisons are not profitable or even possible. Hardy grew up in Dorset and trained as an architect; he spent some years in London as a young man, but was never at home there, and returned to his native county where he spent the rest of his long life. Hardy is a regional novelist, whose imaginary world of 'Wessex' covers a large area of the southern and western counties of England. He was deeply attached to the rural customs and ways of life that he knew as a boy, and which he celebrates in an early novel, *Under the Greenwood Tree* (1872). At the same time he is conscious of the social changes and problems of his day, such as agricultural innovation in *The Mayor of Casterbridge* (1886) or the contradictions of contemporary sexual mores in *Tess of the D'Urbervilles* (1891). Hardy's last novel, *Jude the Obscure* (1896),

WINTER WORK (1883-4). Clausen's painting catches Hardy's feeling for the desperation of rural toil as opposed to its pastoral charm.

is pervaded by a *fin de siècle* sense of crisis and severance with the past. Hardy unfolds the tragic story of his two central characters, who represent new social types: Jude Fawley, the working man who is passionate for education and self-improvement, and the woman he marries, Sue Bridehead, a fascinating but neurotic example of what was known in the 1890s as the 'New Woman'.

A familiar response to Hardy is to call him a fatalist who shows his characters as oppressed and defeated by a malign destiny. There is plenty of evidence in Hardy's fiction to support such an interpretation; but it needs to be balanced or opposed by the view that Hardy's characters struggle bravely against their fates in a spirit of existential defiance, and that they are not always defeated. It is true that there are contradictions at the heart of Hardy's fiction. John Bayley has shown how Hardy is divided between the poetic, intuitive, reticent artist who was moved by places and landscapes, and the fussy craftsman and constructor of elaborate plots, who was given to laboured commentary and intrusive autodidactic opinions about art and ideas. The latter aspect of Hardy is one which can become troublesomely oppressive, despite the general opinion that he was a great novelist. But the best things in Hardy's fiction are splendid and intensely memorable.

Hardy was a poet in many lyrical passages in his novels, and he wrote formal poetry all his life. After the hostile reception of *Jude the Obscure* by critics who found it unacceptably shocking, Hardy gave up fiction, but he continued to write poetry prolifically until his death more than thirty years later. If Hardy is often a poet in his novels, he is a realist in his poetry, not pursuing ideal worlds but soberly and ironically regarding everyday human dramas and hopes and fears. Hardy's craftsmanship is evident, though he was also given to clumsy diction and odd word formations. Though he had not received the conventional education of a gentleman, Hardy had been well trained in Latin at Dorchester grammar school, and his interest in Latin metres led him to experiment with English prosody. His poetry is engrained with a bleak, honest agnosticism that does not flinch from the grimmer sides of the human condition: 'if way to the Better there be, it exacts a full look at the Worst.' Hardy is a good poet, who spoke with a very individual accent, but he can be lowering if read in bulk. Geoffrey Grigson has remarked in an essay on Hardy on the extent to which his poetry is dominated by the word 'if': 'if life was so and so, *if* I had dared, *if* you had loved me or *if* life had continued, *if* you were here and not elsewhere and hadn't broken the appointment, *if* you were not dead'. This sense of regret, taken to a high intensity, inspires some of Hardy's greatest poetry, written after the death of his first wife in 1912. They had been estranged for years, but her death caused him to fall in love again with the young woman he had married long before, and in a sequence of poems bearing the Virgilian epigraph, *Veteris vestigia flammae*, 'ashes of an old fire', he passionately invoked her remembered presence. Hardy kept alive the traditional forms of English poetry in the era of modernist innovation. He has always been something of a poet's poet, and his influence has been acknowledged by W. H. Auden and Philip Larkin, to name only two poets prominent in later generations.

John Gross, in the passage quoted at the beginning of this chapter, remarks that though many writers responded to the uncertainties of the late Victorian mood by retreating into nostalgia and exoticism, others reacted with determined realism. Among these none was more determined than George Gissing (1857–1903), who published his first novel in 1880. Of lesser critical standing than James or Hardy, Gissing was an important novelist, who is still well worth reading. His heroes are studies in alienation, being young men of reasonable education and intellectual abilities, whose lives are thwarted by lack of money. This was Gissing's own situation: his chances of a 'respectable' profession were blighted by a brush with the law when he was a student and he resolved to earn his living by writing novels, though they brought him very little income. A self-destructive streak further complicated his life by leading him into two disastrous marriages. Gissing knew at first hand the shabby-genteel poverty of the unsuccessful urban intellectual, and he knew something, too, of the lives of the desperately poor in the London slums; these experiences provided him with much material for fiction. Though he was convinced that there was something very wrong with the social order, Gissing was a novelist of resentment rather than protest, for he had no faith in political change. His early novel, *Demos* (1886), for instance, is both a moving exploration of the bitter lives of the slum-dwellers and an attack on the socialist movement. The novel ends with an extraordinary manifestation of the spirit of withdrawal and evasion of the real world: the factories that have been polluting a green English valley are physically removed and it is left to resume its former natural state. *The Nether World* (1889) is a better account of London poverty, where Gissing effectively handles a large cast of characters and a fairly complex plot. In *The Odd Women* (1893) he paints a sympathetic picture of the growing contemporary movement for the emancipation of women. But his masterpiece is certainly *New Grub Street* (1891). This is a study of London literary life in the late 1880s, centred on the impecunious but fastidious novelist, Edwin Reardon, who is the vehicle for many of Gissing's own beliefs and attitudes. Reardon wants to make a living by writing novels of some literary seriousness, without compromising with the demands of the market. But the market, in the shape of new publishing ventures catering to the needs of a mass audience, triumphs in the end. The peculiar excellence of *New Grub Street* arises from Gissing's deep personal involvement with its subject. The book also fills one of the traditional functions of the realistic novel by conveying information; in general, about seedy metropolitan life, and in particular, about the changes then affecting the institution of literature.

Gissing is sometimes claimed as an advanced realist of the school of Zola. Although Gissing came to admire Zola at the end of his life, his most

Some Persons of "the Nineties"
little imagining, despite their Proper
Pride and Ornamental aspect,
how much they will interest
Mr. Holbrook Jackson and Mr. Osbert Burdett.

max
1925

MAX BEERBOHM'S RETROSPECTIVE VIEW FROM THE 1920S: 'Some persons of "the nineties" little imagining, despite their proper pride and ornamental aspect, how much they will interest Mr Holbrook Jackson and Mr Osbert Burdett.' Jackson and Burdett had both published books on the 1890s. The persons depicted are, from left to right (*rear row*), Richard Le Gallienne, Walter Sickert, George Moore, John Davidson, Oscar Wilde, W. B. Yeats; (*front row*), Arthur Symons, Henry Harland, Charles Conder, William Rothenstein, Max Beerbohm, Aubrey Beardsley.

unrelentingly realistic fiction, written in the 1880s, was not influenced by him. Gissing's presentation of London owed much to the darker side of Dickens, but it lacked Dickens's imaginative energy and metaphorical power. The faults of Gissing's fiction are obvious, and they partly arise from the pressures on the impoverished writer, as exemplified by Edwin Reardon. Gissing wrote too much, too quickly; his prose is often flat and tired, and his narrative padded. Yet his best work is both intelligent and entertaining; he is an excellent story-teller and, despite his dismal subject-matter, immensely readable.

By the 1890s the extreme and painful realism of the French naturalists such as Zola was beginning to influence English writing though not the pseudo-scientific philosophy that underlay it. The publisher of an English translation of Zola was imprisoned for supposedly disseminating obscenity, but readers and writers of advanced tastes were disposed to take naturalism seriously. One of them was the Irish novelist George Moore (1852–1933); in the 1880s he publicly attacked the powerful circulating library, Mudie's, for refusing to stock his books. By the 1890s novels were becoming shorter and less expensive, escaping from the restraints of publication in three volumes, which for many years had provided the stock-in-trade of the circulating libraries, who had a powerful effect on public taste. Moore took advantage of the new freedom to publish *Esther Waters* (1894), a powerful Zolaesque study of the tribulations and exploitation of a young servant girl. Moore embodied different aspects of the literary *fin de siècle*: aestheticism as well as outspoken realism. He was drawn to the Celtic revival and collaborated with Yeats in the Irish National Theatre.

Another writer who began his career under the influence of the naturalists was Arnold Bennett (1867–1931). His principal subject-matter came from the Potteries area of industrial Staffordshire where he had grown up, and to which he first gave extended fictional treatment in *Anna of the Five Towns* (1902). Bennett was too cheerful and optimistic by temperament to be a consistent literary naturalist, though he wrote about humble lives with great sympathy and understanding. Bennett divided his writing between work which he took with artistic seriousness, and where the French influences are most apparent, and pot-boiling fiction which he wrote simply for money. Bennett produced his best work during the Edwardian years, when he became an established man of letters and unusually wealthy for a writer.

The closing years of the century were a period of literary experiment and innovation. New periodicals were started, directed at the growing popular audience brought into being by universal education; they provided a great opportunity for writers of short stories, such as Arnold Bennett, H. G. Wells, and Rudyard Kipling. The short story, particularly the kind of sad or cynical anecdote influenced by de Maupassant, became a popular form. Traditional literary genres were also directed to new ends. There was a growing taste for the romance, the tale set in other times and other places, which offered imaginative escape from an unlovely present. As we have seen, Stevenson argued that the romance could be more essentially truthful than realistic fiction. One new novelist who was initially regarded as a writer of romances was Joseph Conrad (1857-1924). His first novel *Almayer's Folly* appeared in 1895, and though his reputation was slow to develop, within a few years he was known and enjoyed as a writer of yarns about seafaring life, set in the East Indies and the South Seas. Conrad himself, who had undergone successive transformations, from a Polish gentleman to a merchant seaman to an English novelist, was a personally exotic figure. Knowing what we now know of his development after the turn of the century, when he proved himself to be a great novelist, the early response to Conrad seems ludicrously wide of the mark. Nevertheless, there are elements in his major fiction which continue to reflect his experience as a seaman: the sense that human life is a struggle against arbitrary hostile forces, and that society is a model of threatened and perilously maintained order, like a ship at sea. There is an inescapable and fascinating strangeness about Conrad's writing, as an aristocratic Polish sensibility is mediated through the forms and language of the English novel, in an English prose that is impeccable but idiosyncratic.

Other modes of romance were directed not at remote areas of the present-day world, but at the future. The knowledge that the nineteenth century was in its final years produced a strong and uneasy concern with what the twentieth century would reveal. Sometimes this concern took the form of a utopian projection of a new and better world; more often there were apocalyptic images of future wars and social disasters, and even of the disappearance of the human race in its familiar form. A celebrated instance of the utopian romance was *News from Nowhere* (1891) by William Morris, as mentioned in the previous chapter, who had been active since the late 1850s as a poet, designer, and revolutionary socialist. *News from Nowhere* was written as a reply to an earlier novel set in the future, *Looking Backward* by the American, Edward Bellamy, which Morris found unacceptable as a vision of things to come. Morris's romance evokes a cleaner, finer London, after capitalism has been overthrown and a socialist commonwealth established; machinery, though not abolished, is kept unobtrusively out of sight. The book is more a dream than a blueprint, poetically beautiful rather than intellectually convincing as an analysis of social trends and possibilities; but it has proved an inspiration to many later socialists.

The other kind of fiction about the future was apocalyptic and pessimistic, and its most brilliant practitioner was H. G. Wells (1866-1946). He was a young man of humble origins who had had to struggle against much adversity to make his name as a writer, though when the breakthrough came in the mid-1890s he achieved rapid celebrity. A salient fact about Wells was that unlike most English writers he had received a scientific education; at the Royal College of Science in the 1880s he had read science and attended lectures by

AN ILLUSTRATION BY EDMUND
SULLIVAN TO H. G. WELLS'S 'A STORY
OF THE DAYS TO COME'. Published in a
magazine in 1899 with the caption: 'The
great machine that had come flying
through the air from America that morning
rushed down out of the sky.' A remarkable
combination of *art nouveau* and primitive
science fiction.

the great Thomas Huxley. Throughout a long career as a writer Wells was
very conscious of the power of physical science to transform life, either for the
worse, as he liked to show in his early fiction, or for the better, a possibility
he became more concerned with in his later utopian writings. At the start of
his career Wells combined a scientific background with a remarkably vivid and
ingenious imagination. He gave a new impetus to the genre of the 'scientific
romance'; his writing had something in common with the science fiction of the
Frenchman Jules Verne, but was imaginatively freer and less tied to actual
scientific possibilities. Wells used scientific language as a kind of rhetoric to
give a plausible flavour to episodes and situations which were instances of the
marvellous and the fantastic. Invisibility, for instance, was a traditional folklore

motif, but Wells gave it a rationale in terms of modern physics in *The Invisible Man* (1897). (But as he cheerfully admitted in a letter to Arnold Bennett his explanation would not actually hold water.)

Wells's finest example of the scientific romance is his first sustained essay in the genre, *The Time Machine* (1895). This wonderfully original exploration of the remote future is set in the year 802701, when evolutionary development has divided humanity into two distinct species; one descended from the nineteenth-century bourgeoisie, the other from the proletariat, who live underground and prey on the former. *The Time Machine* is a work of genuinely poetic imagination; at the same time, it projects many of the social doubts and fears of its age. So, indeed, do other scientific romances by Wells, notably *The War of the Worlds* (1898), a harrowing account of the occupation and subjugation of southern England by Martian invaders. As well as being a gripping narrative, *The War of the Worlds* provides an imaginative critique of imperialism, and presents an apocalyptic image of imperial England in a state of collapse and dissolution when attacked by more powerful forces. Wells was also a writer of comic realistic fiction of a broadly Dickensian kind, and in the 1900s he published several immensely popular novels of this kind. His prophesies became more positive and utopian and less imaginatively compelling. Increasingly Wells was less concerned with the literary art that he had practised so memorably at the start of his career, and much more interested in being a public commentator on important social and political questions.

Rudyard Kipling (1865-1936), another writer who became famous in the 1890s, has long been enjoyed by non-literary readers; liberal intellectuals and academics find it harder to come to terms with him. Kipling, an Anglo-Indian imperialist, was a great outsider in late Victorian England. He was born in India in 1865, educated in England, and returned to India in his teens to work as a journalist and become a writer. When he came back to England for good in 1889 he was already famous as the author of *Plain Tales from the Hills* (1888), a collection of pungent short stories in the Maupassant manner, sardonically recounting the lives of the more prosperous Anglo-Indians. In England Kipling was much in demand as a short story writer and he became a master of the genre. He had a wealth of Indian experience to draw on, acquired as a child and young man, and British readers, slowly waking up to the fact that they had an Indian empire, were eager to read what Kipling had to tell them about it. He wrote satirically about the political and administrative classes who ruled India, but drew admiring pictures of a previously invisible section of the British community there, the private soldiers in the army; he celebrated them in short stories and in several collections of poetry, of which the first was *Barrack Room Ballads* (1892). Though a writer of immense gifts with a wide following, Kipling kept apart from established literary circles, and preferred the company of soldiers and men of action to that of literary people. He was an inspired writer of the best kind of children's books—those that are

THE FAIR TOXOPHILITES. W.P. Frith's *English Archers, Nineteenth Century* (1872) shows the English leisured classes at play. This is the sporting, if often intellectually limited, world of George Eliot's *Daniel Deronda* and of Matthew Arnold's aristocratic 'Barbarians'.

IMPERIAL SUPERMAN. A book-cover for a novel by G. A. Henty, a prolific and popular writer of boys' adventure stories about the Empire.

THE AFTERMATH OF BATTLE. The visionary painter Stanley Spencer depicts a bus-load of wounded soldiers arriving at the gates of a hospital. The scene is based on his own experience in 1918.

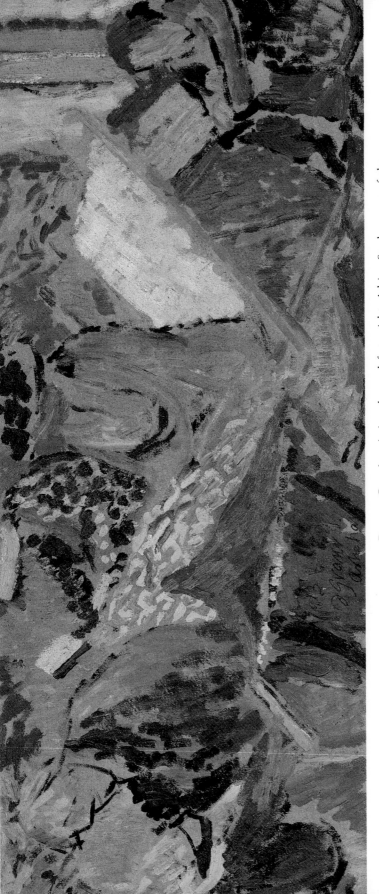

A BLOOMSBURY GROUP, 1913. Duncan Grant's painting shows, left to right, Adrian Stephen, son of the eminent Victorian man of letters, Sir Leslie Stephen; his sisters, Virginia Woolf and Vanessa Bell; and a friend.

also enjoyed by adults—such as *The Jungle Book* (1894) and *Just So Stories* (1902). Though personally reserved, Kipling had a strong sympathy for the common man and his modes of expression, such as music-hall songs and recitations. So celebrated an aphoristic poem as 'If', though wholly unlike the kind of pure poetry pursued by the young Yeats and the Rhymers, has what one might call the nourishing impurity of common proverbial wisdom. Indeed, one of Kipling's achievements as a poet was to give many proverbial phrases to the language, such as 'East is East, and West is West and never the twain shall meet', or 'The female of the species is more deadly than the male', or 'Somewhere East of Suez', or 'The White Man's Burden', or 'You're a better man than I am, Gunga Din!' Kipling was convinced that the British Empire was a great force for good, a conviction which separates him from many readers in a post-imperial age. And there is a brutal absolutism about some of his attitudes that can be repellent.

Even in his heyday Kipling was not universally popular; Max Beerbohm, for instance, savagely caricatured him as a loud-mouthed vulgar patriot. On the other hand, writers ideologically opposed to Kipling, such as the socialist Orwell and the Communist Brecht, have been appreciative of his genius. The

COLONIAL TROOPS AT QUEEN VICTORIA'S DIAMOND JUBILEE (1897). The Empire reached its apogee on this occasion. It was marked by Kipling's poem, 'Recessional', which contained a note of warning as well as triumph.

idea of Kipling as a simple patriot is itself too simple; as a serious imperialist he sharply attacked his fellow countrymen for being unworthy of their imperial mission. This was particularly true after the Boer War. Queen Victoria's Diamond Jubilee of 1897 saw the apogee of the imperial ideal and was marked by Kipling with his poem 'Recessional', which was as much a warning as a celebration. Two years later, in the early months of the Boer War, the British and Imperial forces were at first outsoldiered and badly beaten by the Boer farmers. The result was a scandal and a severe shock to national self-esteem. Kipling eventually responded with a sombre poem, 'The Islanders', which denounced the complacency and martial incompetence of 'the flanneled fools at the wicket and the muddied oafs at the goal'. Kipling's passionate but stoical imperialism, and the generally dignified rectitude of his expression of it, made it seem more a Roman than a late Victorian quality.

Literally the last word on the nineteenth century was uttered by Thomas Hardy in his poem 'The Darkling Thrush', which is dated 31 December 1900 (which Hardy regarded as the last day of the old century). Hardy conveys a sense of chill, shrunken uncertainty on this portentous date; then the mood changes as an old bedraggled thrush begins to sing cheerfully in the winter dusk, as if expressing 'Some blessed hope, whereof he knew / And I was unaware'. A few days later, in the first month of the twentieth century, Queen Victoria died; an era had finally ended.

The Edwardians

Yeats, in his inveterate mythologizing of the past, saw the year 1900 as marking a return to normality after the extravagances of the Decadence: 'Then in 1900 everybody got down off his stilts: henceforth nobody drank absinthe with his black coffee; nobody went mad; nobody committed suicide; nobody joined the Catholic church; or if they did I have forgotten.' Yeats *had* forgotten: in the 1900s Arthur Symons went mad for a time and the poet John Davidson committed suicide. Yet overall the 1900s did seem more ordinary; there was an air of relief that Queen Victoria's long reign was finally over, and King Edward's cheerful materialism set a new social tone.

The anti-Victorian revolt which had begun well before the turn of the century became more assertive. There is a substantial example of it in John Galsworthy's novel *The Man of Property* (1906). Galsworthy (1867–1933) set out to satirize the Victorian upper middle class, whom he saw as reducing everything to property values, including life itself. He introduced the large interlocking clan of the Forsytes in their tall, over-furnished houses in Kensington and Bayswater, with their principal embodiment in Soames Forsyte, a rising solicitor in his thirties, tight-lipped, closely shaven, and supercilious. The story is centred on two pieces of 'property': a country house Soames is building for himself; and his wife Irene, whom he is losing to another man. As social satire

BERNARD SHAW AND H. G. WELLS in about 1905. Though closely associated in the public eye of Edwardian England as socialists and literary iconoclasts, they were often at odds, particularly in disagreement over the running of the Fabian Society. The wily Shaw usually outmanœuvred the impulsive Wells.

The Man of Property is pointed and effective, but Galsworthy was fatally drawn, despite himself, to sympathize with the objects of his satire. D. H. Lawrence remarked: 'Galsworthy had not quite enough of the superb courage of his satire. He faltered and gave into the Forsytes.' When Galsworthy wrote the succeeding volumes in *The Forsyte Saga* he sentimentalized the Forsytes and turned Soames from something very like a villain into the admired and endorsed central intelligence of the sequence.

A cool appraisal of English society is noticeable in Edwardian fiction. H. G. Wells's *Tono-Bungay* (1909) is an impressive example, even though it is too sprawlingly ambitious to be an entirely successful novel in aesthetic terms. It contains strands of Dickensian comedy, realistic description of lower-class life, and a kind of restrained science fiction in the accounts of early aeronautics. The work is dominated by the metaphor which Wells introduces near the beginning, where English society is seen as a large country house, with the lower classes concealed below stairs in the servants' quarters, while the upper classes enjoy life in the elegant drawing-rooms. This model was influenced by Wells's boyhood memories of Uppark in Sussex, where his mother had once been housekeeper; Wells first drew on it in *The Time Machine*. *Tono-Bungay* was admired by many readers, including Ford Madox Ford, who serialized it in the *English Review*, and the young D. H. Lawrence. The book recalls some of the amplitude of the nineteenth-century novel, but it ends on the indeterminate note of post-Victorian fiction.

There is a comparable amplitude in Arnold Bennett's *The Old Wives' Tale* (1908), which is a triumph of fictional realism. He is intensely concerned in this novel with the inexorable passing of time, over many decades, as we follow the story of two sisters growing up in the Potteries district. One, more adventurous, leaves home and goes to France, where she endures the siege of Paris in the Franco-Prussian War. The other sister stays at home leading a quiet uneventful life, which Bennett nevertheless makes interesting. Although *The Old Wives' Tale* does not attempt the sophisticated temporal devices of modernist fiction, it wonderfully conveys a sense of time as a constant process of change: the appearance of friends alters, children outgrow their clothes, familiar buildings are renovated or pulled down.

Bennett, Galsworthy, and Wells enjoyed a large readership and did not think themselves minority artists; in the 1920s they were denounced by Virginia Woolf for their materialism and lack of true insight into human life. Henry James and Joseph Conrad were much less popular, but their novels of the 1900s are held in the highest esteem by present-day critics. In James's novels of what F. O. Matthiessen called the 'major phase'—*The Wings of the Dove* (1902), *The Ambassadors* (1903), and *The Golden Bowl* (1904)—intense aesthetic concentration and the subtle exploration of fine consciousnesses form a single process; their stylistic intricacy is formidable, but there is always an underlying sense of the speaking voice, for James used to dictate his work to a secretary.

In the Edwardian years Joseph Conrad published two major political novels, which make challengingly difficult use of the form of the novel. *Nostromo* (1904) is a long and complex study of human responses to extreme situations, involving the history, politics, and economic life of a small South American republic; its examination of the impact of American capitalism on a backward community retains a topical element after eighty years. *Under Western Eyes* (1911) is a tense though obliquely constructed story set among Russian revolutionaries exiled in Switzerland, which takes a pessimistic view of hopes of political betterment. The novel conducts an implicit dialogue with Dostoevsky's *The Possessed*, its only rival as a fictional enactment of revolutionary consciousness; Conrad, as an anti-Russian Pole, had an inevitably complicated attitude to Dostoevsky's great novel.

Edwardian men of letters were important public figures—the prestige of the literary profession was very high in those years—and they took part in public debates and controversies; in the press, and sometimes on the same platform. Whatever the deep intellectual uncertainties of the age there was plenty of robust conviction on political and ideological questions. Shaw and Wells were quarrelsome but still friendly participants in socialist politics, and both took part in public debates and arguments with Hilaire Belloc (1870–1953) and G. K. Chesterton (1874–1936). Belloc and Chesterton, sometimes known collectively as the 'Chesterbelloc', were combative Roman Catholic apologists (though Chesterton was a Catholic by conviction, he did not formally join the Church until after the First World War), and exponents of a kind of politics which looked for its model to the peasants and smallholders of Catholic Europe, reinforced by a nostalgia for the medieval social order, and which was hostile to both socialism and capitalism. Belloc was a fine prose-writer and a good minor poet; and his satirical novels about political life are still readable; but

'THE OLD AND THE YOUNG SELF: MR G. K. CHESTERTON' by Max Beerbohm (1925). The inscription on the drawing satirizes the excesses of the 'Chesterbelloc':

Young Self: 'Oh yes, I drank some beer only the other day, and rather liked it; and of course the Crusades were glorious. But all this about English public life being honeycombed with corruption, and about the infallibility of the Pope, and the sacramental qualities of beer, and the soul-cleansing powers of Burgundy, and the immaculate conception of France, and the determination of the Jews to enslave us, and the instant need that we should get straight back into the Middle Ages, and'—

Old Self: 'Well, you haven't met Belloc.'

in order to support himself he dissipated his energies into much ephemeral writing. In some respects this is also true of G. K. Chesterton, who was a man of greater literary gifts, though he preferred to think of himself simply as a journalist. He has a strongly individual vision of reality, and a style of thinking and writing which used the paradoxical vein of the *fin de siècle* for Christian ends. His curious but entertaining fictional romances, such as *The Napoleon of Notting Hill* (1904) and *The Man who was Thursday* (1908), are devoted to exposing the unfamiliarity of the seemingly familiar. Some of Chesterton's poems are rewarding, such as the defiantly theatrical 'Lepanto', and he was an excellent literary critic, particularly in his studies of Dickens and other Victorian authors.

In 1903 a small literary time-bomb exploded, enlarging the anti-Victorian revolt. This was Samuel Butler's posthumous novel, *The Way of All Flesh*. Butler (1835-1902) was an iconoclastic Victorian satirist who attacked all the major doctrines of his day, Darwinism as well as Christianity; his most famous book during his lifetime was a utopian fantasy, *Erewhon* (1872). Butler wrote *The Way of all Flesh* well before his death but did not wish it to be published in his lifetime. The novel directs ruthless scorn at Victorian mores, and in particular the hallowed institution of the family; we see one generation of the Pontifex family oppressing and thwarting the next. Ernest Pontifex, the representative of the youngest generation, after enduring a personal disaster, manages to break away from paternal authority; his story contains many of Butler's own experiences. The novel helped to crystallize a particular Edwardian mood of rejection of the bourgeois family and the ideals that inspired it. Bernard Shaw owed a great deal to Butler's mockingly paradoxical style of polemic, and *The Way of All Flesh* was an inspiration to the young E. M. Forster (1879-1970), whose early novels carry on in a mild way Butler's attacks on Victorian convictions. (Forster's personal revolt was reinforced by his homosexuality, though this was not publicly acknowledged during his life.) Forster's major contribution to the English novel is *A Passage to India* (1924), where the subject of his satire shifts from insular English institutions to the Empire itself. His pre-war novels possess considerable charm, and show a surprising capacity to extract melodrama from small-scale social collisions. In Forster's short stories there is a sensitive continuation of the *fin de siècle* taste for myth and fantasy, set against a humdrum background. The most interesting, though not, perhaps, the most successful of the early novels is *Howards End* (1910). It presents a perceptive anatomy of late-Edwardian England, already suffering from motor cars and traffic congestion and urban sprawl. The novel's motto, 'Only Connect', represents Forster's wistful aspiration for a union of hearts and minds between two aspects of the upper middle class: the cultivated and aesthetic, as represented by the Schlegel sisters, and the decision-makers, the people who get things done in the world of 'telegrams and anger', as represented by the men of the Wilcox family.

Towards Modernism

Howards End shows English society in a state of anxious transition. In the year it was published, 1910, King Edward died and George V came to the throne. It was a year when there were two general elections and widespread industrial unrest. The international modernist explosion in the arts came to London in the form of the first Post-Impressionist Exhibition, followed in 1911 by Diaghilev's Russian Ballet with Stravinsky's music. 'In or about December 1910,' Virginia Woolf later observed with deliberate hyperbole, 'human character changed.' The first signs of literary change were modest. A school of young poets emerged and took their name from the new king, calling themselves 'Georgians'. Their first anthology was published in 1912, 'issued in the belief that English poetry is now again putting on a new strength and beauty'. The Georgians favoured English subjects with a rural flavour, as opposed to the indoor exoticism of the 1890s, and they hoped for a large audience; in this they were successful, for the several Georgian anthologies sold widely. The Georgians stood for Little Englandism as against Kipling's imperial ideal. C. K. Stead has

A BANQUET FOR RANJIT NAWANOGAR (1907). Britain's Indian Empire was celebrated by Kipling and later satirized by E. M. Forster in *A Passage to India*.

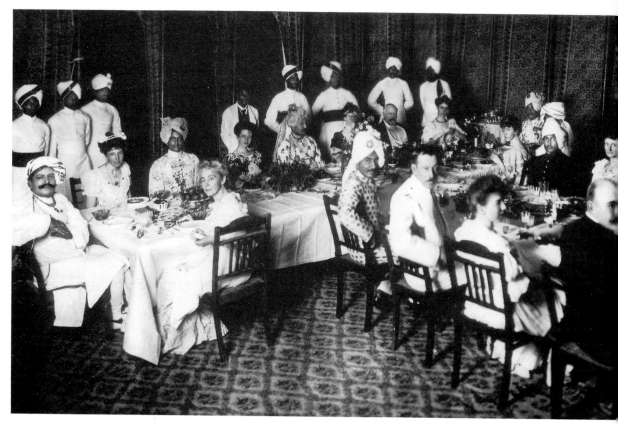

written that the Georgians 'belonged to the new liberal intellectual group that grew steadily in numbers during the first decade of this century, and their type is perhaps best illustrated by the Schlegel sisters in E. M. Forster's novel *Howards End*'. Their poetry was unpretentious and workmanlike, sometimes whimsical, sometimes sentimental, sometimes revealing a satirical edge: Rupert Brooke's 'The Old Vicarage, Grantchester', shows something of all three qualities. Georgian poetry was not committed to the deep refashioning of form and sensibility associated with modernism; it was, however, the tragic destiny of the Georgian poets to become, within a few years, the War Poets: the Georgian idealization of rural England acquired a peculiar poignancy when it was contrasted with a foreign battlefield.

As a concept 'modernism' is easier to employ than to define. At its broadest it refers not just to innovation in literature but to the radical remaking of all the arts that went on in Europe and America in the years before 1914. As an attempt to describe some salient characteristics of modernism in fiction and poetry, one can suggest the following: nothing can be taken for granted in literary form; there must be no unthinking reproduction of what is already familiar; conscious aesthetic attention is essential; our perceptions of reality are necessarily uncertain and provisional; the unparalleled complexity of modern urban life must be reflected in literary form; supposedly primitive myths can help us to grasp and order the chaos of twentieth-century experience; the intense but isolated 'image' or 'moment' or 'epiphany' provides our truest sense of the nature of things; the unconscious life of the mind is as important as the conscious; 'personality' is precarious and fragmentary rather than substantial and unchanging; contradictions in experience can be accommodated in literature by the techniques of ironic juxtaposition or superimposition; literary works can never be given a final or absolute interpretation. These characteristics are not to be found in all those writers we regard as modernist, but many of them will be; we are not dealing with identity of attitudes but with what Wittgenstein called 'family resemblances'. It is certainly not true that the only function of Late Victorian and Edwardian writing was to lead to the eventual triumph of modernism. Literature that is worth reading is worth reading in its own terms and not as a pointer to something else. Yet it is hard not to be affected by some such historicist pressure. The years 1910 to 1930 form one of the richest periods in English literary history, comparable with the end of the sixteenth century or the beginning of the nineteenth. There is an inevitable tension, even a contradiction, between seeing literature as separate works of varying degrees of excellence, and seeing it as schools and movements where one speaks of progress from decadence to renewal. It is not just an academic habit to discuss something so various as literature in these collective terms; the very process of trying to think coherently seems to impose them. The early years of modernism provide an instance of what the historian of science Thomas S. Kuhn has called a 'paradigm shift', when our sense of the very nature of a subject and its possibilities and limitations changes radically. Something like this shift began happening to aesthetic perception in about 1910, which is what Virginia Woolf was trying to imply by saying that human character changed in that year.

One of the most extreme and noisily innovative of continental schools of modernism was Italian Futurism, led by the ebullient F. T. Marinetti, who several times visited London to publicize his ideas and acquire disciples. Futurism wanted an absolute break with the past in poetry, painting, and music, and was fascinated by machinery and the newest forms of technology, such as motor cars and aeroplanes. No English writers went as far as this, but there was a good deal of interest in Futurist theory and practice, which certainly had some influence on Ezra Pound, Wyndham Lewis, and D. H. Lawrence. Anglophone modernism, however, tended not to reject the past as such, but to reject the recent past—that is, the philistine and bourgeois nineteenth century—in favour of remoter periods of history, or a mythologized antiquity. Pound looked to the Provence of the troubadours or the China of Confucius; T. S. Eliot found an ideal order in Dante and in the seventeenth-century England of Donne and Herbert and Lancelot Andrewes; James Joyce used Homer as a way of ordering the chaos of modern existence; and Lawrence aspired to the pure primitive consciousness of American Indians or ancient Etruscans.

After seventy years we are still living with the modernist transformations of lyrical poetry and the realistic novel, and they have not been surpassed or rendered obsolete. Other arts can achieve a kind of permanent revolution by constantly changing their material media, but literature can never free itself from its traditional medium, words, which have a built-in bias towards continuity. Furthermore, modernism did not affect the whole of literature: some major writers such as Hardy and Kipling were unaffected by it. Another important historical consideration is that most of the early modernist writers were not English. James, Pound, and Eliot were American, and Wyndham Lewis was half-American; Conrad was Polish; Yeats and Joyce were Irish, as were Wilde and Shaw, who though not modernists were cultural subverters; Ford was half-German. Virginia Woolf was certainly English; she came from a famous Victorian family, and her father, Leslie Stephen, had been a distinguished man of letters; but as a woman she did not share all the accepted values and assumptions of the English professional classes. Nor, indeed, did D. H. Lawrence, who was intensely English but whose father was a Nottinghamshire miner. One should not make too much of this alien and Celtic invasion of the established literary citadels; similar things had happened before, since London has always been a cosmopolitan centre, hospitable to immigrants. And only a minority of English writers has ever received the traditional education of a gentleman, proceeding from public school to Oxford or Cambridge. Nevertheless, the unfamiliar ethnic and cultural background of the

JAMES JOYCE (1921) AND T. S. ELIOT (1936) (*facing page*), by Wyndham Lewis. Lewis referred to them as the 'Men of 1914', the other two being himself and Ezra Pound. Lewis, Pound, and Eliot appeared in the only two issues of *Blast* which came out, in 1914–15, and Joyce was praised in the opening manifesto.

modernist writers does underline their innovatory significance; in literary-genetic terms the cross-fertilization was clearly beneficial.

In any account of the development of modernism in England the name of Ezra Pound (1885–1972) is bound to be prominent. He is important as a poet and critic, and as a cultural impresario, who generously encouraged painters and sculptors and musicians as well as writers, even when his own resources and prospects were very limited. Pound made a major contribution to English literature by helping to launch Joyce and Eliot when they were unknown. He lived in London from 1908 to 1920 and seemed to be well at home there, though he never ceased playing the part of the brash and *outré* Yankee bohemian, which he clearly enjoyed. But by the end of the war his feelings about Britain had turned very sour, and, like several English writers, he moved to the Continent. Thereafter Pound passed from English literature, or at least the English literary scene, into American literature and perhaps into world literature, with the polyglot *Cantos* occupying him for several decades to come.

Pound began as a poet in a Swinburnean, Pre-Raphaelite mode that was still common enough in Edwardian England but had nothing modernist about it; in old age he dismissed his first collection of poems, *A Lume Spento* (1908),

as 'stale cream puffs'. But Pound had larger talents, energy, and ambition than his young English contemporaries. He also had a great enthusiasm for poetry in other literatures, particularly of the Romance languages, including Provençal. As scholars have been quick to point out, Pound's linguistic abilities were often haphazard; but he compensated for these shortcomings by an intuitive feeling for what a foreign poet was doing. And he had a sure sense of how English poetry might be enriched by other poetries, in a long tradition including Rossetti and Wyatt and Chaucer. Pound restored to English poetry a conviction, which was commonplace in medieval and Renaissance culture but suppressed by Romantic individualism, that poetry is made as much from other poetry as from subjective feelings. Critics have remarked how Pound is most effective as a poet when he is translating, or at least writing with his eye on a foreign original. Much later in his career, after the disasters of the Second World War, Pound began writing a deeply personal kind of poetry; but in his younger days he was at his best when speaking through the *persona* of another man, such as an earlier poet or a figure from history, in a manner developed from Browning's dramatic monologues. His poem 'Near Perigord' is a beautiful example.

Pound is widely credited as the inventor of 'Imagist' poetry. It would be truer to say that he invented the name, and indeed in 1912 he set up a school of Imagist poets, consisting of himself and two friends, Richard Aldington and Hilda Doolittle (who wrote as 'H.D.'). Imagist poetry is essentially an attempt to isolate in a short poem a significant moment, in the Paterian sense, from the flow of life, to crystallize a fleeting experience with an emphasis on its visual aspects, without any overt moral or reflection attached. In fact, something like Imagist poetry had been written in the 1890s, and there were further parallels and anticipations in the tiny forms of Japanese poetry, such as the haiku, which were translated and imitated in the 1900s. T. E. Hulme (1883–1917) wrote some very short poems a few years before Pound formulated Imagism as a doctrine; they were clearly Imagist, as Pound acknowledged. Hulme's poems were dry and whimsical, demystifying stock Romantic sentiment by describing the moon as a red-faced farmer leaning over a hedge or as a child's balloon caught in the rigging of a ship: such images are good examples of what the Russian Formalist critics were to describe a little later as 'defamiliarization', revealing the familiar in a completely fresh way. Hulme was killed in the First World War, and is remembered less as a poet than as a philosopher who wrote some pioneering essays on modernist aesthetics.

Early in 1914 Pound brought out an anthology of poetry called *Des Imagistes*. But by the time the book appeared, his interests were moving in a new direction. He was becoming associated with Vorticism, an aggressive avant-garde movement that was partly a development of Futurism and partly a reaction against it. Vorticism primarily represented the visual arts, though its leader Wyndham Lewis (1882–1957) was both a painter and a writer, and Pound was eager to supply a literary dimension to Vorticism. Lewis was a man of bewilderingly various talents. He wrote fiction and polemical essays, and occasional verse and drama. As a painter he produced between 1912 and 1914 abstract paintings and designs that were very advanced for their time, though many of them are now lost. His writing was equally original, for he brought a painter's eye to whatever he described. Lewis's early writings included a series of short stories about Breton peasants, later revised and collected as *The Wild Body* (1927), a proto-Becketesque play, *The Enemy of the Stars* (1932, revised), and a novel set in pre-war Paris Bohemia, *Tarr* (1918). His prose is abrasive, angular, and not always easy to read, but it is a magnificent medium for defamiliarizing the habitual. Lewis saw life as a black Jonsonian farce, where people customarily act like puppets. The figures in his early writing lack interior lives and simply go through a series of behaviouristic motions. In his later novels, such as *The Revenge for Love* (1937) and *Self Condemned* (1954), his vision mellowed considerably, but his early works have a peculiar hard brilliance; his comic vision is bleak but bracing. Lewis was a man of difficult temperament, intensely paranoid, and a holder of strongly reactionary opinions. But he was some kind of genius. T. S. Eliot once described him as combining the energy of the savage with the mind of a civilized man, which gives a good impression of his contradictory qualities.

In the early summer of 1914 Pound and Lewis collaborated in the production of *Blast*, a large magazine of Vorticist writings and designs, containing a manifesto based on a Futurist original, which aimed 'blasts' at a wide range of Victorian and Edwardian survivals, and 'blessings' at the Vorticists and

1

BLAST First (from politeness) **ENGLAND**

CURSE ITS CLIMATE FOR ITS SINS AND INFECTIONS

DISMAL SYMBOL, SET round our bodies,
of effeminate lout within.
VICTORIAN VAMPIRE, the **LONDON** cloud sucks
the **TOWN'S** heart.

A 1000 MILE LONG, 2 KILOMETER Deep

BODY OF WATER even, is pushed against us
from the Floridas, **TO MAKE US MILD.**

OFFICIOUS MOUNTAINS keep back **DRASTIC WINDS**

SO MUCH VAST MACHINERY TO PRODUCE

THE CURATE of "Eltham"
BRITANNIC ÆSTHETE
WILD NATURE CRANK
DOMESTICATED
POLICEMAN
LONDON COLISEUM
SOCIALIST-PLAYWRIGHT
DALY'S MUSICAL COMEDY
GAIETY CHORUS GIRL
TONKS

11

THE FIRST PAGE OF *BLAST*, No. 1, 1914. *Blast* was a polemical proto-modernist magazine, which attacked English complacency and the Victorian state of mind. It was launched by Wyndham Lewis, who was a major innovator as both artist and writer.

their friends. Its vigorously iconoclastic spirit is still attractive, but as we look at *Blast* we inevitably recall that only a few weeks after it appeared the First World War broke out, and the blasting of civilization began in earnest. With a strange irony *Blast* included reproductions of designs by Lewis called 'Plan of War' and 'Slow Attack'. (Later he became an official war artist.) Vorticism was a promising but short-lived creative moment in English modernist culture that was shortly dispersed by war; the second and last number of *Blast* came out in 1915, and included the first poems of T. S. Eliot to be published in England.

When war came on 4 August 1914 the nation was plunged into patriotic fervour, though few people foresaw the long and destructive conflict that lay ahead. It was the received wisdom of the time that a long war was economically impossible and many people expected it to be over by Christmas. The seventy-year-old Henry James took a broader and deeper view; he saw the war as an absolute disaster, and the decisive end of an era of civilization. On 5 August 1914 he wrote to a friend:

The plunge of civilization into this abyss of blood and darkness by the wanton feat of those two infamous autocrats is a thing that so gives away the whole long age during which we have supposed the world to be, with whatever abatement, gradually bettering, that to have to take it all now for what the treacherous years were all the while really making for and *meaning* is too tragic for any words.

Ezra Pound, as an American and a neutral, took a detached view of the prevailing emotions and tried to preserve his commitment to literature and art. For him the exciting event of the early autumn of 1914 was a visit from a young American, T. S. Eliot (1888–1965), who had come to England from Harvard to do a year's postgraduate work in philosophy at Oxford. Eliot sent him some unpublished poems written several years before, and Pound at once recognized their extraordinary quality, particularly of 'The Love Song of J. Alfred Prufrock', which is one of the first major texts of distinctively modern poetry in English. He wrote to an editor in America: 'He has sent me the best poem that I have yet had or seen from an American.' What most impressed Pound was that Eliot, following his own path, was writing the kind of poetry that Pound had long advocated; Eliot, he wrote, had 'actually trained himself *and* modernized himself *on his own*'.

War and its Aftermath

The First World War, or the Great War as it used to be called, is rightly thought of as bringing cataclysmic changes in life and thought and social forms. Yet in acknowledging these transformations we must remember that revolutionary innovations, particularly in technology, already existed in 1914. The motor car, the aeroplane, the cinema, the telephone, the principles of radio,

DESIGNS BY WYNDHAM LEWIS. (*left*) *Slow Attack* was reproduced in *Blast*, No. 1, just before the outbreak of the First World War. (*below*) *Attack* is a product of Lewis's later work as a war artist.

were quite familiar, though the war greatly speeded their development. Similarly, many of the most radical manifestations of modernism in the arts belong to the immediate pre-war era.

In English literature we need to distinguish between the writing, most often poetry, which directly expresses the personal experiences of the young men who went to war; and the major work by the emerging modernist writers which was published during the war years. The latter was not directly concerned with the war, but represented the continuation and fruition of tendencies from before the war. At the same time the war's presence was increasingly felt, if in oblique or indirect ways, in accentuating the existing modernist sense of crisis and severance with the past.

As Paul Fussell has shown, it was a very literary war. The British nation had achieved a high degree of literacy and before the development of radio and television all mass communication was via the printed page. People read widely and the classics of English literature were in general circulation. Young men of education went into the army as junior officers and, in the conditions of the Western Front, had a short expectation of life. They read poetry as a source of solace and memories of home—*The Oxford Book of English Verse* was a treasured companion—and often they wrote poetry themselves. Much of this 'war poetry' has proved ephemeral and is now of only historical interest. But the work of a few poets has survived to continuing fame and esteem, and in recent years has appeared in new selections and scholarly editions. This is more than a purely academic phenomenon, since it represents a deep continuing preoccupation with the literary witnesses and victims of that great transforming crisis in English life, seventy years after the event.

At the time the most famous of the 'war poets' was the handsome young Georgian, Rupert Brooke (1887-1915), 'the young Apollo, golden-haired' as he was described in a friend's epigram. On the outbreak of war Brooke enlisted in the navy and in the autumn of 1914 he wrote a short sequence of sonnets called '1914', expressing a sense of exalted personal and patriotic dedication (though still a good deal more restrained than many poetic effusions of the first phase of the war). In the spring of 1915, on his way to the Gallipoli campaign, Brooke died of blood-poisoning in the Eastern Mediterranean. His '1914' sonnets achieved immense posthumous fame, particularly the one beginning, 'If I should die, think only this of me'. Brooke caught the popular imagination as a victim and hero. D. H. Lawrence felt something of his mythic appeal, when he wrote: 'The death of Rupert Brooke fills me more and more with the sense of the fatuity of it all. He was slain by bright Phoebus' shaft—it was in keeping with his general sunniness—it was the real climax of his pose.'

If Rupert Brooke was once regarded as the archetypal war poet and victim, that place is now occupied by Wilfred Owen (1893-1918). He served as a young officer on the Western Front and was killed in action in November 1918, one week before the Armistice. As a poet Owen was sensuous and sensitive, Keatsian in the intensity of his responses, and in the brevity of his life, for he was only twenty-five when he was killed. Owen began as a fervent late-Romantic and he never wholly emerged from that mould. But the extremity of front-line experience subjected his poetry to an extraordinarily rapid development, a 'forcing' in the hothouse sense. His poems are preoccupied with the deaths of young men: his attitude to the soldiers in his care was compounded of the young officer's sense of premature paternal responsibility— a common motif in the poetry of the war—and a barely disguised erotic attraction. Though an early 'protest poet', Owen was also a meticulous craftsman and something of a technical innovator, notably in the development of 'pararhyme'. The war made Owen into a major poet, and it was his only real subject.

The extreme experiences undergone by Owen and other soldier poets such as Siegfried Sassoon and Edmund Blunden, strained but did not transform their poetic medium: Sassoon contributed to the Georgian anthologies and Owen said he would be proud to be counted among the Georgians. Edward Thomas (1878-1917) is another poet sometimes regarded as a Georgian, though he was not formally associated with the movement and had too individual a talent to be easily classified. He was already thirty-six when the war broke out, and an established though far from prosperous man of letters, who had written books of travel and literary criticism and studies of the English countryside. The war made Thomas into a poet, though not in the same way as Owen. During the first two years of his military service, which were spent in England, he began writing poetry, crystallizing into verse his feelings about English rural life and tradition. His poetry is not easy to summarize: it is imagistically descriptive, deeply attached to its subjects, lyrical yet restrained. The war is scarcely mentioned in Thomas's poems, but it is a brooding presence, or perhaps a palpable absence. He was killed soon after he arrived in France in 1917.

One of the most interesting victims of the war is Isaac Rosenberg (1890-1918), a Jewish private soldier from the East End of London. He had grown up in poverty, and when his talents as a painter became apparent he was financially supported by some wealthy members of the London Jewish community so that he could attend the Slade School of Art. Despite his lack of formal literary education, Rosenberg read widely, was immersed in poetry, and aspired to be a poet as well as a painter. As a poet of Jewish and urban antecedents he was remote from the gentle, rural English traditionalism of the Georgians (though a short fragment from his verse play *Moses* appeared in one of the Georgian anthologies). Rosenberg's main source of inspiration was Jewish history and legend; and the fact that he was a painter was also an important influence. His poetry was as much symbolic as descriptive. One senses in Rosenberg something of the modernist wish to renovate poetic form,

which again sets him apart from the other war poets. His poetry, in fact, offers an approximate equivalent to the work of the European Expressionist painters: it is energetic, dense, even clotted in verbal texture, emotional and yet somewhat detached in its presentation of its subject. 'Louse Hunters' is a strong painterly rendering of naked soldiers killing lice in their clothes, one of the more down-to-earth aspects of life at the Front. If Owen was consumed by the pity of war, Rosenberg saw the war as an overwhelming, inexplicable, but fascinating spectacle. His 'Break of Day in the Trenches' seems to me not only Rosenberg's finest poem, but one of the finest of all war poems. He is Owen's only rival; if the war was Owen's overwhelming subject in poetry, for Rosenberg it was a topic to be mastered and transcended.

A common theme of the poetry written by serving soldiers was a deep alienation between the fighting man and the civilian, the world of the trenches and the careless, comfortable life of England, only a few hours' journey away by boat and train. In a late poem Owen expressed the feeling that all that was best in England had fled to France, to be buried on the battlefields.

Yet senior and established writers did not ignore the war; they wrote

WAR AND THE ARTIST. (*far left*) *La Mitrailleuse* by the English Futurist painter, C. R. W. Nevinson (1915). This painting of a French machine-gun post emphasizes the mechanized inhumanity of the steel helmet and the gun. (*left*) Isaac Rosenberg's self-portrait in a steel helmet of *c*.1916 presents a more human face.

government propaganda, and some of them visited the Front. H. G. Wells's novel of 1916, *Mr. Britling Sees It Through*, was immensely popular at the time; strongly autobiographical, like most of Wells's later fiction, it presented the disrupting effect of the war on the life of a middle-aged writer and his family and friends. It seemed to sum up the wartime experiences and emotions of many English people not directly involved in fighting; though not outstanding as a novel, it remains an important document of contemporary consciousness. Bernard Shaw's play *Heartbreak House* (1919) is a Chekhovian study of the decline of an upper-class English family, with the war in the background. Shaw uses the family as a metaphor for the breakdown of established values and attitudes, and the play has a melancholy, poetic quality unusual in the brisk, iconoclastic Shaw. The play ends with an air raid and falling bombs.

Ford Madox Ford's (1873–1939) novel *The Good Soldier* (1915) provides an interesting instance of the pre-war sense of crisis. On his fortieth birthday in 1913 he sat down to write a novel that would be an uncompromising work of art. The result was a small masterpiece of aesthetic concentration, 'the finest French novel in English', as a critic described it. The form of the novel is arresting, particularly the fluid treatment of time, suggesting the randomness of memory rather than the fixed forward order of traditional narratives. Yet the artistic force of the novel is involved with specific historical circumstances. Though there are only four major characters, two upper-class couples caught up in an adulterous entanglement that drags on over several years, the book has a representative quality, expressing Ford's conviction that the opulent, arrogant social order of late Victorian and Edwardian England was irredeemably doomed. The book was finished in the summer of 1914, and the opening section appeared in *Blast* under Ford's original title of *The Saddest Story*. After the outbreak of war his publisher complained that such a title sounded too depressing for wartime; Ford sarcastically retorted that the book could be called *The Good Soldier* and was taken at his word. A similar piece of opportunism affected D. H. Lawrence's (1885–1930) first collection of short stories, which was published late in 1914 as *The Prussian Officer*, rather than *Honour and Arms*, his intended title.

In the development of literary modernism 1915 was a significant year for fiction. It saw the publication of *The Good Soldier*; Virginia Woolf's first novel, *The Voyage Out*; and D. H. Lawrence's *The Rainbow*. This is one of Lawrence's greatest works, though it was not well received at the time and was even the object of a trumped-up legal charge of obscenity. (Lawrence, whose wife was German and proud of it, was subject to a good deal of petty persecution during the war.) In structure *The Rainbow* is a 'generations' novel, which follows the fortunes of three generations of a Nottinghamshire family, the Brangwens, during the second half of the nineteenth century. But in spirit it is far removed from the solid characterization and substantial settings of the 'classic realist text': it is epic rather than conventionally novelistic, poetic, symbolic, and ultimately mythic, though the life and landscape of Lawrence's native East Midlands are never wholly lost sight of. *The Rainbow* is the first part of a much longer novel that Lawrence had been planning since 1913. Although he wrote the final draft of *The Rainbow* during the first winter of the war its spirit is still positive and optimistic, inspired by Lawrence's ideal of an organic, unified English culture. It concludes with the overarching rainbow, as a hopeful biblical sign of transformed human life.

In *Women in Love* (1920), which was intended as a continuation of *The Rainbow*, Lawrence carries on the story of his two central characters, Ursula and Gudrun Brangwen. But *Women in Love* is not at all a conventional sequel. In the earlier novel Ursula had been the vehicle for Lawrence's own experiences and attitudes; but in *Women in Love* Rupert Birkin takes over the authorial consciousness. *Women in Love* invites comparison with *The Good Soldier*. In most respects Ford's and Lawrence's novels are very unlike each other; nevertheless, in both works the interaction of two couples comes to have a socially and historically representative quality. Sexuality, and its place in supposedly emancipated human relations, is one of Lawrence's major themes; others are industrialism and art, as respectively exemplified by the negative figures of the coal-owner, Gerald Crich, and the artist, Loerke. Instead of the epic and biblical sweep of *The Rainbow*, *Women in Love* presents a sequence of abrupt, discontinuous episodes and close-ups. Lawrence wrote *Women in Love* during the later part of the war, in poverty and isolation in Cornwall, and in deep bitterness of spirit. As has been observed, the war deepened Lawrence's existing tendency to see the world in polar opposites, by presenting the whole of reality in stark oppositions: friend or enemy, kill or be killed. *Women in Love* is pervaded by such polarities, and Paul Delaney describes it

D. H. LAWRENCE IN 1914. A photograph taken soon after he had grown his beard. He wrote at the time, 'I've grown a red beard, behind which I shall take as much cover henceforth as I can, like a creature under a bush.'

as a remarkable example of a 'war novel' that does not mention the war. Wells and Forster and Ford had shown a social order in crisis; in *Women in Love* things are actually falling apart. It is one of the masterpieces of modern English fiction, of a hard, unconsoling kind.

For many British readers Lawrence is the greatest novelist of the century; this, certainly, was the influential conviction of F. R. Leavis. But globally, both in the English-speaking world and beyond it, that title would be seen as belonging to James Joyce (1882–1941). It is difficult, perhaps impossible, to admire Lawrence and Joyce equally. Lawrence hated art that kept its distance from humanity; in a central line of English Romanticism, he wanted literature to enlarge and extend human sympathies, to make people more fully alive to themselves and each other. And with this end in view, he was never afraid to preach. Joyce's literary origins were in the main continental movements of the late nineteenth century, Naturalism and Symbolism. From the one he took the conviction that literature ought to present, relentlessly and exactly, the minute appearances of things, however banal or distasteful; from the other, the idea that the word and the world are separate, and that language ultimately offers not a representation of reality but reality itself. In the tradition of Flaubert, Joyce believed that life was one thing and art was another, and that it was the business of the writer to impose form and order on the chaos of raw experience.

In 1916 Joyce published his first novel, *A Portrait of the Artist as a Young Man*. It was possible to read it as a straightforward autobiographical novel of an Irish Catholic boyhood and adolescence, which is how H. G. Wells responded to the book in an enthusiastic review. Yet though most things in the book have some correspondence with the events of Joyce's own life, it is quite unlike the conventional autobiographical novel of a young man growing up, of which Lawrence's *Sons and Lovers* had been a distinguished instance. All the nouns in the title of Joyce's novel deserve equal attention: if it is about a young man, it is specifically the young man as *artist*, and it is a *portrait*, which is to say, a distanced, selective, framed treatment of its subject. From the book's opening words its concern with language is evident: 'Once upon a time and a very good time it was there was a moocow coming down along the road and this moocow that was coming down along the road met a nicens little boy named baby tuckoo . . .' The language of the fairy-tale and baby talk are drawn on not just to describe but to enact the infant consciousness of the central figure, Stephen Dedalus. The name 'Dedalus' is not Irish and would have been unusual in Dublin, and thus represents a fracturing of realistic convention, which is usually concerned with the typical and the plausible. The name refers to the mythical Greek craftsman and designer, who is invoked in the novel's epigraph from Ovid's *Metamorphoses*; he made wings to escape from his enforced imprisonment in the Cretan labyrinth, which he had designed. For Joyce, the winged Dedalus was an image of the artist, and the word 'flight' is a key motif in the novel. Near the end, Stephen resolves to fly from the constraints of the religion and language and nationality of his native Ireland. Present-day readers of *A Portrait of the Artist* still find the book a truthful account of growing up, and easily identify with Stephen, high-minded prig though he appears to be (just how far Joyce wanted to ironize him is a matter for critical debate). At the same time, the novel's importance as an innovatory modernist text is hard to exaggerate. To take only one instance, the juxtaposition of classical myth and the modern world was to be extended and developed by Joyce in *Ulysses* and by Eliot in *The Waste Land*.

Ezra Pound, in his valuable role as literary impresario, was largely responsible for the publication of Joyce's *Portrait* in 1916 and T. S. Eliot's first slender collection of poems, *Prufrock and Other Observations* in 1917. As a poet himself Pound was productive during the war years. In 1915 he published a group of poems called *Cathay*, one of his most beautiful achievements in poetry. The poems are loosely based on ancient Chinese originals and exemplify Pound's conviction that translation and adaptation are essential aspects of the poet's craft. *Cathay* seems very remote from wartime London, but as Hugh

Kenner has pointed out, its concern with partings and men exiled from home and the rumours of distant wars, means that it is an authentic if oblique form of 'war poetry'. A little later Pound made another indirect treatment of the contemporary historical situation in *Homage to Sextus Propertius*, where the Rome of Propertius offers an analogue to the wartime crisis of the British Empire. The war is brought closer in Pound's *Hugh Selwyn Mauberley* (1920), a sequence of short, intensely ironic poems exploring the consciousness of a minor poet called 'Mauberley', a survivor of the 1890s who has something in common with Pound himself. In the course of the poem he dwells on the human cost of the war, 'Daring as never before, wastage as never before', with so many young men killed or maimed in the supposed cause of civilization, 'For an old bitch gone in the teeth'.

Most of the poems in T. S. Eliot's first collection had been written before the war. As Pound rightly saw, this work, and particularly 'The Love Song of J. Alfred Prufrock', had established modern poetry in English. 'Prufrock' is ironic, discontinuous, imagistic, frequently dissonant, and yet overall intensely musical and memorable. The 'character' of J. Alfred Prufrock himself—though he is not so much a character as a floating consciousness—has become the social archetype of a not-so-young man who is fastidious, timorous, and yet also relentlessly observant and self-aware. E. M. Forster came upon Eliot's early poetry in wartime Egypt and responded with pleasure: 'Here was a protest and a feeble one, and the more congenial for being feeble. For what, in that world of gigantic horror, was tolerable except the slighter gestures of dissent? . . . he who could turn aside to complain of ladies and drawing-rooms preserved a tiny drop of our self-respect, he carried on the human heritage.'

On the outbreak of war W. B. Yeats was nearly fifty, a well-established poet and dramatist. As an Irishman he felt detached from the European conflict, and something of that detachment inspires his fine short lyric, 'An Irish Airman Foresees His Death'. The airman, drawn by 'a lonely impulse of delight', to serve in a cause that is not his, is poised, literally and figuratively, above the struggle. In 1916 there occurred the Easter Rising when armed bands of Irish nationalists proclaimed a republic, and occupied the central Post Office in Dublin and other parts of the city, holding out against the British troops for several days. After the collapse of the Rising several of its leaders were executed. This tragic event deeply affected Yeats, who felt he might have had some responsibility for it because of his earlier work in arousing Irish national consciousness, and he commemorated it in one of his greatest poems, 'Easter 1916'. In this poem, which is political without being propagandist, Yeats fuses the public and personal; the language is direct, ballad-like in places, but the central symbols of sacrifice and regeneration are complex. By then Yeats had developed far beyond the delicate reveries of the Celtic Twilight. After the end of the European War Ireland underwent first a war of independence against the British, and then, after the establishment of the Free State in 1922, a bloody

LONDON BRIDGE (*above*) AND THE MARTELLO TOWER AT SANDYCOVE, NEAR DUBLIN (*below*): places of importance in the great modernist texts of 1922, *The Waste Land* and *Ulysses*. The photograph of London Bridge, over which in the poem flowed a crowd, 'so many, I had not thought death had undone so many', shows the church of St Magnus Martyr, standing prominently in the background.

civil war between supporters and opponents of the settlement. In the great poetry that he wrote during those events and their aftermath, Yeats, with superb authority and power, made a new unity out of the several strands of his art: the personal, the symbolic, and the historical. 'Prayer for my daughter', 'Meditations in Time of Civil War', and 'Among Schoolchildren' are three celebrated instances.

During the 1920s the modernism which was developing during the previous decade came to final maturity. The year 1922 was the *annus mirabilis*; it saw the appearance of a novel, *Ulysses*, and a poem, *The Waste Land*, which came in time to be seen as two of the major texts of twentieth-century literature, and which had an incalculable effect on the writing that followed them. Discussing *Ulysses* in 1923 Eliot wrote:

In using the myth, in manipulating a continuous parallel between contemporaneity and antiquity, Mr. Joyce is pursuing a method which others must pursue after him . . . It is simply a way of controlling, of ordering, of giving a shape and a significance to the immense panorama of futility and anarchy which is contemporary history. It is a method already adumbrated by Mr. Yeats, and of the need for which I believe Mr. Yeats to have been the first contemporary to be conscious . . . Psychology (such as it is, and whether our reaction to it be comic or serious), ethnology, *The Golden Bough* have concurred to make possible what was impossible even a few years ago. Instead of narrative method we may now use the mythical method.

What Eliot says is true not only of Joyce and Yeats; it applies, also, to D. H. Lawrence, who had no time for Joyce or Eliot. And it is pre-eminently true of Eliot's own practice in *The Waste Land*. Both *Ulysses* and *The Waste Land* take as their starting-point life in a twentieth-century city: Dublin in 1904 and London in about 1921. *Ulysses* was originally conceived as a short story, and for all its elaboration the basic situation is simple: we follow the lives of three lower-middle-class Dubliners during the course of one day, 16 June 1904; they are Leopold Bloom, his unfaithful wife, Molly, and the young poet Stephen Dedalus, who is a more mature and distanced figure than the persona of the young Joyce who had dominated *A Portrait of the Artist as a Young Man*. From the basic human situation Joyce moves into ramifying patterns of Homeric legend, multiple symbolism, and a carnival of linguistic variety. *Ulysses* offers an elaborate, not always easily discernible interface between the fiction of ultra-realism and the self-reflective text, or the tradition of Zola and the tradition of Mallarmé. Critics have been interpreting and reinterpreting *Ulysses* for over sixty years, though in the course of academic debate one of the book's most important aspects has been often overlooked; it is, apart from anything else, a great comic novel.

Leopold Bloom walks the streets of Dublin. Underlying *The Waste Land* is a comparable promenade of London, as the poet walks along the Strand and follows the course of the river eastward to the City and Lower Thames Street, or forms part of the crowd of commuters who flow over London Bridge and up King William Street, past the churches of St Magnus Martyr and St Mary Woolnoth. Counterpointed against contemporary London are many elements from ancient myth and folklore, drawn from *The Golden Bough*, Sir James Frazer's great anthropological compendium, which was one of Eliot's major sources in the poem. *The Waste Land* presents a vivid tapestry of the immediate and the remote, and its language abruptly juxtaposes slangy and colloquial speech with purely lyrical utterance, echoes of the Bible and Shakespeare, and phrases from other languages. Ever since it was published, *The Waste Land*

THE MUSIC HALL was vigorous popular entertainment with a broad appeal. Like many other poets, T. S. Eliot was a devotee; he particularly admired Marie Lloyd (*left*), of whom he wrote after her death that she had a capacity for expressing the soul of the people which made them not so much hilarious as happy.

has been read intently, and differently. The poem is like a kaleidoscope, since the same elements can be seen in many different ways. Once, the poem was regarded as an expression of the disillusionment of the Jazz Age, with interesting affinities with Scott Fitzgerald's *The Great Gatsby*, a novel which Eliot admired. *The Waste Land* has been read as an indictment of twentieth-century civilization, and a lament for the lost wholeness and order of the organic society. More recently, critics have been fascinated by the deeply personal elements, particularly the sexual anguish, that can be traced through the poem's supposedly 'impersonal' surface. Other readers have explored the poem's concern with religious belief, both Christian and Indian, though at that time Eliot's interest was in anthropology and comparative religion; his conversion to Anglican Christianity was some years ahead.

However one interprets it, *The Waste Land* has the capacity of great poetry constantly to renew itself and to present unsuspected aspects. It is densely literary and allusive, elegiac and wistfully erotic; it is also energetic and self-confident in its art, drawing on the minority and popular culture of its time: cubism and Stravinsky, jazz and the music-hall and the cinema. *The Waste Land* is moving; it also *moves*.

Eliot was influential as both poet and critic. In later years he remarked that his early criticism was 'workshop criticism', closely related to his poetry, and directed to training a readership that would be properly responsive to modernist literature; his essay, '*Ulysses*, Order and Myth', quoted above, shows the process at work. Eliot's first two collections of critical essays, *The Sacred Wood* (1920) and *Homage to John Dryden* (1924), were to have an effect on literary opinion far beyond the coteries at which they were first directed. The 1920s were a seminal period for literary criticism. One of Eliot's great admirers was the Cambridge academic, I. A. Richards, whose *Principles of Literary Criticism* (1924) was a pioneering work of theory. Other relevant critical texts of the twenties were the posthumous *Speculations* (1924) of T. E. Hulme and *Time and Western Man* (1927) by the maverick modernist painter and writer, Wyndham Lewis. In a more popularizing way, E. M. Forster's *Aspects of the Novel* (1927) was an example of a novelist's 'workshop criticism' which made an important contribution to the study of fictional form.

As a practising novelist Forster produced his greatest achievement, *A Passage to India*, in 1924; it was also his last novel. *A Passage to India* is a triumph of aesthetic concentration and the balance of parts against whole; it is also, of course, an enduring fictional analysis of the effect of colonialism on rulers and ruled. In 1919 Forster's friend Virginia Woolf (1882–1941) published an essay called 'Modern Fiction', which attacked the conventions of traditional realism, and has become a significant text in modernist criticism. Virginia Woolf's best novel is perhaps *To the Lighthouse*, which appeared in 1927. It shows how, in major modernist fiction, the novel not only approaches poetry, but in a certain sense becomes it. *To the Lighthouse* is set in a holiday house party in the vanished pre-1914 world. It has its basis in the personal experiences of Virginia Woolf and her family and friends (though transposed, a little improbably, from Cornwall to Skye), and particularly in her memories of her father, the eminent Victorian, Leslie Stephen. But these sources are transmuted, with great deliberation, into metaphor and symbol; like other modernist texts, *To the Lighthouse* is much concerned with the nature of art and artistic creation, exemplified in the novel by the painter Lily Briscoe, whose art is clearly meant to be a metaphor for Virginia Woolf's own.

In much writing of the twenties the Great War exists as a pervasive memory, or, with books set in pre-war days, a presentiment of things to come, or a deep fissure in recent historical experience, as it is, for instance, in Thomas Mann's *The Magic Mountain*. Virginia Woolf was far more concerned with personal than with public matters; even so, memories of war left their mark on her fiction of the twenties, in such incidents as the suicide of the shell-shocked survivor Septimus Warren Smith in *Mrs. Dalloway* (1925). In *To the Lighthouse* the war, though it occurs only in a potent parenthetical reference in the 'Time Passes' section, violently removes some of the characters and imposes an absolute break between the opening and closing sections of the novel. Aldous Huxley (1894–1963) is a lesser novelist, who was once widely admired as the essential voice of the twenties. If that reputation has not worn particularly well, his early novels remain admirably light-hearted, witty, and readable, though by *Point Counter Point* in 1928 Huxley's heavily didactic and portentous manner was beginning to affect his fiction adversely. The earlier *Antic Hay* (1923), which expresses the hedonistic relief of the immediate post-war years, is altogether preferable. We see Huxley's characters, partly smart, partly Bohemian, gaily pursuing pleasure and trying to forget the four years of privation and bloodshed. Even so, they cannot be forgotten; Myra Viveash, a bored society beauty, is haunted by her love for Tony Lamb, killed in France in 1917, while she moves from one meaningless affair to another. In 1930 D. H. Lawrence died, and his death marks the conclusion of the major phase of modernism; in 1928, he had published his last novel, *Lady Chatterley's Lover*. Once banned and notorious, it is in fact a gentle, elegiac, lyrical work, where Lawrence finally worked out his ideas about how life should be lived, though the result is a simple moral fable rather than a novel of much complexity. The war casts a shadow, or perhaps a skeleton, in the person of the crippled ex-officer, Sir Clifford Chatterley, the last of Lawrence's various embodiments of negative will and destructive attitudes to life.

Meanwhile, those writers who had fought in the war and been fortunate enough to survive were going back to it in memory and imagination. One of the first to do so was Ford Madox Ford, who had served as a middle-aged subaltern and been gassed. His long novel, *Parade's End*, published in several volumes from 1924 onwards, is the finest fictional re-creation of the war by an English writer, and Ford's second masterpiece of twentieth-century fiction;

VIRGINIA WOOLF. An informal snapshot taken by Lady Ottoline Morrell at Garsington (1923/4), showing Virginia Woolf poised between relaxation and nervousness.

where *The Good Soldier* was intensive, *Parade's End* is expansive. Like other writers before him, particularly in the immediate pre-war period, Ford presents a historical view of a social order at the point of dissolution. His hero, Christopher Tietjens, is Ford's romanticized version of a representative type, the vanishing High Tory, a country gentleman of impossibly high ideals and saintly temperament, who serves in the war with distinction and is victimized by the unworthy representatives of the modern world who surround him.

By the end of the decade there had been many literary re-creations of the war, ranging from straightforward autobiography and memoir, such as Edmund Blunden's *Undertones of War* and Robert Graves's *Goodbye to All That*, and fictionalized autobiography, such as Siegfried Sassoon's *Memoirs of a Fox-Hunting Man* and *Memoirs of an Infantry Officer*, to novels with a strong autobiographical content, such as Richard Aldington's *Death of a Hero* and Frederic Manning's *Her Privates We*. In about 1927 the painter and designer David Jones, who had served as a private soldier in the Welch Regiment, turned to writing and began to collect and order his memories of war. The resulting work *In Parenthesis* did not appear until 1937. It is one of the most distinguished of war books, a combination of verse and prose, a dense, allusive work of high modernist art, much influenced by Eliot and Joyce, where memories of the Front Line in 1916 are mingled with elements from Catholic liturgy and Welsh mythology, and where the experience of war is presented as both transcendent and recurrent. But by the time *In Parenthesis* appeared memories of one war were beginning to be displaced by fears of a new one.

9. Mid-Twentieth-Century Literature

1930–1980

MARTIN DODSWORTH

The Thirties: 'All the Fun'

THE thirties felt, and feel, different from the twenties. It is not merely that already in 1930 the foundations were being laid for the Second World War. The rise to power in Germany of Hitler and the Nazi Party were cause for increasing anxiety, but anxiety is not the sole characteristic of the decade. There went with it a sense of release that at last the worst could be imagined, and beyond it something better. 'Today the struggle', wrote Auden in his stirring poem on behalf of the Spanish republicans, putting off to tomorrow the pleasures very much in his mind at that moment:

> Tomorrow the rediscovery of romantic love;
> The photographing of ravens; all the fun under
> . Liberty's masterful shadow . . .

It is 'all the fun' potential in human life that makes the struggle worthwhile. Sometimes it seems that the struggle is fun in itself.

For most writers and intellectuals in the thirties, the struggle was that for a juster society, and in its international aspect it was a fight against Fascism. This was a highly political decade. The general strike of 1926 and the ensuing depression resulted in a temporary loss of confidence in the Labour Party as far as the country as a whole was concerned—since the end of the war the socialists had made great strides in the quest for public support, had indeed formed their first government in 1924, but suffered heavy losses in the election of 1931—but the new generation of writers was almost entirely committed to the Left. Throughout the decade the Communist Party proselytized in the name of international socialism with success; many of the writers to be mentioned in this first section joined the Party for a while, though few were to remain committed. The Moscow show trials of 1936-8, the defeat of the republican cause in Spain, and especially the non-aggression pact entered into between Soviet Russia and Nazi Germany in 1939 were powerful antidotes to the political enthusiasm at the beginning of the decade. That they were so is perhaps an indication of the extent to which many writers had merely flirted with a dangerous politics whose charm had lain in its very danger. Political commitment in the duller and more sober years following the Second World War becomes hard to find, in literature at least.

The thirties fascination with politics was an aspect of its youth. Especially in literature this was a time for the young. The reason is not far to seek. The

WAR MEMORIAL IN LIVERPOOL. 'We young writers of the middle twenties were all suffering, more or less subconsciously, from a feeling of shame that we hadn't been old enough to take part in the European war' (Christopher Isherwood).

VAUDEVILLE
THEATRE, STRAND, W.C.

Lessees & Managers
A. & S. GATTI
Vaudeville Theatre, Strand, W.C.

BERNARD SHAW'S
GREAT CATHERINE

POSTER for a Shaw play, showing the author as a demon king in Russian costume.

IMAGINING THE WAR TO COME, even after the air-raids of the Spanish Civil War, was not easy. Edward Burra's *War in the Sun* (1938) combines the thirties fascination by the machine with forties fantasy in a picture of war that is both dramatic and equivocal.

ROMANTIC JOY, ROMANTIC GLOOM: the forties move away from irony is evident in these two pictures by Eric Ravilious (*c*.1940). His 'Barrage Balloons outside a British Port' would delight a child, and the little tug-boat too; 'Room 29, Home Security Control Room', its single woman hard at work, revises Coleridge's thoughtful solitude in 'Frost at Midnight'.

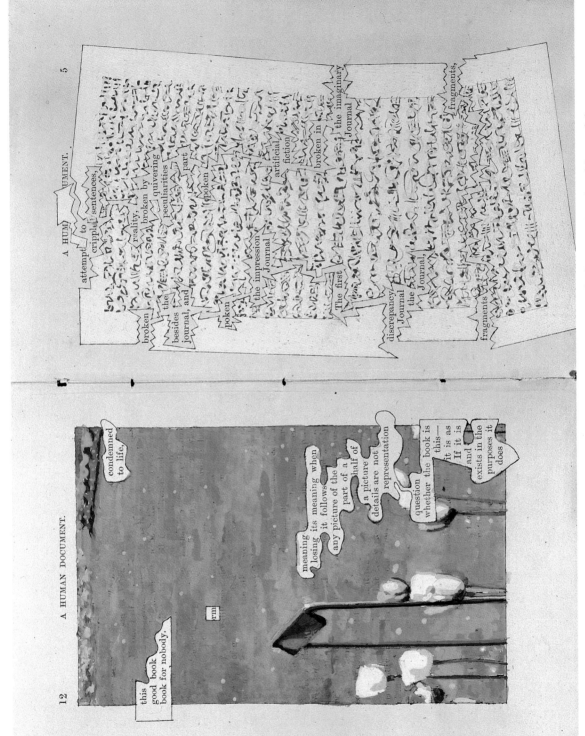

PAGES FROM TOM PHILLIPS'S *A HUMENT* (1980) illustrate not only the aggressive cheerfulness of the later modernism in the visual arts but also the pathetic vulnerability of the printed word.

twenties present the image of a powerfully assured modern literature. Eliot, Joyce, Pound, Lawrence, a refashioned Yeats, stand for the best in the writing of that decade. But Eliot was the only one of these who lived in England itself; and since he had declared himself in 1928 'classicist in literature, royalist in politics and anglo-catholic in religion' he had lost his attraction as a model for the young, though without ceasing to command a more or less qualified respect from them. Joyce's work in progress, like Pound's, was idiosyncratic, fragmentary as yet, and caviare to the intellectual general. Lawrence had died in 1930, his last years' work marred by signs of haste and sickness; his exile had been intellectual as well as physical. Yeats had yet to be recognized as, in his greatest poems, untrammelled by his unorthodox speculations in the spirit-world. The First World War was producing its harvest of memoirs and autobiographical fiction, but its survivors for the most part lived in their past. It was time for the empty citadel of literature to be taken once again. W. H. Auden (1907-73), whose first generally published book *Poems* appeared in 1930 itself, could have taken it single-handed.

His poems of the thirties present powerful versions of the emotion of simultaneous dread and joy that is the mark of the decade. At this time his poems evoke a world of frontiers to be crossed, messages to be delivered, guards to be evaded, and loyalties to be affirmed:

> Control of the passes was, he saw, the key
> To this new district, but who would get it?
> He, the trained spy, had walked into the trap
> For a bogus guide, seduced by the old tricks.
>
> ('The Secret Agent')

We might be in the world of an old-fashioned writer of adventure stories like those of John Buchan (1875-1940) whose heroes, clean-living and athletic public-school men, save England and the Empire from dastardly foreigners in the Highlands of Scotland or the deserts of Asia. But Auden hated his public school, and the loyalties that he affirms are those of the rebels who seek to bring a better life out of the decaying industrial landscape he described so well:

> If we really want to live, we'd better start at once to try;
> If we don't it doesn't matter, but we'd better start to die.
>
> ('Get there if you can . . .')

Auden's poetry was not felt to be conventionally beautiful, but challenging. Its idiom was assiduously modern, even slangy ('Lawrence was brought down by smut-hounds, Blake went *dotty* as he sang'), its characterization economical, even enigmatic, but memorable:

> The old gang to be forgotten in the spring,
> The hard bitch and the riding master
> Stiff underground . . .
>
> ('1929')

W. H. AUDEN, CHRISTOPHER ISHERWOOD, AND STEPHEN SPENDER show the acceptable side of revolution in the thirties. Spender wrote later that if poets of the time seemed to address their work to anyone in particular, it was 'to sixth-formers from their old schools and to one another'.

Under cover of this unconventional technique, the romanticism of his poetry, its sense of love as fated and inevitably failing, of the struggle as necessary but unfulfilling for its participants, *felt* new, and for that reason *was* new.

> Another I, another You,
> Each knowing what to do
> But of no use.
>
>   ('Never Stronger')

The glamour is akin to that of the Byronic hero, but this Byronic hero is thoroughly a child of the twentieth century, with more to know (Freud, Marx) and a greater strength in disillusion.

Auden's poems of the thirties purvey a potent myth. He was a prolific writer, adept in many forms, always surprising. No wonder his dominion in his own generation went unquestioned. Perhaps the best poems are unassuming lyrics like 'That night when joy began' and 'Seen when nights are silent', but everything he writes invites the reader—romantic ballads, comic ballads, the marvellous early 'charade' *Paid on Both Sides*, which combines English pantomime and Icelandic saga in a modern setting, chaotic plays (with Christopher Isherwood) such as *The Ascent of F6*, one of the best of English travel books (with Louis MacNeice), *Letters from Iceland*. The spirit of fun, the spirit of doom intermingle in these works in a way none of his contemporaries could equal.

There are three poets whose work is especially associated with his. Louis MacNeice (1907–63) born in Belfast, educated in England, at first a university teacher of classics, later employed by the BBC, is the best of them, high-spirited and acerbic in his early poems, urbane, almost Horatian in the last ones, but wordy and portentous in his middle patch. His *Autumn Journal* (1939) is soaked in the atmosphere of the Munich year but is over-extended. Its melancholy smacks of self-indulgence. Stephen Spender (b. 1909) wrote a poetry of Shelleyan exuberance and naïvety, never quite capturing the authentically modern idiom of Auden. He is, in fact, a better critic than poet. C. Day-Lewis (1904–72) has most the air of a hanger-on; his poems, far too often hortatory in tone, always sound as if they are being modelled on someone else's. He ended up, incongruously, but not uncharacteristically for a thirties revolutionary, as Poet Laureate.

Auden, MacNeice, Spender, and Day-Lewis were all educated at Oxford; they belonged to the same privileged class, and throve on the sense of complicity in their opposition to the 'old gang'. Not infrequently they wrote for each other, and their poems are littered with allusions to personal circumstance that can never have been easy for the outsider to decipher. They were the new gang, and part of the fascination of their poetry lies in its speaking for a group, a movement, in a new way.

Not everybody felt drawn to the Auden party, and indeed one way and another things had gone sour with it by the time war broke in 1939. About that time William Empson wrote his genial gibe 'Just a Smack at Auden':

> Waiting for the end, boys, waiting for the end,
> What is there to be or do?
> What's become of me or you?
> Are we kind or are we true?
> Sitting two and two, boys, waiting for the end.

WILLIAM EMPSON, a photograph suggesting both the genial English eccentric and the Confucian sage (Empson taught for several years in China).

This hits off the cosy quality of their writing, as well as the sense of doom that in the end predominated, leading Auden to describe the thirties (in his poem 'September 1, 1939') as 'a low dishonest decade', as though it had not been, in its way, his decade especially.

The poetic career of William Empson (1906-84) was virtually confined to the thirties. He published only two books of verse, and they have yet to receive their due from readers. They represent the Cambridge opposition to the successful Oxford school, and, whilst poetry of the Auden kind was written in covert reaction to Eliot's breaking of forms, Empson's derives from one strand in the older poet's critical thinking, his revaluation of the Metaphysical poets. It is a poetry of compacted paradox, whose lines menace the reader with the sense of meaning held in, under pressure: 'Matter includes what must matter enclose'; 'Law makes long spokes of the short stakes of men'; 'Lose is Find with great marsh lights like you.'

Empson's poems lack at first the overt political reference of Auden's, and then are felt to grapple with issues like the arms race and the national sense of crisis rather than to cut through them, as Auden often attempts. But even Empson's early love poems manage to imply the contemporary world as did Donne's, especially in its sense of what relativity has done for our conception of the universe, which parallels Donne's fascination with the spheres and their supposed angelic rulers.

His reputation as an intellectual poet is justified, but is not the whole story. His poetry abounds in direct and musical lines, capable of much explanatory comment, but hardly needing it: 'The waste remains, the waste remains and kills'; 'The heart of standing is you cannot fly'; and (imagining travel through space faster than the speed of light):

> Who moves so among stars their frame unties;
> See where they blur, and die, and are outsoared.
>
> ('Camping Out')

Empson was better known as a critic than as a poet. *Seven Types of Ambiguity* (1930) was published when he was only twenty-four. His poems demonstrate what Eliot meant when he said that 'when a poet's mind is perfectly equipped for its work, it is constantly amalgamating human experience'; his criticism sets out to show by a detailed study of meaning how this could be the case. This stress on meaning leads Empson to emphasize the power of poetry to develop arguments, but in Empson's formulations they are invariably complex and suffused with local circumstance. Empson's work as a critic set up difficult standards for the contemporary writer to meet.

So did that of another writer, the academic F. R. Leavis (1895–1978), another Cambridge man and heavily influenced by Eliot's criticism, though in later life he came to qualify his judgements on Eliot in favour of D. H. Lawrence to the recognition of whose genius in a time of relative neglect, the late forties, he made a great contribution. Leavis is a critic in the tradition of Johnson and Arnold; the criteria for judgement have to do with the critic's understanding of what is to be valued in life itself. He looked for 'maturity' of response in a writer, a quality not to be given categorical definition, but nevertheless recognizable by the reader in terms of his own search for the same quality. This high seriousness is to be admired. Through his influential journal *Scrutiny* (1932–53) Leavis's judgements on literature were widely disseminated. He was sceptical about the poetry of Auden, refusing to be charmed by its boyish qualities—this was not merely the response of a Cambridge critic to an Oxford poet. Leavis's prose, a brilliant extension of the style of Jamesian qualification in the interests of decisive acerbity, was, like Empson's (quick-witted, informal, and funny), a distinguished literary achievement, and his brilliantly cruel attack on the novelist-technocrat C. P. Snow, *Two Cultures?: The Significance of C. P. Snow* (1962), will, when the force of its violent personalities has abated, be recognized as the finest English polemic of the century.

F. R. LEAVIS, teacher and preacher on behalf of a classless élite, enemy of Bloomsbury and the London literary world.

Neither Empson nor Leavis, however, writes what one would instinctively call 'thirties prose'. For that one must turn to the novels of Christopher Isherwood (1904-85), the most famous of which is *Goodbye to Berlin* (1939), based on the author's own experience during the Nazi rise to power in Germany. Its narrator offers this characterization:

I am a camera with its shutter open, quite passive, recording, not thinking. Recording the man shaving at the window opposite and the woman in the kimono washing her hair. Some day all this will have to be developed, carefully printed, fixed.

Isherwood's prose has the clarity and impersonality of a photograph. Like a photograph, it lacks weight; but it can substitute a piercing immediacy of vision for the careful assemblage of words that is style in Dickens or James. Isherwood's master is Forster. If he lacks Forster's comedy, then he also omits Forster's trembling sentimentality.

Like his close friend Auden, Isherwood was a practising homosexual. Auden's fascination with frontiers to be crossed, secrets to be kept, and love's fatality find their unspoken centre in this fact. It explains the marked contrast between the inventive surfaces, the direct outward glance of his poems, and the sense of something not fully revealed in them, inaccessible:

> deep in clear lake
> The lolling bridegroom, beautiful, there.

('1929')

Isherwood's calling as a novelist enabled him to use the homosexual predicament (all male homosexual acts were illegal in Great Britain until 1966) as the basis of human interaction. Its unspoken presence in the novels is like its

CHRISTOPHER ISHERWOOD looks askance at his spry, besuited, youthful self, in a sympathetic portrait by his companion of many years, Don Bachardy (1962).

unacknowledged status in life itself. It works more beneficently in his novels than in Auden's poems.

Although it is the Berlin novels that are most celebrated—there is also *Mr Norris Changes Trains* (1935)—Isherwood's first two stories are equally worthy of attention. *All the Conspirators* (1928) is patently the work of a very young man. Its subject is the futile revolt of brother and sister against a strong-willed bourgeois mother. *The Memorial* (1932) is a more ambitious study of a family disintegrating in the aftermath of the First World War. Both share the hatred for 'Victorian' convention that is the staple of the novels of Ivy Compton-Burnett (1884-1969), though in her case the domestic tyrants who embody this quality are generally male. Isherwood's superiority rests in his lightness of touch and interest in development. Compton-Burnett ornaments her theme in endless, primly witty dialogue, as in the opening to *Manservant and Maidservant* (1947):

> 'Is that fire smoking?' said Horace Lamb.
> 'Yes, it appears to be, my dear boy.'
> 'I am not asking what it appears to be doing. I asked if it was smoking.'
> 'Appearances are not held to be a clue to the truth,' said his cousin. 'But we seem to have no other.'

This hardly presents a photographic illusion. Isherwood generally does. His picture takes in himself in the guise of a young man, innocent, even gauche, but appealingly frank and vulnerable. He is naturally at the centre of his early autobiography, *Lions and Shadows* (1935), an essential comment on the decade. Just how far this innocence is his own creation is made clear in the repugnantly callous picture that replaces it in *Christopher and his Kind* (1977), a late memoir of the same period. Isherwood's best late work is *A Single Man* (1964), the story of a day in the life of an ageing homosexual grieving for his dead partner; but there is a marked falling-off from the work of the thirties, both in style and in a taste for mawkishness and melodrama.

Isherwood belonged to the Auden group and his significance was quickly recognized. Jean Rhys (1890-1979) had to wait until 1966, however, before her great distinction as a novelist came to be generally accepted. Yet she has much in common with Isherwood—a stripped-down unassuming style, an aura of autobiography hanging over every novel, and the use of childishly innocent characters as protagonists. Recognition was slow to come for someone who had not been to public school or Oxford or Cambridge, who was a woman born in Dominica (and always yearning to return to that land of exotically happy childhood), and whose first literary appearances were made under the aegis of the ageing Ford Madox Ford in Paris.

Between 1927 and 1939 she published four novels and a collection of short stories; then there was silence until *Wide Sargasso Sea* (1966). Unusually it is not the story of a twentieth-century woman rather like herself in character and

JEAN RHYS. 'In old age Jean often said that, could the choice be offered her, she would have preferred a life of only average happiness to the greatest literary triumphs' (Francis Wyndham).

situation, but that of the first Mrs Rochester from *Jane Eyre*, exploited and tormented by a husband whom she loves but who understands neither her nor the nature of passion. The fire that burns Thornfield Hall, kills her, and blinds him, is an emblem of the passion he has denied. This gives the book an uncharacteristic neatness. The earlier novels are much more artful formally, and close not with a snap but with calculated hesitation, as, for example, *After Leaving Mr Mackenzie* (1930):

The street was cool and full of grey shadows. Lights were beginning to come out in the cafes. It was the hour between dog and wolf, as they say.

The choice is usually between dog and wolf for Jean Rhys's characters, between one predator and another. These are novels of great painfulness. But their overall effect is complicated by a sense that life is not to be abandoned merely because it is painful. Their heroines see clearly. They are even fair about the men who exploit them because exploiting is the easy and usual thing to do. It is said that the early novels are all alike and there is some truth in that, but of a limited kind. For in each the heroine lives through a different *kind* of experience and affirms her identity in a new way (at the end of *Good Morning, Midnight* (1939): 'Now I am simple and not afraid; now I am myself'). In these novels the mingled dread and joy of thirties youth, innocent and ultimately self-centred, finds expression of tragic force. Perhaps that is why the thirties were, for the most part, indifferent to them.

They were not indifferent to the work of George Orwell (1903–50). He was another public-school boy (Eton this time), but decidedly a member of the awkward squad, not a paid-up member of the 'new gang'. Sometimes regarded as one of the great English radicals, Orwell was somewhat less than that, just as he was somewhat less than 'George Orwell', his real name being Eric Blair. His *reportage* takes him where thirties socialism would have him go. *Down and Out in Paris and London* (1933) and *The Road to Wigan Pier* (1937) give

MINERS AT WORK in good thirties' conditions. Orwell, mapping his Britain, records that a three-mile walk, creep and crawl underground to the coal-face was not impossible; 'it is only because miners sweat their guts out that superior persons can remain superior.'

graphic accounts of that life among the poor and oppressed that Auden and his friends took for granted. But there is something a bit masochistic in Orwell's self-exposure to squalor; it is as though he does not really know why he is doing what he is doing. The difference from Jean Rhys's heroines is that Orwell does not acknowledge his own passivity. Although consciously he works hard at being a decent average sort of fellow (which he was not); the result is something more puzzling, more interesting, and less perfect than the conventional representation of him as a downright saint of the Left.

In the forties Orwell wrote a column for the left-wing weekly *Tribune*; it was called 'As I Please'. The suggestion of something carefree in his independence is entirely false. His novels of the thirties (there are four of them) are depressing but, like the journalism, bring the reader face to face with aspects of the world that are often forgotten—the meanness of ordinary well-intentioned people, for example. Orwell's gloom recedes slightly in *Animal Farm* (1945), the story of the revolution betrayed in Soviet Russia, transferred to an English farm where the animals turf out drunken Mr Jones and run the place 'for themselves'—in fact, for the benefit of the pigs who are now their leaders. It is mordant satire, no doubt. But the sense is inescapable that here self-abnegating Orwell enjoys being in control of his own work. He writes many times about language, is peculiarly sensitive to its manipulations (*Nineteen Eighty-four*, 1949, even has an appendix on the debased language of the 'future'), but only here, where his mind is made up and the burden of being fair-minded removed from him by his form and subject-matter, is he really at ease.

Short sentences, plain diction, brisk narrative—these were not possible in the murky tale of the future *Nineteen Eighty-four*, for it is also, very obviously, a complaint about nineteen forty-eight and post-war austerity, and this ambiguity in the underlying feeling needs a style in which it can hide, even though Orwell himself only wants a style that will tell the truth. A similar internal conflict is at work in his account of his participation in the Spanish Civil War, *Homage to Catalonia* (1938); but it is ungenerous to dwell on it. For this war was the central feature of the myth of thirties international socialism. Orwell was the only author of those dealt with here who went so far as to fight for the republicans (with the Marxist but not Communist POUM—he was in the awkward squad again). This did not prevent him from denouncing the two-faced conduct of the Communists who were largely supported by the intellectual Left in Britain. He should be honoured on both counts.

A socialism that is less than whole-hearted has trouble in defining itself, and a socialism that is opposed to Communism must be un-whole-hearted, craving yet rejecting the ideology of its rival. Orwell was a pragmatic English public-school socialist, and the tensions and contradictions of his work do spring from necessary strains in this self-definition. Life, in a sense, was easier for the writer who declined the call of revolution and reform. Evelyn Waugh (1903–66) makes no bones about his conservatism or his snobbery, and this frankness is very welcome in the literature of the thirties. He is very funny, too, in an equivocal way:

'My boy has been injured in the foot,' said Lady Circumference coldly.
'Dear me! Not badly, I hope? Did he twist his ankle in the jumping?'
'No,' said Lady Circumference, 'he was shot at by one of the assistant masters. But it is kind of you to enquire.'

Waugh is neither witty nor genial, but he respects the absurdity of conventions that help us cope with the chaos of other people ('it is kind of you to enquire').

Waugh's early novels move at a great pace through every aspect of life as it might appear to a member of the upper classes. Since Waugh could only on the most generous terms be described as a member of those classes, public school or not, there is a good deal of fantasy in the novels, a fantasy which he consciously encouraged. The underlying reality is that society is breaking

EVELYN WAUGH, a dashing army officer, whose ability to tell his seniors why they should not smoke their pipes with vintage port perhaps explains why his military career was no more successful than that of his hero, Guy Crouchback. The photograph (1939–40) shows Waugh in Royal Marine Corps uniform.

down because people have not the sense to stick by the old rules of conduct. He relishes the destruction of the newfangled arty aristocrats' possessions by the traditional kind of hunting shooting booby in *Decline and Fall* (1928):

It was a lovely evening. They broke up Mr Austen's grand piano, and stamped Lord Rending's cigars into his carpet, and smashed his china, and tore up Mr Partridge's sheets, and threw the Matisse into his water-jug . . .

Waugh was an aesthete of a kind—his first book was a life of Rossetti—and so a passage like this, not untypical, shows him putting a brave face on things he feared as much as adored. *Brideshead Revisited* (1945) states his positive faith in aristocracy, Roman Catholicism, and sticking together. It is a sentimental melodrama of transparent honesty, but uncharacteristically earnest. The *Sword of Honour* trilogy (1952, 1955, 1961) is more impressive—Guy Crouchback's military career in the Second World War is grotesque, farcical, and pathetic. The books are an elegy for vanished national ideals of Christian decency; the new world is petty, grey, and grim. Crouchback's humanitarian efforts on behalf of a group of displaced Jews in Yugoslavia at the end of the war sound an unusually sympathetic note and give some substance to the view.

Doubtless, Waugh will be remembered as a comic novelist. *Vile Bodies* (1930) and its fellows are worth remembering. But it is the trilogy that most deserves respect.

The Forties: Extravagance and Reason

In January 1939, three months after the British Prime Minister Neville Chamberlain, bearing delusory promises of peace, had returned from his meeting with Hitler in Munich, and nine months before the outbreak of the Second World War, W. H. Auden and Christopher Isherwood set sail for the United States, where both were to settle, Isherwood for life, Auden until 1956, when he returned to spend his last years in England and Austria. Their voyage marks the end of that movement in English literature which had started with the publication of Auden's *Poems* in 1930. The hopes for international comradeship and world reform which had centred on the Spanish Civil War and which had carried Auden and the new gang forward with them, had been dashed. Hitler had annexed Austria and the Sudetenland with the assent of the British government. Franco was about to enter Madrid. This was no country for young men. Yet their departure was ill-timed and ill-managed, a personal decision taking little account of the public world they had courted and castigated. They are subject to pointed ridicule, as Parsnip and Pimpernell, in Evelyn Waugh's novel *Put Out More Flags* (1942). A 'cross, red-headed girl in spectacles from the London School of Economics' puts it bluntly:

What I don't see is how these two can claim to be *Contemporary* if they run away from the biggest event in contemporary history. They were contemporary enough about Spain when no one threatened to come and bomb *them*.

Waugh stands for the solid core of middle-class conservative readers whom the new gang had never been able to impress. He was not the creator of Lord Emsworth, the English aristocrat whose happiest hours are spent in silent communion with his prize-winning sow, Empress of Blandings—that was the enormously successful popular comic novelist P. G. Wodehouse (1881-1975)—but he might have been, because his world was contiguous with that of Wodehouse, just as Wodehouse's rural England of clod-hopping police constables and patrician ninnies borders on the nineteenth-century Barsetshire of Anthony Trollope. Trollope's Mrs Proudie, insufferable wife to the Bishop of Barchester, could figure equally well in Wodehouse or Waugh. When the war came, the English readers whom Auden and his friends had failed to win over turned to their bookshelves and for solace in the guard-post and the air-raid shelter took down the novels of Trollope.

The forties were a colourless and grim decade, in the course of which the hardship of war was merely replaced by the austerities of a peace without plenty. It was natural to dream of other worlds and of more opulent forms of existence. Already in 1938 the Old Etonian belletrist Cyril Connolly (1903-74) had written, in his influential and greatly over-praised *Enemies of Promise*, on behalf of a 'reasoned extravagance' of style, arguing that the development of a 'vernacular prose' in authors such as Isherwood and Orwell had gone too far. Prose-writers of the forties certainly supplied him with extravagance, though its reasoned quality is somewhat in doubt.

Two novelists of fantasy embody this forties taste for extravagance most clearly, though both had to wait some time before they found their most enthusiastic audience. The first of these is Mervyn Peake (1911-68), a brilliant, if mannered, graphic artist, whose trilogy about the imaginary castle of Gormenghast, enormous unmapped citadel of meaningless restrictive ritual, starts with *Titus Groan* (1946). We are certainly a long way from the photographic style of Isherwood here:

Gormenghast, that is, the main massing of the original stone, taken by itself would have displayed a certain ponderous architectural quality were it possible to have ignored the circumfusion of those mean dwellings that swarmed like an epidemic around its outer walls.

'Gormenghast, that is . . .': the main point of such prose is *not* to go straight to the point but to elaborate it to the utmost. The style is in collusion with the antiquated fantastication of Gormenghast which it affects to repudiate. Indeed, as Peake brings his hero Titus out of the grotesquerie that originally surrounds him, his touch becomes less and less sure. The setting for his fantasy engulfs the action for which it should serve only as backcloth.

That can hardly be said of another trilogy which, though it was not published until the fifties, was largely written in the forties, and belongs to them in spirit. J. R. R. Tolkien (1892-1973), an old-fashioned Oxford philologist, used all his

PEAKE'S DRAWING FOR *TITUS GROAN* (1946) leaves it teasingly unclear how far he is indulging Romantic sentiment, how far he is parodying it.

THE HOBBIT (1937): little Bilbo Baggins wanders where the wild things are, anticipating the adventures of his young cousin Frodo by several years.

knowledge of the early European romances to shape the action of *The Lord of the Rings* (three volumes, 1954–5), the story of an epic confrontation between Good and Evil. Frodo Baggins the hobbit, a peaceable *petit bourgeois* dwarf with fur on his feet, has to bring peace to his world by carrying to the Mountain of Fire, in enemy territory, 'the one Ring, ruler of all the Rings of Power' which is, naturally, desired by all the forces of evil and which itself provokes evil desire; there he must cast it into the Crack of Doom where it will be destroyed. This makes a rattling good adventure story with a clear moral, perhaps the reason for its great success at a time when clear morals and, indeed, good adventure stories have become hard to find. It is also a shamefully self-glorying account of how little England defeated the ogre Hitler (Frodo's home-country is The Shire), a fact not mitigated by the circumstance of Frodo's giving in at the last moment to the power of the Ring and declining to throw it away. The exploited creature Gollum turns on him and, biting off his finger, seizes the Ring himself:

. . . Gollum, dancing like a mad thing, held aloft the ring, a finger still thrust within its circle. It shone now as if verily it was wrought of living fire.

'Verily' is the tell-tale emphasis, betraying the author's lack of confidence in the second-hand material he hopes to bring to life. Like Peake's trilogy, *The Lord of the Rings* is a fundamentally ambiguous fiction, refusing, however, to take its own ambiguousness into account.

The war was not a time for new novelists to emerge, but it enabled authors whom the Auden-Isherwood decade had in one way or another inhibited to come into their own. Elizabeth Bowen (1899-1973) is a case in point. By the time war broke out she had published five novels and four collections of stories. They centre upon vulnerable and sensitive young women caught up in an upper-middle-class world of convention that is both menacing and unreal. This description makes them sound like feminine counterparts to Isherwood's first two novels, but the difference is absolute. The pared-down quality of his writing expresses a decisiveness quite lacking in hers. Bowen's tone is elegiac

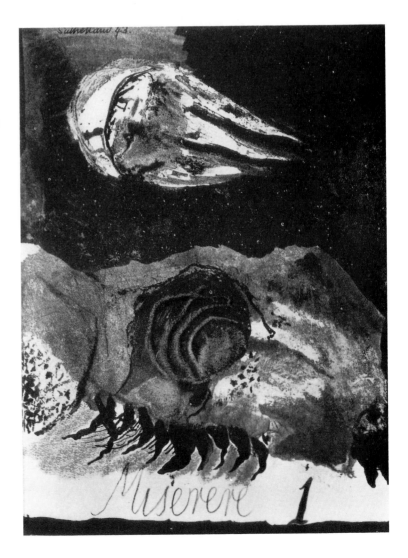

A LITHOGRAPH BY GRAHAM SUTHERLAND for David Gascoyne's *Poems 1937-1942* (1943); the large Romantic gesture towards an apocalyptic sky is exuberant in characteristic forties fashion.

and, in the early novels, Jamesian; it is always literary. It is not surprising then, that her novel of the forties, *The Heat of the Day* (1949), should be an eloquent requiem for the ruins of London after the Blitz. There had always been a hallucinatory quality in her prose which found its true subject in the half-life of that time: 'The Germans no longer came by the full moon. Something more immaterial seemed to threaten, and to be keeping people at home.' Bowen, born into the Anglo-Irish Protestant ascendancy just as it was to lose its power in the formation of the new Irish state, knew the meaning of dispossession well. Her best novel, *The Death of the Heart* (1938), is about a young woman's recognition that the world as it is offers her no possibility of fulfilment. She is a princess whom no prince will ever find. The best that Bowen can do is to lament the past and celebrate, in terms restricted by her own allegiance to her class, life on the edge of destruction. London in wartime was her place especially:

This was the new society of one kind of wealth, resilience, living how it liked—people whom the climate of danger suited, who began, even, all to look a little alike, as they might in the sun, snows and altitude of the same sports station, or browning along the same beach in the south of France. The very temper of pleasures lay in their chanciness . . .

There is something appropriately disquieting about the superposition of images of St Moritz and Nice on that of the ruined city: but there is something exclusive about the manœuvre too, a withdrawal into the privileges of a certain kind of expensive upbringing that leaves too much of life unaccounted for.

Graham Greene (b. 1904) by contrast has a voracious appetite for life in all its forms. *The Confidential Agent* (1939), his ninth novel, uses the novel form to discover the present state of England much as Orwell had used *reportage* and the essay for the same purpose in *The Road to Wigan Pier*. Greene's hero, an agent for the Spanish republicans (though this is not made specific) journeys to the heart of depressed industrial England in search of coal to help a failing war effort; the physical journey is also one that takes the agent through every layer of English society. Bowen's 'climate of danger' already pervades the landscape of this book, where enemy agents and English police join forces to squash the threat to the deadly status quo represented by D's hopeless mission:

. . . the dark was shredding off like a vapour from a long hillside. The light came drably up behind the barn and the field, over the station and the siding, crept up the hill. Brick cottages detached themselves: the stumps of trees reminded him of a battlefield . . .

Five years earlier Greene had published another 'state of England' novel with a similar point of view: *It's a Battlefield* (1934).

Greene is essentially a popular novelist, the nearest thing to Dickens that twentieth-century English literature can offer. He tells a good story, enjoys

WENT THE DAY WELL? (1942) An English heroine prepares for battle. A story by Graham Greene underlay this wartime morale-booster, in which German troops quietly take over an English village and the lady of the manor dies defending the village children.

melodrama and sentiment, and loathes do-gooders. Of course everything moves at a quicker pace than in Dickens, and there are no expansive sub-plots. His central characters are complicated, haunted by guilt and failure, questioning their own ability to feel love, never quite sure that they are in the right. Greene's admiration for Conrad is vulgarized in his hints of doom. But he has no pretensions to be a serious writer in the way that Elizabeth Bowen has. His admirers have laid too much stress on a supposed moral profundity in his work, when what it offers is something smaller, but still valuable: moral suggestiveness. In *The Heart of the Matter* (1948) Scobie has to read to a sick child from an 'improving' book—*A Bishop among the Bantus* (the novel is set in wartime Africa).

'Go on,' the boy said impatiently, 'Anyone can read aloud.'
Scobie found his eyes fixed on an opening paragraph which started, *I shall never forget my first glimpse of the continent where I was to labour for thirty of the best years of my life.* He said slowly, 'From the moment they left Bermuda the low lean rakehelly craft had followed in their wake. The captain was evidently worried, for he watched the strange ship continually through his spy-glass.'

Scobie's substitution of a tale of derring-do for the evangelizing treatise in his hands reflects Greene's own practice of writing stories, often thrillers, through which the moral issues other writers take as guiding lights shine with tantalizing and convincing fitfulness.

Not all Greene's novels are like this. Like Evelyn Waugh, Greene was a convert to Roman Catholicism, and the burden to write as some authoritative Catholic Novelist was heavy upon him. *The Heart of the Matter* is an example: Scobie's adultery ends in his self-murder out of pity for both the women involved, but it is a suicide made to look like death from natural causes. Can God forgive him or not? *The Power and the Glory* (1940) is a gaudy tale built round the paradox of the whisky priest hunted down by the Mexican state—a sinful man, he is nevertheless the means of others' redemption. Though still compelling, these are not Greene at his best; *The Quiet American* (1955) is, the story of a political innocent wreaking havoc as the French fight for Indo-China. Since Greene's Christianity has much in common with Eliot's (and Pascal's), in being a faith founded on doubt, it may be that his religious sense is most powerfully present in the creation of characters without religion such as Fowler, the narrator of *The Quiet American*, whom we leave saying, 'how I wished there existed someone to whom I could say I was sorry.'

Dickens's gusto undergoes metamorphosis in Greene. What he relishes is the seedy and the exotic, and if possible the exotically seedy. He relishes them because if all there is to enjoy is a fallen world, then true enjoyment will involve its fallenness. And then again, he does so because the bizarre in moderation recommends itself. Rowe, in *The Ministry of Fear* (1943), is looking across the Thames to Battersea:

'They can't spoil Whistler's Thames,' a voice said.
'I'm sorry,' Rowe said, 'I didn't catch . . .'
'It's safe underground. Bomb-proof vaults.'

The prose of Dylan Thomas (1914–53) also shows the influence of Dickens, but in more authentically forties style than Greene's, lacks moderation, tends even excessively to excess:

> Mr Farr trod delicately and disgustedly down the dark, narrow stairs like a man on mice. He knew without looking or slipping, that vicious boys had littered the darkest corner with banana peel; and when he reached the lavatory, the basins would be choked and the chains snapped on purpose.

Mr Farr's larger-than-life quality fills his world entirely, extending to the lavatory chains even, snapped 'on purpose' just for him; he is like, for example, Dickens's Mrs Clennam, in *Little Dorrit*, whose house, 'a double house with long, narrow, heavily framed windows . . . leaning on some half-dozen gigantic crutches' is part of *her*, hypocrite, tyrant, and parasite that she is. Thomas in his prose is, however, always in an exuberantly celebratory mood: the stories of *Portrait of the Artist as a Young Dog* (1940) for this reason found, and find, a far wider audience perhaps than anyone else in this chapter. That is certainly true of his radio play *Under Milk Wood*, first performed and published posthumously in 1954, a sentimental grotesque of an imaginary Welsh seaside village, whose weakness may be summed up in no-better-than-than-she-should-be Polly Garter's cry, 'Oh, isn't life a terrible thing, thank God' (which allows little in the way of meaning to God or what is terrible), but whose strength is everywhere evident in its enjoyment of an inexhaustible fantasy. Butcher Beynon tells his wife she is eating cat's liver; 'yesterday we had mole . . . Monday, otter, Tuesday, shrews.' 'He's the biggest liar in town', but his lies make love to the natural world and joke with it. Thomas's achievement in this play was to elevate infantile humour to a grandeur appropriate to its power, subversive and innocent.

THE INTERNATIONAL SURREALIST EXHIBITION, 1936. A young woman with her head in a wire meat-cage covered with red roses stands in a desolate Trafalgar Square. Surrealism largely failed in Britain.

DYLAN THOMAS (1953): 'where a boy / In the listening / Summertime of the dead whispered the truth of his joy' ('Poem in October'). He is standing in the graveyard at Langharne.

And that, after all, is of a piece with Thomas's having been one of the very few English writers of talent to have been interested in surrealism in the thirties. Auden and his friends had turned away from the 'European' qualities of modernism in Joyce and Eliot; it is a mark of how far Thomas was different from them (he was an ex-grammar-school boy with no money and no university education) that he thought he might hitch himself on to the largely French movement. English surrealism came to nothing fairly quickly: by the time it got to England in 1936 it had already been politicized and tidied, and this theatrical aspect to it was no recommendation. The early poems of David Gascoyne (b. 1916) are its finest English memorial, especially the sequence *Hölderlin's Madness* (1938). Thomas shared the surrealist interest in the unconscious mind and the startling image ('When, like a running grave, time tracks you down . . .'), and he has the same liking for the great abstracts of Love and Death, transformed by his sexually obsessive imagination.

Thomas published his first book, *18 Poems* (1934), when he was only twenty, a wild, romantic, and difficult book—still difficult today. His ambitions are best suggested by his only half-mocking self-description as 'the Rimbaud of Cwmdonkin Drive'; his poetry is involved in the impossible endeavour to utter a magically transcendent truth. The poems are charms, openings into the other-worldly. Thomas's unhappy sexuality adds to the turmoil of these weird, musical pieces. A few have won popularity, the early one beginning 'The Force that through the green fuse drives the flower', the late 'Fern Hill', relaxed toward the mode of *Under Milk Wood*, but it is impossible to be at ease with most of them in any sense at all.

Perhaps that is as it should be. Thomas's was a great talent which achieved great things, but which the English culture of his day could only accommodate in the genially vulgarized forms of his prose and drama. Auden's departure for America gave him his chance, but he was not made to assume authority. He had his admirers and his imitators, was identified in the fifties with what, in the poetry of the forties, was to be reacted against, without ever seizing confidently the crown he might have worn. His poverty and alcoholism were the consequences and also the chosen symbols of that failure.

And in any case he was dwarfed by the presence of Eliot, whose always unbiddable poetic gift reasserted its undeniable authority once more with the publication of *Four Quartets*. This had begun with the appearance of what was to be its first part, 'Burnt Norton', as an independent poem in 1936. The other three quartets followed in rapid succession once war had begun: 'East Coker' (1940), 'The Dry Salvages' (1941), and 'Little Gidding' (1942). Each 'quartet' is organized in five sections of which the fourth is always a lyric. The titles refer to places with special meaning for Eliot, but this personal element is only the starting-point for attempts to define matters of universal human importance. These are especially religious poems, but their concept is of a religion localized in space and time:

EAST COKER, left by a seventeenth-century Eliot who settled in America; 'The whole earth is our hospital / Endowed by the ruined millionaire . . .'

> while the light fails
> On a winter's afternoon, in a secluded chapel
> History is now and England.

History is to be made by an acting out of religious faith; religious faith can only exist in history. Eliot takes into his poems a little of the machinery of war, the raiding plane ('the dark dove with the flickering tongue'), the warden at his post, 'undisciplined squads' (of emotion), less certainly 'the drift of the sea and the drifting wreckage', and the poems' courage and contemporaneity were quickly recognized. Doubts—about failures of tone, incomplete responsiveness to the task the poet had set himself—came later, and too late to prevent some passages from entering the common currency:

> Every phrase and every sentence is an end and a beginning,
> Every poem an epitaph. And any action
> Is a step to the block, to the fire, down the sea's throat
> Or to an illegible stone: and that is where we start.

Four Quartets, grand elusive not-quite-statements of belief, effectively and triumphantly mark the end of Eliot's career as a poet, though great success still awaited him in the late verse play *The Cocktail Party* (1949) and its two successors, unsettlingly deadpan adaptations of commercial play forms to higher ends. His best work as a dramatist is *Murder in the Cathedral* (1935), which combines Greek tragedy, mystery, and morality play to tell the martyrdom of Thomas à Becket, and *The Family Reunion* (1939), a play about guilt and pursuit by the Furies set in comfortably upper-class England. Eliot's undeniable artistic assurance and intellectual distinction were a glory but a depressing factor for the poet in England of the thirties and forties.

And were there war poets? Barely. The Second World War was safer for the military than for the civilian stay-at-homes, by and large; it was mobile; it was thoroughly mechanized. Its poets for the most part were, aptly, writers in the alert, observant style of Auden, sobered down by the new circumstances. There are excellent poems about the war by Roy Fuller (b. 1912), Henry Reed (b. 1914), and Alan Ross (b. 1922), quiet, cool, observant, using for the most part a depersonalized version of Auden's style. But these are not poems that embody some new kind of sensibility. For that, one has to turn to the work of Keith Douglas (1920–44).

Of course, there is Auden at work in Douglas too. How could there not be? He was, after all, a member of the same class, though his family was impoverished, who learnt the art of poetry in Auden's decade, and went to Oxford too. He has Auden's assurance and wonderfully interested gaze, but his own awkward independence, even loneliness, replaces the appeal to the group. Douglas always writes a person, not a history or a tone of voice, into his poems. And he undertakes a difficult revision of values, not indulging adolescent rebellion, but judging the old world, the 'obsolescent breed of heroes' whom he fought alongside in the North African desert:

> they are fading into two legends
> in which their stupidity and chivalry are celebrated;
> the fool and the hero will be immortals.

> ('Sportsmen')

His account of service as a junior tank officer in the desert war, *Alamein to Zem Zem* (1946) is one of the best books of its decade. Its intelligence and economy put it in a class above anything by Orwell, from whom he had certainly learned. It is the necessary companion to Waugh's trilogy, confirming and enlightening the novelist's achievement, but standing clear and free itself. Its often-remarked tone of enquiry before the dead Douglas encountered in the

KEITH DOUGLAS'S ILLUSTRATION FOR *ALAMEIN TO ZEM-ZEM* (published 1946) offers a horrific variation on his sardonic line describing a brother officer: 'The noble horse with courage in his eye'.

desert connects with his own sense of himself as possessed of 'a particular monster'—

> the thing I can admit only once to
> anyone, never to those who have not their own.
> Never to those who are happy, whose easy language
> I speak well, though with a stranger's accent.

('The "Bête Noire" Fragments')

Douglas's 'easy language' spoken 'with a stranger's accent' was the appropriate tone for his uneasy time, and his achievement is far greater than the number of surviving poems suggests. He published no book of his own in his short lifetime (he died in Normandy, three days after D-Day); his *Collected Poems* did not appear until 1951.

Douglas's achievement is a personal one; the Second World War did not make a poet of him in the way that the First did Wilfred Owen or Siegfried Sassoon. Instead, he used it to see himself and his English society better. This is typical of the literary experience of that war. Since the twenties, the British had been caught up in great social changes whose nature was unclear to them. What lay ahead? A classless industrialized Paradise or some kind of oligarchy or dictatorship? It is the fear to which this uncertainty gave rise that surfaces in the fantasy and grotesquerie of the forties. The power to transcend this fear by transcending class ideas was given to very few—Thomas, Greene, Douglas, of whom, oddly enough, Douglas, the youngest, seems the most grown-up. Some writers were able if not to achieve transcendence, then at least to see clearly what was to be transcended. Joyce Cary (1888–1957) is one of these.

His first novel appeared in 1932 but it was not until 1941, in *A House of Children*, based on his own childhood in Northern Ireland, that Cary used the first-person style of narrative that seems best suited to him. His novels are racy and shapeless, though the style is economical. There is always room for the reader to be surprised; in the first-person novels, the surprise is shared with the narrator. Cary wrote two trilogies, each novel in which is written as by one of three characters linked by significant events or relationships. In each case the three novels fly apart, held together almost exclusively by our sense that they should not. Though Gulley Jimson, artist-narrator of *The Horse's Mouth* (1944), from the first of these trilogies, is Cary's best-remembered character, the second trilogy (*Prisoner of Grace*, 1952; *Except the Lord*, 1953; *Not Honour More*, 1955) is better. It turns on the life of a Welsh demagogue, Chester Nimmo. Cary's ability to catch a tone of voice is remarkable; it is part of his gusto for life. But at the same time, the single voice becomes predictable. Nina Nimmo in *Prisoner of Grace* is marked too clearly by her use of parenthesis and her self-consciousness about expressions that are slangy. Cary's reckless superficiality at one level, that of style, does enable him at another to confront issues like class and social change without pettiness or sentimentality, and this makes him a more solid author, especially in regard to the forties, than at first he seems.

The merits of Cary's way of doing things come out if he is compared with 'Henry Green' (Henry Yorke, 1905–73). His novels are nervy, deliberated exercises in art, reflecting the experimentalism of Joyce and Woolf. His style is marked, for example by the omission of articles ('They sat round brazier in a circle'), by unidiomatic uses of phrases like 'this one' or 'that man', by repetitions, and by attentive banality in his middle-class dialogue. After Eton and Oxford he worked in the family engineering firm; he became chairman of the British Chemical Plant Manufacturers' Association. His novels show his impatience with conventional middle-class life. *Party Going* (1939) is, for example, a tight little fable about wealthy young people trapped by fog in a railway hotel at one of the London terminals. The mass of people on the concourse outside, now cheerful, now threatening, powerfully symbolize the potential for class conflict in English society. The novel is a tacit recommendation of the mood that produced once more a Labour government in 1945. What it is not is easy or spontaneous; its brilliance strikes the reader as too much under constraint. The earlier novel, *Living* (1929), is about working-class people and the factory they work in. It is well observed, intelligent, and interesting, yet smacks more of ethnography and good intent than of the free imagination. *Caught* (1943), about an upper-class Englishman in the Auxiliary Fire Service in London during the war, is one of the least mannered and least admired of the novels, but by making its subject the gap between himself and the ordinary people who fascinated him Green produced his imaginatively most spacious and successful novel. Apart from *Back* (1946), the story of a returned soldier in civilian life, the later novels show him retreating into a fiction of social satire, sometimes tender (*Loving*, 1945), sometimes not (*Doting*, 1952), but in either case palpably less than he was capable of. The novel was in need of a new beginning in England by the time the fifties came, if, that is, the nation's novel readers were not to stay comfortably settled with Trollope until the end of the century.

The Fifties: Anger and Fear

It is hard to understand what happened in English literature in the fifties without some understanding of the historical circumstances. The determining factor is the return of a Labour government to power in 1945, with enormous popular support. British voters wanted change; their hopes went with their votes, and were not entirely unfulfilled. Under the leadership of Clement Attlee, Labour quickly set about turning promises into action. In 1946 they nationalized the coal industry; transport (1947) and steel (1949) followed soon after, with electricity and domestic gas. In 1946, too, they legislated for a National Health Service, guaranteeing medical treatment for all, irrespective of wealth. Pensions and housing were improved. In 1947 India and Pakistan became independent, leading the way for Britain's divestment of its former colonies.

All these changes were what the people had voted for; but they took place in conditions of economic hardship, the consequences of the war. Britain had to build itself up again at the same time as it was trying to *rebuild* itself. The result was not merely hardship, but also a sense of diminished status in the world. In 1948 Britain accepted invaluable American aid under the European Recovery Plan. It could not have done otherwise; but it was to prove a bitter pill to swallow. Indeed, the Labour government's policies as a whole proved a more powerful medicine than the country was prepared to take. The Labour Party lost favour and by 1951 found itself out of office. The new world was proving to be not quite such a splendid place for the British as they had supposed it would.

This new world required new writers to chart its passages, its deep waters, and its shallows. Those of the thirties and forties, for the most part, had not been close enough to social reality then to make much of a job of grasping it now. Orwell, for example, despite his sympathy for the Left, failed altogether to foresee the Labour victory in 1945, nor did he have any confidence that the party, once elected, would put its policies into practice. The public-school

THE FESTIVAL OF BRITAIN, 1951, made a brave show of welcoming the future in a year when the British people finally rejected its post-war Labour government.

writers of the thirties, the dreamers and fantasists of the forties, needed time to adjust.

Two attempts at adjustment are especially worth considering. C. P. Snow (1905–80), a scientist and civil servant turned novelist, was a grammar-school boy who had benefited from the loosening of the social structure after the First World War. The first volume of his eleven-volume sequence *Strangers and Brothers* was published in 1940, but the series did not really get under way until 1947; the final volumes appeared in 1970. It covers the period from 1914 to 1968 with no great attempt at unity, focusing on the world of scientists, academics, and administrators Snow himself knew well. The world of state enterprise and public affairs to which the Labour Party had contributed so much here finds emphatic expression. So, too, does the cheerlessness of the new age of the fifties. The treatment of the pursuit of power is frank but repulsive. The prose is easy, undemanding both of author and of reader; the plots are solid and unsurprising. A deep complacency stubbornly resists knowledge of the chilling qualities which Snow's account of history wants to reveal.

Anthony Powell (b. 1905), like Snow, started publishing in the thirties; he is a more likeable writer, not only because his novels are predominantly comic. His twelve-novel sequence, *A Dance to the Music of Time* (1951–75), looks at roughly the same period as Snow's, but Powell is an old Etonian, and his story is one of a world of upper-class hard-heads and dimwits going, in their various ways, to the dogs. There is a brilliant accumulation of surface detail,

GRAHAM GREENE'S WASTE LAND: a desolate cemetery in Vienna, last scene of Carol Reed's *The Third Man*, which Greene scripted. The film is a melancholy exploration of post-war tension.

but one can never be sure how much of the book's ponderousness in style is characterization of the limply sensitive narrator, Nicholas Jenkins, and how much is Powell's unconscious addition. His earliest novels—*Afternoon Men* (1931), *Venusberg* (1932)—are crisper and better, because they are less ambitious. The elegiac tone of the sequence sounds not merely for a class that is dying (the monstrous, ludicrous New Man, Widmerpool, ends up a Labour life peer) but also for a talent that cannot immerse itself as it would wish in the life, and the history, it depicts. The gossip, rumour, and chance encounters in which the sequence abounds stand for a distance from historical process which neither the author nor his characters are able to span. Like Snow, Powell writes about social changes he cannot quite understand; unlike Snow, he understands his lack of understanding.

One possible reaction to the failure to understand what is happening to one is anger; and anger, together with fear, was very much an emotion of the fifties. Blankness is not an emotion, but a deep, a troubled, blankness seems also an important element in the work which the fifties produced and to which they responded. Three very different artists, the novelist Kingsley Amis, the poet Philip Larkin, and the dramatist (and novelist in a sense—but for the fifties, a dramatist most of all) Samuel Beckett, show how these qualities interrelate and connect with historical circumstance.

Kingsley Amis (b. 1922), one of the decade's 'angry young men'—the dramatist John Osborne is another—is a comic novelist; anger and the anxiety from which it arises come to terms with the world by perceiving it as ludicrous. In *One Fat Englishman* (1963), a man arranges chairs by a swimming-pool 'in the manner of a sadistic animal-trainer'. His world, and Amis's, is hostile; he serves gin-and-tonic to his guest 'with a glance of ultimate grimness, like a gang-dealer dealing out small arms before a job'. The old cultural certainties mean nothing in Amis's novels, and those who profess them are merely pretenders. The enormous success of his first novel, *Lucky Jim* (1954), depended on the way it vented its nervous tension ostensibly on 'the home-made pottery crowd, the organic husbandry crowd, the recorder-playing crowd', but in fact on the whole world of culture which its shambling hero, a lecturer in history, decides to leave at the end of the novel. *Lucky Jim* is farcical, but its view of life will not be contained within the conventions of farce. Hysteria is imminent throughout. What stays in the memory is not so much the comic set-pieces as the portrait of hapless Jim Dixon's girl-friend, the neurotic, castrating harpy, Margaret. Fear of women and fear of death recur again and again in Amis's novels. One means to cope with them is an attempted bluff common sense; in *I Like It Here* (1958), despite the general hatred for books expressed there, Amis goes out of his way to pay homage to Henry Fielding, in the world of whose novels 'moral seriousness . . . could be made apparent without the aid of evangelical puffing and blowing'. Amis's essential qualities are dampened, however, by the attempt to contain and control his manic humour; his best novels face up to the fact of fear and exploit it, as in *One Fat Englishman*, about an unlovable visitor to the unloved United States, and *Ending Up* (1974), a macabre comedy of old age and death. In these books his resentment of his own anger checks and shapes an impulse that elsewhere proves imperfectly manageable; in them he does not merely appear to be honest (the attraction of *Lucky Jim*) but is so.

The question of honesty is important, for it was the cause of honesty that made Jim's hysterical laughter acceptable to his uncomfortably unsettled first audience. Honesty is also the issue for Amis's close friend Philip Larkin (1922-85), as in his poem on childhood, 'I Remember, I Remember';

> Our garden first: where I did not invent
> Blinding theologies of flowers and fruits,
> And wasn't spoken to by an old hat.
> And here we have that splendid family
>
> I never ran to when I got depressed . . .

PHILIP LARKIN'S HULL: 'the weekday world of those / Who leave at dawn low terraced houses / Timed for factory, yard and site'. He said of the town, characteristically: 'I like it because it's so far from anywhere else.'

Larkin is in control as Amis rarely is. The negatives are carefully deliberated, emphasized by, and with, moderation, and what they deny is represented surprisingly fully: 'Blinding theologies of flowers and fruits' stands blindingly clear in the development of the stanza, asserting the mythical power the poet politely declines. His conclusion, that 'Nothing, like something, happens anywhere' leaves 'nothing' and 'something' in baffling balance.

The bafflement is at least partly a historical sensation, as surfaces in the poem on the First World War, 'MCMXIV'—the very date is passing to a mystery: 'Never such innocence again'. The loss of innocence is what distinguishes Larkin from Hardy, a poet whom he admired and superficially resembles. Hardy knows his mind; when the brass on his friend's coffin, going to the churchyard, flashes out at him from a distance he says, characteristically: 'Looking harder and harder I knew what it meant.' Such innocence is not for Larkin whose poems end with a stunned sense of 'unfenced existence: Facing the sun, untalkative, out of reach', something, like nothing, happening anywhere.

Early in his career Larkin published two novels, *Jill* (1946) and *A Girl in*

Winter (1947). Both are good, both focus on isolation, and on an odd kind of freedom that derives from such isolation. John Kemp, a working-class boy at Oxford invents a girl-friend, Jill, whom he identifies with a girl seen in a bookshop. Reality and fantasy inevitably collide: the lesson is that love dies; fulfilled or unfulfilled, it dies:

Then if there was no difference between love fulfilled and love unfulfilled, how could there be any difference between any other pair of opposites? Was he not freed, for the rest of his life, from choice?

Anxiety gives way to acceptance without even the illusion of disillusionment. For Larkin life is tolerable only so long as it bears no decisive weight of meaning; his religion would be a religion of water, he says in one poem, on its altar

> A glass of water
> Where any-angled light
> Would congregate endlessly.
>
> ('Water')

The image is at once egalitarian and inhuman, a rejoicing in the thing itself, purged of all colour or identity, and it is of a piece with the careful unpossessive attention Larkin gives to the world:

> How separate and unearthly love is,
> Or women are, or what they do,
> Or in our young unreal wishes
> Seem to be . . .
>
> ('The Large Cool Store')

What is perceived changes each moment; this poet celebrates the moments in a deep receptive blankness which is also something to celebrate, which is the lucid forms his poems fill; and if a poem ends, as it well may in Larkin, with 'Get stewed: Books are a load of crap' that too is a point of view to be suffered and made something of.

The Less Deceived (1955) is Larkin's second book of poems, on which his reputation is based, and its rejection of literary stereotype, its rejection of history ('fulfilment's desolate attic') and its rejection of self ('Such attics cleared of me! Such absences!') were all timely. Of course, he looks an old-fashioned poet—he uses rhyme, he is at a basic level easily understood—but he has much in common with the modernist protégé of James Joyce, Samuel Beckett, whose *Waiting for Godot* was the London dramatic sensation of 1955.

Beckett (b. 1906) was an Irishman who, after a short spell teaching at Trinity College, Dublin, settled in France in 1937, his home ever since. His early work was in English—clever, contrived, painfully and irritably sensitive to every aspect of suffering in the world. The comedy of *More Pricks than Kicks* (1934) and *Murphy* (1938) is at once brilliant and chilling. Neither book met with

SHAKESPEARE ON MODERN STAGES. (*Above*) The Royal Shakespeare Company's *Much Ado About Nothing* (1982), I. i; the settings and mirror-floor were by Ralph Koltai. (*Below*) model set by Nicholas Georgiadis for the 1965 Royal Opera House production of Prokoviev's *Romeo and Juliet*. The ballet, composed in 1935-6, originally had a happy ending because, Prokoviev said, dying people cannot dance.

ORWELL'S 'BIG BROTHER' remains a potent image in a country of high unemployment. The 1984 film version of *Nineteen Eighty-Four* makes its point in a chilly representation of comrades without comradeship; Winston drinks his Victory Gin alone at the Chestnut Tree Cafe, though he has company.

great success. In the forties Beckett began to write in French, translating his work later into English. *Godot*, his first play to be performed, was originally composed in French and staged in Paris in 1953.

Two tramps on a country road at evening wait for Godot, who never turns up; the play's two acts are different in many respects, but they have in common the possibility of being summed up in this fashion. *Godot* is a play in which 'nothing happens'. Since all that is needed on stage is a mound and a tree, it might be said that it shows nothing, like something, happening anywhere. Despite its evidently belonging to an alien tradition of symbolic drama, despite its connection with French existentialist philosophy, despite its un-English concern with Christian theology and despite the heartlessness of its humour, it has, then, its affinity with Larkin. The last lines and stage direction are famous:

VLADIMIR: Well? Shall we go?
ESTRAGON: Yes, let's go.
    They do not move.

Going and not moving—two opposites cancel themselves out; Didi and Gogo are 'freed . . . from choice', like Larkin's hero in *Jill*. Both writers arrive at

BECKETT'S *ENDGAME*: 'What's happening, what's happening?'—'Something is taking its course.' The play was first performed in French in 1957. George Divine as Hamm at the Royal Court (1958).

a difficult, blank acceptance of what is, the worth of which depends on our understanding it has not been easy. Beckett's drama develops an extraordinary economy of means: in *That Time* (1974) all that there is to see is the face of a man listening to his own voice; in *Not I* (1973) only a mouth and a barely visible hooded auditor: the woman speaker says she had

> no love . . . spared that . . . no love such as normally vented on the speechless infant . . . in the home . . . no . . . nor indeed for that matter any of any kind . . . no love of any kind . . . at any subsequent stage . . .

How can such a drama work to enrich the sense of life? By requiring attendance, by leaving no possibility of distraction, by asking for judgement exclusively on the basis of what is experienced at the moment of facing that face, that mouth, in a moment of near-religious communion. Beckett is continually drawn to nihilism; when his art succeeds he makes of it something else—a call to human solidarity.

Beckett's later fiction is unlike anyone else's; the *Trilogy* (1950-2 in French) starts as first-person narrative, as though it were *Jane Eyre* or *David Copperfield*, but the fiction disintegrates by intimating that it is a fiction. Then what is it we are reading? Who is responsible for what is on the page?—

> one forgets, I forget, I say I see nothing, or I say it's all in my head, as if I felt a head on me, that's all hypotheses, lies, these gleams too, they were to save me, they were to devour me . . .

The vertiginous glimpse of fictions underlying fictions, lies beneath lies, explains, if it cannot mitigate, the occasional hardening of Beckett's tone, his liking for the schematic, his weakness for the flowery, and it brings out, too, a certain heroism in his humour, of which there is much—not so far distant in tone from Amis's as might be thought: 'Fortunately my father died when I was a boy,' says the speaker in *From an Abandoned Work* (1958), 'otherwise I might have been a professor, he had set his heart on it'. Lucky Jim would have sympathized.

In Amis, Larkin, and Beckett, honesty is always ready to conspire with neurosis. Theirs is a deeply troubled art, obsessive, unruly, requiring of the artist an unrelaxing vigilance to humanize it. That vigilance slips most often in the impatient novels of Amis, most disastrously in Beckett when he makes a sudden dash to simplify the stifling complexity of his would-be blankness, and least noticeably in the poems of Larkin whose mask is that of a modest, self-effacing English fogey (belied by sudden outbursts of petty viciousness: '*You'd care to join us?* In a pig's arse, friend'). Indeed Larkin is associated with a rationality in poetry that is not easily found in his own work—the poetry defined by Robert Conquest's anthology of 1956 *New Lines*: 'empirical in its attitude' and manifesting 'refusal to abandon a rational structure and comprehensible language . . .'

This self-conscious rationality of the 'Movement' poets, as they were called, was in fact only another way of responding to the terrors and anxieties of fifties Britain. In Larkin it is entirely on the surface, a blind for the darker intimations, giving them a benign appearance:

> A sense of falling, like an arrow-shower
> Sent out of sight, somewhere becoming rain.
>
> ('The Whitsun Weddings')

But it is not so different with other poets of the group, the imposed quality of whose 'rational' structures is suggested by Amis's poem 'Masters':

> They only are secure who seem secure;
> Who lose their voice, lose all.

The early poetry of Thom Gunn (b. 1929) is frankly a poetry of will, and exercise of the will is what he admires, as in his poem on the motorcycle gang, 'On the Move': 'They strap in doubt—by hiding it, robust'. It is his own doubt, of personal and sexual identity, that generates the tension in his disciplined verses, where regularity of rhythm and exactitude of rhyme do the strapping in:

> Ferocity existing in the fence
> Built by an exercised intelligence.
>
> ('To Yvor Winters')

In the late fifties Gunn moved to America, and from his third book on (*My Sad Captains*, 1961) a disciplined submission of will to experience has replaced the assertions of *Fighting Terms* (1954) and *The Sense of Movement* (1957). The poetry is no less tense, but more pliably seeks, in a free verse owing much to the American, William Carlos Williams, a

> dark
> wide realm where we
> walk with everyone
>
> ('Touch')

—a poetry set free of the trammels of class and of history.

Donald Davie (b. 1922), another Movement poet, starts off something like Amis and Gunn, all energy and definition:

> A poem is less an orange than a grid:
> It hoists a charge; it does not ooze a juice,
> It has no rind, being entirely hard.
>
> ('Poem as Abstract')

The title of his first book, *Brides of Reason* (1955), is an abbreviated Movement manifesto, but, as he develops, his poetry becomes more relaxed and more various. A distinguished scholar and critic, Davie found himself almost inevitably drawn to consider qualities of Englishness. He is well read in American and Russian poetry and these, together with that of the English eighteenth century, have left their mark on his poetry, which is at once lyric and contemplative, handing itself over to its subject-matter as in 'Green River':

> It exclaims to itself for ever:
> This water is passing by!
> It arrives, and it is leaving!

Indeed, Davie's whole career as a poet manifests creative restlessness, a perpetual turning upon himself in irony or despair and ever different attempts to affirm the kind of positive values still to be won in poems:

> Small clearances, small poems;
> Unlikely now the enormous
> Louring, resonant spaces
> Carved out by a Virgil.
>
> ('Ars Poetica')

Fifties tension finds its most benevolent form in this restlessness.

The ideal of a 'rational' verse put forward by Conquest underlies the fifties admiration for Robert Graves (1895–1985), poet of a much earlier generation, whose fastidiously lucid lyrics won him the admiration and reputation he deserved in this decade. Characteristically, his poems are invested with romantic emotion, but the language used is clear and definite, reflecting ironically on human expectations:

> Why never a warning, either by speech or look,
>   That the love you cruelly gave me could not last?
> Already it was too late: the bait swallowed,
>   The hook fast.
>
> ('The Foreboding')

A poem of the late twenties praises a butterfly's 'honest idiocy of flight'—it has a 'flying-crooked gift'. It was this self-deprecating irony that charmed the fifties, who did not see that, since 1948, when Graves published his exposition of poetic myth, *The White Goddess*, he had been flying crooked to their own line of progress, charting out a poetry of more deeply committed irrationality than they could ever countenance.

The fifties also saw the return to favour of W. H. Auden, who was Oxford Professor of Poetry for five years from 1956, at which time he acquired a permanent summer base in Austria. Auden's arrival in America in 1939 had been quickly followed by a return to practising Christianity: his poetry of the forties shows him adjusting to a new earnestness, and the long poems of the period, apart from the scintillating *New Year Letter* (*The Double Man*) (1940),

are rather cumbersome pieces. *Collected Shorter Poems 1930–1944* (1950) drew attention not only to the revisions Auden had made in his earlier work—were they or were they not signs of betrayal of the thirties common cause?—but also to the impressive elegiac poems (on Yeats, Freud, Ernst Toller, and, belatedly, Henry James) written in the last ten years. *The Shield of Achilles* (1955) confirmed that the new Horatian Auden proclaimed in *Nones* (1951) really had arrived. The tone is now relaxed; it seeks to be urbane and on occasion it is so, as in the opening of 'In Praise of Limestone':

> If it form the one landscape that we, the inconstant ones,
> Are consistently homesick for, this is chiefly
> Because it dissolves in water . . .

'We, the inconstant ones': the rueful acceptance of imperfection is itself gracefully accepted, not dwelt on. There is, of course, something dangerous to the subject about such ease, and late Auden does succumb to complacency and garrulousness, however much spiced up with carefully culled idiom and exotic word ('I'm no photophil who burns / his body brown on beaches . . .'). On the other hand, he remained always an inventive poet, his lighter touches most beguiling, and capable of stabbing home, as in the 1953 lyric, 'The Willow-wren and the Stare':

> She laughed, he laughed, they laughed together,
>   Then they ate and drank:
> *Did he know what he meant?* said the willow-wren—
>   *God only knows*, said the stare.

For all the lucidity of its form, the blankness is very much of its time.

In 1946 Auden had become an American citizen. It is a reminder to us of the way the world was changing in balance of power as well as in enlarged possibility. Auden's Americanness gives his later poetry a special ring. It is not, of course, American in the sense that William Carlos Williams or Wallace Stevens are; but its exploitation of the dictionary, its well-travelled urbanity, do much to purge his poetry of the public-school tones of the thirties. Just as well: literature in England in the fifties starts to adjust to the class-consciousness of the twentieth century, and its writers, though mostly Oxford or Cambridge graduates, tend to play down their middle-class origins. That is part of the meaning of Conquest's 'empirical' attitude; the fifties honestly sought to be free of the stereotypes of class, to get beyond class to some more essential form of life. This aspect is most noticeable in the theatre.

British theatre had been in the doldrums artistically for some time. Management and writers had got into a cosy relationship with their middle-class audience, and the fear of shocking middlebrow sensibility had slowly drained the life out of contemporary drama. Gifted writers such as Noël Coward (1899–1973) frittered their talents away in plays which suggested they might have a content, only to let it evaporate into pleasantry. This happens in his comedy *Private Lives* (1930) which starts as a witty study in boredom and insecurity but ends by averting its eyes from the social implications of its own psychological insights. Eliot's adventures in drama were too few and too specialized (*Murder in the Cathedral* was after all designed specifically for performance in the cathedral at Canterbury) to make much impression on the theatre as a whole. The thirties engagement in drama, encouraged by the success of Auden and Isherwood's political-psychological cocktails, *The Dog Beneath the Skin* (1935) and *The Ascent of F6* (1936), foundered in earnestness and the amateurism of the companies on which it had to depend. By the fifties, however, things had changed and a new theatre came into being, relying not at all on the old middle-class orthodoxies and appealing to far younger audiences. At the Theatre Royal, Stratford, in London's East End, Joan Littlewood, who had worked in street theatre in the thirties, staged classic drama and new plays in an atmosphere of music-hall and melodrama with a popular touch. In 1956 she produced Brendan Behan's *The Quare Fellow* there in an enormously successful production—the play had in fact been first performed two years earlier in Dublin.

Brendan Behan (1923–64) was Irish working-class, eloquent, alcoholic, and much given to song. He attempted a bombing-raid on a Liverpool dockyard in 1939 and was sent to Borstal, that is, a corrective school, in England. In 1942 he went to an Irish gaol for the attempted murder of two detectives, and was released under a general amnesty in 1946. Behan was, as this suggests, passionate, anarchic, and irresponsible; but he knew the life of the underdog and the underdog's view of authority. He gave exuberant expression to both in *The Hostage* (1958) which sets a tragicomic story of IRA politics in a Dublin brothel. Song is more important here than in *The Quare Fellow* which presents an Irish gaol where a man is about to be hanged, but both plays make use of it in a way that underlines affinities with *The Beggar's Opera*, and emphasizes too the differences between this sort of drama—exaggerated, plotless, sentimental, not at all pretending to 'realism'—and the bloodless comedies of meditated infidelity that were the stuff of West End theatre:

many's the time the Bible was a consolation to a fellow all alone in the old cell. The lovely thin paper with a bit of mattress coir in it, and if you could get a match or a bit of tinder or any class of light, was as good a smoke as ever I tasted. Am I right, Dunlavin?

This genial, shrewd comedy in some sense shows up the English agony about class by the ease with which it takes the coexistence of human pettiness and solidarity for granted. *Look Back in Anger* (1956), staged at the Royal Court Theatre, a centre for more overtly ambitious innovation, in the same year as *The Quare Fellow* was at Stratford East, is a full-blown specimen of fifties unease. John Osborne (b. 1929), the playwright, has described himself as educated at 'a rather cheap boarding-school'. The phrase betrays the uncomfortable self-consciousness that makes Jimmy Porter, his angry young man, so gripping a stage character, lacerating himself as he lacerates the shrunken, mean half-life of the Britain he sees around him: 'Nobody thinks, nobody cares. No beliefs, no convictions and no enthusiasm. Just another Sunday evening.' Osborne's skills as a dramatist are primitive; he excels only in the tirade. His plays refuse to develop; they are stuck with their given monologuist. But in *Look Back in Anger* he touched the nerve of the time. Jimmy is a dislikeable woman-hating university graduate who runs a sweet stall in the market and maltreats his wife. Osborne's view of him is different:

He is a disconcerting mixture of sincerity and cheerful malice, of tenderness and freebooting cruelty; restless, importunate, full of pride . . . Blistering honesty, or apparent honesty, like his, makes few friends.

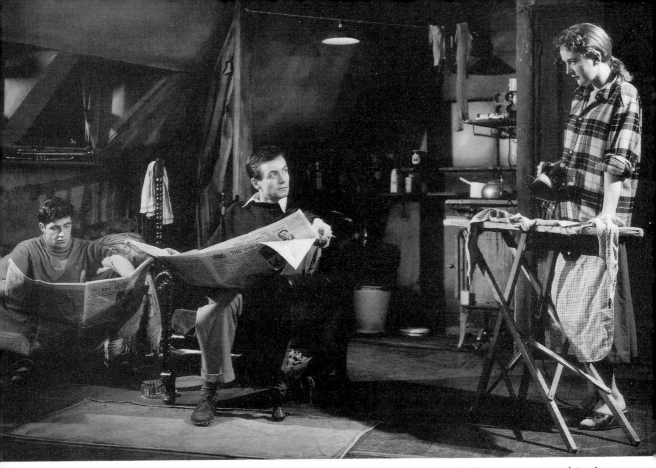

IRONING BOARD AND KITCHEN SINK, the symbols of the new British drama, as presented in the Royal Court theatre's production of *Look Back in Anger* (1956). Note the cleanliness of Osborne's angry young men.

The qualification 'or apparent honesty' points to the ambiguity both of the character and the author's understanding of him. This is, then, a telling example of the doubtful quality of fifties 'honesty'. The play is an explosion of frustration. The social-historical point is made by Jimmy himself:

The old Edwardian brigade do make their brief little world look pretty tempting . . . even I regret it somehow, phoney or not. If you've no world of your own, it's rather pleasant to regret the passing of someone else's.

This was the year of Britain's humiliation in the Suez affair when the Anglo-French attempt to exercise 'authority' of the old-fashioned gunboat kind in reply to the nationalization of the Suez canal led to withdrawal under pressure from both the United Nations Assembly and the United States. The country was, in any case, divided over the issue, and Osborne's second play, his best, *The Entertainer* (1957), caught the mood of frustration and mourning brilliantly in its picture of the superannuated music-hall comedian Archie Rice, ending up with his performance in front of a nude tableau of Britannia:

Don't clap too hard, we're all in a very old building. Yes, very old. Old. What about *that*? What about *her*, eh—Madam with the helmet on? I reckon she's sagging a bit, if you ask me.

Given the bitter feelings to which the present moment could give rise, it is not surprising that the fifties saw various attempts in poetry and fiction to transcend or transfigure the image of contemporary Britain. *The Anathemata* (1952) of David Jones, whose *In Parenthesis* (1937) was considered in the previous chapter, is a case in point, 'fragments of an attempted writing' the purpose of which is to define and preserve a sense of cultural identity at an unfavourable time. Jones, both Welsh and English by inheritance, takes his bearings in history from the Christian empire of the West and its roots in Roman culture. His poem, like Ezra Pound's *Cantos*, opens up large historical vistas, only in his case they are illuminated by a gentle Christian humanism. Like Pound, Jones has much of the amateur scholar about him, and there is something endearingly awkward, perhaps a trifle gimcrack, about his experimentalism, which is indebted to both Joyce and Eliot. But if he is an amateur, he is the amateur in his most committed form, and this, together with an increasing sense of erosion of the national identity, and of western Christianity as beleaguered, explains the gradual elevation of this interesting writer to heights not wholly justified.

The novelist William Golding (b. 1911) though not concerned with national identity is equally taken up with Christianity and with archetypes of human experience. Golding is more concerned with the evil that is in man than with his place at the end of a historic process, a rearguard unconscious 'that dead symbols litter the base of the cult-stone . . . that the stream is very low', as Jones has it. *Lord of the Flies* (1954) is an uncompromising story of the evil that is in men—or, in this case, English schoolboys marooned on a tropical island, who lose their 'civilized' veneer speedily and take to the worship of death. It is an inversion of the famous book for boys by R. M. Ballantyne, *The Coral Island* (1857), all the more effective for its crisp telling, which overlays a complex and disturbing symbolism. Golding's second novel, *The Inheritors* (1955), is a story of the coming of *Homo sapiens*, ousting the gentle Neanderthalers with a cruelty and determination which the novelist pits ironically against the optimistic view of 'progress' in H. G. Wells's *Outline of History*.

Golding is an inventive novelist, and needs to be, as the forays into the present day in *Pincher Martin* (1956), *Free Fall* (1959), and *Darkness Visible* (1979) show. His dialogue in these novels is too often implausibly cumbersome, ill-adapted to the symbolic burden it must carry. The successful novels are those where there is no test of realism possible—as in *The Spire* (1964), about the raising of a cathedral spire, symbol of the longing for God and of the self-regarding pride that frustrates such longing. The remote and medieval

ANTHONY GROSS'S JACKET FOR *PINCHER MARTIN*, a work of art in itself. John Piper and Sidney Nolan have also helped William Golding to proclaim at first glance the serious intentions of his work.

setting mitigates the awkwardly literary quality of the prose and the convincing account of the building process itself gives the book narrative thrust; and these allow its 'moral' to inhabit it with a freedom not at first expected from Golding's novelistic deliberation:

How proud their hope of hell is. There is no innocent work. God knows where God may be.

The sense of sin, the sense of separation from God, the sense that 'there is no innocent work' are fundamental to Golding's deeply pessimistic view of the human race and of its conduct in the twentieth century in particular. In the light of the angry blankness with which others of his contemporaries face their world this theologically well-developed pessimism may appear to have positive values, even to represent a kind of release; but the firm outlines which Golding gives his fictions—'fables' is a word he has on occasion used—exercise a compensatory restraint. The reader is never left to his own devices, but is subject to the always questionable power of the novelist himself—'there is *no* innocent work', and Golding is sunk as deep as his fellows in the morass of fifties uncertainty and panic. His most genial novel, *Rites of Passage* (1980), is, after all, about a man who dies of shame; and the way in which the homosexual encounter which provokes that shame is described disturbs with calculated awkwardness the poise of the book, both as rattling sea adventure and as allegory.

The Sixties and Seventies: Dreams Revived

In 1982 a British military expedition steamed all the way to the South Atlantic in order to restore British rule to the Falkland Islands, which had been for a short time occupied by Argentine forces. The move was enormously popular in Britain. It was as though the humiliation of Britain's last major international intervention at Suez were redeemed. Despite the country's reduced circumstances—in 1968, for example, it had had finally to abandon its role as a world defence power—the British people still yearned for the days when their gunboats went scuttling round the globe keeping good imperial order. They were quite unchastened by their inability to keep themselves in order; there had been continual violence in Northern Ireland since the division between Republicans and Unionists ('Roman Catholics' and 'Protestants') had surfaced again in 1968, an inheritance from the partition of Ireland in 1922 and from unhappy centuries of quasi-colonial rule that had preceded it. Nor did British membership of the European Economic Community, which the country joined in 1973, do anything to establish a new European identity for the former world power; its membership was preceded and followed by continuous bickering, and associated with the large increases in unemployment of the late seventies and eighties. The British people were neither what they had been nor what they truly were. Their crisis of identity is mirrored in the way in which government changed hands every six or seven years in this period. The country just did not know what to make of itself.

Nevertheless, the sixties were a time of important changes, of which the abolition of capital punishment in 1969 is representative. New legislation embodied new, more strictly secular attitudes to morality; 1967 saw the legalization of abortion and of homosexuality within well-defined limits. These changes had an obvious effect on the content of literature; indeed they had been heralded by the judgment in 1960 that Lawrence's *Lady Chatterley's Lover*, banned for almost thirty years, was not after all obscene. In 1968 the censorship of plays for public performance by the Lord Chamberlain's office, a practice going back to 1737, came to an end; whatever the British public wanted to see on the stage it now might see. This was the 'permissive' society reflecting the manners of a young generation. Indeed, Britain in the sixties was represented as a young society, partly in an attempt to throw off the shadows of the fifties, partly as an aspect of the new commercial exploitation of the

ALLEN GINSBERG, an American poet, at the Albert Hall in 1965: poetry in the company of a new patron, modern publicity.

young whose earnings were now worth competing for. London for a brief time became a world fashion centre. But the access of wealth and energy was largely illusory. In 1970, in a final tribute to youth, the age at which people were entitled to vote and to enter into binding contracts was reduced from twenty-one to eighteen, at just about the same time as the economy went into decline, unemployment increasing throughout the seventies and into the eighties.

The new wealth and status of young people in the sixties resulted in a new emphasis on the performing arts. They wanted to be together, at concerts of new popular music especially, but also at poetry readings and plays. The theatrical revival of the fifties took new impetus from this turn in events; poetry was less radically affected. The novel suffered; solitary reading was not to the modern taste, and having withstood bravely the rivalry of radio and the cinema from the twenties on, novelists now found they had to compete in the home with television. Their readership was ageing.

In the theatre the anxieties of the fifties were still at work, notably in the plays of Harold Pinter (b. 1930). These owe a great deal to Beckett; they

PINTER'S *BIRTHDAY PARTY*: the gift of a toy drum precipitates loss of control. Stanley's face should be 'savage and possessed'. Later, he is the object of other people's menace. Bryan Pringle and Doris Hare in the 1964 revival.

confine themselves to very few characters, action is minimal (and where it occurs is hard to explain), place is ill-defined, and symbolic meanings are frequently hinted at. Violence is always a possibility, as in his first substantial piece, *The Birthday Party* (1958), in which two strangers intrude into a seaside boarding-house to torment the hapless Stanley:

GOLDBERG: When did you last pray?
MCCANN: He's sweating!
GOLDBERG: Is the number 846 possible or necessary?
STANLEY: Neither.
GOLDBERG: Wrong! Is the number 864 possible or necessary?
STANLEY: Both.
GOLDBERG: Wrong! It's necessary but not possible.
STANLEY: Both.
GOLDBERG: Wrong! Why do you think the number 846 is necessarily possible?
STANLEY: Must be.
GOLDBERG: Wrong! It's only necessarily necessary . . .

The inert language is used like a blunt instrument to beat Stanley about the head; and indeed later in the play his interrogators do beat him up physically. A similar sort of verbal and physical violence is on display in *The Caretaker* (1960). Mick's first act towards the down-and-out Davies, whom his brother Aston has brought home, is to take him unawares and force him to the floor before subjecting him to interrogation. At the end of the play Davies is driven out by Mick's menacing use of language:

Honest. I can take nothing you say at face value. Every word you speak is open to any number of different interpretations. Most of what you say is lies. You're violent, you're erratic, you're just completely unpredictable.

But Mick also is violent, erratic, and unpredictable, and his brother Aston, who has undergone brain surgery, though not violent, has small rationality in his actions. This is bleaker and emptier than anything in Beckett. It is, certainly, good theatre; the actors inscribe what they please on the blank features of Pinter's prose. But where Beckett gets us to attend to the human presence, Pinter insists on insubstantiality, on the unpredictable course of a performance.

Outside the theatre his plays barely exist; and this is another of their troubling qualities. They are, of course, open to interpretation, and archetype and myth have been invoked in order to explain their power. These explanations tend to distort the action, however, by reducing our sense of its unexpectedness. Pinter depends on his work exceeding our grasp by the very fragility of its structure. In later plays he has focused on sexual feeling as the catalyst for unexpected horrors. In *Old Times* (1971), for example, there is no violence; husband, wife, and woman friend mix memory and desire in an unsettling way, until the wife 'remembers' seeing her friend dead. It is an assertion of hostility that, in a way characteristic of Pinter's plays, seems to come from nowhere. Its sudden emergence contrasts with the nauseatingly familiar materials of cliché and euphemism out of which characters manufacture their dull lives and ordinary fantasies: 'He thought I was going to be sexually forthcoming, that I was about to take a long-promised initiative.' Uncertainties of tone in later plays such as *Old Times* and its successor *No Man's Land* (1975) show how difficult is the abstention from expressiveness on which this style is based. The consistently spare style of *Betrayal* (1978), however, implies a reassertion of the writer's authority over his material. The subject is a man's adultery with his best friend's wife. It is told backwards, but the effect is to emphasize how little is to be understood by going back to the beginning. When Jerry declares himself, he does so in a language already stale with use, despite his insistence that it is entirely new: 'You're lovely. I'm crazy about you. All these words I'm using, don't you see, they've never been said before. Can't you see? I'm crazy about you.' The affair starts from nowhere; but it is already old when it is born. Like all Pinter's plays, it is a non-naturalistic piece. It depends on compelling acquiescence from the audience in its glimpse at the horror underlying the present moment. Pinter's grasp of pace and acting possibilities makes sure that it does.

These plays are classless in a way that was new to the British stage. Characters are conspicuously detached from the class structure, whether they have money or not. Their isolation and anxiety belong with a sense of unrootedness (significantly Arnold Wesker's *Roots*, an attack on the enclosed values of rural society, had been a great success in 1959). Pinter himself was the son of an East End tailor whose literary career detached him from his class origins. Joe Orton (1933–67), son of a gardener, evidently responded to this aspect of Pinter's work; his first full-length play, *Entertaining Mr Sloane* (1964), owes a great deal to him in its story of a young man, Sloane, who intrudes into the life of a brother and sister. This is, however, comedy, or rather a comic reworking of Pinter's violence. Sloane, who has already killed once, batters old Kemp to death, but Kath and Ed are so besotted with his smooth skin they cover up their father's murder in order to share his favours between them.

All three of Orton's major plays had a rough reception at first. Their mixture of brutality and absurd, amoral humour was hard even for the permissive society to take. It was helped down by the change in his second play, *Loot*

JOE ORTON. Postcard reproductions of this drawing by Patrick Procktor were given away with the programme at the original performances of *Crimes of Passion* (1967). A few months later Orton was dead, killed by his lover Kenneth Halliwell.

(1967), to a more exuberant dialogue with Wildean hints: 'Your explanation had the ring of truth. Naturally I disbelieved it.' The contrast with Orton's lavishly bad taste is piquant. *Loot* is a farce about a young man who hides the proceeds of a robbery in his mother's coffin; in transferring her body to a cupboard one of her glass eyes falls out. Much play is made with it subsequently. Christianity is a favourite target for Orton: 'A mendicant monk objected to something I'd said. Made a terrible mess of my face with his crucifix.' Sex takes the place of love, and is always in demand. It has no serious consequences; rape is therefore a comic subject. So are all forms of authority or pretensions to it. Orton releases the anarchism of a child on the little world of the theatre.

Despite his avowed intention to upset middle-class complacency, this anarchism hardly threatens revolution. The non-naturalistic quality of farce insulates the plays from the real world. When someone complains, 'The British police force used to be run by men of integrity,' and gets the reply, 'That is a mistake that has been rectified,' the criticism possible in the exchange remains dormant. Orton respects rules too much to suggest they could be dispensed with. His last play, *What the Butler Saw* (1969), is a brilliant farce set in a psychiatrist's nursing home. Incest, blackmail, and rape are essential to the plot, yet the overall effect is genial and comic. Mrs Prentice has slept with her own son, Dr Prentice wants to seduce his own daughter—the themes of Freudian psychology are found to be entirely appropriate to the conventions of farce, the confusions of identity, women in their underclothes, and men in women's dress. Laughter, the purging of fear, is the natural successor to the mysterious horrors of Pinter. Orton's comedy, in its equivocal way, reflects enough of the fear to be therapeutic, thriving on the business of playing with fire.

Another dramatist, Tom Stoppard (b. 1937) carried on this comic mood into the seventies. The bad taste of Orton is missing, however. Stoppard's plays succeed by surprising and imaginative stage-effects—sections of *Hamlet* mix with Stoppard's own writing in *Rosencrantz and Guildenstern are Dead* (1966). *Jumpers* (1972) starts with the building and collapse of a mysterious human pyramid. *Travesties* (1974) has James Joyce make his entry with a limerick, and the dialogue continues in this form for some time. Stoppard replaces Orton's Freudian and sexual concerns with philosophical ones. Rosencrantz and Guildenstern pass the time in debating probability and chance; in *Jumpers* George, a professional philosopher, grapples with the possibility of God's existence; in *The Real Inspector Hound* (1968), where the 'audience' become involved in a stage 'crime', the theme, as often, is illusion and the construction of rival realities. The philosophy does not give the plays intellectual depth; it distances anxiety by placing it on a remote, metaphysical plane. In later plays, such as the story of dissidence and a philosophical conference, *Professional Foul* (1977), Stoppard takes himself uncomfortably seriously. His dramatic gift is adapted not to criticism but, like Orton's, to accommodation.

THE POPE'S WEDDING in its successful revival of 1984–5; Bond's village lads, nowhere to go, nothing to do, gaze out into nothingness.

Naturally a counter-tendency manifested itself in the theatre, falling in with the radical sympathies of the new young liberal audience. Edward Bond (b. 1934) has become a dramatist of Brechtian pretensions, using Brecht's brisk narrative technique, his exposure of the conventional nature of drama, and his point-making songs. He began as something much more interesting and original. *The Pope's Wedding* (1962) and *Saved* (1965) are studies in the intellectual and emotional poverty of working-class life. The dialogue has its Pinter qualities ('No one 'ome?'—'No'—'Live on yer tod?'—'No'—'O'), but the social dimension is to the fore. In *Saved* a group of youths stone a baby to death in its pram, but the casual violence is all too comprehensible a product of their empty lives. What is remarkable is the representation of ethical heroism in this setting as Len acts to reaffirm the meaning of life in a final scene that has almost abandoned words altogether. Bond's third play *Early Morning* (1968), a deliberately grotesque fantasy about the persistence of 'Victorian' values, begins his decline into predictability. But both *The Narrow Road to the Deep North* (1968) and *The Sea* (1973), the former a Brechtian comedy set in an imaginary Japan, the latter an updated Shavian *Tempest*, are impressive and exciting.

Other plays suffer from their lack of surprise. *Restoration* (1981) is a class-conscious Restoration comedy, but the wit suffers at the hands of speciously theoretical politics. *Lear* (1971), a violent transposal of Shakespeare's play, though brilliant in conception, offers an extravagance that is finally both boring and repellent. By the eighties the steam was running down in British theatre.

The same might also be said of the novel. The causes here are more obvious. The reading public for serious fiction declined after the war with the rise of television; this meant that novelists took greater risks and had to compromise more if they wanted to live by writing. Improved communications on the other hand led to the quicker publication of novels from elsewhere. Since the fifties the novel has been especially strong in America (Nabokov, Bellow, Malamud, Bashevis Singer) and Russia (Pasternak, Solzhenitsyn, Sinyavsky). In the late sixties Latin America joined them, first with the anglophile Argentine Borges, then with García Márquez and Vargas Llosa. The result was a sapping of confidence, a flight from large themes. Within the English tradition Commonwealth writers such as Nadine Gordimer, Doris Lessing, and V. S. Naipaul represented, by their talent, a new threat.

One novelist who survives is Muriel Spark (b. 1918). Her novels interestingly reflect the development in the theatre from horror to comedy. She is a witty writer. In *Memento Mori* (1959) a group of old people receive anonymous telephone calls reminding them of inevitable death; the author regards their reluctance to take the message with a cool eye:

'Lisa Brooke be damned,' said Dame Lettie, which would have been an alarming statement if intended seriously, for Lisa Brooke was not many moments dead . . .

Spark's Roman Catholicism makes her comedy very different from that of the theatre, however. Her novels celebrate the affirmation of faith and the exercise of choice. In *The Girls of Slender Means* (1963) Nicholas Farringdon, anarchist and poet, is turned to the religious life by a revelation of evil in someone else's indifference to suffering. Spark likes to set her novels in enclosed communities, deriving comedy from the juxtaposition of differences which her characters conspire to overlook as long as possible; the novels have a musical quality in the way they weave voices together, each identified by its own leitmotif. Only *The Mandelbaum Gate* (1965) sets out to explore character. Exploration is too hesitant a practice for Spark for whom, crisply, a novelist has conviction or is no novelist. Hallucination recurs in her novels, from *The Comforters* (1957) to *Loitering with Intent* (1981); it is the spur to self-determination. Later novels show some coarsening of perception—*The Abbess of Crewe* (1974) attempts mordancy in its satire on modern religious politics, and achieves rancour—but they are remarkably various in form and setting, each book a new start, a new confession of what there is to be believed.

Distinguished examples of the realist novel become hard to find. However, *The Lonely Passion of Miss Judith Hearne* (1955), a remarkable novel by Brian

Moore (b. 1921) heralded an impressive career. It is the story of an unattractive, lonely Belfast spinster driven by drink from boarding-house to boarding-house to nursing home. The style and subject-matter owe much to Joyce, but Moore elicits a sympathy that was no part of Joyce's aim, in *Dubliners* at least. Moore was born an Ulster Catholic, but emigrated to Canada in the late forties and now lives in California; his novels hover between the English and American traditions in style and subject-matter. *Catholics* (1972) recalls Spark in its story of the extirpation of the Latin Mass in a remote island monastery

MURIEL SPARK speaks her mind in a setting of modest luxury. Her novels comparably house a disposition not to mince words in their elegant structures.

off the coast of Ireland; *The Temptation of Eileen Hughes* (1981), set in London and Belfast, is about a man driven crazy by his obsession with a young girl whom he sees as an image of purity. Moore's remarkable quality is his ability to concentrate on psychological and ethical issues; the social reality is not skimped or ignored, but it is kept in its place. His Irish origins and life of exile give his form of classless creation a strength lacking in the theatre.

Indeed, in the post-war period Ireland fostered a great deal of talent, especially in its poets. First the shadow of Yeats had to be cast off; it was Austin Clarke (1896-1974) who in his later years showed that another Irish style than the Yeatsian was possible. It is adumbrated in *Night and Morning* (1938) but does not realize itself fully until *Ancient Lights* (1955) and its many successors—a rough wild poetry deeply engaged with the local issues of Irish religion and politics but, because these issues are taken up with ethical seriousness, reaching beyond them as in the scorn he brings to plans for the removal of Nelson's Pillar in Dublin:

> No, let him watch the sky
> With those who rule. Stone eye
> And telescope can prove
> Our blessings are above . . .
>
> ('Nelson's Pillar, Dublin')

Clarke's adaptation of Gaelic verse forms to such material and in such a tone were a revelation to Irish poets of the possibilities in a situation that had often enough been seen as circumscribed.

Two poets of a younger generation to realize some of these possibilities were Thomas Kinsella (b. 1928) and John Montague (b. 1929). Kinsella is an unaccommodating poet of passionate and anguished inner life; an early poem speaks of the unconscious process that gives birth to poetry as

> the alien
> Garrison in my own blood
> Keeps constant contact with the main
> Mystery, not to be understood.
>
> ('Baggot Street Deserta')

Later poems explore the idea of self in poems that mingle memories of childhood with dream-images (Clarke, alive to the complications of modern psychology, also wrote two poems from 'a diary of dreams'). Kinsella is a disturbing and lonely figure in poetry, witness to a pain that permeates all, so that even love is likened to the binding together of two trees (like Baucis and Philemon in the classical legend): 'their join / A slowly twisted scar, that I recognise . . .' Montague's concern is with history, personal and national, couched in a style that is unemphatic, translucent, and yet achieved. Gaelic culture and language underlie Montague's English as the objects of understanding, and as what eludes the poet's understanding too, as in 'The Grafted Tongue':

> To grow
> a second tongue, as
> harsh a humiliation
> as twice to be born.
> Decades later
> that child's grandchild's
> speech stumbles over lost
> syllables of an old order.

This is from *The Rough Field* (1972), an ambitious attempt to write about Ulster and the causes of violence. The verse form reflects American free verse, but its expressive hesitances at the line-ending are peculiarly Montague's.

Seamus Heaney (b. 1939), like Montague, comes from Ulster Catholic stock. His first collection, *Death of a Naturalist* (1966), might recall the nature poetry of someone like Edward Thomas, were it not closer to the horrors of childhood; in 'The Barn'

SEAMUS HEANEY, the poet with his feet on the ground, behind him a jungle of alien life. 'I rhyme / To see myself, to set the darkness echoing' ('Personal Helicon'). The portrait is by Edward McGuire (1974).

> I lay face-down to shun the fear above.
> The two-legged sacks moved in like great blind rats.

He is a poet of correspondences: the door of *Door into the Dark* (1969) is the door of a smithy but it is also that of the forge of imagination. His profound appreciation of physical skills and tasks and the sensuous quality of his verse combine in celebration of the creativity of ordinary human acts. But the killings and counter-killings in Ulster put him under pressure: *North* (1975) is a record of tides of rape and pillage in Ireland ending with the poet's self-characterization as 'An inner emigré, grown long-haired And thoughtful'. Yet his success was such that he could not simply retire into himself: later poems show strain and anxiety in his relation to his audience, and then, in *Station Island* (1984), a new release.

Among contemporary English poets, Heaney is closest to Ted Hughes (b. 1930) a prolific, near-demonic poet, possessed with the life of nature—'A life subdued to its instrument' as he says of pike in an early poem. The first two books, *The Hawk in the Rain* (1957) and *Lupercal* (1960), retain the trappings of conventionality in their use of rhyme and stanza form, but their message is one of impatience with human intellect and deviousness. With his third book, *Wodwo* (1967), style itself becomes freer, recalling the impulsive spurts (and the droll irony) of D. H. Lawrence:

> I suppose you just gape and let your gaspings
> Rip in and out through your voicebox
> > > > O lark
>
> .   .   .   .
>
> The larks carry their tongues to the last atom
> Battering and battering their last sparks out at the limit . . .
> > > > > > ('Skylarks')

Hughes's great quality as a poet shows in the freshness and directness of his diction, having *gaspings* rip in and out, seeing larks battering *sparks* out— these are audacious usages but entirely within the spoken idiom.

What Heaney responds to in Hughes is the way his poems voice a psychic drama, often violent and distressing, as in the poems of *Crow* (1970), fragments of a sequence which was intended overall to be comic but which in what we have of it truly horrifies. Crow is the survivor, the black instinctive heart of the self for whom love is meaningless:

> God tried to teach Crow how to talk.
> 'Love', said God. 'Say, Love'.
> Crow gaped, and the white shark crashed into the sea
> And went rolling downwards, discovering its own depth.
> > > > ('Crow's First Lesson')

Much of this poetry is anti-human. It reflects the experience of human cruelty

CROW
TED HUGHES

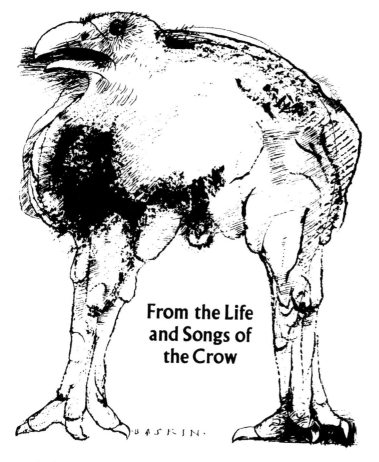

BASKIN'S CROW, more reptile than bird, unnaturally massive, defiantly obscene, a horrific talisman for the late twentieth century.

From the Life and Songs of the Crow

·BASKIN·

underlying the work of contemporary East European poets such as Pilinszky and Popa, both admired by Hughes. But it would be wrong to see it as wholly negative in emphasis. *River* (1983), a celebration of the alien life of the river, and of the fisherman's hunt for his prey, also celebrates community, even that of other people; the river can lead one to

> Try to speak and nearly succeed
> Heal into time and other people.
> ('Go Fishing')

Hughes tells out his life in the force and simplicity of his poetry.

OFFA, KING OF ALL ENGLAND, the 'presiding figure' of Geoffrey Hill's *Mercian Hymns*, from an eighth-century coin (enlarged). 'Ringed by its own lustre, the masterful head emerges, kempt and jutting, out of England's well.'

No greater contrast than that with Geoffrey Hill (b. 1932) could be imagined. Hill's poetry is deliberated, an embodiment of thinking-with-feeling; it cannot forget that the individual is conditioned by history as well as by temperament. Insight is, then, never simple. Where Hughes is prolific, Hill is ascetically sparing. Where Hughes's master is Lawrence, Hill's is Eliot. Hughes's concern with religion is reflected in his construction of an anti-Christian myth based partly on Graves's *White Goddess*, partly on his own studies in anthropology— in this respect *Crow* was only the forerunner for *Cave Birds* (1975) and *Gaudete* (1977). But Hill is concerned with the meaning of Christianity for a society that rejects it but is still indebted to it; his poetry affirms the present force of an absent Christ in verse of metaphysical paradox and Empsonian difficulty, telling Christ

> You are beyond me, innermost true light,
>
> uttermost exile for no exile's sake,
> King of our earth not caring to unclasp
> its void embrace, the semblance of your quiet.

('Lachrimae Coactae')

This can hardly be a popular poetry, but it is nevertheless a poetry of immediate and general concern. The loss of faith is crucial to British experience since the war, and it has its religious dimension; not to know oneself is not to know one's God, the idea one serves. Hill's concern with power and right government has to do with this; for what is the basis for authority but some kind of belief in it? *Mercian Hymns* (1971) is a sequence of prose poems in which memories of the poet's childhood mingle with evocations of the eighth-century King of the Mercians, Offa; it tells a story which is that of the child's becoming a poet and Offa's outgrowing his power. It commemorates the continuity of English history, juxtaposing the pride in suburban homes with the old pride of battle:

> Coiled entrenched England: brickwork and paintwork stalwart above hacked marl. The clashing primary colours—'Ethandune', 'Catraeth', 'Maldon', 'Pengwern'. Steel against yew and privet. Fresh dynasties of smiths.

And, of course, Smiths, the commonplace essential surname of England. Tender and humorous, sober and assured, *Mercian Hymns* revises the dream of empire that has haunted so many British writers, exchanging it for a more complex valuation of both the present and the past—

> the mannerly extortions, languid praise,
> all that devotion long since bought and sold . . .
>
> ('The Laurel Axe')

As for the future, that depends not merely on writers. For the present, there is life in the old dog of English literature yet.

PLACES OF GENERAL LITERARY INTEREST

FURTHER READING

1. OLD AND MIDDLE ENGLISH

GENERAL WORKS

D. Pearsall, *Old English and Middle English Poetry* (Routledge History of English Poetry, vol. 1) (London, 1977), a detailed and lively survey.

K. Malone and A. C. Baugh, *The Middle Ages* (A Literary History of England, vol. 1) (2nd edn., London, 1967), useful for facts.

E. R. Curtius, *European Literature and the Latin Middle Ages*, trans. W. R. Trask (London, 1953), a pioneering study of the Latin traditions behind medieval vernacular literatures.

C. S. Lewis, *The Allegory of Love: A Study of Medieval Tradition* (Oxford, 1936), still valuable, though to be used with caution on courtly love.

M. T. Clanchy, *From Memory to Written Record: England 1066-1307* (London, 1979), excellent historical study of the growth of literacy.

R. M. Wilson, *The Lost Literature of Medieval England* (2nd edn., London, 1970), a salutary reminder of the works which do not survive.

OLD ENGLISH LITERATURE

C. L. Wrenn, *A Study of Old English Literature* (London, 1967), a general account.

E. G. Stanley (ed.), *Continuations and Beginnings: Studies in Old English Literature* (London, 1966), notable essays on major authors and genres.

T. A. Shippey, *Old English Verse* (London, 1972), the best introduction to the subject.

A. G. Brodeur, *The Art of Beowulf* (Berkeley, Calif., 1959), a general study of the poem.

K. Sisam, *The Structure of Beowulf* (Oxford, 1965), bracingly sceptical about everything, not least the structure.

MIDDLE ENGLISH LITERATURE

D. Everett, *Essays on Middle English Literature*, ed. P. M. Kean (Oxford, 1955), sober and penetrating.

B. Ford (ed.), *Medieval Literature: Chaucer and the Alliterative Tradition* (New Pelican Guide to English Literature, vol. 1, pt. 1) (London, 1982), essays by various hands, with a useful anthology of texts.

A. C. Spearing, *Criticism and Medieval Poetry* (2nd edn., London, 1972), stimulating critical discussions.

T. Turville-Petre, *The Alliterative Revival* (Cambridge, 1977), the best study of an obscure subject.

J. A. Burrow, *Ricardian Poetry: Chaucer, Gower, Langland and the Gawain Poet* (London, 1971), treats the age of Richard II as a literary period.

D. S. Brewer (ed.), *Chaucer and Chaucerians* (London, 1966), essays by various hands on Chaucer and his successors.

J. A. W. Bennett, *The Parlement of Foules: An Interpretation* (Oxford, 1957), a learned exposition of Chaucer's reading and thought.

E. T. Donaldson, *Speaking of Chaucer* (London, 1970), various essays by Chaucer's best recent critic.

C. Muscatine, *Chaucer and the French Tradition* (Berkeley, Calif., 1957), wide-ranging and influential study of Chaucer in relation to French medieval poetry.

D. W. Robertson, *A Preface to Chaucer: Studies in Medieval Perspectives* (Princeton, NJ, 1962), controversial but salutary attack on complacent modern views of Chaucer, in the name of 'historical criticism'.

A. C. Spearing, *The Gawain-Poet: A Critical Study* (Cambridge, 1970), perceptive discussions of the four poems ascribed to this writer.

R. W. Frank, *Piers Plowman and the Scheme of Salvation* (New Haven, Conn., 1957), the most helpful study of *Piers*.

R. Woolf, *The English Religious Lyric in the Middle Ages* (Oxford, 1968), the standard comprehensive work.

—— *The English Mystery Plays* (London, 1972), a general study.

V. A. Kolve, *The Play Called Corpus Christi* (London, 1967), intelligent and interesting discussion of mystery plays.

D. Mehl, *The Middle English Romances of the Thirteenth and Fourteenth Centuries* (London, 1968), useful survey.

D. Gray, *Robert Henryson* (Leiden, 1980), the best study of a fine poet.

2. TUDOR LITERATURE

SURVEYS AND HISTORIES

C. S. Lewis, *English Literature in the Sixteenth Century, Excluding Drama* (Oxford, 1954), a formidable literary history: provocative and still the best place to begin reading about Tudor writers.

E. R. Curtius, *European Literature and the Latin Middle Ages*, trans. Willard R. Trask (London, 1953), essential for the advanced student of literary forms.

J. Burckhardt, *The Civilisation of the Renaissance* (a convenient translation is the one by S. G. C. Middlemore, revised by Irene Gordon, New York, 1960), at various times, revered, attacked, and dismissed, but still an important account of that major Renaissance art-form, the modern state.

J. Huizinga, *The Waning of the Middle Ages*, trans. F. Hopman (London, 1927), controversial but outstanding.

F. A. Yates, *Astraea: the Imperial Theme in the Sixteenth Century* (London, 1975), readings of the political, religious, and iconographic history of early European courts.

J. Hollander, *Vision and Resonance* (New Haven and London, 2nd edn. 1985), on poetry and music, with special attention to several Renaissance poets (Campion, Jonson, etc.).

WAYS OF READING

R. Tuve, *Elizabethan and Metaphysical Imagery* (Chicago and London, 1947), a useful guide to what the Elizabethans expected of poetic devices.

W. J. Ong, *Rhetoric, Romance and Technology* (Ithaca and London, 1971), enviable knowledge and easy delivery in discussing Tudor rhetoric, poetics, and education.

A. Fowler, *Conceitful Thought* (Edinburgh, 1975), essays in historical and generic criticism (on Wyatt, Spenser, etc.): the best of its kind. ·

R. Lanham, *The Motives of Eloquence* (New Haven and London, 1976), an interesting introduction to the significance of rhetoric in the Renaissance and its implications for the western notion of the self.

BOOKS OF ARGUMENT

H. A. Mason, *Humanism and Poetry in the Early Tudor Period* (London, 1959), informed, sensitive, and as argumentative as possible. Mason has literary taste and judgement, even if it now looks a little dated. The same is true of:

J. Buxton, *Elizabethan Taste* (London, 1963), an excellent guide to the connections between Elizabethan literature and the other arts.

R. Southall, *The Courtly Maker: an Essay on the Poetry of Wyatt and his Contemporaries* (Oxford, 1964), helpful on the emerging Protestant imagination.

S. Greenblatt, *Renaissance Self-Fashioning* (Chicago and London, 1980), convincing readings of texts in terms of social and individual power, desire, and consciousness: especially good on More.

ESSAYS

A useful compilation is *Elizabethan Poetry: Lyrical and Narrative*, ed. G. Hammond (London, 1984) ('Casebook' series); the extracts from Coleridge, Winters, Richards, and Hunter all get the mind moving. Other essays well worth reading:

D. Jones, 'The Myth of Arthur', in *Epoch and Artist: Selected Writings* (London, 1959).

D. Davie, 'A Reading of "The Ocean's Love to Cynthia"', in *Elizabethan Poetry*, ed. J. R. Brown and B. Harris (London, 1960).

C. S. Lewis, *Spenser's Images of Life*, ed. Alastair Fowler (Cambridge, 1967).

Ted Hughes, Introduction and 'Note' to his Faber selection, *A Choice of Shakespeare's Verse* (London, 1971), the most intelligent, if wayward, essay written on *Venus and Adonis*, and Shakespeare's personal mythology, since Coleridge.

3. WILLIAM SHAKESPEARE

(*Prepared by Stanley Wells*)

THE ELIZABETHAN AND JACOBEAN THEATRE

E. K. Chambers, *The Elizabethan Stage*, 4 vols. (Oxford, 1923).

G. E. Bentley, *The Jacobean and Caroline Stage*, 7 vols. (Oxford, 1941-68).

A. J. Gurr, *The Shakespearean Stage*, 1574-1642 (Cambridge, 2nd edn., 1980), a concise digest of information.

A. Harbage, *Annals of English Drama*, rev. S. Schoenbaum (London, 1964).

M. Hattaway, *Elizabethan Popular Theatre* (London, 1982).

P. Thompson, *Shakespeare's Theatre* (London, 1983).

The Revels History of Drama in English, vol. 3 (by J. L. Barroll, A. Leggatt, R. Hosley, A. Kernan) (London, 1975); vol. 4 (by P. Edwards, G. E. Bentley, K. McLuskie, L. Potter) (London, 1981).

WILLIAM SHAKESPEARE

Reference works

G. Bullough, *Narrative and Dramatic Sources of Shakespeare*, 8 vols. (London, 1957-75), a valuable anthology, with well-considered critical introductions.

E. K. Chambers, *William Shakespeare: A Study of Facts and Problems*, 2 vols. (Oxford, 1930).

K. Muir, *The Sources of Shakespeare's Plays* (London, 1977).

G. C. D. Odell, *Shakespeare from Betterton to Irving*, 2 vols. (New York, 1920, repr. 1963), critically outdated, but still a valuable survey.

S. Schoenbaum, *William Shakespeare: A Documentary Life* (Oxford, 1975; compact edition, 1977).

S. Wells, ed., *The Cambridge Companion to Shakespeare Studies* (Cambridge, 1986).

Texts

Facsimiles
Shakespeare's Plays in Quarto, ed. M. J. B. Allen and K. Muir (Berkeley, Calif., 1981).
The First Folio of Shakespeare (The Norton Facsimile), ed. C. Hinman (London, 1968).

Complete works
The Complete Works, ed. P. Alexander (London, 1951).
The Riverside Shakespeare, ed. G. B. Evans *et al.* (Boston, 1974), a conservatively edited, annotated text with ancillary material.
The Complete Works, ed. S. Wells, G. Taylor, *et al.* (Oxford, 1986), a new view of Shakespeare's text; in both modern-spelling and old-spelling versions.

Annotated editions of individual works
The Arden Shakespeare (London, 1951–).
The Oxford Shakespeare (Oxford, 1982–).
The New Cambridge Shakespeare (Cambridge, 1984–).
The New Penguin Shakespeare (Harmondsworth, 1967–).

Criticism

The vast body of critical literature is concisely surveyed in the new *Cambridge Companion* (see above). *Shakespeare Survey* (Cambridge, annually) includes critical surveys of each year's criticism and scholarship. Some of the soundest criticism is in introductions to the annotated editions listed above. More general studies include:
C. L. Barber, *Shakespeare's Festive Comedy* (Princeton, 1959), a well-written, anthropologically based study.
A. C. Bradley, *Shakespearean Tragedy* (London, 1904), a classic of criticism.
P. Edwards, *Shakespeare: A Writer's Progress* (Oxford, 1986), a critical survey of the corpus.
A. Righter, *Shakespeare and the Idea of the Play* (London, 1962).
E. M. W. Tillyard, *Shakespeare's Histories* (London, 1944), needs to be supplemented by later studies.

OTHER DRAMATISTS

Texts

Most editions of the complete works of individual dramatists are either out of date or of specialist interest to textual scholars. The general reader is best served by editions of individual plays in the Revels Plays series (London, 1958–76; Manchester 1976–) and by the Regents Renaissance Drama series (Lincoln, Nebr., 1963–77) and the New Mermaid series (London, 1964–).

Criticism

Even more than with Shakespeare, introductions to editions of single plays often form the best guide. More general works include:
A. Barton, *Ben Jonson, Dramatist* (Cambridge, 1984).
M. C. Bradbrook, *The Growth and Structure of Elizabethan Comedy* (London, 1955); *Themes and Conventions of Elizabethan Tragedy* (Cambridge, 1935); *John Webster: Citizen and Dramatist* (London, 1980).
M. Doran, *Endeavours of Art: a Study of Form in Elizabethan Drama* (Madison, Wis., 1954).
M. Heinemann, *Puritanism and Theatre: Thomas Middleton and Opposition Drama under the Early Stuarts* (Cambridge, 1980).
G. K. Hunter, *John Lyly, The Humanist as Courtier* (London, 1962).

Jacobean Theatre, ed. B. Harris and J. R. Brown (London, 1960).
Elizabethan Theatre, ed. B. Harris and J. R. Brown (London, 1966).
H. Levin, *Christopher Marlowe: The Over-reacher* (Cambridge, Mass., 1952).

4. THE SEVENTEENTH CENTURY

GENERAL

The *Oxford English Dictionary* remains our major source of information about the language in this period. A useful adaptation of it, listing new words as they are recorded, year by year, is *A Chronological English Dictionary* (Heidelberg, 1970), ed. T. Finkenstaedt *et. al.*

D. Bush, *English Literature in the Earlier Seventeenth Century 1600–1660*, 2nd rev. edn.
 (Oxford, 1962), the fullest literary history with excellent bibliographies, unsympathetic
 to Donne.
H. J. C. Grierson and G. Bullough (eds.), *The Oxford Book of Seventeenth Century Verse*
 (Oxford, 1934), the fullest anthology.
G. Saintsbury (ed.), *Minor Poets of the Caroline Period*, 3 vols. (Oxford, 1905, 1968),
 indispensable: a combination of catholic taste and literary enquiry unthinkable today.
H. Kenner (ed.), *Seventeenth Century Poetry. The Schools of Donne and Jonson* (New York,
 1964), good selection, intelligent comment.
R. Freeman, *English Emblem Books* (London, 1948), still the best introduction.
F. P. Wilson, *Elizabethan and Jacobean* (Oxford, 1945), pithy, challenging.
Basil Willey, *The Seventeenth-Century Background* (London, 1934), a pioneering work for its
 day, slanted towards a rather narrow philosophical tradition.
W. R. Keast (ed.), *Seventeenth Century English Poetry. Modern Essays in Criticism* (New
 York, 1971).
S. E. Fish (ed.), *Seventeenth Century Prose. Modern Essays in Criticism* (New York, 1971).
F. Saxl and R. Wittkower, *British Art and the Mediterranean* (Oxford, 1948; 1969), English
 debts to the classicizing of the European Renaissance.
M. Corbett and R. Lightbown, *The Comely Frontispiece. The Emblematic Title-Page in
 England, 1550–1660* (London, 1979).
G. Williamson, *The Donne Tradition* (Cambridge, Mass., 1930).
—— *Seventeenth Century Contexts* (London, 1960).
A. Alvarez, *The School of Donne* (London, 1961).
L. L. Martz, *The Poetry of Meditation: A Study in English Religious Literature of the
 Seventeenth Century* (New Haven, 1954), valuable reconstruction of meditative procedures,
 but tends to force the poems to conform to them.
R. F. Jones *et al.*, *The Seventeenth Century* (Stanford, Calif., 1951), influential essays on prose
 style and science, which now need considerable qualification.
R. Tuve, *Elizabethan and Metaphysical Imagery* (Chicago, 1947), difficult but important.
P. Delany, *British Autobiography in the Seventeenth Century* (London, 1969).

INDIVIDUAL AUTHORS

C. Hunt, *Donne's Poetry* (New Haven, 1954).
A. Stein, *John Donne's Lyrics* (Minneapolis, 1962).
R. S. Peterson, *Imitation and Praise in the Poems of Ben Jonson* (New Haven, 1981).
J. Summers, *George Herbert. His Religion and Art* (Cambridge, Mass., 1954).
H. Vendler, *The Poetry of George Herbert* (Cambridge, Mass., 1975).
B. Vickers, *Francis Bacon and Renaissance Prose* (Cambridge, 1968).

F. L. Huntley, *Sir Thomas Browne* (Ann Arbor, 1962).

L. Babb, *Sanity in Bedlam* (East Lansing, Mich., 1959), on Robert Burton.

S. Mintz, *The Hunting of Leviathan* (Cambridge, 1962), Hobbes and his critics.

T. A. Spragens, Jr., *The Politics of Motion. The World of Thomas Hobbes* (Lexington, Ky., 1973).

John Evelyn, *Diary*, ed. E. S. de Beer, 6 vols. (Oxford, 1955); one vol. edn. (Oxford, 1959), invaluable document, exemplary edition.

J. Summers, *The Muse's Method. An Introduction to 'Paradise Lost'* (London, 1962).

D. Burden, *The Logical Epic* (London, 1967).

G. K. Hunter, *Paradise Lost* (London, 1980).

M. Lieb and J. T. Shawcross (eds.), *Achievements of the Left Hand: Essays on the Prose of John Milton* (Amherst, Mass., 1974).

J. W. Binns (ed.), *The Latin Poetry of English Poets* (London, 1974).

L. L. Martz, *The Paradise Within* (New Haven, 1964).

P. Legouis, *Andrew Marvell, Poet, Puritan, Patriot* (Oxford, 1968).

5. RESTORATION AND EIGHTEENTH CENTURY

GENERAL

P. Earle, *The World of Defoe* (London, 1976), an engaging book, by a historian not a literary scholar, on the conditions of life as Defoe depicted them in fiction.

A. S. Turberville (ed.), *Johnson's England, An Account of the Life and Manners of his Age*, 2 vols. (Oxford, 1933), which, with the next work, is extremely good though dated in various attitudes and assumptions.

A. R. Humphreys, *The Augustan World, Life and Letters in Eighteenth-Century England* (London, 1954, 2nd edn. 1964).

R. B. Schwartz, *Daily Life in Johnson's London* (Madison, Wisc., 1984), vivid, detailed, and closely enough in touch with the literature.

P. Holland, *The Ornament of Action, Text and Performance in Restoration Comedy* (Cambridge, 1979), a most illuminating account of theatre history and conditions of performance.

J. W. Krutch, *Comedy and Conscience after the Restoration* (Columbia, 1924), despite the very considerable shift of attitudes since this book was written, still the best and clearest account of the effects of the movement against the drama.

J. Loftis, *Comedy and Society from Congreve to Fielding* (Stanford, Calif., 1959).

J. Sutherland, *A Preface to Eighteenth-Century Poetry* (Oxford, 1948), often reprinted.

J. D. Hunt, *The Figure in the Landscape* (London, 1976).

J. Hagstrum, *The Sister Arts* (Chicago, 1958), descriptive poetry seen in relation to the visual arts and criticism on them.

I. Watt, *The Rise of the Novel, Studies in Defoe, Richardson, and Fielding* (London, 1957), a pioneering account of the development of social realism.

A. D. McKillop, *The Early Masters of English Fiction* (Lawrence, Kan., 1967).

E. Rothstein, *Systems of Order and Inquiry in Later Eighteenth-Century Fiction* (Berkeley, Calif., 1975), an interesting new look at informing principles in the novel's second stage.

C. McIntosh, *The Choice of Life* (New Haven, 1973).

W. B. Carnochan, *Confinement and Flight, An Essay on English Literature of the Eighteenth Century* (Berkeley, Calif., 1977), stimulating and wide-ranging pursuit of a theme.

INDIVIDUAL AUTHORS

D. Wykes, *A Preface to Dryden* (London, 1977).

P. Ramsey, *The Art of John Dryden* (Lexington, Ky., 1969), sensitive and enthusiastic, an analysis of Dryden's poetry in critical rather than historical terms.

D. H. Griffin, *Satires Against Mankind: The Poems of Rochester* (Berkeley, Calif., 1973), weighty, detailed, and demanding.

N. Dennis, *Jonathan Swift: A Short Character* (London, 1964).

D. Nokes, *Jonathan Swift, A Hypocrite Reversed* (Oxford, 1985).

K. Williams, *Jonathan Swift and the Age of Compromise* (Lawrence, Kan., 1958).

P. Rogers, *An Introduction to Pope* (London, 1975).

R. A. Brower, *Alexander Pope, The Poetry of Allusion* (Oxford, 1959), not only relates Pope to his ancient masters, but provides a satisfyingly complex yet clear reading of the range of his works.

M. Mack, *The Garden and the City: Retirement and Politics in the Later Poetry of Pope* (Toronto, 1969).

J. Sutherland, *Daniel Defoe: A Critical Study* (Cambridge, Mass., 1971).

M. Kinkead-Weekes, *Samuel Richardson, Dramatic Novelist* (London, 1973).

R. Alter, *Fielding and the Nature of the Novel* (Cambridge, Mass., 1968).

D. Thomson, *Wild Excursions: The Life and Fiction of Laurence Sterne* (London, 1972), an unusual, responsive, acutely critical biography.

W. J. Bate, *The Achievement of Samuel Johnson* (New York, 1955).

P. Fussell, *Samuel Johnson and the Life of Writing* (London, 1972).

6. THE ROMANTIC PERIOD

GENERAL

W. L. Renwick, *English Literature 1789-1815* (Oxford, 1963), with the next entry, volumes of *The Oxford History of English Literature*. Besides dealing with major and minor authors they have chapters on biography, autobiography, journalism, and travel writing.

I. Jack, *English Literature 1815-1832* (Oxford, 1963).

M. Butler, *Romantics, Rebels and Reactionaries: English Literature and its background 1760-1830* (Oxford, 1981).

M. Praz, *The Romantic Agony*, trans. from the Italian by A. Davidson (London, 1933), on 'the pathology of Romanticism'.

C. M. Bowra, *The Romantic Imagination* (Cambridge, Mass., 1950), deals especially with the major Romantic poets.

M. H. Abrams, *The Mirror and the Lamp: romantic theory and the critical tradition* (New York, 1953).

S. Prickett (ed.), *The Romantics* (London, 1981), in The Context of English Literature series, with chapters on art, religion, philosophy, literature, and the historical context 1782-1832.

Thomas de Quincey, *Recollections of the Lakes and the Lake Poets* (1834-40), ed. D. Wright (Harmondsworth, 1970).

M. R. Booth, R. Southern, Frederick and Lise-Lone Marker, and R. Davies, *The Revels History of Drama in English*, vol. vi, *1750-1880* (London, 1975), deals with theatres and actors as well as plays and playwrights.

J. M. S. Tompkins, *The Popular Novel in England 1770-1800* (London, 1932), an unexpectedly delightful book.

William Cobbett, *Rural Rides*, ed. G. D. H. and Margaret Cole, 3 vols. (London, 1930), travels through Britain by an agriculturalist and reformer, which first appeared in the *Political Register* between 1821 and 1834.

INDIVIDUAL AUTHORS

M. Lascelles, *Jane Austen and her Art* (Oxford, 1939).

M. Kirkham, *Jane Austen, Feminism and Fiction* (Brighton, 1983), sees Jane Austen's novels in the context of eighteenth-century feminism.

K. Raine, *William Blake* (London, 1970), an illustrated introduction to Blake by a modern poet and disciple.

D. V. Erdman, *Blake: Prophet against Empire, a Poet's Interpretation of the History of his Own Times* (Princeton, 1954).

T. Crawford, *Burns, A Study of the Poems and Songs* (Edinburgh and London, 1960).

Byron's Letters and Journals, ed. L. A. Marchand, 12 vols. (London, 1973-82).

A. Rutherford, *Byron, A Critical Study* (Edinburgh and London, 1961).

J. Barrell, *The Idea of Landscape and the Sense of Place 1730-1840. An Approach to the Poetry of John Clare* (Cambridge, 1972).

J. S. Hill, *A Coleridge Companion: An Introduction to the Major Poems and the 'Biographia Literaria'* (London, 1983).

J. L. Lowes, *The Road to Xanadu: A Study in the Ways of the Imagination* (London, 1927), an exploration of what 'The Ancient Mariner' and 'Kubla Khan' owed to Coleridge's reading, especially in Renaissance travel books.

S. Prickett, *Coleridge and Wordsworth and the Poetry of Growth* (Cambridge, 1970).

R. Gittings, *John Keats* (London, 1968), a biography.

S. M. Sperry, *Keats the Poet* (Princeton, 1973).

Lord David Cecil, *A Portrait of Charles Lamb* (London, 1983).

T. Crawford, *Walter Scott* (Edinburgh, 1982).

R. Holmes, *Shelley, The Pursuit* (London, 1974), a biography.

D. King-Hele, *Shelley, His Thought and Work* (London, 1960).

M. Moorman, *William Wordsworth, a biography*, 2 vols. (Oxford, 1957-65).

M. Jacobus, *Tradition and Experiment in Wordsworth's 'Lyrical Ballads' (1798)* (Oxford, 1976).

7. HIGH VICTORIAN LITERATURE

GENERAL

W. E. Houghton, *The Victorian Frame of Mind 1830-1870* (New Haven and London, 1957), a standard study of attitudes and ideas in the period.

R. D. Altick, *Victorian People and Ideas* (New York, 1973), a useful complement to Houghton's survey.

L. Stone, *The Family, Sex and Marriage in England 1500-1800* (London, 1977), a discussion of changes in family structure, manners, and emotions. The final chapter considers developments post 1800.

O. Chadwick, *The Victorian Church*, 2 vols. (London, 1966), the definitive survey of the Victorian churches and churchmen.

U. C. Knoepflmacher and G. B. Tennyson (eds.), *Nature and the Victorian Imagination* (Berkeley, Los Angeles, and London, 1977), an excellent collection of essays haunted by the tutelary spirit of Ruskin.

J. Gross, *The Rise and Fall of the Man of Letters: Aspects of Literary Life since 1800* (London, 1969), a stimulating study of some of the major contributors to the journals.

K. Tillotson, *Novels of the Eighteen-Forties* (London, 1954), still the most able account of the early Victorian literary world.

G. Beer, *Darwin's Plots: Evolutionary Narrative in Darwin, George Eliot and Nineteenth-Century Fiction* (London 1983), an illuminating study of Darwin and his influence on literature.

INDIVIDUAL AUTHORS

Elizabeth Gaskell, *The Life of Charlotte Brontë* (London, 1857), consistently reprinted.

W. Gérin, *Charlotte Brontë: The Evolution of Genius* (Oxford, 1967); the two essential biographies.

—— *Emily Brontë: A Biography* (Oxford, 1971).

W. Irvine and P. Honan, *The Ring, The Book, and The Poet: A Biography of Robert Browning* (London, 1975).

J. A. Froude, *Thomas Carlyle: A History of the first Forty years of his Life 1795-1835.*

—— *Thomas Carlyle: A History of his Life in London 1834-1881*, 4 vols. (London, 1882, 1884), the exhaustive but indispensable study of the master by a disciple.

F. Kaplan, *Thomas Carlyle: A Biography* (Cambridge, 1983), a scrupulous updating of Froude's *Life.*

J. Forster, *The Life of Charles Dickens*, 3 vols. (London, 1872-4), the annotated edition by J. W. T. Ley remains useful, still the standard life of Dickens despite its omissions.

J. Butt and K. Tillotson, *Dickens at Work* (London, 1957), an invaluable account of Dickens's working methods.

G. S. Haight, *George Eliot: A Biography* (Oxford, 1968), the standard modern life by the editor of the novelist's letters.

W. Gérin, *Elizabeth Gaskell: A Biography* (Oxford, 1976).

J. W. Mackail, *The Life of William Morris*, 2 vols. (London, 1899), an important source for studies of Morris and his circle.

E. T. Cook, *The Life of Ruskin*, 2 vols. (London, 1911).

H. Tennyson, *Alfred Lord Tennyson: A Memoir*, 2 vols. (London 1897), a standard, if somewhat pious, *Life* by the poet's son.

R. B. Martin, *Tennyson: The Unquiet Heart* (Oxford, 1980), a sympathetic and perceptive rereading of the biographical evidence.

G. N. Ray, *Thackeray: The Uses of Adversity 1811-1846* (London, 1955).

—— *Thackeray: The Age of Wisdom 1847-1863* (London, 1958); the standard biography by the editor of Thackeray's superb letters.

8. LATE VICTORIAN TO MODERNIST

GENERAL

J. Batchelor, *The Edwardian Novelists* (London, 1982).

Q. Bell, *Bloomsbury* (London, 1968), a short but well-informed study by the nephew and biographer of Virginia Woolf.

B. Bergonzi, *Heroes' Twilight: a study of the literature of the Great War*, 2nd edn. (London, 1980).

M. Bradbury, *The Social Context of Modern English Literature* (London, 1971).

—— and J. McFarlane (eds.), *Modernism* (Harmondsworth, 1976), a large collection of essays on modernism, both anglophone and continental.

J. A. V. Chapple, *Documentary and Imaginative Literature 1880-1920* (London, 1970).

R. Ellmann (ed.), *Edwardians and Late Victorians* (New York, 1960).

—— and C. Fiedelson (eds.), *The Modern Tradition: Backgrounds of Modern Literature* (New York, 1965).

P. Faulkner, *Modernism* (London, 1977).

B. Ford (ed.), *From James to Eliot* (New Pelican Guide to English Literature, vol. 7) (Harmondsworth, 1983).

A. Friedman, *The Turn of the Novel* (New York, 1966).

P. Fussell, *The Great War and Modern Memory* (London, 1975), an outstanding book on the interaction of historical and literary experience.

J. Gross, *The Rise and Fall of the Man of Letters* (London, 1969).

J. B. Harmer, *Victory in Limbo: Imagism 1908-1917* (London, 1975).

G. Hough, *The Last Romantics* (London, 1949), a standard work on the aesthetic movement.

S. Hynes, *The Edwardian Turn of Mind* (Princeton, 1968), an excellent account of the intellectual and cultural history of Edwardian England.

—— *Edwardian Occasions* (London, 1972).

H. Jackson, *The Eighteen Nineties* (London, 1913; new edn. 1976), still indispensable.

H. Kenner, *The Pound Era* (London, 1972), a detailed but idiosyncratic account.

F. Kermode, *Romantic Image* (London, 1957), a suggestive study of the late-Romantic origins of modernist ideas.

D. Perkins, *A History of Modern Poetry: from the 1890s to the High Modernist Mode* (Cambridge, Mass., 1976).

E. Rickword, *Essays and Opinions 1921-31*, ed. Alan Young (Cheadle, 1974), collected criticism of a central intelligence of the decade.

R. H. Ross, *The Georgian Revolt: rise and fall of a poetic ideal 1910-1922* (London, 1967).

C. K. Stead, *The New Poetic* (London, 1964), a brilliant discussion of the origins of modern poetry.

J. I. M. Stewart, *Eight Modern Writers* (Oxford History of English Literature, vol. 12) (Oxford, 1963).

R. K. R. Thornton, *The Decadent Dilemma* (London, 1983).

INDIVIDUAL AUTHORS

A. N. Wilson, *Hilaire Belloc* (London, 1984).

M. Drabble, *Arnold Bennett: a biography* (London, 1974).

C. Hassall, *Rupert Brooke: a biography* (London, 1964).

P. Henderson, *Samuel Butler: the incarnate bachelor* (London, 1953).

M. Ward, *Gilbert Keith Chesterton* (London, 1944).

J. Baines, *Joseph Conrad: a critical biography* (London, 1960).

P. Ackroyd, *T. S. Eliot* (London, 1984).

A. Mizener, *The Saddest Story: a biography of Ford Madox Ford* (London, 1971).

P. N. Furbank, *E. M. Forster: a life*, 2 vols. (London, 1977-8).

D. Barker, *The Man of Principle: a view of Galsworthy* (London, 1963).

J. Korg, *George Gissing: a critical biography* (Seattle, 1963).

R. Gittings, *Young Thomas Hardy* and *The Older Hardy* (London, 1975, 1978).

B. Bergonzi, *Gerard Manley Hopkins* (London and New York, 1977).

N. Page, *A. E. Housman: a critical biography* (London, 1983).

A. R. Jones, *The Life and Opinions of T. E. Hulme* (London, 1960).

S. Bedford, *Aldous Huxley: a biography*, 2 vols. (London, 1973-4).

L. Edel, *The Life of Henry James*, 2 vols. (Harmondsworth, 1977).

R. Ellmann, *James Joyce* (2nd edn., Oxford, 1984).

C. Carrington, *Rudyard Kipling: his life and work* (London, 1955).

H. T. Moore, *The Priest of Love: a life of D. H. Lawrence* (London, 1974).

J. Myers, *The Enemy: a biography of Wyndham Lewis* (London, 1980).

E. P. Thompson, *William Morris: romantic to revolutionary* (2nd edn., London, 1977).

J. Stallworthy, *Wilfred Owen: a biography* (London, 1974).

T. Wright, *The Life of Walter Pater*, 2 vols. (London, 1907).

N. Stock, *The Life of Ezra Pound* (London, 1970).

J. Cohen, *Journey to the Trenches: the life of Isaac Rosenberg* (London, 1975).

St. John Ervine, *Bernard Shaw: his life, work and friends* (London, 1956).

J. P. Hennessy, *Robert Louis Stevenson* (London, 1974).
R. George Thomas, *Edward Thomas: A Portrait* (Oxford, 1985).
N. and J. Mackenzie, *The Time Traveller: the Life of H. G. Wells* (London, 1973).
H. Pearson, *The Life of Oscar Wilde* (London, 1946).
Q. Bell, *Virginia Woolf: a biography*, 2 vols. (London, 1972).
A. N. Jeffares, *W. B. Yeats: Man and Poet* (2nd edn., London, 1962).

9. MID-TWENTIETH-CENTURY LITERATURE

SOCIAL AND POLITICAL HISTORY

C. L. Mowatt, *Britain between the Wars, 1918-1940* (London, 1955).
R. Graves and A. Hodge, *The Long Weekend: A Social History of Great Britain, 1918-1939* (London, 1940), especially interesting for its closeness to the period discussed.
C. M. Woodhouse, *Post-War Britain* (London, 1966).
M. Sissons and P. French (eds.), *The Age of Austerity, 1945-51* (London, 1963).
V. Bogdanov and R. Skidelsky (eds.), *The Age of Affluence, 1951-64* (London, 1970).

THE CLIMATE OF OPINION

H. Nicolson, *Diaries and Letters*, ed. Nigel Nicolson, 3 vols. (London, 1966-8).
Sir H. Channon, *Chips: The Diaries of Sir Henry Channon*, ed. R. Rhodes James (London, 1966), like Nicolson, Channon was a Member of Parliament with an interest in the arts. Their diaries show clearly and entertainingly what that meant in the period up to about 1950.
George Orwell, *The Collected Journalism, Essays and Letters*, ed. Sonia Orwell and Ian Angus, 4 vols. (London, 1968).
Evelyn Waugh, *The Letters*, ed. M. Amory (London, 1980), makes a piquant contrast with the Orwell.

INDIVIDUAL AUTHORS

H. Carpenter, *W. H. Auden: A Biography* (London, 1981).
B. Crick, *George Orwell: A Life* (London, 1980).
D. Jones, *Dai Greatcoat: A Self-portrait of David Jones in his Letters*, ed. René Hague (London, 1980).
Dylan Thomas, *Selected Letters*, ed. Constantine Fitzgibbon (London, 1966).
D. Bair, *Samuel Beckett: A Biography* (London, 1978).
D. Graham, *Keith Douglas: A Biography* (London, 1974).
J. Maclaren-Ross, *Memoirs of the Forties* (London, 1967), includes a selection of his fine stories from that period.
Donald Davie, *These the Companions: Recollections* (London, 1982).

LITERARY HISTORY AND CRITICISM

The New Pelican Guide to English Literature, ed. B. Ford, vol. 7, *From James to Eliot;* vol. 8, *The Present* (Harmondsworth, 1983).
W. W. Robson, *Modern English Literature* (London, 1970), does not go much beyond 1950.
G. S. Fraser, *The Modern Writer and his World* (London, 1953, rev. 1964).
W. Y. Tindall, *Forces in Modern British Literature 1885-1946* (New York, 1947), an interesting American point of view.
R. Hewison, *Under Siege: Literary Life in London 1939-1945* (London, 1977).
—— *In Anger: Culture in the Cold War 1945-60* (London, 1981); both Hewison's books place literary history in a wider view of the cultural scene.

J. R. Taylor, *Anger and After: A Guide to the New British Drama* (London, 1962, rev. 1969), starts in the early fifties and ends with Pinter.

—— *The Second Wave: British Drama for the Seventies* (London, 1971), continues the story.

B. Bergonzi, *The Situation of the Novel* (London, 1970).

A. Burgess, *The Novel Now* (London, 1967, rev. 1971), like Bergonzi, Burgess looks outside Britain as well as inwards.

S. Hynes, *The Auden Generation: Literature and Politics in England in the 1930s* (London, 1976).

C. H. Sisson, *English Poetry 1900-1950: An Assessment* (London, 1981).

B. Morrison, *The Movement: English Poetry and Fiction of the 1950's* (London, 1980).

D. Davie, *Thomas Hardy and British Poetry* (London, 1973), the second half is largely concerned with poetry of the fifties and after.

CHRONOLOGY

THE works in the right-hand column are listed selectively: not all books of a given writer are included, especially in the case of the more prolific authors. Except in a few cases (duly noted), the date given is that of publication rather than composition or performance. Some dates are approximate, and no attempt has been made to fix Shakespeare's plays to a single year with what could only be spurious precision in many instances.

EVENTS	LITERARY WORKS
450 Traditional date of the coming of the 'Saxons' to England	
597 St Augustine's mission arrives in Kent	
	c.720 Lindisfarne Gospels
	731 Bede, *Ecclesiastical History of the English People*
871 Alfred becomes king of Wessex	
899 Death of Alfred	
991 The battle of Maldon: Byrhtnoth defeated by the Danes	
	992 Ælfric, *Catholic Homilies*
	c.1000 The four major surviving manuscripts of Anglo-Saxon poetry: Vercelli, Exeter, Cædmon, and *Beowulf* MSS
1066 Norman Conquest	
	c.1138 Geoffrey of Monmouth, *History of the Kings of Britain*
1154 Accession of Henry II	
1189 Death of Henry II	
	c.1200 *The Owl and the Nightingale;* Laȝamon, *Brut*
1215 Magna Carta	
	c.1220 *Ancrene Wisse*
1221–4 Arrival of Dominican and Franciscan Friars in England	
1265 Death of Simon de Montfort	
1327 Accession of Edward III	
	c.1330 Auchinleck MS and MS Harley 2253
1337 Beginning of the Hundred Years War	
c.1343 Birth of Geoffrey Chaucer	
1348 First occurrence of the Black Death in England	
	c.1370 Chaucer, *Book of the Duchess*

EVENTS	LITERARY WORKS
1377 Death of Edward III, accession of Richard II	*c.*1377 Langland, *Piers Plowman* (B Text)
1381 The Peasants' Revolt	
	*c.*1385 Chaucer, *Troilus and Criseyde*
	*c.*1387 Chaucer begins work on *The Canterbury Tales*
	1390 Gower, *Confessio Amantis*
1394 Birth of Charles of Orleans and James I of Scotland	
1399 Deposition of Richard II; accession of Henry IV	
1400 Death of Chaucer	*c.*1400 Sole surviving MS of *Sir Gawain*, *Pearl*, *Cleanness*, and *Patience*
1408 Death of John Gower	
1415 Battle of Agincourt	
1426 Death of Thomas Hoccleve	
1449 Death of John Lydgate	
1455 The first battle in the Wars of the Roses	
	1473–4 Caxton, *History of Troy*, the first book printed in English
1485 Richard III defeated at Battle of Bosworth; succeeded by Henry VII	1485 Malory, *Morte Darthur*
1492–1504 Voyages of Columbus	1500 Skelton, *Bouge of Court*; Erasmus, *Adagia*
1504 Colet made Dean of St Paul's	*c.*1504 Skelton, *Philip Sparrow*
1509 Henry VII dies; accession of Henry VIII, who marries Katherine of Aragon	
1513 Battle of Flodden	1513 Skelton, *Ballad of Scottish King*; Douglas, translation of *Aeneid*; Machiavelli, *Il Principe* ('The Prince')
	1516 More, *Utopia*; Skelton, *Magnificence*
	1517 Luther's Wittemberg theses
	1519 Erasmus, *Moriae encomium* ('Praise of Folly')
1520 Field of Cloth of Gold	
	1523 Skelton, *Garland of Laurel*
1525 Battle of Pavia	
1529 Fall of Wolsey; rise of Thomas Cromwell; More becomes Chancellor	
	1531 Elyot, *Book of the Governor*
1533–5 Henry excommunicated; Acts of Succession and Supremacy; Henry makes himself Supreme Head of the Church; More executed	
1536–9 Abbeys suppressed; breaking of images; English Bible in every church	
1537 Beginning of Calvin's Theocracy at Geneva	1537 Cranmer, *Institution of a Christian Man*

EVENTS	LITERARY WORKS
1540 Institution of the Jesuits; Cromwell executed	
1542 Roman Inquisition established	
1545 Council of Trent opens	
1547 Henry VIII dies; accession of Edward VI; Surrey executed	1547 Cranmer, Bonner, Grindal, etc., *Certain Sermons or Homilies*
1549 Book of Common Prayer	
1553 Edward VI dies; accession of Mary	
	1557 Tottel's edition, *Songs and Sonnets* ('Tottel's Miscellany'); Surrey's translation of *Aeneid*, II and IV; North, *Dial of Princes*
1558 Mary dies; accession of Elizabeth I	
	1559 *Mirror for Magistrates*
	1560 Geneva Bible
	1561 Hoby's translation of Castiglione, *Book of the Courtier*; Norton's translation of Calvin, *Institution*
	1563 Foxe, *Acts and Monuments*
	1568 Bishops' Bible
1570 Elizabeth excommunicated by Pope Pius V	1570 Ascham, *The Schoolmaster*
1571 Battle of Lepanto	
1577 Drake begins voyage around the world	1577 Sidney, 'Old' *Arcadia* (1577–80)
	1578 Lyly, *Euphues, the Anatomy of Wit*
	1579 Spenser, *Shepheardes Calender*; North, *Plutarch's Lives*
	1581–6 Sidney, *Astrophil and Stella* (1581–3); *Defence of Poetry* (*c*.1582) 'New' *Arcadia* (three books, uncompleted *c*.1584)
1586 Sidney killed at battle of Zutphen	
1587 Execution of Mary Queen of Scots	
1588 Spanish Armada defeated	1588–92 Shakespeare's early plays, including *1, 2, 3 Henry VI*; *Taming of the Shrew*; *Comedy of Errors*; *Love's Labour's Lost*; *Richard III*
	1589 Puttenham, *Art of English Poesy*
	1590 Spenser, *Faerie Queene* (I–III); Sidney, 'New' *Arcadia*; Lodge, *Rosalynde*
1592 Plague closes theatres for two years	1592 Daniel, *Delia* and *The Complaint of Rosamond*; Ralegh, *Ocean to Scinthia*
	1593 Marlowe, *Hero and Leander*; Shakespeare, *Venus and Adonis*; Drayton, *Idea, the Shepherd's Garland*; Hooker, *Laws of Ecclesiastical Polity* (I–IV)
1594 Lord Chamberlain's Men (theatre company) established	1594 Shakespeare, *Rape of Lucrece*; Nashe, *Unfortunate Traveller*
	c.1594 Shakespeare, *Sonnets* (composed)

EVENTS	LITERARY WORKS
	1594-1600 Shakespeare, plays including *Midsummer Night's Dream*; *Romeo and Juliet*; *1, 2 Henry IV*; *As You Like It*; *Merry Wives of Windsor*; *Julius Caesar*
	1595 Daniel, *Civil Wars* (I-IV); Spenser, *Amoretti*; *Epithalamion*
1596 Essex storms Cadiz	1596 Spenser, *Faerie Queene* (enlarged to six books); *Prothalamion*; Davies, *Orchestra*
	1597 Drayton, *England's Heroical Epistles*; Hooker, *Laws of Ecclesiastical Polity*, V; Bacon's *Essays*
	1598 Chapman-Marlowe, *Hero and Leander*; Florio, *World of Words*
1599 Essex goes to Ireland as Lord Deputy, returns and is imprisoned. Globe theatre built	1599 Daniel, *Poetical Essays* (including *Musophilus*); Nashe, *Lenten Stuff*
1600 Bruno burnt at Rome; East India Company founded	
1601 Essex rebellion	1601-4 Shakespeare, plays including *Hamlet, Twelfth Night, All's Well That Ends Well, Measure for Measure*
1603 Death of Elizabeth; accession of James I	
	1604-8 Shakespeare, plays including *Othello, King Lear, Macbeth, Antony and Cleopatra, Coriolanus*
1605 Gunpowder plot; Jonson's first court masque, with Inigo Jones	1605 Bacon, *Advancement of Learning*
1609 Virginian expedition wrecked in the Bermudas	1608-13 Shakespeare, plays including *Cymbeline, Winter's Tale, Tempest, Henry VIII*
c.1610 Plantation of Ulster commences	
1611 King James Bible published	
1613 Marriage of Princess Elizabeth to Elector Palatine; Globe theatre burned	
1614 The Globe rebuilt	
	1616 Ben Jonson, *Works*
1618 Execution of Ralegh; Thirty Years War begins	
	1623 Shakespeare, First Folio
	1627 Bacon, *New Atlantis*
	1628 William Harvey, *De motu cordis et sanguinis*
1629 Charles begins personal rule with dissolution of Parliament	
	1633 Donne, *Poems*; Herbert, *The Temple*
	1634 Milton, *Comus*, performed
	1637 Milton, *Lycidas*
1640 Long Parliament summoned	
1642 Civil War; closing of the theatres	

EVENTS	LITERARY WORKS
1644 Victory of parliamentary army at Marston Moor	1644 Milton, *Areopagitica*
1646 King surrenders to the Scots	
1649 Trial and execution of Charles I	
1649–52 Oliver Cromwell conquers Ireland and Scotland	
	1650 Marvell, *Horatian Ode* (composed)
	1651 Hobbes, *Leviathan*
1653 Cromwell becomes Lord Protector	
1655–60 War with Spain	
1658 Cromwell dies; succeeded by his son Richard	
1659 Richard overthrown by the army; Rump Parliament recalled	
1660 Charles II restored; reopening of the theatres	1660 Dryden, *Astraea Redux*
1662 Church of England restored; Royal Society receives its charter	
1665 Second Dutch War begins; Great Plague in London	
1666 London destroyed in the Great Fire; Wren's plan for a totally new city comes too late to be used	
	1667 Dryden, *Annus Mirabilis*; Milton, *Paradise Lost*
	1675 Wycherley, *The Country Wife*
	1677 Dryden, *All for Love*
	1678 Bunyan, *The Pilgrim's Progress*, pt. 1
	1680 Rochester, *Poems*
1681 Lord Shaftesbury tried for High Treason: acquitted	
	1682 Dryden, *Mac Flecknoe* (written *c*.1678), *Religio Laici*
1685 Charles II dies; James II succeeds; Monmouth invades and is crushed	
1688 Glorious Revolution: James II flees, William III and Mary succeed	
1694 Mary dies	
	1695 Congreve, *Love for Love*
	1700 Congreve, *The Way of the World*
1701 War of Spanish Succession begins: Britain and allies against France	
1702 William dies; Anne succeeds	
	1704 Defoe, *The Review* (begun); Swift, *The Battle of the Books* and *A Tale of a Tub*
	1706 Farquhar, *The Recruiting Officer*
1707 Union of England and Scotland	1707 Farquhar, *The Beaux Stratagem*
	1709 Pope, *Pastorals*

EVENTS	LITERARY WORKS
	1709-11 Steele (and others), *The Tatler*
	1711-12 *The Spectator*
	1712 Pope, *The Rape of the Lock*
1713 Peace of Utrecht ends War of Spanish Succession	
1714 Anne dies; George I, summoned from Hanover, succeeds	
1715 Jacobite rebellion in favour of James Edward, the 'Old Pretender'	
	1717 Pope, *Works* (including 'Eloisa to Abelard')
	1719 Defoe, *Robinson Crusoe*
1720 South Sea Bubble: thousands lose money; directors and government accused of corruption	
1721 Walpole forms ministry	
	1722 Defoe, *Moll Flanders*
	1726 Swift, *Gulliver's Travels*; Thomson, *Winter*
1727 George I dies; George II succeeds; Walpole retains power	
	1728 Gay, *The Beggar's Opera*; Pope, *The Dunciad* (first version)
1733 Walpole's ministry survives excise crisis	1733 Pope, first imitation of Horace; first epistle in *An Essay on Man*
1737 Queen Caroline dies; Licensing Act	
	1738 Pope, *Epilogue to the Satires*; Johnson, *London*
1739 War against Spain, long resisted by Walpole, begins	
1740 War of Austrian Succession begins	1740 Richardson, *Pamela*, pt. 1
1742 Walpole falls	1742 Fielding, *Joseph Andrews*
	1743 Pope, *The Dunciad* (final version)
1745 Second Jacobite Rebellion, led by Charles Edward, the 'Young Pretender': harshly put down	
	1747-8 Richardson, *Clarissa*
1748 Peace of Aix-la-Chapelle ends War of Austrian Succession	
	1749 Johnson, *The Vanity of Human Wishes*; Fielding, *Tom Jones*
	1750-2 Johnson, *The Rambler*
	1755 Johnson, *Dictionary*
1757 Pitt-Newcastle ministry	
1759 Wolfe takes Quebec	1759 Johnson, *Rasselas*
	1759-67 Sterne, *Tristram Shandy*
1760 George II dies; his grandson George III succeeds	
1762 Lord Bute's ministry, unpopular, begins	

EVENTS	LITERARY WORKS
1763 Peace of Paris ends Seven Years War; British gains in India and North America	
	1766 Goldsmith, *The Vicar of Wakefield*
1770 North's ministry begins	1770 Goldsmith, *The Deserted Village*
	1773 Goldsmith, *She Stoops to Conquer*
	1775 Sheridan, *The Rivals*; Johnson, *Journey to the Western Isles*
1776 American Declaration of Independence	1776–88 Gibbon, *Decline and Fall*
	1777 Sheridan, *The School for Scandal*
	1778 Burney, *Evelina*
	1779–81 Johnson, *The Lives of the Poets*
1780 Gordon Riots	
1781 British forces defeated by Americans at Yorktown	1781 Sheridan, *The Critic*; Rousseau, *Confessions*; Schiller, *The Robbers*; Kant, *A Critique of Pure Reason*
1783 Peace of Versailles at which Britain recognizes the independence of the American colonies	1783 Blake, *Poetical Sketches*
1784 James Watt invents the steam engine	
1785 Cartwright invents the power loom	1785 Cowper, *The Task*
	1786 Beckford, *Vathek*; Burns, *Poems, Chiefly in the Scottish Dialect*
1787 Association for the Abolition of the Slave Trade formed	1787 Mary Wollstonecraft, *Thoughts on the Education of Daughters*
1788–9 Regency Crisis	1788 *Daily Universal Register* (started 1785) becomes *The Times*
1789 The French Revolution. The Fall of the Bastille, 14 July; the Declaration of the Rights of Man, 4 August	1789 Blake, *Songs of Innocence*; Gilbert White, *Natural History of Selborne*
	1790 Blake, *The Marriage of Heaven and Hell*; Burke, *Reflections on the Revolution in France*
1791 Flight of Louis XVI	1791 Boswell, *The Life of Samuel Johnson*; Paine, *The Rights of Man*, pt. 1
1792 French royal family imprisoned; September massacres	1792 Wollstonecraft, *A Vindication of the Rights of Woman*
1793 Execution of Louis XVI; The Terror; murder of Marat; Britain joins the war against France	1793 Blake, *Visions of the Daughters of Albion*; *America*; Godwin, *Political Justice*
1794 Danton and Robespierre executed; in Britain Habeas Corpus Act suspended; Tooke, Holcroft, and Thelwall acquitted	1794 Blake, *Songs of Experience*; *The Book of Urizen*; Godwin, *Caleb Williams*; Ann Radcliffe, *The Mysteries of Udolpho*
1795 The French Directory established. The Speenhamland system for poor relief	1795 Lewis, *The Monk*
1796 Bonaparte's Italian campaign	1796 Fanny Burney, *Camilla*
	1797 Ann Radcliffe, *The Italian*
1798 The battle of the Nile; revolt in Ireland	1798 Wordsworth and Coleridge, *Lyrical Ballads*
1799 Bonaparte becomes First Consul	

EVENTS	LITERARY WORKS
1800 Union with Ireland	1800 Maria Edgeworth, *Castle Rackrent*
1802 Peace of Amiens	1802 Scott, *The Minstrelsy of the Scottish Border*; *The Edinburgh Review* begun
1803 War with France renewed	
1804 Bonaparte becomes Emperor Napoleon I	1804 Blake, *Milton*; his *Jerusalem* begun
1805 Battle of Trafalgar	1805 Scott, *The Lay of the Last Minstrel*; Wordsworth at work on a version of *The Prelude*
1807 Abolition of the slave trade in the British Empire	1807 Byron, *Hours of Idleness*; Wordsworth, *Poems*
1808 Peninsular War begins	1808 Hunt, *The Examiner*; Scott, *Marmion*; Goethe, *Faust*
1809 Moore killed at Corunna	1809 Byron, *English Bards and Scotch Reviewers*; *Quarterly Review* founded; Hannah More, *Coelebs in Search of a Wife*
	1810 Crabbe, *The Borough*; Scott, *The Lady of the Lake*
1811 Prince of Wales becomes Regent; Luddite riots	1811 Jane Austen, *Sense and Sensibility*
1812 French retreat from Moscow	1812 Crabbe, *Tales*; Byron, *Childe Harold's Pilgrimage*
	1813 Byron, *The Giaour*; Shelley, *Queen Mab*; Austen, *Pride and Prejudice*
1814 Napoleon abdicates and retreats to Elba; Stephenson's steam locomotive	1814 Wordsworth, *The Excursion*; Byron, *The Corsair*; Austen, *Mansfield Park*; Scott, *Waverley*
1815 Battle of Waterloo; Corn law passed	1815 Wordsworth, *The White Doe of Rylstone* and *Poems*; Scott, *Guy Mannering*
1816 Elgin marbles bought by British Museum	1816 Coleridge, *Christabel* and *Kubla Khan*; Shelley, *Alastor*; Austen, *Emma*; Scott, *The Antiquary* and *Old Mortality*; Peacock, *Headlong Hall*
	1817 Coleridge, *Sibylline Leaves* and *Biographia Literaria*; Byron, *Manfred*; Keats, *Poems*; Hazlitt, *The Characters of Shakespeare's Plays*; *Blackwood's Edinburgh Magazine* founded
	1818 Byron, *Beppo*; Keats, *Endymion*; Austen, *Northanger Abbey* and *Persuasion*; Peacock, *Nightmare Abbey*; Scott, *Rob Roy* and *The Heart of Midlothian*; Mary Shelley, *Frankenstein*; Hazlitt, *Lectures on the English Poets*
1819 Peterloo massacre	1819 Crabbe, *Tales of the Hall*; Byron, *Don Juan*; Wordsworth, *Peter Bell*; Scott, *The Bride of Lammermoor*
1820 Death of George III	1820 Shelley, *The Cenci* and *Prometheus Unbound*; Keats, *Lamia, Isabella, The Eve*

EVENTS

LITERARY WORKS

of St. Agnes and Other Poems; Clare, *Poems Descriptive of Rural Life*; Scott, *Ivanhoe*; Lamb, *Essays of Elia* begun

1821 Greeks rise against Turks

1821 Byron, *Cain*; Shelley, *Epipsychidion* and *Adonais*; Clare, *The Village Minstrel*; De Quincey, *Confessions of an English Opium-Eater*; Hazlitt, *Table Talk*

1822 Wordsworth, *Ecclesiastical Sketches*; Byron, *The Vision of Judgment*

1824 National Gallery opened

1824 Scott, *Redgauntlet*; Hogg, *Private Memoirs and Confessions of a Justified Sinner*; *Westminster Review* founded

1825 Financial crisis; Trade Unions legalized; Stockton to Darlington railway

1825 Hazlitt, *The Spirit of the Age*; Pepys' diary published

1827 Battle of Navarino; Scott acknowledges authorship of the Waverley novels

1827 Clare, *The Shepherd's Calendar*; Keble, *The Christian Year*

1828 Repeal of the Test and Corporation Acts

1828 Scott, *The Fair Maid of Perth*

1829 Catholic emancipation

1830 Death of George IV; Greek independence; Agitation for Reform; Manchester and Liverpool Railway

1830 Cobbett, *Rural Rides*; Tennyson, *Poems, chiefly lyrical*

1831 Unsuccessful introduction of Reform Bills; Bristol Riots

1832 Reform Act

1832 Tennyson, *Poems* (dated 1833)

1833 Abolition of Slavery; Keble's Assize Sermon

1833 Carlyle, *Sartor Resartus*; first 'Tract for the Times'

1834 New Poor Law; burning of Houses of Parliament; Fox Talbot's first photograph

1835 Municipal Reform Act

1835 Browning, *Paracelsus*

1836 Dickens, *Sketches by Boz* and first number of *Pickwick Papers* (1836–7)

1837 Death of William IV; accession of Victoria

1837 Carlyle, *The French Revolution*; Dickens, *Oliver Twist*

1838 London–Birmingham Railway; 'People's Charter' published

1838 Dickens, *Nicholas Nickleby*

1839 Penny Postage Act

1839 Carlyle, *Chartism*

1840 Opium War; new Houses of Parliament begun; first presentation of the People's Charter to Parliament

1840 Dickens, *Master Humphrey's Clock* (containing *Old Curiosity Shop* and *Barnaby Rudge*, 1840–1); Browning, *Sordello*

1841 Carlyle, *On Heroes & Hero Worship*; J. H. Newman, *Tract XC*; *Punch* founded

1842 Chartist riots; second presentation of the People's Charter to Parliament; Copyright Act

1842 Tennyson, *Poems*; Browning, *Dramatic Lyrics*

1843 Theatre Regulations Bill (monopoly removed from Covent Garden and Drury Lane theatres)

1843 Macaulay, *Essays*; Carlyle, *Past and Present*; Ruskin, *Modern Painters* (vol. 1); Dickens, *A Christmas Carol*, *Martin Chuzzlewit*

EVENTS	LITERARY WORKS
	1843–4 Disraeli, *Coningsby*
1844 Royal Commission on Health in Towns	1844 Thackeray, *Barry Lyndon*
1845 Failure of Irish potato crop	1845 Disraeli, *Sybil*; Browning, *Dramatic Romances and Lyrics*
1846 Famine in Ireland; Repeal of Corn Laws	
	1846–8 Dickens, *Dombey and Son*
1847 Ten Hours Factory Act	1847 Tennyson, *The Princess*; Charlotte Brontë, *Jane Eyre*; Emily Brontë, *Wuthering Heights*; Anne Brontë, *Agnes Grey*
	1847–8 Thackeray, *Vanity Fair*
1848 Chartist Demonstration in London (third presentation of Charter); Public Health Act; foundation of Pre-Raphaelite Brotherhood; revolutions in France, Germany, Poland, Hungary, and Italy; Second Republic in France; Roman Republic	1848 Elizabeth Gaskell, *Mary Barton*; Anne Brontë, *The Tenant of Wildfell Hall*
	1848–9 Thackeray, *Pendennis*
	1849 Charlotte Brontë, *Shirley*; Ruskin, *Seven Lamps of Architecture*
	1849–50 Dickens, *David Copperfield*
	1849–61 Macaulay, *History of England*
1850 'Papal Aggression' (following re-establishment of Roman Catholic hierarchy in England)	1850 Tennyson, *In Memoriam AHH*; Carlyle, *Latter-Day Pamphlets*; E. B. Browning, *Sonnets from the Portuguese*
1851 Great Exhibition; Louis Napoleon III's *coup d'état*	1851 Elizabeth Gaskell, *Cranford*
	1851–3 Ruskin, *The Stones of Venice*
	1852 Thackeray, *Henry Esmond*; Matthew Arnold, *Empedocles on Etna*
	1852–3 Dickens, *Bleak House*
	1853 Charlotte Brontë, *Villette*; Elizabeth Gaskell, *Ruth*; Matthew Arnold, *Poems*
1854 Crimean War breaks out; Battles of Alma, Inkerman, and Balaclava; Preston cotton spinners' strike; Working Man's College opened	1854 Dickens, *Hard Times*
1855 Fall of Sebastopol; Metropolitan Board of Works; repeal of Stamp Duty on newspapers	1855 Tennyson, *Maud*; Kingsley, *Westward Ho!*; Browning, *Men and Women*; Elizabeth Gaskell, *North and South*; Trollope, *The Warden*
	1855–7 Dickens, *Little Dorrit*
1856 Peace of Paris (ending Crimean War)	
1857 Indian Mutiny	1857 E. B. Browning, *Aurora Leigh*; Trollope, *Barchester Towers*; Elizabeth Gaskell, *Life of Charlotte Brontë*; Charlotte Brontë, *The Professor*; George Eliot, *Scenes of Clerical Life*

EVENTS	LITERARY WORKS
	1857–9 Thackeray, *The Virginians*
1858 Peace in India; India transferred to British Crown	1858 Clough, *Amours de Voyage*
	1858–65 Carlyle, *Frederick the Great*
	1859 George Eliot, *Adam Bede*; Meredith, *The Ordeal of Richard Feverel*; Darwin, *The Origin of Species*; J. S. Mill, *On Liberty*
	1859–72 Tennyson, *Idylls of the King*
1860 Garibaldi's campaign in Sicily and Naples	1860 Wilkie Collins, *The Woman in White*; Ruskin, *Unto This Last*
	1860–1 Dickens, *Great Expectations*
1861 Victor Emmanuel, King of United Italy; outbreak of American Civil War; death of Prince Consort	1861 George Eliot, *Silas Marner*; Trollope, *Framley Parsonage*
	1862 C. Rossetti, *Goblin Market*; Meredith, *Modern Love*
	1862–3 George Eliot, *Romola*
1863 Lancashire 'cotton famine'	1863 Elizabeth Gaskell, *Sylvia's Lovers*
1864 Geneva Convention	1864 Elizabeth Gaskell, *Wives and Daughters*; J. H. Newman, *Apologia pro vita sua*
	1864–5 Dickens, *Our Mutual Friend*
1865 Suppression of Jamaican rebellion by Governor Eyre; assassination of Lincoln	1865 Matthew Arnold, *Essays in Criticism*; J. H. Newman, *Dream of Gerontius*; Carroll, *Alice in Wonderland*; Swinburne, *Atalanta in Calydon*
1866 Austro-Prussian War	1866 George Eliot, *Felix Holt*; Kingsley, *Hereward the Wake*; Swinburne, *Poems and Ballads*
1867 Representation of People Act (Second Reform Act)	1867 Matthew Arnold, *New Poems*; Trollope, *The Last Chronicle of Barset*
	1868 Wilkie Collins, *The Moonstone*
	1868–9 Browning, *The Ring and the Book*
	1868–70 Morris, *The Earthly Paradise*
1869 First Vatican Council (1869–70)	1869 Trollope, *Phineas Finn*; J. S. Mill, *The Subjection of Women*
1870 Married Woman's Property Act; Franco-Prussian War; Papal States incorporated into Kingdom of Italy; Forster's Education Act	1870 Dickens, *Edwin Drood*; D. G. Rossetti, *Poems*
1871 Paris Commune (Mar.–May)	1871–2 George Eliot, *Middlemarch*
	1873 Matthew Arnold, *Literature and Dogma*; J. S. Mill, *Autobiography*
	1874–5 Trollope, *The Way We Live Now*
1875 Agricultural Depression	
	1876 George Eliot, *Daniel Deronda*
1877 Victoria, Empress of India	
1878 Congress of Berlin	
	1879 Meredith, *The Egoist*

EVENTS	LITERARY WORKS
1880 Gladstone Prime Minister	
	1881 Henry James, *The Portrait of a Lady*
1885 Radio waves discovered; internal combustion engine invented	
	1888 Rudyard Kipling, *Plain Tales from the Hills*
	1889 W. B. Yeats, *The Wanderings of Oisin*
	1890 Kipling, *Barrack Room Ballads*
	1891 Thomas Hardy, *Tess of the D'Urbervilles*; George Gissing, *New Grub Street*
1895 X-rays discovered	1895 H. G. Wells, *The Time Machine*
1896 Wireless telegraphy invented	1896 A. E. Housman, *A Shropshire Lad*; Hardy, *Jude the Obscure*
1897 Queen Victoria's Diamond Jubilee	
	1899 Oscar Wilde, *The Importance of Being Earnest*
1899-1902 Boer War	
1901 Death of Queen Victoria	
1903 First aeroplane flight	1903 Samuel Butler, *The Way of all Flesh*; James, *The Ambassadors*; Bernard Shaw, *Man and Superman*
	1904 Joseph Conrad, *Nostromo*; James, *The Golden Bowl*
1906 Liberal government elected	
	1907 J. M. Synge, *The Playboy of the Western World*
	1908 Arnold Bennett, *The Old Wives' Tale*
1909 English channel flown	1909 Wells, *Tono-Bungay*
1910 Death of Edward VII; George V king; first Post-Impressionist Exhibition	1910 E. M. Forster, *Howards End*
	1911 Conrad, *Under Western Eyes*
	1913 D. H. Lawrence, *Sons and Lovers*
	1914 *Blast*. James Joyce, *Dubliners*; W. B. Yeats, *Responsibilities*
1914-18 First World War	
	1915 Ford Madox Ford, *The Good Soldier*; Lawrence, *The Rainbow*
1916 Easter Rising, Dublin; Battle of the Somme	1916 Joyce, *A Portrait of the Artist as a Young Man*
1917 Russian Revolution	1917 T. S. Eliot, *Prufrock and Other Observations*
	1918 Wyndham Lewis, *Tarr*; Gerard Manley Hopkins, *Poems*
1919 Atlantic flown	
	1920 Wilfred Owen, *Poems*; Lawrence, *Women in Love*; Shaw, *Heartbreak House*; Eliot, *The Sacred Wood*

EVENTS	LITERARY WORKS
1921 Irish Free State established	1921 Aldous Huxley, *Crome Yellow*
1922 Fascism takes power in Italy	1922 Eliot, *The Waste Land*; Joyce, *Ulysses*
	1923 Huxley, *Antic Hay*
1924 First Labour government	1924 Forster, *A Passage to India*; Ford, *Some Do Not*
	1925 Virginia Woolf, *Mrs Dalloway*
1926 General Strike	
	1927 Woolf, *To the Lighthouse*
	1928 Yeats, *The Tower*; Lawrence, *Lady Chatterley's Lover*; Evelyn Waugh, *Decline and Fall*
1930 World economic depression	1930 W. H. Auden, *Poems*; Eliot, *Ash Wednesday*; Waugh, *Vile Bodies*; Coward, *Private Lives*; Empson, *Seven Types of Ambiguity*
1931 Fall of Labour government	1931 Anthony Powell, *Afternoon Men*
	1932 Isherwood, *The Memorial*; Powell, *Venusberg*; *Scrutiny* first appears
1933 Hitler becomes Chancellor of Germany	1933 George Orwell, *Down and Out in Paris and London*
	1934 Samuel Beckett, *More Pricks than Kicks*; Graham Greene, *It's a Battlefield*
	1935 Isherwood, *Mr Norris Changes Trains* and *Lions and Shadows*; Auden and Isherwood, *The Dog Beneath the Skin*; Eliot, *Murder in the Cathedral*
1936 Civil War breaks out in Spain; first of the Moscow show trials	1936 Eliot, 'Burnt Norton'; Auden and Isherwood, *The Ascent of F6*
	1937 Auden and MacNeice, *Letters from Iceland*; David Jones, *In Parenthesis*; Orwell, *The Road to Wigan Pier*
1938 German occupation of Austria; Munich agreement	1938 Beckett, *Murphy*; Elizabeth Bowen, *The Death of the Heart*; Orwell, *Home to Catalonia*
1939 End of the Civil War in Spain; outbreak of the Second World War; Russo-German pact agreed	1939 MacNeice, *Autumn Journal*; Green, *Party Going*; Greene, *The Confidential Agent*; Isherwood, *Goodbye to Berlin*; Jean Rhys, *Good Morning Midnight*; Eliot, *The Family Reunion*
	1940 Auden, *New Year Letter*; Eliot, 'East Coker'; Greene, *The Power and the Glory*; C. P. Snow, *Strangers and Brothers* (first volume of the series so named); Dylan Thomas, *Portrait of the Artist as a Young Dog*
	1941 Eliot, 'The Dry Salvages'
	1942 Eliot, 'Little Gidding'; Waugh, *Put Out More Flags*
	1944 Joyce Cary, *The Horse's Mouth*

EVENTS	LITERARY WORKS
1945 End of the Second World War; Labour government returns to power	1945 Henry Green, *Loving*; Orwell, *Animal Farm*; Waugh, *Brideshead Revisited*
1946 Nationalization of the coal industry; foundation of a national health service	1946 Green, *Back*; Philip Larkin, *Jill*; Mervyn Peake, *Titus Groan*
1947 Nationalization of transport; independence of India and Pakistan	1947 Ivy Compton-Burnett, *Manservant and Maidservant*; Larkin, *A Girl in Winter*
1948 Britain accepts American aid	1948 Greene, *The Heart of the Matter*; Graves, *The White Goddess*
1949 Steel industry nationalized	1949 Bowen, *The Heat of the Day*; Orwell, *Nineteen Eighty-four*; Eliot, *The Cocktail Party*
1950 Labour government returned to office with a substantially reduced majority	1950 Auden, *Collected Shorter Poems 1930–1944*; Beckett, *Molloy* (in French, the first volume of his *Trilogy*)
1951 Conservative Party returned to power	1951 Keith Douglas, *Collected Poems*; Powell, *A Question of Upbringing* (first volume of *A Dance to the Music of Time*)
	1952 D. Jones, *The Anathemata*; Waugh, *Men at Arms*
	1953 Cary, *Except the Lord*
	1954 Thom Gunn, *Fighting Terms*; Golding, *Lord of the Flies*; J. R. R. Tolkien, *The Fellowship of the Ring* (first volume of *The Lord of the Rings*); Dylan Thomas, *Under Milk Wood*; Kingsley Amis, *Lucky Jim*
	1955 Auden, *The Shield of Achilles*; Donald Davie, *Brides of Reason*; Larkin, *The Less Deceived*; Golding, *The Inheritors*; Greene, *The Quiet American*; Brian Moore, *The Lonely Passion of Judith Hearne*; Waugh, *Officers and Gentlemen*; Beckett, *Waiting for Godot* (first English performance)
1956 Egypt nationalizes the Suez Canal; Britain, France, and Israel intervene and are obliged to withdraw	1956 Robert Conquest (ed.), *New Lines*; Golding, *Pincher Martin*; Brendan Behan, *The Quare Fellow* (first English performance); John Osborne, *Look Back in Anger*
	1957 Gunn, *The Sense of Movement*; Hughes, *The Hawk in the Rain*; Muriel Spark, *The Comforters*; Osborne, *The Entertainer*
	1958 Amis, *I Like it Here*; Behan, *The Hostage*; Pinter, *The Birthday Party*
	1959 Spark, *Memento Mori*; A. Wesker, *Roots*; Golding, *Free Fall*
1960 Unexpurgated text of *Lady Chatterley's Lover* found not obscene in court of law	1960 Hughes, *Lupercal*; Pinter, *The Caretaker*
	1961 Gunn, *My Sad Captains*; Waugh, *Sword of Honour*

EVENTS	LITERARY WORKS
	1962 F. R. Leavis, *Two Cultures?*
	1963 Amis, *One Fat Englishman*; Spark, *The Girls of Slender Means*
	1964 Isherwood, *A Single Man*; Joe Orton, *Entertaining Mr Sloane*; Golding, *The Spire*
	1965 Edward Bond, *Saved*
	1966 Seamus Heaney, *Death of a Naturalist*; Jean Rhys, *Wide Sargasso Sea*; Tom Stoppard, *Rosencrantz and Guildenstern are Dead*
1967 Legalization within limits of homosexuality and abortion	1967 Orton, *Loot*; Hughes, *Wodwo*
1968 Britain abandons her role in world-wide defence; hostility between 'Catholic' and 'Protestant' groups in Northern Ireland is renewed and remains a continuing problem; censorship of the theatre by the Lord Chamberlain's office comes to an end	1968 Stoppard, *The Real Inspector Hound*
1969 Abolition of capital punishment	1969 Heaney, *Door into the Dark*; Orton, *What the Butler Saw*
1970 Age of majority reduced from 21 to 18	1970 Hughes, *Crow*
	1971 Geoffrey Hill, *Mercian Hymns*; Bond, *Lear*; Pinter, *Old Times*
	1972 John Montague, *The Rough Field*; Moore, *Catholics*; Stoppard, *Jumpers*
1973 United Kingdom enters the European Economic Community	1973 Beckett, *Not I*; Bond, *The Sea*
	1974 Amis, *Ending Up*; Spark, *The Abbess of Crewe*; Beckett, *That Time*; Stoppard, *Travesties*
	1975 Pinter, *No Man's Land*
	1977 Hughes, *Gaudete*; Stoppard, *Professional Foul*; Isherwood, *Christopher and his Kind*
	1978 Pinter, *Betrayal*
	1979 Golding, *Darkness Visible*
	1980 Golding, *Rites of Passage*
	1981 Moore, *The Temptation of Eileen Hughes*; Spark, *Loitering with Intent*; Bond, *Restoration*
	1983 Hughes, *River*
	1984 Heaney, *Station Island*

ACKNOWLEDGEMENTS

THE illustrations on the following pages are reproduced by Gracious Permission of Her Majesty the Queen 76; 250 and 251 (Crown Copyright reserved).

Photographs and illustrations were supplied by, or are reproduced by kind permission of, the following: George Allen & Unwin 447 (right); Keith Anderson 463; Ashmolean Museum, Oxford 365, 396, 405; Auckland City Art Gallery 149; Marquess of Bath, Longleat House, Warminster, Wiltshire 136; BBC Hulton Picture Library 339, 387, 388 (both), 401, 407, 421, 426 (both), 442; Birmingham City Art Gallery 326; Bodleian Library, Oxford 2, 67 (right), 225, 266; Janet and Colin Bord 5; British Library 23, 28, 49, 51, 55, 78, 152 (top), 185, 320, 457; British Museum 6, 9, 66, 139, 217, 219, 230, 241, 242, 262, 264, 270, 273, 276, 284, 301, 314, 371; Brontë Society, photo N. K. Howarth 352; Buckingham County Museum 247; Cambridge University Library 213; Camera Press 436, 438, 469; Christie's 249, 392; Condé Nast, photo John Deakin 453; Donald Cooper 157, 465, 481; Corpus Christi College, Cambridge 42; Courtauld Institute of Art 87, 280 (left), 376, 377, 384; Department of Environment, Crown Copyright reserved 38, 357; André Deutsch 441; Dickens House and Museum, London 346; Patric Dickinson 419; Zoë Dominic 477.

Entwistle Photographic Services 35 (both); Faber & Faber Ltd. (and estate of Anthony Gross) 474, (and Leonard Baskin) 487; Fitzwilliam Museum, Cambridge 257 (bottom), 280 (right); Folger Shakespeare Library 114 (bottom), 132; Fotomas Index 214-15; Garrick Club, photo E. T. Archive 348; Mark Gerson 483; Guildhall Library and Art Gallery, London 114 (top), 152 (middle), 228-9, 306, 329; Houghton Library, Harvard University 424 (top); Humanities Research Center, Texas 381, 390; Huntington Library, California 46 (both); International Museum of Photography at George Eastman House 403;

Peter Jackson 72; Jesus College, Cambridge 260; A. F. Kersting 18, 32, 58, 108; Jorge Lewinski 424 (bottom); © Estate of Mrs G. A. Wyndham Lewis. By permission 410, 411, 413, 415 (both); London Borough of Richmond-on-Thames, Orleans House 236; Mander and Mitchenson Theatre Collection 137; Mansell Collection 100, 119, 126, 254, 268, 297, 344 (both); Merseyside County Art Galleries, Liverpool 147, 252; Methuen (and Don Bachardy 439, (and estate of Mervyn Peake) 447 (left); Walter Michel 415; Museum of Fine Arts, Boston 198, 202; Museum of London 47.

National Film Archive, London 130, 450, 461; National Galleries of Scotland 322; National Gallery of Ireland 410; National Maritime Museum 69; National Monuments Record 25, 432; National Portrait Gallery 134, 208, 289, 304, 315 (both), 355; National Trust 92, 109, 335, 363; Nicholson and Watson, from David Gascoyne's *Poems 1937-42* © AGADP, Paris & Cosmopress, Geneva 1987, 448; The Pierpont Morgan Library 259; Edward Piper 455; Duke of Portland, photo National Portrait Gallery 115; Post Office 460; Patrick Procktor 479; Private Collection, photo National Portrait Gallery 193; Public Record Office 152 (bottom); Bertram Rota Ltd. 439, 474; Royal Albert Hall 476; Marquess of Salisbury 299; Science Museum, London 331; Shakespeare Birthplace Trust 154, 158 (right); Shakespeare Centre, Stratford-upon-Avon 123; Tate Gallery 145 (top), 278, 337, 350, 393, 418; Marquess of Tavistock & the Trustees of the Bedford Estate 97, 166; Theatre Museum, photos Houston Rogers 142, 472; Ulster Museum, Belfast 485; Victoria and Albert Museum 67 (left), 145 (bottom), 238, 287, 310, 341, 452; Mrs Julian Vinogradoff 429; Warburg Institute 61; Auberon Waugh, photo Weidenfeld & Nicolson 444; Weidenfeld & Nicolson 434; Winchester City Museum 15; York Archaeological Trust 12.

INDEX

In longer entries, major references are listed first, with secondary references grouped together after the word 'also'. Multiple references on a page are indicated by a figure in parentheses after the page number. Numbers in italics refer to black and white illustrations and their captions. Colour plates (which are unpaginated) are located by reference to the nearest page of text (usually opposite) and printed in bold. Titles of individual works are not indexed, except for anonymous works, periodicals, and the plays and poems of Shakespeare.

J. A. V.